ELIZABETHAN DRAMA:
Eight Plays

ELIZABETHAN DRAMA:
Eight Plays

A New Edition

Edited and with Introductions
by
John Gassner
and
William Green

Elizabethan Drama: Eight Plays
Copyright © 1967, 1990 by Mrs. John Gassner &
William Green

Library of Congress Cataloging-In-Publication Data

Elizabethan drama: eight plays / edited and with introductions
by John Gassner and William Green. —A new ed.
    p.   cm.
    Bibliography: p.
    Contents: Arden of Feversham / Anonymous — The Span-
ish tragedy / by Thomas Kyd — Friar Bacon and Friar Bungay
/ by Robert Greene — Doctor Faustus / by Christopher Marlowe — Edward II / by Christopher Marlowe — Everyman in
his humour / by Ben Jonson — The shoemaker's holiday / by
Thomas Dekker — A woman killed with kindness / by Thomas Heywood.
    ISBN 1-55783-028-2 : $12.95
    1. English drama—Early modern and Elizabethan, 1500-
1600.
I. Gassner, John, 1903-1967. II. Green, William, 1926- .
PR1263.E54 1989
822'.3'08--dc19   88-38841
                                            CIP

APPLAUSE THEATRE BOOK PUBLISHERS
211 West 71st Street
New York, NY 10023
(212) 595-4735

FOR

GEORGE B. PARKS

amicus humani generis

Contents

Elizabethan Drama

1558–1603

BY JOHN GASSNER

No one with even the slightest interest in English literature needs to be told that its greatest period is the Elizabethan Age, and no one familiar with that period is likely to depart from the consensus that its major literary achievement is the drama.

Although the term "Elizabethan drama" has often been used loosely to cover the dramatic literature of the second half of the sixteenth century and the first third of the seventeenth, it is here applied only to the productions of Queen Elizabeth's reign, from her accession to the throne of England in 1558 to her death in 1603.. Even when strictly—and somewhat arbitrarily—confined to the reign of Henry VIII's celebrated daughter, the Virgin Queen, the Elizabethan Age defies simple definition. It is said with some justice that it marks the high point of the Renaissance in England; but the Middle Ages were not miraculously abolished by the coronation of Elizabeth, and it is a mistake to overlook the persistence of strong medieval elements in Elizabethan culture and theatre. A residue is observable, for instance, in the popularity of the *De Casibus* "Fall of Princes" theme in tragedy, as in Marlowe's *Edward II* and Shakespeare's *Richard II* ("For God's sake, let us sit upon the ground / And tell sad stories of the death of kings," says Richard II), and the persistence of medieval morality-play figures, such as the prankish devil or "Vice," the struggles of the Good and the Bad Angel for the soul of the hero, and the presence of the Seven Deadly Sins in Marlowe's *Doctor Faustus*. Memories of feudal warfare abound in the "chronicle plays," or "histories," of Shakespeare and his colleagues. Fancy and superstition color the comedies and tragedies; the Middle Ages account for the elves and witches in Shakespeare's otherwise sophisticated artistry. The very playhouses of England, like its domestic architecture, retained medieval features.

ix

The Renaissance, blended with vestigial medievalism, was itself no novelty during Elizabeth's reign but was already almost a century old in England by the time she became queen. By the 1550's it was no longer a question of introducing the "learning" or humanism of the Italian Renaissance into England but of giving it wider dissemination, of assimilating it, and of translating Renaissance learning into English creativeness.

The same thing may be said of English nationalism. Aspirations to a unified and stable government had long been present in England, and efforts to achieve it had been made with noteworthy success by Elizabeth's forebears, Henry VII and Henry VIII. The main threat to national unity had been Mary Tudor's pious efforts to turn back the clock of history by instituting in England a counterreformation after the triumph of the Protestant Reformation; the threat ended with her death. When her Protestant sister Elizabeth succeeded her, even the presence of a Catholic underground did not seriously affect the stability of the government, which was loyally supported in a crisis by such prominent Catholics as Lord Howard, the commander of the British fleet, who repelled the Spanish Armada in 1588.

The unity and prestige of the English nation was only fortified by danger from foreign quarters, which reached a climax with the fiasco of Philip II's attempted invasion of England. With the disaster that overwhelmed the Spanish Armada, England attained the security needed for peaceful economic development, and Britannia began to rule the waves. National confidence and pride were assured. Less than a decade later, in *Richard II*, Shakespeare was speaking of a nation conscious of its manifest destiny when he made John of Gaunt acclaim

> This royal throne of kings, this scepter'd isle,
> This earth of majesty, this seat of Mars,
> This other Eden, demi-paradise,
> This fortress built by Nature for herself
> Against infection and the hand of war,
> This happy breed of men, this little world,
> This precious stone set in the silver sea
> Which serves it in the office of a wall . . .
> This blessed plot, this earth, this realm, this England.

This patriotic fervor was no elite-nationalism confined to the court. John of Gaunt's lines were intended to be heard in the theatre by groundlings and noblemen alike. And while there was no lack of courtiers in England, and while a number of them were, like Raleigh, noted for valor and vanity as well as for conspicuous service to their Queen and country, the power of England was broadly based on the enterprise of the middle classes. Many of Elizabeth's most influential councillors, including her great chancellor, Lord Burghley, were of middle-class origin. A fiery young poet like Christopher Marlowe, at the beginning of his career, might be inebriated by visions of imperial glory, but English power rested on a firm economic foundation. Anyone troubled by this unromantic conclusion will do well to reflect that the Periclean age and the Italian Renaissance had equally mundane, middle-class bases.

Dramatic literature, in fact, paralleled an expansion of England which profited the middle class without assuring the nation democratic government or even greatly mitigating the absolutism of the Tudor monarchy. The course of Elizabethan drama can be traced as an advance from courtly literature to plays written mainly to be performed for the multitude—or rather, for a cross-section of the population of London and its environs. And it is one of the paradoxes of art that the most distinguished plays characterized, among other things, by the greatest dramatic poetry were mainly written for that public. The masterpieces of Greek drama were likewise originally produced for a mixed, rather than an exclusive, audience. So far as the theatre is concerned, the greatest art is apt to be the least secluded art. It is also significant, as Professor Alfred Harbage observed in *Shakespeare and the Rival Traditions* (New York, 1952), that the plays written for the open-air "public" theatres expressed healthier attitudes than those written for production in the expensive and therefore more exclusive "private" theatres.

These circumstances do not, of course, mean that those who wrote for the private theatres invariably fell below the moral and dramatic standards of those who wrote for the "public" theatres. The same writers often lent their talents to both enterprises, as Shakespeare did. Ultimately, after the death of Queen Elizabeth—which marks the close of the period covered in this volume—it was the audiences for the "private" theatres which prevailed with the authors, while the "public" theatre lost much of its following and influence as a result of the growth of Puritan hostility to the stage as an ungodly institution. The example of courtly or "coterie" playwriting by no means was unmitigatedly deplorable. On the contrary, courtly writing helped to refine popular playwriting by enriching its language and adding grace of manner and expression to its

vigor of feeling and action. Professor Harbage plausibly sur-
mises that Shakespeare owed a portion of his literary education to the coterie writers ("he may have owed something to
Marston as he certainly owed something to Lyly"). And it is
noteworthy that university-bred Elizabethan playwrights were
by no means content to be coterie writers; the most effective of
them, led by Christopher Marlowe, were responsible for many
triumphs of the popular stage—triumphs achieved without
renouncing the pretensions to learning, triumphs which called
attention to them as university men. In fact, Elizabethan
writers in general liked to associate themselves with humanistic
learning and embellish their writings with classical allusions.

The best Elizabethan plays therefore represent a fusion of
popular and learned elements, producing both theatre and
literature. In the best work of the age theatrical élan does
not banish the literary flair, and the authors' literary ambitions
do not inhibit theatrical vivacity and dramatic action. This
rare entente cordiale between dramatic literature and "theatre"
is apparent in the very structure and texture of the plays; most
thoroughly in the work of Shakespeare, who is not represented
in this volume, but conspicuously enough in much of the work
of his fellow playwrights. The progress of Elizabethan drama
from the courtly ventures of Lyly to the sturdier labors of
Kyd, Greene, Marlowe, Dekker, Heywood, and Jonson is
essentially a movement toward this synthesis of nonliterary
and literary constituents of drama and is reflected in Elizabethan drama's characteristic mingling of prose and verse
(and in the growing dramatic flexibility and expressiveness
of the latter), action and reflection, refined sensibility and raw
experience, tragedy and horseplay.

To these qualities we must add one more attribute: the
relatively free form or loose structure of most of the plays.
Their most obvious structural feature is their freedom of
movement. In this respect they were still medieval, following
the episodic organization of the passion plays or "mystery
play" cycles. Efforts to restrict the action and to tighten the
structure of Elizabethan plays were made in the name of the
unities of time, place, and action, for which Renaissance
scholars on the Continent had invoked the sanction of Aristotle, but the attempt was frustrated by the exuberance of the
Elizabethan age as reflected in the theatre by its playwrights,
performers, and audiences. Despite some lip service to classic
example, the ruling spirit of the Elizabethan stage was notably
romantic, manifesting itself in a flair for action, adventure,

and violence even in the midst of the highest literary intentions. In supplying plays for the popular theatre the playwrights did not shrink from showing even the most savage actions (the gouging out of Gloucester's eyes in *King Lear* is an example) instead of merely reporting them, as was the custom in classic drama. Thus they activated the rhetorical turbulence of Seneca, whom the Elizabethans acclaimed as the exemplary classic playwright and whom they presumably followed in favoring themes of revenge, sententious comment, and the agency of ghosts. This same tendency toward histrionic extravagance appeared in the dramatic posture and dialogue of typical Elizabethan characters.

Within a century the Elizabethan period in theatre was viewed with mixed feelings of admiration and dismay as an age of genius and poor taste. Even Shakespeare was not exempted from such censure, and it was considered essential to tamper with his dramatic action as well as his language for the benefit of presumably more refined audiences than he had been obliged to please in his day.

The content of Elizabethan plays conformed to the spirit of the age. Playwrights and their audiences were attracted to tales of comic or tragicomic adventure drawn from foreign literature; these were often folksy manners and beliefs, racy realistic speech, and vivid character drawing. The Elizabethans were also partial to chronicles of the English nation such as Holinshed's, replete with accounts of feudal warfare, national pacification, and the fatal course of lords and monarchs. The "history play," as exemplified by Marlowe's *Edward II* and Shakespeare's *Henry IV,* became a major genre. Parallel situations derived mainly from Roman history and recent events across the English Channel also occupied the theatre. The high tragedies of the age often had a context of history or legend that passed for history. This is true of Shakespeare's tragedies, with the exception of *Othello*—which, unlike *Hamlet, Macbeth, King Lear,* and *Antony and Cleopatra,* derives from an Italian *novella,* or tale, published in 1565. A strong pulse was provided by the vogue of revenge tragedies abounding in fury, intrigue, and bloodshed, in the manner of the first and greatest popular success in this genre, *The Spanish Tragedy,* and culminating in *Hamlet,* which for all its profundity contains more violence of passion and action (and more corpses) than most great tragedies of any other period. The more mundane substance of middle-class dramas such as *Arden of Feversham* was also far from placid, and the London life

exhibited in such plays as *The Shoemaker's Holiday* reveled
in the confident heartiness of the ordinary man.

A commonly entertained set of values provided a stimulus
to Elizabethan drama and an explicit or implicit rationale for
its action. A political and moral principle of proportion—or,
in Elizabethan parlance, "degree"—was official doctrine.
Everybody was to have, and keep, his place in the human world
ruled by kings as well as in the universe ruled by God to
ensure the stability and civil order of England. This principle
of "degree" received its clearest formulation from Shakespeare
in *Troilus and Cressida* when Ulysses undertakes to heal the
rift in the ranks of the Greek chieftains besieging Troy. In that
famous long speech (Act I, Scene 3, lines 81-137) the best
remembered lines define the ideal of "degree" as divinely ordained:

> The heavens themselves, the planets, and this centre
> Observe degree, priority, and place,
> Insisture, course, proportion, season, form,
> Office and custom, in all line of order . . . but when the planets
> In evil mixture to disorder wander,
> What plagues and what portents! what mutiny!
> What raging of the sea! shaking of earth!
> Commotion in the winds! frights, changes, horrors,
> Divert and crack, rend and deracinate
> The unity and married calm of states
> Quite from their fixture. O, when degree is shaked,
> Which is the ladder to all high designs,
> Then enterprise is sick! How could communities,
> Degrees in Schools and brotherhoods in cities
> Peaceful commerce from dividable shores,
> The primogenitive and due of birth,
> Prerogative of age, crowns, sceptres, laurels,
> But by degree, stand in authentic place?
> Take but degree away, untune that string,
> And hark, what discord follows. Each thing meets
> In mere oppugnancy. The bounded waters
> Should lift their bosoms higher than the shores
> And make a sop of all this solid globe.

Shakespeare was saying poetically not only what the English
humanist Sir Thomas Elyot had maintained much earlier in
prose in the first chapter of his influential *Book of the Governor*—"Take away order from all things, what should then remain"—but also what nearly everyone supposedly believed.

Exemplified in many a history play and many a tragedy too
(crudely in the early *Gorboduc* and superbly in *Macbeth* and
King Lear), "degree" was good monarchical dogma and gave
an ethical, as well as a metaphysical, coloring to Tudor absolutism. An entire nation, weary of civil strife and still mindful

of the fifteenth-century Wars of the Roses before the Tudor dynasty ascended the throne of England, could assent to the doctrine. Encapsulated in it, moreover, was the worth and self-respect of individuals on the lower rungs of the social ladder.

At the same time, with God's will, or as a result of a favorable turn of "Fortune's wheel," the doctrine of degree did not, and indeed could not, inhibit lawful ambition. Although the place occupied by man was justified as part of the world order known as the "great chain of being," Elizabethan man was constantly striving to leave *his* place in that chain—and succeeding. He could derive encouragement from the familiar spectacle of common men acquiring great wealth and social status even as poor farmers were simultaneously being reduced to beggary and vagabondage because the landed gentry was enclosing the common pasture land to satisfy the increasing market for wool. Enterprise in trade, augmented by profitable piracy called privateering and underwritten by sound business-men, spoliation of the land, and land grabbing, exploitation of monopolies, rivalries at court for patronage and political appointments, social climbing, and lavish displays of wealth and power characterized England as it moved out of the Middle Ages.

Elizabethan drama could not but reflect the dynamism of Elizabethan society. In it the sense of individual worth possessed even by the lowly characters we meet in the plays of Shakespeare and his contemporaries often translates itself into ambition, the will to self-realization, or the "will to power." Normal self-regard constitutes the vitality of the common man and the charm of romantic heroines in the comedies; overweening egotism or unlawful ambition is the *hamartia,* or tragic flaw, in the tragedies. Since Greek drama has been called "tragedy of fate," serious Elizabethan drama may, with as much warrant, be called "tragedy of the will." In many an Elizabethan play the action of an energetic will to a considerable degree accounts for the presence of protagonists who, for better or worse, are among the most arresting characters in all dramatic literature.

The dramatic interest of the age appeared, moreover, in the dual content of aristocratic and popular, literary and non-literary, entertainment. On the one hand the age luxuriated in courtly pageantry wherever the Queen resided or was entertained during her excursions to the country seat of some great nobleman. On the other hand the villages and country towns abounded in folk festivities, May-games, morris dancers, mummings, and other seasonal festivities not yet extirpated, although already severely deplored, by the Puritan sects which also frowned upon the theatrical profession. The passion for literary expression provoked the refined sonneteering of the age and the preciosity—known as euphuism and Arcadianism —of much of its prose and verse, as well as the vulgarity of humor and language.

For the theatre the ultimate result of regard for literary expression was the development of blank verse (unrhymed iambic pentameter verse with a shifting pause or "caesura") into the most distinguished and effective instrument of dramatic speech. At the same time a common penchant for traditional merrymaking, festivities, dances, jigs, popular ballads, jest books, folklore, buffoonery or clowning, sports, and pranks undoubtedly enlivened both dramatic action and dialogue and peopled the plays with the rustics or clowns who counterpoint the romantic sentiments of upper-class characters. Commoners also supplied farcical subplots to the exalted literary matter of Elizabethan comedies and tragedies.

This marriage of tastes, subject, and genres became an accepted convention in the courtliest of entertainments, approved by the Queen herself and by her "Master of Revels"; that Elizabeth should have had such an official in her menage is itself characteristic of the age. And characteristic, too, was the fact that in courtly revels such as those with which Elizabeth was entertained by her favorite, the Earl of Leicester, at his country seat Kenilworth, hearty rustic pastimes commingled with the mythological pageants. If a carefree blending of styles, plots, and character types could cause considerable confusion or inchoateness in Elizabethan drama, it also accounted for the variety and liveliness associated with the theatre of the age. A general spirit of holiday was one of the Elizabethan theatre's most characteristic features, as pleasing to its patrons as it was dismaying to its Puritan censors.

The theatre shared in this common interest, so that ample and attractive playhouses, such as the Globe and the Fortune, began to be erected in the environs of London. (Not in the city proper because of the opposition of the city fathers, the London Council, and the enmity of Puritan preachers who considered the theatre a corrupting influence, but on the south bank of the Thames, which lay outside the jurisdiction of the Council.) In the last quarter of the sixteenth century London had become an important center of European trade and manufacture, and playgoing was one of its principal sources of entertainment. From two to five stage companies supplied the growing demand for it, keeping many writers occupied writing new plays for the actors. During the three years 1598–1600 it is known that the playwright Thomas Dekker supplied one company, the Lord Admiral's Men, with eight plays (at about six pounds per play) and collaborated on twenty-four others. Speed of composition was always a desideratum during the period, plays apparently being fabricated in a fortnight when the demand was urgent. (Division of the public into common playgoers and gentlemen did not become marked until the reign of Elizabeth's successor, James I, when "public" theatres began to lose their audience while "private" theatres such as the Blackfriars, owned by Shakespeare's company, attracted the fashionable part of London's population.)

The expansion of theatrical activity in England was associated with the growth of theatrical companies, patronage to give them respectability and status, and playhouses to accommodate their performances. First, in 1574, the Earl of Leicester enabled his players, or "servants," to acquire a patent (or license) to perform plays. In 1576, opposition to productions within London proper led the manager of Leicester's Company, James Burbage, to build his playhouse, called the Theatre, outside the city boundaries, in Shoreditch; and another theatre, the Curtain, rose by its side in 1577. Some years later England's theatrical center shifted from Shoreditch to the south side of the Thames. About 1587 the theatrical manager Philip Henslowe built the Rose on the Bankside, and the Swan was also erected there in 1595. In 1599 James Burbage's two sons, Cuthbert and Richard, the famous actor who played Shakespeare's tragic roles, pulled down their late father's Theatre in Shoreditch and with its timbers built the Globe on the Bankside. And in 1600 the theatrical entrepreneur Philip Henslowe, and the actor Edward Alleyn, who played the heroic roles in Marlowe's *Tamburlaine* and *Doctor Faustus,* built the Fortune near the northwest boundary of London. Other public playhouses were erected after Queen Elizabeth's death—the Red Bull in 1606 and the Hope in 1613.

The theatre, as L. G. Salingar of Cambridge University puts it, was indeed "the point of closest contact between humanism and popular taste." (*The Age of Shakespeare,* London, 1955.) Although some plays were written especially for the universities, the law schools known as the Inns of Court, and the court, most of them were produced by commercial managements for the general public in the so-called public theatres. Here the majority of the playgoers, called the ground-lings, stood on the ground in the pit for a penny while the better-suited public occupied the balconies, and some gallants sat on the stage itself. The playhouse, a tall wooden structure accommodating several galleries, was itself a small world with respect to many of its features as well as its mixed audiences. Open to the sky except for a roof over the top gallery and a portion of the stage, the "yard" where the groundlings stood was uncovered and the stage, on which the performances were given in the afternoon, was illuminated by natural light. (Artificial light was used only in the completely covered "private" theatres.) No curtain separated spectators from the raised stage, and the platform on which most of the stage action was played projected into the auditorium far enough to be surrounded on three sides by the public.

Actor and playgoer were, then, on terms of considerable intimacy, and this relationship was especially emphasized whenever the actor spoke a monologue, soliloquized, or delivered himself of an "aside." Whatever the author's motivation for employing these standard devices of Elizabethan playwriting (and they were conducive to the writing and successful delivery of superb poetry and sparkling wit as well as to the efficient revelation of a character's intentions, uncertainties, and inner struggles), their prevalence was plainly encouraged by the thrust of the platform stage and the arenalike character of the playhouse. At the same time, this stage provided several acting levels and areas at the back of the platform, by the doors opening on to it, and by a gallery above it, which could serve as an upper stage.

Specific features once ascribed to the Elizabethan stage have been called into question by contemporary scholarship, and it is a mistake to assume that there was one single, unvarying pattern for the Elizabethan playhouse. But whether or not it included an actual alcove or so-called inner stage and a real upper stage, there can be little question that it provided ample opportunity for effective movement by the actors and opportunities for stage processions. The illusion of a setting such as the battlements of a castle or walled city, the prow of a ship, or a balcony in Juliet's house could be formed from the various levels of the stage structure. A scene could be localized by movable set pieces and three-dimensionally built pieces, by a pavillion in the back of the stage, and by other stage properties, such as bedsteads, arbors, and tents, as were employed in the fifth act of *Richard III,* as well as by arranging groups of appropriately costumed actors with or without heraldic insignia, banners, and weapons. Localization was also established by dialogue and descriptive passages, which facilitated "scene changes" without requiring any laborious realistic alteration of settings and insured the rapid progress of dramatic action, one of the chief characteristics of Elizabethan drama.

Organized into companies of players under the protection of royalty or some powerful lord (Shakespeare's troupe was known as the Lord Chamberlain's Men until the new monarch, James I, took the actors into his own service in 1603 as the King's Men), the Elizabethan theatre flourished in London except in the period of the plague, when they were closed down. Hardly handicapped, it would seem, by restrictive measures, the absence of actresses (female roles were played by young apprentices to actors), and the necessity of submitting manuscripts of new plays to the scrutiny of the Master of the Revels, the players managed to present plays more outspoken, frivolous or weighty, complex and exacting than most modern pieces. Apparently directed by the playwrights themselves in many instances, the plays benefited from expert productions. Efficiently organized backstage, and well supplied with stage properties, lavishly costumed, and possessing means for producing sound effects and pyrotechnic displays, the Elizabethan acting companies won the approbation of the public and the esteem of the educated. Some of the actors gained a prestige comparable to that of the stars of the modern stage. Outstanding were Edward Alleyn, of the Lord Admiral's Men, and Richard Burbage, chief actor in Shakespeare's company, as tragedians; Thomas Pope (succeeded in 1603 by John Lowin) as a comedian; Robert Tarleton (?–1588), Will Kempe, and, after 1599, Robert Armin as farceurs, clowns, and vaudevillians. Apparently highly skilled in stage action, forceful in speech and gestures, and at their best combining character plausibility and a show of naturalness with stylization, they evidently made even moderately competent playwriting prevail on the stage; otherwise the success of much gimcrack dramaturgy and extravagances of plot and speech cannot be accounted for. The actors' importance cannot be overstated. They carried the Elizabethan drama forward from crude beginnings to later memorable, if often to our taste flawed, achievements. Ultimately, of course, the lasting worth of the plays depends on the literary as well as the dramatic talent and enterprise of their authors.

In mid-century dramatic writing there are two noteworthy

humanistic efforts to imitate Roman comedy, the schoolmaster Nicholas Udall's *Ralph Roister Doister,* produced between 1552 and 1554 at the Westminster School of which the scholarly Udall was headmaster, and *Gammer Gurton's Needle,* a more homespun work attributed to William Stevenson, a fellow of Christ's College, Cambridge. And one adaptation from the Italian poet Ariosto's *Gli Suppositi* made by George Gascoigne under the title of *The Supposes,* which was performed at Gray's Inn in 1566, makes vivacious use of disguises such as appear in later Elizabethan comedies, including Shakespeare's. One tragedy, *Gorboduc,* patterned by Thomas Norton and Thomas Sackville after Senecan drama for performance by the law students of the Inner Temple before the Queen in 1562, is noteworthy among the Senecan imitations favored by the educated before the advent of Marlowe and Shakespeare. *Gorboduc* was political drama and a warning against possible chaos in England if Elizabeth failed to marry and leave an heir to the throne. Most importantly, the play introduced blank verse to the British stage. Of all the early plays following Senecan play structure, *Gorboduc* was the most vigorous even if it too suffered from Senecan rhetoric and from the customary substitution of lengthy and turgid Messengers' reports for actual stage action.

A quarter of a century after the productions of *Gorboduc* and *The Supposes* begins the new age, when tragedy acquired its typical Elizabethan energy and comedy its no less characteristic vivacity. The tragic gambit is first played successfully by Thomas Kyd, whose *Spanish Tragedy* (*circa* 1587) activated all the impedimenta of Senecan revenge tragedy, and then by Christopher Marlowe, whose first produced play, *Tamburlaine,* studded its gory chronicle of a conqueror's climb to power with intoxicating dramatic poetry. Comedy is given stylistic grace about the same time by John Lyly (1554–1606), author of the early romantic play *Alexander and Campaspe* (c. 1584) in which Alexander the Great renounces his passion for the beautiful Campaspe when he discovers that she loves the painter Apelles, and *Endymion* (1587), in which Lyly flattered Queen Elizabeth by comparing her to the mythological figure of Cynthia, the virgin moon goddess, who falls in love with the young shepherd Endymion. The designer of pageants, George Peele (*circa* 1556–96), also known for an elevated Biblical drama, *David and Bethsabe,* enriches pastoral comedy with lyrical passages, mostly in riming measures, in his masquelike play *The Arrangement of Paris* (c. 1581-83), in which the judgment of Paris is reversed; the golden apple is awarded by the virgin goddess Diana to one of her nymphs called Eliza—a compliment, no doubt intentional, to Queen Elizabeth. Peele's livelier folk-play, *The Old Wives' Tale* (*circa* 1593) is also replete with musical verse and graceful fantasy.

Joining Lyly and Peele in the 1580's, the bohemian man about town and man of letters Robert Greene (1558–1592) cultivates a virtually new genre of romantic comedy in his two best-known dramatic pieces, *Friar Bacon and Friar Bungay* and *James IV*, by maneuvering two plots in the same work and thus attaining variety of interest. This kind of multiple structure, plot and subplot, became a favorite form of play construction in the Elizabethan theatre. In *Friar Bacon and Friar Bungay*, Greene blends a homely comedy of magic with a love story; in *James IV,* a pseudohistorical romance, he combines a variety of elements, including pageantry, song, and a wedding masque, as well as moral symbolism, to keep his public entertained and, presumably, instructed.

In brief, the operalike qualities of romantic Elizabethan comedy are quickly established in the work of these writers at the same time that the high matter and exalted tone of Elizabethan tragedy are realized in the serious plays. Also at this early period, comedy acquires charming characters, such as Greene's country girl Margaret in *Friar Bacon and Friar Bungay*, who may be considered prototypes of Shakespeare's delightful young heroines. With these works and some others—such as Henry Porter's brisk comedy *The Two Angry Women of Abington* and the anonymous crime play *Arden of Feversham* (published in 1592), which has the flavor of later Elizabethan middle-class drama, and a number of early examples of the Elizabethan genre of patriotic history plays, of which the anonymous *Famous Victories of Henry V* (*circa* 1588) is the best known—we get a comprehensive view of the landscape of Elizabethan dramatic literature. If it shows but few peaks, such as Marlowe's masterpieces, *Doctor Faustus* and *Edward II* (to which we could add substantially if we included the comedies, tragedies, and histories written by Shakespeare before the death of his Queen), all of it comprises an essential portion of the English heritage. *The Famous Victories of Henry V* is the predecessor of Shakespeare's Henry IV and Henry V plays. Other insufficiently known anonymous plays, such as *Woodstock* (*circa* 1592), and *The True Chronicle History of King Leir and His Three Daughters* (*circa* 1594) anticipated Shakespeare's *Richard III* and *King Lear.* These transitional works bear a relationship to the late medieval morality plays. Shakespeare himself reflects this transition and retains vestiges of this genre in *Richard III,* whose hero compares himself to the "Vice" character in the moralities when he says, in the first scene of Act III, "Thus, like the formal Vice, Iniquity, I moralize two meanings in one word."

The Elizabethan forerunners, moreover, were soon accompanied by the men of genius who made the age so illustrious. Among the forerunners themselves, Christopher Marlowe went on from the popular success of *Tamburlaine* to writing *Doctor Faustus* and *Edward II,* plays which exemplify his development of the Renaissance tragedy of intellectual ambition in the former and his deepening of the history play into character drama in the latter. By the time Marlowe's young flame is extinguished in 1593, Shakespeare has already won a reputation with a number of plays, and he is soon joined by other prominent successors of the generation of Lyly, Greene, Kyd, and Marlowe—most notably by Ben Jonson, whose early plays, *Every Man in His Humour* (1598) and *Every Man out of His Humour* (1599), carry realistic comedy and morality drama to a climactic intensity and satiric penetration unique in the history of the drama. With these youthful but immensely inventive and vigorous pieces Jonson is at the threshold of his fame as the author of his masterpieces *Volpone* (1606), *The Alchemist* (1610), and *Bartholomew Fair* (1614) during the reign of James I. Shakespeare, too, arrives at the zenith of his power in 1601 with the advent of *Hamlet,* while Gloriana still occupies the throne of England.

The achievement of this great age was *dual*—unbounded *theatrical* inventiveness and a virtuosity of *language,* combining uncommonly racy colloquial speech with majestic poetry, never again attained in the English-speaking theatre.

Elizabethan Drama

Arden of Feversham

ANONYMOUS

A genre of domestic, mainly middle-class drama arose early in the Elizabethan theatre, not too surprisingly when we consider the middle-class character of much religious and didactic drama of the medieval theatre which preceded the Elizabethan. *Arden of Feversham,* once attributed to Shakespeare and with more reason to Thomas Kyd, is the outstanding early representative of this subtragic species of drama.

It has been easy to underrate this play on the grounds of poor structure (a novelistic one), common if at times vivid characters, and the mediocrity of their motives and means: it is a sordid story they enact. The substance of the action, consisting of the efforts of an unfaithful wife and her lover to do away with the woman's husband with the help of hired murderers, brings the play closer to sensational journalism than to tragedy. But this atypical early work has over the years rightly acquired champions, such as the distinguished scholar Hardin Craig, who refers to it as "the great anonymous play" and declares that the story told by the Elizabethan chronicle writer Holinshed has in this play been transfigured "into moving tragedy, a masterpiece of psychological interpretation, which foreshadows *Macbeth*." (*The Literature of the English Renaissance*, New York, 1962, pp. 81-82). Earlier, Frederick S. Boas, who entertained a similar opinion (in *An Introduction to Tudor Drama*, Oxford, 1933), called the play "a deeply moving work of art" and especially praised the characterizations.

Moreover, this earliest extant domestic tragedy or quasi-tragedy may be regarded with approval, as Ashley Thorndike does (*Tragedy*, p. 110), for its "reaction from the royalties, marvels, and unrealities of the contemporary tragedy" of the last quarter of the sixteenth century. The Epilogue can be cited as a conscious "defiance of romanticism and the since well-worn creed of the realist":

1

> Gentlemen, we hope you'll pardon this naked tragedy,
> Wherein no filèd points are foisted in
> To make it gracious to the ear or eye;
> For simple truth is gracious enough,
> And needs no other points of glossing stuff.

This program is not followed effectively in all particulars, but it is realized especially well in the characterization of Arden's adulterous wife; "the greatest merit of the play lies in the portrait of Alice Arden, absorbed in a despicable passion, but cunning and unabashed, incomparably the most lifelike evil woman up to this time depicted in the drama." (Thorndike). Frederick S. Boas also gave special praise to the portrait of Alice Arden, "the bourgeoise Clytemnestra, as she has been called, who dares everything to satisfy her guilty passion" (p. 107), and who never falters in her determination to rid herself of her husband when, as he lies dying, she finishes him off with a dagger "for hindering Mosbie's love and mine."

To these claims of interest may be added the moral, if also somewhat flatly moralizing, stress on Arden's culpability as an economic malefactor (see especially Act IV, Scene 4, lines 211-63). Arden does not feel guilty for having seized a parcel of land by means that evidently have a thin show of legality, but he is guilty in the sight of heaven, and his murder is looked upon as divine retribution by the anonymous author. The intrusion of an economic factor into the play is a modern detail and an element of realism in the Elizabethan age, which was only too familiar with the enclosure of common land for private gain and with questionable monopolistic practices.

J. G.

Authorship. The authorship of *The Lamentable and True Tragedy of Master Arden of Feversham in Kent,* to give the play its full title, is open to conjecture. Edward Jacob, in his preface to the 1770 reprint, attributed the authorship to Shakespeare on rather scanty evidence. This view is no longer accepted. Modern scholars believe either that the play was written by an imitator of Thomas Kyd or that it was written by Kyd himself.

Date. The play was entered in the Stationers' Register on April 3, 1592, and printed later that year. This is the only factual evidence for ascertaining the date. About 1592, therefore, appears a reasonable date.

Text and Publishing Data. The first quarto (1592) was printed anonymously for Edward White. In 1599 a second quarto appeared, followed by a third quarto in 1633. This was the last printing of the play until Edward Jacob made his late-eighteenth century reprint, using the first quarto (Q1) as his source.

Sources. Arden of Feversham is based on an actual notorious murder committed in 1551. In the first edition of his *Chronicles* (1577) Holinshed gives a lengthy account of the murder, and it is this account which *Arden's* author used as his chief source. However, the play contains material not present in Holinshed's account: the role of Master Franklin, Arden's attitude of discounting any suggestions that his wife may be unfaithful, and the device of the fog to thwart the plans of the murderers. These suggest that either other accounts may have been used or that local legend added elements to the story.

Genre. The play is a domestic tragedy, the first extant example of this genre in Elizabethan drama. Domestic tragedy deals with tragic events in the lives of middle- or low-class families, usually centering on stories of murder or adultery drawn from actual happenings of the day.

W. G.

DRAMATIS PERSONAE

THOMAS ARDEN, Gentleman, of Feversham
FRANKLIN, his Friend
MOSBIE
CLARKE, a Painter
ADAM FOWLE, Landlord of the Flower-de-Luce
BRADSHAW, a Goldsmith
MICHAEL, Arden's Servant
GREENE
RICHARD REEDE, a Sailor
BLACK WILL } Murderers
SHAKEBAG
A PRENTICE
A FERRYMAN
LORD CHEINY
MAYOR OF FEVERSHAM
ALICE, Arden's Wife
SUSAN, Mosbie's Sister
ATTENDANTS ON LORD CHEINY
THE WATCH

ACT I

(Before and in ARDEN'S *house. Enter* ARDEN *and* FRANKLIN.)

FRANKLIN. Arden, cheer up thy spirits, and droop no more!
My gracious Lord, the Duke of Somerset,
Hath freely given to thee and to thy heirs,
By letters patents from his Majesty,[1]
All the lands of the Abbey of Feversham.
Here are the deeds,
  (Gives them.)
Sealed and subscribed with his name and the king's:
Read them, and leave this melancholy mood.

ARDEN. Franklin, thy love prolongs my weary life;
And but for thee how odious were this life,
That shows me nothing but torments my soul,
And those foul objects that offend mine eyes!
Which makes me wish that for this veil of heaven
The earth hung over my head and covered me.
Love-letters pass 'twixt Mosbie and my wife,
And they have privy meetings in the town:
Nay, on his finger did I spy the ring
Which at our marriage-day the priest put on.
Can any grief be half so great as this?

FRANKLIN. Comfort thyself, sweet friend; it is not strange
That women will be false and wavering.

ARDEN. Aye, but to dote on such a one as he
Is monstrous, Franklin, and intolerable.

FRANKLIN. Why, what is he?

ARDEN. A botcher,* and no better at the first;   a mender
Who, by base brokage getting some small stock,   or tailor
Crept into service of a nobleman,
And by his servile flattery and fawning
Is now become the steward of his house,
And bravely jets it* in his silken gown.   struts

FRANKLIN. No nobleman will countenance such a peasant.

ARDEN. Yes, the Lord Clifford, he that loves not me.

---

[1] The murder on which this play is based took place in 1551;
the king alluded to is Edward VI. Since at this time Edward was
a minor, the Duke of Somerset served as Lord Protector.

But through his favour let him not grow proud;
For were he by the Lord Protector backed,
He should not make me to be pointed at.
I am by birth a gentleman of blood,[2]
And that injurious ribald, that attempts
To violate my dear wife's chastity
(For dear I hold her love, as dear as heaven)
Shall on the bed which he thinks to defile
See his dissevered joints and sinews torn,
Whilst on the planchers* pants his weary body,   floor planks
Smeared in the channels of his lustful blood.
    FRANKLIN. Be patient, gentle friend, and learn of me
To ease thy grief and save her chastity:
Intreat her fair; sweet words are fittest engines
To race* the flint walls of a woman's breast.   raze
In any case be not too jealous,
Nor make no question of her love to thee;
But, as securely, presently* take horse,   immediately
And lie with me at London all this term;
For women, when they may, will not,
But, being kept back, straight grow outrageous.
    ARDEN. Though this abhors from reason,[3] yet I'll try it,
And call her forth and presently take leave.
How! Alice!

    (*Enter* ALICE.)

    ALICE. Husband, what mean you to get up so early?
Summer nights are short, and yet you rise ere day.
Had I been wake, you had not risen so soon.
    ARDEN. Sweet love, thou knowest that we two, Ovid-like,
Have often chid the morning when it 'gan to peep,
And often wished that dark night's purblind steeds
Would pull her by the purple mantle back,
And cast her in the ocean to her love.
But this night, sweet Alice, thou hast killed my heart:
I heard thee call on Mosbie in thy sleep.
    ALICE. 'Tis like I was asleep when I named him,
For being awake he comes not in my thoughts.
    ARDEN. Ay, but you started up and suddenly,
Instead of him, caught me about the neck.

      [2] From a good family.
      [3] Goes contrary to my reasoning.

ALICE. Instead of him? why, who was there but you?
And where but one is, how can I mistake?
   FRANKLIN. Arden, leave to urge her over-far.
   ARDEN. Nay, love, there is no credit in a dream;
Let it suffice I know thou lovest me well.
   ALICE. Now I remember whereupon it came:
Had we no talk of Mosbie yesternight?
   FRANKLIN. Mistress Alice, I heard you name him once
     or twice.
   ALICE. And thereof came it, and therefore blame not me.
   ARDEN. I know it did, and therefore let it pass.
I must to London, sweet Alice, presently.
   ALICE. But tell me, do you mean to stay there long?
   ARDEN. No longer there till my affairs be done.
   FRANKLIN. He will not stay above a month at most.
   ALICE. A month? ay me! Sweet Arden, come again
Within a day or two, or else I die.
   ARDEN. I cannot long be from thee, gentle Alice.
Whilst Michael fetch our horses from the field,
Franklin and I will down unto the quay;
For I have certain goods there to unload.
Meanwhile prepare our breakfast, gentle Alice;
For yet ere noon we'll take horse and away.

              (*Exeunt* ARDEN *and* FRANKLIN.)

   ALICE. Ere noon he means to take horse and away!
Sweet news is this. O that some airy spirit
Would in the shape and likeness of a horse
Gallop with Arden 'cross the Ocean,
And throw him from his back into the waves!
Sweet Mosbie is the man that hath my heart:
And he usurps it, having nought but this,
That I am tied to him by marriage.
Love is a God, and marriage is but words;
And therefore Mosbie's title is the best.
Tush! whether it be or no, he shall be mine,
In spite of him, of Hymen,* and of rites.   god of marriage

   (*Enter* ADAM *of the Flower-de-luce.*)

And here comes Adam of the Flower-de-luce;
I hope he brings me tidings of my love.
—How now, Adam, what is the news with you?
Be not afraid; my husband is now from home.

ADAM. He whom you wot* of, Mosbie, Mistress Alice, know
Is come to town, and sends you word by me
In any case you may not visit him.
　　ALICE. Not visit him?
　　ADAM. No, nor take no knowledge of his being here.
　　ALICE. But tell me, is he angry or displeased?
　　ADAM. It should seem so, for he is wondrous sad.
　　ALICE. Were he as mad as raving Hercules,
I'll see him, I; and were thy house of force,*　　　　　fortified
These hands of mine should race* it to the ground,　　　raze
Unless that thou wouldst bring me to my love.
　　ADAM. Nay, and you be so impatient, I'll be gone.
　　ALICE. Stay, Adam, stay; thou wert wont to be my friend.
Ask Mosbie how I have incurred his wrath;
Bear him from me these pair of silver dice
With which we played for kisses many a time,
And when I lost, I won, and so did he;—
Such winning and such losing Jove send me!
And bid him, if his love do not decline,
To come this morning but along my door,
And as a stranger but salute me there:
This may he do without suspect* or fear.　　　　　　suspicion
　　ADAM. I'll tell him what you say, and so farewell.

　　　　　　　　　　　　　　　　　　　　(*Exit* ADAM.)

　　ALICE. Do, and one day I'll make amends for all.—
I know he loves me well, but dares not come,
Because my husband is so jealous,
And these my narrow-prying neighbours blab,
Hinder our meetings when we would confer.
But, if I live, that block shall be removed,
And, Mosbie, thou that comes to me by stealth,
Shalt neither fear the biting speech of men,
Nor Arden's looks; as surely shall he die
As I abhor him and love only thee.

　　(*Enter* MICHAEL.)

How now, Michael, whither are you going?
　　MICHAEL. To fetch my master's nag.
I hope you'll think on me.
　　ALICE. Ay; but, Michael, see you keep your oath,
And be as secret as you are resolute.

MICHAEL. I'll see he shall not live above a week.

ALICE. On that condition, Michael, here's my hand:
None shall have Mosbie's sister but thyself.

MICHAEL. I understand the painter here hard by
Hath made report that he and Sue is sure.*   betrothed

ALICE. There's no such matter, Michael; believe it not.

MICHAEL. But he hath sent a dagger sticking in a heart,
With a verse or two stolen from a painted cloth,
The which I hear the wench keeps in her chest.
Well, let her keep it! I shall find a fellow
That can both write and read and make rhyme too.
And if I do—well, I say no more:
I'll send from London such a taunting letter
As* she shall eat the heart he sent with salt   that
And fling the dagger at the painter's head.

ALICE. What needs all this? I say that Susan's thine.

MICHAEL. Why, then I say that I will kill my master,
Or anything that you will have me do.

ALICE. But, Michael, see you do it cunningly.

MICHAEL. Why, say I should be took, I'll ne'er confess
That you know anything; and Susan, being a maid,
May beg me from the gallows of the sheriff.

ALICE. Trust not to that, Michael.

MICHAEL. You cannot tell me, I have seen it, I.
But, mistress, tell her, whether I live or die,
I'll make more worth than twenty painters can;
For I will rid mine elder brother away,
And then the farm of Bolton is mine own.
Who would not venture upon house and land,
When he may have it for a right down* blow?   downright

(*Enter* MOSBIE.)

ALICE. Yonder comes Mosbie. Michael, get thee gone,
And let not him nor any know thy drifts.

        (*Exit* MICHAEL.)

Mosbie, my love!

MOSBIE. Away, I say, and talk not to me now.

ALICE. A word or two, sweet heart, and then I will.

'Tis yet but early days,* thou needst not fear.   early in the day
   MOSBIE. Where is your husband?
   ALICE. 'Tis now high water, and he is at the quay.
   MOSBIE. There let him be; henceforward know me not.
   ALICE. Is this the end of all thy solemn oaths?
Is this the fruit thy reconcilement buds?
Have I for this given thee so many favours,
Incurred my husband's hate, and, out alas!
Made shipwreck of mine honour for thy sake?
And dost thou say "henceforward know me not"?
Remember, when I lock'd thee in my closet,*   private room
What were thy words and mine; did we not both
Decree to murder Arden in the night?
The heavens can witness, and the world can tell,
Before I saw that falsehood look of thine,
'Fore I was tangled with thy 'ticing* speech,   enticing
Arden to me was dearer than my soul,—
And shall be still: base peasant, get thee gone,
And boast not of thy conquest over me,
Gotten by witchcraft and mere* sorcery!   absolute
For what hast thou to countenance my love,
Being descended of a noble house,
And matched already with a gentleman
Whose servant thou may'st be!—and so farewell.
   MOSBIE. Ungentle and unkind Alice, now I see
That which I ever feared, and find too true:
A woman's love is as the lightning-flame,
Which even in bursting forth consumes itself.
To try thy constancy have I been strange;
Would I had never tried, but lived in hope!
   ALICE. What need'st thou try me whom thou ne'er
     found false?
   MOSBIE. Yet pardon me, for love is jealous.
   ALICE. So lists* the sailor to the mermaid's song,   listens
So looks the traveller to the basilisk:
I am content for to be reconciled,
And that, I know, will be mine overthrow.
   MOSBIE. Thine overthrow? first let the world dissolve.
   ALICE. Nay, Mosbie, let me still enjoy thy love,
And happen what will, I am resolute.
My saving husband hoards up bags of gold
To make our children rich, and now is he
Gone to unload the goods that shall be thine,
And he and Franklin will to London straight.

MOSBIE. To London, Alice? if thou'lt be ruled by me,
We'll make him sure enough for coming there.
    ALICE. Ah, would we could!
    MOSBIE. I happened on a painter yesternight,
The only cunning man of Christendom;
For he can temper poison with his oil,
That whoso looks upon the work he draws
Shall, with the beams that issue from his* sight,   its
Suck venom to his breast and slay himself.
Sweet Alice, he shall draw thy counterfeit,
That Arden may, by gazing on it, perish.
    ALICE. Ay, but Mosbie, that is dangerous,
For thou, or I, or any other else,
Coming into the chamber where it hangs, may die.
    MOSBIE. Ay, but we'll have it covered with a cloth
And hung up in the study for himself.
    ALICE. It may not be, for when the picture's drawn,
Arden, I know, will come and show it me.
    MOSBIE. Fear not; we'll have that shall serve the turn.
    (*They cross the stage.*)
This is the painter's house; I'll call him forth.
    ALICE. But, Mosbie, I'll have no such picture, I.
    MOSBIE. I pray thee leave it to my discretion.
How! Clarke!

    (*Enter* CLARKE.)

Oh, you are an honest man of your word! you served me well.
    CLARKE. Why, sir, I'll do it for you at any time,
Provided, as you have given your word,
I may have Susan Mosbie to my wife.
For, as sharp-witted poets, whose sweet verse
Make heavenly gods break off their nectar draughts
And lay their ears down to the lowly earth,
Use humble promise to their sacred Muse,
So we that are the poets' favourites
Must have a love: ay, Love is the painter's muse,
That makes him frame a speaking countenance,
A weeping eye that witnesses heart's grief.
Then tell me, Master Mosbie, shall I have her?
    ALICE. 'Tis pity but he should; he'll use her well.
    MOSBIE. Clarke, here's my hand: my sister shall be thine.
    CLARKE. Then, brother, to requite this courtesy,
You shall command my life, my skill, and all.

ALICE. Ah, that thou couldst be secret.

MOSBIE. Fear him not; leave; I have talked sufficient.

CLARKE. You know not me that ask such questions.
Let it suffice I know you love him well,
And fain would have your husband made away:
Wherein, trust me, you show a noble mind,
That rather than you'll live with him you hate,
You'll venture life, and die with him you love.
The like will I do for my Susan's sake.

ALICE. Yet nothing could enforce me to the deed
But Mosbie's love. Might I without control
Enjoy thee still, then Arden should not die:
But seeing I cannot, therefore let him die.

MOSBIE. Enough, sweet Alice; thy kind words makes
    me melt.
Your trick of poisoned pictures we dislike;
Some other poison would do better far.

ALICE. Ay, such as might be put into his broth,
And yet in taste not to be found at all.

CLARKE. I know your mind, and here I have it for you.
Put but a dram of this into his drink,
Or any kind of broth that he shall eat,
And he shall die within an hour after.

ALICE. As I am a gentlewoman, Clarke, next day
Thou and Susan shall be married.

MOSBIE. And I'll make her dowry more than I'll talk of,
    Clarke.

CLARKE. Yonder's your husband. Mosbie, I'll be gone.

(*Enter* ARDEN *and* FRANKLIN.)

ALICE. In good time see where my husband comes.
Master Mosbie, ask him the question yourself.

                                              (*Exit* CLARKE.)

MOSBIE. Master Arden, being at London yesternight,
The Abbey lands, whereof you are now possessed,
Were offered me on some occasion
By Greene, one of Sir Antony Ager's men:
I pray you, sir, tell me, are not the lands yours?
Hath any other interest herein?

ARDEN. Mosbie, that question we'll decide anon.
Alice, make ready my breakfast, I must hence.

                                               (*Exit* ALICE.)

As for the lands, Mosbie, they are mine

By letters patents from his Majesty.
But I must have a mandate for my wife;
They say you seek to rob me of her love:
Villain, what makes thou in her company?
She's no companion for so base a groom.

MOSBIE. Arden, I thought not on her, I came to thee;
But rather than I pocket up this wrong——

FRANKLIN. What will you do, sir?

MOSBIE. Revenge it on the proudest of you both.

(ARDEN *draws forth* MOSBIE'S *sword*.)

ARDEN. So, sirrah; you may not wear a sword,
The statute makes against artificers;[4]
I warrant that I do.[5] Now use your bodkin,
Your Spanish needle, and your pressing iron,
For this shall go with me; and mark my words,
You goodman botcher, 'tis to you I speak:
The next time that I take thee near my house,
Instead of legs I'll make thee crawl on stumps.

MOSBIE. Ah, Master Arden, you have injured me:
I do appeal to God and to the world.

FRANKLIN. Why, canst thou deny thou wert a botcher once?

MOSBIE. Measure me what I am, not what I was.

ARDEN. Why, what art thou now but a velvet drudge,
A cheating steward, and base-minded peasant?

MOSBIE. Arden, now thou hast belched and vomited
The rancorous venom of thy mis-swoll'n heart,
Hear me but speak: as I intend to live
With God and his elected saints in heaven,
I never meant more to solicit her;
And that she knows, and all the world shall see.
I loved her once;—sweet Arden, pardon me,
I could not choose, her beauty fired my heart!
But time hath quenched these over-raging coals;
And, Arden, though I now frequent thy house,
'Tis for my sister's sake, her waiting-maid,
And not for hers. Mayest thou enjoy her long:
Hell-fire and wrathful vengeance light on me,
If I dishonour her or injure thee.

ARDEN. Mosbie, with these thy protestations
The deadly hatred of my heart's appeased,

---

[4] The law forbids craftsmen to wear swords.
[5] The law justifies what I am doing.

And thou and I'll be friends, if this prove true.
As for the base terms I gave thee late,
Forget them, Mosbie: I had cause to speak,
When all the knights and gentlemen of Kent
Make common table-talk of her and thee.

   MOSBIE. Who lives that is not touched with slanderous
     tongues?

   FRANKLIN. Then, Mosbie, to eschew the speech of men,
Upon whose general bruit* all honour hangs,   **report**
Forbear his house.

   ARDEN. Forbear it! nay, rather frequent it more:
The world shall see that I distrust her not.
To warn him on the sudden from my house
Were to confirm the rumour that is grown.

   MOSBIE. By my faith, sir, you say true,
And therefore will I sojourn here a while,
Until our enemies have talked their fill;
And then, I hope, they'll cease, and at last confess
How causeless they have injured her and me.

   ARDEN. And I will lie at London all this term
To let them see how light I weigh their words.

   (*They go into the house. Enter* ALICE.)

   ALICE. Husband, sit down; your breakfast will be cold.
   ARDEN. Come, Master Mosbie, will you sit with us?
   MOSBIE. I cannot eat, but I'll sit for company.
   ARDEN. Sirrah Michael, see our horse be ready.
   ALICE. Husband, why pause ye? why eat you not?
   ARDEN. I am not well; there's something in this broth
That is not wholesome; didst thou make it, Alice?
   ALICE. I did, and that's the cause it likes not you.
   (*She throws the broth on the ground.*)
There's nothing that I do can please your taste;
You were best to say I would have poisoned you.
I cannot speak or cast aside my eye,
But he imagines I have stepped awry.
Here's he that you cast in my teeth so oft:
Now will I be convinced or purge myself.
I charge thee speak to this mistrustful man,
Thou that wouldst see me hang, thou, Mosbie, thou:
What favour hast thou had more than a kiss,[6]

     [6] Kissing during this period was frequently nothing more than
an act of greeting.

At coming or departing from the town?

MOSBIE. You wrong yourself and me to cast these doubts:
Your loving husband is not jealous.

ARDEN. Why, gentle Mistress Alice, cannot I be ill
But you'll accuse yourself?
Franklin, thou hast a box of mithridate;*   antidote
I'll take a little to prevent the worst.   against poison

FRANKLIN. Do so, and let us presently* take horse; immediately
My life for yours, ye shall do well enough.

ALICE. Give me a spoon, I'll eat of it myself;
Would it were full of poison to the brim,
Then should my cares and troubles have an end.
Was ever silly* woman so tormented?   simple

ARDEN. Be patient, sweet love; I mistrust not thee.

ALICE. God will revenge it, Arden, if thou dost;
For never woman loved her husband better
Than I do thee.

ARDEN. I know it, sweet Alice; cease to complain,
Lest that in tears I answer thee again.

FRANKLIN. Come, leave this dallying, and let us away.

ALICE. Forbear to wound me with that bitter word;
Arden shall go to London in my arms.

ARDEN. Loth am I to depart, yet I must go.

ALICE. Wilt thou to London, then, and leave me here?
Ah, if thou love me, gentle Arden, stay.
Yet, if thy business be of great import
Go, if thou wilt, I'll bear it as I may;
But write from London to me every week,
Nay, every day, and stay no longer there
Than thou must needs, lest that I die for sorrow.

ARDEN. I'll write unto thee every other tide,*   that is,
And so farewell, sweet Alice, till we meet next.   frequently

ALICE. Farewell, husband, seeing you'll have it so;
And, Master Franklin, seeing you take him hence,
In hope you'll hasten him home, I'll give you this.
(*She kisses him.*)

FRANKLIN. And if he stay, the fault shall not be mine.
Mosbie, farewell, and see you keep your oath.

MOSBIE. I hope he is not jealous of me now.

ARDEN. No, Mosbie, no; hereafter think of me
As of your dearest friend, and so farewell.
         (*Exeunt* ARDEN, FRANKLIN, *and* MICHAEL.)

ALICE. I am glad he is gone; he was about to stay,
But did you mark me then how I brake off?

MOSBIE. Ay, Alice, and it was cunningly performed.
But what a villain is that painter Clarke!

ALICE. Was it not a goodly poison that he gave?
Why, he's as well now as he was before.
It should have been some fine confection
That might have given the broth some dainty taste:
This powder was too gross and populous.*   thick

MOSBIE. But had he eaten but three spoonfuls more,
Then had he died and our love continued.

ALICE. Why, so it shall, Mosbie, albeit he live.

MOSBIE. It is impossible, for I have sworn
Never hereafter to solicit thee,
Or, whilst he lives, once more importune thee.

ALICE. Thou shalt not need, I will importune thee.
What? shall an oath make thee forsake my love?
As if I have not sworn as much myself
And given my hand unto him in the church!
Tush, Mosbie; oaths are words, and words is wind,
And wind is mutable: then, I conclude,
'Tis childishness to stand upon an oath.

MOSBIE. Well proved, Mistress Alice; yet by your leave
I'll keep mine unbroken whilst he lives.

ALICE. Ay, do, and spare not, his time is but short;
For if thou beest as resolute as I,
We'll have him murdered as he walks the streets.
In London many alehouse ruffians keep,*   lodge
Which, as I hear, will murder men for gold.
They shall be soundly fee'd to pay him home.

(*Enter* GREENE.)

MOSBIE. Alice, what's he that comes yonder? knowest thou
   him?

ALICE. Mosbie, be gone: I hope 'tis one that comes
To put in practice our intended drifts.

                                            (*Exit* MOSBIE.)

GREENE. Mistress Arden, you are well met.
I am sorry that your husband is from home,
When as my purposed journey was to him:
Yet all my labour is not spent in vain,
For I suppose that you can full discourse
And flat resolve* me of the thing I seek.   clearly answer

ALICE. What is it, Master Greene? If that I may
Or can with safety, I will answer you.

GREENE. I heard your husband hath the grant of late,
Confirmed by letters patents from the king,

Of all the lands of the Abbey of Feversham,
Generally intitled,* so that all former grants   deeded
Are cut off; whereof I myself had one;
But now my interest by that is void.
This is all, Mistress Arden; is it true or no?
    ALICE. True, Master Greene; the lands are his in state,
And whatsoever leases were before
Are void for term of Master Arden's life;
He hath the grant under the Chancery seal.
    GREENE. Pardon me, Mistress Arden, I must speak,
For I am touched. Your husband doth me wrong
To wring me from the little land I have.
My living is my life, and only that
Resteth remainder of my portion.
Desire of wealth is endless in his mind,
And he is greedy-gaping still* for gain;   always
Nor cares he though young gentlemen do beg,
So he may scrape and hoard up in his pouch.
But, seeing he hath ta'en my lands, I'll value life
As careless as he is careful for to get:
And tell him this from me, I'll be revenged,
And so as he shall wish the Abbey lands
Had rested still within their former state.
    ALICE. Alas, poor gentleman, I pity you,
And woe is me that any man should want!
God knows 'tis not my fault; but wonder not
Though he be hard to others, when to me,—
Ah, Master Greene, God knows how I am used.
    GREENE. Why, Mistress Arden, can the crabbed churl
Use you unkindly? respects he not your birth,
Your honourable friends, nor what you brought?
Why, all Kent knows your parentage and what you are.
    ALICE. Ah, Master Greene, be it spoken in secret here,
I never live good day with him alone:
When he's at home, then have I froward* looks,   wicked
Hard words and blows to mend the match withal;
And though I might content as good a man,
Yet doth he keep in every corner trulls;
And when he's weary with his trugs* at home,   prostitutes
Then rides he straight to London; there, forsooth,
He revels it among such filthy ones
As counsels him to make away his wife.
Thus live I daily in continual fear,
In sorrow; so despairing of redress

As every day I wish with hearty prayer
That he or I were taken forth the world.

    GREENE. Now trust me, Mistress Alice, it grieveth me
So fair a creature should be so abused.
Why, who would have thought the civil sir so sullen?
He looks so smoothly. Now, fie upon him, churl!
And if he live a day, he lives too long.
But frolic, woman! I shall be the man
Shall set you free from all this discontent;
And if the churl deny my interest
And will not yield my lease into my hand,
I'll pay him home, whatever hap to me.*   regardless of risk
    ALICE. But speak you as you think?
    GREENE. Ay, God's my witness, I mean plain dealing,
For I had rather die than lose my land.
    ALICE. Then, Master Greene, be counsellèd by me:
Endanger not yourself for such a churl,
But hire some cutter* for to cut him short,   cutthroat
And here's ten pound to wager them withal;
When he is dead, you shall have twenty more,
And the lands whereof my husband is possess'd
Shall be intitled as they were before.
    GREENE. Will you keep promise with me?
    ALICE. Or count me false and perjured whilst I live.
    GREENE. Then here's my hand, I'll have him so dispatched.
I'll up to London straight, I'll thither post,
And never rest till I have compassed* it.   accomplished
Till then farewell.
    ALICE. Good fortune follow all your forward thoughts.
                   (*Exit* GREENE.)
And whosoever doth attempt the deed,
A happy hand I wish, and so farewell.—
All this goes well: Mosbie, I long for thee
To let thee know all that I have contrived.

(ALICE *stands before the house. Enter* MOSBIE *and* CLARKE.)

    MOSBIE. How, now, Alice, what's the news?
    ALICE. Such as will content thee well, sweetheart.
    MOSBIE. Well, let them pass a while, and tell me, Alice,
How have you dealt and tempered with* my sister? worked upon
What, will she have my neighbour Clarke, or no?
    ALICE. What, Master Mosbie! let him woo himself!
Think you that maids look not for fair words?

Go to her, Clarke; she's all alone within;
Michael my man is clean out of her books.

CLARKE. I thank you, Mistress Arden, I will in;
And if fair Susan and I can make a gree,[7]
You shall command me to the uttermost,
As far as either goods or life may stretch.
(*Goes into the house.*)

MOSBIE. Now, Alice, let's hear thy news.

ALICE. They be so good that I must laugh for joy,
Before I can begin to tell my tale.

MOSBIE. Let's hear them, that I may laugh for company.

ALICE. This morning, Master Greene, Dick Greene, I mean,
From whom my husband had the Abbey land,
Came hither, railing, for to know the truth
Whether my husband had the lands by grant.
I told him all, whereat he stormed amain*   violently
And swore he would cry quittance with* the churl   get even with
And, if he did deny his interest,
Stab him, whatsoever did befall himself.
Whenas* I saw his choler thus to rise,   when
I whetted on the gentleman with words;
And, to conclude, Mosbie, at last we grew
To composition for my husband's death.
I gave him ten pound for to hire knaves,
By some device to make away the churl;
When he is dead, he should have twenty more
And repossess his former lands again.
On this we 'greed, and he is ridden straight
To London, for to bring his death about.

MOSBIE. But call you this good news?

ALICE. Ay, sweetheart, be they not?

MOSBIE. 'Twere cheerful news to hear the churl were dead;
But trust me, Alice, I take it passing ill
You would be so forgetful of our state
To make recount of it to every groom.
What! to acquaint each stranger with our drifts,
Chiefly in case of murder, why, 'tis the way
To make it open unto Arden's self
And bring thyself and me to ruin both.
Forewarned, forearmed; who threats his enemy,
Lends him a sword to guard himself withal.

ALICE. I did it for the best.

[7] Come to an agreement.

MOSBIE. Well, seeing 'tis done, cheerly* let it pass.   cheerfully
You know this Greene; is he not religious?*   conscientious
A man, I guess, of great devotion?
    ALICE. He is.
    MOSBIE. Then, sweet Alice, let it pass: I have a drift*   scheme
Will quiet all, whatever is amiss.

(*Enter* CLARKE *and* SUSAN.)

    ALICE. How now, Clarke? have you found me false?
Did I not plead the matter hard for you?
    CLARKE. You did.
    MOSBIE. And what? wilt be a match?
    CLARKE. A match, i' faith, sir: ay, the day is mine.
The painter lays his colours to the life,
His pencil draws no shadows in his love.
Susan is mine.
    ALICE. You make her blush.
    MOSBIE. What, sister, is it Clarke must be the man?
    SUSAN. It resteth in your grant; some words are past,
And haply* we be grown unto a match,   perhaps
If you be willing that it shall be so.
    MOSBIE. Ah, Master Clarke, it resteth at my grant:
You see my sister's yet at my dispose,
But, so you'll grant me one thing I shall ask,
I am content my sister shall be yours.
    CLARKE. What is it, Master Mosbie?
    MOSBIE. I do remember once in secret talk
You told me how you could compound by art
A crucifix impoisoned,
That whoso look upon it should wax* blind   become
And with the scent be stifled, that ere long
He should die poisoned that did view it well.
I would have you make me such a crucifix,
And then I'll grant my sister shall be yours.
    CLARKE. Though I am loth, because it toucheth life,
Yet, rather or* I'll leave sweet Susan's love,   before
I'll do it, and with all the haste I may.
But for whom is it?
    ALICE. Leave that to us. Why, Clarke, is it possible
That you should paint and draw it out yourself,
The colours being baleful and impoisoned,
And no ways prejudice* yourself withal?   endanger

MOSBIE. Well questioned, Alice; Clarke, how answer you
    that?
CLARKE. Very easily: I'll tell you straight
How I do work of these impoisoned drugs.
I fasten on my spectacles so close
As nothing can any way offend my sight;
Then, as I put a leaf within my nose,
So put I rhubarb to avoid the smell,
And softly as another work I paint.
    MOSBIE. 'Tis very well; but against when shall I have it?
    CLARKE. Within this ten days.
    MOSBIE.   'Twill serve the turn.
Now, Alice, let's in and see what cheer you keep.
I hope, now Master Arden is from home,
You'll give me leave to play your husband's part.
    ALICE. Mosbie, you know, who's master of my heart,
He well may be the master of the house.

                                   (*Exeunt.*)

ACT II

Scene 1

(*Country between Feversham and London. Enter* GREENE
and BRADSHAW.)

BRADSHAW. See you them that comes yonder, Master
    Greene?
GREENE. Ay, very well: do you know them?

(*Enter* BLACK WILL *and* SHAKEBAG.)

BRADSHAW. The one I know not, but he seems a knave
Chiefly for bearing the other company;
For such a slave, so vile a rogue as he,
Lives not again upon the earth.
Black Will is his name. I tell you, Master Greene,
At Boulogne he and I were fellow-soldiers,
Where he played such pranks
As all the camp feared him for his villainy.
I warrant you he bears so bad a mind
That for a crown he'll murder any man.
    GREENE. The fitter is he for my purpose, marry!
    WILL. How now, fellow Bradshaw? Whither away so early?
    BRADSHAW. O Will, times are changed: no fellows now,

Though we were once together in the field;
Yet thy friend to do thee any good I can.

WILL. Why, Bradshaw, was not thou and I fellow-soldiers
at Boulogne, where I was a corporal, and thou but a base mercenary groom? No fellows now! because you are a goldsmith
and have a little plate in your shop! You were glad to call me
"fellow Will," and with a curtsey to the earth, "One snatch,
good corporal," when I stole the half ox from John the vic-
tualer, and domineer'd* with it amongst good fellows in   feasted
one night.

BRADSHAW. Ay, Will, those days are past with me.

WILL. Ay, but they be not past with me, for I keep that
same honourable mind still. Good neighbour Bradshaw, you
are too proud to be my fellow; but were it not that I see more
company coming down the hill, I would be fellows with you
once more, and share crowns with you too. But let that pass,
and tell me whither you go.

BRADSHAW. To London, Will, about a piece of service,
Wherein haply thou mayest pleasure me.

WILL. What is it?

BRADSHAW. Of late Lord Cheiny lost some plate,
Which one did bring and sold it at my shop,
Saying he served Sir Antony Cooke.
A search was made, the plate was found with me,
And I am bound to answer at the 'size.*   assizes
Now, Lord Cheiny solemnly vows, if law
Will serve him, he'll hang me for his plate.
Now I am going to London upon hope
To find the fellow. Now, Will, I know
Thou art acquainted with such companions.

WILL. What manner of man was he?

BRADSHAW. A lean-faced writhen* knave,   twisted
Hawk-nosed and very hollow-eyed,
With mighty furrows in his stormy brows;
Long hair down his shoulders curled;
His chin was bare, but on his upper lip
A mutchado,* which he wound about his ear.   mustache

WILL. What apparel had he?

BRADSHAW. A watchet* satin doublet all-to* torn,   light blue/
The inner side did bear the greater show;   completely
A pair of thread-bare velvet hose, seam rent,
A worsted stocking rent above the shoe,
A livery cloak, but all the lace was off;
'Twas bad, but yet it served to hide the plate.

WILL. Sirrah Shakebag, canst thou remember since we trolled the bowl[8] at Sittingburgh, where I broke the tapster's head of the Lion with a cudgel stick?

SHAKEBAG. Ay, very well, Will.

WILL. Why, it was with the money that the plate was sold for. Sirrah Bradshaw, what wilt thou give him that can tell thee who sold thy plate?

BRADSHAW. Who, I pray thee, good Will?

WILL. Why, 'twas one Jack Fitten. He's now in Newgate for stealing a horse, and shall be arraigned the next 'size.

BRADSHAW. Why, then let Lord Cheiny seek Jack Fitten forth,
For I'll back and tell him who robbed him of his plate.
This cheers my heart; Master Greene, I'll leave you,
For I must to the Isle of Sheppy with speed.

GREENE. Before you go, let me entreat you
To carry this letter to Mistress Arden of Feversham
And humbly recommend me to herself.

BRADSHAW. That will I, Master Greene, and so farewell.
Here, Will, there's a crown for thy good news.

(*Exit* BRADSHAW.)

WILL. Farewell, Bradshaw; I'll drink no water for thy sake whilst this lasts.—Now, gentlemen, shall we have your company to London?

GREENE. Nay, stay, sirs:
A little more I needs must use your help,
And in a matter of great consequence,
Wherein if you'll be secret and profound,
I'll give you twenty angels for your pains.

WILL. How? twenty angels? give my fellow George Shakebag and me twenty angels? And if thou'lt have thy own father slain, that thou may'st inherit his land, we'll kill him.

SHAKEBAG. Ay, thy mother, thy sister, thy brother, or all thy kin.

GREENE. Well, this is it: Arden of Feversham
Hath highly wronged me about the Abbey land,
That no revenge but death will serve the turn.
Will you two kill him? here's the angels down,
And I will lay the platform* of his death.   plan

WILL. Plat me no platforms; give me the money, and I'll stab him as he stands pissing against a wall, but I'll kill him.

SHAKEBAG. Where is he?

---

[8] Passed the drinking cup.

GREENE. He is now at London, in Aldersgate Street.

SHAKEBAG. He's dead as if he had been condemned by an
Act of Parliament, if once Black Will and I swear his death.

GREENE. Here is ten pound, and when he is dead,
Ye shall have twenty more.

WILL. My fingers itches to be at the peasant. Ah, that I
might be set a work thus through the year, and that murder
would grow to an occupation, that a man might follow without danger of law:—zounds, I warrant I should be warden of
the company! Come, let us be going, and we'll bait*stop for food
at Rochester, where I'll give thee a gallon of sack to
handsel* the match withal.   confirm

(*Exeunt.*)

Scene 2

(*London. A street near St. Paul's. A stall at one side. Enter*
MICHAEL.)

MICHAEL. I have gotten such a letter as will touch the
     painter:
And thus it is:

(*Enter* ARDEN *and* FRANKLIN *and hear* MICHAEL *read this
letter.*)

"My duty remembered, Mistress Susan, hoping in God you
be in good health, as I Michael was at the making hereof.
This is to certify you that as the turtle* true, when   turtledove
she hath lost her mate, sitteth alone, so I, mourning for your
absence, do walk up and down Paul's till one day I fell asleep
and lost my master's pantofles.* Ah, Mistress Susan,   slippers
abolish that paltry painter, cut him off by the shins with a
frowning look of your crabbed countenance, and think upon
Michael, who, drunk with the dregs of your favour, will cleave
as fast to your love as a plaster of pitch to a galled horse-back.
Thus hoping you will let my passions penetrate, or rather im-
petrate* mercy of your meeks hands, I end   obtain by entreaty
               "Yours, Michael, or else not Michael."

ARDEN. Why, you paltry knave,
Stand you here loitering, knowing my affairs,
What haste my business craves to send to Kent?

FRANKLIN. Faith, friend Michael, this is very ill,
Knowing your master hath no more but you,
And do ye slack his business for your own?

ARDEN. Where is the letter, sirrah? let me see it.
(*He gives him the letter.*)
See, Master Franklin, here's proper stuff:
Susan my maid, the painter, and my man,
A crew of harlots,[9] all in love, forsooth;
Sirrah, let me hear no more of this,
Nor for thy life once write to her a word.

(*Enter* GREENE, WILL, *and* SHAKEBAG.)

Wilt thou be married to so base a trull?*   prostitute
'Tis Mosbie's sister: come I once at home,
I'll rouse her from remaining in my house.
Now, Master Franklin, let us go walk in Paul's;
Come but a turn or two, and then away.

(*Exeunt.*)

GREENE. The first is Arden, and that's his man,
The other is Franklin, Arden's dearest friend.
WILL. Zounds, I'll kill them all three.
GREENE. Nay, sirs, touch not his man in any case;
But stand close, and take you fittest standing,*   the best position
And at his coming forth speed* him: kill
To the Nag's Head, there is this coward's haunt.
But now I'll leave you till the deed be done.

(*Exit* GREENE.)

SHAKEBAG. If he be not paid his own, ne'er trust Shakebag.
WILL. Sirrah Shakebag, at his coming forth I'll run him through, and then to the Blackfriars, and there take water and away.
SHAKEBAG. Why, that's the best; but see thou miss him not.
WILL. How can I miss him, when I think on the forty angels I must have more?

(*They conceal themselves against the stall. Enter a* PRENTICE.)

PRENTICE. 'Tis very late; I were best shut up my stall, for here will be old* filching, when the press* comes excessive/crowd
forth of Paul's.
(*Lets down his window, and it breaks* BLACK WILL'S *head.*)
WILL. Zounds, draw, Shakebag, I am almost killed.
PRENTICE. We'll tame you, I warrant.
WILL. Zounds, I am tame enough already.

[9] Unworthy individuals of either sex.

(*Enter* ARDEN, FRANKLIN, *and* MICHAEL.)

ARDEN. What troublesome fray or mutiny is this?

FRANKLIN. 'Tis nothing but some brabling paltry fray,
Devised to pick men's pockets in the throng.

ARDEN. Is't nothing else? come, Franklin, let's away.

(*Exeunt.*)

WILL. What 'mends* shall I have for my broken   amends
head?

PRENTICE. Marry, this 'mends, that if you get you not away
all the sooner, you shall be well beaten and sent to the Coun-
ter.*   a London prison

(*Exit* PRENTICE.)

WILL. Well, I'll be gone, but look to your signs, for I'll put
them down all. Shakebag, my broken head grieves me not so
much as by this means Arden hath escaped.

(*Enter* GREENE.)

GREENE. I had a glimpse of him and his companion. Why,
sirs, Arden's as well as I; I met him and Franklin going merrily
to the ordinary.* What, dare you not do it?   tavern

WILL. Yes, sir, we dare do it; but, were my consent to give
again, we would not do it under ten pound more. I value every
drop of my blood at a French crown. I have had ten pound
to steal a dog, and we have no more here to kill a man; but
that a bargain is a bargain, and so forth, you should do it
yourself.

GREENE. I pray thee, how came thy head broke?

WILL. Why, thou seest it is broke, dost thou not?

SHAKEBAG. Standing against a stall, watching Arden's coming, a boy let down his shop-window, and broke his head;
whereupon arose a brawl, and in the tumult Arden escaped
us and passed by unthought on. But forbearance is no acquittance; another time we'll do it, I warrant thee.

GREENE. I pray thee, Will, make clean thy bloody brow,
And let us bethink us on some other place
Where Arden may be met with handsomely.
Remember how devoutly thou hast sworn
To kill the villain; think upon thine oath.

WILL. Tush, I have broken five hundred oaths!
But wouldst thou charm me to effect this deed,
Tell me of gold, my resolution's fee;
Say thou seest Mosbie kneeling at my knees,

Offering me service for my high attempt,
And sweet Alice Arden, with a lap of crowns,
Comes with a lowly curtsey to the earth,
Saying "Take this but for thy quarterage,* quarterly payment
Such yearly tribute will I answer* thee."   pay
Why, this would steel soft-mettled cowardice,
With which Black Will was never tainted yet.
I tell thee, Greene, the forlorn traveller,
Whose lips are glued with summer's parching heat,
Ne'er longed so much to see a running brook
As I to finish Arden's tragedy.
Seest thou this gore that cleaveth to my face?
From hence ne'er will I wash this bloody stain,
Till Arden's heart be panting in my hand.
 GREENE. Why, that's well said; but what saith Shakebag?
 SHAKEBAG. I cannot paint my valour out with words:
But, give me place and opportunity,
Such mercy as the starven lioness,
When she is dry sucked of her eager young,
Shows to the prey that next encounters her,
On Arden so much pity would I take.
 GREENE. So should it fare with men of firm resolve.
And now, sirs, seeing that this accident
Of meeting him in Paul's hath no success,
Let us bethink us of some other place
Whose earth may swallow up this Arden's blood.

 (*Enter* MICHAEL.)

See, yonder comes his man: and wot* you what? know
The foolish knave's in love with Mosbie's sister,
And for her sake, whose love he cannot get
Unless Mosbie solicit his suit,
The villain hath sworn the slaughter of his master.
We'll question him, for he may stead* us much.—— help
How now, Michael, whither are you going?
 MICHAEL. My master hath new supped,
And I am going to prepare his chamber.
 GREENE. Where supped Master Arden?
 MICHAEL. At the Nag's Head, at the eighteen pence ordinary.
How now, Master Shakebag? what, Black Will! God's dear
lady, how chance your face is so bloody?
 WILL. Go to, sirrah, there is a chance in it; this sauciness
in you will make you be knocked.

MICHAEL. Nay, an you be offended, I'll be gone.

GREENE. Stay, Michael, you may not escape us so.
Michael, I know you love your master well.

MICHAEL. Why, so I do; but wherefore urge you that?

GREENE. Because I think you love your mistress better.

MICHAEL. So think not I; but say; i'faith, what, if I should?

SHAKEBAG. Come to the purpose, Michael; we hear
You have a pretty love in Feversham.

MICHAEL. Why, have I two or three, what's that to thee!

WILL. You deal too mildly with the peasant. Thus it is:
'Tis known to us that you love Mosbie's sister;
We know besides that you have ta'en your oath
To further Mosbie to your mistress' bed,
And kill your master for his sister's sake.
Now, sir, a poorer coward than yourself
Was never fostered in the coast of Kent:
How comes it then that such a knave as you
Dare swear a matter of such consequence?

GREENE. Ah, Will——

WILL. Tush, give me leave, there's no more but this:
Sith* thou has sworn, we dare discover all;   since
And hadst thou or should'st thou utter it,
We have devised a complat* under hand,   plot
Whatever shall betide to any of us,
To send thee roundly to the devil of hell.
And therefore thus: I am the very man,
Marked in my birth-hour by the destinies,
To give an end to Arden's life on earth;
Thou but a member but to whet the knife
Whose edge must search the closet of his breast:
Thy office is but to appoint the place,
And train* the master to his tragedy;   decoy
Mine to perform it when occasion serves.
Then be not nice,* but here devise with us   foolish
How and what way we may conclude his death.

SHAKEBAG. So shalt thou purchase Mosbie for thy friend,
And by his friendship gain his sister's love.

GREENE. So shall thy mistress be thy favourer,*   that is
And thou disburdened of the oath thou made.   favor you

MICHAEL. Well, gentlemen, I cannot but confess,
Sith you have urged me so apparently,
That I have vowed my master Arden's death;
And he whose kindly love and liberal hand
Doth challenge nought but good deserts of me,

I will deliver over to your hands.
This night come to his house at Aldersgate:
The doors I'll leave unlock'd against you come.
No sooner shall ye enter through the latch,
Over the threshold to the inner court,
But on your left hand shall you see the stairs
That leads directly to my master's chamber:
There take him and dispose him as ye please.
Now it were good we parted company;
What I have promised, I will perform.
   WILL. Should you deceive us, 'twould go wrong with you.
   MICHAEL. I will accomplish all I have revealed.
   WILL. Come, let's go drink: choler makes me as dry
as a dog.

             (*Exeunt* WILL, GREENE, *and* SHAKEBAG.)
   MICHAEL. Thus feeds the lamb securely on the down,
Whilst through the thicket of an arbour brake
The hunger-bitten wolf o'erpries* his haunt   **looks over**
And takes advantage for to eat him up.
Ah, harmless Arden, how hast thou misdone,
That thus thy gentle life is levelled at?
The many good turns that thou hast done to me,
Now must I quittance* with betraying thee.   **repay**
I that should take the weapon in my hand
And buckler* thee from ill-intending foes,   **defend**
Do lead thee with a wicked fraudful smile,
As unsuspected, to the slaughter-house.
So have I sworn to Mosbie and my mistress,
So have I promised to the slaughtermen;
And should I not deal currently* with them,   **genuinely**
Their lawless rage would take revenge on me.
Tush, I will spurn at mercy for this once:
Let pity lodge where feeble women lie,
I am resolved, and Arden needs must die.

                   (*Exit* MICHAEL.)

ACT III

Scene 1

(*A room in* FRANKLIN'S *house, at Aldersgate. Enter* ARDEN *and* FRANKLIN.)

ARDEN. No, Franklin, no: if fear or stormy threats,

If love of me or care of womanhood,
If fear of God or common speech of men,
Who mangle credit with their wounding words,
And couch dishonour as dishonour buds,
Might join repentance in her wanton thoughts,
No question then but she would turn the leaf
And sorrow for her dissolution;*   degeneration
But she is rooted in her wickedness,
Perverse and stubborn, not to be reclaimed;
Good counsel is to her as rain to weeds,
And reprehension* makes her vice to grow   censure
As Hydra's head that plenished* by decay.   replenished
Her faults, methink, are painted in my face,
For every searching eye to overread;
And Mosbie's name, a scandal unto mine,
Is deeply trenchèd in my blushing brow.
Ah, Franklin, Franklin, when I think on this,
My heart's grief rends my other powers
Worse than the conflict at the hour of death.
    FRANKLIN. Gentle Arden, leave this sad lament:
She will amend, and so your griefs will cease;
Or else she'll die, and so your sorrows end.
If neither of these two do haply fall,
Yet let your comfort be that others bear
Your woes, twice doubled all, with patience.
    ARDEN. My house is irksome; there I cannot rest.
    FRANKLIN. Then stay with me in London; go not home.
    ARDEN. Then that base Mosbie doth usurp my room
And makes his triumph of my being thence.*   absent
At home or not at home, where'er I be,
Here, here it lies, ah Franklin, here it lies
That will not out till wretched Arden dies.

    (*Enter* MICHAEL.)

    FRANKLIN. Forget your griefs a while; here comes your man.
    ARDEN. What a-clock is't, sirrah?
    MICHAEL. Almost ten.
    ARDEN. See, see, how runs away the weary time!
Come, Master Franklin, shall we go to bed?
    FRANKLIN. I pray you, go before: I'll follow you.
                        (*Exeunt* ARDEN *and* MICHAEL.)
—Ah, what a hell is fretful jealousy!
What pity-moving words, what deep-fetched sighs,

What grievous groans and overlading woes
Accompanies this gentle gentleman!
Now will he shake his care-oppressèd head,
Then fix his sad eyes on the sullen earth,
Ashamed to gaze upon the open world;
Now will he cast his eyes up towards the heavens,
Looking that ways for redress of wrong:
Sometimes he seeketh to beguile his grief
And tells a story with his careful tongue;
Then comes his wife's dishonour in his thoughts
And in the middle cutteth off his tale,
Pouring fresh sorrow on his weary limbs.
So woe-begone, so inly charged with woe,
Was never any lived and bare it so.

(*Enter* MICHAEL.)

MICHAEL. My master would desire you come to bed.
FRANKLIN. Is he himself already in his bed?
MICHAEL. He is, and fain* would have the light away.   gladly
(*Exit* FRANKLIN.)
—Conflicting thoughts, encampèd in my breast,
Awake me with the echo of their strokes,
And I, a judge to censure either side,
Can give to neither wishèd victory.
My master's kindness pleads to me for life
With just demand, and I must grant it him:
My mistress she hath forced me with an oath,
For Susan's sake, the which I may not break,
For that is nearer than a master's love:
That grim-faced fellow, pitiless Black Will,
And Shakebag, stern in bloody stratagem,
—Two rougher ruffians never lived in Kent,—
Have sworn my death, if I infringe my vow,
A dreadful thing to be considered of.
Methinks I see them with their bolstered* hair   disheveled
Staring and grinning in thy gentle face,
And in their ruthless hands their daggers drawn,
Insulting o'er thee with a peck of oaths,
Whilst thou submissive, pleading for relief,
Art mangled by their ireful instruments.
Methinks I hear them ask where Michael is,
And pitiless Black Will cries: "Stab the slave!
The peasant will detect* the tragedy!"   disclose

The wrinkles in his foul death-threat'ning face
Gapes open wide, like graves to swallow men.
My death to him is but a merriment,
And he will murder me to make him sport.
He comes, he comes! ah, Master Franklin, help!
Call on the neighbours, or we are but dead!

(*Enter* FRANKLIN *and* ARDEN.)

FRANKLIN. What dismal outcry calls me from my rest?
ARDEN. What hath occasioned such a fearful cry?
Speak, Michael: hath any injured thee?
MICHAEL. Nothing, sir; but as I fell asleep,
Upon the threshold leaning to the stairs,
I had a fearful dream that troubled me,
And in my slumber thought I was beset
With murderer thieves that came to rifle me.
My trembling joints witness my inward fear:
I crave your pardons for disturbing you.
ARDEN. So great a cry for nothing I ne'er heard.
What? are the doors fast locked and all things safe?
MICHAEL. I cannot tell; I think I locked the doors.
ARDEN. I like not this, but I'll go see myself.—
Ne'er trust me but the doors were all unlocked:
This negligence not half contenteth me.
Get you to bed, and if you love my favour,
Let me have no more such pranks as these.
Come, Master Franklin, let us go to bed.
FRANKLIN. Ay, by my faith; the air is very cold.
Michael, farewell; I pray thee dream no more.

(*Exeunt.*)

Scene 2

(*Outside* FRANKLIN'S *house. Enter* WILL, GREENE, *and*
SHAKEBAG.)

SHAKEBAG. Black night hath hid the pleasures of the day,
And sheeting darkness overhangs the earth,
And with the black fold of her cloudy robe
Obscures us from the eyesight of the world,
In which sweet silence such as we triumph.
The lazy minutes linger on their time,
As loth to give due audit to the hour,

Till in the watch[10] our purpose be complete
And Arden sent to everlasting night.
Greene, get you gone, and linger here about,
And at some hour hence come to us again,
Where we will give you instance* of his death.   proof
    GREENE. Speed to my wish, whose will so e'er says no;[11]
And so I'll leave you for an hour or two.

                       (*Exit* GREENE.)
    WILL. I tell thee, Shakebag, would this thing were done:
I am so heavy that I can scarce go;
This drowsiness in me bodes little good.
    SHAKEBAG. How now, Will? become a precisian?*   Puritan
Nay, then let's go sleep, when bugs* and fears   bugaboos
Shall kill our courages with their fancy's* work.   imagination's
    WILL. Why, Shakebag, thou mistakes me much,
And wrongs me too in telling me of fear.
Were't not a serious thing we go about,
It should be slipt* till I had fought with thee,   put aside
To let thee know I am no coward, I.
I tell thee, Shakebag, thou abusest me.
    SHAKEBAG. Why, thy speech bewrayed* an inly kind revealed
    of fear,
And savoured of a weak relenting spirit.
Go forward now in that we have begun,
And afterwards attempt* me when thou darest.   attack
    WILL. And if I do not, heaven cut me off!
But let that pass, and show me to this house,
Where thou shalt see I'll do as much as Shakebag.
    SHAKEBAG. This is the door; but soft, methinks 'tis shut.
The villain Michael hath deceived us.
    WILL. Soft, let me see, Shakebag; 'tis shut indeed.
Knock with thy sword, perhaps the slave will hear.
    SHAKEBAG. It will not be; the white-livered peasant
Is gone to bed, and laughs us both to scorn.
    WILL. And he shall buy his merriment as dear
As ever coistril* bought so little sport: cowardly knave
Ne'er let this sword assist me when I need,
But rust and canker after I have sworn,
If I, the next time that I meet the hind,*   fellow
Lop not away his leg, his arm, or both.

       [10] One of the time divisions of the night.
       [11] That is, no matter who wishes the opposite.

SHAKEBAG. And let me never draw a sword again,
Nor prosper in the twilight, cockshut light,[12]
When I would fleece the wealthy passenger,
But lie and languish in a loathsome den,
Hated and spit at by the goers-by,
And in that death may die unpitied,
If I, the next time that I meet the slave,
Cut not the nose from off the coward's face
And trample on it for this villainy.

WILL. Come, let's go seek out Greene; I know he'll swear.

SHAKEBAG. He were a villain, an he would not swear.
'Twould make a peasant swear among his boys,
That ne'er durst say before but "yea" and "no,"
To be thus flouted of a coistril.

WILL. Shakebag, let's seek out Greene, and in the morning
At the alehouse butting* Arden's house   abutting on
Watch the out-coming of that prick-eared cur,
And then let me alone to handle him.

                                                    (*Exeunt.*)

                            Scene 3

(*Room in* FRANKLIN'S *house as before. Enter* ARDEN,
FRANKLIN, *and* MICHAEL.)

ARDEN. Sirrah, get you back to Billingsgate
And learn what time the tide will serve our turn;
Come to us in Paul's. First go make the bed,
And afterwards go hearken for the flood.*   flood tide
                                        (*Exit* MICHAEL.)
Come, Master Franklin, you shall go with me.
This night I dreamt that, being in a park,
A toil* was pitched to overthrow the deer,   net
And I upon a little rising hill
Stood whistly* watching for the herd's approach.   silently
Even there, methoughts, a gentle slumber took me,
And summoned all my parts to sweet repose;
But in the pleasure of this golden rest
An ill-thewed foster* had removed the toil,   roguish forester
And rounded me with that beguiling home[13]

---

[12] "The time when poultry are shut up"(?)—O.E.D.
[13] Ensnared me in the net.

Which late, methought, was pitched to cast* the deer.   throw
With that he blew an evil-sounding horn,
And at the noise another herdman came,
With falchion* drawn, and bent it at my breast,   sword
Crying aloud, "Thou art the game we seek!"
With this I woke and trembled every joint,
Like one obscured in a little bush,
That sees a lion foraging about,
And, when the dreadful forest-king is gone,
He pries about with timorous suspect*   looks suspiciously
Throughout the thorny casements of the brake,
And will not think his person dangerless,
But quakes and shivers, though the cause be gone:
So, trust me, Franklin, when I did awake,
I stood in doubt whether I waked or no:
Such great impression took* this fond* surprise.   gave/
God grant this vision bedeem me any good.[14]   foolishly credulous
   FRANKLIN. This fantasy doth rise from Michael's fear,
Who being awaked with the noise he made,
His troubled senses yet could take no rest;
And this, I warrant you, procured your dream.
   ARDEN. It may be so, God frame* it to the best: contrive
But oftentimes my dreams presage too true.
   FRANKLIN. To such as note their nightly fantasies,
Some one in twenty may incur belief;
But use it not, 'tis but a mockery.
   ARDEN. Come, Master Franklin; we'll now walk in Paul's
And dine together at the ordinary,*   inn
And by my man's direction draw to the quay,
And with the tide go down to Feversham.
Say, Master Franklin, shall it not be so?
   FRANKLIN. At your good pleasure, sir; I'll bear you
    company.

                              (*Exeunt.*)

Scene 4

(*Aldersgate. Enter* MICHAEL *at one door. Enter* GREENE, WILL, *and* SHAKEBAG *at another door.*)

WILL. Draw, Shakebag, for here's that villain Michael.
GREENE. First, Will, let's hear what he can say.

  [14] That is, does not herald evil for me.

WILL. Speak, milksop slave, and never after speak.
MICHAEL. For God's sake, sirs, let me excuse myself:
For here I swear, by heaven and earth and all,
I did perform the utmost of my task,
And left the doors unbolted and unlocked.
But see the chance: Franklin and my master
Were very late conferring in the porch,
And Franklin left his napkin where he sat
With certain gold knit in it, as he said.
Being in bed, he did bethink himself,
And coming down he found the doors unshut:
He locked the gates, and brought away the keys,
For which offence my master rated* me.   scolded
But now I am going to see what flood it is,
For with the tide my master will away;
Where you may front* him well on Rainham Down,   confront
A place well-fitting such a stratagem.
WILL. Your excuse hath somewhat mollified my choler.
Why now, Greene, 'tis better now nor e'er it was.
GREENE. But, Michael, is this true?
MICHAEL. As true as I report it to be true.
SHAKEBAG. Then, Michael, this shall be your penance,
To feast us all at the Salutation,
Where we will plat* our purpose thoroughly.   plot
GREENE. And, Michael, you shall bear no news of this tide,
Because* they two may be in Rainham Down   in order that
Before your master.
MICHAEL. Why, I'll agree to anything you'll have me,
So you will except of my company.[15]

                                                   (*Exeunt.*)

                        Scene 5

(ARDEN'S *house at Feversham. Enter* MOSBIE.)

MOSBIE. Disturbèd thoughts drives me from company
And dries my marrow with their watchfulness;
Continual trouble of my moody brain
Feebles my body by excess of drink,
And nips me as the bitter north-east wind
Doth check the tender blossoms in the spring.
Well fares the man, howe'er his cates* do taste,   dainties
That tables* not with foul suspicion;   dines

    [15] Excuse me from accompanying you.

And he but pines amongst his delicates,
Whose troubled mind is stuffed with discontent.
My golden time was when I had no gold;
Though then I wanted, yet I slept secure;
My daily toil begat me night's repose,
My night's repose made daylight fresh to me.
But since I climbed the top-bough of the tree
And sought to build my nest among the clouds,
Each gentle stirry[16] gale doth shake my bed,
And makes me dread my downfall to the earth.
But whither doth contemplation carry me?
The way I seek to find, where pleasure dwells,
Is hedged behind me that I cannot back,
But needs must on, although to danger's gate.
Then, Arden, perish thou by that decree;
For Greene doth ear* the land and weed thee up   plow
To make my harvest nothing but pure corn.
And for his pains I'll hive him up a while,
And after smother him to have his wax:
Such bees as Greene must never live to sting.
Then is there Michael and the painter too,
Chief actors to Arden's overthrow;
Who when they shall see me sit in Arden's seat,
They will insult upon me for my meed,[17]
Or fright me by detecting of* his end.   revealing
I'll none of that, for I can cast a bone
To make these curs pluck out each other's throat,
And then am I sole ruler of mine own.
Yet Mistress Arden lives; but she's myself,
And holy Church rites makes us two but one.
But what for that? I may not trust you, Alice:
You have supplanted Arden for my sake,
And will extirpen* me to plant another.   extirpate
'Tis fearful sleeping in a serpent's bed,
And I will cleanly rid my hands of her.

(*Enter* ALICE.)

But here she comes, and I must flatter her.
—How now, Alice? what, sad and passionate?

[16] Stirry = stirring (active) [?].
[17] That is, They will assail me disrespectfully for my corrupt gain.

Make me partaker of thy pensiveness:
Fire divided burns with lesser force.

    ALICE. But I will dam that fire in my breast
Till by the force thereof my part consume.[18]
Ah, Mosbie!

    MOSBIE. Such deep pathaires,* like to a cannon's burst _{moving sighs}
Discharged against a ruinated wall,[19]
Breaks my relenting heart in thousand pieces.
Ungentle* Alice, thy sorrow is my sore;   unkind
Thou know'st it well, and 'tis thy policy
To forge distressful looks to wound a breast
Where lies a heart that dies when thou art sad.
It is not love that loves to anger love.

    ALICE. It is not love that loves to murder love.

    MOSBIE. How mean you that?

    ALICE. Thou knowest how dearly Arden loved me.

    MOSBIE. And then?

    ALICE. And then—conceal the rest, for 'tis too bad,
Lest that my words be carried with the wind,
And published in the world to both our shames.
I pray thee, Mosbie, let our springtime wither;
Our harvest else will yield but loathsome weeds.
Forget, I pray thee, what hath passed betwixt us,
For how I blush and tremble at the thoughts!

    MOSBIE. What? are you changed?

    ALICE. Ay, to my former happy life again,
From title of an odious strumpet's name
To honest Arden's wife, not Arden's honest* wife.   chaste
Ha, Mosbie! 'tis thou has rifled me of that
And made me slanderous to all my kin;
Even in my forehead is thy name engraven,
A mean artificer, that low-born name.
I was bewitched: woe worth the hapless* hour   unlucky
And all the causes that enchanted me!

    MOSBIE. Nay, if you ban,* let me breathe curses forth, curse
And if you stand so nicely* at your fame,   fastidiously
Let me repent the credit I have lost.
I have neglected matters of import
That would have stated* me above thy state,   placed

---

[18] Contemplating a separation from Mosbie, Alice states that
she will keep her ardor within herself in an attempt to smother it.
[19] That is, a wall that is to be destroyed.

Forslowed* advantages, and spurned at time: lost
Ay, Fortune's right hand Mosbie hath forsook
To take a wanton giglot* by the left.   lascivious woman
I left the marriage of an honest* maid,   chaste
Whose dowry would have weighed down all thy wealth,
Whose beauty and demeanour far exceeded thee:
This certain good I lost for changing bad,
And wrapt my credit in thy company.
I was bewitched,—that is no theme of thine,
And thou unhallowed has enchanted me.
But I will break thy spells and exorcisms,
And put another sight upon these eyes
That showed my heart a raven for a dove.
Thou art not fair, I viewed thee not till now;
Thou art not kind, till now I knew thee not;
And now the rain hath beaten off thy gilt,
Thy worthless copper shows thee counterfeit.
It grieves me not to see how foul thou art,
But mads me that ever I thought thee fair.
Go, get thee gone, a copesmate* for thy hinds;*companion/servants
I am too good to be thy favourite.
   ALICE. Ay, now I see, and too soon find it true,
Which often hath been told me by my friends,
That Mosbie loves me not but for my wealth,
Which too incredulous I ne'er believed.
Nay, hear me speak, Mosbie, a word or two;
I'll bite my tongue if it speak bitterly.
Look on me, Mosbie, or I'll kill myself:
Nothing shall hide me from thy stormy look.
If thou cry war, there is no peace for me;
I will do penance for offending thee,
And burn this prayer-book, where I here use
The holy word that had converted me.
See, Mosbie, I will tear away the leaves,
And all the leaves, and in this golden cover
Shall thy sweet phrases and thy letters dwell;
And thereon will I chiefly meditate,
And hold no other sect but such devotion.
Wilt thou not look? is all thy love o'erwhelmed?
Wilt thou not hear? what malice stops thine ears?
Why speaks thou not? what silence ties thy tongue?
Thou hast been sighted* as the eagle is,   endowed with sight
And heard* as quickly* as the fearful* hare,   endowed with
                                                      hearing/sharp/
                                                            timid
And spoke* as smoothly as an orator,   endowed with speech

When I have bid thee hear or see or speak,
And art thou sensible in none of these?
Weigh all thy good turns with this little fault,
And I deserve not Mosbie's muddy looks.
A fence of trouble is not thickened still:[20]
Be clear again, I'll ne'er more trouble thee.

MOSBIE. O no, I am a base artificer:
My wings are feathered for a lowly flight.
Mosbie? fie! no, not for a thousand pound.
Make love to you? why, 'tis unpardonable;
We beggars must not breathe where gentles are.

ALICE. Sweet Mosbie is as gentle as a king,
And I too blind to judge him otherwise.
Flowers do sometimes spring in fallow lands,
Weeds in gardens, roses grow on thorns;
So, whatsoe'er my Mosbie's father was,
Himself is valued gentle by his worth.

MOSBIE. Ah, how you women can insinuate,
And clear a trespass with your sweet-set tongue!
I will forget this quarrel, gentle Alice,
Provided I'll be tempted so no more.

(*Enter* BRADSHAW.)

ALICE. Then with thy lips seal up this new-made match.
MOSBIE. Soft, Alice, here comes somebody.
ALICE. How now, Bradshaw, what's the news with you?
BRADSHAW. I have little news, but here's a letter
That Master Greene importuned me to give you.
ALICE. Go in, Bradshaw; call for a cup of beer;
'Tis almost supper-time, thou shalt stay with us.

(*Exit* BRADSHAW.)

(*Reads the letter.*)
"We have missed of our purpose at London, but shall per-
form it by the way. We thank our neighbour Bradshaw.—
Yours, Richard Greene."
How likes my love the tenor of this letter?
MOSBIE. Well, were his date completed and expired.

[20] "A troubled pool is not always turbid." (?)—Baskervill's
gloss.

ALICE. Ah, would it were! Then comes my happy hour:
Till then my bliss is mixed with bitter gall.
Come, let us in to shun suspicion.
    MOSBIE. Ay, to the gates of death to follow thee.

                                      (*Exeunt.*)

Scene 6

(*Country near Rochester. Enter* GREENE, WILL, *and*
SHAKEBAG.)

    SHAKEBAG. Come, Will, see thy tools be in a readiness!
Is not thy powder dank, or will thy flint strike fire?
    WILL. Then ask me if my nose be on my face,
Or whether my tongue be frozen in my mouth.
Zounds, here's a coil!*   fuss
You were best swear me on the interrogatories[21]
How many pistols I have took in hand,
Or whether I love the smell of gunpowder,
Or dare abide the noise the dag* will make,   pistol
Or will not wink at flashing of the fire.
I pray thee, Shakebag, let this answer thee,
That I have took more purses in this down
Than e'er thou handledst pistols in thy life.
    SHAKEBAG. Ay, haply thou has picked more in a throng:
But, should I brag what booties I have took,
I think the overplus that's more than thine
Would mount to a greater sum of money
Then* either thou or all thy kin are worth.   than
Zounds, I hate them as I hate a toad
That carry a muscado* in their tongue,   musket
And scarce a hurting weapon in their hand.
    WILL. O Greene, intolerable!
It is not for mine honour to bear this.
Why, Shakebag, I did serve the king at Boulogne,
And thou canst brag of nothing that thou hast done.
    SHAKEBAG. Why, so can Jack of Feversham,
That sounded* for a fillip* of the nose,   swooned/blow
When he that gave it him holloed in his ear,
And he supposed a cannon-bullet hit him.
    (*They fight.*)

---

[21] Formal questioning, in law, of an accused person.

GREENE. I pray you, sirs, list* to Æsop's talk: listen
Whilst two stout dogs were striving for a bone,
There comes a cur and stole it from them both;
So, while you stand striving on these terms of manhood,
Arden escapes us, and deceives us all.
  SHAKEBAG. Why, he begun.
  WILL.   And thou shalt find I'll end;
I do but slip it until better time:
But, if I do forget——
  (*He kneels down and holds up his hands to heaven.*)
  GREENE. Well, take your fittest standings,*   prepared positions
        and once more
Lime well your twigs to catch this wary bird.[22]
I'll leave you, and at your dag's discharge
Make towards, like the longing water-dog
That coucheth till the fowling-piece be off,
Then seizeth on the prey with eager mood.
Ah, might I see him stretching forth his limbs,
As I have seen them beat their wings ere now!
  SHAKEBAG. Why, that thou shalt see, if he come this way.
  GREENE. Yes, that he doth, Shakebag, I warrant thee:
But brawl not when I am gone in any case.
But, sirs, be sure to speed* him when he comes,   kill
And in that hope I'll leave you for an hour.
                                        (*Exit* GREENE.)

(*Enter* ARDEN, FRANKLIN, *and* MICHAEL.)

  MICHAEL. 'Twere best that I went back to Rochester:
The horse halts downright,* it were not good   limps badly
He travelled in such pain to Feversham;
Removing of a shoe may haply help it.
  ARDEN. Well, get you back to Rochester; but, sirrah, see
Ye o'ertake us ere we come to Rainham Down,
For 't will be very late ere we get home.
  MICHAEL (*aside*). Ay, God he knows, and so doth Will
        and Shakebag,
That thou shalt never go further than that down;
And therefore have I pricked the horse[23] on purpose,

----

[22] That is, prepare your trap well. Bird lime is a sticky substance that was spread on twigs to catch birds.

[23] Pierced the foot of the horse to the flesh.

Because I would not view the massacre.

                                        (*Exit* MICHAEL.)
ARDEN. Come, Master Franklin, onwards with your tale.
FRANKLIN. I do assure you, sir, you task me much:
A heavy blood is gathered at my heart,
And on the sudden is my wind so short
As hindereth the passage of my speech;
So fierce a qualm yet ne'er assailed me.
   ARDEN. Come, Master Franklin, let us go softly:*   slowly
The annoyance of the dust or else some meat
You ate at dinner cannot brook* with you.   agree
I have been often so, and soon amended.*   recovered
   FRANKLIN. Do you remember where my tale did leave?
   ARDEN. Ay, where the gentleman did check* his wife. rebuke
   FRANKLIN. She being reprehended* for the fact,* censured/deed
Witness produced that took her with the deed,
Her glove brought in which there she left behind,
And many other assured arguments,
Her husband asked her whether it were not so.
   ARDEN. Her answer then? I wonder how she looked,
Having forsworn it with such vehement oaths,
And at the instant so approved* upon her.   proved
   FRANKLIN. First did she cast her eyes down to the earth,
Watching the drops that fell amain* from thence;   violently
Then softly draws she forth her handkerchief,
And modestly she wipes her tear-stained face;
Them hemmed she out, to clear her voice should seem,
And with a majesty addressed herself
To encounter all their accusations.—
Pardon me, Master Arden, I can no more;
This fighting at my heart makes short my wind.
   ARDEN. Come, we are almost now at Rainham Down:
Your pretty tale beguiles the weary way;
I would you were in state to tell it out.
   SHAKEBAG. Stand close, Will, I hear them coming.

(*Enter* LORD CHEINY *with his men.*)

WILL. Stand to it, Shakebag, and be resolute.
   LORD CHEINY. Is it so near night as it seems,
Or will this black-faced evening have a shower?
—What, Master Arden? you are well met,
I have longed this fortnight's day to speak with you:
You are a stranger, man, in the Isle of Sheppy.

ARDEN. Your honour's always! bound to do you service.
LORD CHEINY. Come you from London, and ne'er a man
    with you?
ARDEN. My man's coming after, but here's
My honest friend that came along with me.
LORD CHEINY. My Lord Protector's man I take you to be.
FRANKLIN. Ay, my good lord, and highly bound to you.
LORD CHEINY. You and your friend come home and sup
    with me.
ARDEN. I beseech your honour pardon me;
I have made a promise to a gentleman,
My honest friend, to meet him at my house;
The occasion is great, or else would I wait on you.
LORD CHEINY. Will you come to-morrow and dine with me,
And bring your honest friend along with you?
I have divers matters to talk with you about.
    ARDEN. To-morrow we'll wait upon your honour.
LORD CHEINY. One of you stay my horse at the top of the
    hill.
—What! Black Will? for whose purse wait you?
Thou wilt be hanged in Kent, when all is done.
    WILL. Not hanged, God save your honour;
I am your bedesman,[24] bound to pray for you.
LORD CHEINY. I think thou ne'er said'st prayer in all thy
    life.—
One of you give him a crown:—
And, sirrah, leave this kind of life;
If thou beest tainted* for a penny-matter,   accused
And come in question, surely thou wilt truss.*   hang
—Come, Master Arden, let us be going;
Your way and mine lies four miles together.

        (*Exeunt.* BLACK WILL *and* SHAKEBAG *remain.*)
    WILL. The devil break all your necks at four miles' end!
Zounds, I could kill myself for very anger!
His lordship chops me in,*   interrupts suddenly
Even when my dag was levelled at his heart.
I would his crown were molten down his throat.
    SHAKEBAG. Arden, thou hast wondrous holy luck.
Did ever man escape as thou hast done?
Well, I'll discharge my pistol at the sky,
For by this bullet Arden might not die.

    [24] A beadsman; one who says prayers for hire or for charity.

(*Enter* GREENE.)

GREENE. What, is he down? is he dispatched?

SHAKEBAG. Ay, in health towards Feversham, to shame us all.

GREENE. The devil he is! why, sirs, how escaped he?

SHAKEBAG. When we were ready to shoot,
Comes my Lord Cheiny to prevent his death.

GREENE. The Lord of Heaven hath preserved him.

WILL. Preserved a fig! The Lord Cheiny hath preserved him,
And bids him to a feast to his house at Shorlow.
But by the way once more I'll meet with him,
And, if all the Cheinies in the world say no,
I'll have a bullet in his breast to-morrow.
Therefore come, Greene, and let us to Feversham.

GREENE. Ay, and excuse ourselves to Mistress Arden:
O, how she'll chafe when she hears of this!

SHAKEBAG. Why, I'll warrant you she'll think we dare not do it.

WILL. Why, then let us go, and tell her all the matter,
And plat the news[25] to cut him off to-morrow.

(*Exeunt.*)

ACT IV

Scene 1

(ARDEN'S *house at Feversham. Enter* ARDEN *and his wife,* FRANKLIN, *and* MICHAEL.)

ARDEN. See how the hours, the gardant* of   guardian
heaven's gate,
Have by their toil removed the darksome clouds,
That Sol may well discern the trampled path
Wherein he wont* to guide his golden car;   is accustomed
The season fits; come, Franklin, let's away.

ALICE. I thought you did pretend* some special hunt,   intend
That made you thus cut short the time of rest.

ARDEN. It was no chase that made me rise so early,
But, as I told thee yesternight, to go
To the Isle of Sheppy, there to dine with my Lord Cheiny;

    [25] Prepare a new plan.

For so his honour late commanded me.

ALICE. Ay, such kind husbands seldom want excuses;
Home is a wild cat to a wandering wit.
The time hath been,—would God it were not past,—
That honour's title nor a lord's command
Could once have drawn you from these arms of mine.
But my deserts or your desires decay,
Or both; yet if true love may seem desert,
I merit still to have thy company.

FRANKLIN. Why, I pray you, sir, let her go along with us;
I am sure his honour will welcome her
And us the more for bringing her along.

ARDEN. Content; sirrah, saddle your mistress' nag.

ALICE. No, begged favour merits little thanks;
If I should go, our house would run away,
Or else be stolen; therefore I'll stay behind.

ARDEN. Nay, see how mistaking you are! I pray thee, go.

ALICE. No, no, not now.

ARDEN. Then let me leave thee satisfied in this,
That time nor place nor persons alter me,
But that I hold thee dearer than my life.

ALICE. That will be seen by your quick return.

ARDEN. And that shall be ere night, and if I live.
Farewell, sweet Alice, we mind to sup with thee.

                                            (*Exit* ALICE.)

FRANKLIN. Come, Michael, are our horses ready?

MICHAEL. Ay, your horse are ready, but I am not ready, for
I have lost my purse, with six and thirty shillings in it, with
taking up of my master's nag.

FRANKLIN. Why, I pray you, let us go before,
Whilst he stays behind to seek his purse.

ARDEN. Go to, sirrah, see you follow us to the Isle of
    Sheppy
To my Lord Cheiny's, where we mean to dine.

                                (*Exeunt* ARDEN *and* FRANKLIN.)

MICHAEL. So, fair weather after you, for before you lies
Black Will and Shakebag in the broom close,[26] too close for
you: they'll be your ferrymen to long home.[27]

(*Enter* CLARKE.)

[26] In the patch of broom shrubs.
[27] That is, They will fetch you to the grave.

But who is this? the painter, my corrival, that would needs win
Mistress Susan.

CLARKE. How now, Michael? how doth my mistress and all
at home?

MICHAEL. Who? Susan Mosbie? she is your mistress, too?

CLARKE. Ay, how doth she and all the rest?

MICHAEL. All's well but Susan; she is sick.

CLARKE. Sick? Of what disease?

MICHAEL. Of a great fear.

CLARKE. A fear of what?

MICHAEL. A great fever.

CLARKE. A fever? God forbid!

MICHAEL. Yes, faith, and of a lordaine,* too, as big   lout
as yourself.

CLARKE. O, Michael, the spleen prickles you. Go to, you
carry an eye over Mistress Susan.

MICHAEL. I' faith, to keep her from the painter.

CLARKE. Why more from a painter than from a serving creature like yourself?

MICHAEL. Because you painters make but a painting table
of a pretty wench, and spoil her beauty with blotting.

CLARKE. What mean you by that?

MICHAEL. Why, that you painters paint lambs in the lining
of wenches' petticoats, and we serving-men put horns to them
to make them become sheep.

CLARKE. Such another word will cost you a cuff or a knock.

MICHAEL. What, with a dagger made of a pencil? Faith, 'tis
too weak, and therefore thou too weak to win Susan.

CLARKE. Would Susan's love lay upon this stroke.

(*He breaks* MICHAEL'S *head.*)

(*Enter* MOSBIE, GREENE, *and* ALICE.)

ALICE. I'll lay my life, this is for Susan's love.
Stayed you behind your master to this end?
Have you no other time to brabble* in   squabble
But now when serious matters are in hand?—
Say, Clarke, hast thou done the thing thou promised?

CLARKE. Ay, here it is; the very touch is death.

ALICE. Then this, I hope, if all the rest do fail,
Will catch Master Arden,
And make him wise in death that lived a fool.
Why should he thrust his sickle in our corn,
Or what hath he to do with thee, my love,

Or govern me that am to rule myself?
Forsooth, for credit sake, I must leave thee!
Nay, he must leave to live that we may love,
May live, may love; for what is life but love?
And love shall last as long as life remains,
And life shall end before my love depart.
    MOSBIE. Why, what is love without true constancy?
Like to a pillar built of many stones,
Yet neither with good mortar well compact*   firmly put
                                      together
Nor with cement to fasten it in the joints,
But that it shakes with every blast of wind,
And, being touched, straight falls unto the earth,
And buries all his* haughty pride in dust.   its
No, let our love be rocks of adamant,
Which time nor place nor tempest can asunder.
    GREENE. Mosbie, leave protestations now,
And let us bethink us what we have to do.
Black Will and Shakebag I have placed
In the broom close, watching Arden's coming;
Let's to them and see what they have done.

                                    (*Exeunt.*)

Scene 2

    (*The Kentish coast opposite the Isle of Sheppy. Enter* ARDEN *and* FRANKLIN.)

    ARDEN. Oh, ferryman, where art thou?

    (*Enter the* FERRYMAN.)

    FERRYMAN. Here, here, go before to the boat, and I will fol-
low you.
    ARDEN. We have great haste; I pray thee, come away.
    FERRYMAN. Fie, what a mist is here!
    ARDEN. This mist, my friend, is mystical,
Like to a good companion's smoky brain,
That was half drowned with new ale overnight.
    FERRYMAN. 'Twere pity but his skull were opened to make
more chimney room.
    FRANKLIN. Friend, what's thy opinion of this mist?
    FERRYMAN. I think 'tis like to a curst* wife in a little   cross
house, that never leaves her husband till she have driven him

out at doors with a wet pair of eyes; then looks he as if his
house were a-fire, or some of his friends dead.

ARDEN. Speaks thou this of thine own experience?

FERRYMAN. Perhaps, ay; perhaps, no: For my wife is as
other women are, that is to say, governed by the moon.

FRANKLIN. By the moon? how, I pray thee?

FERRYMAN. Nay, thereby lies a bargain, and you shall not
have it fresh and fasting.*   for nothing(?)

ARDEN. Yes, I pray thee, good ferryman.

FERRYMAN. Then for this once; let it be midsummer moon,[28]
but yet my wife has another moon.

FRANKLIN. Another moon?

FERRYMAN. Ay, and it hath influences and eclipses.

ARDEN. Why, then, by this reckoning you sometimes play
the man in the moon?

FERRYMAN. Ay, but you had not best to meddle with that
moon, lest I scratch you by the face with my bramble-bush.

ARDEN. I am almost stifled with this fog; come, let's away.

FRANKLIN. And, sirrah, as we go, let us have some more of
your bold yeomanry.*   homely speech

FERRYMAN. Nay, by my troth, sir, but flat knavery.

                                                    (*Exeunt.*)

Scene 3

(*Another place on the coast. Enter* WILL *from one side, and*
SHAKEBAG *from the other.*)

SHAKEBAG. Oh, Will, where art thou?

WILL. Here, Shakebag, almost in hell's mouth, where I cannot see my way for smoke.

SHAKEBAG. I pray thee speak still that we may meet by the
sound, for I shall fall into some ditch or other, unless my feet
see better than my eyes.

WILL. Didst thou ever see better weather to run away with
another man's wife, or play with a wench at pot finger?

SHAKEBAG. No; this were a fine world for chandlers, if this
weather would last; for then a man should never dine nor sup
without candle-light. But, sirrah Will, what horses are those
that passed?

WILL. Why, didst thou hear any?

[28] In folklore, a time associated with a prevalence of lunacy.

SHAKEBAG. Ay, that I did.

WILL. My life for thine, 'twas Arden, and his companion, and then all our labour's lost.

SHAKEBAG. Nay, say not so, for if it be they, they may haply lose their way as we have done, and then we may chance meet with them.

WILL. Come, let us go on like a couple of blind pilgrims. (SHAKEBAG *falls into a ditch.*)

SHAKEBAG. Help, Will, help. I am almost drowned.

(*Enter the* FERRYMAN.)

FERRYMAN. Who's that that calls for help?

WILL. 'Twas none here, 'twas thou thyself.

FERRYMAN. I came to help him that called for help. Why, how now? who is this that's in the ditch? You are well enough served to go without a guide such weather as this.

WILL. Sirrah, what companies hath passed your ferry this morning?

FERRYMAN. None but a couple of gentlemen, that went to dine at my Lord Cheiny's.

WILL. Shakebag, did not I tell thee as much?

FERRYMAN. Why, sir, will you have any letters carried to them?

WILL. No, sir; get you gone.

FERRYMAN. Did you ever see such a mist as this?

WILL. No, nor such a fool as will rather be hought* hamstrung than get his way.

FERRYMAN. Why, sir, this is no Hough-Monday;²⁹ you are deceived.—What's his name, I pray you, sir?

SHAKEBAG. His name is Black Will.

FERRYMAN. I hope to see him one day hanged upon a hill.
(*Exit* FERRYMAN.)

SHAKEBAG. See how the sun hath cleared the foggy mist, Now we have missed the mark of our intent.

(*Enter* GREENE, MOSBIE, *and* ALICE.)

MOSBIE. Black Will and Shakebag, what make* you   do
here?

²⁹ Hock Monday, a festival day coming shortly after Easter.

What, is the deed done? is Arden dead?
WILL. What could a blinded man perform in arms?
Saw you not how till now the sky was dark,
That neither horse nor man could be discerned?
Yet did we hear their horses as they passed.
    GREENE. Have they escaped you, then, and passed the ferry?
    SHAKEBAG. Ay, for a while; but here we two will stay,
And at their coming back meet with them once more.
Zounds, I was ne'er so toiled* in all my life   fatigued
In following so slight a task as this.
    MOSBIE. How cam'st thou so berayed?*   mud-bespattered
    WILL. With making false footing in the dark;
He needs would follow them without a guide.
    (ALICE *gives them some coins.*)
    ALICE. Here's to pay for a fire and good cheer:
Get you to Feversham to the Flower-de-luce,
And rest yourselves until some other time.
    GREENE. Let me alone; it most concerns my state.
    WILL. Ay, Mistress Arden, this will serve the turn,
In case we fall into a second fog.
                    (*Exeunt* GREENE, WILL, *and* SHAKEBAG.)
    MOSBIE. These knaves will never do it, let us give it over.
    ALICE. First tell me how you like my new device:*   plan
Soon, when my husband is returning back,
You and I both marching arm in arm,
Like loving friends, we'll meet him on the way,
And boldly beard and brave him to his teeth.[30]
When words grow hot and blows begin to rise,
I'll call those cutters* forth your tenement,   cutthroats
Who, in a manner to take up the fray,
Shall wound my husband Hornsby* to the death. cuckolded husband
    MOSBIE. A fine device! why, this deserves a kiss.
                                        (*Exeunt.*)

Scene 4

(*The open country. Enter* DICK REEDE *and a* SAILOR.)

    SAILOR. Faith, Dick Reede, it is to little end:
His conscience is too liberal,[31] and he too niggardly

---

[30] That is, We'll openly defy him.
[31] That is, He is completely indifferent.

To part from any thing may do thee good.

REEDE. He is coming from Shorlow as I understand;
Here I'll intercept him, for at his house
He never will vouchsafe to speak with me.
If prayers and fair entreaties will not serve,
Or make no battery in his flinty breast,

(*Enter* FRANKLIN, ARDEN, *and* MICHAEL.)

I'll curse the carle,* and see what that will do.   villain
See where he comes to further my intent!—
Master Arden, I am now bound to the sea;
My coming to you was about the plat*   plot
Of ground which wrongfully you detain from me.
Although the rent of it be very small,
Yet it will help my wife and children,
Which here I leave in Feversham, God knows,
Needy and bare: for Christ's sake, let them have it!

ARDEN. Franklin, hearest thou this fellow speak?
That which he craves I dearly bought of him,
Although the rent of it was ever mine.—
Sirrah, you that ask these questions,
If with thy clamorous impeaching* tongue   accusing
Thou rail on me, as I have heard thou dost,
I'll lay thee up so close³² a twelve-month's day,
As thou shalt neither see the sun nor moon.
Look to it, for, as surely as I live,
I'll banish pity if thou use me thus.

REEDE. What, wilt thou do me wrong and threat me too,
Nay, then, I'll tempt thee, Arden, do thy worst.
God, I beseech thee, show some miracle
On thee or thine, in plaguing thee for this.
That plot of ground which thou detains from me,
I speak it in an agony of spirit,
Be ruinous and fatal unto thee!
Either there be butchered by thy dearest friends,
Or else be brought for men to wonder at,
Or thou or thine miscarry* in that place,   come to harm
Or there run mad and end thy cursèd days!

FRANKLIN. Fie, bitter knave, bridle thine envious*   spiteful
     tongue;
For curses are like arrows shot upright,

³² I'll put you away so tightly.

Which falling down light on the shooter's head.

REEDE. Light where they will! Were I upon the sea,
As oft I have in many a bitter storm,
And saw a dreadful southern flaw* at hand,   gust
The pilot quaking at the doubtful* storm,   dreaded
And all the sailors praying on their knees,
Even in that fearful time would I fall down,
And ask of God, whate'er betide of me,
Vengeance on Arden or some misevent*   mischance
To show the world what wrong the carle hath done.
This charge I'll leave with my distressful wife,
My children shall be taught such prayers as these;
And thus I go, but leave my curse with thee.

             (*Exeunt* REEDE *and* SAILOR.)

ARDEN. It is the railingest knave in Christendom,
And oftentimes the villain will be mad;
It greatly matters not what he says,
But I assure you I ne'er did him wrong.

    FRANKLIN. I think so, Master Arden.

    ARDEN. Now that our horses are gone home before,
My wife may haply meet me on the way.
For God knows she is grown passing kind of late,
And greatly changed from
The old humour of her wonted frowardness,[33]
And seeks by fair means to redeem old faults.

    FRANKLIN. Happy the change that alters for the best!
But see in any case you make no speech
Of the cheer we had at my Lord Cheiny's,
Although most bounteous and liberal,
For that will make her think herself more wronged,
In that we did not carry her along;
For sure she grieved that she was left behind.

    ARDEN. Come, Franklin, let us strain to mend our pace,
And take her unawares playing the cook;

        (*Enter* ALICE *and* MOSBIE.)

For I believe she'll strive to mend our cheer.

    FRANKLIN. Why, there's no better creatures in the world,
Than women are when they are in good humours.*   moods

    ARDEN. Who is that? Mosbie? what, so familiar?
Injurious strumpet, and thou ribald knave,

        [33] That is, she is greatly changed from her former perverse temperament.

Untwine those arms.

ALICE. Ay, with a sugared kiss let them untwine.

ARDEN. Ah, Mosbie! perjured beast! bear this and all!

MOSBIE. And yet no horned beast; the horns are thine.[34]

FRANKLIN. O monstrous! Nay, then it is time to draw.

ALICE. Help, help! they murder my husband.

(ARDEN, FRANKLIN, *and* MOSBIE *fight.*)

(*Enter* WILL *and* SHAKEBAG.)

SHAKEBAG. Zounds, who injures Master Mosbie?

(WILL *and* SHAKEBAG *join* MOSBIE. *The three are driven off
        by* ARDEN *and* FRANKLIN.)

                            Help, Will! I am hurt.

MOSBIE. I may thank you, Mistress Arden, for this wound.

                    (*Exeunt* MOSBIE, WILL, *and* SHAKEBAG.)

    ALICE. Ah, Arden, what folly blinded thee?

Ah, jealous harebrained man, what hast thou done!

When we, to welcome thee with intended sport,

Came lovingly to meet thee on thy way,

Thou drew'st thy sword, enraged with jealousy,

And hurt thy friend whose thoughts were free from harm:

All for a worthless kiss and joining arms,

Both done but merrily to try thy patience.

And me unhappy that devised the jest,

Which, though begun in sport, yet ends in blood!

    FRANKLIN. Marry, God defend me from such a jest!

    ALICE. Could'st thou not see us friendly smile on thee,

When we joined arms, and when I kissed his cheek?

Hast thou not lately found me over-kind?

Did'st thou not hear me cry "they murder thee"?

Called I not help to set my husband free?

No, ears and all were witched; ah me accursed

To link in liking with a frantic man!

Henceforth I'll be thy slave, no more thy wife,

For with that name I never shall content thee.

If I be merry, thou straightways thinks me light;

If sad, thou sayest the sullens* trouble me;   gloomy ill-humor

If well attired, thou thinks I will be gadding;

If homely, I seem sluttish* in thine eye: untidy

Thus am I still, and shall be while* I die.   until

Poor wench abused by thy misgovernment!

[34] The reference is to the horns of a cuckold.

ARDEN. But is it for truth that neither thou nor he
Intendedst malice in your misdemeanour?

ALICE. The heavens can witness of our harmless thoughts.

ARDEN. Then pardon me, sweet Alice, and forgive this fault!
Forget but this and never see the like.
Impose me penance, and I will perform it,
For in thy discontent I find a death,—
A death tormenting more than death itself.

ALICE. Nay, had'st thou loved me as thou dost pretend,
Thou wouldst have marked the speeches of thy friend,
Who going wounded from the place, he said
His skin was pierced only through my device;
And if sad sorrow taint thee for this fault,
Thou would'st have followed him, and seen him dressed,
And cried him mercy whom thou hast misdone:*   injured
Ne'er shall my heart be eased till this be done.

ARDEN. Content thee, sweet Alice, thou shalt have thy will,
Whate'er it be. For that I injured thee,
And wronged my friend, shame scourgeth my offence;
Come thou thyself, and go along with me,
And be a mediator 'twixt us two.

FRANKLIN. Why, Master Arden! know you what you do?
Will you follow him that hath dishonoured you?

ALICE. Why, canst thou prove I have been disloyal?

FRANKLIN. Why, Mosbie taunted your husband with the
horn.

ALICE. Ay, after he had reviled him
By the injurious name of perjured beast:
He knew no wrong could spite a jealous man
More than the hateful naming of the horn.

FRANKLIN. Suppose 'tis true; yet is it dangerous
To follow him whom he hath lately hurt.

ALICE. A fault confessed is more than half amends;
But men of such ill spirit as yourself
Work crosses and debates 'twixt man and wife.

ARDEN. I pray thee, gentle Franklin, hold thy peace:
I know my wife counsels me for the best.
I'll seek out Mosbie where his wound is dressed,
And salve this hapless quarrel if I may.

(*Exeunt* ARDEN *and* ALICE.)

FRANKLIN. He whom the devil drives must go
        perforce.*   of necessity
Poor gentleman, how soon he is bewitched!

And yet, because his wife is the instrument,
His friends must not be lavish in their speech.

(*Exit* FRANKLIN.)

ACT V

Scene 1

(*Before and in* ARDEN'S *house. Enter* WILL, SHAKEBAG, *and* GREENE.)

WILL. Sirrah Greene, when was I so long in killing a man?

GREENE. I think we shall never do it; let us give it over.

SHAKEBAG. Nay, Zounds! we'll kill him, though we be hanged at his door for our labour.

WILL. Thou knowest, Greene, that I have lived in London this twelve years, where I have made some go upon wooden legs for taking the wall on me;[35] divers with silver noses for saying "There goes Black Will!" I have cracked as many blades as thou hast nuts.

GREENE. O monstrous lie!

WILL. Faith, in a manner I have. The bawdy-houses have paid me tribute; there durst not a whore set up, unless she have agreed with me first for opening her shop-windows. For a cross word of a tapster I have pierced one barrel after another with my dagger, and held him by the ears till all his beer hath run out. In Thames Street a brewer's cart was like to have run over me: I made no more ado, but went to the clerk and cut all the notches of his tallies,[36] and beat them about his head. I and my company have taken the constable from his watch, and carried him about the fields on a coltstaff.[37] I have broken a sergeant's head with his own mace, and bailed whom I list* with my sword and buckler. All the ten-   wished penny-alehouses-men would stand every morning with a quart-pot in their hand, saying, "Will it please your worship drink?" He that had not done so, had been sure to have had his sign pulled down and his lattice borne away the next night. To conclude, what have I not done? yet cannot do this; doubtless, he is preserved by miracle.

[35] For forcing me into the street.
[36] The accounts were kept by making notches in sticks.
[37] Cowlstaff, a strong stick used to carry tubs.

(*Enter* ALICE *and* MICHAEL *from the house.*)

GREENE. Hence, Will! here comes Mistress Arden.

ALICE. Ah, gentle Michael, art thou sure they're friends?

MICHAEL. Why, I saw them when they both shook hands.
When Mosbie bled, he even wept for sorrow,
And railed on Franklin that was cause of all.
No sooner came the surgeon in at doors,
But my master took to his purse and gave him money,
And, to conclude, sent me to bring you word
That Mosbie, Franklin, Bradshaw, Adam Fowle,
With divers of his neighbours and his friends,
Will come and sup with you at our house this night.

ALICE. Ah, gentle Michael, run thou back again,
And, when my husband walks into the fair,
Bid Mosbie steal from him and come to me;
And this night shall thou and Susan be made sure.

MICHAEL. I'll go tell him.

ALICE. And as thou goest, tell John cook of our guests,
And bid him lay it on, spare for no cost.

(*Exit* MICHAEL.)

WILL. Nay, and there be such cheer, we will bid ourselves.—
Mistress Arden, Dick Greene and I do mean to sup with you.

ALICE. And welcome shall you be.

(*Leading them into the house.*)
Ah, gentlemen,
How missed you of your purpose yesternight?

GREENE. 'Twas long of* Shakebag, that   because of
unlucky villain.

SHAKEBAG. Thou dost me wrong; I did as much as any.

WILL. Nay then, Mistress Arden, I'll tell you how it was:
When he should have locked with both his hilts,
He in a bravery* flourished o'er his head;   bravado
With that comes Franklin at him lustily,
And hurts the slave; with that he slinks away.
Now his way had been to have come hand and feet, one and
two round, at his costard;* he like a fool bears his   head
sword-point half a yard out of danger. I lie here for my life;
if the devil come, and he brave no more strength than
fence,* he shall never beat me from this ward.*   fencing skill/
defense
I'll stand to it; a buckler in a skilful hand is as good
as a castle; nay, 'tis better than a sconce,* for I have   fort
tried it.

Mosbie, perceiving this, began to faint:
With that comes Arden with his arming sword,*   two-handed
And thrust him through the shoulder in a trice.   sword
   ALICE. Ay, but I wonder why you both stood still.
   WILL. Faith, I was so amazed, I could not strike.
   ALICE. Ah, sirs, had he yesternight been slain,
For every drop of his detested blood
I would have crammed in angels* in thy fist,   coins
And kissed thee, too, and hugged thee in my arms.
   WILL. Patient yourself, we cannot help it now.
Greene and we two will dog him through the fair,
And stab him in the crowd, and steal away.

   (*Enter* MOSBIE.)

   ALICE. It is unpossible; but here comes he
That will, I hope, invent some surer means.
Sweet Mosbie, hide thy arm, it kills my heart.
   MOSBIE. Ay, Mistress Arden, this is your favour.*   love token
   ALICE. Ah, say not so; for when I saw thee hurt,
I could have took the weapon thou let'st fall,
And run at Arden; for I have sworn
That these mine eyes, offended with his sight,
Shall never close till Arden's be shut up.
This night I rose and walked about the chamber,
And twice or thrice I thought to have murdered him.
   MOSBIE. What, in the night? then had we been undone.
   ALICE. Why, how long shall he live?
   MOSBIE. Faith, Alice, no longer than this night.—
Black Will and Shakebag, will you two perform
The complot* that I have laid?   plot
   WILL. Ay, or else think me a villain.
   GREENE. And rather than you shall want, I'll help myself.
   MOSBIE. You, Master Greene, shall single Franklin forth,
And hold him with a long tale of strange news,
That he may not come home till supper-time.
I'll fetch Master Arden home, and we like friends
Will play a game or two at tables* here.   backgammon
   ALICE. But what of all this? how shall he be slain?
   MOSBIE. Why, Black Will and Shakebag locked within the
      counting-house*   office
Shall at a certain watchword given rush forth.
   WILL. What shall the watchword be?
   MOSBIE. "Now I take you"; that shall be the word:

But come not forth before in any case.

WILL. I warrant you. But who shall lock me in?

ALICE. That will I do; thou'st keep the key thyself.

MOSBIE. Come, Master Greene, go you along with me.
See all things ready, Alice, against we come.

ALICE. Take no care for that; send you him home.

(*Exeunt* MOSBIE *and* GREENE.)

And if he e'er go forth again, blame me.
Come, Black Will, that in mine eyes art fair;
Next unto Mosbie do I honour thee;
Instead of fair words and large promises
My hands shall play you golden harmony:
How like you this? say, will you do it, sirs?

WILL. Ay, and that bravely,* too. Mark my device: splendidly
Place Mosbie, being a stranger, in a chair,
And let your husband sit upon a stool,
That I may come behind him cunningly,
And with a towel pull him to the ground,
Then stab him till his flesh be as a sieve;
That done, bear him behind the Abbey,
That those that find him murdered may suppose
Some slave or other killed him for his gold.

ALICE. A fine device! you shall have twenty pound,
And, when he is dead, you shall have forty more,
And, lest you might be suspected staying here,
Michael shall saddle you two lusty geldings;
Ride whither you will, to Scotland, or to Wales,
I'll see you shall not lack, where'er you be.

WILL. Such words would make one kill a thousand men!
Give me the key: which is the counting-house?

ALICE. Here would I stay and still encourage you;
But that I know how resolute you are.

SHAKEBAG. Tush, you are too faint-hearted; we must do it.

ALICE. But Mosbie will be there, whose very looks
Will add unwonted courage to my thought,
And make me the first that shall adventure on him.

WILL. Tush, get you gone; 'tis we must do the deed.
When this door opens next, look for his death.

(*Exeunt* WILL *and* SHAKEBAG.)

ALICE. Ah, would he now were here that it might open!
I shall no more be closed in Arden's arms,
That like the snakes of black Tisiphone[38]

---

[38] One of the Furies; she was represented with snakes encircling
her arms like bracelets and with one reptile in her hair.

Sting me with their embracings! Mosbie's arms
Shall compass* me, and, were I made a star,   encircle
I would have none other spheres but those.
There is no nectar but in Mosbie's lips!
Had chaste Diana* kissed him, she like me   the moon goddess
Would grow love-sick, and from her watery bower
Fling down Endymion[39] and snatch him up:
Then blame not me that slay a silly* man   .   insignificant
Not half so lovely as Endymion.

(*Enter* MICHAEL.)

MICHAEL. Mistress, my master is coming hard by.
ALICE. Who comes with him?
MICHAEL. Nobody but Mosbie.
ALICE. That's well, Michael. Fetch in the
tables,* and when thou hast done, stand   the backgammon
before the counting-house door.   tables
MICHAEL. Why so?
ALICE. Black Will is locked within to do the deed.
MICHAEL. What? shall he die to-night?
ALICE. Ay, Michael.
MICHAEL. But shall not Susan know it?
ALICE. Yes, for she'll be as secret as ourselves.
MICHAEL. That's brave.* I'll go fetch the tables.   splendid
ALICE. But, Michael, hark to me a word or two:
When my husband is come in, lock the street-door;
He shall be murdered or* the guests come in.   before

(*Exit* MICHAEL.)

(*Enter* ARDEN *and* MOSBIE.)

Husband, what mean you to bring Mosbie home?
Although I wished you to be reconciled,
'Twas more for fear of you than love of him.
Black Will and Greene are his companions,
And they are cutters,* and may cut you short: cutthroats
Therefore I thought it good to make you friends.
But wherefore do you bring him hither now?

[39] Enamored of the handsome youth Endymion, Diana visited
him nightly as he slept on Mount Latmus, covering him with
kisses.

You have given me my supper with his sight.[40]

MOSBIE. Master Arden, methinks your wife would have
    me gone.

ARDEN. No, good master Mosbie; women will be prating.
Alice, bid him welcome; he and I are friends.

ALICE. You may enforce* me to it, if you will;   compel
But I had rather die than bid him welcome.
His company hath purchased me ill friends,
And therefore will I ne'er frequent it more.

MOSBIE (*aside*).—Oh, how cunningly she can dissemble!

ARDEN. Now he is here, you will not serve me so.

ALICE. I pray you be not angry or displeased;
I'll bid him welcome, seeing you'll have it so.
You are welcome, Master Mosbie; will you sit down?

(ALICE *motions* MOSBIE *into a chair which faces the counting-house door. She then calls for* MICHAEL. *He enters with
the tables, and sets them before* MOSBIE.)

MOSBIE. I know I am welcome to your loving husband;
But for yourself, you speak not from your heart.

ALICE. And if I do not, sir, think I have cause.

MOSBIE. Pardon me, Master Arden; I'll away.

ARDEN. No, good Master Mosbie.

ALICE. We shall have guests enough, though you go hence.

MOSBIE. I pray you, Master Arden, let me go.

ARDEN. I pray thee, Mosbie, let her prate her fill.

ALICE. The doors are open, sir, you may be gone.

MICHAEL (*aside*).—Nay, that's a lie, for I have locked the
    doors.

ARDEN. Sirrah, fetch me a cup of wine, I'll make them
    friends.

                    (*Exit* MICHAEL.)

And, gentle Mistress Alice, seeing you are so stout,*   unyielding
You shall begin! frown not, I'll have it so.

ALICE. I pray you meddle with that you have to do.

ARDEN. Why, Alice! how can I do too much for him
Whose life I have endangered without cause?

(MICHAEL *returns with the cup of wine.*)

ALICE. 'Tis true; and, seeing 'twas partly through my means,
I am content to drink to him for this once.
Here, Master Mosbie! and I pray you, henceforth
Be you as strange to me as I to you.

    [40] That is, ruined my appetite.

Your company hath purchased me ill friends,
And I for you, God knows, have undeserved
Been ill spoken of in every place;
Therefore henceforth frequent my house no more.
    MOSBIE. I'll see your husband in despite of you.
Yet, Arden, I protest to thee by heaven,
Thou ne'er shalt see me more after this night,
I'll go to Rome rather than be forsworn.
    ARDEN. Tush, I'll have no such vows made in my house.
    ALICE. Yes, I pray you, husband, let him swear;
And, on that condition, Mosbie, pledge me here.
    MOSBIE. Ay, as willingly as I mean to live.
    ARDEN. Come, Alice, is our supper ready yet?
    ALICE. It will by then you have played a game at tables.
(She motions MICHAEL to draw up a stool for ARDEN. He does so and then takes his position before the counting-house door.)
    ARDEN. Come, Master Mosbie, what shall we play for?
    MOSBIE. Three games for a French crown, sir,
      and please* you.   if it pleases
    ARDEN. Content.

(They play at the tables.[41] Enter WILL and SHAKEBAG.)

WILL. —Can he not take him yet? what a spite is that?
    ALICE. —Not yet, Will; take heed he see thee not.
    WILL. —I fear he will spy me as I am coming.
    MICHAEL. —To prevent that, creep betwixt my legs.
    MOSBIE. One ace, or else I lose the game.
    ARDEN. Marry, sir, there's two for failing.[42]
    MOSBIE. Ah, Master Arden, "now I can take you."
(WILL pulls him down with a towel.)
    ARDEN. Mosbie! Michael! Alice! what will you do?
    WILL. Nothing but take you up, sir, nothing else.
    MOSBIE. There's for the pressing iron you told me of.
(Stabs him.)
    SHAKEBAG. And there's for the ten pound in my sleeve.
(Stabs him.)

---

[41] According to the account in Holinshed, Michael at this point "stood at his master's back, holding a candle in his hand, to shadow Black Will, that Arden might by no means perceive him coming forth."

[42] If one is insufficient.

ALICE. What! groans thou? nay, then give me the weapon!
Take this for hindering Mosbie's love and mine.
(*She stabs him.*)
MICHAEL. O, mistress!
WILL. Ah, that villain will betray us all.
MOSBIE. Tush, fear him not; he will be secret.
MICHAEL. Why, dost thou think I will betray myself?
SHAKEBAG. In Southwark dwells a bonny northern lass,
The widow Chambly; I'll to her house now,
And if she will not give me harborough,*   harbor
I'll make booty of the quean* even to her smock.   ill-behaved
                                                    woman
WILL. Shift for yourselves; we two will leave you now.
ALICE. First lay the body in the counting-house.
(*They lay the body in the counting-house.*)
WILL. We have our gold; Mistress Alice, adieu;
Mosbie, farewell, and Michael, farewell too.

                                        (*Exeunt.*)

(*Enter* SUSAN.)

SUSAN. Mistress, the guests are at the doors.
Hearken, they knock: what, shall I let them in?
ALICE. Mosbie, go thou and bear them company.
                                    (*Exit* MOSBIE.)
And, Susan, fetch water and wash away this blood.
SUSAN. The blood cleaveth to the ground and will not out.
ALICE. But with my nails I'll scrape away the blood;—
The more I strive, the more the blood appears!
SUSAN. What's the reason, Mistress, can you tell?
ALICE. Because I blush not at my husband's death.

(*Enter* MOSBIE.)

MOSBIE. How now? what's the matter? is all well?
ALICE. Ay, well, if Arden were alive again.
In vain we strive, for here his blood remains.
MOSBIE. Why, strew rushes on it, can you not?
This wench doth nothing: fall unto the work.
ALICE. 'Twas thou that made me murder him.
MOSBIE. What of that?
ALICE. Nay, nothing, Mosbie, so it be not known.
MOSBIE. Keep thou it close,* and 'tis unpossible.   secret
ALICE. Ah, but I cannot! was he not slain by me?

My husband's death torments me at the heart.
  MOSBIE. It shall not long torment thee, gentle Alice;
I am thy husband, think no more of him.

(*Enter* ADAM FOWLE *and* BRADSHAW.)

BRADSHAW. How now, Mistress Arden? what ail you weep?[43]
  MOSBIE. Because her husband is abroad so late.
A couple of ruffians threatened him yesternight,
And she, poor soul, is afraid he should be hurt.
  ADAM. Is't nothing else? tush, he'll be here anon.

(*Enter* GREENE.)

GREENE. Now, Mistress Arden, lack you any guests?
  ALICE. Ah, Master Greene, did you see my husband lately?
  GREENE. I saw him walking behind the Abbey even now.

(*Enter* FRANKLIN.)

  ALICE. I do not like this being out so late.—
Master Franklin, where did you leave my husband?
  FRANKLIN. Believe me I saw him not since morning.
Fear you not, he'll come anon; meantime
You may do well to bid his guests sit down.
  ALICE. Ay, so they shall; Master Bradshaw, sit you there;
I pray you, be content, I'll have my will.
Master Mosbie, sit you in my husband's seat.
  MICHAEL. —Susan, shall thou and I wait on them?
Or, an thou sayest the word, let us sit down too.
  SUSAN. —Peace, we have other matters now in hand.
I fear me, Michael, all will be bewrayed.*   revealed
  MICHAEL. —Tush, so it be known that I shall marry thee
in the morning, I care not though I be hanged ere night. But
to prevent the worst, I'll buy some ratsbane.
  SUSAN. —Why, Michael, wilt thou poison thyself?
  MICHAEL. —No, but my mistress, for I fear she'll tell.
  SUSAN. —Tush, Michael; fear not her, she's wise enough.
  MOSBIE. Sirrah Michael, gives a cup of beer.—
Mistress Arden, here's to your husband.
  ALICE. My husband!

[43] That is, What ails you that you weep?

FRANKLIN. What ails you, woman, to cry so suddenly?

ALICE. Ah, neighbours, a sudden qualm came o'er my heart;
My husband being forth torments my mind.
I know something's amiss, he is not well;
Or else I should have heard of him ere now.

MOSBIE (*aside*).—She will undo us through her
foolishness.

GREENE. Fear not, Mistress Arden, he's well enough.

ALICE. Tell not me; I know he is not well:
He was not wont for to stay thus late.
Good Master Franklin, go and seek him forth,
And if you find him, send him home to me,
And tell him what a fear he hath put me in.

FRANKLIN (*aside*).—I like not this; I pray God all be well.
I'll seek him out, and find him if I can.

(*Exeunt* FRANKLIN, MOSBIE, *and* GREENE.)

ALICE (*aside to* MICHAEL).—Michael, how shall I do to
rid the rest away?

MICHAEL (*aside to* ALICE).—Leave that to my charge,
let me alone.
'Tis very late, Master Bradshaw,
And there are many false knaves abroad,
And you have many narrow lanes to pass.

BRADSHAW. Faith, friend Michael, and thou sayest true.
Therefore I pray thee light's forth and lend's a link.

(*Exeunt* BRADSHAW, ADAM, *and* MICHAEL.)

ALICE. Michael, bring them to the doors, but do not stay;
You know I do not love to be alone.
—Go, Susan, and bid thy brother come:
But wherefore should he come? Here is nought but fear;
Stay, Susan, stay, and help to counsel me.

SUSAN. Alas, I counsel! fear frights away my wits.

(*They open the counting-house door, and look upon*
ARDEN.)

ALICE. See, Susan, where thy quondam master lies,
Sweet Arden, smeared in blood and filthy gore.

SUSAN. My brother, you, and I shall rue this deed.

ALICE. Come, Susan, help to lift his body forth,
And let our salt tears be his obsequies.

(*Enter* MOSBIE *and* GREENE.)

MOSBIE. Now now, Alice, whither will you bear him?

ALICE. Sweet Mosbie, art thou come? Then weep that will:

I have my wish in that I joy thy sight.
  GREENE. Well, it behoves us to be circumspect.
  MOSBIE. Ay, for Franklin thinks that we have murdered him.
  ALICE. Ay, but he cannot prove it for his life.
We'll spend this night in dalliance and in sport.

  (*Enter* MICHAEL.)

  MICHAEL. O mistress, the Mayor and all the watch
Are coming towards our house with glaives and bills. *swords and
                                                       halberds
  ALICE. Make the door fast; let them not come in.
  MOSBIE. Tell me, sweet Alice, how shall I escape?
  ALICE. Out at the back-door, over the pile of wood,
And for one night lie at the Flower-de-luce.
  MOSBIE. That is the next way to betray myself.
  GREENE. Alas, Mistress Arden, the watch will take me here,
And cause suspicion, where else would be none.
  ALICE. Why, take that way that Master Mosbie doth;
But first convey the body to the fields.
  MOSBIE. Until to-morrow, sweet Alice, now farewell:
And see you confess nothing in any case.
  GREENE. Be resolute, Mistress Alice, betray us not
But cleave to us as we will stick to you.
(*Exeunt* MOSBIE, GREENE, MICHAEL, *and* SUSAN *with the
            body, leaving* ALICE *alone for a short interval.*)
  ALICE. Now, let the judge and juries do their worst:
My house is clear, and now I fear them not.
  SUSAN. As we went, it snowed all the way,
Which makes me fear our footsteps will be spied.
  ALICE. Peace, fool, the snow will cover them again.
  SUSAN. But it had done before we came back again.
  ALICE. Hark, hark, they knock! go, Michael, let them in.

  (*Enter the* MAYOR *and the* WATCH.)

How now, Master Mayor, have you brought my husband
      home?
  MAYOR. I saw him come into your house an hour ago.
  ALICE. You are deceived; it was a Londoner.
  MAYOR. Mistress Arden, know you not one that is called
      Black Will?
  ALICE. I know none such: what mean these questions?

MAYOR. I have the Council's warrant to apprehend him.
ALICE (*aside*).—I am glad it is no worse.
Why, Master Mayor, think you I harbour any such?
MAYOR. We are informed that here he is;
And therefore pardon us, for we must search.
ALICE. Ay, search, and spare you not, through every room:
Were my husband at home, you would not offer this.

(*Enter* FRANKLIN.)

Master Franklin, what mean you come so sad?
FRANKLIN. Arden, thy husband, and my friend, is slain.
ALICE. Ah, by whom? Master Franklin, can you tell?
FRANKLIN. I know not; but behind the Abbey
There he lies murdered in most piteous* case.   **brutally**
MAYOR. But, Master Franklin, are you sure 'tis he?
FRANKLIN. I am too sure; would God I were deceived.
ALICE. Find out the murderers, let them be known.
FRANKLIN. Ay, so they shall: come you along with us.
ALICE. Wherefore?
FRANKLIN. Know you this hand-towel and this knife?
SUSAN (*aside to* MICHAEL).—Ah, Michael, through this thy
   negligence
Thou hast betrayed and undone us all.
MICHAEL (*aside to* SUSAN).—I was so afraid I knew not
   what I did:
I thought I had thrown them both into the well.
ALICE. It is the pig's blood we had to supper.
But wherefore stay you? find out the murderers.
MAYOR. I fear me you'll prove one of them yourself.
ALICE. I one of them? what mean such questions?
FRANKLIN. I fear me he was murdered in this house
And carried to the fields; for from that place
Backwards and forwards may you see
The print of many feet within the snow.
And look about this chamber where we are,
And you shall find part of his guiltless blood;
For in his slipshoe* did I find some rushes,   **slipper**
Which argueth he was murdered in this room.
MAYOR. Look in the place where he was wont to sit.
See, see! his blood! it is too manifest.
ALICE. It is a cup of wine that Michael shed.

MICHAEL. Ay, truly.

FRANKLIN. It is his blood, which, strumpet, thou hast shed.
But if I live, thou and thy 'complices
Which have conspired and wrought his death shall rue it.

ALICE. Ah, Master Franklin, God and heaven can tell
I loved him more than all the world beside.
But bring me to him, let me see his body.

FRANKLIN. Bring that villain and Mosbie's sister too;
And one of you go to the Flower-de-luce,
And seek for Mosbie, and apprehend him too.

(*Exeunt.*)

Scene 2

(*An obscure street in London. Enter* SHAKEBAG.)

SHAKEBAG. The widow Chambly in her husband's days I
    kept;
And now he's dead, she is grown so stout
She will not know her old companions.
I came thither, thinking to have had harbour
As I was wont,
And she was ready to thrust me out at doors;
But whether she would go or no, I got me up,
And as she followed me, I spurned* her down the stairs,   kicked
And broke her neck, and cut her tapster's throat,
And now I am going to fling them in the Thames.
I have the gold; what care I though it be known!
I'll cross the water and take sanctuary.

(*Exit.*)

Scene 3

(ARDEN'S *house at Feversham. Enter the* MAYOR, MOSBIE,
FRANKLIN, MICHAEL, *and* SUSAN.)

MAYOR. See, Mistress Arden, where your husband lies;
Confess this foul fault and be penitent.

ALICE. Arden, sweet husband, what shall I say?
The more I sound his name, the more he bleeds;[44]
This blood condemns me, and in gushing forth
Speaks as it falls, and asks me why I did it.

---

[44] According to superstition, the body of the victim began
bleeding again in the presence of the murderer, thereby pointing
out the criminal.

Forgive me, Arden: I repent me now,
And, would my death save thine, thou should'st not die.
Rise up, sweet Arden, and enjoy thy love,
And frown not on me when we meet in heaven:
In heaven I'll love thee, though on earth I did not.
    MAYOR. Say, Mosbie, what made thee murder him?
    FRANKLIN. Study not for an answer; look not down:
His purse and girdle[45] found at thy bed's head
Witness sufficiently thou didst the deed;
It bootless* is to swear thou didst it not.   useless
    MOSBIE. I hired Black Will and Shakebag, ruffians both,
And they and I have done this murderous deed.
But wherefore stay we? Come and bear me hence.
    FRANKLIN. Those ruffians shall not escape; I will up to
      London,
And get the Council's warrant to apprehend them.

                                                          (*Exeunt.*)

Scene 4

(*The Kentish coast. Enter* WILL.)

    WILL. Shakebag, I hear, hath taken sanctuary,
But I am so pursued with hues and cries
For petty robberies that I have done,
That I can come unto no sanctuary.
Therefore must I in some oyster-boat
At last be fain* to go on board some hoy,*   content/small
And so to Flushing. There is no staying here.   boat
At Sittingburgh the watch was like to take me,
And had not I with my buckler covered my head,
And run full blank at all adventures,*   taken all risks
I am sure I had ne'er gone further than that place;
For the constable had twenty warrants to apprehend me,
Besides that, I robbed him and his man once at Gadshill.
Farewell, England; I'll go to Flushing now.

                                                           (*Exit.* WILL)

Scene 5

(*Justice-room at Feversham. Enter* MAYOR, MOSBIE, ALICE,
MICHAEL, SUSAN, *and* BRADSHAW.)

    [45] Belt for carrying a purse.

MAYOR. Come, make haste, and bring away the prisoners.

BRADSHAW. Mistress Arden, you are now going to God,
And I am by the law condemned to die
About a letter I brought from Master Greene.
I pray you, Mistress Arden, speak the truth:
Was I ever privy to your intent or no?[46]

ALICE. What should I say? You brought me such a letter,
But I dare swear thou knewest not the contents.
Leave now to trouble me with wordly things,
And let me meditate upon my saviour Christ,
Whose blood must save me for the blood I shed.

MOSBIE. How long shall I live in this hell of grief?
Convey me from the presence of that strumpet.

ALICE. Ah, but for thee I had never been a strumpet.
What cannot oaths and protestations do,
When men have opportunity to woo?
I was too young to sound* thy villainies,   penetrate
But now I find it and repent too late.

SUSAN. Ah, gentle brother, wherefore should I die?
I knew not of it till the deed was done.

MOSBIE. For thee I mourn more than for myself;
But let it suffice, I cannot save thee now.

MICHAEL. And if your brother and my mistress
Had not promised me you in marriage,
I had ne'er given consent to this foul deed.

MAYOR. Leave to accuse each other now,
And listen to the sentence I shall give.
Bear Mosbie and his sister to London straight,
Where they in Smithfield must be executed;
Bear Mistress Arden unto Canterbury,
Where her sentence is she must be burnt;
Michael and Bradshaw in Feversham must suffer death.

ALICE. Let my death make amends for all my sins.

MOSBIE. Fie upon women! this shall be my song;
But bear me hence, for I have lived too long.

SUSAN. Seeing no hope on earth, in heaven is my hope.

MICHAEL. Faith, I care not, seeing I die with Susan.

BRADSHAW. My blood be on his head that gave the sentence.

MAYOR. To speedy execution with them all!

(Exeunt.)

[46] Although Bradshaw was not implicated in the murder, the
Holinshed *Chronicle's* account indicates that he was not a particularly reputable individual. The author of the play is following the source in sentencing him to death along with his companions.

EPILOGUE

(*Enter* FRANKLIN.)

FRANKLIN. Thus have you seen the truth of Arden's death.
As for the ruffians, Shakebag and Black Will,
The one took sanctuary, and, being sent for out,
Was murdered in Southwark as he passed
To Greenwich, where the Lord Protector lay.
Black Will was burned in Flushing on a stage;
Greene was hanged at Osbridge in Kent;
The painter fled and how he died we know not.
But this above the rest is to be noted:
Arden lay murdered in that plot of ground
Which he by force and violence held from Reede;
And in the grass his body's print was seen
Two years and more after the deed was done.
Gentlemen, we hope you'll pardon this naked tragedy,
Wherein no filèd points are foisted in[47]
To make it gracious to the ear or eye;
For simple truth is gracious enough,
And needs no other points of glosing stuff.*   palliatives
(*Exit.*)

[47] That is, which has not been touched up.

The Spanish Tragedy

BY THOMAS KYD

One of the first playwrights who wrote for the popular Elizabethan stage (rather than for the schools or for the Inns of Court, where gentlemen studied for the legal profession), was Thomas Kyd (1558–1594). Although none of the early texts actually bear his name, Kyd leaped into fame with the 1586–87 production of *The Spanish Tragedy*. The son of a London scrivener or notary, he was sent in 1565 to the Merchant Taylors' School, where the great Elizabethan poet Edmund Spenser was his schoolmate. Apparently Kyd's formal education ended there, but although he did not attend either of England's two universities, he acquired a working knowledge of Latin, a taste for Seneca's Roman tragedies, and a talent for writing exciting theatre which the school productions of his formative years may well have awakened. He probably wrote or contributed to other plays, including the anonymous *Arden of Feversham,* and translated from the French a sixteenth-century Senecan imitation, *Cornélie* by Robert Garnier. (Kyd appears to have been proficient in French and Italian as well as in Latin.) He is also believed to have been the author of the lost play of *Hamlet* upon which Shakespeare apparently based his masterpiece.

The Spanish Tragedy had an enormous success and enrolled Kyd in the ranks of the literary profession then rarely pursued with any success by men who had not attended either Oxford or Cambridge. One of his acquaintances was Christopher Marlowe, with whom he shared quarters in London for a short time—an association that was to cost him dearly. Accused of atheism when incriminating antireligious papers were seized in their home, Kyd was arrested and tortured, but he was freed after maintaining that the papers belonged to Marlowe, who was consequently apprehended and ordered to appear before the Privy Council. But Kyd lost his patron as a result of this investigation, and having failed to obtain finan-

73

cial assistance from the Lord Chancellor, he died a year later
in great poverty.

The Spanish Tragedy is noteworthy both as a play and an
influence. Although Kyd was a mediocre poet, he was an accomplished rhetorician and dramatist. Moreover, his gifts
suited *The Spanish Tragedy,* so that the rhetoric matches the
action, and the action is apropriate to the high-tension state
of mind and feeling that justify and at times even require the
rhetoric. The latter consists of the highflown style known as
Senecan, because associated with Seneca, the most influential
classical playwright. Seneca's work became accessible even
to Elizabethans who, like Shakespeare, had "small Latin" or
none at all, in an English translation. His plays were published
in 1581 under the title *Seneca His Tenne Tragedies* (one of
the ten, *Octavia,* was actually not Seneca's).

Replete with sonorous tirades and exclamations, the style
suited the melodrama of revenge, disguise, and surprise that
make up Kyd's plot. At the same time his classical allusions
gave the plot dignity, and his Senecan maxims, known as *sen-
tentiae* or "sentences," added a philosophical tinge that goes
far toward justifying the word "Tragedy" in the title. Further
justification is supplied by Kyd's focus on characters who may
be extreme in love and hate but who are not cardboard figures, especially the protagonist, Hieronimo, whose motivation
—a grieving father's desire to avenge the foul murder of his
son—is not only comprehensible but compelling. The play
also has interesting secondary characters, especially the proud
beauty Bel-imperia and her ruthlessly designing brother Lorenzo, who contrives the murder of Bel-imperia's lover Horatio
in order to give her to the Prince of Portugal who can advance
his fortunes. Stiff though they be, the characters are impelled
by genuine feeling and, in the case of Lorenzo, by mentally
acute villainy. In the case of Hieronimo, as in that of Hamlet,
inner conflict and mental disturbance, usually feigned but
sometimes real, are arresting, even if Hieronimo himself is too
prolix and his conduct at times unclear.

An even more important achievement for the inchoate early
Elizabethan drama was Kyd's command of structure. Though
turgid, the play is organized into a dramatic whole by division
into scenes and acts, by action and counteraction, and by the
inception and development of a plot that suspensefully hurtles
toward its catastrophic conclusion. A good part of the action,
moreover, is presented on the stage rather than narrated in
the customary Senecan imitations. In this respect Kyd served

and advanced the cause of popular, as opposed to academic, theatre and set a pattern for playwrights who invigorated the drama with their "unclassical" shows of violence on the stage to replace discreet reports by a Senecan Messenger, or *Nuntius*.

Paradoxically Kyd served Seneca better than did the academicians and literati who paid him the dubious compliment of strict imitation. The success of *The Spanish Tragedy* established the popularity of the "revenge tragedy" genre which reached its literary and dramatic zenith with Shakespeare's *Hamlet* and had a period of renascence during the reign of James I. Kyd's effective mingling of prose passages with blank verse also set a profitable example of variety and relative realism in tragedy. Kyd was probably not unique in adopting such Senecan dramatic elements as a chorus and a ghost who calls for revenge at the beginning of a play, but he was unique in making them work theatrically in the "public" theatre, even at the cost of a sensationalism which invited parody from more sophisticated successors. Into the revenge-tragedy genre he also introduced the vacillating revenger (like Hamlet, Hieronimo dallies) and the "play-within-the-play" device for promoting vengeance, which in *Hamlet* consists of "The Mousetrap" piece with which Hamlet detects his uncle's guilt. Shakespeare postponed the revenge; Kyd brings the play to a conclusion by having the characters carry out their revenge during the "play-within-the-play" episode, while the spectators think that the murders are merely feigned.

The crudities of *The Spanish Tragedy*, especially noticeable in its excessively narrative exposition, are minor by comparison with the skill Kyd exhibited in the invention of stage situations, as in the scene in which Hieronimo is roused from his bed and led to discover his son's body hanging in his arbor and the ingenious use of the play-within-the-play scene to carry out the revenge. On balance, it is possible to agree with Ashley Thorndike's judgment (in *Tragedy,* p. 104) that the play cannot be "pushed aside as mere blood and thunder tirade" and that "Beneath its absurdities there lies the conception of an inner struggle against overwhelming responsibility, and of the conflict of the individual against evil and fate."

J. G.

Authorship. Early editions of the play bear no author's name. Attribution to Thomas Kyd comes from an allusion of Thomas Heywood's in his *Apology for Actors* (1612). Heywood prefaces a quotation from Act IV, Scene 1, of the play with the statement, "Therefore M[aster] Kid, in his *Spanish Tragedy,* upon occasion presenting itself, thus writes. . . ." There are no grounds for doubting Heywood's statement.

Date. Conclusive evidence for establishing a date still remains to be discovered. The play has been placed anywhere from 1582 to 1590, most scholars favoring 1586–87. Evidence for 1582 as the initial date stems from the observation that the opening of Act II, Scene 1, imitates Sonnet XLVII from Thomas Watson's *Hecatompathia,* a work which was entered in the Stationers' Register on March 31, 1582. The terminal date is 1592. The play was entered in the Stationers' Register on October 6 of that year and had previously been acted at the Rose earlier in the year, as entries in Henslowe's *Diary* indicate.

Text and Publishing Data. The earliest extant edition is that of 1592, printed by Edward Allde and published by Edward White. It claims to be a corrected version of an earlier one published by Abel Jeffes, who held the copyright. Since White had no legal right to publish his version, the Stationers Company fined him, confiscated the stock, and sold the copies for the benefit of the poor of the company. This 1592 edition, technically "an octavo in fours," is a good one and has become the authoritative text of the play. In 1594 Jeffes brought out another octavo-in-fours edition, which was nothing more than a sloppy reprint of White's 1592 edition. In 1599 Jeffes assigned his copyright to William White, who late in the year brought out his quarto reprint of the 1594 edition. The copyright passed in 1600 to Thomas Pavier, who two years later published a version which though based on the 1599 edition contains the famous "Additions." Remaining seventeenth century quartos are those of 1603, 1610, 1615, 1618, 1623, and 1633.

The Additions. Two entries in Henslowe's *Diary,* in 1601 and 1602 respectively, record payments of sums to Ben Jonson for "additions" to *The Spanish Tragedy.* There are five such additions running to a total of about 320 lines. On the basis of a comparison of Jonson's literary style with that in the additions, coupled with the observations that the high sum recorded in the *Diary* seems incompatible with the slight work involved and that the short time lapse between payment and publication raises questions about sufficient time for composition, scholars have amassed evidence to question Jonson as the author of the additions. Since no other candidate is forthcoming and the *Diary* entries have to be reckoned with, the matter can be probed no further at present.

Sources. There is no known source. Investigation into political relationships between Spain and Portugal in the 1580's does not produce evidence for any mirroring of historical events in the play. Incidental materials from the writings of Robert Garnier, particularly *Cornélie,* and from Virgil have been worked into the script. Further, the influence of Senecan tragedy is apparent.

Stage History. The play was a popular one. Aside from the ten extant early editions, the play had thirteen performances in the 1592–93 season by Lord Strange's Men at the Rose; was revived at the Rose by the Lord Admiral's Men for thirteen performances in 1596–97; and made its way to the Continent as early as 1601 with a performance recorded at Frankfurt-am-Main. References by other playwrights and parodies further indicate that the play was popular through about 1615.

W. G.

DRAMATIS PERSONAE

THE GHOST OF ANDREA ⎱ Chorus
REVENGE ⎰

THE KING OF SPAIN
DON CYPRIAN, Duke of Castile, the King's brother
LORENZO, the Duke's son
HIERONIMO, Marshal of Spain
HORATIO, his son
THE VICEROY OF PORTUGAL
BALTHAZAR, his son
DON PEDRO, the Viceroy's brother
ALEXANDRO ⎱ Portuguese Nobles
VILLUPPO ⎰
SPANISH GENERAL
PORTUGUESE AMBASSADOR
DEPUTY TO THE MARSHAL
DON BAZULTO, an old man
PEDRINGANO, Bel-imperia's servant
SERBERINE, Balthazar's servant
CHRISTOPHIL, jailor of Bel-imperia
PAGE TO LORENZO
THREE WATCHMEN
MESSENGER
HANGMAN
THREE CITIZENS
BEL-IMPERIA, Don Cyprian's daughter
ISABELLA, Hieronimo's wife
MAID TO ISABELLA
THREE KINGS ⎱
THREE KNIGHTS ⎬ First dumb show
A DRUMMER ⎰
HYMEN ⎱ Second dumb show
TWO TORCHBEARERS ⎰

		Characters of Hieronimo's play
Soliman, Sultan of Turkey...	BALTHAZAR	
Erasto, Knight of Rhodes...	LORENZO	
The Bashaw	HIERONIMO	
Perseda, a Christian captive.	BEL-IMPERIA	

78

Soldiers, Nobles, Retinue, Halberdiers, Trumpeters, etc.
In the additions:
BAZARDO, a painter
PEDRO $\Big\}$ Hieronimo's servants
JAQUES

Note: The original stage directions and punctuation have been
modified here and there for clearer reading and staging.

ACT I

Induction

(*Enter the* GHOST OF ANDREA, *and with him* REVENGE.)

GHOST. When this eternal substance of my soul
Did live imprisoned in my wanton flesh,
Each in their function serving other's need,
I was a courtier in the Spanish Court.
My name was Don Andrea; my descent,
Though not ignoble, yet inferior far
To gracious fortunes of my tender youth:
For there in prime and pride of all my years,
By duteous service and deserving love,
In secret I possessed a worthy dame,
Which hight* sweet Bel-imperia by name.   was called
But in the harvest of my summer joys
Death's winter nipped the blossoms of my bliss,
Forcing divorce betwixt my love and me.
For in the late conflict with Portingale*   Portugal
My valor drew me into danger's mouth
Till life to death made passage through my wounds.
When I was slain, my soul descended straight[1]
To pass the flowing stream of Acheron;*   river in Hell
But churlish Charon,* only boatman there,   ferryman in Hell
Said that, my rites of burial not performed,
I might not sit amongst his passengers.
Ere Sol had slept three nights in Thetis' lap,*   sea goddess
And slaked his smoking chariot in her flood,
By Don Horatio, our Knight Marshal's son,
My funerals and obsequies were done.
Then was the ferryman of hell content
To pass me over to the slimy strand
That leads to fell Avernus'* ugly waves.   lake in Hell
There, pleasing Cerberus* with honeyed speech,   Hell guard

[1] This and the following 67 lines give a description of the underworld based on Virgil's *Aeneid,* Book VI.

I passed the perils of the foremost porch.
Not far from hence, amidst ten thousand souls,
Sat Minos, Aeacus, and Rhadamanth,*   judges in Hell
To whom no sooner gan I make approach,
To crave a passport for my wand'ring ghost,
But Minos, in graven leaves of lottery,[2]
Drew forth the manner of my life and death.
"This knight," quoth he, "both lived and died in love,
And for his love tried fortune of the wars,
And by war's fortune lost both love and life."
"Why then," said Aeacus, "convey him hence
To walk with lovers in our fields of love,
And spend the course of everlasting time
Under green myrtle trees and cypress shades."
"No, no," said Rhadamanth, "it were not well
With loving souls to place a martialist,*   soldier
He died in war and must to martial fields,
Where wounded Hector lives in lasting pain,
And Achilles' Myrmidons* do scour the plain." Achilles' followers
Then Minos, mildest censor* of the three,   judge
Made this device* to end the difference: plan
"Send him," quoth he, "to our infernal King,
To doom* him as best seems his majesty."   judge
To this effect my passport straight was drawn.
In keeping on my way to Pluto's* Court,   god of the
                                               underworld
Through dreadful shades of ever-glooming night,
I saw more sights than thousand tongues can tell,
Or pens can write, or mortal hearts can think.
Three ways there were: that on the right-hand side
Was ready way unto the 'foresaid fields
Where lovers live and bloody martialists,
But either* sort* contained within his bounds.   each/group
The left-hand path, declining fearfully,
Was ready downfall to the deepest hell,*   Tartarus
Where bloody Furies shake their whips of steel,
And poor Ixion* turns an endless wheel;   punished by Zeus
Where usurers are choked with melting gold,
And wantons* are embraced with ugly snakes,   licentious
                                                   individuals
And murderers groan with never-killing wounds,
And perjured wights* scalded in boiling lead,   persons
And all foul sins with torments overwhelmed.

[2] The lottery slip on which was engraved the record of Andrea's life.

'Twixt these two ways I trod the middle path,
Which brought me to the fair Elysian green,*   Elysium
In midst whereof there stands a stately tower,
The walls of brass, the gates of adamant.
Here finding Pluto with his Proserpine,*   goddess of Hell
I showed my passport, humbled on my knee;
Whereat fair Proserpine began to smile,
And begged that only she might give my doom.*   sentence
Pluto was pleased and sealed it with a kiss.
Forthwith, Revenge, she rounded* thee in th'ear,   whispered
And bade thee lead me through the gates of Horn* gates of sleep
Where dreams have passage in the silent night.
No sooner had she spoke but we were here,
I wot* not how, in twinkling of an eye.   know
   REVENGE. Then know, Andrea, that thou art arrived
Where thou shalt see the author of thy death,
Don Balthazar, the prince of Portingale,
Deprived of life by Bel-imperia.
Here sit we down to see the mystery,
And serve for Chorus in this tragedy.

Scene 1

(*Before a castle of the Spanish King. Enter* SPANISH KING,
GENERAL, CASTILE, HIERONIMO.)

KING. Now say, Lord General, how fares our camp?*   army
   GENERAL. All well, my sovereign liege, except some few
That are deceased by fortune of the war.
   KING. But what portends thy cheerful countenance,
And posting to our presence thus in haste?
Speak, man, hath fortune given us victory?
   GENERAL. Victory, my liege, and that with little loss.
   KING. Our Portingals will pay us tribute then?
   GENERAL. Tribute and wonted homage therewithal.
   KING. Then blest be heaven and guider of the heavens,
From whose fair influence such justice flows.
   CASTILE. *O multum dilecte Deo, tibi militat aether,*
Et conjuratae curvato poplite gentes
Succumbunt: recti soror est victoria juris.[3]

    [8] "O much loved of God, Heaven fights for thee, and the con-
spiring nations fall on bended knee: victory is the sister of just
law." (Adapted from an address of Claudian. Most of the Latin
passages in the play are patchwork adaptations from Roman
writers.)

KING. Thanks to my loving brother of Castile.—
But, General, unfold in brief discourse
Your form of battle and your war's success,
That, adding all the pleasure of thy news
Unto the height of former happiness,
With deeper wage* and greater dignity   reward
We may reward thy blissful chivalry.
    GENERAL. Where Spain and Portingale do jointly knit
Their frontiers, leaning on each other's bound,
There met our armies in their proud array;
Both furnished well, both full of hope and fear,
Both menacing alike with daring shows,
Both vaunting sundry colors of device,[4]
Both cheerly sounding trumpets, drums, and fifes,
Both raising dreadful clamors to the sky,
That valleys, hills, and rivers made rebound,
And heaven itself was frighted with the sound.
Our battles* both were pitched in squadron form,*   armies/form
Each corner strongly fenced with wings of shot;   of a square
But ere we joined and came to push of pike,
I brought a squadron of our readiest shot
From out our rearward to begin the fight.
They brought another wing to encounter us.
Meanwhile, our ordnance played on either side,
And captains strove to have their valors tried.
Don Pedro, their chief horsemen's corlonell,*   colonel
Did with his cornet* bravely make attempt   troop
To break the order of our battle ranks;
But Don Rogero, worthy man of war,
Marched forth against him with our musketeers,
And stopped the malice of his fell approach.
While they maintain hot skirmish to and fro,
Both battles join and fall to handy-blows,*   hand-to-hand
Their violent shot resembling th'ocean's rage,   fighting
When, roaring loud, and with a swelling tide,
It beats upon the rampires* of huge rocks   ramparts
And gapes to swallow neighbor-bounding lands.
Now while Bellona* rageth here and there,   goddess of war
Thick storms of bullets rain like winter's hail,
And shivered lances dark the troubled air.
Pede pes et cuspide cuspis;

---

[4] Proudly displaying their heraldic banners.

Arma sonant armis, vir petiturque viro.[5]
On every side drop captains to the ground,
And soldiers, some ill maimed, some slain outright:
Here falls a body sundered from his head,
There legs and arms lie bleeding on the grass,
Mingled with weapons and unbowelled steeds,
That scattering overspread the purple plain.
In all this turmoil, three long hours and more,
The victory to neither part inclined,
Till Don Andrea, with his brave lanciers,*   lancers
In their main battle made so great a breach
That, half dismayed, the multitude retired;
But Balthazar, the Portingals' young Prince,
Brought rescue and encouraged them to stay.
Here-hence[6] the fight was eagerly renewed,
And in that conflict was Andrea slain,
Brave man at arms, but weak to* Balthazar.   compared to
Yet while the Prince, insulting* over him,   exulting
Breathed out proud vaunts, sounding to our reproach,
Friendship and hardy valor, joined in one,
Pricked* forth Horatio, our Knight Marshal's son,   spurred
To challenge forth that Prince in single fight.
Not long between these twain the fight endured,
But straight the prince was beaten from his horse,
And forced to yield him prisoner to his foe.
When he was taken, all the rest they fled,
And our carbines pursued them to the death,
Till, Phoebus waving to the western deep,*   that is,
                                                          the sun setting
Our trumpeters were charged to sound retreat.
     KING. Thanks, good Lord General, for these good news,
And for some argument* of more to come,   token
Take this and wear it for thy sovereign's sake.
     (*Gives him his chain.*)
But tell me now, hast thou confirmed a peace?
     GENERAL. No peace, my liege, but peace conditional,
That if with homage tribute be well paid,
The fury of your forces will be stayed;

---

     [5] "Foot against foot and lance against lance; arms clash on
arms, and man rushes on man."

     [6] As a result of this.

And to this peace their Viceroy hath subscribed,
(*Gives the* KING *a paper.*)
And made a solemn vow that during life
His tribute shall be truly paid to Spain.
    KING. These words, these deeds, become thy person
      well.—
But now, Knight Marshal, frolic* with thy king,   be gay
For 'tis thy son that wins this battle's prize.
    HIERONIMO. Long may he live to serve my sovereign liege,
And soon decay unless he serve my liege.
    KING. Nor thou nor he shall die without reward.
    (*A tucket* afar off.*)   flourish of
                                            trumpets
What means this warning of this trumpet's sound?
    GENERAL. This tells me that your grace's men of war,
Such as war's fortune hath reserved from death,
Come marching on towards your royal seat
To show themselves before your majesty;
For so I gave in charge at my depart.
Whereby by demonstration shall appear
That all (except three hundred or few more)
Are safe returned, and by their foes enriched.

    (*The* "ARMY" *enters;* BALTHAZAR *appears between* LORENZO
    and HORATIO, *captive.*)

    KING. A gladsome sight! I long to see them here.

    (*They enter and pass by.*)

Was that the warlike Prince of Portingale
That by our nephew was in triumph led?
    GENERAL. It was, my liege, the Prince of Portingale.
    KING. But what was he that on the other side
Held him by th'arm, as partner of the price?
    HIERONIMO. That was my son, my gracious sovereign;
Of whom though from his tender infancy
My loving thoughts did never hope but well,
He never pleased his father's eyes till now,
Nor filled my heart with overcloying joys.
    KING. Go, let them march once more about these walls,
That, staying them, we may confer and talk

With our brave prisoner and his double guard.

(*Exit a messenger.*)

Hieronimo, it greatly pleaseth us
That in our victory thou have a share,
By virtue of thy worthy son's exploit.

(*Enter the Army again.*)

Bring hither the young Prince of Portingale;
The rest march on; but ere they be dismissed
We will bestow on every soldier
Two ducats, and on every leader ten,
That they may know our largess welcomes them.

(*Exeunt all the Army but* BALTHAZAR,
LORENZO, *and* HORATIO.)

Welcome Don Balthazar! welcome nephew!
And thou, Horatio, thou art welcome too.
Young Prince, although thy father's hard misdeeds,
In keeping back the tribute that he owes,
Deserve but evil measure at our hands,
Yet shalt thou know that Spain is honorable.

BALTHAZAR. The trespass that my father made in peace
Is now controlled* by fortune of the wars;   checked
And cards once dealt, it boots not ask, "Why so?"
His men are slain, a weakening to his realm;
His colors seized, a blot unto his name;
His son distressed, a corsive* to his heart: corrosive
These punishments may clear his late offence.

KING. Ay, Balthazar, if he observe this truce,
Our peace will grow the stronger for these wars.
Meanwhile live thou, though not in liberty,
Yet free from bearing any servile yoke;
For in our hearing thy deserts were great,
And in our sight thyself art gracious.

BALTHAZAR. And I shall study to deserve this grace.

KING. But tell me (for their holding makes me doubt)
To which of these twain art thou prisoner?

LORENZO. To me, my liege.

HORATIO.   To me, my sovereign.

LORENZO. This hand first took his courser by the reins.

HORATIO. But first my lance did put him from his horse.

LORENZO. I seized his weapon and enjoyed*   possessed
    it first.   (with delight)

HORATIO. But first I forced him lay his weapons down.

KING. Let go his arm, upon our privilege.*   royal right
(*They let him go.*)

Say, worthy Prince, to whether* didst thou yield?   which one

BALTHAZAR. To him* in courtesy, to this perforce: that is,
                                                                                     Lorenzo
He spake me fair, this other gave me strokes;
He promised life, this other threatened death;
He won my love, this other conquered me;
And truth to say, I yield myself to both.

HIERONIMO. But that I know your grace for just and wise,
And might seem partial in this difference,
Enforced by nature and by law of arms
My tongue should plead for young Horatio's right.
He hunted well that was a lion's death,
Not he that in a garment wore his skin;
So hares may pull dead lions by the beard.

KING. Content thee, Marshal, thou shalt have no wrong,
And, for thy sake, thy son shall want no right.—
Will both abide the censure* of my doom?*   judgment/sentence

LORENZO. I crave no better than your grace awards.

HORATIO. Nor I, although I sit beside* my right.   forego

KING. Then by my judgment thus your strife shall end:
You both deserve, and both shall have reward.
Nephew, thou took'st his weapon and his horse;
His weapons and his horse are thy reward.
Horatio, thou didst force him first to yield;
His ransom therefore is thy valor's fee;
Appoint the sum as ye shall both agree.
But, nephew, thou shalt have the Prince in guard
For thine estate best fitteth such a guest;
Horatio's house were small for all his train.
Yet, in regard thy substance passeth his,
And that just guerdon* may befall desert,   reward
To him we yield the armor of the Prince.
How likes Don Balthazar of this device?*   plan

BALTHAZAR. Right well, my liege, if this proviso were,
That Don Horatio bear us company,
Whom I admire and love for chivalry.

KING. Horatio, leave him not that loves thee so.
Now let us hence to see our soldiers paid,
And feast our prisoner as our friendly guest.

(*Exeunt.*)

Scene 2

(*The Portuguese Court. Enter* VICEROY, ALEXANDRO, VIL-
LUPPO, *and Attendants.*)

VICEROY. Is our ambassador dispatched for Spain?
ALEXANDRO. Two days, my liege, are past since his depart.
VICEROY. And tribute payment gone along with him?
ALEXANDRO. Ay, my good lord.
VICEROY. Then rest we here awhile in our unrest,
And feed our sorrows with some inward sighs,
For deepest cares break never into tears.
But wherefore sit I in a regal throne?
    (*Falls to the ground.*)
This better fits a wretch's endless moan.
Yet this is higher than my fortunes reach
And therefore better than my state deserves.
Ay, ay, this earth, image of melancholy,
Seeks him whom fates adjudge to misery.
Here let me lie; now am I at the lowest.
Qui jacet in terra non habet unde cadat.
In me consumpsit vires fortuna nocendo;
Nil superest ut jam possit, obesse magis.[7]
Yes, Fortune may bereave* me of my crown: deprive
    (*Takes off the crown.*)
Here, take it now; let Fortune do her worst,
She will not rob me of this sable weed.*   garment
O no, she envies none but pleasant things.
Such is the folly of despiteful chance.
Fortune is blind and sees not my deserts;
So is she deaf and hears not my laments;
And could she hear, yet is she wilful-mad,
And therefore will not pity my distress.
Suppose that she could pity me, what then?
What help can be expected at her hands
Whose foot is standing on a rolling stone,
And mind more mutable than fickle winds?
Why wail I then, where's hope of no redress?
O yes, complaining* makes my grief seem less.   lamenting
My late ambition hath distained* my faith;   soiled or tarnished

---

[7] "Who lies on the ground can fall no further. Fortune has
used up her power to hurt me; nothing is left that now can harm
me more."

My breach of faith occasioned bloody wars;
Those bloody wars have spent my treasure;
And with my treasure my people's blood;
And with their blood, my joy and best beloved,
My best beloved, my sweet and only son.
O wherefore went I not to war myself?
The cause was mine; I might have died for both.
My years were mellow, his but young and green;
My death were natural, but his was forced.

ALEXANDRO. No doubt, my liege, but still the Prince sur-
vives.
VICEROY. Survives! Ay, where?
ALEXANDRO. In Spain, a prisoner by mischance of war.
VICEROY. Then they have slain him for his father's fault.
ALEXANDRO. That were a breach to common law of arms.
VICEROY. They reck no laws that meditate revenge.
ALEXANDRO. His ransom's worth will stay from foul re-
venge.
VICEROY. No; if he lived the news would soon be here.
ALEXANDRO. Nay, evil news fly faster still* than good.   always
VICEROY. Tell me no more of news, for he is dead.
VILLUPPO. My sovereign, pardon the author of ill news,
And I'll bewray* the fortune of thy son.   reveal
VICEROY. Speak on; I'll guerdon* thee, what ere it be.   reward
Mine ear is ready to receive ill news,
My heart grown hard 'gainst mischief's battery.
Stand up, I say, and tell thy tale at large.
VILLUPPO. Then hear that truth which these mine eyes
have seen.
When both the armies were in battle joined,
Don Balthazar, amidst the thickest troops,
To win renown did wondrous feats of arms.
Amongst the rest I saw him hand to hand
In single fight with their Lord General;
Till Alexandro, that here counterfeits
Under the color of a duteous friend,
Discharged his pistol at the Prince's back,
As though he would have slain their general.
But therewithal Don Balthazar fell down,
And when he fell, then we began to fly;
But, had he lived, the day had sure been ours.
ALEXANDRO. O wicked forgery!* O traitorous   falsification
miscreant!
VICEROY. Hold thy peace!—but now, Villuppo, say

Where then became* the carcass of my son?   <small>what became of</small>
   VILLUPPO. I saw them drag it to the Spanish tents.
   VICEROY. Ay, ay, my nightly dreams have told me this.
Thou false, unkind, unthankful, traitorous beast,
Wherein had Balthazar offended thee
That thou shouldst thus betray him to our foes?
Was't Spanish gold that blearèd so thine eyes
That thou couldst see no part of our deserts?
Perchance, because thou art Terserae's lord,[8]
Thou hadst some hope to wear this diadem,
If first my son and then myself were slain;
But thy ambitious thought shall break thy neck.
Ay, this was it that made thee spill his blood;
   (*Takes the crown and puts it on again.*)
But I'll now wear it till thy blood be spilt.
   ALEXANDRO. Vouchsafe, dread sovereign, to hear me speak.
   VICEROY. Away with him! His sight is second hell.
Keep him till we determine of his death.
                   (ALEXANDRO *is taken away.*)
If Balthazar be dead, he shall not live.
Villuppo, follow us for thy reward.
                        (*Exit* VICEROY.)

   VILLUPPO. Thus have I with an envious* forgèd tale   <small>malicious</small>
Deceived the King, betrayed mine enemy,
And hope for guerdon of my villainy.

                            (*Exit.*)

Scene 3

(*The Spanish Court. Enter* HORATIO *and* BEL-IMPERIA.)

   BEL-IMPERIA. Signior Horatio, this is the place and hour
Wherein I must entreat thee to relate
The circumstance of Don Andrea's death,
Who, living, was my garland's sweetest flower,
And in his death hath buried my delights.
   HORATIO. For love of him and service to yourself,
I nill* refuse this heavy doleful charge;   <small>will not</small>
Yet tears and sighs, I fear, will hinder me.
When both our armies are enjoined in fight,
Your worthy chevalier amidst the thick'st,
For glorious cause still aiming at the fairest,
Was at the last by young Don Balthazar

    [8] Terceira is in the Azores. Under Portuguese political tradition,
its ruler would have had great power.

Encountered hand to hand. Their fight was long,
Their hearts were great, their clamors menacing,
Their strength alike, their strokes both dangerous.
But wrathful Nemesis,* that wicked power,   goddess of retribution
Envying at Andrea's praise and worth,
Cut short his life to end his praise and worth.
She, she herself, disguised in armor's mask
(As Pallas was before proud Pergamus)[9]
Brought in a fresh supply of halberdiers,
Which paunched* his horse and dinged* him   stabbed in the
    to the ground.   belly/knocked
Then young Don Balthazar, with ruthless rage
Taking advantage of his foe's distress,
Did finish what his halberdiers begun,
And left not till Andrea's life was done.
Then, though too late, incensed with just remorse,
I with my band set forth against the Prince,
And brought him prisoner from his halberdiers.
    BEL-IMPERIA. Would thou hadst slain him that so slew my
        love.
But then was Don Andrea's carcass lost?
    HORATIO. No, that was it for which I chiefly strove;
Nor stepped I back till I recovered him.
I took him up and wound him in mine arms,
And wielding* him unto my private tent   carrying
There laid down and dewed him with my tears,
And sighed and sorrowed as became a friend.
But neither friendly sorrow, sighs, nor tears
Could win pale Death from his usurpèd right.
Yet this I did and less I could not do:
I saw him honored with due funeral.
This scarf I plucked from off his lifeless arm,
And wear it in remembrance of my friend.
    BEL-IMPERIA. I know the scarf; would he had kept it still!
For had he lived he would have kept it still
And worn it for his Bel-imperia's sake,
For 'twas my favor at his last depart.
But now wear thou it both for him and me,
For after him thou hast deserved it best.
But for thy kindness in his life and death,
Be sure while Bel-imperia's life endures
She will be Don Horatio's thankful friend.

    [9] See *Aeneid*, II, 615–16.

HORATIO. And, madam, Don Horatio will not slack
Humbly to serve fair Bel-imperia.
But now, if your good liking stand thereto,
I'll crave your pardon to go seek the Prince,
For so the Duke, your father, gave me charge.

(*Exit.*)

BEL-IMPERIA. Ay, go, Horatio; leave me here alone;
For solitude best fits my cheerless mood.
Yet what avails to wail Andrea's death,
From whence Horatio proves my second love?
Had he not loved Andrea as he did,
He could not sit in Bel-imperia's thoughts.
But how can love find harbor in my breast,
Till I revenge the death of my beloved?
Yes, second love shall further my revenge;
I'll love Horatio, my Andrea's friend,
The more to spite the Prince that wrought his end.
And where Don Balthazar that slew my love,
Himself now pleads for favor at my hands,
He shall, in rigor of my just disdain,
Reap long repentance for his murderous deed.
For what was't else but murderous cowardice,
So many to oppress* one valiant knight   overpower
Without respect of honor in the fight?
And here he comes that murdered my delight.

(*Enter* LORENZO *and* BALTHAZAR.)

LORENZO. Sister, what means this melancholy walk?
BEL-IMPERIA. That for a while I wish no company.
LORENZO. But here the Prince is come to visit you.
BEL-IMPERIA. That argues that he lives in liberty.
BALTHAZAR. No, madam, but in pleasing servitude.
BEL-IMPERIA. Your prison then, belike, is your
    conceit.*   fancy
BALTHAZAR. Ay, by conceit my freedom is enthralled.
BEL-IMPERIA. Then with conceit enlarge* yourself   set free
    again.
BALTHAZAR. What if conceit have laid my heart to
    gage?*   as a pledge
BEL-IMPERIA. Pay that you borrowed, and recover it.
BALTHAZAR. I die if it return from whence it lies.
BEL-IMPERIA. A heartless man and live? A miracle!

BALTHAZAR. Ay, lady, love can work such miracles.
LORENZO. Tush, tush, my lord, let go these
    ambages,*   circumlocutions
And in plain terms acquaint her with your love.
BEL-IMPERIA. What boots complaint, when there's no
    remedy?
BALTHAZAR. Yes, to your gracious self must I complain,
In whose fair answer lies my remedy,
On whose perfection all my thoughts attend,
On whose aspect mine eyes find beauty's bower,
In whose translucent breast my heart is lodged.
BEL-IMPERIA. Alas, my lord, these are hot words of
    course,*   conventional phrases
And but device to drive me from this place.

(*She, in going in, lets fall her glove, which* HORATIO, *coming out, takes up.*)

HORATIO. Madam, your glove.
BEL-IMPERIA. Thanks, good Horatio; take it for thy pains.
BALTHAZAR. Signior Horatio stooped in happy time.
HORATIO. I reaped more grace than I deserved or hoped.
LORENZO. My lord, be not dismayed for what is past;
You know that women oft are humorous;*   capricious
These clouds will overblow with little wind.
Let me alone; I'll scatter them myself.
Meanwhile, let us devise to spend the time
In some delightful sports and revelling.
HORATIO. The King, my lords, is coming hither straight
To feast the Portingal ambassador;
Things were in readiness before I came.
BALTHAZAR. Then here it fits us to attend the King
To welcome hither our ambassador,
And learn my father and my country's health.

(*Enter the banquet,* TRUMPETS, *the* KING, *his Court and* AMBASSADOR.)

KING. See, Lord Ambassador, how Spain entreats*   treats
Their prisoner Balthazar, thy Viceroy's son;
We pleasure more in kindness than in wars.
AMBASSADOR. Sad is our King, and Portingale laments,
Supposing that Don Balthazar is slain.
BALTHAZAR (*aside*). So am I slain, by beauty's tyranny.

You see, my lord, how Balthazar is slain:
I frolic with the Duke of Castile's son,
Wrapped every hour in pleasures of the court,
And graced* with favors of his majesty.   honored
    KING. Put off your greetings till our feast be done;
Now come and sit with us, and taste our cheer.
    (*They sit down to the banquet.*)
Sit down, young Prince; you are our second guest.
Brother, sit down, and, nephew, take your place.
Signior Horatio, wait thou upon our cup,
For well thou hast deserved to be honored.
Now, lordings, fall to; Spain is Portugal,
And Portugal is Spain: we both are friends,
Tribute is paid, and we enjoy our right.
But where is old Hieronimo, our Marshal?
He promised us, in honor of our guest,
To grace our banquet with some pompous
        jest.*   courtly entertainment

    (*Enter* HIERONIMO, *with a* DRUMMER *and three* KNIGHTS,
each with his scutcheon; then he fetches three Kings; the
KNIGHTS *take their crowns and them captive.*)

Hieronimo, this masque contents mine eye,
Although I sound not well the mystery.[10]
    HIERONIMO. The first armed knight that hung his scutch-
      eon up
    (*He takes the scutcheon and gives it to the* KING.)
Was English Robert, Earl of Gloucester,
Who, when King Stephen bore sway in Albion,
Arrived with five and twenty thousand men
In Portingale, and by success of war
Enforced* the King, then but a Saracen,   forced
To bear the yoke of the English monarchy.[11]
    KING. My Lord of Portingale, by this you see
That which may comfort both your King and you,

    [10] That is, I do not fully comprehend the allegory.
    [11] The accounts of English victories over the Spanish and Por-
tuguese are not historically accurate. The first refers to the capture of Lisbon in 1147, but there is no evidence that Robert of
Gloucester was ever in Portugal. The second refers to Edmund
Langley's 1381 expedition, in which Langley sided with Portugal
against Spain. He became Duke of York for service against the
Scots. Though the historical evidence for the third account is not
clear, it appears that John of Gaunt was defeated in his Spanish
campaign of 1386–87.

And make your late discomfort seem the less.
But say, Hieronimo, what was the next?
   HIERONIMO. The second knight that hung his scutcheon up
   (*He does as he did before.*)
Was Edmund, Earl of Kent in Albion,
When English Richard wore the diadem.
He came likewise, and razèd Lisbon walls,
And took the King of Portingale in fight.
For which and other such like service done
He after was created Duke of York.
   KING. This is another special argument
That Portingale may deign to bear our yoke,
When it by little England hath been yoked.
But now, Hieronimo, what were the last?
   HIERONIMO. The third and last, not least in our account,
   (*Doing as before.*)
Was, as the rest, a valiant Englishman,
Brave John of Gaunt, the Duke of Lancaster,
As by his scutcheon plainly may appear.
He with a puissant army came to Spain
And took our King of Castile prisoner.
   AMBASSADOR. This is an argument for our Viceroy
That Spain may not insult for her success,
Since English warriors likewise conquered Spain,
And made them bow their knees to Albion.
   KING. Hieronimo, I drink to thee for this device,*   ^{that is,}
Which hath pleased both the ambassador and me.   ^{entertainment}
Pledge me, Hieronimo, if thou love the King.
   (*Takes the cup of* HORATIO.)
My lord, I fear we sit but overlong,
Unless our dainties were more delicate,
But welcome are you to the best we have.
Now let us in, that you may be dispatched;
I think our council is already set.

                          (*Exeunt omnes.*)

CHORUS

(*Consisting of* ANDREA *and* REVENGE.)
   ANDREA. Come we for this from depth of underground,
To see him feast that gave me my death's wound?
These pleasant sights are sorrow to my soul:
Nothing but league, and love, and banqueting.
   REVENGE. Be still, Andrea; ere we go from hence,

I'll turn their friendship into fell despite,*   terrible ill will
Their love to mortal hate, their day to night,
Their hope into despair, their peace to war,
Their joys to pain, their bliss to misery.

ACT II

Scene 1

(*The palace of* DON CYPRIAN. *Enter* LORENZO *and* BAL-
THAZAR.)

LORENZO. My lord, though Bel-imperia seem thus coy,
Let reason hold you in your wontèd joy.
In time the savage bull sustains the yoke.[12]
In time all haggard hawks will stoop to lure,[13]
In time small wedges cleave the hardest oak,
In time the flint is pierced with softest shower,
And she in time will fall from her disdain
And rue the sufferance of your friendly pain.
BALTHAZAR. No, she is wilder and more hard withal
Than beast, or bird, or tree, or stony wall.
But wherefore blot I Bel-imperia's name?
It is my fault, not she, that merits blame.
My feature* is not to content her sight;   shape
My words are rude and work her no delight.
The lines I send her are but harsh and ill,
Such as do drop from Pan and Marsyas' quill.[14]
My presents are not of sufficient cost,
And, being worthless all my labor's lost.
Yet might she love me for my valiancy,
Ay, but that's slandered* by captivity.   brought into
                                                   disrepute
Yet might she love me to content her sire,
Ay, but her reason masters his desire.
Yet might she love me as her brother's friend,

---

[12] This and the next seven lines interweave lines from Thomas
Watson's *Hecatompathia* (1582), Sonnet 47.

[13] That is, untamed hawks, in the course of being trained, can
be enticed to come down for recapture through use of baited
devices.

[14] Pan and Marsyas were gods who challenged Apollo to a
flute-playing contest, but they were inferior musicians. The
"quill" is the reed flute.

Ay, but her hopes aim at some other end.
Yet might she love me to uprear her state,
Ay, but perhaps she hopes some nobler mate.
Yet might she love me as her beauty's thrall,
Ay, but I fear she cannot love at all.
    LORENZO. My lord, for my sake leave these extasies* _{anxieties}
And doubt not but we'll find some remedy.
Some cause there is that lets you not be loved;
First that must needs be known and then removed.
What if my sister love some other knight?
    BALTHAZAR. My summer's day will turn to winter's night.
    LORENZO. I have already found a stratagem
To sound the bottom of this doubtful theme.
My lord, for once you shall be ruled by me:
Hinder me not, whate'er you hear or see.
By force or fair means will I cast about
To find the truth of all this question out.
Ho, Pedringano.
    PEDRINGANO (*within*). *Signior.*
    LORENZO.   *Vien qui presto.*[15]

(*Enter* PEDRINGANO.)

    PEDRINGANO. Hath your lordship any service to command
      me?
    LORENZO. Ay, Pedringano, service of import,
And, not to spend the time in trifling words,
Thus stands the case. It is not long, thou know'st,
Since I did shield thee from my father's wrath
For thy conveyance* in Andrea's love,   _{service as}
For which thou wert adjudged to punishment.   _{go-between}
I stood betwixt thee and thy punishment,
And since, thou knowest how I have favored thee.
Now to these favors will I add reward,
Not with fair words, but store of golden coin,
And lands and living joined with dignities,
If thou but satisfy my just demand.
Tell truth and have me for thy lasting friend.
    PEDRINGANO. Whate'er it be your lordship shall demand,
My bounden duty bids me tell the truth,
If* case it lie in me to tell the truth.   _{in}
    LORENZO. Then, Pedringano, this is my demand:

    [15] "Come here quickly."

Whom loves my sister Bel-imperia?
For she reposeth all her trust in thee.
Speak, man, and gain both friendship and reward.
I mean, whom loves she in Andrea's place?
    PEDRINGANO. Alas, my lord, since Don Andrea's death
I have no credit with her as before,
And therefore know not if she love or no.
    LORENZO. Nay, if thou dally, then I am thy foe,
    (*Draws his sword.*)
And fear shall force what friendship cannot win.
Thy death shall bury what thy life conceals;
Thou diest for more esteeming her than me.
    PEDRINGANO. O stay, my lord.
    LORENZO. Yet speak the truth, and I will guerdon*   reward
    thee,
And shield thee from whatever can ensue,
And will conceal whate'er proceeds from thee;
But if thou dally once again, thou diest.
    PEDRINGANO. If madam Bel-imperia be in love—
    LORENZO. What, villain,—if's and and's?
    (*Makes a move to kill him.*)
    PEDRINGANO. O stay, my lord; she loves Horatio.
    (BALTHAZAR *starts back.*)
    LORENZO. What, Don Horatio, our Knight Marshal's son?
    PEDRINGANO. Even him, my lord.
    LORENZO. Now say but how knowest thou he is her love,
And thou shalt find me kind and liberal.
Stand up, I say, and fearless tell the truth.
    PEDRINGANO. She sent him letters, which myself perused,
Full fraught with lines and arguments of love,
Preferring him before Prince Balthazar.
    LORENZO. Swear on this cross* that what thou   that is,
    sayest is true,   his sword-hilt
And that thou wilt conceal what thou hast told.
    PEDRINGANO. I swear to both, by Him that made us all.
    LORENZO. In hope thine oath is true, here's thy reward;
But if I prove thee perjured and unjust,
This very sword whereon thou took'st thine oath
Shall be the worker of thy tragedy.
    PEDRINGANO. What I have said is true, and shall, for me,
Be still concealed from Bel-imperia.
Besides, your honor's liberality
Deserves my duteous service, even till death.

LORENZO. Let this be all that thou shalt do for me:
Be watchful when and where these lovers meet,
And give me notice in some secret sort.
  PEDRINGANO. I will, my lord.
  LORENZO. Then shalt thou find that I am liberal.
Thou know'st that I can more advance thy state
Than she; be therefore wise, and fail me not.
Go and attend her, as thy custom is,
Lest absence make her think thou dost amiss.

(Exit PEDRINGANO.)

Why so! *Tam armis quam ingenio:*[16]
Where words prevail not, violence prevails;
But gold doth more than either of them both.
How likes Prince Balthazar this stratagem?
  BALTHAZAR. Both well and ill; it makes me glad and sad.
Glad, that I know the hinderer of my love,
Sad, that I fear she hates me whom I love;
Glad, that I know on whom to be revenged,
Sad, that she'll fly me if I take revenge.
Yet must I take revenge, or die myself,
For love resisted grows impatient.
I think Horatio be my destined plague:
First, in his hand he brandishèd a sword,
And with that sword he fiercely wagèd war,
And in that war he gave me dangerous wounds,
And by those wounds he forcèd me to yield,
And by my yielding I became his slave.
Now in his mouth he carries pleasing words,
Which pleasing words do harbor sweet conceits,
Which sweet conceits are limed* with sly deceits,   baited
Which sly deceits smooth* Bel-imperia's ears,   flatter
And through her ears dive down into her heart,
And in her heart set him where I should stand.
Thus hath he tane* my body by his force,   taken
And now by sleight would captivate my soul;
But in his fall I'll tempt the destinies,
And either lose my life or win my love.
  LORENZO. Let's go, my lord; your staying stays revenge.
Do you but follow me, and gain your love;
Her favor must be won by his remove.

(Exeunt.)

---

[16] "As much by arms as by guile."

Scene 2

(*Another room in the palace. Enter* HORATIO *and* BEL-IMPERIA.)

HORATIO. Now, madam, since by favor of your love
Our hidden smoke is turned to open flame,
And that with looks and words we feed our thoughts,
Two chief contents, where more cannot be had.
Thus in the midst of love's fair blandishments,
Why show you sign of inward languishments?
    (PEDRINGANO *shows all to the* PRINCE *and* LORENZO, *placing them in secret.*) [17]
BEL-IMPERIA. My heart, sweet friend, is like a ship at sea:
She wisheth port, where, riding all at ease
She may repair what stormy times have worn,
And leaning on the shore may sing with joy
That pleasure follows pain, and bliss annoy.
Possession of thy love is th'only port
Wherein my heart, with fears and hopes long tossed,
Each hour doth wish and long to make resort,
There to repair the joys that it hath lost,
And, sitting safe, to sing in Cupid's choir
That sweetest bliss is crown of love's desire.

(BALTHAZAR *and* LORENZO *stand above observing.*)

BALTHAZAR. O sleep, mine eyes, see not my love profaned;
Be deaf, my ears, hear not my discontent;
Die, heart, another joys* what thou deservest.   enjoys
    LORENZO. Watch still, mine eyes, to see this love disjoined;
Hear still, mine ears, to hear them both lament;
Live, heart, to joy at fond* Horatio's fall.   foolish, infatuated
    BEL-IMPERIA. Why stands Horatio speechless all this while?
    HORATIO. The less I speak, the more I meditate.
    BEL-IMPERIA. But whereon dost thou chiefly meditate?
    HORATIO. On dangers past, and pleasures to ensue.
    BALTHAZAR (*repeating, above*). On pleasures past, and dangers to ensue.
    BEL-IMPERIA. What dangers and what pleasures dost thou mean?

    [17] They probably were standing on the balcony over the inner stage.

HORATIO. Dangers of war, and pleasures of our love.

LORENZO (*repeating, above*). Dangers of death, but pleasures none at all.

BEL-IMPERIA. Let dangers go, thy war shall be with me,
But such a war, as breaks no bond of peace.
Speak thou fair words, I'll cross them with fair words;
Send thou sweet looks, I'll meet them with sweet looks;
Write loving lines, I'll answer loving lines;
Give me a kiss, I'll countercheck thy kiss:
Be this our warring peace, or peaceful war.

HORATIO. But, gracious madam, then appoint the field
Where trial of this war shall first be made.

BALTHAZAR. Ambitious villain, how his boldness grows!

BEL-IMPERIA. Then be thy father's pleasant bower the field,
Where first we vowed a mutual amity.
The Court were dangerous; that place is safe.
Our hour shall be when Vesper* 'gins to rise,   the evening star
That summons home distressful travelers.*   laborers
There none shall hear us but the harmless birds;
Happily the gentle nightingale
Shall carol us asleep, ere we be 'ware,
And, singing with the prickle* at her breast,   thorn
Tell our delight and mirthful dalliance.
Till then each hour will seem a year and more.

HORATIO. But, honey sweet and honorable love,
Return we now into your father's sight;
Dangerous suspicion waits on our delight.

LORENZO (*above*). Ay, danger mixed with jealous despite
Shall send thy soul into eternal night.

(*Exeunt.*)

Scene 3

(*The royal palace. Enter the* KING OF SPAIN, *Portingale* AMBASSADOR, DON CYPRIAN, *etc.*)

KING. Brother of Castile, to the Prince's love
What says your daughter, Bel-imperia?

CYPRIAN. Although she coy it,* as becomes her   affect shyness
   kind,
And yet dissemble that she loves the Prince,
I doubt not, I, but she will stoop in time.
And were she froward,* which she will not be,   perverse
Yet herein shall she follow my advice,

Which is to love him, or forgo my love.

KING. Then, Lord Ambassador of Portingale,
Advise thy King to make this marriage up,
For strengthening of our late confirmèd league;
I know no better means to make us friends.
Her dowry shall be large and liberal;
Besides that she is daughter and half heir
Unto our brother here, Don Cyprian,
And shall enjoy the moiety* of this land,   half
I'll grace her marriage with an uncle's gift,
And this it is: in case the match go forward,
The tribute which you pay shall be released,
And if by Balthazar she have a son,
He shall enjoy the kingdom after us.

AMBASSADOR. I'll make the motion to my sovereign liege,
And work it if my counsel may prevail.

KING. Do so, my lord, and if he give consent,
I hope his presence here will honor us
In celebration of the nuptial day;
And let himself determine of the time.

AMBASSADOR. Wilt please your grace command me aught
    beside?

KING. Commend me to the King, and so farewell.
But where's Prince Balthazar to take his leave?

AMBASSADOR. That is performed already, my good lord.

KING. Amongst the rest of what you have in charge,
The Prince's ransom must not be forgot.
That's none of mine but his that took him prisoner,
And well his forwardness* deserves reward.   courage
It was Horatio, our Knight Marshal's son.

AMBASSADOR. Between us there's a price already
    pitched,*   settled
And shall be sent with all convenient speed.

KING. Then once again farewell, my lord.

AMBASSADOR. Farewell, my Lord of Castile, and the rest.
                                                    (*Exit.*)

KING. Now, brother, you must take some little pains
To win fair Bel-imperia from her will.
Young virgins must be ruled by their friends.
The Prince is amiable, and loves her well;
If she neglect him and forgo his love,
She both will wrong her own estate and ours.
Therefore, whiles I do entertain the Prince
With greatest pleasure that our Court affords,

Endeavor you to win your daughter's thought:
If she give back,* all this will come to naught.   refuses
                                                    (*Exeunt.*)

Scene 4

(HIERONIMO'S *garden. Enter* HORATIO, BEL-IMPERIA, *and*
PEDRINGANO.)

HORATIO. Now that the night begins with sable wings
To overcloud the brightness of the sun,
And that in darkness pleasures may be done,
Come, Bel-imperia, let us to the bower,
And there in safety pass a pleasant hour.
   BEL-IMPERIA. I follow thee, my love, and will not back,
Although my fainting heart controls* my soul.   wars with
   HORATIO. Why, make you doubt of Pedringano's faith?
   BEL-IMPERIA. No, he is as trusty as my second self.
Go, Pedringano, watch without the gate,
And let us know if any make approach.
   PEDRINGANO (*aside*). Instead of watching, I'll deserve more
    gold
By fetching Don Lorenzo to this match.
                                        (*Exit* PEDRINGANO.)
   HORATIO. What means my love?
   BEL-IMPERIA.   I know not what myself;
And yet my heart foretells me some mischance.
   HORATIO. Sweet, say not so; fair Fortune is our friend,
And heavens have shut up day to pleasure us.
The stars, thou seest, hold back their twinkling shine,
And Luna* hides herself to pleasure us.   moon goddess
   BEL-IMPERIA. Thou hast prevailed; I'll conquer my mis-
    doubt,
And in thy love and counsel drown my fear.
I fear no more; love now is all my thoughts.
Why sit we not? for pleasure asketh ease.
   HORATIO. The more thou sitt'st within these leafy bowers
The more will Flora* deck it with her flowers.   goddess of flowers
   BEL-IMPERIA. Ay, but if Flora spy Horatio here,
Her jealous eye will think I sit too near.
   HORATIO. Hark, madam, how the birds record* by night   sing
For joy that Bel-imperia sits in sight.
   BEL-IMPERIA. No, Cupid counterfeits the nightingale,
To frame sweet music to Horatio's tale.

HORATIO. If Cupid sing, then Venus is not far;
Ay, thou art Venus, or some fairer star.
BEL-IMPERIA. If I be Venus, thou must needs be Mars;
And where Mars reigneth there must needs be wars.
HORATIO. Then thus begin our wars: put forth thy hand
That it may combat with my ruder hand.
BEL-IMPERIA. Set forth thy foot to try the push of mine.
HORATIO. But first my looks shall combat against thine.
BEL-IMPERIA. Then ward* thyself; I dart this kiss   protect
at thee.
HORATIO. Thus I retort the dart thou threw'st at me.
BEL-IMPERIA. Nay then, to gain the glory of the field,
My twining arms shall yoke and make thee yield.
HORATIO. Nay then, my arms are large and strong withal;
Thus elms by vines are compassed, till they fall.
BEL-IMPERIA. O let me go, for in my troubled eyes
Now mayst thou read that life in passion dies.
HORATIO. O stay awhile, and I will die with thee;
So shalt thou yield, and yet have conquered me.
BEL-IMPERIA. Who's there, Pedringano? we are betrayed!

(*Enter* LORENZO, BALTHAZAR, SERBERINE, *and* PEDRINGANO,
disguised.)

LORENZO. My lord, away with her; take her aside.
O sir, forbear; your valor is already tried.
(HORATIO *struggles.*)
Quickly dispatch, my masters.
(*They hang him in the arbor.*)
HORATIO. What, will you murder me?
LORENZO. Ay, thus, and thus! these are the fruits of love.
(*They stab him.*)
BEL-IMPERIA. O save his life, and let me die for him!
O save him, brother; save him, Balthazar!
I loved Horatio but he loved not me.
BALTHAZAR. But Balthazar loves Bel-imperia.
LORENZO. Although his life were still ambitious proud,
Yet is he at the highest now he is dead.
BEL-IMPERIA. Murder! murder! help, Hieronimo, help!
LORENZO. Come, stop her mouth; away with her.
                                          (*Exeunt.*)

Scene 5

(*The same. Enter* HIERONIMO *in his nightshirt.*)

HIERONIMO. What outcries pluck me from my naked bed,
And chill my throbbing heart with trembling fear,
Which never danger yet could daunt before?
Who calls Hieronimo? speak, here I am.
I did not slumber, therefore 'twas no dream.
No, no, it was some woman cried for help,
And here within this garden did she cry,
And in this garden must I rescue her.
But stay, what murd'rous spectacle is this?
A man hanged up and all the murderers gone,
And in my bower, to lay the guilt on me.
This place was made for pleasure, not for death.
  (*He cuts the body down.*)
Those garments that he wears I oft have seen—
Alas, it is Horatio, my sweet son!
O no, but he that whilom* was my son!   formerly
O was it thou that call'dst me from my bed?
O speak, if any spark of life remain!
I am thy father. Who hath slain my son?
What savage monster, not of human kind,
Hath here been glutted with thy harmless blood,
And left thy bloody corpse dishonored here,
For me, amidst these dark and deathful shades,
To drown thee with an ocean of my tears?
O heavens, why made you night to cover sin?
By day this deed of darkness had not been.
O earth, why didst thou not in time devour
The vild* profaner of this sacred bower?   vile
O poor Horatio, what hadst thou misdone,
To lose thy life ere life was new begun?
O wicked butcher, whatsoe'er thou wert,
How could thou strangle virtue and desert?
Ay me most wretched, that have lost my joy,
In losing my Horatio, my sweet boy!

(*Enter* ISABELLA.)

ISABELLA. My husband's absence makes my heart to throb.
Hieronimo!

HIERONIMO. Here, Isabella, help me to lament;
For sighs are stopped, and all my tears are spent.
ISABELLA. What world of grief! my son, Horatio!
O, where's the author of this endless woe?
HIERONIMO. To know the author were some ease of grief,
For in revenge my heart should find relief.
ISABELLA. Then is he gone? and is my son gone too?
O, gush out, tears, fountains and floods of tears;
Blow, sighs, and raise an everlasting storm;
For outrage* fits our cursèd wretchedness.   fury
[*Beginning of first of 1602 Addition*:]
Ay me, Hieronimo, sweet husband, speak.
HIERONIMO. He supped with us to-night, frolic and merry,
And said he would go visit Balthazar
At the Duke's Palace; there the Prince doth lodge.
He had no custom to stay out so late;
He may be in his chamber; some go see.
Roderigo, ho!

(*Enter* PEDRO *and* JAQUES.)

ISABELLA. Ay me, he raves! Sweet Hieronimo!
HIERONIMO. True, all Spain takes note of it.
Besides, he is so generally beloved;
His majesty the other day did grace him
With waiting on his cup. These be favors
Which do assure me he cannot be short lived.
ISABELLA. Sweet Hieronimo!
HIERONIMO. I wonder how this fellow got his clothes?
Sirrah, sirrah, I'll know the truth of all!
Jaques, run to the Duke of Castile's presently
And bid my son Horatio to come home.
I and his mother have had strange dreams to-night.
Do ye hear me, sir?
JAQUES.   Ay, sir.
HIERONIMO.   Well sir, begone.
Pedro, come hither; knowest thou who this is?
PEDRO. Too well, sir.
HIERONIMO. Too well, who is it? Peace, Isabella.
Nay, blush not, man.
PEDRO.   It is my Lord Horatio.
HIERONIMO. Ha, ha, Saint James, but this doth make me
    laugh,
That there are more deluded than myself.

PEDRO. Deluded?

HIERONIMO. Ay, I would have sworn myself, within this
  hour,
That this had been my son Horatio;
His garments are so like.
Ha, are they not great persuasions?

ISABELLA. O would to God it were not so.

HIERONIMO. Were not, Isabella? dost thou dream it is?
Can thy soft bosom entertain a thought,
That such a black deed of mischief should be done
On one so pure and spotless as our son?
Away, I am ashamed.

ISABELLA.   Dear Hieronimo,
Cast a more serious eye upon thy grief;
Weak apprehension gives but weak belief.

HIERONIMO. It was a man, sure, that was hanged up here;
A youth, as I remember. I cut him down.
If it should prove my son now after all?
Say you? say you? Light, lend me a taper;
Let me look again. O God,
Confusion, mischief, torment, death and hell,
Drop all your stings at once in my cold bosom,
That now is stiff with horror; kill me quickly.
Be gracious to me, thou infective* night,   infectious
And drop this deed of murder down on me;
Gird in my waste of grief with thy large darkness,
And let me not survive; to see the light
May put me in the mind I had a son.

ISABELLA. O sweet Horatio, O my dearest son.

HIERONIMO. How strangely had I lost my way to grief.
[*End of the Addition.*]

HIERONIMO.[18] Sweet, lovely rose, ill-plucked before thy
  time,
Fair, worthy son, not conquered, but betrayed,
I'll kiss thee now, for words with tears are stayed.

ISABELLA. And I'll close up the glasses of his sight,
For once these eyes were only my* delight.   that is,
                                                             my only
HIERONIMO. Seest thou this handkercher besmeared with
  blood?
It shall not from me till I take revenge.
Seest thou those wounds that yet are bleeding fresh?

---

[18] The name is repeated as a convenience to the reader in re-
constructing the original script.

I'll not entomb them till I have revenged.
Then will I joy amidst my discontent,
Till then my sorrow never shall be spent.

ISABELLA. The heavens are just; murder cannot be hid;
Time is the author both of truth and right,
And time will bring this treachery to light.

HIERONIMO. Meanwhile, good Isabella, cease thy plaints,
Or, at the least, dissemble them awhile;
So shall we sooner find the practice out,
And learn by whom all this was brought about.
Come, Isabel, now let us take him up.
(*They lift the body up.*)
And bear him in from out this cursèd place.
I'll say his dirge; singing fits not this case.
O aliquis mihi quas pulchrum ver educat herbas,
    (HIERONIMO *sets his breast to his sword.*)
Misceat, et nostro detur medicina dolori:
Aut, si qui faciunt annorum obliva, succos
Praebeat; ipse metam magnum quaecunque per orbem
Gramina Sol pulchras effert in luminis oras;
Ipse bibam quicquid meditatur saga veneni,
Quicquid et herbarum vi caeca nenia nectit:
Omnia perpetiar, lethum quoque, dum semel omnis
Noster in extincto moriatur pectore sensus.
Ergo tuos oculos nunquam (mea vita) videbo,
Et tua perpetuus sepelivit lumina somnus?
Emoriar tecum: sic, sic juvat ire sub umbras.
At tamen absistam properato cedere letho,
Ne mortem vindicta tuam tam nulla sequatur.[19]

(*He throws the sword from him and bears the body away.*)

CHORUS

ANDREA. Brought'st thou me hither to increase my pain?
I looked that Balthazar should have been slain;

[19] "Oh let someone mix me herbs which beautiful spring brings forth, and let medicine be given for our pain; or let him offer potions, if there be any which cause forgetfulness of the years; may I myself throughout the great world gather whatever plants the sun brings forth into the beauteous realms of light; may I myself drink whatever poison the sorceress concocts and whatever herbs her incantation unites through occult power. Let me endure all, even death, provided that all feeling may die in a heart already dead. Shall I then never again see your eyes, my life, and has eternal sleep buried your light? Let me die with you; thus, thus would I go to the shades below. But nevertheless I shall refrain from yielding to hasty death, lest then no vengeance should follow your death."

But 'tis my friend Horatio that is slain,
And they abuse fair Bel-imperia,
On whom I doted more than all the world,
Because she loved me more than all the world.
    REVENGE. Thou talkest of harvest when the corn is green:
The end is crown of every work well done;
The sickle comes not till the corn be ripe.
Be still, and ere I lead thee from this place,
I'll show thee Balthazar in heavy case.

ACT III

Scene 1

(The Portuguese Court. Enter VICEROY OF PORTINGALE,
NOBLES, *and* VILLUPPO.)

    VICEROY. Infortunate condition of kings,
Seated amidst so many helpless doubts.
First, we are placed upon extremest height,
And oft supplanted with exceeding hate,
But ever subject to the wheel of chance,
And at our highest never joy we so
As we both doubt* and dread our overthrow.   fear
So striveth not the waves with sundry winds
As Fortune toileth in the affairs of kings,
That would be feared, yet fear to be beloved,
Sith* fear or love to kings is flattery.   since
For instance, lordings, look upon your King,
By hate deprivèd of his dearest son,
The only hope of our successive line.
    NOBLEMAN. I had not thought that Alexandro's heart
Had been envenomed with such extreme hate;
But now I see that words have several works,
And there's no credit in the countenance.
    VILLUPPO. No; for, my lord, had you beheld the train* deceit
That feignèd love had colored in his looks,
When he in camp consorted* Balthazar,   accompanied
Far more inconstant had you thought the sun,
That hourly coasts* the center of the earth,   moves around
Than Alexandro's purpose to the Prince.
    VICEROY. No more, Villuppo, thou hast said enough,
And with thy words thou slayest our wounded thoughts.
Nor shall I longer dally with the world,

Procrastinating Alexandro's death.
Go, some of you, and fetch the traitor forth,

                        (*Exit a* NOBLEMAN.)

That, as he is condemnèd, he may die.

    (*Enter* ALEXANDRO *with a* NOBLEMAN *and Halberdiers.*)

    NOBLEMAN. In such extremes will nought but patience
      serve.
    ALEXANDRO. But in extremes what patience shall I use?
Nor discontents it me to leave the world
With whom there nothing can prevail but wrong.
    NOBLEMAN. Yet hope the best.
    ALEXANDRO.   'Tis Heaven is my hope.
As for the earth, it is too much infect*   infected
To yield me hope of any of her mold.
    VICEROY. Why linger ye? bring forth that daring fiend,
And let him die for his accursèd deed.
    ALEXANDRO. Not that I fear the extremity of death
(For nobles cannot stoop to servile fear)
Do I, O King, thus discontented live.
But this, O this torments my laboring soul,
That thus I die suspected of a sin
Whereof, as heavens have known my secret thoughts,
So am I free from this suggestion.*   false charge
    VICEROY. No more, I say; to the tortures, when!* (ejaculation of
Bind him, and burn his body in those flames   impatience)
    (*They bind him to the stake.*)
That shall prefigure those unquenchèd fires
Of Phlegethon,[20] preparèd for his soul.
    ALEXANDRO. My guiltless death will be avenged on thee,
On thee, Villuppo, that hath maliced* thus,   entertained malice
Or for thy meed* hast falsely me accused.   reward
    VILLUPPO. Nay, Alexandro, if thou menace me,
I'll lend a hand to send thee to the lake*   that is,
Where those thy words shall perish with thy works. Avernus
Injurious traitor! monstrous homicide!

    (*Enter* AMBASSADOR *and Attendants.*)

    AMBASSADOR. Stay, hold awhile,
And here, with pardon of his majesty,

      [20] River of fire in hell.

Lay hands upon Villuppo.
 VICEROY.   Ambassador,
What news hath urged this sudden entrance?
 AMBASSADOR. Know, sovereign lord, that Balthazar doth
  live.
 VICEROY. What sayest thou? liveth Balthazar, our son?
 AMBASSADOR. Your highness' son, Lord Balthazar, doth
  live;
And, well entreated* in the Court of Spain,   treated
Humbly commends him to your majesty.
These eyes beheld, and these my followers;
With these, the letters of the King's commends,*   greetings
 (*Gives him letters.*)
Are happy witnesses of his highness' health.
 (*The* KING *looks on the letters, and proceeds.*)
 VICEROY. "Thy son doth live, your tribute is received,
Thy peace is made, and we are satisfied.
The rest resolve upon as things proposed
For both our honors and thy benefit."
 AMBASSADOR. These are his highness' farther articles.
 (*He gives him more letters.*)
 VICEROY. Accursèd wretch, to intimate these ills
Against the life and reputation
Of noble Alexandro. Come, my lord, unbind him.
Let him unbind thee that is bound to death,
To make a quital* for thy discontent.   requital
 (*They unbind him.*)
 ALEXANDRO. Dread lord, in kindness* you could do by nature
  no less
Upon report of such a damnèd fact;*   deed
But thus we see our innocence hath saved
The hopeless life which thou, Villuppo, sought
By thy suggestions to have massacred.
 VICEROY. Say, false Villuppo, wherefore didst thou thus
Falsely betray Lord Alexandro's lfe?
Him whom thou knowest that no unkindness else
But even the slaughter of our dearest son
Could once have moved us to have misconceived.
 ALEXANDRO. Say, treacherous Villuppo, tell the King—:
Or wherein hath Alexandro used thee ill?
 VILLUPPO. Rent with remembrance of so foul a deed,
My guilty soul submits me to thy doom;*   judgment
For not for Alexandro's injuries,
But for reward and hope to be preferred.*   advanced

Thus have I shamelessly hazarded his life.

   VICEROY. Which, villain, shall be ransomed with thy
     death,
And not so mean* a torment as we here   moderate
Devised for him who, thou said'st, slew our son,
But with the bitterest torments and extremes
That may be yet invented for thine end.

   (ALEXANDRO *seems to entreat.*)

Entreat me not; go, take the traitor hence.

              (*Exit* VILLUPPO *and Guards.*)

And, Alexandro, let us honor thee
With public notice of thy loyalty.
To end those things articulated* here   specified in
By our great lord, the mighty King of Spain,   articles
We with our council will deliberate.
Come, Alexandro, keep us company.

                   (*Exeunt.*)

Scene 2

(*The Spanish Court. Enter* HIERONIMO.)

   HIERONIMO. O eyes! no eyes, but fountains fraught with
     tears;
O life! no life, but lively form of death;
O world! no world, but mass of public wrongs,
Confused and filled with murder and misdeeds.
O sacred heavens! if this unhallowed deed,
If this inhuman and barbarous attempt,
If this incomparable murder thus
Of mine, but now no more my son,
Shall unrevealed and unrevengèd pass,
How should we term your dealings to be just,
If you unjustly deal with those that in your justice trust?
The night, sad secretary* to my moans,   confidant
With direful visions wakes my vexèd soul,
And with the wounds of my distressful son
Solicits me for notice of his death.
The ugly fiends do sally forth of hell,
And frame my steps to unfrequented paths,
And fear* my heart with fierce inflamèd thoughts.   frighten
The cloudy day my discontents records,
Early begins to register my dreams
And drive me forth to seek the murderer.

Eyes, life, world, heavens, hell, night and day,
See, search, show, send some man, some mean, that may—
    (*A letter falls.*)
What's here? a letter? tush! it is not so,
A letter written to Hieronimo.
"For want of ink, receive this bloody writ.
Me hath my hapless brother hid from thee;
Revenge thyself on Balthazar and him,
For these were they that murderèd thy son.
Hieronimo, revenge Horatio's death,
And better fare than Bel-imperia doth."
    HIERONIMO. What means this unexpected miracle?
My son slain by Lorenzo and the Prince.
What cause had they Horatio to malign?*   plot against
Or what might move thee, Bel-imperia,
To accuse thy brother, had he been the mean?
Hieronimo, beware, thou art betrayed,
And to entrap thy life this train* is laid.   plot
Advise thee therefore; be not credulous:
This is devisèd to endanger thee,
That thou, by this, Lorenzo shouldst accuse,
And he, for thy dishonor done, should draw
Thy life in question and thy name in hate.
Dear was the life of my belovèd son,
And of his death behoves me be revenged.
Then hazard not thine own, Hieronimo,
But live t'effect thy resolution.
I therefore will by circumstances* try   indirect means
What I can gather to confirm this writ;
And, hark'ning near the Duke of Castile's house,
Close,* if I can, with Bel-imperia,   meet
To listen more, but nothing to bewray.*   betray

    (*Enter* PEDRINGANO.)

Now, Pedringano.
    PEDRINGANO.   Now, Hieronimo.
    HIERONIMO. Where's thy lady?
    PEDRINGANO.   I know not; here's my lord.

    (*Enter* LORENZO.)

    LORENZO. How now, who's this? Hieronimo?
    HIERONIMO.   My lord.

PEDRINGANO. He asketh for my Lady Bel-imperia.

LORENZO. What to do, Hieronimo? The Duke, my father, hath
Upon some disgrace awhile removed her hence;
But if it be aught I may inform her of,
Tell me, Hieronimo, and I'll let her know it.

HIERONIMO. Nay, nay, my lord, I thank you; it shall not need.
I had a suit unto her, but too late,
And her disgrace makes me unfortunate.

LORENZO. Why so, Hieronimo? Use me.

HIERONIMO. O no, my lord, I dare not; it must not be.
I humbly thank your lordship.

[*Beginning of second 1602 Addition.*]

HIERONIMO.   Who? you, my lord?
I reserve your favor for a greater honor;
This is a very toy,* my lord, a toy.   trifle

LORENZO. All's one, Hieronimo, acquaint me with it.

HIERONIMO. I' faith, my lord, it is an idle thing;
I must confess I ha' been too slack, too tardy,
Too remiss unto your honor.

LORENZO.   How now, Hieronimo?

HIERONIMO. In troth, my lord, it is a thing of nothing;
The murder of a son, or so;
A thing of nothing, my lord.

[*End of Addition.*]

LORENZO.   Why then, farewell.

HIERONIMO. My grief no heart, my thoughts no tongue can tell.

                                              (*Exit.*)

LORENZO. Come hither, Pedringano; seest thou this?

PEDRINGANO. My lord, I see it, and suspect it too.

LORENZO. This is that damnèd villain, Serberine,
That hath, I fear, revealed Horatio's death.

PEDRINGANO. My lord, he could not, 'twas so lately done,
And since, he hath not left my company.

LORENZO. Admit he have not, his condition's* such   nature
As fear or flattering words may make him false.
I know his humor* and therewith repent   disposition
That ere I used him in this enterprise.
But, Pedringano, to prevent the worst,
And 'cause I know thee secret as my soul,
Here, for thy further satisfaction, take thou this.

    (*Gives him more gold.*)

And harken to me; thus it is devised.
This night thou must, and prithee so resolve,
Meet Serberine at Saint Luigi's Park—
Thou knowest 'tis here hard by behind the house—
There take thy stand, and see thou strike him sure;
For die he must, if we do mean to live.

PEDRINGANO. But how shall Serberine be there, my lord?

LORENZO. Let me alone; I'll send to him to meet
The Prince and me, where thou must do this deed.

PEDRINGANO. It shall be done, my lord, it shall be done;
And I'll go arm myself to meet him there.

LORENZO. When things shall alter, as I hope they will,
Then shalt thou mount for this; thou knowest my mind.

(*Exit* PEDRINGANO.)

Che le Ieron![21]

(*Enter* PAGE.)

PAGE.　　　　My lord?

LORENZO.　　　　　　　Go, sirrah, to Serberine,
And bid him forthwith meet the Prince and me
At Saint Luigi's Park, behind the house,
This evening, boy.

PAGE.　　　　　　I go, my lord.

LORENZO. But, sirrah, let the hour be eight a'clock.
Bid him not fail.

PAGE.　　　　　　I fly, my lord.

(*Exit*.)

LORENZO. Now to confirm the complot*　　　plot
　　thou hast cast*　　　　　　　　　　contrived
Of all these practices,* I'll spread the watch,　schemes
Upon precise commandment from the King,
Strongly to guard the place where Pedringano
This night shall murder hapless Serberine.
Thus must we work that will avoid distrust;
Thus must we practise to prevent mishap,
And thus one ill another must expulse.
This sly enquiry of Hieronimo
For Bel-imperia breeds suspicion,
And this suspicion bodes a further ill.
As for myself, I know my secret fault,*　　　offense
And so do they; but I have dealt for them.

[21] "An unintelligible expression, possibly a corruption of the page's name" (Boas).

They that for coin their souls endangerèd,
To save my life for coin shall venture theirs;
And better it's that base companions* die   fellows
Than by their life to hazard our good haps.*   fortunes
Nor shall they live, for me to fear their faith.
I'll trust myself, myself shall be my friend;
For die they shall; slaves are ordained to no other end.

                                                   (*Exit.*)

Scene 3

   (*St. Luigi's Park. Enter* PEDRINGANO, *with a pistol.*)

PEDRINGANO. Now, Pedringano, bid thy pistol hold;
And hold on, Fortune, once more favor me;
Give but success to mine attempting spirit,
And let me shift for taking of mine aim.[22]
Here is the gold, this is the gold proposed;
It is no dream that I adventure for,
But Pedringano is possessed thereof.
And he that would not strain his conscience
For him that thus his liberal purse hath stretched,
Unworthy such a favor, may he fail,
And, wishing, want, when such as I prevail.
As for the fear of apprehension,
I know, if need should be, my noble lord
Will stand between me and ensuing harms.
Besides, this place is free from all suspect.*   suspicion
Here therefore will I stay and take my stand.

   (*Enter the* WATCH *unseen by* PEDRINGANO.)

1 WATCH. I wonder how much to what intent it is
That we are thus expressly charged to watch.
   2 WATCH. 'Tis by commandment in the King's own name.
   3 WATCH. But we were never wont to watch and ward* patrol
So near the Duke his brother's house before.
   2 WATCH. Content yourself, stand close, there's somewhat
in't.

   (*Enter* SERBERINE.)

SERBERINE. Here, Serberine, attend and stay thy pace;
For here did Don Lorenzo's page appoint

     [22] That is, and leave it to me to aim the pistol.

That thou by his command shouldst meet with him.
How fit a place, if one were so disposed,
Methinks this corner is to close* with one.   meet
   PEDRINGANO. Here comes the bird that I must seize upon.
Now, Pedringano, or never, play the man.
   SERBERINE. I wonder that his lordship stays so long,
Or wherefore should he send for me so late.
   PEDRINGANO. For this, Serberine, and thou shalt ha't.* have it
   (*Shoots the pistol.*)
So, there he lies; my promise is performed.
   (*The* WATCH *advances.*)
   1 WATCH. Hark, gentlemen, this is a pistol shot.
   2 WATCH. And here's one slain; stay the murderer.
   PEDRINGANO. Now by the sorrows of the souls in hell,
   (*He strives with the* WATCH.)
Who first lays hand on me, I'll be his priest.[23]
   3 WATCH. Sirrah, confess, and therein play the priest.
Why hast thou thus unkindly* killed the man?   unnaturally
   PEDRINGANO. Why? because he walked abroad so late.
   3 WATCH. Come sir, you had been better kept your bed
Than have committed this misdeed so late.
   2 WATCH. Come, to the Marshal's with the murderer.
   1 WATCH. On to Hieronimo's; help me here
To bring the murdered body with us too.
   PEDRINGANO. Hieronimo? Carry me before whom you will.
Whate'er he be, I'll answer him and you,
And do your worst, for I defy you all.

(Exeunt.)

Scene 4

   (*The palace of* DON CYPRIAN. *Enter* LORENZO *and* BALTHA-
ZAR.)

   BALTHAZAR. How now, my lord, what makes you rise so
    soon?
   LORENZO. Fear of preventing our mishaps too late.
   BALTHAZAR. What mischief is it that we not
    mistrust?*   do not suspect
   LORENZO. Our greatest ills we least mistrust, my lord,
And inexpected harms do hurt us most.
   BALTHAZAR. Why, tell me, Don Lorenzo, tell me, man,
If aught concerns our honor and your own.

   [23] That is, assist his passage to the next world—kill him.

LORENZO. Nor you, nor me, my lord, but both in one;
For I suspect, and the presumption's great,
That by those base confederates in our fault
Touching the death of Don Horatio,
We are betrayed to old Hieronimo.
BALTHAZAR. Betrayed, Lorenzo? Tush, it cannot be.
LORENZO. A guilty conscience, urgèd with the thought
Of former evils, easily cannot err.
I am persuaded, and dissuade me not,
That all's revealèd to Hieronimo,
And therefore know that I have cast* it thus—   planned

(Enter PAGE.)

But here's the page. How now, what news with thee?
PAGE. My lord, Serberine is slain.
BALTHAZAR. Who? Serberine, my man?
PAGE. Your highness' man, my lord.
LORENZO. Speak, page, who murdered him?
PAGE. He that is apprehended for the fact.*   deed
LORENZO. Who?
PAGE. Pedringano.
BALTHAZAR. Is Serberine slain that loved his lord so well?
Injurious villain, murderer of his friend.
LORENZO. Hath Pedringano murdered Serberine?
My lord, let me entreat you to take the pains
To exasperate* and hasten his revenge   make severe
With your complaints unto my lord the King.
This their dissension breeds a greater doubt.
BALTHAZAR. Assure thee, Don Lorenzo, he shall die,
Or else his highness hardly shall deny.[24]
Meanwhile I'll haste the Marshal sessions.
For die he shall for this his damnèd deed.
                                    (Exit BALTHAZAR.)
LORENZO. Why so, this fits our former policy,
And thus experience bids the wise to deal.
I lay the plot; he prosecutes the point.*   executes
                                                      the deed
I set the trap; he breaks the worthless twigs,
And sees not that wherewith the bird was limed.*   trapped
Thus hopeful men, that mean to hold their own,
Must look like fowlers to their dearest friends.

[24] That is, otherwise his highness will be dealing harshly in denying me this.

He runs to kill whom I have holpe* to catch, helped
And no man knows it was my reaching fatch.* carefully
prepared plan
'Tis hard to trust unto a multitude,
Or any one, in mine opinion,
When men themselves their secrets will reveal.

(*Enter a* MESSENGER *with a letter.*)

Boy!
   PAGE. My lord.
   LORENZO. What's he?
   MESSENGER.   I have a letter to your lordship.
   LORENZO. From whence?
   MESSENGER.   From Pedringano, that's imprisonèd.
   LORENZO. So, he is in prison then?
   MESSENGER.   Ay, my good lord.
   LORENZO. What would he with us? He writes us here,
To stand good lord,* and help him in distress. be a good
patron
Tell him I have his letters, know his mind,
And what we may, let him assure him of.
Fellow, be gone; my boy shall follow thee.

(Exit MESSENGER.)

(*Aside.*) This works like wax; yet once more try thy wits.
Boy, go, convey this purse to Pedringano;
Thou knowest the prison; closely* give it him, secretly
And be advised that none be thereabout.
Bid him be merry still, but secret;
And though the Marshal sessions be today,
Bid him not doubt of his delivery.
Tell him his pardon is already signed,
And thereon bid him boldly be resolved;
For, were he ready to be turnèd off,* hanged
As 'tis my will the uttermost be tried,
Thou with his pardon shalt attend him still.
Show him this box, tell him his pardon's in't;
But open't not, and if thou lovest thy life;
But let him wisely keep his hopes unknown.
He shall not want while Don Lorenzo lives.
Away!
   PAGE.   I go, my lord, I run.
   LORENZO. But, sirrah, see that this be cleanly* done. cleverly

(Exit PAGE.)

Now stands our fortune on a tickle* point, precariously
balanced

And now or never ends Lorenzo's doubts.
One only thing is uneffected yet,
And that's to see the executioner.
But to what end? I list not* trust the air   do not want to
With utterance of our pretence* therein,   intention
For fear the privy whisp'ring of the wind
Convey our words amongst unfriendly ears
That lie too open to advantages.

> *E quel che voglio io, nessun lo sa;*
> *Intendo io: quel mi basterà.*[25]

                                              (*Exit.*)

Scene 5

(*A street. Enter* BOY *with the box.*)

BOY. My master hath forbidden me to look in this box, and
by my troth, 'tis likely, if he had not warned me, I should not
have had so much idle time; for we men's-kind in our minority
are like women in their uncertainty: that they are most forbidden, they will soonest attempt. So I now. By my bare honesty,
here's nothing but the bare empty box. Were it not sin against
secrecy, I would say it were a piece of gentlemanlike knavery.
I must go to Pedringano, and tell him his pardon is in this
box; nay, I would have sworn it, had I not seen the contrary.
I cannot choose but smile to think how the villain will flout the
gallows, scorn the audience, and descant* on the hang- comment
man, and all presuming of his pardon from hence. Will't not be
an odd jest for me to stand and grace every jest he makes,
pointing my finger at this box, as who would say, "Mock on;
here's thy warrant." Is't not a scurvy jest that a man should
jest himself to death? Alas! poor Pedringano, I am in a sort
sorry for thee; but if I should be hanged with thee, I cannot
weep.

                                              (*Exit.*)

Scene 6

(*Hall of Justice. Enter* HIERONIMO *and the* DEPUTY.)

HIERONIMO. Thus must we toil in other men's extremes,
That know not how to remedy our own,
And do them justice, when unjustly we,

> [25] "And what I wish, no one knows; I know, which is enough
> for me."

For all our wrongs, can compass* no redress.   devise
But shall I never live to see the day
That I may come, by justice of the heavens,
To know the cause that may my cares allay?
This toils my body, this consumeth age,
That only I to all men just must be,
And neither gods nor men be just to me.
    DEPUTY. Worthy Hieronimo, your office asks
A care to punish such as do transgress.
    HIERONIMO. So is't my duty to regard his death
Who, when he lived, deserved my dearest blood.
But come; for what we came for let's begin,
For here[26] lies that which bids me to be gone.

    (*Enter* Officers, HANGMAN, BOY, *and* PEDRINGANO, *with a
letter in his hand, bound.*)

    DEPUTY. Bring forth the prisoner, for the court is set.
    PEDRINGANO. Gramercy, boy, but it was time to come;
For I had written to my lord anew
A nearer matter that concerneth him,
For fear his lordship had forgotten me;
But sith* he hath remembered me so well,   since
Come, come, come on, when shall we to this gear?*   business
    HIERONIMO. Stand forth, thou monster, murderer of men,
And here, for satisfaction of the world,
Confess thy folly, and repent thy fault;
For there's thy place of execution.
    PEDRINGANO. This is short work. Well, to your Marshalship
First I confess, nor fear I death therefore,
I am the man; 'twas I slew Serberine.
But, sir, then you think this shall be the place
Where we shall satisfy you for this gear?
    DEPUTY. Ay, Pedringano.
    PEDRINGANO.   Now I think not so.
    HIERONIMO. Peace, impudent, for thou shalt find it so;
For blood with blood shall, while I sit as judge,
Be satisfied, and the law discharged.
And though myself cannot receive the like,
Yet will I see that others have their right.
Dispatch; the fault's approved* and confessed,   proved
And by our law he is condemned to die.

    [26] The antecedent of *here* is uncertain, possibly Horatio's
bloody handkerchief.

HANGMAN. Come on, sir, are you ready?

PEDRINGANO. To do what, my fine, officious knave?

HANGMAN. To go to this gear.

PEDRINGANO. O sir, you are too forward: thou wouldst fain furnish me with a halter, to disfurnish me of my habit.[27] So I should go out of this gear, my raiment, into that gear, the rope. But, hangman, now I spy your knavery, I'll not change without boot,* that's flat.   additional payment

HANGMAN. Come, sir.

PEDRINGANO. So then, I must up?

HANGMAN. No remedy.

PEDRINGANO. Yes, but there shall be for my coming down.

HANGMAN. Indeed, here's a remedy for that.

PEDRINGANO. How? be turned off?*   hanged

HANGMAN. Ay, truly. Come, are you ready? I pray, sir, dispatch; the day goes away.

PEDRINGANO. What, do you hang by the hour? If you do, I may chance to break your old custom.

HANGMAN. Faith, you have reason; for I am like to break your young neck.

PEDRINGANO. Dost thou mock me, hangman? Pray God, I be not preserved to break your knave's pate for this.

HANGMAN. Alas, sir, you are a foot too low to reach it, and I hope you will never grow so high while I am in the office.

PEDRINGANO. Sirrah, dost see yonder boy with the box in his hand?

HANGMAN. What, he that points to it with his finger?

PEDRINGANO. Ay, that companion.

HANGMAN. I know him not, but what of him?

PEDRINGANO. Dost thou think to live till his old doublet will make thee a new truss?*   jacket

HANGMAN. Ay, and many a fair year after, to truss up many an honester man than either thou or he.

PEDRINGANO. What hath he in his box, as thou think'st?

HANGMAN. Faith, I cannot tell, nor I care not greatly. Methinks you should rather harken to your soul's health.

PEDRINGANO. Why, sirrah hangman, I take it that that is good for the body is likewise good for the soul, and it may be in that box is balm for both.

HANGMAN. Well, thou art even the merriest piece of man's flesh that e'er groaned at my office door.

[27] A reference to the custom of giving the hangman the clothes of those he executes.

PEDRINGANO. Is your roguery become an office with a knave's name?

HANGMAN. Ay, and that shall all they witness that see you seal it with a thief's name.

PEDRINGANO. I prithee, request this good company to pray with me.

HANGMAN. Ay, marry, sir, this is a good motion.*   proposal
My masters, you see here's a good fellow.

PEDRINGANO. Nay, nay, now I remember me, let them alone till some other time, for now I have no great need.

HIERONIMO. I have not seen a wretch so impudent.
O monstrous times, where murder's set so light,
And where the soul, that should be shrined in heaven,
Solely delights in interdicted things,
Still wand'ring in the thorny passages
That intercepts itself of* happiness.   bars
Murder! O bloody monster! God forbid
A fault so foul should scape unpunishèd.
Dispatch, and see this execution done.
This makes me to remember thee, my son.

                  (*Exit* HIERONIMO.)

PEDRINGANO. Nay, soft, no haste.

DEPUTY. Why, wherefore stay you? Have you hope of
    life?

PEDRINGANO. Why, ay.

HANGMAN. As how?

PEDRINGANO. Why, rascal, by my pardon from the King.

HANGMAN. Stand you on that? Then you shall off with this.
(*He pushes him off the ladder.*)

DEPUTY. So, executioner, convey him hence,
But let his body be unburied:
Let not the earth be chokèd or infect
With that which heavens contemns, and men neglect.

                  (*Exeunt.*)

Scene 7

(HIERONIMO's *house. Enter* HIERONIMO.)

HIERONIMO. Where shall I run to breathe abroad my woes,
My woes whose weight hath wearièd the earth?
Or mine exclaims, that have surcharged the air
With ceaseless plaints for my deceasèd son?
The blust'ring winds, conspiring with my words,

At my lament have moved the leafless trees,
Disrobed the meadows of their flow'rèd green,
Made mountains marsh with spring tides of my tears,
And broken through the brazen gates of hell.
Yet still tormented is my tortured soul
With broken sighs and restless passions,
That wingèd, mount and, hovering in the air,
Beat at the windows of the brightest heavens,
Soliciting for justice and revenge.
But they are placed in those empyreal* heights,   celestial
Where, countermured* with walls of diamond,   doubly walled
I find the place impregnable, and they
Resist my woes, and give my words no way.

(*Enter* HANGMAN *with a letter.*)

HANGMAN. O Lord, sir, God bless you, sir, the man, sir,
Petergade, sir, he that was so full of merry conceits—
HIERONIMO. Well, what of him?
HANGMAN. O Lord, sir, he went the wrong way; the fellow
had a fair commission to the contrary. Sir, here is his passport;
I pray you, sir, we have done him wrong.
HIERONIMO. I warrant thee; give it me.
HANGMAN. You will stand between the gallows and me?
HIERONIMO. Ay, ay.
HANGMAN. I thank your lord worship.

(*Exit* HANGMAN.)

HIERONIMO. And yet, though somewhat nearer me concerns,
I will, to ease the grief that I sustain,
Take truce with sorrow while I read on this.
    My lord, I write as mine extremes required,
    That you would labor my delivery.
    If you neglect, my life is desperate,
    *And in my death I shall reveal the troth.**   truth
    You know, my lord, I slew him for your sake,
    And was confederate with the Prince and you;
    Won by rewards and hopeful promises,
    *I holpe** to murder Don Horatio too.*   helped
Holpe he to murder mine Horatio?
And actors in th'accursèd tragedy
Wast thou, Lorenzo, Balthazar and thou,
Of whom my son, my son, deserved so well?
What have I heard? what have mine eyes beheld?

O sacred heavens, may it come to pass
That such a monstrous and detested deed,
So closely smothèred, and so long concealed,
Shall thus by this be vengèd* or revealed?   a\
Now see I what I durst not then suspect,
That Bel-imperia's letter was not feigned.
Nor feignèd she, though falsely they have wronged
Both her, myself, Horatio, and themselves.
Now may I make compare 'twixt hers and this,
Of every accident; I ne'er could find
Till now, and now I feelingly perceive,
They did what heaven unpunished would not leave.
O false Lorenzo, are these thy flattering looks?
Is this the honor that thou didst my son?
And Balthazar, bane to thy soul and me,
Was this the ransom he reserved thee for?
Woe to the cause of these constrainèd wars!
Woe to thy baseness and captivity;
Woe to thy birth, thy body, and thy soul,
Thy cursèd father, and thy conquered self;
And banned with bitter execrations be
The day and place where he did pity thee.
But wherefore waste I mine unfruitful words,
When naught but blood will satisfy my woes?
I will go plain me* to my lord the King,   complain
And cry aloud for justice through the Court,
Wearing the flints with these my witherèd feet,
And either purchase justice by entreats
Or tire them all with my revenging threats.

                                  (Exit.)

ACT IV

Scene 1

(The same. Enter ISABELLA *and her* MAID.)

ISABELLA. So that you say this herb will purge the eye,
And this, the head?
Ah, but none of them will purge the heart.
No, there's no medicine left for my disease,
Nor any physic to recure the dead.
    (She runs lunatic.)

Horatio! O, where's Horatio?

MAID. Good madam, affright not thus yourself
With outrage for your son Horatio.
He sleeps in quiet in the Elysian fields.

ISABELLA. Why, did I not give you gowns and goodly things,
Bought you a whistle and a whipstalk* too,   whip handle
To be revengèd on their villainies?

MAID. Madam, these humors* do torment my soul.   ravings

ISABELLA. "My soul," poor soul, thou talks of things
Thou know'st not what; my soul hath silver wings
That mounts me up unto the highest heavens.
To heaven? Ay, there sits my Horatio,
Backed with a troop of fiery cherubins
Dancing about his newly healèd wounds,
Singing sweet hymns and chanting heavenly notes;
Rare harmony to greet his innocence,
That died, ay died, a mirror in our days.
But say, where shall I find the men, the murderers,
That slew Horatio? whither shall I run
To find them out that murderèd my son?

                                                    (*Exeunt.*)

Scene 2

(*The palace of* DON CYPRIAN. BEL-IMPERIA, *at a window.*)

BEL-IMPERIA. What means this outrage that is offered me?
Why am I thus sequestered from the court?
No notice; shall I not know the cause
Of this my secret and suspicious ills?
Accursèd brother, unkind* murderer,   unnatural
Why bends thou thus thy mind to martyr me?
Hieronimo, why writ I of thy wrongs,
Or why art thou so slack in thy revenge?
Andrea, O Andrea, that thou sawest
Me for thy friend Horatio handled thus,
And him for me thus causeless murderèd.
Well, force perforce, I must constrain myself
To patience and apply me to the time,*   accept the
                                                            situation
'll Heaven, as I have hoped, shall set me free.

CHRISTOPHIL.)

OPHIL. Come, Madam Bel-imperia, this may not be.
                                                    (*Exeunt.*)

Scene 3

(*The same. Enter* LORENZO, BALTHAZAR, *and the* l____,

LORENZO. Boy, talk no further; thus far things go well.
Thou art assurèd that thou sawest him dead?
PAGE. Or else, my lord, I live not.
LORENZO. That's enough.
As for his resolution in his end,
Leave that to him with whom he sojourns now.
Here, take my ring and give it Christophil,
And bid him let my sister be enlarged,*   freed
And bring her hither straight.

(*Exit* PAGE.)

This that I did was for a policy,
To smooth and keep the murder secret,
Which, as a nine-days' wonder,[28] being o'erblown,
My gentle sister will I now enlarge.
BALTHAZAR. And time, Lorenzo; for my lord the Duke,
You heard, inquired for her yesternight.
LORENZO. Why, and my lord, I hope you heard me say
Sufficient reason why she kept away.
But that's all one. My lord, you love her?
BALTHAZAR. Ay.
LORENZO. Then in your love beware, deal cunningly,
Salve all suspicions, only soothe me up;*   back up
                    my story
And if she hap to stand on terms* with us, make difficulties
As for her sweetheart and concealment so,
Jest with her gently; under feignèd jest
Are things concealed that else would breed unrest.
But here she comes.

(*Enter* BEL-IMPERIA.)

Now, sister—
BEL-IMPERIA. Sister? no!
Thou art no brother, but an enemy;
Else wouldst thou not have used thy sister so:
First, to affright me with thy weapons drawn
And with extremes abuse my company;
And then to hurry me, like whirlwind's rage,

[28] Refers to the length of time a novelty is supposed to hold
one's attention.

Amidst a crew of thy confederates,
And clap me up* where none might come at me,   imprison me
Nor I at any to reveal my wrongs.
What madding fury did possess thy wits?
Or wherein is't that I offended thee?

LORENZO. Advise you better, Bel-imperia,
For I have done you no disparagement;
Unless, by more discretion than deserved,
I sought to save your honor and mine own.

BEL-IMPERIA. Mine honor? Why, Lorenzo, wherein is't
That I neglect my reputation so
As you, or any, need to rescue it?

LORENZO. His highness and my father were resolved
To come confer with old Hieronimo
Concerning certain matters of estate
That by the Viceroy was determinèd.

BEL-IMPERIA. And wherein was mine honor touched in
    that?

BALTHAZAR. Have patience, Bel-imperia; hear the rest.

LORENZO. Me, next in sight, as messenger they sent
To give him notice that they were so nigh.
Now when I came, consorted with* the Prince,   accompanied by
And unexpected in an arbor there
Found Bel-imperia with Horatio—

BEL-IMPERIA. How then?

LORENZO. Why, then, rememb'ring that old disgrace
Which you for Don Andrea had endured,
And now were likely longer to sustain
By being found so meanly accompanied,
Thought rather, for I know no readier mean,
To thrust Horatio forth* my father's way.   out of

BALTHAZAR. And carry you obscurely somewhere else,
Lest that his highness should have found you there.

BEL-IMPERIA. Even so, my lord? And you are witness
That this is true which he entreateth of?
You, gentle brother, forged this for my sake,
And you, my lord, were made his instrument.
A work of worth, worthy the noting too.
But what's the cause that you concealed me since?

LORENZO. Your melancholy, sister, since the news
Of your first favorite Don Andrea's death,
My father's old wrath hath exasperate.*   intensified

BALTHAZAR. And better was't for you, being in disg
To absent yourself and give his fury place.

BEL-IMPERIA. But why had I no notice of his ire?

LORENZO. That were to add more fuel to your fire,
Who burnt like Aetna for Andrea's loss.

BEL-IMPERIA. Hath not my father then inquired for me?

LORENZO. Sister, he hath, and thus excused I thee.
(*He whispers in her ear.*)
But Bel-imperia, see the gentle Prince;
Look on thy love, behold young Balthazar,
Whose passions by thy presence are increased;
And in whose melancholy thou mayest see
Thy hate, his love; thy flight, his following thee.

BEL-IMPERIA. Brother, you are become an orator—
I know not, I, by what experience—
Too politic* for me, past all compare,   cunning
Since last I saw you; but content yourself;
The Prince is meditating higher things.

BALTHAZAR. 'Tis of thy beauty then, that conquers kings;
Of those thy tresses, Ariadne's twines,[29]
Wherewith my liberty thou hast surprised;
Of that thine ivory front,* my sorrow's map,   face
Wherein I see no haven to rest my hope.

BEL-IMPERIA. To love and fear, and both at once, my lord,
In my conceit,* are things of more import   opinion
Than women's wits are to be busied with.

BALTHAZAR. 'Tis I that love.

BEL-IMPERIA.   Whom?

BALTHAZAR.   Bel-imperia.

BEL-IMPERIA. But I that fear.

BALTHAZAR.   Whom?

BEL-IMPERIA.   Bel-imperia.

LORENZO. Fear yourself?

BEL-IMPERIA.   Ay, brother.

LORENZO.   How?

BEL-IMPERIA.   As those
That what they love are loth and fear to lose.

BALTHAZAR. Then, fair, let Balthazar your keeper be.

BEL-IMPERIA. No, Balthazar doth fear as well as we:

[29] That is, her braids are the bonds by which he has been made captive. The reference to Ariadne, who guided Theseus through the Labyrinth by using a thread, may, it has been suggested, be an error for Arachne, the Lydian girl whom Athena turned into a spider for daring to compete with her in weaving.

Et tremulo metui pavidum iunxere timorem,
Est vanum stolidae proditionis opus.[30]

LORENZO. Nay, and you argue things so cunningly,
We'll go continue this discourse at court.

BALTHAZAR. Led by the loadstar of her heavenly looks,
Wends poor oppressèd Balthazar,
As o'er the mountains walks the wanderer,
Incertain to effect* his pilgrimage.   uncertain of
                                                          completing
                                                          (*Exeunt.*)

Scene 4

(*A street. Enter two* PORTINGALES, *and* HIERONIMO *meets
them.*)

1 PORTINGALE. By your leave, sir.
[*Beginning of third 1602 Addition.*]

HIERONIMO. 'Tis neither as you think, nor as you think,
Nor as you think; you're wide all.
These slippers are not mine, they were my son Horatio's.
My son—and what's a son? A thing begot
Within a pair of minutes, thereabout;
A lump bred up in darkness, and doth serve
To ballace* these light creatures we call women;   ballast
And, at nine months' end, creeps forth to light.
What is there yet in a son,
To make a father dote, rave, or run mad?
Being born, it pouts, cries, and breeds teeth.
What is there yet in a son? He must be fed,
Be taught to go,* and speak. Ay, or yet   walk
Why might not a man love a calf as well?
Or melt in passion o'er a frisking kid,
As for a son? Methinks a young bacon,*   pig
Or a fine little smooth-horse-colt,
Should move a man as much as doth a son.
For one of these, in very little time,
Will grow to some good use; whereas a son,
The more he grows in stature and in years
The more unsquared, unbevelled, he appears;
Reckons his parents among the rank of fools,
Strikes care upon their heads with his mad riots,

[30] "And I feared to add trembling fear to a fearful man, vain
is the work of senseless treachery."

Makes them look old before they meet with age.
This is a son! And what a loss were this,
Considered truly?—O, but my Horatio
Grew out of reach of these insatiate humours:
He loved his loving parents;
He was my comfort and his mother's joy,
The very arm that did hold up our house;
Our hopes were storèd up in him.
None but a damnèd murderer could hate him.
He had not seen the back of nineteen year,
When his strong arm unhorsed
The proud Prince Balthazar and his great mind,*   spirit
Too full of honor, took him unto mercy
That* valiant but ignoble Portingale.   for that
Well, heaven is heaven still,
And there is Nemesis, and Furies,
And all things called whips,
And they sometimes do meet* with murderers;   catch up with
They do not always scape;* that's some comfort.   escape
Ay, ay, ay; and then time steals on,
And steals, and steals, till violence leaps forth
Like thunder wrappèd in a ball of fire,
And so doth bring confusion to them all.
    [*End of Addition.*]
Good leave have you; nay, I pray go,
For I'll leave you, if you can leave me so.
    2 PORTINGALE. Pray you, which is the next way to my lord
      the Duke's?
    HIERONIMO. The next way from me.
    1 PORTINGALE.   To his house we mean.
    HIERONIMO. O, hard by; 'tis yon house that you see.
    2 PORTINGALE. You could not tell us if his son were there?
    HIERONIMO. Who, my Lord Lorenzo?
    1 PORTINGALE   Ay sir.
    (HIERONIMO *goes in at one door and comes out at another.*)
    HIERONIMO.   O, forbear,
For other talk for us far fitter were.
But if you be importunate to know
The way to him and where to find him out,
Then list to me and I'll resolve your doubt.
There is a path upon your left-hand side
That leadeth from a guilty conscience
Unto a forest of distrust and fear.

A darksome place and dangerous to pass.
There shall you meet with melancholy thoughts,
Whose baleful humors if you but uphold,*   maintain
It will conduct you to despair and death;
Whose rocky cliffs when you have once beheld,
Within a hugy* dale of lasting night,   huge
That, kindled with the world's iniquities,
Doth cast up filthy and detested fumes.
Not far from thence, where murderers have built
A habitation for their cursèd souls,
There, in a brazen cauldron fixed by Jove,
In his fell wrath, upon a sulphur flame,
Yourselves shall find Lorenzo bathing him*   himself
In boiling lead and blood of innocents.
    1 PORTINGALE. Ha, ha, ha!
    HIERONIMO. Ha, ha, ha!
Why, ha, ha, ha! Farewell, good ha, ha, ha!

                                              (*Exit.*)

    2 PORTINGALE. Doubtless this man is passing lunatic,
Or imperfection of his age doth make him dote.
Come, let's away to seek my lord the Duke.

                                              (*Exeunt.*)

Scene 5

(*The Spanish Court. Enter* HIERONIMO, *with a poniard in
one hand and a rope in the other.*)[31]

HIERONIMO. Now, sir, perhaps I come and see the King;
The King sees me, and fain* would hear my suit.   gladly
Why, is not this a strange and seld-seen* thing,   seldom seen
That standers-by with toys should strike me mute.
Go to, I see their shifts, and say no more.
Hieronimo, 'tis time for thee to trudge.
Down by the dale that flows with purple gore
Standeth a fiery tower; there sits a judge
Upon a seat of steel and molten brass,
And 'twixt his teeth he holds a firebrand,
That leads unto the lake where hell doth stand.
Away, Hieronimo, to him be gone.
He'll do thee justice for Horatio's death.

────────────

    [31] These have been noted as "the stock 'properties' of a would-
be suicide."

Turn down this path*—thou shalt be with him   that is,
the poniard
    straight—
Or this,* and then thou need'st not take thy breath.   the rope
This way or that way? Soft and fair, not so.
For if I hang or kill myself, let's know
Who will revenge Horatio's murther then?
No, no! fie, no! pardon me, I'll none of that.
    (*He flings away the dagger and halter.*)
This way I'll take, and this way comes the King,
    (*He takes them up again.*)
And here I'll have a fling at him; that's flat.
And, Balthazar, I'll be with thee to bring,*   have you
punished
And thee, Lorenzo. Here's the King—nay, stay;
And here, ay here—there goes the hare away.[32]

    (*Enter* KING, AMBASSADOR, CASTILE, *and* LORENZO.)

KING. Now show, ambassador, what our Viceroy saith.
Hath he received the articles we sent?
    HIERONIMO. Justice, O justice to Hieronimo.
    LORENZO. Back! seest thou not the King is busy?
    HIERONIMO. O, is he so?
    KING. Who is he that interrupts our business?
    HIERONIMO. Not I.—(*Aside.*) Hieronimo, beware; go by,
    go by.*   remain unnoticed
AMBASSADOR. Renownèd King, he hath received and read
Thy kingly proffers and thy promised league;
And, as a man extremely overjoyed
To hear his son so princely entertained,
Whose death he had so solemnly bewailed,
This for thy further satisfaction
And kingly love, he kindly lets thee know:
First, for the marriage of his princely son
With Bel-imperia, thy belovèd niece,
The news are more delightful to his soul
Than myrrh or incense to the offended heavens.
In person, therefore, will he come himself,
To see the marriage rites solemnizèd,
And, in the presence of the Court of Spain,
To knit a sure inexplicable* band   inextricable
Of kingly love and everlasting league
Betwixt the crowns of Spain and Portingal.

    [32] That is, the chase is under way.

There will he give his crown to Balthazar,
And make a queen of Bel-imperia.
    KING. Brother, how like you this our Viceroy's love?
    CASTILE. No doubt, my lord, it is an argument
Of honorable care to keep his friend,
And wondrous zeal to Balthazar his son;
Nor am I least indebted to his grace,
That bends his liking to my daughter thus.
    AMBASSADOR. Now last, dread lord, here hath his highness
        sent,
Although he send not that his son return,
His ransom due to Don Horatio.
    HIERONIMO. Horatio? who calls Horatio?
    KING. And well remembered; thank his majesty.
Here, see it given to Horatio.
    HIERONIMO. Justice, O, justice, justice, gentle King.
    KING. Who is that? Hieronimo?
    HIERONIMO. Justice, O, justice! O, my son, my son,
My son, whom naught can ransom or redeem!
    LORENZO. Hieronimo, you are not well advised.
    HIERONIMO. Away, Lorenzo, hinder me no more;
For thou hast made me bankrupt of my bliss.
Give me my son; you shall not ransom him!
Away! I'll rip the bowels of the earth.
    (*He digs with his dagger.*)
And ferry over to th'Elysian plains,
And bring my son to show his deadly wounds.
Stand from about me!
I'll make a pickaxe of my poniard,
And here surrender up my Marshalship;
For I'll go marshal up the fiends in hell,
To be avengèd on you all for this.
    KING. What means this outrage?*   outburst
Will none of you restrain his fury?
    HIERONIMO. Nay, soft and fair; you shall not need to strive.
Needs must he go that the devils drive.
                                             (*Exit.*)

    KING. What accident hath hapt Hieronimo?
I have not seen him to demean him* so.   behave himself
    LORENZO. My gracious lord, he is with extreme pride,
Conceived of young Horatio, his son,
And covetous of having to himself
The ransom of the young Prince Balthazar,
Distract, and in a manner lunatic.

KING. Believe me, nephew, we are sorry for't;
This is the love that fathers bear their sons.
But, gentle brother, go give to him this gold,
The Prince's ransom; let him have his due.
For what he hath, Horatio shall not want;
Happily* Hieronimo hath need thereof.   perhaps
   LORENZO. But if he be thus helplessly distract,
'Tis requisite his office be resigned,
And given to one of more discretion.
   KING. We shall increase his melancholy so;
'Tis best that we see further in it first,
Till when, ourself will exempt him the place.[33]
And, brother, now bring in the ambassador,
That he may be a witness of the match
'Twixt Balthazar and Bel-imperia,
And that we may prefix* a certain time   set
Wherein the marriage shall be solemnized,
That we may have thy lord, the Viceroy, here.
   AMBASSADOR. Therein your highness highly shall content
His majesty, that longs to hear from hence.
   KING. On then, and hear you, Lord Ambassador—
                           (*Exeunt.*)

[*Beginning of fourth 1602 Addition.*]

Scene 6

(HIERONIMO's *garden. Enter* JAQUES *and* PEDRO.)

JAQUES. I wonder, Pedro, why our master thus
At midnight sends us with our torches light,
When man and bird and beast are all at rest,
Save those that watch for rape and bloody murder.
   PEDRO. O Jaques, know thou that our master's mind
Is much distraught, since his Horatio died,
And—now his agèd years should sleep in rest,
His heart in quiet—like a desperate man,
Grows lunatic and childish for his son.
Sometimes, as he doth at his table sit,
He speaks as if Horatio stood by him;
Then starting in a rage, falls on the earth,
Cries out, "Horatio, where is my Horatio?"

   [33] This is a corrupt line which means "I will not relieve him of
his post without further investigation."

So that with extreme grief and cutting sorrow
There is not left in him one inch of man.
See, where he comes.

(*Enter* HIERONIMO.)

HIERONIMO. I pry through every crevice of each wall,
Look on each tree, and search through every brake,*   thicket
Beat at the bushes, stamp our grandam earth,
Dive in the water, and stare up to heaven,
Yet cannot I behold my son Horatio.
How now, who's there? Sprites, sprites?
  PEDRO. We are your servants, that attend you, sir.
  HIERONIMO. What make you with your torches in the dark?
  PEDRO. You bid us light them, and attend you here.
  HIERONIMO. No, no, you are deceived!—not I; you are
     deceived!
Was I so mad to bid you light your torches now?
Light me your torches at the mid of noon,
Whenas* the sun god rides in all his glory;   when
Light me your torches then.
  PEDRO.   Then we burn daylight.
  HIERONIMO. Let it be burnt; Night is a murderous slut,
That would not have her treasons to be seen;
And yonder pale-faced Hecate there, the moon,
Doth give consent to that is done in darkness;
And all those stars that gaze upon her face,
Are aglets* on her sleeve, pins on her train;   metal ornaments
And those that should be powerful and divine
Do sleep in darkness when they most should shine.
  PEDRO. Provoke them not, fair sir, with tempting words;
The heavens are gracious, and your miseries
And sorrow makes you speak you know not what.
  HIERONIMO. Villain, thou liest, and thou doest nought
But tell me I am mad: thou liest; I am not mad;
I know thee to be Pedro, and he Jaques.
I'll prove it[34] to thee; and were I mad, how could I?
Where was she that same night when my Horatio
Was murdered? She should have shone; search thou the book.
Had the moon shone, in my boy's face there was a kind of
     grace,

     [34] That is, prove that the moon and stars colluded in making
     the murder possible.

That I know—nay, I do know—had the murderer seen him,
His weapon would have fall'n and cut the earth,
Had he been framed of nought but blood and death.
Alack, when mischief doth it knows not what,
What shall we say to mischief?

(*Enter* ISABELLA.)

ISABELLA. Dear Hieronimo, come in a doors;
O, seek not means so to increase thy sorrow.
HIERONIMO. Indeed, Isabella, we do nothing here;
I do not cry: ask Pedro, and ask Jaques;
Not I, indeed; we are very merry, very merry.
ISABELLA. How? Be merry here, be merry here?
Is not this the place, and this the very tree,
Where my Horatio died, where he was murderèd?
HIERONIMO. Was—do not say what; let her weep it out.
This was the tree; I set it of a kernel;
And when our hot Spain could not let it grow,
But that the infant and the human sap
Began to wither, duly twice a morning
Would I be sprinkling it with fountain water.
At last it grew and grew, and bore and bore,
Till at the length
It grew a gallows and did bear our son;
It bore thy fruit and mine. O wicked, wicked plant.
(*One knocks within at the door.*)
See who knocks there.
PEDRO.   It is a painter, sir.
HIERONIMO. Bid him come in and paint some comfort,
For surely there's none lives but painted comfort.
Let him come in; one knows not what may chance:
God's will that I should set this tree!—but even so
Masters ungrateful servants rear from nought,
And then they hate them that did bring them up.

(*Enter the* PAINTER.)

PAINTER. God bless you, sir.
HIERONIMO. Wherefore, why, thou scornful villain?
How, where, or by what means should I be blessed?
ISABELLA. What wouldst thou have, good fellow?
PAINTER.   Justice, madam.
HIERONIMO. O, ambitious beggar, wouldest thou have that

That lives not in the world?
Why, all the undelvèd mines cannot buy
An ounce of justice, 'tis a jewel so inestimable.
I tell thee,
God hath engrossed* all justice in his hands,   collected .
And there is none but what comes from him.
    PAINTER. O then I see
That God must right me for my murd'red son.
    HIERONIMO. How, was thy son murderèd?
    PAINTER. Ay, sir; no man did hold a son so dear.
    HIERONIMO. What, not as thine? that's a lie
As massy* as the earth. I had a son,   massive
Whose least unvalued hair did weigh
A thousand of thy sons; and he was murdered.
    PAINTER. Alas, sir, I had no more but he.
    HIERONIMO. Nor I, nor I; but this same one of mine
Was worth a legion; but all is one.
Pedro, Jaques, go in a doors; Isabella, go;
And this good fellow here and I
Will range this hideous orchard up and down,
Like to two lions reavèd* of their young.   robbed
Go in a doors, I say.
                (Exeunt. The PAINTER *and he sit down.)*
                Come, let's talk wisely now.
Was thy son murderèd?
    PAINTER.   Ay, sir.
    HIERONIMO.   So was mine.
How doo'st take it? Art thou not sometimes mad?
Is there no tricks* that comes before thine eyes?   illusions
    PAINTER. O Lord, yes, sir.
    HIERONIMO. Art a painter? Canst paint me a tear, or a
wound, a groan, or a sigh? Canst paint me such a tree as this?
    PAINTER. Sir, I am sure you have heard of my painting;
my name's Bazardo.
    HIERONIMO. Bazardo, afore God, an excellent fellow. Look
you, sir, do you see, I'd have you paint me my gallery in your
oil colors matted,* and draw me five years younger than   dulled
I am—do ye see, sir, let five years go, let them go—like the
Marshal of Spain, my wife Isabella standing by me, with a
speaking look to my son Horatio, which should intend to this
or some such like purpose: "God bless thee, my sweet son";
and my hand leaning upon his head, thus, sir, do you see? May
it be done?
    PAINTER. Very well, sir.

HIERONIMO. Nay, I pray, mark me, sir. Then, sir, would I have you paint me this tree, this very tree. Canst paint a doleful cry?

PAINTER. Seemingly, sir.

HIERONIMO. Nay, it should cry; but all is one. Well, sir, paint me a youth run through and through with villains' swords, hanging upon this tree. Canst thou draw a murderer?

PAINTER. I'll warrant you, sir; I have the pattern of the most notorious villains that ever lived in all Spain.

HIERONIMO. O let them be worse, worse; stretch thine art, and let their beards be of Judas his own color,* and   that is, red let their eyebrows jutty over*—in any case observe   project that. Then, sir, after some violent noise, bring me forth in my shirt, and my gown under mine arm, with my torch in my hand, and my sword reared up thus; and with these words:

"What noise is this? Who calls Hieronimo?"

May it be done?

PAINTER. Yea, sir.

HIERONIMO. Well, sir, then bring me forth, bring me through alley* and alley, still with a distracted countenance   garden walk going along, and let my hair heave up my nightcap. Let the clouds scowl, make the moon dark, the stars extinct, the winds blowing, the bells tolling, the owl shrieking, the toads croaking, the minutes jarring,* and the clock striking twelve.   ʒuᴉppon And then at last, sir, starting, behold a man hanging, and tottering and tottering, as you know the wind will wave a man, and I with a trice* to cut him down. And looking upon   instantly him by the advantage of my torch, find it to be my son Horatio. There you may show a passion, there you may show a passion! Draw me like old Priam of Troy, crying, "The house is afire, the house is afire, as the torch over my head!" Make me curse, make me rave, make me cry, make me mad, make me well again, make me curse hell, invocate heaven, and in the end leave me in a trance—and so forth.

PAINTER. And is this the end?

HIERONIMO. O no, there is no end; the end is death and madness. As I am never better than when I am mad; then methinks I am a brave fellow; then I do wonders; but reason abuseth me, and there's the torment, there's the hell. At the last, sir, bring me to one of the murderers; were he as strong as Hector, thus would I tear and drag him up and down.

(*He beats the* PAINTER *in, then comes out again with a book in his hand.*)

[*End of Addition.*]

(*Enter* HIERONIMO, *with a book in his hand.*)

Vindicta mihi![35]
Ay, heaven will be revenged of every ill,
Nor will they suffer murder unrepaid.
Then stay, Hieronimo, attend their will,
For mortal men may not appoint their time.
  Per scelus semper tutum est sceleribus iter.[36]
Strike, and strike home, where wrong is offered thee;
For evils unto ills conductors be.
And death's the worst of resolution,
For he that thinks with patience to contend*   achieve
To quiet life his life shall easily end.
  Fata si miseros juvant, habes salutem:
  Fata si vitam negant, habes sepulchrum.[37]
If destiny thy miseries do ease,
Then hast thou health and happy shalt thou be.
If destiny deny thee life, Hieronimo,
Yet shalt thou be assurèd of a tomb;
If neither, yet let this thy comfort be:
Heaven covereth him that hath no burial.
And to conclude, I will revenge his death.
But how? not as the vulgar wits of men,
With open, but inevitable ills,
As by a secret, yet a certain mean,*   means
Which under kindship* will be cloakèd best.   kindness
Wise men will take their opportunity,
Closely and safely fitting things to time.
But in extremes, advantage hath no time;
And therefore all times fit not for revenge.
Thus therefore will I rest me in unrest,
Dissembling quiet in unquietness,
Not seeming that I know their villainies,
That my simplicity* may make them think   stupidity
That ignorantly* I will let all slip;   unknowingly

   [35] "Vengeance is mine."
   [36] "The safe course through crime is always more crime."
   [37] Translated in next four lines.

For ignorance, I wot,* and well they know,   know
    Remedium malorum iners est.[38]
Nor aught avails it me to menace them,
Who, as a wintry storm upon a plain,
Will bear me down with their nobility.
No, no, Hieronimo, thou must enjoin
Thine eyes to observation, and thy tongue
To milder speeches than thy spirit affords,
Thy heart to patience, and thy hands to rest,
Thy cap to courtesy, and thy knee to bow,
Till to revenge thou know when, where, and how.
    (*A noise within.*)
How now, what noise? what coil* is that you keep?   disturbance

    (*Enter a* SERVANT.)

    SERVANT. Here are a sort* of poor petitioners   group
That are importunate,* and it shall please you, sir,   persistently
That you should plead their cases to the King.   solicitous
    HIERONIMO. That I should plead their several actions?
Why, let them enter, and let me see them.

    (*Enter three* CITIZENS *and an* Old Man.)

    1 CITIZEN. So, I tell you this: for learning and for law,
There is not any advocate in Spain
That can prevail, or will take half the pain
That he will in pursuit of equity.
    HIERONIMO. Come near, you men, that thus importune me.
(*Aside.*) Now must I bear a face of gravity;
For thus I used, before my Marshalship,
To plead in causes as Corregidor.*   advocate
Come on, sirs, what's the matter?
    2 CITIZEN. Sir, an action.
    HIERONIMO. Of battery?
    1 CITIZEN. Mine of debt.
    HIERONIMO. Give place.
    2 CITIZEN. No, sir, mine is an action of the case.[39]
    3 CITIZEN. Mine an *ejectione firmae*[40] by a lease.

    [38] "Is an idle remedy for ills."
    [39] An action involving matters not specifically covered by existing law.
    [40] A writ to eject a tenant.

HIERONIMO. Content you, sirs; are you determinèd
That I should plead your several actions?
   1 CITIZEN. Ay, sir, and here's my declaration.
   2 CITIZEN. And here is my band.*   bond
   3 CITIZEN. And here is my lease.
   (*They give him papers.*)
   HIERONIMO. But wherefore stands yon silly* man so   lowly
   mute,
With mournful eyes and hands to heaven upreared?
Come hither, father, let me know thy cause.
   SENEX. O worthy sir, my cause, but slightly known,
May move the hearts of warlike Myrmidons,*   subjects of
                                            Achilles
And melt the Corsic* rocks with ruthful tears.   Corsican
   HIERONIMO. Say, father, tell me, what's thy suit?
   SENEX. No, sir; could my woes
Give way unto my most distressful words,
Then should I not in paper, as you see,
With ink bewray* what blood began in me.   reveal
   HIERONIMO. What's here? "The humble supplication
Of Don Bazulto for his murdered son."
   SENEX. Ay, sir.
   HIERONIMO. No, sir; it was my murdered son.
O my son, my son, O my son Horatio!
But mine, or thine, Bazulto, be content.
Here, take my handkercher and wipe thine eyes,
Whiles wretched I in thy mishaps may see
The lively portrait of my dying self.
   (*He draws out a bloody handkerchief.*)
O no, not this; Horatio, this was thine;
And when I dyed it in thy dearest blood,
This was a token 'twixt thy soul and me
That of thy death revengèd I should be.
But here, take this, and this—what, my purse?—
Ay, this, and that, and all of them are thine,
For all as one are our extremities.*   extravagances
   1 CITIZEN. O, see the kindness of Hieronimo.
   2 CITIZEN. This gentleness shows him a gentleman.
   HIERONIMO. See, see, O see thy shame, Hieronimo!
See here a loving father to his son;
Behold the sorrows and the sad laments
That he delivereth for his son's decease.
If love's effects so strives in lesser things,
If love enforce such moods in meaner wits,
If love express such power in poor estates,

Hieronimo, when as a raging sea,
Tossed with the wind and tide, o'erturnest then
The upper billows, course of waves to keep,
Whilst lesser waters labor in the deep,
Then shamest thou not, Hieronimo, to neglect
The sweet revenge of thy Horatio?
Though on this earth justice will not be found,
I'll down to hell, and in this passion
Knock at the dismal gates of Pluto's Court,
Getting by force, as once Alcides* did,   Hercules
A troop of Furies and tormenting hags
To torture Don Lorenzo and the rest.
Yet, lest the triple-headed porter* should   Cerberus
Deny my passage to the slimy strond,*   shore
The Thracian poet* thou shalt counterfeit.*   Orpheus/imitate
Come on, old father, be my Orpheus,
And if thou canst* no notes upon the harp,   know
Then sound the burden of thy sore heart's grief,
Till we do gain that Proserpine* may grant   Goddess of Hell
Revenge on them that murderèd my son.
Then will I rent* and tear them, thus, and thus,   rend
Shivering their limbs in pieces with my teeth.
    (*Tears the papers.*)
    1 CITIZEN. O sir, my declaration!
                (*Exit* HIERONIMO, *followed by* CITIZENS.)
    2 CITIZEN.   Save my bond!

    (*Re-enter* HIERONIMO.)

    2 CITIZEN. Save my bond!
    3 CITIZEN. Alas, my lease! it cost me ten pound,
And you, my lord, have torn the same.
    HIERONIMO. That cannot be; I gave it never a wound;
Show me one drop of blood fall from the same.
How is it possible I should slay it then?
Tush, no; run after, catch me if you can.
                (*Exeunt all but the* Old Man.)

    (BAZULTO *remains till* HIERONIMO *enters again, who, star-
ing him in the face, speaks.*)

    HIERONIMO. And art thou come, Horatio, from the depth,
To ask for justice in this upper earth,
To tell thy father thou art unrevenged,

To wring more tears from Isabella's eyes,
Whose lights are dimmed with overlong laments?
Go back, my son; complain to Aeacus,*   judge in Hell
For here's no justice; gentle boy, begone,
For justice is exiled from the earth;
Hieronimo will bear thee company.
Thy mother cries on righteous Rhadamanth*   judge in Hell
For just revenge against murderers.
    SENEX. Alas, my lord, whence springs this troublèd speech?
    HIERONIMO. But let me look on my Horatio.
Sweet boy, how art thou changed in death's black shade!
Had Proserpine no pity on thy youth,
But suffered thy fair crimson-colored spring
With withered winter to be blasted thus?
Horatio, thou art older than thy father.
Ah, ruthless fate, that favor* thus transforms!   appearance
    BAZULTO. Ah, my good lord, I am not your young son.
    HIERONIMO. What, not my son? Thou then a Fury art,
Sent from the empty kingdom of black night
To summon me to make appearance
Before grim Minos and just Rhadamanth,
To plague Hieronimo that is remiss,
And seeks not vengeance for Horatio's death.
    BAZULTO. I am a grievèd man, and not a ghost,
That came for justice for my murdered son.
    HIERONIMO. Ay, now I know thee, now thou namest thy
      son.
Thou art the lively image of my grief;
Within thy face my sorrows I may see.
Thy eyes are gummed with tears, thy cheeks are wan,
Thy forehead troubled, and thy mutt'ring lips
Murmur sad words abruptly broken off
By force of windy sighs thy spirit breathes;
And all this sorrow riseth for thy son,
And selfsame sorrow feel I for my son.
Come in, old man, thou shalt to Isabel.
Lean on my arm; I thee, thou me, shalt stay,
And thou, and I, and she will sing a song,
Three parts in one, but all of discords framed.
Talk not of chords, but let us now be gone,
For with a cord Horatio was slain.

                                          (Exeunt.)

Scene 7

(The Spanish Court. Enter, on the one side, the KING OF
SPAIN, *the* DUKE, LORENZO, BALTHAZAR, BEL-IMPERIA, *and*
ATTENDANTS; *and, on the other,* VICEROY, DON PEDRO, *and*
ATTENDANTS.)*

KING. Go, brother, it is the Duke of Castile's cause;
Salute the Viceroy in our name.

CASTILE.   I go.

VICEROY. Go forth, Don Pedro, for thy nephew's sake,
And greet the Duke of Castile.

PEDRO.   It shall be so.

KING. And now to meet these Portuguese;
For as we now are, so sometimes were these,
Kings and commanders of the western Indies.
Welcome, brave Viceroy, to the Court of Spain,
And welcome all his honorable train.
'Tis not unknown to us for why you come,
Or have so kingly crossed the seas.
Sufficeth it, in this we note the troth
And more than common love you lend to us.
So is it that mine honorable niece
(For it beseems us now that it be known)
Already is betrothed to Balthazar,
And by appointment and our condescent*   consent
Tomorrow are they to be married.
To this intent we entertain thyself,
Thy followers, their pleasure, and our peace.
Speak, men of Portingale, shall it be so?
If ay, say so; if not, say flatly no.

VICEROY. Renowned King, I come not as thou think'st,
With doubtful followers, unresolvèd men,
But such as have upon thine articles
Confirmed thy motion and contented me.
Know, sovereign, I come to solemnize
The marriage of thy belovèd niece,
Fair Bel-imperia, with my Balthazar,
With thee, my son; whom sith* I live to see,   since
Here take my crown; I give it her and thee;
And let me live a solitary life,
In ceaseless prayers,
To think how strangely heaven hath thee preserved.

KING. See, brother, see, how nature strives in him.
Come, worthy Viceroy, and accompany
Thy friend with thine extremities;*   intensity of
A place more private fits this princely mood.   emotion
    VICEROY. Or here, or where your highness thinks it good.
                    (*Exeunt all but* CASTILE *and* LORENZO.)
    CASTILE. Nay, stay, Lorenzo; let me talk with you.
Seest thou this entertainment of these kings?
    LORENZO. I do, my lord, and joy to see the same.
    CASTILE. And knowest thou why this meeting is?
    LORENZO. For her, my lord, whom Balthazar doth love.
And to confirm their promised marriage.
    CASTILE. She is thy sister?
    LORENZO.   Who, Bel-imperia?
Ay, my gracious lord, and this is the day
That I have longed so happily to see.
    CASTILE. Thou wouldst be loth that any fault of thine
Should intercept her in her happiness?
    LORENZO. Heavens will not let Lorenzo err so much.
    CASTILE. Why then, Lorenzo, listen to my words:
It is suspected, and reported too,
That thou, Lorenzo, wrong'st Hieronimo,
And in his suits towards his majesty
Still keep'st him back and seeks to cross his suit.
    LORENZO. That I, my lord?
    CASTILE. I tell thee, son, myself have heard it said,
When, to my sorrow, I have been ashamed
To answer for thee, though thou art my son.
Lorenzo, knowest thou not the common love
And kindness that Hieronimo hath won
By his deserts within the Court of Spain?
Or seest thou not the King my brother's care
In his behalf, and to procure his health?
Lorenzo, shouldst thou thwart his passions,
And he exclaim against thee to the King,
What honor were't in this assembly,
Or what a scandal were't among the kings
To hear Hieronimo exclaim on thee?
Tell me, and look thou tell me truly too,
Whence grows the ground of this report in Court?
    LORENZO. My lord, it lies not in Lorenzo's power
To stop the vulgar,* liberal of their tongues.   common people
A small advantage makes a water-breach,
And no man lives that long contenteth all.

CASTILE. Myself have seen thee busy to keep back
Him and his supplications from the King.
 LORENZO. Yourself, my lord, hath seen his passions
That ill beseemed the presence of a king;
And, for* I pitied him in his distress,   *because*
I held him thence with kind and courteous words
As free from malice to Hieronimo
As to my soul, my lord.
 CASTILE. Hieronimo, my son, mistakes thee then.
 LORENZO. My gracious father, believe me, so he doth.
But what's a silly* man, distract in mind   *poor*
To think upon the murder of his son?
Alas, how easy is it for him to err!
But for his satisfaction and the world's,
'Twere good, my lord, that Hieronimo and I
Were reconciled, if he misconster* me.   *misconstrue*
 CASTILE. Lorenzo, thou hast said; it shall be so.
Go one of you, and call Hieronimo.
 (*Calls off stage.*)

 (*Enter* BALTHAZAR *and* BEL-IMPERIA.)

 BALTHAZAR. Come, Bel-imperia, Balthazar's content,
My sorrow's ease and sovereign of my bliss,
Sith* heaven hath ordained thee to be mine;   *since*
Disperse those clouds and melancholy looks,
And clear them up with those thy sun-bright eyes,
Wherein my hope and heaven's fair beauty lies.
 BEL-IMPERIA. My looks, my lord, are fitting for my love,
Which, new-begun, can show no brighter yet.
 BALTHAZAR. New-kindled flames should burn as morning
    sun.
 BEL-IMPERIA. But not too fast, lest heat and all be done.
I see my lord, my father.
 BALTHAZAR.   Truce, my love;
I will go salute him.
 CASTILE.   Welcome, Balthazar,
Welcome, brave Prince, the pledge of Castile's peace;
And welcome, Bel-imperia. How now, girl?
Why comest thou sadly to salute us thus?
Content thyself, for I am satisfied.
It is not now as when Andrea lived;
We have forgotten and forgiven that,

And thou art gracèd with a happier love.
But, Balthazar, here comes Hieronimo;
I'll have a word with him.

(*Enter* HIERONIMO *and a* SERVANT.)

HIERONIMO. And where's the Duke?
SERVANT.   Yonder.
HIERONIMO.   Even so.
(*Aside.*) What new device have they devisèd,
    trow?*   do you suppose
*Pocas palabras,** mild as the lamb,   "few words"
Is't I will be revenged? No, I am not the man.
    CASTILE. Welcome, Hieronimo.
    LORENZO. Welcome, Hieronimo.
    BALTHAZAR. Welcome, Hieronimo.
    HIERONIMO. My lords, I thank you for Horatio.
    CASTILE. Hieronimo, the reason that I sent
To speak with you, is this.
    HIERONIMO.   What, so short?
Then I'll be gone; I thank you for't.
    CASTILE. Nay, stay, Hieronimo;—go, call him, son.
    LORENZO. Hieronimo, my father craves a word with you.
    HIERONIMO. With me, sir? Why, my lord, I thought you
    had done.
    LORENZO. No. Would he had!
    CASTILE.   Hieronimo, I hear
You find yourself aggrievèd at my son,
Because you have not access unto the King,
And say 'tis he that intercepts your suits.
    HIERONIMO. Why, is not this a miserable thing, my lord?
    CASTILE. Hieronimo, I hope you have no cause,
And would be loth that one of your deserts
Should once have reason to suspect my son,
Considering how I think of you myself.
    HIERONIMO. Your son Lorenzo? Whom, my noble lord?
The hope of Spain, mine honorable friend?
Grant me the combat of them, if they dare.
    (*Draws out his sword.*)
I'll meet him face to face, to tell me so.
These be the scandalous reports of such
As love not me, and hate my lord too much.
Should I suspect Lorenzo would prevent
Or cross my suit, that loved my son so well?

My lord, I am ashamed it should be said.

LORENZO. Hieronimo, I never gave you cause.

HIERONIMO. My good lord, I know you did not.

CASTILE.   There then pause;

And for the satisfaction of the world,

Hieronimo, frequent my homely* house,   simple

The Duke of Castile, Cyprian's ancient seat;

And when thou wilt, use me, my son, and it;

But here, before Prince Balthazar and me,

Embrace each other, and be perfect friends.

HIERONIMO. Ay, marry, my lord, and shall.

Friends, quoth he? See, I'll be friends with you all,

Specially with you, my lovely lord;

For divers* causes it is fit for us   several

That we be friends: the world is suspicious,

And men may think what we imagine not.

BALTHAZAR. Why, this is friendly done, Hieronimo.

LORENZO. And thus, I hope, old grudges are forgot.

HIERONIMO. What else? It were a shame it should not be so.

CASTILE. Come on, Hieronimo, at my request;

Let us entreat your company today.

(*Exeunt all but* HIERONIMO.)

HIERONIMO. Your lordship's to command.

Pha! keep your way:

> *Chi mi fa più carezze che non suole,*
> *Tradito mi ha, o tradir mi vuole.*[41]

(*Exit.*)

CHORUS

GHOST. Awake, Erichtho![42] Cerberus, awake!

Solicit Pluto, gentle Proserpine!

To combat, Acheron and Erebus![43]

For ne'er, by Styx and Phlegethon in hell,

O'er-ferried Charon to the fiery lakes

Such fearful sights as poor Andrea sees.

Revenge, awake!

[41] "He who caresses me more than he was accustomed to, has betrayed me, or wants to betray me."

[42] A Thessalian sorceress. Kyd mistakes her for one of the Furies.

[43] Son of Chaos. Erebus was that portion of the underworld through which the dead passed as soon as they died.

REVENGE.   Awake? For why?

GHOST. Awake, Revenge; for thou art ill-advised
To sleep away what thou art warned to watch.

REVENGE. Content thyself, and do not trouble me.

GHOST. Awake, Revenge; if love—as love hath had—
Have yet the power or prevalence in hell.
Hieronimo with Lorenzo is joined in league,
And intercepts our passage to revenge.
Awake, Revenge, or we are woebegone.

REVENGE. Thus worldlings ground what they have dreamed
          upon.*   build on dreams
Content thyself, Andrea; though I sleep,
Yet is my mood* soliciting their souls.   anger
Sufficeth thee that poor Hieronimo
Cannot forget his son Horatio.
Nor dies Revenge, although he sleep awhile;
For in unquiet, quietness is feigned,
And slumbering is a common worldly wile.
Behold, Andrea, for an instance, how
Revenge hath slept, and then imagine thou
What 'tis to be subject to destiny.

(Enter a Dumb Show.)

GHOST. Awake, Revenge; reveal this mystery.

REVENGE. The two first the nuptial torches bore
As brightly burning as the mid-day's sun;
But after them doth Hymen* hie as fast,   god of marriage
Clothed in sable and a saffron robe,
And blows them out and quencheth them with blood,
As discontent that things continue so.

GHOST. Sufficeth me; thy meaning's understood,
And thanks to thee and those infernal powers
That will not tolerate a lover's woe.
Rest thee, for I will sit to see the rest.

REVENGE. Then argue not, for thou hast thy request.

ACT V

Scene 1

(The palace of DON CYPRIAN. *Enter* BEL-IMPERIA *and*
HIERONIMO.)

BEL-IMPERIA. Is this the love thou bear'st Horatio?
Is this the kindness that thou counterfeits?
Are these the fruits of thine incessant tears?
Hieronimo, are these thy passions,
Thy protestations and thy deep laments
That thou wert wont* to weary men withal?   accustomed
O unkind father! O deceitful world!
With what excuses canst thou show thyself
From this dishonor and the hate of men,
Thus to neglect the loss and life of him
Whom both my letters and thine own belief
Assures thee to be causeless slaughterèd?
Hieronimo, for shame, Hieronimo,
Be not a history to after times
Of such ingratitude unto thy son.
Unhappy mothers of such children then,
But monstrous fathers to forget so soon
The death of those whom they with care and cost
Have tendered so, thus careless should be lost.
Myself, a stranger in respect of thee,
So loved his life as still I wish their deaths.
Nor shall his death be unrevenged by me,
Although I bear it out for fashion's sake.[44]
For here I swear, in sight of heaven and earth,
Shouldst thou neglect the love thou shouldst retain,
And give it over and devise no more,
Myself should send their hateful souls to hell
That wrought his downfall with extremest death.
     HIERONIMO. But may it be that Bel-imperia
Vows such revenge as she hath deigned to say?
Why then I see that heaven applies our drift,*   assists our plan
And all the saints do sit soliciting
For vengeance on those cursèd murderers.
Madam, 'tis true, and now I find it so:
I found a letter written in your name,
And in that letter, how Horatio died.
Pardon, O pardon, Bel-imperia,
My fear and care* in not believing it;   caution
Nor think I thoughtless think upon a mean*   means
To let his death be unrevenged at full.
And here I vow, so you but give consent
And will conceal my resolution,

[44] That is, pretend to accept the situation.

I will ere long determine of their deaths
That causeless thus have murderèd my son.

    BEL-IMPERIA. Hieronimo, I will consent, conceal,
And aught that may effect for thine avail
Join with thee to revenge Horatio's death.

    HIERONIMO. On, then; whatsoever I devise,
Let me entreat you, grace* my practices;   support
Forwhy* the plot's already in mine head.   because
Here they are.

    (*Enter* BALTHAZAR *and* LORENZO.)

    BALTHAZAR.   How now, Hieronimo?
What, courting Bel-imperia?

    HIERONIMO.   Ay, my lord;
Such courting as, I promise you,
She hath my heart; but you, my lord, have hers.

    LORENZO. But now, Hieronimo, or never, we
Are to entreat your help.

    HIERONIMO.   My help?
Why, my good lords, assure yourselves of me;
For you have given me cause; ay, by my faith have you.

    BALTHAZAR. It pleased you, at the entertainment of the
        ambassador,
To grace the King so much as with a show.
Now, were your study so well furnishèd,
As, for the passing of the first night's sport,
To entertain my father with the like,
Or any such like pleasing motion,*   entertainment
Assure yourself, it would content them well.

    HIERONIMO. Is this all?

    BALTHAZAR. Ay, this is all.

    HIERONIMO. Why then, I'll fit you; say no more.
When I was young, I gave my mind
And plied myself to fruitless poetry;
Which though it profit the professor* naught   practitioner
Yet is it passing pleasing to the world.

    LORENZO. And how for that?

    HIERONIMO.   Marry, my good lord, thus:——
And yet methinks you are too quick with us——
When in Toledo there I studied,
It was my chance to write a tragedy,
See here, my lords,

    (*He shows them a book.*)

Which, long forgot, I found this other day.
Now would your lordships favor me so much
As but to grace me with your acting it,
I mean each one of you to play a part,
Assure you it will prove most passing strange
And wondrous plausible* to that assembly.   pleasing
    BALTHAZAR. What? Would you have us play a tragedy?
    HIERONIMO. Why, Nero thought it no disparagement,
And kings and emperors have tane* delight   taken
To make experience* of their wits in plays.   trial
    LORENZO. Nay, be not angry, good Hieronimo;
The Prince but asked a question.
    BALTHAZAR.   In faith, Hieronimo,
And you be in earnest,
I'il make one.
    LORENZO. And I another.
    HIERONIMO. Now, my good lord, could you entreat
Your sister, Bel-imperia, to make one?
For what's a play without a woman in it?
    BEL-IMPERIA. Little entreaty shall serve me, Hieronimo,
For I must needs be employed in your play.
    HIERONIMO. Why, this is well. I tell you, lordings,
It was determined to have been actèd
By gentlemen and scholars too,
Such as could tell what to speak.
    BALTHAZAR.   And now
It shall be played by princes and courtiers,
Such as can tell how to speak
If, as it is our country manner,
You will but let us know the argument.
    HIERONIMO. That shall I roundly.* The chronicles of   plainly
    Spain
Record this written of a Knight of Rhodes:
He was betrothed, and wedded at the length,
To one Perseda, an Italian dame,
Whose beauty ravished all that her beheld,
Especially the soul of Soliman,
Who at the marriage was the chiefest guest.
By sundry means sought Soliman to win
Perseda's love, and could not gain the same.
Then 'gan he break* his passions to a friend,   tell
One of his bashaws,* whom he held full dear.   pashas
He had this bashaw long solicited,
And saw she was not otherwise to be won

But by her husband's death, this Knight of Rhodes,
Whom presently by treachery he slew.
She, stirred with an exceeding hate therefore
As cause of this, slew Soliman;
And, to escape the bashaw's tyranny,
Did stab herself, and this the tragedy.
    LORENZO. O, excellent!
    BEL-IMPERIA.   But say, Hieronimo,
What then became of him that was the bashaw?
    HIERONIMO. Marry, thus: moved with remorse of his mis-
       deeds,
Ran to a mountain top, and hung himself.
    BALTHAZAR. But which of us is to perform that part?
    HIERONIMO. O, that will I, my lords; make no doubt of it:
I'll play the murderer, I warrant you,
For I already have conceited* that.   planned
    BALTHAZAR. And what shall I?
    HIERONIMO. Great Soliman, the Turkish Emperor.
    LORENZO. And I?
    HIERONIMO.   Erastus, the Knight of Rhodes.
    BEL-IMPERIA. And I?
    HIERONIMO.   Perseda, chaste and resolute.
And here, my lords, are several abstracts drawn,
For each of you to note your parts,
And act it as occasion's offered you.
You must provide a Turkish cap,
A black mustachio, and a fauchion;*   curved broadsword
    (*Gives a paper to* BALTHAZAR.)
You, with a cross, like to a Knight of Rhodes;
    (*Gives another to* LORENZO.)
And, madam, you must attire yourself
    (*He gives* BEL-IMPERIA *another.*)
Like Phoebe, Flora, or the Huntress,*   Diana
Which to your discretion shall seem best.
And as for me, my lords, I'll look to one,
And with the ransom that the Viceroy sent
So furnish and perform this tragedy
As all the world shall say Hieronimo
Was liberal in gracing of it so.
    BALTHAZAR. Hieronimo, methinks a comedy were better.
    HIERONIMO. A comedy?
Fie! comedies are fit for common wits;
But to present a kingly troop withal,

Give me a stately written tragedy;
*Tragedia cothurnata,** fitting kings,   high tragedy
Containing matter, and not common things.
My lords, all this must be performed
As fitting for the first night's revelling.
The Italian tragedians were so sharp of wit,
That in one hour's meditation
They would perform anything in action.
    LORENZO. And well it may;* for I have seen the like   may be true
In Paris 'mongst the French tragedians.
    HIERONIMO. In Paris? Mass,* and well   (an oath)
      remembered.
There's one thing more that rests for us to do.
    BALTHAZAR. What's that, Hieronimo? Forget not anything.
    HIERONIMO. Each one of us
Must act his part in unknown languages,
That it may breed the more variety:
As you, my lord, in Latin, I in Greek,
You in Italian; and, for because I know
That Bel-imperia hath practisèd the French,
In courtly French shall all her phrases be.
    BEL-IMPERIA. You mean to try my cunning then, Hiero-
      nimo?
    BALTHAZAR. But this will be a mere confusion
And hardly shall we all be understood.
    HIERONIMO. It must be so; for the conclusion
Shall prove the invention and all was good.
And I myself in an oration,
And with a strange and wondrous show besides,
That I will have there behind a curtain,
Assure yourself, shall make the matter known;
And all shall be concluded in one scene,
For there's no pleasure tane* in tediousness.   taken
    BALTHAZAR (*aside to* LORENZO). How like you this?
    LORENZO.   Why, thus, my lord,
We must resolve to soothe his humours up.*   humor him
    BALTHAZAR. On then, Hieronimo; farewell till soon.
    HIERONIMO. You'll ply this gear?[45]

    LORENZO.   I warrant you.
                     (*Exeunt all but* HIERONIMO.)

[45] That is, You'll employ yourselves in this undertaking?

HIERONIMO.   Why so!
Now shall I see the fall of Babylon,
Wrought by the heavens in this confusion.
And if the world like not this tragedy,
Hard is the hap* of old Hieronimo.   fortune
                                                               (*Exit.*)

                        Scene 2

(HIERONIMO's *garden. Enter* ISABELLA *with a weapon.*)

ISABELLA. Tell me no more!—O monstrous homicides!
Since neither piety nor pity moves
The King to justice or compassion,
I will revenge myself upon this place,
Where thus they murdered my belovèd son.
     (*She cuts down the arbor.*)
Down with these branches and these loathsome boughs
Of this unfortunate and fatal pine.
Down with them, Isabella; rent* them up,   rend
And burn the roots from whence the rest is sprung.
I will not leave a root, a stalk, a tree,
A bough, a branch, a blossom, nor a leaf,
No, not an herb within this garden plot,
Accursèd complot* of my misery.   accomplice
Fruitless for ever may this garden be,
Barren the earth, and blissless whosoever
Imagines not to keep it unmanured.*   uncultivated
An eastern wind, commixed with noisome airs,
Shall blast the plants and the young saplings;
The earth with serpents shall be pesterèd,
And passengers,* for fear to be infect,   passers-by
Shall stand aloof, and, looking at it, tell:
"There, murdered, died the son of Isabel."
Ay, here he died, and here I him embrace.
See, where his ghost solicits with his wounds
Revenge on her that should revenge his death.
Hieronimo, make haste to see thy son,
For sorrow and despair hath cited* me   summoned
To hear Horatio plead with Rhadamanth.
Make haste, Hieronimo, to hold excused
Thy negligence in pursuit of their deaths
Whose hateful wrath bereaved him of his breath.
Ah, nay, thou dost delay their deaths,

Forgives the murderers of thy noble son,
And none but I bestir me—to no end.
And as I curse this tree from further fruit,
So shall my womb be cursèd for his sake;
And with this weapon will I wound the breast,
The hapless breast that gave Horatio suck.
   (*She stabs herself.*)

Scene 3

(*The palace of* DON CYPRIAN. *Enter* HIERONIMO; *he strikes
the curtain. Enter the* DUKE OF CASTILE.)

CASTILE. How now, Hieronimo, where's your fellows
That you take all this pain?
   HIERONIMO. O sir, it is for the author's credit
To look that all things may go well.
But, good my lord, let me entreat your grace
To give the King the copy of the play;
This is the argument of what we show.
   CASTILE. I will, Hieronimo.
   HIERONIMO. One thing more, my good lord.
   CASTILE. What's that?
   HIERONIMO. Let me entreat your grace
That, when the train are passed into the gallery,
You would vouchsafe to throw me down the key.[46]
   CASTILE. I will, Hieronimo.
                                        (*Exit* CASTILE.)
   HIERONIMO. What, are you ready, Balthazar?
Bring a chair and a cushion for the King.

(*Enter* BALTHAZAR, *with a chair.*)

Well done, Balthazar; hang up the title;* our scene is   title board
Rhodes. What, is your beard on?
   BALTHAZAR. Half on; the other is in my hand.

---

   [46] The locale of the gallery is in dispute. Most scholars believe
that on the Elizabethan stage it was the balcony over the inner
stage. Philip Edwards convincingly suggests that the gallery here
does not mean a balcony but the hall itself. Later events of the
scene help to confirm this view; the audience for the "play-
within-the-play," according to Professor Edwards, was seated on
the platform stage—on the same level as the actors in Hieronimo's play. Professor Edwards interprets *"throw me down the
key"* as meaning "throw the key down [on the floor] for me."
—W. G.

HIERONIMO. Dispatch for shame; are you so long?

(*Exit* BALTHAZAR.)

Bethink thyself, Hieronimo,
Recall thy wits, recount thy former wrongs
Thou hast received by murder of thy son;
And lastly, not least, how Isabel,
Once his mother and thy dearest wife,
All woebegone for him, hath slain herself.
Behoves thee then, Hieronimo, to be revenged.
The plot is laid of dire revenge;
On, then, Hieronimo, pursue revenge,
For nothing wants but acting of revenge.

(*Enter* SPANISH KING, VICEROY, DUKE OF CASTILE, DON
PEDRO, *and their train. Exit* HIERONIMO.)

KING. Now, Viceroy, shall we see the tragedy
Of Soliman, the Turkish Emperor,
Performed of pleasure by your son the Prince,
My nephew Don Lorenzo, and my niece.

VICEROY. Who? Bel-imperia?

KING. Ay, and Hieronimo, our Marshal,
At whose request they deign to do't themselves.
These be our pastimes in the Court of Spain.
Here, brother, you shall be the bookkeeper;*   prompter
This is the argument of that they show.

(*He gives him a book.*)

Gentlemen, this play of HIERONIMO, *in sundry languages,
was thought good to be set down in English, more largely
for the easier understanding to every public reader.*[47]

(*Enter* BALTHAZAR, BEL-IMPERIA, *and* HIERONIMO.)

BALTHAZAR. *Bashaw, that Rhodes is ours, yield heavens
    the honor,
And holy Mahomet, our sacred prophet;
And be thou graced with every excellence
That Soliman can give, or thou desire.
But thy desert in conquering Rhodes is less*

---

[47] The "play-within-the-play" that follows is a summary of an
anonymous tragedy, *Soliman and Perseda*, which Kyd may have
written.

Than in reserving this fair Christian nymph,
Perseda, blissful lamp of excellence,
Whose eyes compel, like powerful adamant,
The warlike heart of Soliman to wait.

KING. See, Viceroy, that is Balthazar, your son,
That represents the Emperor Soliman:
How well he acts his amorous passion.

VICEROY. Ay, Bel-imperia hath taught him that.

CASTILE. That's because his mind runs all on Bel-imperia.

HIERONIMO. *Whatever joy earth yields betide** *your*   fall on
majesty.

BALTHAZAR. *Earth yields no joy without Perseda's love.*

HIERONIMO. *Let then Perseda on your grace attend.*

BALTHAZAR. *She shall not wait on me, but I on her;*
Drawn by the influence of her lights,* I yield.   eyes
But let my friend, the Rhodian knight, come forth,
Erasto, dearer than my life to me,
That he may see Perseda, my beloved.

(*Enter* ERASTO.)

KING. Here comes Lorenzo: Look upon the plot,*   script
And tell me, brother, what part plays he?

BEL-IMPERIA. *Ah, my Erasto, welcome to Perseda.*

LORENZO. *Thrice happy is Erasto that thou livest;*
Rhodes' loss is nothing to Erasto's joy;
Sith his Perseda lives, his life survives.

BALTHAZAR. *Ah, Bashaw, here is love betwixt Erasto*
And fair Perseda, sovereign of my soul.

HIERONIMO. *Remove Erasto, mighty Soliman,*
And then Perseda will be quickly won.

BALTHAZAR. *Erasto is my friend; and while he lives,*
Perseda never will remove her love.

HIERONIMO. *Let not Erasto live to grieve great Soliman.*

BALTHAZAR. *Dear is Erasto in our princely eye.*

HIERONIMO. *But if he be your rival, let him die.*

BALTHAZAR. *Why, let him die; so love commandeth me;*
Yet grieve I that Erasto should so die.

HIERONIMO. *Erasto, Soliman saluteth thee,*
And lets thee wit* by me his highness' will,   know
Which is, thou shouldest be thus employed.

(*Stabs him.*)

BEL-IMPERIA. *Ay me! Erasto! see, Soliman; Erasto's slain!*

BALTHAZAR. *Yet liveth Soliman to comfort thee.*

Fair queen of beauty, let not favor die,
But with a gracious eye behold his grief,
That with Perseda's beauty is increased,
If by Perseda his grief be not released.
 BEL-IMPERIA. *Tyrant, desist soliciting vain suits;*
Relentless are mine ears to thy laments,
As thy butcher is pitiless and base,
Which seized on my Erasto, harmless knight.
Yet by thy power thou thinkest to command,
And to thy power Perseda doth obey;
But, were she able, thus she would revenge
Thy treacheries on thee, ignoble Prince:
 (Stabs him.)
And on herself she would be thus revenged.
 (Stabs herself.)
 KING. Well said,*—Old Marshal, this was   well presented
  bravely done.
 HIERONIMO. But Bel-imperia plays Perseda well.
 VICEROY. Were this in earnest, Bel-imperia,
You would be better to my son than so.
 KING. But now what follows for Hieronimo?
 HIERONIMO. Marry, this follows for Hieronimo:
Here break we off our sundry languages,
And thus conclude I in our vulgar tongue.
Haply* you think, but bootless* are your   perhaps/in vain
  thoughts,
That this is fabulously counterfeit,*   a fictitious
                 representation
And that we do as all tragedians do:
To die today, for fashioning our scene,
The death of Ajax or some Roman peer
And in a minute, starting up again,
Revive to please tomorrow's audience.
No, princes: know I am Hieronimo,
The hopeless father of a hapless son,
Whose tongue is tuned to tell his latest* tale,   last
Not to excuse gross errors in the play.
I see your looks urge instance* of these words;   demand
                   explanation
Behold the reason urging me to this:
 (Shows his dead son.)
See here my show; look on this spectacle.
Here lay my hope, and here my hope hath end.
Here lay my heart, and here my heart was slain.
Here lay my treasure, here my treasure lost.
Here lay my bliss, and here my bliss bereft.

But hope, heart, treasure, joy, and bliss,
All fled, failed, died, yea, all decayed with this.
From forth these wounds came breath that gave me life;
They murdered me that made these fatal marks.
The cause was love, whence grew this mortal hate;
The hate, Lorenzo and young Balthazar;
The love, my son to Bel-imperia.
But night, the coverer of accursèd crimes,
With pitchy silence hushed these traitors' harms,
And lent them leave, for they had sorted leisure*   ample chance
To take advantage in my garden plot
Upon my son, my dear Horatio.
There merciless they butchered up my boy,
In black, dark night, to pale, dim, cruel death.
He shrieks; I heard, and yet, methinks, I hear,
His dismal outcry echo in the air.
With soonest speed I hasted to the noise,
Where hanging on a tree I found my son,
Through-girt* with wounds, and slaughtered as you see.   pierced
And grieved I, think you, at this spectacle?
Speak, Portuguese, whose loss resembles mine;
If thou canst weep upon thy Balthazar,
'Tis like I wailed for my Horatio.
And you, my lord, whose reconcilèd son
Marched in a net,* and thought himself unseen,   practiced deceit
And rated me for brainsick lunacy,
With "God amend that mad Hieronimo!"
How can you brook* our play's catastrophe?   bear
And here behold this bloody handkercher,
Which at Horatio's death I weeping dipped
Within the river of his bleeding wounds.
It, as propitious, see, I have reserved,
And never hath it left my bloody heart,
Soliciting remembrance of my vow
With these, O, these accursèd murderers.
Which now performed, my heart is satisfied.
And to this end the Bashaw I became
That might revenge me on Lorenzo's life,
Who therefore was appointed to the part,
And was to represent the Knight of Rhodes,
That I might kill him more conveniently.
So, Viceroy, was this Balthazar, thy son,
That Soliman which Bel-imperia,
In person of Perseda, murdered,

Solely appointed to that tragic part
That she might slay him that offended her.
Poor Bel-imperia missed her part in this:
For though the story saith she should have died,
Yet I of kindness, and of care to her,
Did otherwise determine of her end.
But love of him whom they did hate too much
Did urge her resolution to be such.
And, princes, now behold Hieronimo,
Author and actor in this tragedy,
Bearing his latest fortune in his fist,
And will as resolute conclude his part
As any of the actors gone before.
And, gentles, thus I end my play;
Urge no more words; I have no more to say.
      (*He runs to hang himself.*)
      KING. O hearken, Viceroy!—hold, Hieronimo!
Brother, my nephew and thy son are slain!
      VICEROY. We are betrayed; my Balthazar is slain!
Break ope the doors; run, save Hieronimo.
      (*They break in, and hold* HIERONIMO.)
Hieronimo, do but inform the King of these events;
Upon mine honor, thou shalt have no harm.
      HIERONIMO. Viceroy, I will not trust thee with my life,
Which I this day have offered to my son.
Accursèd wretch,
Why stayest thou him that was resolved to die?
      KING. Speak, traitor; damned, bloody murderer, speak!
For now I have thee, I will make thee speak.
Why hast thou done this undeserving* deed?   undeserved
      VICEROY. Why hast thou murderèd my Balthazar?
      CASTILE. Why has thou butchered both my children thus?
      HIERONIMO. O, good words!
As dear to me was my Horatio
As yours, or yours, or yours, my lord, to you.
My guiltless son was by Lorenzo slain,
And by Lorenzo and that Balthazar
Am I at last revengèd thoroughly,
Upon whose souls may heavens be yet avenged
With greater far than these afflictions.
      CASTILE. But who were thy confederates in this?
      VICEROY. That was thy daughter, Bel-imperia;
For by her hand my Balthazar was slain:

I saw her stab him.

KING.   Why speakest thou not?

HIERONIMO. What lesser liberty can kings afford
Than harmless silence? then afford it me.
Sufficeth, I may not, nor I will not tell thee.

KING. Fetch forth the tortures.
Traitor as thou art, I'll make thee tell.

HIERONIMO. Indeed,
Thou mayest torment me as his wretched son
Hath done in murd'ring my Horatio;
But never shalt thou force me to reveal
The thing which I have vowed inviolate.
And therefore, in despite of all thy threats,
Pleased with their deaths, and eased with their revenge,
First take my tongue, and afterwards my heart.
    [*Beginning of fifth 1602 Addition, a substitution for pre-
    ceding 25 lines.*]

HIERONIMO. But are you sure they are dead?

CASTILE.   Ay, slave, too sure.

HIERONIMO. What, and yours too?

VICEROY. Ay, all are dead; not one of them survive.

HIERONIMO. Nay, then I care not; come, and we shall
    be friends;
Let us lay our heads together:
See, here's a goodly noose will hold them all.

VICEROY. O damnèd devil, how secure* he is.   unconcerned

HIERONIMO. Secure? why, doest thou wonder at it?
I tell thee, Viceroy, this day I have seen revenge,
And in that sight am grown a prouder monarch
Than ever sat under the crown of Spain.
Had I as many lives as there be stars,
As many heavens to go to as those lives
I'd give them all, ay, and my soul to boot
But I would see thee ride in this red pool.

CASTILE. Speak! who were thy confederates in this?

VICEROY. That was thy daughter Bel-imperia;
For by her hand my Balthazar was slain:
I saw her stab him.

HIERONIMO. O, good words!
As dear to me was my Horatio
As yours, or yours, or yours, my lord, to you.

My guiltless son was by Lorenzo slain,
And by Lorenzo and that Balthazar
Am I at last revengèd thoroughly;
Upon whose souls may heavens yet be revenged
With greater far than these afflictions.
Methinks, since I grew inward* with revenge,   intimate
I cannot look with scorn enough on death.
    KING. What, doest thou mock us, slave?—Bring tortures
      forth.
    HIERONIMO. Do, do, do; and meantime I'll torture you.
You* had a son, as I take it, and your son   (the Viceroy)
Should ha' been married to your* daughter; ha, (Don Cyprian's)
    was't not so?
You* had a son too; he was my liege's nephew.   (Don Cyprian)
He was proud and politic,* had he lived,   cunning
He might a come to wear the crown of Spain.
I think 'twas so: 'twas I that killed him;
Look you, this same hand, 'twas it that stabbed
His heart. Do you see? This hand—
For one Horatio, if you ever knew him,
A youth, one that they hanged up in his father's garden;
One that did force your* valiant son to yield,   (the Viceroy's)
While your* more valiant son did take him   (Don Cyprian's)
    prisoner.
    VICEROY. Be deaf, my senses; I can hear no more.
    KING. Fall, heaven, and cover us with thy sad ruins.
    CASTILE. Roll all the world within thy pitchy cloud.
    HIERONIMO. Now do I applaud what I have acted.
    Nunc iners cadat manus.[48]
Now to express the rupture of my part,
First take my tongue, and afterward my heart.
    (*He bites out his tongue.*)
    [*End of Addition.*]
    KING. O monstrous resolution of a wretch.
See, Viceroy, he hath bitten forth his tongue,
Rather than to reveal what we required.
    CASTILE. Yet can he write.
    KING. And if in this he satisfy us not,
We will devise th'extremest kind of death
That ever was invented for a wretch.
    (*Then* HIERONIMO *makes signs for a knife to mend his pen.*)

---

[48] "Now let the hand fall idle."

CASTILE. O, he would have a knife to mend his pen.
VICEROY. Here, and advise thee that thou write the troth.
(HIERONIMO *stabs the* DUKE *and himself.*)
KING. Look to my brother; save Hieronimo!
What age hath ever heard such monstrous deeds?
My brother, and the whole succeeding hope
That Spain expected after my decease.
Go, bear his body hence, that we may mourn
The loss of our belovèd brother's death;
That he may be entombed, whate'er befall.
I am the next, the nearest, last of all.
    VICEROY. And thou, Don Pedro, do the like for us;
Take up our hapless* son, untimely slain;   unfortunate
Set me with him, and he with woeful me,
Upon the mainmast of a ship unmanned,
And let the wind and tide haul me along
To Scylla's barking and untamed gulf,[49]
Or to the loathsome pool of Acheron,
To weep my want for my sweet Balthazar;
Spain hath no refuge for a Portingale.
    (*Trumpets sound a dead march, with the* KING OF SPAIN
mourning over his brother's body and the KING OF PORTU-
GAL *bearing the body of his son.*)[50]

CHORUS

(GHOST *and* REVENGE.)
    GHOST. Ay, now my hopes have end in their effects,
When blood and sorrow finish my desires:
Horatio murdered in his father's bower,
Vild* Serberine by Pedringano slain,   vile
False Pedringano hanged by quaint device,*   a cunning trick
Fair Isabella by herself misdone,
Prince Balthazar by Bel-imperia stabbed,
The Duke of Castile and his wicked son
Both done to death by old Hieronimo,
My Bel-imperia fall'n as Dido* fell,   Queen of
                                     Carthage
And good Hieronimo slain by himself.

[49] Scylla was both a treacherous rock on the Italian coast opposite Sicily and the name of a female monster living on the rock.

[50] Kyd contradicts his own directions of the first two lines of the Viceroy's last speech.

Ay, these were spectacles to please my soul.
Now will I beg at lovely Proserpine
That, by the virtue of her princely doom,*   sentence
I may consort* my friends in pleasing sort,*   accompany/company
And on my foes work just and sharp revenge.
I'll lead my friend Horatio through those fields
Where never-dying wars are still inured;*   waged
I'll lead fair Isabella to that train*   way of life
Where pity weeps but never feeleth pain;
I'll lead my Bel-imperia to those joys
That vestal virgins and fair queens possess;
I'll lead Hieronimo where Orpheus plays,
Adding sweet pleasure to eternal days.
But say, Revenge, for thou must help, or none,
Against the rest how shall my hate be shown?
   REVENGE. This hand shall hale them down to
     deepest hell,
Where none but furies, bugs,* and tortures dwell.   terrors
   GHOST. Then, sweet Revenge, do this at my request:
Let me be judge, and doom* them to unrest.   sentence
Let loose poor Tityus[51] from the vulture's gripe,*   grip
And let Don Cyprian supply his room;
Place Don Lorenzo on Ixion's wheel,[52]
And let the lover's* endless pains surcease   (Ixion's)
(Juno forgets old wrath, and grants him ease);
Hang Balthazar about Chimaera's* neck,   fire-breathing
                                     monster
And let him there bewail his bloody love,
Repining at our joys that are above;
Let Serberine go roll the fatal stone,
And take from Sisyphus[53] his endless moan;
False Pedringano, for his treachery,
Let him be dragged through boiling Acheron,*   river in Hell
And there live, dying still in endless flames,
Blaspheming gods and all their holy names.
   REVENGE. Then haste we down to meet thy friends
     and foes:

     [51] A giant punished for sinning by having two vultures devour
his liver.
     [52] Ixion's punishment for sin was to be bound on an endlessly
revolving wheel.
     [53] Sisyphus eternally had to roll a stone uphill.

To place thy friends in ease, the rest in woes;
For here though death hath end their misery,
I'll there begin their endless tragedy.

(*Exeunt.*)

Friar Bacon and Friar Bungay

BY ROBERT GREENE

Robert Greene (1558-92) was one of the most colorful personalities of the Elizabethan literary scene. Combining a university education with a taste for raw life, of which there was an abundance in London, Greene acquired notoriety in bohemian circles after coming down from Cambridge, where he had acquired two degrees. Born in Norwich, he returned there for a while, married, and fathered a son. But, abandoning his wife and child, he became one of the most prolific as well as dissipated of the "university wits" who tried to make a living by writing without benefit of the upper-class patronage which had previously sustained men of letters. In the pursuit of an extremely precarious independent career Greene published nearly thirty pamphlets, consisting chiefly of love stories and more or less lurid tracts on London life and its various degrees of roguery, to which he added toward the end of his makeshift life some confessional literature.

Like other "university wits" he found employment in the theatre, which had a great need for new playwrights. He began with an imitation of Marlowe's *Tamburlaine*; next, about 1590, he collaborated with Thomas Lodge, the author of the pastoral romance *Rosalynde* (Shakespeare's source for *As You Like It*), on a Biblical drama entitled *A Looking-Glass for London and England* (published in 1594), a domesticated version of the story of Jonah, drawing a parallel between the sins of Assyrian Nineveh and England's capital city; and shortly after this he burlesqued both Marlowe's *Tamburlaine* and Kyd's *The Spanish Tragedy* in *Orlando Furioso*. He arrived at maturity in the theatre with *Friar Bacon and Friar Bungay*, aptly described as "the first well planned and skillfully executed romantic comedy in English" (Thomas Marc Parrott and Robert Hamilton Ball, *A Short View of Elizabethan Drama*, New York, 1943, p. 71). To the romantic substance

169

of Prince Edward's love for Margaret, the rustic maiden of Fressingfield, and her own love for his friend and go-between, Lord Lacy, Greene added the fanciful comedy of the thirteenth-century English scientist "magician" Friar Bacon's dabbling in the black art. He enriched this vivid part of the play with the homely comic characters of Miles, the inept clown whose negligence ruined the magic-working Friar Bacon's Brazen Head and who was carried away to hell on the back of a roaring devil, and a professional Fool, Ralph, who has been considered the prototype of Shakespeare's Touchstone and Feste.

Greene wrote a second and more unified romantic play, the tragi-comedy *James IV*, which revolves around an idealized young wife and medieval "Patient Griselda" figure who, disguised as a youth, flees from her royal husband because he, infatuated with another woman, decides to murder her. Ultimately everything turns out well when she averts a conflict between her father, the English king, and her husband, the king of Scotland, and recovers her husband. The constant Dorothea is plainly the forerunner of Shakespeare's Viola, Rosalind, and Imogen, antedating their charm, their protective resort to masculine attire, and their persistence in the pursuit of love. Unfortunately the text of *James IV* has come down only in a corrupt state.

Greene, sinking rapidly into debauchery and poverty, did not further capitalize on his dramatic talent. Consequently we must turn to *Friar Bacon and Friar Bungay* to find him at his best as a professional playwright. The attractiveness of its love story and the public interest in magic or conjuring won Greene a singular success, and the play is also noteworthy in theatrical history for possessing in the country girl Margaret the first fully developed romantic heroine of the Elizabethan theatre.

J. G.

Date. Scholars have dated this play between 1589 and 1592. Henslowe notes in his *Diary* that when it was performed in February, 1592, *Friar Bacon* was already an "old play." But how old? Henslowe's notation simply meant that the play was not having a premiere performance. No factual evidence exists for ascertaining an initial date; however, the strongest inferential evidence places the play about 1591-92.

Text and Publishing Data. The play was entered in the Stationers' Register on May 14, 1594. The first quarto appeared during the year, with Edward White as the printer. The second quarto, Q2, published in 1630, merely reprinted Q1. The only other early text is a third quarto, which appeared in 1655. A playhouse manuscript furnished the copy for Q1. There are no act or scene divisions in the early texts.

Sources. Many similarities exist between *Friar Bacon* and Marlowe's *Doctor Faustus*. It is impossible to determine the exact relationship between the two plays because the date of each cannot be precisely determined. One need not, however, seek further than *The Famous History of Friar Bacon,* a late-sixteenth-century work, to find the source for Greene's play. The magic story and the feud of the two neighbors and their sons can be found in *The Famous History.* . . . (The earliest extant edition of the work is 1627.) The love story of Margaret of Fressingfield is original. Although historical personages play a major role in the play, Greene's historical background is entirely fictitious.

Stage History. Henslowe's *Diary* records performances by Lord Strange's Men in 1592 and 1593, and by the combined Queen's and Sussex's Men in 1594. In 1602, the Lord Admiral's Men revived the play with a specially written prologue and epilogue by Thomas Middleton, whose additions have not survived. According to the title page of the 1630 quarto, the Prince Palatine's company "lately" played *Friar Bacon.*

W. G.

DRAMATIS PERSONAE

KING HENRY THE THIRD
EDWARD, PRINCE OF WALES, his son
EMPEROR OF GERMANY
KING OF CASTILE
LACY, Earl of Lincoln
WARREN, Earl of Sussex
ERMSBY, a gentleman
RALPH SIMNELL, the King's Fool
FRIAR BACON
MILES, Friar Bacon's poor scholar
FRIAR BUNGAY
JAQUES VANDERMAST, a German magician
BURDEN,
MASON,   } Doctors of Oxford
CLEMENT,
LAMBERT, } gentlemen
SERLSBY,
TWO SCHOLARS, sons to Lambert and Serlsby
KEEPER of Fressingfield
FRIEND TO THE KEEPER
THOMAS,   } Rustics
RICHARD,
CONSTABLE, POST, LORDS, COUNTRY CLOWNS, etc.
ELINOR, daughter to the King of Castile
MARGARET, the Keeper's daughter (of Fressingfield)
JOAN, a farmer's daughter
HOSTESS of the Bell at Henley
A DEVIL, a fiend like HERCULES
A DRAGON, shooting fire, etc.

Scene 1

(*Framlingham. Enter* PRINCE EDWARD *malcontented, with* LACY, WARREN, ERMSBY, *and* RALPH SIMNELL, *the Fool of the play.*)

LACY. Why looks my lord like to a troubled sky
When heaven's bright shine is shadowed with a fog?
Alate* we ran the deer, and through the lawns* lately/glades
Stripped* with our nags the lofty frolic bucks   outstripped
That scudded 'fore the teasers* like the wind.   hounds
Ne'er was the deer of merry Fressingfield
So lustily pulled down by jolly mates,
Nor shared the farmers such fat venison,
So frankly dealt,* this hundred years before;   liberally
                 distributed
Nor have I seen my lord more frolic in the chase,
And now—changed to a melancholy dump.* low in spirit
 WARREN. After the prince got to the Keeper's lodge,
And had been jocund in the house awhile,
Tossing off ale and milk in country cans,
Whether it was the country's sweet content,
Or else the bonny damsel filled us drink
That seemed so stately in her stammel* red, coarse woolen
                   cloth
Or that a qualm did cross his stomach then,
But straight he fell into his passions.*   moodiness
 ERMSBY. Sirrah Ralph, what say you to your master,
Shall he thus all amort* live malcontent?   spiritless
 RALPH. Hearest thou, Ned?—Nay, look if he will speak to me!
 PRINCE EDWARD. What say'st thou to me, fool?
 RALPH. I prithee, tell me, Ned, art thou in love with the Keeper's daughter?
 PRINCE EDWARD. How if I be, what then?
 RALPH. Why, then, sirrah, I'll teach thee how to deceive Love.
 PRINCE EDWARD. How, Ralph?
 RALPH. Marry, Sirrah Ned, thou shalt put on my cap and my coat and my dagger, and I will put on thy clothes and thy sword; and so thou shalt be my fool.
 PRINCE EDWARD. And what of this?
 RALPH. Why, so thou shalt beguile Love; for Love is such a

proud scab,* that he will never meddle with fools nor   rascal
children. Is not Ralph's counsel good, Ned?

    PRINCE EDWARD. Tell me, Ned Lacy, didst thou mark the
       maid,
How lively in her country-weeds* she looked?   country clothes
A bonnier wench all Suffolk cannot yield:
All Suffolk? Nay, all England holds none such.

    RALPH. Sirrah Will Ermsby, Ned is deceived.

    ERMSBY. Why, Ralph?

    RALPH. He says all England hath no such, and I say, and
I'll stand to it, there is one better in Warwickshire.

    WARREN. How provest thou that, Ralph?

    RALPH. Why, is not the abbot a learned man, and hath
read many books, and thinkest thou he hath not more learning
than thou to choose a bonny wench? Yes, I warrant thee, by
his whole grammar.*   that is,
                                         learning

    ERMSBY. A good reason, Ralph.

    PRINCE EDWARD. I tell thee, Lacy, that her sparkling eyes
Do lighten forth sweet love's alluring fire;
And in her tresses she doth fold the looks
Of such as gaze upon her golden hair;
Her bashful white, mixed with the morning's red,
Luna* doth boast upon her lovely cheeks;   that is,
                                   the moon
Her front* is beauty's table, where she paints   forehead
The glories of her gorgeous excellence;
Her teeth are shelves of precious marguerites,*   pearls
Richly enclosed with ruddy coral cliffs.
Tush, Lacy, she is beauty's over-match,
If thou survey'st her curious imagery.*   exquisite
                                 appearance

    LACY. I grant, my lord, the damsel is as fair
As simple Suffolk's homely towns can yield;
But in the court be quainter* dames than she,   more exquisite
Whose faces are enriched with honor's tint,
Whose beauties stand upon the stage of fame,
And vaunt their trophies in the courts of love.

    PRINCE EDWARD. Ned, but hadst thou watched her as myself,
And seen the secret beauties of the maid,
Their courtly coyness were but foolery.

    ERMSBY. Why, how watched you her, my lord?

    PRINCE EDWARD. Whenas* she swept like Venus   when
       through the house.
And in her shape fast folded up my thoughts,
Into the milk-house went I with the maid,
And there amongst the cream-bowls she did shine

As Pallas* 'mongst her princely huswifery.*   Pallas Athena/
housekeeping
She turned her smock over her lily arms,
And dived them into milk to run her cheese;
But whiter than the milk her crystal skin,
Checked with lines of azure, made her blush[1]
That art or nature durst* bring for compare.   dared
Ermsby, if thou hadst seen, as I did note it well,
How beauty played the huswife, how this girl,
Like Lucrece, laid her fingers to the work,
Thou wouldst, with Tarquin, hazard Rome and all[2]
To win the lovely maid of Fressingfield.

RALPH. Sirrah Ned, would'st fain have her?

PRINCE EDWARD. Ay, Ralph.

RALPH. Why, Ned, I have laid the plot in my head; thou
shalt have her already.

PRINCE EDWARD. I'll give thee a new coat, an learn* me that.
if you teach

RALPH. Why Sirrah Ned, we'll ride to Oxford to Friar
Bacon. O, he is a brave scholar, sirrah; they say he is a brave
necromancer, that he can make women of devils, and he can
juggle cats into costermongers.*   street vendors

PRINCE EDWARD. And how then, Ralph?

RALPH. Marry, sirrah, thou shalt go to him; and because*
in order that
thy father Harry shall not miss thee, he shall turn me into thee;
and I'll to the court, and I'll prince it out; and he shall make
thee either a silken purse full of gold, or else a fine wrought
smock.

PRINCE EDWARD. But how shall I have the maid?

RALPH. Marry, sirrah, if thou be'st a silken purse full of
gold, then on Sundays she'll hang thee by her side, and you
must not say a word. Now, sir, when she comes into a great
press* of people, for fear of the cutpurse,*   crowd/pickpocket
a sudden she'll swap* thee into her plackerd;* then, sweep/placket
sirrah, being there, you may plead for yourself.

ERMSBY. Excellent policy!*   scheme

PRINCE EDWARD. But how if I be a wrought smock?

RALPH. Then she'll put thee into her chest and lay thee into
lavender, and upon some good day she'll put thee on; and at

---

[1] Would have made that woman blush that art . . . compare.

[2] Lucretia, wife of Lucius Tarquinius Collatinus, was noted for
her great virtue. Raped by Sextus Tarquinius, she denounced her
attacker to her family, demanded revenge, and then stabbed herself. As a result the Tarquins were banished from Rome, an act
which led to the establishment of the Roman Republic.

night when you go to bed, then being turned from a smock to
a man, you may make up the match.

LACY. Wonderfully wisely counseled, Ralph.

PRINCE EDWARD. Ralph shall have a new coat.

RALPH. God thank you when I have it on my back, Ned.

PRINCE EDWARD. Lacy, the Fool hath laid a perfect plot;
For why* our country Margaret is so coy,*   because/reserved
And stands so much upon her honest points,*   that is, chastity
That marriage or no market with the maid.
Ermsby, it must be necromantic spells
And charms of art that must enchain her love,
Or else shall Edward never win the girl.
Therefore, my wags, we'll horse us in the morn,
And post to Oxford to this jolly friar:
Bacon shall by his magic do this deed.

WARREN. Content, my lord; and that's a speedy way
To wean these headstrong puppies from the teat.

PRINCE EDWARD. I am unknown, not taken for the prince;
They only deem us frolic courtiers,
That revel thus among our liege's game;
Therefore I have devised a policy:
Lacy, thou know'st next Friday is Saint James',*   July 25
And then the country flocks to Harleston fair;
Then will the Keeper's daughter frolic there,
And over-shine the troop of all the maids
That come to see and to be seen that day.
Haunt thee disguised among the country-swains,*   rustics
Feign thou'rt a farmer's son, not far from thence,
Espy her loves, and who she liketh best;
Cote* him, and court her to control the clown;*   outstrip/rustic
Say that the courtier 'tired* all in green,   attired
That helped her handsomely to run her cheese,
And filled her father's lodge with venison,
Commends him, and sends fairings* to herself.   gifts
Buy something worthy of her parentage,
Not worth her beauty; for, Lacy, then the fair
Affords no jewel fitting for the maid.
And when thou talk'st of me, note if she blush;
O, then she loves; but if her cheeks wax pale,
Disdain it is. Lacy, send how she fares,
And spare no time nor cost to win her loves.

LACY. I will, my lord, so execute this charge
As if that Lacy were in love with her.

PRINCE EDWARD. Send letters speedily to Oxford of the news.

RALPH. And, Sirrah Lacy, buy me a thousand thousand million of fine bells.

LACY. What wilt thou do with them, Ralph?

RALPH. Marry, every time that Ned sighs for the Keeper's daughter, I'll tie a bell about him, and so within three or four days I will send word to his father Harry, that his son and my master Ned is become Love's morris-dance.

PRINCE EDWARD. Well, Lacy, look with care unto thy charge,
And I will haste to Oxford to the friar,
That he by art and thou by secret gifts
Mayst make me lord of merry Fressingfield.

LACY. God send your honor your heart's desire.

(Exeunt.)

Scene 2

(FRIAR BACON'S *cell at Oxford. Enter* FRIAR BACON, *with* MILES, *his poor scholar, with books under his arm; with them are* BURDEN, MASON, CLEMENT, *three* DOCTORS.)

BACON. Miles, where are you?

MILES. *Hic sum, doctissime et reverendissime doctor.*

BACON. *Attulisti nos libros meos de necromantia?*

MILES. *Ecce quam bonum et quam jucundum habitare libros in unum!*[3]

BACON. Now, masters of our academic state,
That rule in Oxford, viceroys in your place,
Whose heads contain maps of the liberal arts,
Spending your time in depth of learned skill,
Why flock you thus to Bacon's secret cell,
A friar newly stalled* in Brazen-nose?   installed
Say what's your mind, that I may make reply.

BURDEN. Bacon, we hear that* long we have   that which
    suspect,
That thou art read in magic's mystery;
In pyromancy, to divine by flames;
To tell, by hydromatic, ebbs and tides;

---

[3] MILES. Here I am, learned and reverend doctor.
BACON. Have you brought us my books on necromancy?
MILES. Behold, how good and pleasant it is for books to dwell in one place.
(An echo of Psalm 133: "Behold, how good and how pleasant it is for brethren to dwell together in unity!")

By aeromancy to discover doubts,*   solve difficulties
To plain out* questions, as Apollo did.   explain
    BACON. Well, Master Burden, what of all this?
    MILES. Marry, sir, he doth but fulfil, by rehearsing of these
names, the fable of the Fox and the Grapes; that which is
above us pertains nothing to us.
    BURDEN. I tell thee, Bacon, Oxford makes report,
Nay, England, and the court of Henry says,
Thou'rt making of a brazen head by art,
Which shall unfold strange doubts and aphorisms,[4]
And read a lecture in philosophy;
And, by the help of devils and ghastly fiends,
Thou mean'st ere many years or days be past,
To compass* England with a wall of brass.   encircle
    BACON. And what of this?
    MILES. What of this, master! Why, he doth speak mys-
tically; for he knows, if your skill fail to make a brazen head,
yet Mother Waters' strong ale will fit his turn to make him
have a copper nose.
    CLEMENT. Bacon, we come not grieving at thy skill,
But joying that our academy yields
A man supposed the wonder of the world;
For if thy cunning work these miracles,
England and Europe shall admire thy fame,
And Oxford shall in characters of brass,
And statues, such as were built up in Rome,
Eternize Friar Bacon for his art.
    MASON. Then, gentle friar, tell us thy intent.
    BACON. Seeing you come as friends unto the friar,
Resolve you,* doctors, Bacon can by books   be assured
Make storming Boreas* thunder from his cave,   North Wind
And dim fair Luna to a dark eclipse.
The great arch-ruler, potentate of hell,
Trembles when Bacon bids him or his fiends,
Bow to the force of his pentagonon.[5]
What art can work, the frolic friar knows;
And therefore will I turn my magic books,
And strain out necromancy to the deep.
I have contrived and framed a head of brass
(I made Belcephon hammer out the stuff),

      [4] Statements of scientific principles.
      [5] Pentagram, a five-rayed star having magical powers.

And that by art shall read philosophy;
And I will strengthen England by my skill,
That if ten Caesars lived and reigned in Rome,
With all the legions Europe doth contain,
They should not touch a grass of English ground.
The work that Ninus[6] reared at Babylon,
The brazen walls framed by Semiramis,[7]
Carved out like to the portal of the sun,
Shall not be such as rings the English strand
From Dover to the market-place of Rye.

BURDEN. Is this possible?

MILES. I'll bring ye two or three witnesses.

BURDEN. What be those?

MILES. Marry, sir, three or four as honest devils and good companions as any be in hell.

MASON. No doubt but magic may do much in this;
For he that reads but mathematic rules
Shall find conclusions that avail to work
Wonders that pass the common sense of men.

BURDEN. But Bacon roves a bow[8] beyond his reach,
And tells of more than magic can perform,
Thinking to get a fame by fooleries.
Have I not passed as far in state of schools,*   that is, degrees
And read of many secrets? Yet to think
That heads of brass can utter any voice,
Or more, to tell of deep philosophy,
This is a fable Æsop had forgot.

BACON. Burden, thou wrong'st me in detracting thus;
Bacon loves not to stuff himself with lies.
But tell me 'fore these doctors, if thou dare,
Of certain questions I shall move to thee.

BURDEN. I will; ask what thou can.

MILES. Marry, sir, he'll straight be on your pick-pack,* to
know whether the feminine or the masculine   pick-a-back,
gender be most worthy.   shoulders

BACON. Were you not yesterday, Master Burden, at Henley
upon the Thames?

---

[6] Legendary founder of Nineveh and the Assyrian empire; husband to Semiramis.

[7] Assyrian queen noted for her great beauty and accomplishments.

[8] Shoots at a target.

BURDEN. I was; what then?

BACON. What book studied you thereon all night?

BURDEN. I! None at all; I read not there a line.

BACON. Then, doctors, Friar Bacon's art knows naught.

CLEMENT. What say you to this, Master Burden? Doth he not touch you?

BURDEN. I pass not of* his frivolous speeches.   care not for

MILES. Nay, Master Burden, my master, ere he hath done with you, will turn you from a doctor to a dunce, and shake you so small, that he will leave no more learning in you than is in Balaam's ass.

BACON. Master, for that learned Burden's skill is deep,
And sore he doubts of Bacon's cabalism,*   occult art
I'll show you why he haunts to Henley oft:
Not, doctors, for to taste the fragrant air,
But there to spend the night in alchemy,
To multiply with secret spells of art;
Thus private steals he learning from us all.
To prove my sayings true, I'll show you straight
The book he keeps at Henley for himself.

MILES. Nay, now my master goes to conjuration, take heed.

BACON. Masters, stand still, fear not, I'll show you but his book.

(*Here he conjures.*)
Per omnes deos infernales, Belcephon![9]

(*Enter a woman with a shoulder of mutton on a spit, and a* DEVIL.)

MILES. O, master, cease your conjuration, or you spoil all; for here's a she-devil come with a shoulder of mutton on a spit. You have marred the devil's supper; but no doubt he thinks our college fare is slender, and so hath sent you his cook with a shoulder of mutton, to make it exceed.*   better

HOSTESS. O, where am I, or what's become of me?

BACON. What art thou?

HOSTESS. Hostess at Henley, mistress of the Bell.

BACON. How camest thou here?

HOSTESS. As I was in the kitchen 'mongst the maids,
Spitting the meat 'gainst supper for my guests,
A motion* moved me to look forth of door: impulse

---

[9] By all the infernal gods, Belcephon.

No sooner had I pried into the yard,
But straight a whirlwind hoisted me from thence,
And mounted me aloft unto the clouds.
As in a trance I thought nor feared naught,
Nor know I where or whither I was ta'en,
Nor where I am nor what these persons be.

BACON. No? Know you not Master Burden?

HOSTESS. O, yes, good sir, he is my daily guest.—
What, Master Burden! 'twas but yesternight
That you and I at Henley played at cards.

BURDEN. I know not what we did.—A pox of all conjuring
friars!

CLEMENT. Now, jolly friar, tell us, is this the book
That Burden is so careful to look on?

BACON. It is.— But, Burden, tell me now,
Think'st thou that Bacon's necromantic skill
Cannot perform his head and wall of brass,
When he can fetch thine hostess in such post?

MILES. I'll warrant you, master, if Master Burden could
conjure as well as you, he would have his book every night
from Henley to study on at Oxford.

MASON. Burden, what, are you mated* by this   checkmated
frolic friar?—
Look how he droops; his guilty conscience
Drives him to 'bash,* and makes his hostess blush.   be abashed

BACON. Well, mistress, for I will not have you missed,
You shall to Henley to cheer up your guests
'Fore supper 'gin.*—Burden, bid her adieu;   begins
Say farewell to your hostess 'fore she goes.—
Sirrah, away, and set her safe at home.

HOSTESS. Master Burden, when shall we see you at Henley?

BURDEN. The devil take thee and Henley too.

                    (*Exeunt* HOSTESS *and* DEVIL.)

MILES. Master, shall I make a good motion?

BACON. What's that?

MILES. Marry, sir, now that my hostess is gone to provide
supper, conjure up another spirit, and send Doctor Burden
flying after.

BACON. Thus, rulers of our academic state,
You have seen the friar frame his art by proof;
And as the college called Brazen-nose
Is under him, and he the master there,

So surely shall this head of brass be framed,
And yield forth strange and uncouth* aphorisms;   unknown
And hell and Hecate shall fail the friar,
But I will circle England round with brass.

    MILES. So be it *et nunc et semper;*[10] amen.

                                         (*Exeunt.*)

Scene 3

    (*Harleston Fair. Enter* MARGARET, *the fair maid of Fressing-field, and* JOAN; THOMAS, RICHARD, *and other* CLOWNS; *and* LACY *disguised in country apparel.*)

    THOMAS. By my troth, Margaret, here's a weather is able to make a man call his father "whoreson"; if this weather hold, we shall have hay good cheap* and butter   at a low price
and cheese at Harleston will bear no price.

    MARGARET. Thomas, maids when they come to see the fair
Count not to make a cope* for dearth of hay;   bargain
When we have turned our butter to the salt,
And set our cheese safely upon the racks,
Then let our fathers price it as they please.
We country sluts* of merry Fressingfield   girls
Come to buy needless naughts to make us fine,
And look that young men should be frank* this day,   generous
And court us with such fairings* as they can.   gifts
Phoebus is blithe, and frolic looks from heaven,
As when he courted lovely Semele,[11]
Swearing the pedlars shall have empty packs,
If that fair weather may make chapmen* buy.   customers

    LACY. But, lovely Peggy, Semele is dead,
And therefore Phoebus from his palace pries,
And, seeing such a sweet and seemly saint,
Shows all his glories for to court yourself.

    MARGARET. This is a fairing, gentle sir, indeed,
To soothe me up with such smooth flattery;
But learn of me, your scoff's too broad before.[12]
Well, Joan, our beauties must abide their jests;
We serve the turn in jolly Fressingfield.

---

[10] And now and always.
[11] It was Zeus who courted Semele, a Theban princess.
[12] That is, you are mocking me in too obvious a manner.

JOAN. Margaret, a farmer's daughter for a farmer's son;
I warrant you, the meanest of us both
Shall have a mate to lead us from the church.
But, Thomas, what's the news? What, in a dump?
Give me your hand, we are near a pedlar's shop;
Out with your purse, we must have fairings now.

THOMAS. Faith, Joan, and shall. I'll bestow a fairing on you, and then we will to the tavern, and snap off a pint of wine or two.

(*All this while* LACY *whispers in* MARGARET'S *ear.*)

MARGARET. Whence are you, sir? Of Suffolk? For your terms
Are finer than the common sort of men.

LACY. Faith, lovely girl, I am of Beccles by,
Your neighbor, not above six miles from hence,
A farmer's son, that never was so quaint*   fastidious
But that he could do courtesy to such dames.
But trust me, Margaret, I am sent in charge
From him that reveled in your fathers' house,
And filled his lodge with cheer and venison,
'Tired in green. He sent you this rich purse,
His token that he helped you run your cheese,
And in the milkhouse chatted with yourself.

MARGARET. To me? You forget yourself.*   you are mistaken
LACY. Women are often weak in memory.

MARGARET. O, pardon, sir, I call to mind the man.
'Twere little manners to refuse his gift,
And yet I hope he sends it not for love;
For we have little leisure to debate of that.

JOAN. What, Margaret! Blush not; maids must have their loves.

THOMAS. Nay, by the mass, she looks pale as if she were angry.

RICHARD. Sirrah, are you of Beccles? I pray, how doth Goodman Cob? My father bought a horse of him.—I'll tell you, Margaret, 'a* were good to be a gentleman's jade,*   he/horse
for of all things the foul hilding* could not   worthless
abide a dung-cart.   creature

MARGARET (*aside*). How different is this farmer from the
    rest
That erst as yet have pleased my wandering sight!
His words are witty, quickened with a smile,
His courtesy gentle, smelling of the court;

Facile and debonair in all his deeds;
Proportioned as was Paris, when, in gray,[18]
He courted Œnon in the vale by Troy.
Great lords have come and pleaded for my love;
Who but the Keeper's lass of Fressingfield?
And yet methinks this farmer's jolly son
Passeth the proudest that hath pleased mine eye.
But, Peg, disclose not that thou art in love,
And show as yet no sign of love to him,
Although thou well wouldst wish him for thy love;
Keep that to thee till time doth serve thy turn,
To show the grief wherein thy heart doth burn.—
Come, Joan and Thomas, shall we to the fair?—
You, Beccles man, will not forsake us now?

    LACY. Not whilst I may have such quaint* girls as   attractive
    you.

    MARGARET. Well, if you chance to come by Fressingfield,
Make but a step into the Keeper's lodge,
And such poor fare as woodmen can afford,
Butter and cheese, cream and fat venison,
You shall have store, and welcome therewithal.

    LACY. Gramercies, Peggy; look for me ere long.

                             (*Exeunt omnes.*)

Scene 4

(*Hampton Court. Enter* KING HENRY THE THIRD, *the* EM-
PEROR, *the* KING OF CASTILE, ELINOR, *his daughter, and*
VANDERMAST, *a German magician.*)

    KING HENRY. Great men of Europe, monarchs of the west,
Ringed with the walls of old Oceanus,
Whose lofty surge is like the battlements
That compassed high-built Babel in with towers,
Welcome, my lords, welcome, brave western kings,
To England's shore, whose promontory cliffs
Show Albion is another little world;
Welcome, says English Henry to you all;
Chiefly unto the lovely Elinor,
Who dared for Edward's sake cut through the seas,
And venture as Agenor's damsel* through the deep,   Europa
To get the love of Henry's wanton* son.   amorous

    [18] Traditional color for a shepherd's garb.

KING OF CASTILE. England's rich monarch, brave Plantag-
  enet,
The Pyren Mounts swelling above the clouds,
That ward the wealthy Castile in with walls,
Could not detain the beauteous Elinor;
But, hearing of the fame of Edward's youth,
She dared to brook Neptunus' haughty pride,
And bide the brunt of froward* Æolus.*   perverse/King
                                                          of Winds
Then may fair England welcome her the more.
  ELINOR. After that English Henry by his lords
Had sent Prince Edward's lovely counterfeit,*   picture
A present to the Castile Elinor,
The comely portrait of so brave a man,
The virtuous fame discoursed of his deeds,
Edward's courageous resolution,
Done at the Holy Land 'fore Damas'* walls,[14]   Damascus
Led both mine eye and thoughts in equal links
To like so of the English monarch's son,
That I attempted perils for his sake.
  EMPEROR. Where is the prince, my lord?
  KING HENRY. He posted down, not long since, from the
      court,
To Suffolk side, to merry Framlingham,
To sport himself amongst my fallow deer;
From thence, by packets sent to Hampton-house,[15]
We hear the prince is ridden with his lords,
To Oxford, in the academy there
To hear dispute amongst the learned men.
But we will send forth letters for my son,
To will him come from Oxford to the court.
  EMPEROR. Nay, rather, Henry, let us, as we be,
Ride for to visit Oxford with our train.
Fain would I see your universities,
And what learned men your academy yields.
From Hapsburg have I brought a learned clerk*   scholar
To hold dispute with English orators.
This doctor, surnamed Jaques Vandermast,
A German born, passed into Padua,
To Florence and to fair Bologna,
To Paris, Rheims, and stately Orleans,

---

[14] This reference is not historically accurate.
[15] Historically, Hampton Court was built much later, during
the reign of Henry VIII.

And, talking there with men of art, put down
The chiefest of them all in aphorisms,[16]
In magic, and the mathematic rules.
Now let us, Henry, try him in your schools.

 KING HENRY. He shall, my lord; this motion*   proposal
likes me well.
We'll progress straight to Oxford with our trains,
And see what men our academy brings.—
And, wonder* Vandermast, welcome to me.   wondrous
In Oxford shalt thou find a jolly friar,
Called Friar Bacon, England's only flower;
Set him but nonplus in his magic spells,
And make him yield in mathematic rules,
And for thy glory I will bind thy brows,
Not with a poet's garland made of bays,
But with a coronet of choicest gold.
Whilst then* we set to Oxford with our troops,   until
Let's in and banquet in our English court.

               (*Exeunt.*)

Scene 5

(*Oxford. Enter* RALPH SIMNELL, *in* PRINCE EDWARD'S *apparel; and* EDWARD, WARREN, *and* ERMSBY, *disguised.*)

 RALPH. Where be these vagabond knaves, that they attend
no better on their master?

 PRINCE EDWARD. If it please your honor, we are all ready at
an inch.*   at short notice

 RALPH. Sirrah Ned, I'll have no more post-horse to ride on.
I'll have another fetch.*   trick

 ERMSBY. I pray you, how is that, my lord?

 RALPH. Marry, sir, I'll send to the Isle of Ely for four or
five dozen of geese, and I'll have them tied six and six together
with whip-cord. Now upon their backs will I have a fair field-
bed[17] with a canopy; and so, when it is my pleasure, I'll flee
into what place I please. This will be easy.

 WARREN. Your honor hath said well; but shall we to Brazen-
nose College before we pull off our boots?

 ERMSBY. Warren, well motioned; we will to the friar
Before we revel it within the town.—
Ralph, see you keep your countenance like a prince.

   [16] Statements of scientific principles.
   [17] A bed for use in the field.

RALPH. Wherefore have I such a company of cut- _{swaggering} ting* knaves to wait upon me, but to keep and defend my countenance against all mine enemies? Have you not good swords and bucklers?

ERMSBY. Stay, who comes here?

(*Enter* FRIAR BACON *and* MILES.)

WARREN. Some scholar; and we'll ask him where Friar Bacon is.

BACON. Why, thou arrant dunce, shall I never make thee a good scholar? Doth not all the town cry out and say, Friar Bacon's subsizer[18] is the greatest blockhead in all Oxford? Why, thou canst not speak one word of true Latin.

MILES. No, sir? Yes, what is this else? *Ego sum tuus homo,* "I am your man"; I warrant you, sir, as good Tully's phrase* as any is in Oxford. _{Ciceronian Latin}

BACON. Come on, sirrah; what part of speech is *Ego*?

MILES. *Ego,* that is "I"; marry, *nomen substantivo.*

BACON. How prove you that?

MILES. Why, sir, let him prove himself an 'a will; I can be heard, felt, and understood.[19]

BACON. O gross dunce!

(*Here beats him.*)

PRINCE EDWARD. Come, let us break off this dispute between these two.—

Sirrah, where is Brazen-nose College?

MILES. Not far from Coppersmith's Hall.

PRINCE EDWARD. What, dost thou mock me?

MILES. Not I, sir; but what would you at Brazen-nose?

ERMSBY. Marry, we would speak with Friar Bacon.

MILES. Whose men be you?

ERMSBY. Marry, scholar, here's our master.

RALPH. Sirrah, I am the master of these good fellows; mayst thou not know me to be a lord by my reparrel?* _{apparel}

MILES. Then here's good game for the hawk; for here's the master-fool and a covey of coxcombs. One wise man, I think, would spring you all.* _{that is, flush you out}

PRINCE EDWARD. Gog's* wounds! Warren, kill _{God's} him!

---

[18] A student who received free board and tuition in return for performing menial chores.

[19] "A humorous condensation of the definition of a noun substantive" (Ward).

WARREN. Why, Ned, I think the devil be in my sheath; I cannot get out my dagger.

ERMSBY. Nor I mine. 'Swounds, Ned, I think I am bewitched.

MILES. A company of scabs!* The proudest of you   scoundrels all draw your weapon, if he can.—(*Aside.*) See how boldly I speak, now my master is by.

PRINCE EDWARD. I strive in vain; but if my sword be shut
And conjured fast by magic in my sheath,
Villain, here is my fist.

(*Strikes* MILES *a box on the ear.*)

MILES. O, I beseech you conjure his hands too, that he may not lift his arms to his head, for he is light-fingered!

RALPH. Ned, strike him; I'll warrant* thee by mine   support
     honor.

BACON. What means the English prince to wrong my man?

PRINCE EDWARD. To whom speak'st thou?

BACON. To thee.

PRINCE EDWARD. Who art thou?

BACON. Could you not judge when all your swords grew
     fast,
That Friar Bacon was not far from hence?
Edward, King Henry's son and Prince of Wales,
Thy fool disguised cannot conceal thyself.
I know both Ermsby and the Sussex Earl,
Else Friar Bacon had but little skill.
Thou com'st in post from merry Fressingfield,
Fast-fancied* to the Keeper's bonny lass,   bound by love
To crave some succor of the jolly friar;
And Lacy, Earl of Lincoln, hast thou left
To treat* fair Margaret to allow thy loves;   entreat
But friends are men, and love can baffle lords;
The earl both woos and courts her for himself.

WARREN. Ned, this is strange; the friar knoweth all.

ERMSBY. Apollo could not utter more than this.

PRINCE EDWARD. I stand amazed to hear this jolly friar
Tell even the very secrets of my thoughts.—
But, learned Bacon, since thou know'st the cause
Why I did post so fast from Fressingfield,
Help, friar, at a pinch, that I may have
The love of lovely Margaret to myself,
And, as I am true Prince of Wales, I'll give

Living and lands to strength thy college state.*   estate
   WARREN. Good friar, help the prince in this.
   RALPH. Why, servant Ned, will not the friar do it? Were not
my sword glued to my scabbard by conjuration, I would cut
off his head, and make him do it by force.
   MILES. In faith, my lord, your manhood and your sword is
all alike; they are so fast conjured that we shall never see them.
   ERMSBY. What, doctor, in a dump!* Tush, help the   lost in
     prince,   thought
And thou shalt see how liberal he will prove.
   BACON. Crave not such actions greater dumps than these?
I will, my lord, strain out my magic spells;
For this day comes the earl to Fressingfield,
And 'fore that night shuts in the day with dark,
They'll be betrothed each to other fast.
But come with me; we'll to my study straight,
And in a glass prospective* I will show   magic glass
What's done this day in merry Fressingfield.
   PRINCE EDWARD. Gramercies, Bacon; I will 'quite*   requite
     thy pain.
   BACON. But send your train, my lord, into the town;
My scholar shall go bring them to their inn;
Meanwhile we'll see the knavery of the earl.
   PRINCE EDWARD. Warren, leave me; and, Ermsby, take the
     fool;
Let him be master, and go revel it,
Till I and Friar Bacon talk awhile.
   WARREN. We will, my lord.
   RALPH. Faith, Ned, and I'll lord it out till thou comest.
I'll be Prince of Wales over all the black-pots*   leather wine jugs
     in Oxford.

                                                 (Exeunt.)

Scene 6

(FRIAR BACON'S *cell.* FRIAR BACON *and* PRINCE EDWARD *go
into the study.*)

   BACON. Now, frolic Edward, welcome to my cell;
Here tempers* Friar Bacon many toys,*   devises/triflers
And holds this place his consistory-court,
Wherein the devils plead homage to his words.
Within this glass prospective thou shalt see

This day what's done in merry Fressingfield
'Twixt lovely Peggy and the Lincoln Earl.
    PRINCE EDWARD. Friar, thou glad'st me. Now shall Edward
    try
How Lacy meaneth to his sovereign Lord.
    BACON. Stand there and look directly in the glass.

    (*Enter* MARGARET *and* FRIAR BUNGAY.)

What sees my lord?
    PRINCE EDWARD. I see the Keeper's lovely lass appear,
As brightsome as the paramour of Mars,*   Venus
Only attended by a jolly friar.
    BACON. Sit still, and keep the crystal in your eye.
    MARGARET. But tell me, Friar Bungay, is it true
That this fair courteous country swain,
Who says his father is a farmer nigh,
Can be Lord Lacy, Earl of Lincolnshire?
    BUNGAY. Peggy, 'tis true, 'tis Lacy for my life,
Or else mine art and cunning both do fail,
Left by Prince Edward to procure his loves;
For he in green, that holp* you run your cheese,   helped
Is son to Henry, and the Prince of Wales.
    MARGARET. Be what he will, his lure is but for lust.
But did Lord Lacy like poor Margaret,
Or would he deign to wed a country lass,
Friar, I would his humble handmaid be,
And for great wealth 'quite* him with courtesy.   requite
    BUNGAY. Why, Margaret, dost thou love him?
    MARGARET. His personage, like the pride of vaunting
    Troy,*   that is, Paris
Might well avouch to shadow Helen's scape:[20]
His wit is quick and ready in conceit,*   with ideas
As Greece afforded in her chiefest prime.
Courteous, ah friar, full of pleasing smiles!
Trust me, I love too much to tell thee more;
Suffice to me he's England's paramour.
    BUNGAY. Hath not each eye that viewed thy pleasing face
Surnamed thee Fair Maid of Fressingfield?
    MARGARET. Yes, Bungay; and would God the lovely earl
Had that in *esse** that so many sought.   in actuality

[20] Might well certify to excuse Helen's transgression.

BUNGAY. Fear not, the friar will not be behind
To show his cunning to entangle love.
PRINCE EDWARD. I think the friar courts the bonny wench;[21]
Bacon, methinks he is a lusty churl.*   lustful fellow
BACON. Now look, my lord.

(*Enter* LACY.)

PRINCE EDWARD. Gog's wounds, Bacon, here comes Lacy!
FRIAR BACON. Sit still, my lord, and mark the comedy.
FRIAR BUNGAY. Here's Lacy, Margaret; step aside awhile.
(*They withdraw.*)
LACY. Daphne, the damsel that caught Phoebus* fast,   Apollo
And locked him in the brightness of her looks,
Was not so beauteous in Apollo's eyes
As is fair Margaret to the Lincoln Earl.
Recant thee, Lacy, thou art put in trust.
Edward, thy sovereign's son, hath chosen thee,
A secret friend, to court her for himself,
And dar'st thou wrong thy prince with treachery?
Lacy, love makes no exception of a friend,
Nor deems it of a prince but as a man.
Honor bids thee control him in his lust;
His wooing is not for to wed the girl,
But to entrap her and beguile the lass.
Lacy, thou lov'st, then brook not such abuse,
But wed her, and abide thy prince's frown;
For better die than see her live disgraced.
MARGARET. Come, friar, I will shake him from his
    dumps.*   depression
(*Comes forward.*)
How cheer you, sir? A penny for your thought.
You're early up, pray God it be the near.[22]
What, come from Beccles in a morn so soon?
LACY. Thus watchful are such men as live in love,
Whose eyes brook broken slumbers for their sleep.
I tell thee, Peggy, since last Harleston fair
My mind hath felt a heap of passions.
MARGARET. A trusty man, that court it for your friend.
Woo you still for the courtier all in green?
(*Aside.*) I marvel that he sues not for himself.

[21] Edward cannot hear their conversation.
[22] Favorable; cf. the proverb "Early up and never the nearer."

LACY. Peggy, I pleaded first to get your grace for him;
But when mine eyes surveyed your beauteous looks,
Love, like a wag,* straight dived into my heart,   mischievous boy
And there did shrine the idea* of yourself.   image
Pity me, though I be a farmer's son,
And measure not my riches, but my love.
 MARGARET. You are very hasty; for to garden well,
Seeds must have time to sprout before they spring:
Love ought to creep as doth the dial's shade,
For timely* ripe is rotten too too soon.   too early
 BUNGAY (*advancing*). *Deus hic;** room for a merry God here
  friar!
What, youth of Beccles, with the Keeper's lass?
'Tis well; but tell me, hear you any news?
 LACY. No, friar. What news?
 FRIAR BUNGAY. Hear you not how the pursuivants do post
With proclamations through each country-town?
 LACY. For what, gentle friar? Tell the news,
 BUNGAY. Dwell'st thou in Beccles, and hear'st not of these
  news?
Lacy, the Earl of Lincoln, is late fled
From Windsor court, disguised like a swain,*   rustic
And lurks about the country here unknown.
Henry suspects him of some treachery,
And therefore doth proclaim in every way,
That who can take the Lincoln Earl shall have,
Paid in the Exchequer, twenty thousand crowns.
 LACY. The Earl of Lincoln! Friar, thou art mad.
It was some other; thou mistak'st the man.
The Earl of Lincoln! Why, it cannot be.
 MARGARET. Yes, very well, my lord, for you are he.
The Keeper's daughter took you prisoner.
Lord Lacy, yield, I'll be your jailer once.
 PRINCE EDWARD. How familiar they be, Bacon!
 BACON. Sit still, and mark the sequel of their loves.
 LACY. Then am I double prisoner to thyself.
Peggy, I yield. But are these news in jest?
 MARGARET. In jest with you, but earnest unto me;
For-why* these wrongs do wring me at the heart.   because
Ah, how these earls and noblemen of birth
Flatter and feign to forge poor women's ill!
 LACY. Believe me, lass, I am the Lincoln Earl.
I not deny, but, 'tired thus in rags,

I lived disguised to win fair Peggy's love.

MARGARET. What love is there where wedding ends not love?

LACY. I meant, fair girl, to make thee Lacy's wife.

MARGARET. I little think that earls will stoop so low.

LACY. Say, shall I make thee countess ere I sleep?

MARGARET. Handmaid unto the earl, so please himself;
A wife in name, but servant in obedience.

LACY. The Lincoln Countess, for it shall be so;
I'll plight the bands,[23] and seal it with a kiss.

PRINCE EDWARD. Gog's wounds, Bacon, they kiss! I'll stab them.

BACON. O, hold your hands, my lord, it is the glass!

PRINCE EDWARD. Choler to see the traitors 'gree* so well   agree
Made me think the shadows substances.

BACON. 'Twere a long poniard, my lord, to reach between
Oxford and Fressingfield; but sit still and see more.

BUNGAY. Well, Lord of Lincoln, if your loves be knit,
And that your tongues and thoughts do both agree,
To avoid ensuing jars,* I'll hamper up* the match.   quarrels/fasten
I'll take my portace* forth and wed you here,   breviary
Then go to bed and seal up your desires.

LACY. Friar, content. Peggy, how like you this?

MARGARET. What likes my lord is pleasing unto me.

BUNGAY. Then hand-fast* hand, and I will to my book.   join

BACON. What sees my lord now?

PRINCE EDWARD. Bacon, I see the lovers hand in hand,
The friar ready with his portace there
To wed them both; then am I quite undone.
Bacon, help now, if e'er thy magic served;
Help, Bacon; stop the marriage now,
If devils or necromancy may suffice,
And I will give thee forty thousand crowns.

BACON. Fear not, my lord, I'll stop the jolly friar
For mumbling up* his orisons* this day.   from completing/
                                    prayers

LACY. Why speak'st not, Bungay? Friar, to thy book.

(*But* BUNGAY *is mute, crying* "Hud, hud.")

MARGARET. How look'st thou, Friar, as a man distraught?
Reft of thy senses, Bungay? Show by signs,
If thou be dumb, what passion holdeth thee.

LACY. He's dumb indeed. Bacon hath with his devils
Enchanted him, or else some strange disease

---

[23] That is, I'll pledge matrimony.

Or apoplexy hath possessed his lungs.
But, Peggy, what he cannot with his book,
We'll 'twixt us both unite it up in heart.
    MARGARET. Else let me die, my lord, a miscreant.
    PRINCE EDWARD. Why stands Friar Bungay so amazed?
    BACON. I have struck him dumb, my lord; and, if your
      honor please,
I'll fetch this Bungay straightway from Fressingfield,
And he shall dine with us in Oxford here.
    PRINCE EDWARD. Bacon, do that, and thou contentest me.
    LACY. Of courtesy, Margaret, let us lead the friar
Unto thy father's lodge, to comfort him
With broths, to bring him from this hapless* trance.   unfortunate
    MARGARET. Or else, my lord, we were passing unkind
To leave the friar so in his distress.

    (*Enter a* DEVIL, *and carries* BUNGAY *on his back.*)

O, help, my lord; A devil, a devil, my lord!
Look how he carries Bungay on his back!
Let's hence, for Bacon's spirits be abroad.
                         (*Exit with* LACY.)
    PRINCE EDWARD. Bacon, I laugh to see the jolly friar
Mounted upon the devil, and how the earl
Flees with his bonny lass for fear.
As soon as Bungay is at Brazen-nose,
And I have chatted with the merry friar,
I will in post hie me to Fressingfield,
And 'quite* these wrongs on Lacy ere 't be long.   requite, pay back
    BACON. So be it, my lord; but let us to our dinner;
For ere we have taken our repast awhile,
We shall have Bungay brought to Brazen-nose.
                         (*Exeunt.*)

Scene 7

(*The Regent-house at Oxford. Enter three* DOCTORS, BUR-
DEN, MASON *and* CLEMENT.)

    MASON. Now that we are gathered in the Regent-house,
It fits us talk about the king's repair,*   visit
For he, trooped with* all the western kings,   accompanied by
That lie alongst the Dantzic seas by east,

North by the clime of frosty Germany,
The Almain* monarch, and the Saxon duke,   German
Castile and lovely Elinor with him,
Have in their jests[24] resolved for Oxford town.

    BURDEN. We must lay plots of stately tragedies,
Strange comic shows, such as proud Roscius[25]
Vaunted before the Roman emperors,
To welcome all the western potentates.

    CLEMENT. But more; the king by letters hath foretold
That Frederick, the Almain emperor,
Hath brought with him a German of esteem,
Whose surname is Don Jaques Vandermast,
Skilful in magic and those secret arts.

    MASON. Then must we all make suit unto the friar,
To Friar Bacon, that he vouch this task,
And undertake to countervail* in skill   counterbalance
The German; else there's none in Oxford can
Match and dispute with learned Vandermast.

    BURDEN. Bacon, if he will hold the German play,
Will teach him what an English friar can do.
The devil, I think, dare not dispute with him.

    CLEMENT. Indeed, Mas'* doctor, he displeasured   master
     you,
In that he brought your hostess with her spit,
From Henley, posting unto Brazen-nose.

    BURDEN. A vengeance on the friar for his pains!
But leaving that, let's hie to Bacon straight,
To see if he will take this task in hand.

    CLEMENT. Stay, what rumor* is this? The town is up   noise
     in a mutiny.
What hurly-burly is this?

(*Enter a* CONSTABLE, *with* RALPH SIMNELL, WARREN,
ERMSBY, *all still disguised, and* MILES.)

    CONSTABLE. Nay, masters, if you were ne'er so good, you
shall before the doctors to answer your misdemeanor.

    BURDEN. What's the matter, fellow?

    CONSTABLE. Marry, sir, here's a company of ruf-
flers,* that, drinking in the tavern, have made a   troublemakers
great brawl and almost killed the vintner.

---

    [24] *Jest* = *gest,* a royal journey.
    [25] Famous actor of ancient Rome.

MILES. *Salve,** Doctor Burden!   Hail
        This lubberly lurden*   worthless fellow
        Ill-shaped and ill-faced,
        Disdained and disgraced,
        What he tells unto *vobis*
        Mentitur de nobis.[26]

BURDEN. Who is the master and chief of this crew?

MILES. *Ecce asinum mundi*
        Figura rotundi,[27]
        Neat, sheat;* and fine,   trim
        As brisk as a cup of wine.

BURDEN. What are you?

RALPH. I am, father doctor, as a man would say, the bell-wether of this company; these are my lords, and I the Prince of Wales.

CLEMENT. Are you Edward, the king's son?

RALPH. Sirrah Miles, bring hither the tapster that drew the wine, and, I warrant, when they see how soundly I have broke his head, they'll say 'twas done by no less man than a prince.

MASON. I cannot believe that this is the Prince of Wales.

WARREN. And why so, sir?

MASON. For they say the prince is a brave and a wise gentleman.

WARREN. Why, and think'st thou, doctor, that he is not so?
Dar'st thou detract and derogate from him,
Being so lovely and so brave a youth?

ERMSBY. Whose face, shining with many a sugared smile,
Bewrays* that he is bred of princely race.   reveals

MILES. And yet, master doctor,
        To speak like a proctor,
        And tell unto you
        What is veriment* and true;   truth
        To cease of this quarrel,
        Look but on his apparel;
        Then mark but my talis,
        He is great Prince of Walis,
        The chief of our *gregis,**   band
        And *filius regis,**   king's son
        Then 'ware what is done,
        For he is Henry's white* son.   darling

[26] You, he lies about us.
[27] Behold the ass of the world, round in shape.

RALPH. Doctors, whose doting night-caps are not capable
of my ingenious dignity, know that I am Edward Plantagenet,
whom if you displease will make a ship that shall hold all your
colleges, and so carry away the niniversity with a fair wind to
the Bankside in Southwark. How sayest thou, Ned Warren,
shall I not do it?

WARREN. Yes, my good lord; and, if it please your lordship,
I will gather up all your old pantofles,* and cork-soled slippers
with the cork make you a pinnace of five-hundred ton, that
shall serve the turn marvelous well, my lord.

ERMSBY. And I, my lord, will have pioners* to under- diggers
mine the town, that the very gardens and orchards be carried
away for your summer-walks.

MILES. And I, with *scientia*
  And great *diligentia,*
  Will conjure and charm,
  To keep you from harm;
  That *utrum horum mavis,*[28]
  Your very great *navis,**   ship
  Like Barclay's ship,[29]
  From Oxford do skip
  With colleges and schools,
  Full-loaden with fools.
  Quid dicis ad hoc,[30]
  Worshipful *Domine* Dawcock?*   Lord Dolt

CLEMENT. Why, hair-brained courtiers, are you drunk or
  mad,
To taunt us up with such scurrility?
Deem you us men of base and light esteem,
To bring us such a fop for Henry's son?—
Call out the beadles and convey them hence
Straight to Bocardo;[31] let the roisters lie
Close clapt in bolts, until their wits be tame.

ERMSBY. Why, shall we to prison, my lord?

RALPH. What sayest, Miles, shall I honor the prison with my
  presence?

MILES. No, no; out with your blades,
  And hamper these jades,*   worthless fellows
  Have a flurt* and a crash,   quick throw

---

[28] Which of these you prefer.
[29] *The Ship of Fools.*
[30] What do you say to this?
[31] An Oxford prison located in the old North Gate.

Now play revel-dash,*   rowdy game
And teach these sacerdos*   priests
That the Bocardos,
Like peasants and elves,
Are meet for themselves.

MASON. To the prison with them, constable.

WARREN. Well, doctors, seeing I have sported me
With laughing at these mad and merry wags,
Know that Prince Edward is at Brazen-nose,
And this, attired like the Prince of Wales,
Is Ralph, King Henry's only loved fool;
I, Earl of Sussex, and this Ermsby,
One of the privy-chamber to the king;
Who, while the prince with Friar Bacon stays,
Have reveled it in Oxford as you see.

MASON. My lord, pardon us, we knew not what you were;
But courtiers may make greater scapes* than these.   escapades
Wilt please your honor dine with me today?

WARREN. I will, Master doctor, and satisfy the vintner for
his hurt; only I must desire you to imagine him*   that is, Ralph
all this forenoon the Prince of Wales.

MASON. I will, sir.

RALPH. And upon that I will lead the way; only I will have
Miles go before me, because I have heard Henry say that
wisdom must go before majesty.

(*Exeunt.*)

Scene 8

(*Fressingfield. Enter* PRINCE EDWARD *with his poniard in
his hand,* LACY, *and* MARGARET.)

PRINCE EDWARD. Lacy, thou canst not shroud thy traitorous
      thoughts,
Nor cover, as did Cassius, all his wiles;
For Edward hath an eye that looks as far
As Lynceus[32] from the shores of Graecia.
Did not I sit in Oxford by the friar,
And see thee court the maid of Fressingfield,
Sealing thy flattering fancies* with a kiss?   amorous
Did not proud Bungay draw his portace forth,   inclinations
And joining hand in hand had married you,
If Friar Bacon had not struck him dumb,

[32] An Argonaut famed for his sharp eyesight.

And mounted him upon a spirit's back,
That we might chat at Oxford with the friar?
Traitor, what answer'st? Is not all this true?

LACY. Truth all, my lord; and thus I make reply:
At Harleston fair, there courting for your grace,
Whenas* mine eye surveyed her curious* shape,   when/exquisite
And drew the beauteous glory of her looks
To dive into the center of my heart,
Love taught me that your honor did but jest,
That princes were in fancy* but as men;   love
How that the lovely maid of Fressingfield
Was fitter to be Lacy's wedded wife
Than concubine unto the Prince of Wales.

PRINCE EDWARD. Injurious Lacy, did I love thee more
Than Alexander his Hephæstion?
Did I unfold the passions of my love,
And lock them in the closet of thy thoughts?
Wert thou to Edward second to himself,
Sole friend, and partner of his secret loves?
And could a glance of fading beauty break
Th' enchained fetters of such private friends?
Base coward, false, and too effeminate
To be corrival* with a prince in thoughts!   partner
From Oxford have I posted since I dined,
To 'quite a traitor 'fore that Edward sleep.

MARGARET. 'Twas I, my lord, not Lacy stept awry;
For oft he sued and courted for yourself,
And still wooed for the courtier all in green;
But I, whom fancy made but over-fond,*   excessively foolish
Pleaded myself with looks as if I loved;
I fed mine eye with gazing on his face,
And still bewitched loved Lacy with my looks;
My heart with sighs, mine eyes pleaded with tears,
My face held pity and content at once,
And more I could not cipher-out by signs,
But that I loved Lord Lacy with my heart.
Then, worthy Edward, measure with thy mind
If women's favors will not force men fall,
If beauty, and if darts of piercing love,
Are not of force to bury thoughts of friends.

PRINCE EDWARD. I tell thee, Peggy, I will have thy loves;
Edward or none shall conquer Margaret.

In frigates bottomed with rich Sethin* planks,   shittim
Topt with the lofty firs of Lebanon,
Stemmed and incased with burnished ivory,
And over-laid with plates of Persian wealth,
Like Thetis* shalt thou wanton* on the waves,   sea goddess/sport
And draw the dolphins to thy lovely eyes,
To dance lavoltas* in the purple streams;   lively dances
Sirens, with harps and silver psalteries,
Shall wait with music at thy frigate's stem,
And entertain fair Margaret with their lays.
England and England's wealth shall wait on thee;
Britain shall bend unto her prince's love,
And do due homage to thine excellence,
If thou wilt be but Edward's Margaret.

    MARGARET. Pardon, my lord; if Jove's great royalty
Sent me such presents as to Danæ;[33]
If Phœbus, 'tired in Latona's web,*   fabrics
Come courting from the beauty of his lodge;
The dulcet tunes of frolic Mercury,
Nor all the wealth heaven's treasury affords,
Should make me leave Lord Lacy or his love.

    PRINCE EDWARD. I have learned at Oxford, then, this point
      of schools,*—   principle of / argument
Ablata causa, tollitur effectus.[34]
Lacy, the cause that Margaret cannot love
Nor fix her liking on the English prince,
Take him away, and then th' effects will fail.
Villain, prepare thyself; for I will bathe
My poniard in the bosom of an earl.

    LACY. Rather than live, and miss fair Margaret's love,
Prince Edward, stop not at the fatal doom,*   judgment
But stab it home; end both my loves and life.

    MARGARET. Brave Prince of Wales, honored for royal deeds,
'Twere sin to stain fair Venus' courts with blood;
Love's conquest ends, my lord, in courtesy.
Spare Lacy, gentle Edward; let me die,
For so both you and he do cease your loves.

    PRINCE EDWARD. Lacy shall die as traitor to his lord.

---

[33] Jove (Zeus) fathered Danae's son Perseus. Phoebus and Mercury (in the following lines) also were sired by Zeus. Phoebus's mother was Latona and Mercury's mother, Maia.

[34] If the cause is removed, the effect is taken away.

LACY. I have deserved it, Edward; act it well.

MARGARET. What hopes the prince to gain by Lacy's death?

PRINCE EDWARD. To end the loves 'twixt him and Margaret.

MARGARET. Why, thinks King Henry's son that Margaret's love
Hangs in th' uncertain balance of proud time?
That death shall make a discord of our thoughts?
No, stab the earl, and, 'fore the morning sun .
Shall vaunt him* thrice over the lofty east,   proudly present himself
Margaret will meet her Lacy in the heavens.

LACY. If aught betides to lovely Margaret
That wrongs or wrings her honor from content,
Europe's rich wealth nor England's monarchy
Should not allure Lacy to over-live.*   live after her
Then, Edward, short my life, and end her loves.

MARGARET. Rid* me, and keep a friend worth   get rid of
many loves.

LACY. Nay, Edward, keep a love worth many friends.

MARGARET. An if thy mind be such as fame hath blazed,
Then, princely Edward, let us both abide
The fatal resolution of thy rage.
Banish thou fancy,* and embrace revenge,   love
And in one tomb knit both our carcasses,
Whose hearts were linked in one perfect love.

PRINCE EDWARD (*aside*). Edward, art thou that famous Prince of Wales,
Who at Damasco beat the Saracens,
And brought'st home triumph on thy lance's point?
And shall thy plumes be pulled by Venus down?
Is't princely to dissever lovers' leagues,
To part such friends as glory in their loves?
Leave, Ned, and make a virtue of this fault,
And further Peg and Lacy in their loves;
So in subduing fancy's passion,
Conquering thyself, thou gett'st the richest spoil.—
Lacy, rise up. Fair Peggy, here's my hand.
The Prince of Wales hath conquered all his thoughts,
And all his loves he yields unto the earl.
Lacy, enjoy the maid of Fressingfield;
Make her thy Lincoln Countess at the church,
And Ned, as he is true Plantagenet,
Will give her to thee frankly* for thy wife.   unreservedly

LACY. Humbly I take her of my sovereign,
As if that Edward gave me England's right,
And riched me with the Albion diadem.
MARGARET. And doth the English prince mean true;
Will he vouchsafe to cease his former loves,
And yield the title of a country maid
Unto Lord Lacy?
    PRINCE EDWARD. I will, fair Peggy, as I am true lord.
    MARGARET. Then, lordly sir, whose conquest is as great,
In conquering love, as Caesar's victories,
Margaret, as mild and humble in her thoughts
As was Aspasia unto Cyrus' self,[35]
Yields thanks, and, next Lord Lacy, doth enshrine
Edward the second secret in her heart.[36]
    PRINCE EDWARD. Gramercy, Peggy. Now that vows are past,
And that your loves are not to be revolt,*   overturned
Once, Lacy, friends again. Come, we will post
To Oxford; for this day the king is there,
And brings for Edward Castile Elinor.
Peggy, I must go see and view my wife;
I pray God I like her as I loved thee.
Beside, Lord Lincoln, we shall hear dispute
'Twixt Friar Bacon and learned Vandermast.
Peggy, we'll leave you for a week or two.
    MARGARET. As it please Lord Lacy; but love's foolish looks
Think footsteps miles and minutes to be hours.
    LACY. I'll hasten, Peggy, to make short return.
But please your honor go unto the lodge,
We shall have butter, cheese, and venison;
And yesterday I brought for Margaret
A lusty* bottle of neat* claret-wine;   strong/undiluted
Thus can we feast and entertain your grace.
    PRINCE EDWARD. 'Tis cheer, Lord Lacy, for an emperor,
If he respect the person and the place.
Come, let us in; for I will all this night
Ride post until I come to Bacon's cell.

                                            (*Exeunt.*)

[35] See Plutarch's Life of Artaxerxes.
[36] That is, in second place in her affection.

Scene 9

(*Oxford. Enter* KING HENRY, *the* EMPEROR, *the* KING OF CASTILE, ELINOR, VANDERMAST, *and* BUNGAY.)

EMPEROR. Trust me, Plantagenet, these Oxford schools
Are richly seated near the river-side;
The mountains full of fat and fallow deer,
The battling* pastures lade* with kine and flocks,   fertile/laden
The town gorgeous with high-built colleges,
And scholars seemly in their grave attire,
Learned in searching principles of art.
What is thy judgment, Jaques Vandermast?

VANDERMAST. That lordly are the buildings of the town,
Spacious the rooms, and full of pleasant walks;
But for the doctors, how that they be learned,
It may be meanly, for aught I can hear.

BUNGAY. I tell thee, German, Hapsburg holds none such,
None read so deep as Oxenford contains:
There are within our academic state
Men that may lecture it in Germany
To all the doctors of your Belgic* schools.   Belgian

KING HENRY. Stand to him, Bungay, charm this Vander-
    mast,
And I will use thee as a royal king.

VANDERMAST. Wherein dar'st thou dispute with me?

BUNGAY. In what a doctor and a friar can.

VANDERMAST. Before rich Europe's worthies put thou forth
The doubtful question unto Vandermast.

BUNGAY. Let it be this,—Whether the spirits of pyromancy
or geomancy be most predominant in magic?

VANDERMAST. I say, of pyromancy.

BUNGAY. And I, of geomancy.

VANDERMAST. The cabalists that write of magic spells,
As Hermes,[87] Melchie,[88] and Pythagoras,
Affirm that, 'mongst the quadruplicity
Of elemental essence,* *terra* is but thought   that is, the
To be a *punctum** squared* to the rest;   four elements
And that the compass* of ascending elements   atom/compared
Exceed in bigness as they do in height;   sizes

[87] Hermes Trismegistus.
[88] Porphyry (Malchus), a neo-Platonist.

Judging the concave circle of the sun
To hold the rest in his circumference.
If, then, as Hermes says, the fire be greatest,
Purest, and only giveth shape to spirits,
Then must these dæmones that haunt that place
Be every way superior to the rest.

   BUNGAY. I reason not of elemental shapes,
Nor tell I of the concave latitudes,
Noting their essence nor their quality,
But of the spirits that pyromancy calls,
And of the vigor of the geomantic fiends.
I tell thee, German, magic haunts the ground,
And those strange necromantic spells,
That work such shows and wondering in the world,
Are acted by those geomantic spirits
That Hermes calleth *terræ filii*.[39]
The fiery spirits are but transparent shades,
That lightly pass as heralds to bear news;
But earthly fiends, closed in the lowest deep,
Dissever mountains, if they be but charged,
Being more gross and massy* in their power.   heavy

   VANDERMAST. Rather these earthly geomantic spirits
Are dull and like the place where they remain;
For when proud Lucifer fell from the heavens,
The spirits and angels that did sin with him,
Retained their local essence as their faults,
All subject under Luna's continent.
They which offended less hung in the fire,
And second* faults did rest within the air;   that is, lesser
But Lucifer and his proud-hearted fiends
Were thrown into the center of the earth,
Having less understanding than the rest,
As having greater sin and lesser grace.
Therefore such gross and earthly spirits do serve
For jugglers, witches, and vile sorcerers;
Whereas the pyromantic genii
Are mighty, swift, and of far-reaching power.
But grant that geomancy hath most force;
Bungay, to please these mighty potentates,
Prove by some instance what thy art can do.
   BUNGAY. I will.

     [39] Sons of the earth.

EMPEROR. Now, English Harry, here begins the game;
We shall see sport between these learned men.
VANDERMAST. What wilt thou do?
BUNGAY. Show thee the tree, leaved with refined gold,
Whereon the fearful dragon held his seat,
That watched the garden called Hesperides,
Subdued and won by conquering Hercules.
   (*Here* BUNGAY *conjures, and the tree appears with the
   dragon shooting fire.*)
VANDERMAST. Well done!
KING HENRY. What say you, royal lordings, to my friar?
Hath he not done a point of cunning skill?
VANDERMAST. Each scholar in the necromantic spells
Can do as much as Bungay hath performed.
But as Alcmena's bastard razed this tree,
So will I rise him up as when he lived,
And cause him pull the dragon from his seat,
And tear the branches piecemeal from the root.
Hercules! *Prodi, prodi,** Hercules!   , come forth
   (HERCULES *appears in his lion's skin.*)
HERCULES. *Quis me vult?*[40]
VANDERMAST. Jove's bastard son, thou Libyan Hercules,
Pull off the sprigs from off th' Hesperian tree,
As once thou didst to win the golden fruit.
HERCULES. *Fiat.*[41]
   (*He begins to break the branches.*)
VANDERMAST. Now Bungay, if thou canst by magic charm
The fiend, appearing like great Hercules,
From pulling down the branches of the tree,
Then art thou worthy to be counted learned.
BUNGAY. I cannot.
VANDERMAST. Cease, Hercules, until I give thee charge.
Mighty commander of this English isle,
Henry, come from the stout Plantagenets,
Bungay is learned enough to be a friar;
But to compare with Jaques Vandermast,
Oxford and Cambridge must go seek their cells
To find a man to match him in his art.
I have given non-plus to the Paduans,
To them of Sien,* Florence, and Bologna,   Siena
Rheims, Louvain, and fair Rotterdam,

---

[40] Who wishes me?
[41] Let it be done.

Frankfort, Lutetia,* and Orleans; Paris
And now must Henry, if he do me right,
Crown me with laurel, as they all have done.

(*Enter* BACON.)

BACON. All hail to this royal company,
That sit to hear and see this strange dispute!
Bungay, how stand'st thou as a man amazed?
What, hath the German acted more than thou?
VANDERMAST. What are thou that question'st thus?
BACON. Men call me Bacon.
VANDERMAST. Lordly thou look'st, as if that thou were
learned;
Thy countenance as if science held her seat
Between the circled arches of thy brows.
KING HENRY. Now, monarchs, hath the German found his
match.
EMPEROR. Bestir thee, Jaques, take not now the foil,
Lest thou dost lose what foretime thou didst gain.
VANDERMAST. Bacon, wilt thou dispute?
BACON. No.
Unless he were more learned than Vandermast;
For yet, tell me, what hast thou done?
VANDERMAST. Raised Hercules to ruinate that tree
That Bungay mounted by his magic spells.
BACON. Set Hercules to work.
VANDERMAST. Now Hercules, I charge thee to thy task;
Pull off the golden branches from the root.
HERCULES. I dare not. See'st thou not great Bacon here,
Whose frown doth act more than my magic can?
VANDERMAST. By all the thrones, and dominations,
Virtues, powers, and mighty hierarchies,
I charge thee to obey to Vandermast.
HERCULES. Bacon, that bridles headstrong Belcephon,
And rules Asmenoth, guider of the north,
Binds me from yielding unto Vandermast.
KING HENRY. How now, Vandermast! Have you met with
your match?
VANDERMAST. Never before was't known to Vandermast
That men held devils in such obedient awe.
Bacon doth more than art, or else I fail.* am mistaken
EMPEROR. Why, Vandermast, art thou overcome?

Bacon, dispute with him, and try his skill.

BACON. I come not, monarchs, for to hold dispute
With such a novice as is Vandermast;
I came to have your royalties to dine
With Friar Bacon here in Brazen-nose;
And, for* this German troubles but the place,   since
And holds this audience with a long suspense,
I'll send him to his academy hence.
Thou Hercules, whom Vandermast did raise,
Transport the German unto Hapsburg straight,
That he may learn by travail, 'gainst* the spring,   by
More secret dooms* and aphorisms* of art.   pronouncements/
Vanish the tree, and thou away with him!   principles

(*Exit the spirit of* HERCULES, *with* VANDERMAST *and the tree.*)

EMPEROR. Why, Bacon, whither dost thou send him?

BACON. To Hapsburg; there your highness at return
Shall find the German in his study safe.

KING HENRY. Bacon, thou hast honored England with thy
  skill,
And made fair Oxford famous by thine art;
I will be English Henry to thyself.
But tell me, shall we dine with thee today?

BACON. With me, my lord; and while I fit my cheer,
See where Prince Edward comes to welcome you,
Gracious as the morning-star of Heaven.

(*Exit.*)

(*Enter* EDWARD, LACY, WARREN, *and* ERMSBY.)

EMPEROR. Is this Prince Edward, Henry's royal son?
How martial is the figure of his face!
Yet lovely and beset with amorets.*   love-kindling
                                                           looks
KING HENRY. Ned, where hast thou been?

PRINCE EDWARD. At Framlingham, my lord, to try your
  bucks
If they could 'scape the teasers* or the toil.*   that is,
But hearing of these lordly potentates   hunters/trap
Landed, and progressed up to Oxford town,
I posted to give entertain to them;
Chief to the Almain monarch; next to him,
And joint with him, Castile and Saxony
Are welcome as they may be to the English court.
Thus for the men: but see, Venus appears,

Or one that overmatcheth Venus in her shape!
Sweet Elinor, beauty's high-swelling pride,
Rich nature's glory and her wealth at once,
Fair of all fairs, welcome to Albion;
Welcome to me, and welcome to thine own,
If that thou deign'st the welcome from myself.

ELINOR. Martial Plantagenet, Henry's high-minded son,
The mark that Elinor did count her aim,
I liked thee 'fore I saw thee; now I love,
And so as in so short a time I may;
Yet so as time shall never break that so,
And therefore so accept of Elinor.

KING OF CASTILE. Fear not, my lord, this couple will agree,
If love may creep into their wanton* eyes: unmanageable
And therefore, Edward, I accept thee here,
Without suspense, as my adopted son.

KING HENRY. Let me that joy in these consorting
    greets,*   accompanying
                                                  greetings
And glory in these honors done to Ned,
Yield thanks for all these favors to my son,
And rest a true Plantagenet to all.

(*Enter* MILES *with a cloth and trenchers and salt.*)

MILES. *Salvete, omnes reges,*[42]
          That govern your *greges**   people
          In Saxony and Spain,
          In England and in Almain!
          For all this frolic rabble
          Must I cover the table
          With trenchers, salt, and cloth;
          And then look for your broth.

EMPEROR. What pleasant fellow is this?

KING HENRY. 'Tis, my lord, Doctor Bacon's poor scholar.

MILES (*aside*). My master hath made me sewer* of   waiter
these great lords; and, God knows, I am as serviceable at a
table as a sow is under an apple-tree. 'Tis no matter; their
cheer shall not be great, and therefore what skills where the salt
stand, before or behind?[43]

                                                  (*Exit.*)

[42] Greetings, all kings.
[43] What does it matter where . . . behind; an allusion to the
custom of separating the more important from the less important guests according to the position of a large saltcellar on the
table.

KING OF CASTILE. These scholars know more skill in axioms,
How to use quips and sleights of sophistry,
Than for to cover* courtly for a king.   set a table

(MILES *re-enters, bringing a mess of pottage and broth; and,
after him, comes* BACON.)

MILES. Spill, sir? Why, do you think I never carried two-
    penny chop* before in my life?   that is,
                                       a meat dish
By your leave, *nobile decus,**   your noble grace
For here comes Doctor Bacon's *pecus,**   beast
Being in his full age
To carry a mess of pottage.
    BACON. Lordings, admire* not if your cheer be this.   wonder
For we must keep our academic fare;
No riot where philosophy doth reign:
And therefore, Henry, place these potentates,
And bid them fall unto their frugal cates.*   delicacies
    EMPEROR. Presumptuous friar! What, scoff'st thou at a king?
What, dost thou taunt us with thy peasant's fare,
And give us cates* fit for country swains?   food
Henry, proceeds this jest of thy consent,
To twit us with a pittance of such price?
Tell me, and Frederick will not grieve thee long.
    KING HENRY. By Henry's honor, and the royal faith
The English monarch beareth to his friend,
I knew not of the friar's feeble fare,
Nor am I pleased he entertains you thus.
    BACON. Content thee, Frederick, for I showed the cates,
To let thee see how scholars used to feed;
How little meat refines our English wits.
Miles, take away, and let it be thy dinner.
    MILES. Marry, sir, I will.
This day shall be a festival day with me;
For I shall exceed in the highest degree.

(*Exit* MILES.)
    BACON. I tell thee, monarch, all the German peers
Could not afford thy entertainment such,
So royal and so full of majesty,
As Bacon will present to Frederick.
The basest waiter that attends thy cups
Shall be in honors greater than thyself;
And for thy cates, rich Alexandria drugs,*   spices

Fetched by carvels* from Ægypt's richest straits,   small, fast ships
Found in the wealthy strand of Africa,
Shall royalize the table of my king;
Wines richer than th' Ægyptian courtesan
Quaffed to Augustus' kingly countermatch,*   rival; that
                                                      is, Antony
Shall be caroused in English Henry's feast;
Candy* shall yield the richest of her canes;   Candia
Persia, down her Volga by canoes,
Send down the secrets of her spicery;
The Afric dates, mirabolans* of Spain,   plums
Conserves and suckets* from Tiberias,   sweetmeats
Cates from Judæa, choicer than the lamp[44]
That fired Rome with sparks of gluttony,
Shall beautify the board for Frederick:
And therefore grudge not at a friar's feast.

                                                      (*Exeunt.*)

Scene 10

(*Fressingfield. Enter two gentlemen,* LAMBERT *and* SERLS-
BY, *with the* KEEPER.)

LAMBERT. Come, frolic Keeper of our liege's game,
Whose table spread hath ever venison
And jacks* of wine to welcome passengers,   pitchers
Know I'm in love with jolly Margaret,
That overshines our damsels as the moon
Darkeneth the brightest sparkles of the night.
In Laxfield here my land and living lies;
I'll make thy daughter jointer* of it all,   jointure
So thou consent to give her to my wife;
And I can spend five hundred marks a-year.
   SERLSBY. I am the lands-lord, Keeper, of thy holds,
By copy all thy living lies in me;[45]
Laxfield did never see me raise my due;*   rent
I will enfeoff fair Margaret in all,
So she will take her to a lusty squire.

   [44] Possibly *lamprey;* possibly *torch,* meaning that the delicacies
described "are choicer than [those] which in ancient times gave
fire to [incited] Roman gluttony" (H. Spencer).
   [45] That is, your income is derived solely from my land, which
you occupy only through "copyhold"—a former type of owner-
ship of land confirmed by a copy of the manor roll establishing
the title to the land.

KEEPER. Now, courteous gentles, if the Keeper's girl
Hath pleased the liking fancy of you both,
And with her beauty hath subdued your thoughts,
'Tis doubtful to decide the question.
It joys me that such men of great esteem
Should lay their liking on this base estate,
And that her state should grow so fortunate
To be a wife to meaner men* than you.   men of
                                                         less means
But sith* such squires will stoop to keeper's fee,*   since/estate
I will, to avoid displeasure of you both,
Call Margaret forth, and she shall make her choice.
    LAMBERT. Content, Keeper; send her unto us.
                        (*Exit* KEEPER.)
Why, Serlsby, is thy wife so lately dead,
Are all thy loves so lightly passed over,
As thou canst wed before the year be out?
    SERLSBY. I live not, Lambert, to content the dead,
Nor was I wedded but for life to her;
The grave ends and begins a married state.

    (*Enter* MARGARET.)

    LAMBERT. Peggy, the lovely flower of all towns,
Suffolk's fair Helen, and rich England's star,
Whose beauty, tempered with her huswifery,
Makes England talk of merry Fressingfield!
    SERLSBY. I cannot trick it up with poesies,
Nor paint my passions with comparisons,*   similes
Nor tell a tale of Phœbus and his loves;
But this believe me,—Laxfield here is mine,
Of ancient rent seven hundred pounds a-year.
And if thou canst but love a country squire,
I will enfeoff thee, Margaret, in all.
I cannot flatter; try me, if thou please.
    MARGARET. Brave neighboring squires, the stay of Suffolks'
      clime,
A keeper's daughter is too base in 'gree*   degree
To match with men accounted of such worth;
But might I not displease, I would reply.
    LAMBERT. Say, Peggy; naught shall make us discontent.
    MARGARET. Then, gentles, note that love hath
      little stay,*   steadiness

Nor can the flames that Venus sets on fire
Be kindled but by fancy's motion.
Then pardon, gentles, if a maid's reply
Be doubtful, while* I have debated with myself,   until
Who, or of whom, love shall constrain me like.

    SERLSBY. Let it be me; and trust me, Margaret,
The meads environed with the silver streams,
Whose battling* pastures fatten all my flocks,   fertile
Yielding forth fleeces stapled with such wool*   of such quality
As Lempster* cannot yield more finer stuff,   Leominster
And forty kine with fair and burnished heads,
With strouting* dugs that paggle* to the ground,   swelling/hang
Shall serve thy dairy, if thou wed with me.

    LAMBERT. Let pass the country wealth, as flocks and kine,
And lands that wave with Ceres'* golden sheaves,   goddess of grain
Filling my barns with plenty of the fields;
But, Peggy, if thou wed thyself to me,
Thou shalt have garments of embroidered silk,
Lawns,* and rich net-works for thy head-attire.   linenlike fabrics
Costly shall be thy fair habiliments,
If thou wilt be but Lambert's loving wife.

    MARGARET. Content you, gentles, you have proffered fair,
And more than fits a country maid's degree;
But give me leave to counsel me a time
For fancy blooms not at the first assault;
Give me—but ten days' respite, and I will reply,
Which or to whom myself affectionates.

    SERLSBY. Lambert, I tell thee, thou'rt importunate;
Such beauty fits not such a base esquire;
It is for Serlsby to have Margaret.

    LAMBERT. Think'st thou with wealth to overreach me?
Serlsby, I scorn to brook thy country braves;*   boasts
I dare thee, coward, to maintain this wrong,
At dint of rapier, single in the field.

    SERLSBY. I'll answer, Lambert, what I have avouched.
Margaret, farewell; another time shall serve.

                           (Exit SERLSBY.*)*

    LAMBERT. I'll follow.—Peggy, farewell to thyself;
Listen how well I'll answer for thy love.

                           (Exit LAMBERT.*)*

    MARGARET. How fortune tempers lucky haps* with   happenings
    frowns

And wrongs me with the sweets of my delight!
Love is my bliss and love is now my bale.
Shall I be Helen in my froward* fates,   adverse
As I am Helen in my matchless hue,
And set rich Suffolk with my face afire?
If lovely Lacy were but with his Peggy,
The cloudy darkness of his bitter frown,
Would check the pride of these aspiring squires.
Before the term of ten days be expired,
Whenas* they look for answer of their loves,   when
My lord will come to merry Fressingfield,
And end their fancies and their follies both.
Till when, Peggy, be blithe and of good cheer.

(*Enter a* POST *with a letter and a bag of gold.*)

POST. Fair lovely damsel, which way leads this path?
How might I post me unto Fressingfield?
Which footpath leadeth to the Keeper's lodge?
MARGARET. Your way is ready, and this path is right;
Myself do dwell hereby in Fressingfield;
And if the Keeper be the man you seek,
I am his daughter. May I know the cause?
POST. Lovely, and once beloved of my lord,—
No marvel if his eye was lodged so low,
When brighter beauty is not in the heavens,—
The Lincoln Earl hath sent you letters here,
And, with them, just an hundred pounds in gold.
Sweet, bonny wench, read them, and make reply.
MARGARET. The scrolls that Jove sent Danaë,
Wrapt in rich closures* of fine burnished gold,   coverings
Were not more welcome than these lines to me.
Tell me, whilst that I do unrip the seals,
Lives Lacy well? How fares my lovely lord?
POST. Well, if that wealth may make men to live well.
(*Gives the letter, and* MARGARET *reads it.*)
MARGARET. The blooms of the almond-tree grow in a night,
and vanish in a morn; the flies hæmeræ,* fair Peggy,   ephemeral
take life with the sun, and die with the dew; fancy that slippeth
in with a gaze goeth out with a wink; and too timely*   premature
loves have ever the shortest length. I write this as thy grief,
and my folly, who at Fressingfield loved that which time hath

taught me to be but mean* dainties. Eyes are dis- common, cheap
semblers, and fancy is but queasy;* therefore know, hazardous
Margaret, I have chosen a Spanish lady to be my wife, chief
waiting-woman to the Princess Elinor; a lady fair, and no less
fair than thyself, honorable and wealthy. In that I forsake
thee, I leave thee to thine own liking; and for thy dowry I
have sent thee an hundred pounds; and ever assure thee of
my favor, which shall avail thee and thine much.

    Farewell.   Not thine, nor his own,
                                          EDWARD LACY.

Fond* Até, doomer of bad-boding fates,   affectionate
That wrapp'st proud Fortune in thy snaky locks,
Didst thou enchant my birthday with such stars
As lightened mischief from their infancy?
If heavens had vowed, if stars had made decree,
To show on me their froward* influence,   adverse
If Lacy had but loved, heavens, hell, and all,
Could not have wronged the patience of my mind.

    POST. It grieves me, damsel; but the earl is forced
To love the lady by the king's command.

    MARGARET. The wealth combined within the English
      shelves,*   coasts
Europe's commander, nor the English king,
Should not have moved the love of Peggy from her lord.

    POST. What answer shall I return to my lord?

    MARGARET. First, for thou cam'st from Lacy whom
      I loved,—
Ah, give me leave to sigh at every thought!
Take thou, my friend, the hundred pound he sent;
For Margaret's resolution craves no dower.
The world shall be to her as vanity;
Wealth, trash; love, hate; pleasure, despair—
For I will straight to stately Framlingham,
And in the abbey there be shorn a nun,
And yield my loves and liberty to God.
Fellow, I give thee this, not for the news,
For those be hateful unto Margaret,
But for thou'rt Lacy's man, once Margaret's love.

    POST. What I have heard, what passions I have seen,
I'll make report of them unto the earl.

    MARGARET. Say that she joys his fancies be at rest,
And prays that his misfortune may be hers.

                                          (Exeunt.)

Scene 11

(FRIAR BACON'S *cell. Enter* FRIAR BACON *drawing the curtains with a white stick, a book in his hand, and a lamp lighted by him, and the* BRAZEN HEAD, *and* MILES, *with weapons by him.*)

BACON. Miles, where are you?

MILES. Here, sir.

BACON. How chance you tarry so long?

MILES. Think you that the watching of the Brazen Head craves no furniture?* I warrant you, sir, I have so   apparatus armed myself that if all your devils come, I will not fear them an inch.

BACON. Miles, thou know's that I have dived into hell,
And sought the darkest palaces of fiends;
That with my magic spells great Belcephon
Hath left his lodge and kneeled at my cell;
The rafters of the earth rent from the poles,
And three-formed Luna[46] hid her silver looks,
Trembling upon her concave continent,
When Bacon read upon his magic book.
With seven years' tossing* necromantic charms,   turning over
Poring upon dark Hecat's* principles,   goddess of
      witchcraft
I have framed out a monstrous head of brass,
That, by the enchanting forces of the devil,
Shall tell out strange and uncouth* aphorisms,*   unknown/principles
And girt fair England with a wall of brass.
Bungay and I have watched these threescore days,
And now our vital spirits crave some rest.
If Argus lived, and had his hundred eyes,
They could not over-watch Phobetor's* night.   son of Morpheus
Now, Miles, in thee rests Friar Bacon's weal:
The honor and renown of all his life
Hangs in the watching of this Brazen Head;
Therefore I charge thee by the immortal God,
That holds the souls of men within his fist,
This night thou watch; for ere the morning-star
Sends out his glorious glister on the north,
The head will speak; then, Miles, upon thy life,

[46] Selene in heaven, Artemis on earth, Hecate in the lower world.

Wake me; for then by magic art I'll work
To end my seven years' task with excellence.
If that a wink but shut thy watchful eye,
Then farewell Bacon's glory and his fame!
Draw close the curtains, Miles: now for thy life,
Be watchful, and—

    (*Here he falls asleep.*)

    MILES. So; I thought you would talk yourself asleep anon;
and 'tis no marvel, for Bungay on the days, and he on the
nights, have watched just these ten and fifty days; now this
is the night, and 'tis my task, and no more. Now, Jesus bless
me, what a goodly head it is! And a nose! You talk of *nos
autem glorificare;*[47] but here's a nose that I warrant may be
called *nos autem populare* for the people of the parish. Well,
I am furnished with weapons; now, sir, I will set me down by
a post, and make it as good as a watchman to wake me, if
I chance to slumber. I thought, Goodman Head, I would call
you out of your *memento* . . . (*Sits down and knocks his
head.*) Passion o' God, I have almost broke my pate! Up,
Miles, to your task; take your brown-bill* in your hand; halberd
here's some of your master's hobgoblins abroad.

    (*With this a great noise is heard, and* THE HEAD *speaks.*)

    THE BRAZEN HEAD. Time is!

    MILES. Time is! Why, Master Brazen-head, have you such
a capital nose, and answer you with syllables, "Time is"?
Is this all my master's cunning, to spend seven years' study
about "Time is"? Well, sir, it may be we shall have some
better orations of it anon. Well, I'll watch you as narrowly
as ever you were watched, and I'll play with you as the
nightingale with the slow-worm; I'll set a prick against my
breast. (*Places the brown bill against his chest.*) Now rest
there, Miles. Lord have mercy upon me, I have almost killed
myself! Up, Miles; list how they rumble.

    THE BRAZEN HEAD. Time was!

    MILES. Well, Friar Bacon, you have spent your seven-years'
study well, that can make your head speak but two words at
once, "Time was." Yea, marry, time was when my master
was a wise man, but that was before he began to make the
Brazen Head. You shall lie while* your arse ache, an your until
head speak no better. Well, I will watch, and walk up and
down, and be a peripatetian and a philosopher of Aristotle's
stamp. What, a fresh noise? Take thy pistols in hand, Miles.

---

[47] Miles puns on the word *nos* with which an introit opens.

(*Here* THE HEAD *speaks, and a lightning flashes forth; and a hand appears that breaks down* THE HEAD *with a hammer.*)

THE BRAZEN HEAD. Time is past!

MILES. Master, master, up! Hell's broken loose; your head speaks; and there's such a thunder and lightning, that I warrant all Oxford is up in arms. Out of your bed, and take a brown-bill in your hand; the latter day is come.

BACON. Miles, I come. (*Rises and comes forward.*) O, passing warily watched!
Bacon will make thee next himself in love.
When spake the head?

MILES. When spake the head! Did not you say that he should tell strange principles of philosophy? Why, sir, it speaks but two words at a time.

BACON. Why, villain, hath it spoken oft?

MILES. Oft! ay, marry, hath it, thrice; but in all those three times it hath uttered but seven words.

BACON. As how?

MILES. Marry, sir, the first time he said "Time is," as if Fabius Commentator* should have pronounced a Cunctator sentence; the second-time he said "Time was"; and the third time, with thunder and lightning, as in great choler, he said, "Time is past."

BACON. 'Tis past indeed. Ah, villain! time is past.
My life, my fame, my glory, all are past.
Bacon, the turrets of thy hope are ruined down,
Thy seven years' study lieth in the dust;
Thy Brazen Head lies broken through a slave
That watched, and would not when the head did will.
What said the head first?

MILES. Even, sir, "Time is."

BACON. Villain, if thou hadst called to Bacon then,
If thou hadst watched, and waked the sleepy friar,
The Brazen Head had uttered aphorisms,
And England had been circled round with brass;
But proud Asmenoth, ruler of the north,
And Demogorgon, master of the fates,
Grudge that a mortal man should work* so much.   accomplish
Hell trembled at my deep-commanding spells,
Fiends frowned to see a man their over-match;
Bacon might boast more than a man might boast.
But now the braves* of Bacon have an end,   boasts
Europe's conceit* of Bacon hath an end,   image

His seven years' practice sorteth to* ill end: results in
.And, villain, sith* my glory hath an end,   since
I will appoint thee to some fatal end.
Villain, avoid! Get thee from Bacon's sight!
Vagrant, go roam and range about the world,
And perish as a vagabond on earth!
    MILES. Why, then, sir, you forbid me your service?
    BACON. My service, villain, with a fatal curse,
That direful plagues and mischief fall on thee.
    MILES. 'Tis no matter, I am against you with the old
proverb,—The more the fox is cursed, the better he fares.[48]
God be with you, sir. I'll take but a book in my hand, a
wide-sleeved gown on my back, and a crowned cap on my
head, and see if I can want* promotion.   lack
    BACON. Some fiend or ghost haunt on thy weary steps,
Until they do transport thee quick* to hell;   alive
For Bacon shall have never merry day,
To lose the fame and honor of his head.

                                           (Exeunt.)

Scene 12

(*Court. Enter the* EMPEROR, *the* KING OF CASTILE, KING
HENRY, ELINOR, PRINCE EDWARD, LACY, *and* RALPH SIM-
NELL.)

    EMPEROR. Now, lovely prince, the prime of Albion's wealth,
How fare the Lady Elinor and you?
What, have you courted and found Castile fit
To answer England in equivalence?
Will't be a match 'twixt bonny Nell and thee?
    PRINCE EDWARD. Should Paris enter in the courts of Greece,
And not lie fettered in fair Helen's looks?
Or Phœbus 'scape those piercing amorets*   love glances
That Daphne glanced at his deity?
Can Edward, then, sit by a flame and freeze,
Whose heat puts Helen and fair Daphne down?
Now, monarchs, ask the lady if we 'gree.
    KING HENRY. What, madam, hath my son found grace
      or no?
    ELINOR. Seeing, my lord, his lovely counterfeit,*   picture
And hearing how his mind and shape agreed,

    [48] Miles puns on *coursed* (*pursued*) and *fares* (*goes*).

I came not, trooped with all this warlike train,
Doubting of love, but so affectionate
As* Edward hath in England what he won in Spain.   that
> KING OF CASTILE. A match, my lord; these wantons*   lively ones
>   needs must love;

Men must have wives, and women will be wed.
Let's haste the day to honor up the rites.
> RALPH. Sirrah Harry, shall Ned marry Nell?
> KING HENRY. Ay, Ralph; how then?
> RALPH. Marry, Harry, follow my counsel. Send for Friar
Bacon to marry them, for he'll so conjure him and her with
his necromancy, that they shall love together like pig and lamb
whilst they live.
> KING OF CASTILE. But hearest thou, Ralph, art thou content
>   to have Elinor to thy lady?
> RALPH. Ay, so she will promise me two things.
> KING OF CASTILE. What's that, Ralph?
> RALPH. That she will never scold with Ned, nor fight with
>   me.—

Sirrah Harry, I have put her down with a thing unpossible.
> KING HENRY. What's that, Ralph?
> RALPH. Why, Harry, didst thou ever see that a woman could
both hold her tongue and her hands? No; but when egg-pies
grow on apple-trees, then will thy gray mare prove a bag-
piper.
> EMPEROR. What say the Lord of Castile and the Earl of Lin-
coln, that they are in such earnest and secret talk?
> KING OF CASTILE. I stand, my lord, amazed at his talk,

How he discourseth of the constancy
Of one surnamed, for beauty's excellence,
The Fair Maid of merry Fressingfield.
> KING HENRY. 'Tis true, my lord, 'tis wondrous for to hear;

Her beauty passing Mars's paramour,*   Venus
Her virgin's right as rich as Vesta's* was.   virgin goddess
Lacy and Ned have told me miracles.
> KING OF CASTILE. What says Lord Lacy? Shall she be his
>   wife?
> LACY. Or else Lord Lacy is unfit to live.

May it please your highness give me leave to post
To Fressingfield, I'll fetch the bonny girl,
And prove, in true appearance at the court,
What I have vouched often with my tongue.
> KING HENRY. Lacy, go to the 'querry* of my stable,   equerry

And take such coursers as shall fit thy turn;

Hie thee to Fressingfield, and bring home the lass;
And, for* her fame flies through the English coast,   because
If it may please the Lady Elinor,
One day shall match your excellence and her.

 ELINOR. We Castile ladies are not very coy;*   distant
Your highness may command a greater boon;
And glad were I to grace the Lincoln Earl
With being partner of his marriage-day.

 PRINCE EDWARD. Gramercy, Nell, for I do love the lord,
As he that's second to thyself in love.

 RALPH. You love her?—Madame Nell, never believe him
you, though he swears he loves you.

 ELINOR. Why, Ralph?

 RALPH. Why, his love is like unto a tapster's glass that is
broken with every touch; for he loved the fair maid of Fressingfield once out of all ho*—Nay, Ned, never wink   greatly
upon me; I care not, I.

 KING HENRY. Ralph tells all; you shall have a good
  secretary* of him.   confidant
But, Lacy, haste thee post* to Fressingfield;   quickly
For ere thou hast fitted all things for her state,
The solemn marriage-day will be at hand.

 LACY. I go, my lord.

             (Exit.)

 EMPEROR. How shall we pass this day, my lord?

 KING HENRY. To horse, my lord; the day is passing fair,
We'll fly the partridge, or go rouse the deer.
Follow, my lords; you shall not want for sport.

            (Exeunt.)

Scene 13

(FRIAR BACON'S *cell. Enter* FRIAR BACON *with* FRIAR BUN-
GAY *to his cell.*)

 BUNGAY. What means the friar that frolicked it of late
To sit as melancholy in his cell
As if he had neither lost nor won today?

 BACON. Ah, Bungay, . . . my Brazen Head is spoiled,
My glory gone, my seven years' study lost!
The fame of Bacon, bruited through the world,
Shall end and perish with this deep disgrace.

 BUNGAY. Bacon hath built foundation of his fame
So surely on the wings of true report,

With* acting* strange and uncouth* miracles,   by/performing/
                                                 unusual
As this cannot infringe what he deserves.

    BACON. Bungay, sit down, for by prospective* skill   that is,
                                                            prophesying
I find this day shall fall out ominous;

Some deadly act shall 'tide* me ere I sleep;   betide

But what and wherein little can I guess.

    BUNGAY. My mind is heavy, whatsoe'er shall hap.

(*Enter* TWO SCHOLARS, *sons of* LAMBERT *and* SERLSBY.)

    BACON. Who's that knocks?

    BUNGAY. Two scholars that desire to speak with you.

    BACON. Bid them come in.

Now, my youths, what would you have?

    FIRST SCHOLAR. Sir, we are Suffolk-men and neighboring
        friends;

Our fathers in their countries lusty squires;

Their lands adjoin; in Cratfield mine doth dwell,

And his in Laxfield. We are college-mates,

Sworn brothers, as our fathers live as friends.

    BACON. To what end is all this?

    SECOND SCHOLAR. Hearing your worship kept within your
        cell

A glass prospective, wherein men might see

Whatso their thoughts or hearts' desire could wish,

We come to know how that our fathers fare.

    BACON. My glass is free for every honest man.

Sit down, and you shall see ere long, how

Or in what state your friendly fathers live.

Meanwhile, tell me your names.

    FIRST SCHOLAR. Mine Lambert.

    SECOND SCHOLAR. And mine Serlsby.

    BACON. Bungay, I smell there will be a tragedy.

(*Enter* LAMBERT *and* SERLSBY *with rapiers and daggers.*)

    LAMBERT. Serlsby, thou hast kept thine hour like a man;

Thou'rt worthy of the title of a squire,

That durst, for proof of thy affection

And for thy mistress' favor, prize* thy blood.   risk

Thou know'st what words did pass at Fressingfield,

Such shameless braves* as manhood cannot brook.   boasts

Ay, for I scorn to bear such piercing taunts,

Prepare thee, Serlsby; one of us will die.

    SERLSBY. Thou see'st I single meet thee in the field,
And what I spake, I'll maintain with my sword.
Stand on thy guard, I cannot scold it out.
An if thou kill me, think I have a son,
That lives in Oxford in the Broadgates-hall,
Who will revenge his father's blood with blood.

    LAMBERT. And, Serlsby, I have there a lusty boy,
That dares at weapon buckle with thy son,
And lives in Broadgates too, as well as thine.
But draw thy rapier, for we'll have a bout.

    BACON. Now, lusty younkers,* look within the   young gentlemen
    glass,
And tell me if you can discern your sires.

    FIRST SCHOLAR. Serlsby, 'tis hard; thy father offers wrong,
To combat with my father in the field.

    SECOND SCHOLAR. Lambert, thou liest, my father's is th'
    abuse,*   injury
And thou shalt find it, if my father harm.*   come to harm

    BUNGAY. How goes it, sirs?

    FIRST SCHOLAR. Our fathers are in combat hard by Fressing-
    field.

    BACON. Sit still, my friends, and see the event.

    LAMBERT. Why stand'st thou, Serlsby? Doubt'st thou of thy
    life?
A veney,* man! Fair Margaret craves so much.   bout

    SERLSBY. Then this for her.

    FIRST SCHOLAR. Ah, well thrust!

    SECOND SCHOLAR. But mark the ward.*   parry
    (LAMBERT *and* SERLSBY *fight and kill each other.*)

    LAMBERT. O, I am slain!
    (*Dies.*)

    SERLSBY. And I,—Lord have mercy on me!
    (*Dies.*)

    FIRST SCHOLAR. My Father slain!—Serlsby, ward that.

    SECOND SCHOLAR. And so is mine!—Lambert, I'll 'quite thee
    well.
    (*The* TWO SCHOLARS *stab one another and die.*)

    BUNGAY. O strange stratagem!*   deed of
                                            violence

    BACON. See, friar, where the fathers both lie dead!
Bacon, thy magic doth effect this massacre.
This glass prospective worketh many woes;
And therefore seeing these brave lusty Brutes,*   Britons
These friendly youths, did perish by thine art,

End all thy magic and thine art at once.
The poniard that did end their fatal* lives,   fated
Shall break the cause efficient of* their woes.   effecting
So fade the glass, and end with it the shows
That necromancy did infuse the crystal with.
    (*He breaks the glass.*)
    BUNGAY. What means learned Bacon thus to break his glass?
    BACON. I tell thee, Bungay, it repents me sore
That ever Bacon meddled in this art.
The hours I have spent in pyromantic spells,
The fearful tossing* in the latest night   turning over
Of papers full of necromantic charms,
Conjuring and adjuring devils and fiends,
With stole and alb and strong pentagonon;
The wresting of the holy name of God,[49]
As Sother, Eloim, and Adonai,
Alpha, Manoth, and Tetragrammaton,
With praying to the five-fold powers of heaven,
Are instances* that Bacon must be damned   reasons
For using devils to countervail* his God.   equal
Yet, Bacon, cheer thee, drown not in despair;
Sins have their salves, repentance can do much.
Think Mercy sits where Justice holds her seat,
And from those wounds those bloody Jews did pierce,
Which by thy magic oft did bleed afresh,
From thence for thee the dew of mercy drops,
To wash the wrath of high Jehovah's ire,
And make thee as a new-born babe from sin.
Bungay, I'll spend the remnant of my life
In pure devotion, praying to my God
That he would save what Bacon vainly lost.

                            (*Exeunt.*)

Scene 14

    (*Fressingfield. Enter* MARGARET *in nun's apparel, the* KEEPER, *her father, and their* FRIEND.)

    KEEPER. Margaret, be not so headstrong in these vows;
O, bury not such beauty in a cell,
That England hath held famous for the hue!
Thy father's hair, like to the silver blooms

      [49] These lines refer to twisting variations of the name of God in order to make pentacles (magical symbols).

That beautify the shrubs of Africa,
Shall fall before the dated time of death,
Thus to forego his lovely Margaret.
    MARGARET. Ah, father, when the harmony of heaven
Soundeth the measures of a lively faith,
The vain illusions of this flattering world
Seem odious to the thoughts of Margaret.
I loved once,—Lord Lacy was my love,
And now I hate myself for that I loved,
And doted more on him than on my God,
For this I scourge myself with sharp repents.
But now the touch of such aspiring sins
Tells me all love is lust but love of heavens;
That beauty used for love is vanity.
The world contains naught but alluring baits,
Pride, flattery, and inconstant thoughts.
To shun the pricks of death, I leave the world,
And vow to meditate on heavenly bliss,
To live in Framlingham a holy nun,
Holy and pure in conscience and in deed;
And for to wish all maids to learn of me
To seek heaven's joy before earth's vanity.
    FRIEND. And will you, then, Margaret, be shorn a nun, and
so leave us all?
    MARGARET. Now farewell world, the engine of all woe!
Farewell to friends and father! Welcome Christ!
Adieu to dainty robes! This base attire
Better befits an humble mind to God
Than all the show of rich habiliments.
Farewell, O love! and, with fond love, farewell
Sweet Lacy, whom I loved once so dear!
Ever be well, but never in my thoughts,
Lest I offend to think on Lacy's love:
But even to that, as to the rest, farewell!

    (*Enter* LACY, WARREN, *and* ERMSBY, *booted and spurred.*)

    LACY. Come on, my wags, we're near the Keeper's lodge.
Here have I oft walked in the watery meads,
And chatted with my lovely Margaret.
    WARREN. Sirrah Ned, is not this the Keeper?
    LACY. 'Tis the same.
    ERMSBY. The old lecher hath gotten holy mutton* loose woman
    to him; a nun, my lord.

LACY. Keeper, how far'st thou? Holla, man, what cheer?
How doth Peggy, thy daughter and my love?

KEEPER. Ah, good my lord! O, woe is me for Peggy!
See where she stands clad in her nun's attire,
Ready for to be shorn in Framlingham;
She leaves the world because she left your love.
O, good my lord, persuade her if you can!

LACY. Why, how now, Margaret! What, a malcontent?
A nun? What holy father taught you this,
To ask yourself to such a tedious life
As die a maid? 'Twere injury to me,
To smother up such beauty in a cell.

MARGARET. Lord Lacy, thinking of thy former miss,[50]
How fond* the prime of wanton years were spent   foolishly
In love (O, fie upon that fond conceit,
Whose hap and essence hangeth in the eye!),
I leave both love and love's content at once,
Betaking me to Him that is true love,
And leaving all the world for love of Him.

LACY. Whence, Peggy, comes this metamorphosis?
What, shorn a nun, and I have from the court
Posted with coursers to convey thee hence
To Windsor, where our marriage shall be kept!
Thy wedding-robes are in the tailor's hands.
Come, Peggy, leave these peremptory vows.

MARGARET. Did not my lord resign his interest,
And make divorce 'twixt Margaret and him?

LACY. 'Twas but to try sweet Peggy's constancy.
But will fair Margaret leave her love and lord?

MARGARET. Is not heaven's joy before earth's fading bliss,
And life above sweeter than life in love?

LACY. Why, then, Margaret will be shorn a nun?

MARGARET. Margaret hath made a vow which may not be
revoked.

WARREN. We cannot stay, my lord; an if she be so strict,
Our leisure grants us not to woo afresh.

ERMSBY. Choose you, fair damsel; yet the choice is yours:
Either a solemn nunnery or the court,
God or Lord Lacy. Which contents you best,
To be a nun or else Lord Lacy's wife?

LACY. A good motion.*—Peggy, your answer must   proposal
be short.

[50] That is, your former mistaken love for me.

MARGARET. The flesh is frail; my lord doth know it well
That when he comes with his enchanting face,
Whatsoe'er betide, I cannot say him nay.
Off goes the habit* of a maiden's heart,   garb
And, seeing fortune will, fair Framlingham,
And all the show of holy nuns, farewell!
Lacy for me, if he will be my lord.

LACY. Peggy, thy lord, thy love, thy husband.
Trust me, by truth of knighthood, that the king
Stays for to marry matchless Elinor,
Until I bring thee richly to the court,
That one day may both marry her and thee.
How say'st thou, Keeper? Art thou glad of this?

KEEPER. As if the English king had given
The park and deer of Fressingfield to me.

ERMSBY. I pray thee, my Lord of Sussex, why art thou in a
        brown study?*   meditative

WARREN. To see the nature of women; that be they never
        so near
God, yet they love to die in a man's arms.

LACY. What have you fit for breakfast? We have hied
And posted all this night to Fressingfield.

MARGARET. Butter and cheese, and umbles[51] of a deer,
Such as poor keepers have within their lodge.

LACY. And not a bottle of wine?

MARGARET. We'll find one for my lord.

LACY. Come, Sussex, let us in; we shall have more,
For she speaks least, to hold her promise sure.

                                                          (*Exeunt.*)

Scene 15

(FRIAR BACON's *cell. Enter a* DEVIL *to seek* MILES.)

DEVIL. How restless are the ghosts of English spirits
When every charmer with his magic spells
Calls us from nine-fold-trenched Phlegethon,*   underworld river
To scud and over-scour the earth in post
Upon the speedy wings of swiftest winds!
Now Bacon hath raised me from the darkest deep,
To search about the world for Miles his man,
For Miles, and to torment his lazy bones

---

[51] Numbles: heart, liver, kidneys, etc.

For careless watching of his Brazen Head.
See where he comes. O, he is mine.

(*Enter* MILES *with a gown and a corner-cap.**)   academic cap

MILES. A scholar, quoth you! Marry, sir, I would I had been
a bottle-maker when I was made a scholar; for I can get neither
to be a deacon, reader, nor schoolmaster, no, not the clerk of a
parish. Some call me a dunce; another saith, my head is as full
of Latin as an egg's full of oatmeal. Thus I am tormented,
that the devil and Friar Bacon haunt me.—Good Lord, here's
one of my master's devils! I'll go speak to him.—What, Master Plutus, how cheer you?

DEVIL. Dost thou know me?

MILES. Know you, sir! Why, are not you one of my master's devils, that were wont to come to my master, Doctor
Bacon, at Brazen-nose?

DEVIL. Yes, marry, am I.

MILES. Good Lord, Master Plutus, I have seen you a thousand times at my master's, and yet I had never the manners to
make you drink. But, sir, I am glad to see how conformable
you are to the statute.[52] (*To the audience.*) I warrant you, he's
as yeomanly a man as you shall see; mark you, masters, here's
a plain, honest man, without welt or guard.*—But I pray   lacings
you sir, do you come lately from hell?

DEVIL. Ay, marry; how then?

MILES. Faith, 'tis a place I have desired long to see. Have
you not good tippling-houses there? May not a man have a
lusty fire there, a pot of good ale, a pair* of cards, a   pack
swinging piece of chalk,[53] and a brown toast that will clap a
white waistcoat* on a cup of good drink?   foam

DEVIL. All this you may have there.

MILES. You are for me, friend, and I am for you. But I pray
you, may I not have an office there?

DEVIL. Yes, a thousand. What wouldst thou be?

MILES. By my troth, sir, in a place where I may profit myself. I know hell is a hot place, and men are marvelous dry,
and much drink is spent there; I would be a tapster.

DEVIL. Thou shalt.

MILES. There's nothing lets* me from going with you,   stops
but that 'tis a long journey, and I have never a horse.

---

[52] The statute against wearing dress above one's station.
[53] *Swinging:* large—the chalk was used to keep a record of the
ale bought on credit.

DEVIL. Thou shalt ride on my back.

MILES. Now surely here's a courteous devil, that, for to pleasure his friend, will not stick to make a jade of himself.— But I pray you, goodman friend, let me move a question to you.

DEVIL. What's that?

MILES. I pray you, whether is your pace a trot or an amble?

DEVIL. An amble.

MILES. 'Tis well; but take heed it be not a trot. But 'tis no matter, I'll prevent it.

DEVIL. What dost?

MILES. Marry, friend, I put on my spurs; for if I find your pace either a trot or else uneasy, I'll put you to a false gallop;* I'll make you feel the benefit of my spurs.   canter

DEVIL. Get up upon my back.

MILES. O Lord, here's even a goodly marvel, when a man rides to hell on the devil's back!

                              (*Exeunt, roaring.*)

Scene 16

(*The Court. Enter the* EMPEROR *with a pointless sword;*[54] *next the* KING OF CASTILE *carrying a sword with a point;*[55] LACY *carrying the Globe;* PRINCE EDWARD; WARREN *carrying a rod of gold with a dove on it;*[56] ERMSBY *with a crown and scepter;* PRINCESS ELINOR *with the fair maid of Fressingfield on her left hand;* KING HENRY; BACON; *with other* LORDS *attending.*)

PRINCE EDWARD. Great potentates, earth's miracles for state,
Think that Prince Edward humbles at your feet,
And, for these favors, on his martial sword
He vows perpetual homage to yourselves,
Yielding these honors unto Elinor.

KING HENRY. Gramercies, lordings; old Plantagenet,
That rules and sways the Albion diadem,
With tears discovers these conceived joys,
And vows requital, if his men-at-arms,
The wealth of England, or due honors done
To Elinor, may 'quite* his favorites.   requite
But all this while what say you to the dames
That shine like to the crystal lamps of heaven?

[54] Sword of mercy.
[55] Sword of justice.
[56] "Rod of equity."

EMPEROR. If but a third were added to these two,
They did surpass those gorgeous images
That gloried Ida with rich beauty's wealth.[57]

MARGARET. 'Tis I, my lords, who humbly on my knee
Must yield her orisons* to mighty Jove   prayers
For lifting up his handmaid to this state;
Brought from her homely cottage to the court,
And graced with kings, princes, and emperors,
To whom (next to the noble Lincoln Earl)
I vow obedience, and such humble love
As may a handmaid to such mighty men.

PRINCESS ELINOR. Thou martial man that wears the Almain
     crown,
And you the western potentates of might,
The Albion princess, English Edward's wife,
Proud that the lovely star of Fressingfield,
Fair Margaret, Countess to the Lincoln Earl,
Attends on Elinor,—gramercies, lord, for her,—
'Tis I give thanks for Margaret to you all,
And rest* for her due bounden to yourselves.   remain

KING HENRY. Seeing the marriage is solemnized,
Let's march in triumph to the royal feast.—
But why stands Friar Bacon here so mute?

BACON. Repentant for the follies of my youth,
That magic's secret mysteries misled,
And joyful that this royal marriage
Portends such bliss unto this matchless realm.

KING HENRY. Why, Bacon,
What strange event shall happen to this land?
Or what shall grow from Edward and his queen?

BACON. I find by deep prescience of mine art,
Which once I tempered in my secret cell,
That here where Brute[58] did build his Troynovant,*   London
From forth the royal garden of a king
Shall flourish out so rich and fair a bud,[59]
Whose brightness shall deface proud Phœbus' flower,
And over-shadow Albion with her leaves.
Till then Mars shall be master of the field,

[57] The Judgment of Paris, involving the goddesses Aphrodite, Hera, and Pallas Athena, took place on Mount Ida.

[58] Brute: the legendary Brutus of Troy, thought to be the first king of Britain.

[59] Elizabeth I. She was a descendant of Henry III through the line of John of Gaunt.

But then the stormy threats of wars shall cease;
The horse shall stamp as careless of the pike,
Drums shall be turned to timbrels of delight;
With wealthy favors plenty shall enrich
The strand that gladded wandering Brute to see,
And peace from heaven shall harbor in these leaves
That gorgeous beautify this matchless flower;
Apollo's heliotropion* then shall stoop,   heliotrope
And Venus' hyacinth shall vail* her top;   lower
Juno shall shut her gilliflowers up,
And Pallas' bay shall 'bash her brightest green;
Ceres' carnation, in consort* with those,   company
Shall stoop and wonder at Diana's rose.
    KING HENRY. This prophecy is mystical.
But, glorious commanders of Europa's love,
That make fair England like that wealthy isle
Circled with Gihon and swift Euphrates,
In royalizing Henry's Albion
With presence of your princely mightiness,
Let's march: the tables all are spread,
And viands, such as England's wealth affords,
Are ready set to furnish out the boards.
You shall have welcome, mighty potentates;
It rests* to furnish up this royal feast,   remains
Only your hearts be frolic; for the time
Craves that we taste of naught but jouissance.*   enjoyment
Thus glories England over all the west.
                         (*Exeunt omnes.*)

Omne tulit punctum qui miscuit utile dulci.[60]

[60] "He has won every vote who has combined profit with pleasure."—Horace.

Doctor Faustus

BY CHRISTOPHER MARLOWE

More is known about Christopher Marlowe (1564–93) than about most other Elizabethan playwrights. The son of a master shoemaker in the cathedral city of Canterbury, he received an excellent classical education there at the King's School before going up to Cambridge. After distinguishing himself as a university student, he went on missions to the Continent for Walsingham, the head of Elizabeth's secret service, and gained the esteem of distinguished Elizabethan personages as well as the admiration of some of his fellow writers. Shakespeare apostrophized him after his untimely death in 1593 in *As You Like It,* quoting a line from the dead poet's unfinished narrative masterpiece, *Hero and Leander* (completed by George Chapman in 1598), when Rosalind exclaims,

> Dear shepherd, now I find thy saw of might,
> "Who ever loved that loved not at first sight?"

There is nevertheless not enough data to build a reliable analysis of Marlowe's work on a biographical foundation. It is reasonably certain that he was a young man of high spirits and intellectual daring who acquired notoriety in his day as a brawler and "atheist." (At a later date he might have been described, perhaps more correctly, as an agnostic or "free-thinker" rather than as an atheist.) A minority view, entertained by such scholars as Roy W. Battenhouse (*Marlowe's Tamburlaine: A Study in Renaissance Moral Philosophy,* Nashville, Tenn., 1941) and Douglas Cole (*Suffering and Evil in the Plays of Christopher Marlowe,* Princeton, N. J., 1962), has tried to redeem him for religious orthodoxy. But it is far more likely that Marlowe earned his reputation as a free-thinker, or as an iconoclast, innovator, and essentially original thinker and artist, as Harry Levin has cogently defined him in his distinguished book *The Overreacher: A Study of Christopher Marlowe* (Cambridge, Mass., 1952). Earlier studies,

231

such as Una Ellis-Fermor's *Christopher Marlowe* (London, 1926) and Paul H. Kocher's *Christopher Marlowe, A Study of His Thought, Learning, and Character* (Chapel Hill, N. C., 1946), also opted for the romantic view of Marlowe as a skeptic and a Byronic figure.

A list of charges drawn up against him by a disreputable informer Richard Baines should not be taken at face value but should not be entirely ignored. The fact that only his death in a tavern in the village of Deptford near London saved Marlowe from interrogation by the Star Chamber confirms the impression many passages in his plays would have created—that he was at least strongly drawn to unorthodox opinions. Of all his plays and poems, *Doctor Faustus* confirms this viewpoint most, even if Faustus is punished for resorting to magic and selling his soul to the devil, as well as for being incapable of believing in the mercy of God.

Marlowe's first produced work, the two-part chronicle play, *Tamburlaine* (1587–88), concerned itself and evidently showed empathy with an amoral conqueror whom Marlowe endowed with a poet's sensibility in his worship of success and kingship (*Tamburlaine* has been called "an archetypal Noble Savage"). Other plays which may have been written between *Tamburlaine* and *Doctor Faustus,* most notably *The Jew of Malta* (1588–89?), were also involved with the theme of evil in conflict with morality. With *The Jew of Malta* we are drawn into the world of the grotesque, whether we regard the play as essentially melodrama or, as T. S. Eliot surmised, as farce. Here the protagonist is a much put-upon but insatiably revengeful merchant, who despite his boundless villainy is something of a poet—at least about riches—and a man of spirit. In view of the strength of this character study, it is especially regrettable that the only extant manuscript of the play is so corrupt.

With *Doctor Faustus* we ascend into the world of tragedy. In *Doctor Faustus* the protagonist is also materialistic up to a point, in that he uses magic to satisfy a desire for power; but Faustus is essentially a quasi-Promethean figure, consumed with a passion to know the secrets of the universe and to gain mastery of its powers. Faustus is, so to speak, the new man of the Renaissance, a synthesis of humanist and scientist in a still superstitious world. His tragedy as an overreaching scholar-poet is what the play unfolds. In the nature of his aims, personality, inner struggles, and ultimate fate Faustus straddles the Middle Ages and the modern world, and his errors and defeat stem from his transitional role: his flight is Icarian; he flies recklessly into the sun of knowledge and consequently falls into the pit of damnation. But in his impatience with the limitations of human knowledge, in the boldness of his attempt to soar above the bounds of ordinary ambition and accomplishment, Faustus has a captivating magnificence as a stage character. And he appears in the proper frame of a Moralitylike drama, in which a man's soul is at stake.

A spiritualized and intellectualized Tamburlaine, Marlowe's wonder-working hero is endowed with suitable language for daring inquiry and high spirit. In spite of the scenes of Faustus' anguish, his struggle with Christian conscience, and the dire ending, the play is in its best passages, such as the rhapsody on Helen, a work of reckless rapture and soaring imagination. Marlowe amply deserved the tribute paid him (for *Hero and Leander,* actually, rather than for his plays) by the contemporary poet Michael Drayton:

> Marlowe, bathed in the Thespian springs,
> Had in him those brave translunary things
> That our first poets had: his raptures were
> All air and fire, which made his verse clear.
> For that fine madness still he did retain
> Which rightly should possess a poet's brain.

Doctor Faustus, however, has properly earned other designations. It is a play of wonder—or, as the Elizabethans would say, "bewonderment"—and, bearing on such scenes as the last, a tragedy of "awe." As C. L. Barber puts it (in *Tulane Drama Review,* summer 1964): ". . . in presenting a search for magical dominion, Marlowe makes blasphemy a Promethean enterprise, heroic and tragic, an expression of the Renaissance." After making allowances for some of the horseplay, uncertainly ascribed to Marlowe, and the mangled text that has come down to us, one can only conclude that *Doctor Faustus* is the first great English tragedy.

J. G.

Authorship. Christopher Marlowe is credited with the authorship of the play; however, the prose farce scenes and certain blank-verse scenes appear to be the work of another writer. Scholarly consensus holds that Marlowe worked with an unknown collaborator or collaborators, but that the design of the play is Marlowe's. Candidates for collaboration are Thomas Nashe, Samuel Rowley, and Thomas Dekker, but insufficient evidence exists to pinpoint any Elizabethan dramatist.

Date. In the absence of documentary evidence to establish a date, two theories have been considered. One holds that *Doctor Faustus* was written early in Marlowe's brief career, c. 1588-89. The other that the play came at the end of his career, in 1592 or 1593. Modern scholarship tends to support this latter dating, although the question remains open.

Text and Publishing Data. The earliest extant edition of *The Tragicall History of D. Faustus* is the quarto of 1604, of which only one copy has survived. Inasmuch as the play was entered in the Stationers' Register in January 1601, there is a strong probability that earlier editions existed. Thomas Bushell, who published the 1604 quarto—known as the A-text—transferred his copyright to John Wright, who in 1609 brought out a reprint edition with the title expanded to *The Tragicall History of the Horrible Life and Death of Doctor Faustus.* This text was reissued in 1611. It and its predecessors are known as A1, A2, and A3. In 1616 Wright published a different version entitled *The Tragicall History of the Life and Death of Doctor Faustus.* This text, known as the B-text, was reissued in five subsequent editions: 1619, 1620, 1624, 1628, and 1631. No significant differences appear in these various B-text editions.

The A-text is shorter than the B, containing 1517 lines against 2121. In November 1602, Philip Henslowe paid William Birde and Samuel Rowley four pounds for additions to *Doctor Faustus,* but scholars, mainly through the studies of W. W. Greg, discount these additions as the explanation for the longer text. At present the B-text is considered closer to the original version of the play, the A-text being a cut-down, inferior version made before the 1602 additions (now apparently lost). The A-text, therefore, may be a "bad" quarto. The present text relies mainly on the B-text.

Sources. The historical Johannes Faustus was a German itinerant scholar and magician active around 1510-40. Gradually his reputation spread, and legends grew up describing his activities. In 1587 a book entitled *Historia von D. Johann Fausten* by an anonymous author was published in Frankfurt-am-Main. Within a few years it was translated into English by one P. F., who has never been further identified. P. F.'s version, entitled *The Historie of the Damnable Life, and Deserved Death of Doctor John Faustus,* contains passages which do not appear in the German text. Marlowe's *Doctor*

Faustus is based on the *Damnable Life* with some minor material drawn from contemporary witchcraft literature and from John Foxe's *Acts and Monuments*. The English version of the Faust story, which appeared in 1592, and the dating problem are closely entwined, for on the interpretation of complicated bibliographical information dealing with the publication of the *Damnable Life* hangs most of the case for making the play early or late Marlowe.

Stage History. The play was popular. Nine quarto editions appeared through 1631. Its first recorded stage performance occurred at the Rose, where the Lord Admiral's Men presented it in September 1594. Inasmuch as Henslowe did not mark this performance as "new" in his *Diary*, earlier performances had probably taken place. There is a continuous record of performances from 1594 through 1597. Sporadic records indicate that *Doctor Faustus* was revived periodically until the closing of the theaters during the Commonwealth period. It was back in the repertory during the Restoration and then disappeared from the stage until the nineteenth century. At that time it ran into serious competition from Goethe's *Faust* and various operatic versions. *Doctor Faustus* came into its own again in the early twentieth century and has since had a fairly frequent record of amateur and professional revivals throughout the world. In Elizabethan times the great actor-manager Edward Alleyn played Faustus.

W. G.

THE TRAGICAL HISTORY OF DOCTOR FAUSTUS

BY CHRISTOPHER MARLOWE

DRAMATIS PERSONAE

THE CHORUS
DOCTOR FAUSTUS
WAGNER, his servant
VALDES } friends to
CORNELIUS } Faustus
THREE SCHOLARS
AN OLD MAN
THE POPE
RAYMOND, King of Hungary
BRUNO, the rival Pope
TWO CARDINALS
ARCHBISHOP OF RHEIMS
CARDINAL OF LORRAINE
CHARLES V, Emperor of
   Germany
MARTINO }
FREDERICK } Gentlemen
BENVOLIO } of his Court
A KNIGHT
DUKE OF SAXONY
DUKE OF ANHOLT [Vanholt]
DUCHESS OF ANHOLT
   [Vanholt]

BISHOPS, MONKS, FRIARS,
   SOLDIERS and ATTENDANTS
ROBIN, an ostler
   (also called the CLOWN)
DICK
A VINTNER
A HORSE-COURSER
A CARTER
HOSTESS
GOOD ANGEL
BAD ANGEL
MEPHISTOPHILIS
LUCIFER
BELZEBUB
DEVILS
THE SEVEN DEADLY SINS
PIPER
ALEXANDER THE GREAT }
PARAMOUR }
   OF ALEXANDER }
DARIUS } Apparitions
HELEN }
TWO CUPIDS }

ACT I

Prologue

(*Enter* CHORUS.)

CHORUS. Not marching in the fields of Thrasimen,[1]
Where Mars did mate* the warlike Carthagens;   join with
Nor sporting in the dalliance of love,
In courts of kings, where state is over-turn'd;
Nor in the pomp of proud audacious deeds,
Intends our Muse to vaunt his heavenly verse.
Only this, Gentles—we must now perform
The form of Faustus' fortunes, good or bad:
And now to patient judgments we appeal,
And speak for Faustus in his infancy.
Now is he born, of parents base of stock,
In Germany, within a town call'd Rhode:[2]
At riper years, to Wittenberg he went,
Whereas* his kinsmen chiefly brought him up.   where
So much he profits in divinity,
The fruitful plot of scholarism grac'd,[3]
That shortly he was grac'd[4] with Doctor's name,
Excelling all and sweetly can dispute
In th' heavenly matters of theology;
Till swoln with cunning of a self-conceit,[5]
His waxen wings did mount above his reach,

[1] Hannibal defeated the Romans in the battle of Lake Trasimene (217 B.C.).

[2] Roda, in the Duchy of Saxe-Altenburg.

[3] That is, having graced the fruitful garden of scholarship.

[4] Punning on the official "grace" by which a Cambridge University student was permitted to take his degree.

[5] "Intellectual pride engendered by arrogance" (Greg).

And, melting, heavens conspir'd his over-throw;[6]
For, falling to a devilish exercise,
And glutted now with learning's golden gifts,
He surfeits upon cursed necromancy;
Nothing so sweet as magic is to him,
Which he prefers before his chiefest bliss:*   that is, salvation
And this* the man that in his study sits.   this is

                                             (*Exit.*)

Scene 1

(FAUSTUS *in his study.*)

FAUSTUS. Settle thy studies, Faustus, and begin
To sound the depth of that thou wilt profess:*   teach
Having commenc'd,* be a divine in show,   taken a degree
Yet level* at the end of every art,   aim
And live and die in Aristotle's works.
Sweet Analytics, 'tis thou hast ravish'd me!
Bene disserere est finis logices.[7]
Is to dispute well logic's chiefest end?
Affords this art no greater miracle?
Then read no more; thou hast attain'd that end.
A greater subject fitteth Faustus' wit:*   understanding
Bid ὂν καὶ μὴ ὂν [8] farewell; and Galen[9] come;
Seeing, *Ubi desinit philosophus ibi incipit medicus,*[10]
Be a physician, Faustus; heap up gold,
And be eternis'd for some wondrous cure!
Summum bonum medicinæ sanitas,[11]
The end of physic is our body's health.
Why, Faustus, hast thou not attain'd that end?
Is not thy common talk sound aphorisms?*   that is, medical precepts
Are not thy bills* hung up as monuments,   prescriptions
Whereby whole cities have escap'd the plague,
And thousand desp'rate maladies been cur'd?
Yet art thou still but Faustus, and a man.
Couldst thou make men to live eternally,

[6] Marlowe refers to the myth of Icarus.

[7] "To argue well is the end of logic."

[8] "Being and not being."

[9] Ancient Greek physician who was the leading authority on medicine for practitioners in the Middle Ages.

[10] "Where the philosopher stops, there the physician begins."

[11] "The greatest good of medicine is health."

Or, being dead, raise them to life again,
Then this profession were to be esteem'd.
Physic, farewell! Where is Justinian?
   (*Reads.*)
'*Si una eademque res legatur duobus*
Alter rem, alter valorem rei,' *etc.*[12]
A petty case of paltry legacies!
   (*Reads.*)
'*Exhæreditare filium non potest pater nisi*'[13]—
Such is the subject of the Institute,*   Justinian's
And universal body of the law.   *Institutes*
This study fits a mercenary drudge,
Who aims at nothing but external trash;
Too servile and illiberal for me.
When all is done, divinity is best:
Jeromë's Bible, Faustus; view it well.
   (*Reads.*)
'*Stipendium peccati mors est.*[14] Ha! '*Stipendium,*' *etc.*
The reward of sin is death: that's hard.
   (*Reads.*)
'*Si peccasse negamus, fallimur*
Et nulla est in nobis veritas.'
If we say that we have no sin,
We deceive ourselves, and there is no truth in us.
Why, then, belike we must sin,
And so consequently die:
Ay, we must die an everlasting death.
What doctrine call you this, *Che sera, sera:*
What will be, shall be? Divinity, adieu!
These metaphysics* of magicians,   supernatural arts
And necromantic books are heavenly;
Lines, circles, letters, and characters;
Ay, these are those that Faustus most desires.
O, what a world of profit and delight,
Of power, of honour, and omnipotence,
Is promised to the studious artisan!*   master of
                                        learning
All things that move between the quiet* poles   fixed
Shall be at my command: emperors and kings

[12] "If the same thing is willed to two persons, one shall have the thing, the other the value of the thing."

[13] "A father cannot disinherit his son except—"

[14] In this and the five following lines, Faustus reads and translates from Romans, vi:23 and I St. John, i:8.

Are but obey'd in their several* provinces,   individual
Nor can they raise the wind, or rend the clouds;
But his dominion that exceeds in this,*   that is,
                                                               necromancy
Stretcheth as far as doth the mind of man;
A sound magician is a demi-god:
Here, tire my brain to get a deity!
   (*Enter* WAGNER.)
Wagner, commend me to my dearest friends,
The German Valdes and Cornelius;
Request them earnestly to visit me.
   WAGNER. I will, sir.

                                     (*Exit.*)

   FAUSTUS. Their conference* will be a greater help   conversation
     to me
Than all my labours, plod I ne'er so fast.

   (*Enter the* GOOD ANGEL *and* BAD ANGEL.)

   GOOD ANGEL. O, Faustus, lay that damned book aside,
And gaze not on it, lest it tempt thy soul,
And heap God's heavy wrath upon thy head!
Read, read the Scriptures:—that is blasphemy.
   BAD ANGEL. Go forward, Faustus, in that famous art
Wherein all Nature's treasure is contain'd:
Be thou on earth as Jove is in the sky,
Lord and commander of these elements.

                       (*Exeunt* ANGELS.)
   FAUSTUS. How am I glutted with conceit of this!*   this notion
Shall I make spirits fetch me what I please,
Resolve me of all ambiguities,
Perform what desperate enterprise I will?
I'll have them fly to India for gold,
Ransack the ocean for orient pearl,
And search all corners of the new-found world
For pleasant fruits and princely delicates;*   delicacies
I'll have them read me strange philosophy,
And tell the secrets of all foreign kings;
I'll have them wall all Germany with brass,
And make swift Rhine circle fair Wittenberg.
I'll have them fill the public schools* with silk,   university
                                                          lecture rooms
Wherewith the students shall be bravely* clad;   handsomely
I'll levy soldiers with the coin they bring,

And chase the Prince of Parma[15] from our land,
And reign sole king of all the Provinces;
Yea, stranger engines for the brunt* of war,   violence
Than was the fiery keel at Antwerpe bridge,[16]
I'll make my servile spirits to invent.
   (*He calls within.*)

   (*Enter* VALDES *and* CORNELIUS.)

Come, German Valdes, and Cornelius,
And make me blest with your sage conference!
Valdes, sweet Valdes, and Cornelius,
Know that your words have won me at the last
To practise magic and concealed arts:
Yet not your words only, but mine own fantasy,*   imagination
That will receive no object;* for my head   usual academic
But ruminates on necromantic skill.   subject
Philosophy is odious and obscure;
Both law and physic are for petty wits;
Divinity is basest of the three,*   baser than
Unpleasant, harsh, contemptible, and vile: the others
'Tis magic, magic, that hath ravish'd me.
Then, gentle friends, aid me in this attempt
And I, that have with subtle syllogisms
Gravell'd* the pastors of the German church,   confounded
And made the flowering pride of Wittenberg
Swarm to my problems,* as the infernal spirits   lectures
On sweet Musæus[17] when he came to hell,
Will be as cunning as Agrippa[18] was,
Whose shadows made all Europe honour him.
   VALDES. Faustus, these books, thy wit, and our experience
Shall make all nations to canonize us.
As Indian Moors* obey their Spanish lords,   American
So shall the spirits of every element   Indians
Be always serviceable* to us three;   obedient
Like lions shall they guard us when we please;
Like Almaine rutters* with their horsemen's staves,   German
                                                            cavalrymen

---

   [15] Spanish governor-general of the Netherlands (1579-92).

   [16] A Dutch fire-ship used to damage Parma's bridge over the
Scheldt river in April 1585.

   [17] Pre-Homeric Greek poet. See *Aeneid*, vi, 667.

   [18] Henry Cornelius Agrippa von Nettesheim, Renaissance magician thought to have the power of calling up the shadows of
the dead.

Or Laplana giants, trotting by our sides;
Sometimes like women, or unwedded maids,
Shadowing* more beauty in their airy brows   having
Than has the white breasts of the queen of love:
From Venice shall they drag huge argosies,
And from America the golden fleece
That yearly stuffs old Philip's treasury;
If learned Faustus will be resolute.
    FAUSTUS. Valdes, as resolute am I in this
As thou to live: therefore object* it not.   mention
    CORNELIUS. The miracles that magic will perform
Will make thee vow to study nothing else.
He that is grounded in astrology,
Enrich'd with tongues,* well seen* in minerals,   languages/
                                                      knowledgeable
Hath all the principles magic doth require:
Then doubt not, Faustus, but to be renown'd,
And more frequented* for this mystery   sought out
Than heretofore the Delphian oracle.
The spirits tell me they can dry the sea,
And fetch the treasure of all foreign wrecks,
Yea, all the wealth that our forefathers hid
Within the massy* entrails of the earth: massive
Then tell me, Faustus, what shall we three want?
    FAUSTUS. Nothing, Cornelius. O, this cheers my soul!
Come, show me some demonstrations magical,
That I may conjure in some bushy grove,
And have these joys in full possession.
    VALDES. Then haste thee to some solitary grove,
And bear wise Bacon's and Albertus'[19] works,
The Hebrew Psalter, and New Testament;
And whatsoever else is requisite
We will inform thee ere our conference cease.
    CORNELIUS. Valdes, first let him know the words of art;
And then, all other ceremonies learn'd,
Faustus may try his cunning* by himself.   skill
    VALDES. First I'll instruct thee in the rudiments,
And then wilt thou be perfecter than I.
    FAUSTUS. Then come and dine with me, and, after meat,
We'll canvass every quiddity* thereof;   essential
                                                        point (crux)?
For, ere I sleep, I'll try what I can do:

    [19] Roger Bacon and Albertus Magnus, thirteenth-century sci-
entists who supposedly dabbled in magic. Albertus may be a
misprint for Albanus (Pietro d'Albano), a thirteenth-century
alchemist.

This night I'll conjure, though I die therefore.

(Exeunt omnes.)

Scene 2

(Before FAUSTUS'S *house. Enter* TWO SCHOLARS.*)*

FIRST SCHOLAR. I wonder what's become of Faustus, that was wont to make our schools ring with *sic probo.*[20]

(Enter WAGNER.*)*

SECOND SCHOLAR. That shall we presently know; here comes his boy.

FIRST SCHOLAR. How now, sirrah! where's thy master?

WAGNER. God in heaven knows.

SECOND SCHOLAR. Why, dost not thou know, then?

WAGNER. Yes, I know; but that follows not.

FIRST SCHOLAR. Go to, sirrah! leave your jesting, and tell us where he is.

WAGNER. That follows not by force of argument, which you, being Licentiates,[21] should stand upon; therefore acknowledge your error, and be attentive.

SECOND SCHOLAR. Then you will not tell us?

WAGNER. You are deceiv'd, for I will tell you: yet, if you were not dunces you would never ask me such a question; for is he not *corpus naturale?* and is not that *mobile?*[22] Then wherefore should you ask me such a question? But that I am by nature phlegmatic, slow to wrath, and prone to lechery (to love, I would say), it were not for you to come within forty foot of the place of execution,* although I the dining room do not doubt but to see you both hanged the next sessions. Thus having triumph'd over you, I will set my countenance like a precisian* and begin to speak thus:—Truly, my puritan dear brethren, my master is within at dinner, with Valdes and Cornelius, as this wine, if it could speak, would inform your worships: and so, the Lord bless you, preserve you, and keep you, my dear brethren.

(Exit.)

FIRST SCHOLAR. O Faustus. Then I fear that which I have long suspected,

[20] "Thus I prove it." A scholastic term.

[21] Qualified for master's or doctor's degrees.

[22] " 'Corpus naturale seu mobile' was the current scholastic expression for the subject-matter of physics" (Ward).

That thou art fallen into that damned art
For which they two are infamous through the world.
   SECOND SCHOLAR. Were he a stranger, not allied to me,
The danger of his soul would make me mourn.
But, come, let us go and inform the Rector,*   university head
It may be his grave counsel may reclaim him.
   FIRST SCHOLAR. I fear me nothing will reclaim him now!
   SECOND SCHOLAR. Yet let us see what we can do.
                              (*Exeunt.*)

Scene 3

(*A grove. Enter* FAUSTUS *to conjure.*)

   FAUSTUS. Now that the gloomy shadow of the night,
Longing to view Orion's drizzling look,
Leaps from th' antarctic world unto the sky,
And dims the welkin* with her pitchy breath,   sky
Faustus, begin thine incantations,
And try if devils will obey thy hest,*   call
Seeing thou hast pray'd and sacrific'd to them.
Within this circle is Jehovah's name,
Forward and backward anagrammatiz'd;
Th' abbreviated names of holy saints,
Figures of every adjunct* to the heavens,   star affixed to
And characters of signs* and erring stars,* the Zodiac/planets
By which the spirits are enforc'd to rise:
Then fear not, Faustus, to be resolute,
And try the utmost magic can perform.
   (*Thunder.*)
'Sint mihi Dei Acherontis propitii! Valeat numen triplex
Jehovæ! Ignis, aeris, aquæ, terræ spiritus, salvete! Orientis
princeps, Belzebub, inferni ardentis monarcha, et Demo-
gorgon, propitiamus vos, ut appareat et surgat Mephisto-
philis. (Enter DRAGON above.) Quid tu moraris? per Jehovam,
Gehennam, et consecratam aquam quam nunc spargo, sig-
numque crucis quod nunc facio, et per vota nostra, ipse nunc
surgat nobis dicatus Mephistophilis!*[23]

    [23] "May the Gods of Acheron be favorable to me. Farewell to
the triple spirit of Jehovah! Spirits of fire, air, water, earth, hail!
[Lucifer] Prince of the East, Beelzebub monarch of burning hell,
and Demorgorgon, we ask your favor that Mephistophilis may
appear and rise. Why do you delay? By Jehovah, hell and the
holy water which I now sprinkle, and the sign of the cross which
I now make, and by our prayers, may Mephistophilis himself now
rise to do us service."

(*Enter* MEPHISTOPHILIS.)

I charge thee to return, and change thy shape;
Thou art too ugly to attend on me:
Go, and return an old Franciscan friar;
That holy shape becomes a devil best.

(*Exit* MEPHISTOPHILIS.)

I see there's virtue in my heavenly* words: scriptural
Who would not be proficient in this art?
How pliant is this Mephistophilis,
Full of obedience and humility!
Such is the force of magic and my spells:
Now, Faustus, thou art conjuror laureat,*   that is,
                                      expert conjuror
That canst command great Mephistophilis.
Quin redis, Mephistophilis, fratris imagine![24]

(*Re-enter* MEPHISTOPHILIS *like a Franciscan friar.*)

MEPHISTOPHILIS. Now, Faustus, what would'st thou have
    me do?
FAUSTUS. I charge thee wait upon me whilst I live,
To do whatever Faustus shall command,
Be it to make the moon drop from her sphere,
Or the ocean to overwhelm the world.
MEPHISTOPHILIS. I am a servant to great Lucifer,
And may not follow thee without his leave;
No more than he commands must we perform.
FAUSTUS. Did not he charge thee to appear to me?
MEPHISTOPHILIS. No, I came now hither of mine own
    accord.
FAUSTUS. Did not my conjuring raise thee? speak.
MEPHISTOPHILIS. That was the cause, but yet
    *per accidens,**   only incidentally
For, when we hear one rack* the name   torment into anagrams
    of God,
Abjure the Scriptures and his Saviour Christ,
We fly, in hope to get his glorious soul;
Nor will we come, unless he use such means

    [24] "Why don't you return, Mephistophilis, in the likeness of a
friar!"

Whereby he is in danger to be damn'd.
Therefore the shortest cut for conjuring
Is stoutly to abjure the Trinity,
And pray devoutly to the prince of hell.
    FAUSTUS. So Faustus hath
Already done; and holds this principle,
There is no chief but only Belzebub;
To whom Faustus doth dedicate himself.
This word 'damnation' terrifies not me,
For I confound hell in Elysium:[25]
My ghost be with the old philosophers!
But, leaving these vain trifles of men's souls,
Tell me what is that Lucifer thy lord?
    MEPHISTOPHILIS. Arch-regent and commander of all spirits.
    FAUSTUS. Was not that Lucifer an angel once?
    MEPHISTOPHILIS. Yes, Faustus, and most dearly lov'd of
      God.
    FAUSTUS. How comes it then that he is prince of devils?
    MEPHISTOPHILIS. O, by aspiring pride and insolence;
For which God threw him from the face of heaven.
    FAUSTUS. And what are you that live with Lucifer?
    MEPHISTOPHILIS. Unhappy spirits that fell with Lucifer,
Conspir'd against our God with Lucifer,
And are for ever damn'd with Lucifer.
    FAUSTUS. Where are you damn'd?
    MEPHISTOPHILIS.   In hell.
    FAUSTUS. How comes it then that thou art out of hell?
    MEPHISTOPHILIS. Why this is hell, nor am I out of it:
Think'st thou that I, that saw the face of God,
And tasted the eternal joys of Heaven,
Am not tormented with ten thousand hells,
In being depriv'd of everlasting bliss?
O, Faustus, leave these frivolous demands,
Which strikes a terror to my fainting soul!
    FAUSTUS. What, is great Mephistophilis so
      passionate*   sorrowful
For being deprived of the joys of heaven?
Learn thou of Faustus manly* fortitude,   that is, earthly
And scorn those joys thou never shalt possess.
Go bear these tidings to great Lucifer:
Seeing Faustus hath incurr'd eternal death

[25] That is, I do not distinguish between hell and Elysium.

By desperate thoughts against Jove's deity,*   that is, the
                                               Christian God
Say, he surrenders up to him his soul,
So* he will spare him four-and-twenty years,   provided that
Letting him live in all voluptuousness;
Having thee ever to attend on me,
To give me whatsoever I shall ask,
To tell me whatsoever I demand,
To slay mine enemies, and to aid my friends,
And always be obedient to my will.
Go, and return to mighty Lucifer,
And meet me in my study at midnight,
And then resolve me of thy master's mind.
    MEPHISTOPHILIS. I will, Faustus.

                                                     (Exit.)

    FAUSTUS. Had I as many souls as there be stars,
I'd give them all for Mephistophilis.
By him I'll be great Emperor of the world,
And make a bridge through the moving air,
To pass the ocean with a band of men;
I'll join the hills that bind* the Afric shore,   enclose
And make that country continent to* Spain,   continuous with
And both contributory to my crown:
The Emperor shall not live but by my leave,
Nor any potentate of Germany.
Now that I have obtain'd what I desir'd,
I'll live in speculation* of this art,   contemplation
Till Mephistophilis return again.
                                                     (Exit.)

Scene 4

(Enter WAGNER *and* ROBIN, *the* CLOWN.*)*

WAGNER. Come hither, sirrah boy.

CLOWN. Boy! O disgrace to my person. Zounds, boy in
your face! You have seen many boys with beards, I am sure.

WAGNER. Sirrah, hast thou no comings in?*   income

CLOWN. Yes, and goings out too, you may see, sir.

WAGNER. Alas, poor slave! see how poverty jests in his
nakedness! I know the villain's out of service, and so hungry,
that I know he would give his soul to the devil for a shoulder
of mutton, though it were blood-raw.

CLOWN. Not so, neither. I had need to have it well roasted, and good sauce to it, if I pay so dear, I can tell you.

WAGNER. Sirrah, wilt thou be my man and wait on me, and I will make thee go like *Qui mihi discipulus?*[26]

CLOWN. What, in verse?

WAGNER. No slave; in beaten* silk and staves-   embroidered
acre.[27]

CLOWN. Staves-acre! that's good to kill vermin, Then, belike, if I serve you, I shall be lousy.

WAGNER. Why, so thou shalt be, whether thou do'st it or no. For, Sirrah, if thou do'st not presently bind thyself to me for seven years, I'll turn all the lice about thee into familiars,* and make them tear thee in pieces.   attendant spirits

CLOWN. Nay, sir, you may save yourself a labour, for they are as familiar with me as if they had paid for their meat and drink, I can tell you.

WAGNER. Well, sirrah, leave your jesting and take these guilders.*   Dutch coins

CLOWN. Yes, marry, sir, and I thank you too.

WAGNER. So, now thou art to be at an hour's warning, whensoever and wheresoever the devil shall fetch thee.

CLOWN. Here, take your guilders again, I'll none of 'em.

WAGNER. Not I, thou art pressed,* for I will pres-   engaged
ently raise up two devils to carry thee away—Banio, Belcher!

CLOWN. Belcher! and Belcher come here, I'll belch him. I am not afraid of a devil.

(*Enter two* DEVILS.)

WAGNER. How now, sir, will you serve me now?

CLOWN. Ay, good Wagner, take away the devil then.

WAGNER. Spirits, away! Now, sirrah, follow me.

                                        (*Exeunt* DEVILS.)

CLOWN. I will, sir, but hark you, master, will you teach me this conjuring occupation?

WAGNER. Ay, sirrah, I'll teach thee to turn thyself to a dog, or a cat, or a mouse, or a rat, or any thing.

CLOWN. A dog, or a cat, or a mouse, or a rat, O brave Wagner!

WAGNER. Villain, call me Master Wagner, and see that you

---

[26] "You who are my student," that is, a model student.
[27] A type of plant used in killing lice.

walk attentively and let your right eye be always dia-
metrally* fixed upon my left heel, that thou may'st   directly
quasi vestigias nostras insistere.[28]

CLOWN. Well, sir, I warrant you.

(*Exeunt.*)

ACT II

Scene 1

(*Enter* FAUSTUS *in his study.*)

FAUSTUS. Now, Faustus, must
Thou needs be damn'd, and canst thou not be sav'd.
What boots* it, then, to think on God or heaven?   profits
Away with such vain fancies, and despair;
Despair in God, and trust in Belzebub:
Now go not backward; Faustus, be resolute:
Why waver'st thou? O, something soundeth in mine ear,
'Abjure this magic, turn to God again!'
Ay, and Faustus will turn to God again.
To God? he loves thee not;
The God thou serv'st is thine own appetite,
Wherein is fix'd the love of Belzebub:
To him I'll build an altar and a church,
And offer lukewarm blood of new-born babes.
   (*Enter* GOOD ANGEL *and* BAD ANGEL.)
BAD ANGEL. Go forward, Faustus, in that famous art.
GOOD ANGEL. Sweet Faustus, leave that execrable art.
FAUSTUS. Contrition, prayer, repentance—what of these?
GOOD ANGEL. O, they are means to bring thee unto heaven!
BAD ANGEL. Rather illusions, fruits of lunacy,
That make them foolish that do use them most.
   GOOD ANGEL. Sweet Faustus, think of heaven and heavenly
things.
   BAD ANGEL. No, Faustus; think of honour and of wealth.
                    (*Exeunt* ANGELS.)
FAUSTUS. Wealth! Why, the signiory* of Embden[29]   territory
   shall be mine.

----

[28] "As if to tread in our tracks."

[29] Emden, an important port in northwest Germany in the sixteenth century.

When Mephistophilis shall stand by me,
What power can hurt me? Faustus, thou art safe:
Cast no more doubts—Mephistophilis, come!
And bring glad tidings from great Lucifer;—
Is't not midnight?—come, Mephistophilis,
Veni, veni, Mephistophile!

(*Enter* MEPHISTOPHILIS.)

Now tell me what saith Lucifer, thy lord?
    MEPHISTOPHILIS. That I shall wait on Faustus while he lives,
So he will buy my service with his soul.
    FAUSTUS. Already Faustus hath hazarded that for thee.
    MEPHISTOPHILIS. But now thou must bequeath it solemnly,
And write a deed of gift with thine own blood;
For that security craves Lucifer.
If thou deny it, I must back to hell.
    FAUSTUS. Stay, Mephistophilis, tell me what good
Will my soul do thy lord?
    MEPHISTOPHILIS. Enlarge his kingdom.
    FAUSTUS. Is that the reason why he tempts us thus?
    MEPHISTOPHILIS. *Solamen miseris socios habuisse doloris.*[30]
    FAUSTUS. Why, have you any pain that torture*   (that is, you
        others?   who torture)
    MEPHISTOPHILIS. As great as have the human souls of men.
But tell me, Faustus, shall I have thy soul?
And I will be thy slave, and wait on thee,
And give thee more than thou hast wit to ask.
    FAUSTUS. Ay, Mephistophilis, I'll give it him.
    MEPHISTOPHILIS. Then, Faustus, stab thy arm courageously,
And bind thy soul, that at some certain day
Great Lucifer may claim it as his own;
And then be thou as great as Lucifer.
    FAUSTUS (*stabbing his arm*). Lo, Mephistophilis, for love
        of thee,
I cut mine arm, and with my proper* blood   .   own
Assure my soul to be great Lucifer's,
Chief lord and regent of perpetual night!
View here this blood that trickles from mine arm,
And let it be propitious for my wish.
    MEPHISTOPHILIS. But, Faustus,
Write it in manner of a deed or gift.
    FAUSTUS. Ay, so I do. (*Writes.*) But, Mephistophilis,

    [30] That is, "Misery loves company."

My blood congeals, and I can write no more.
MEPHISTOPHILIS. I'll fetch thee fire to dissolve it straight.
(*Exit.*)

FAUSTUS. What might the staying of my blood portend?
Is it unwilling I should write this bill?* deed
Why streams it not, that I may write afresh?
Faustus gives to thee his soul: oh, there it stay'd!
Why shouldst thou not? is not thy soul thine own?
Then write again, *Faustus gives to thee his soul.*

(*Re-enter* MEPHISTOPHILIS *with a chafer of coals.*)

MEPHISTOPHILIS. See, Faustus, here is fire, set it* on. the blood
FAUSTUS. So, now the blood begins to clear again;
Now will I make an end immediately.
(*Writes.*)
MEPHISTOPHILIS (*aside*). What will not I do to obtain his
soul?
FAUSTUS. *Consummatum est;*[31] this bill is ended,
And Faustus hath bequeath'd his soul to Lucifer.
But what is this inscription on mine arm?
*Homo, fuge!** Whither should I fly? "man, fly!"
If unto God, he'll throw me down to hell.
My senses are deceiv'd; here's nothing writ:—
O yes, I see it plain; even here is writ,
Homo, fuge! Yet shall not Faustus fly.
MEPHISTOPHILIS. I'll fetch him somewhat to delight his
mind.
(*Aside, and then exit.*)

(*Enter* DEVILS, *giving crowns and rich apparel to* FAUSTUS.
They dance, and then depart. Enter MEPHISTOPHILIS.)

FAUSTUS. What means this show? Speak, Mephistophilis.
MEPHISTOPHILIS. Nothing, Faustus, but to delight thy mind,
And let thee see what magic can perform.
FAUSTUS. But may I raise such spirits when I please?
MEPHISTOPHILIS. Ay, Faustus, and do greater things than
these.
FAUSTUS. Then there's enough for a thousand souls.
Here, Mephistophilis, receive this scroll,
A deed of gift of body and of soul:

[31] "It is finished." Faustus blasphemously utters Christ's last
words (St. John xix:30).

But yet conditionally that thou perform
All articles prescrib'd between us both.
    MEPHISTOPHILIS. Faustus, I swear by hell and Lucifer
To effect all promises between us made!
    FAUSTUS. Then hear me read it, Mephistophilis.

On these conditions following.
First, that Faustus may be a spirit in form and substance.
Secondly, that Mephistophilis shall be his servant, and at his
    command.
Thirdly, that Mephistophilis shall do for him, and bring him
    whatsoever.*   anything
Fourthly, that he* shall be in his chamber or house Mephistophilis
    invisible.
Lastly, that he shall appear to the said John Faustus at all
    times, in what form or shape soever he please.
I, John Faustus, of Wittenberg, Doctor, by these presents, do
    give both body and soul to Lucifer Prince of the East, and
    his minister Mephistophilis; and furthermore grant unto
    them that, four and twenty years being expired, and these
    articles above written being inviolate, full power to fetch or
    carry the said John Faustus, body and soul, flesh, blood, or
    goods, into their habitation wheresoever.
                                   By me, John Faustus.

    MEPHISTOPHILIS. Speak, Faustus, do you deliver this as your
      deed?
    FAUSTUS. Ay, take it, and the devil give thee good of it!
    MEPHISTOPHILIS. So, now, Faustus, ask me what thou wilt.
    FAUSTUS. First I will question with thee about hell.
Tell me, where is the place that men call hell?
    MEPHISTOPHILIS. Under the heavens.
    FAUSTUS. Ay, so are all things else, but whereabouts?
    MEPHISTOPHILIS. Within the bowels of these elements,
Where we are tortur'd and remain for ever:
Hell hath no limits, nor is circumscrib'd
In one self place; but where we are is hell,
And where hell is, there must we ever be:
And, to be short, when all the world dissolves,
And every creature shall be purified,
All places shall be hell that is not heaven.
    FAUSTUS. I think hell's a fable.
    MEPHISTOPHILIS. Ay, think so, till experience change thy
      mind.

FAUSTUS. Why, dost thou think that Faustus shall be
   damn'd?
MEPHISTOPHILIS. Ay, of necessity, for here's the scroll
In which thou hast given thy soul to Lucifer.
FAUSTUS. Ay, and body too: but what of that?
Think'st thou that Faustus is so fond* to imagine   foolish
That, after this life, there is any pain?
No, these are trifles and mere old wives' tales.
   MEPHISTOPHILIS. But I am an instance to prove the
      contrary;
For I tell thee I am damn'd, and now in hell.
   FAUSTUS. Nay, and this be hell, I'll willingly be damn'd:
What! sleeping, eating, walking, and disputing!
But, leaving off this, let me have a wife,
The fairest maid in Germany, for I
Am wanton and lascivious
And cannot live without a wife.
   MEPHISTOPHILIS. Well, Faustus, thou shalt have a wife.

(*He fetches in a* WOMAN-DEVIL.)

FAUSTUS. What sight is this?
MEPHISTOPHILIS. Now, Faustus, wilt thou have a wife?
FAUSTUS. Here's a hot whore indeed! No, I'll no wife.
MEPHISTOPHILIS. Marriage is but a ceremonial toy;
And if thou lovest me, think no more of it.
I'll cull* thee out the fairest courtesans,   choose
And bring them ev'ry morning to thy bed:
She whom thine eye shall like, thy heart shall have,
Were she as chaste as was Penelope,*   Ulysses' wife
As wise as Saba,* or as beautiful   Queen of Sheba
As was bright Lucifer before his fall.
Here, take this book, and peruse it well:
The iterating of these lines brings gold;
The framing of this circle on the ground
Brings thunder, whirlwinds, storm and lightning;
Pronounce this thrice devoutly to thyself,
And men in harness* shall appear to thee,   armor
Ready to execute what thou command'st.
   FAUSTUS. Thanks, Mephistophilis, for this sweet book.
This will I keep as chary* as my life.   carefully
                                                           (*Exeunt.*[32])

   [32] Some scholars believe there is a missing scene which follows
here.

Scene 2

(FAUSTUS *in his study and* MEPHISTOPHILIS.)

FAUSTUS. When I behold the heavens, then I repent,
And curse thee, wicked Mephistophilis,
Because thou hast depriv'd me of those joys.
    MEPHISTOPHILIS. 'Twas thine own seeking, Faustus, thank
    thyself.
But think'st thou heaven is such a glorious thing?
I tell thee, Faustus, it is not half so fair
As thou, or any man that breathes on earth.
    FAUSTUS. How prov'st thou that?
    MEPHISTOPHILIS. 'Twas made for man; then he's more
    excellent.
    FAUSTUS. If heaven was made for man, 'twas made for me:
I will renounce this magic and repent.

(*Enter the two* ANGELS.)

GOOD ANGEL. Faustus, repent; yet God will pity thee.
BAD ANGEL. Thou art a spirit; God cannot pity thee.
FAUSTUS. Who buzzeth in mine ears, I am a spirit?
Be I a devil, yet God may pity me;
Yea, God will pity me, if I repent.
    BAD ANGEL. Ay, but Faustus never shall repent.
                            (*Exeunt* ANGELS.)
    FAUSTUS. My heart is harden'd, I cannot repent:
Scarce can I name salvation, faith, or heaven,
But fearful echoes thunders in mine ears,
'Faustus, thou art damn'd!' Then swords, and knives,
Poison, guns, halters, and envenom'd steel
Are laid before me to despatch myself;
And long ere this I should have done the deed,
Had not sweet pleasure conquer'd deep despair,
Have not I made blind Homer sing to me
Of Alexander's* love and Oenon's* death?   Paris's/Oenone's
And hath not he,* that built the walls of Thebes,   Amphion
With ravishing sound of his melodious harp,
Made music with my Mephistophilis?

Why should I die, then, or basely despair?
I am resolv'd; Faustus shall not repent.—
Come, Mephistophilis, let us dispute again,
And reason of divine astrology.
Speak, are there many spheres above the moon?[33]
Are all celestial bodies but one globe,
As is the substance of this centric earth?[34]

MEPHISTOPHILIS. As are the elements, such are the heavens,
Even from the moon unto the imperial orb,
Mutually folded in each others' spheres,
And jointly move upon one axletree,
Whose termine* is termed the world's wide pole;   end
Nor are the names of Saturn, Mars, or Jupiter
Feign'd, but are erring stars.*   planets

FAUSTUS.   But have they all
One motion, both *situ et tempore?*[35]

MEPHISTOPHILIS. All move from east to west in four and
twenty hours upon the poles of the world; but differ in their
motions upon the poles of the zodiac.

FAUSTUS. These slender questions Wagner can decide:
Hath Mephistophilis no greater skill?
Who knows not the double motion of the planets?
That the first is finish'd in a natural day;
The second thus: Saturn in 30 years;
Jupiter in 12; Mars in 4; the Sun, Venus, and Mercury in a
year; the Moon in 28 days. These are freshmen's questions.
But, tell me, hath every sphere a dominion or intelligen-
tia?*   ruling spirit

MEPHISTOPHILIS. Ay.

FAUSTUS. How many heavens or spheres are there?

MEPHISTOPHILIS. Nine; the seven planets, the firmament,
and the imperial heaven.

FAUSTUS. But is there not *coelum igneum, et cristallinum?*[36]

MEPHISTOPHILIS. No, Faustus, they be but fables.

---

[33] What follows is a technical discussion of Renaissance astro-
nomical concepts.

[34] In the center of the universe.

[35] "In position and in time"; that is, Do they move in the same
direction, and is the duration of their revolutions the same?

[36] "The fiery and crystalline spheres."

FAUSTUS. Resolve me then in this one question: why are not conjunctions, oppositions, aspects, eclipses, all at one time, but in some years we have more, in some less?

MEPHISTOPHILIS. *Per inaequalem motum respectu totius.*[37]

FAUSTUS. Well, I am answer'd. Now tell me who made the world.

MEPHISTOPHILIS. I will not.

FAUSTUS. Sweet Mephistophilis, tell me.

MEPHISTOPHILIS. Move me not, Faustus.

FAUSTUS. Villain, have not I bound thee to tell me any thing?

MEPHISTOPHILIS. Ay, that is not against our kingdom.
This is: thou art damn'd; think thou of hell.

FAUSTUS. Think, Faustus, upon God that made the world.

MEPHISTOPHILIS. Remember this.

(Exit.)

FAUSTUS. Ay, go, accursed spirit, to ugly hell!
'Tis thou hast damn'd distressed Faustus' soul.
Is't not too late?

(Enter the two ANGELS.)

BAD ANGEL. Too late.

GOOD ANGEL. Never too late, if Faustus will repent.

BAD ANGEL. If thou repent, devils will tear thee in pieces.

GOOD ANGEL. Repent, and they shall never raze* thy   graze
skin.

(Exeunt ANGELS.)

FAUSTUS. O, Christ, my Saviour, my Saviour,
Help to save distressed Faustus' soul!

(Enter LUCIFER, BELZEBUB, and MEPHISTOPHILIS.)

LUCIFER. Christ cannot save thy soul, for he is just:
There's none but I have interest* in the same.   legal title

FAUSTUS. O, what art thou that look'st so terribly?

LUCIFER. I am Lucifer,
And this is my companion prince in hell.

FAUSTUS. O, Faustus, they are come to fetch thy soul!

BELZEBUB. We are come to tell thee thou dost injure us.

LUCIFER. Thou call'st on Christ, contrary to thy promise.

[37] "Because of their unequal motion with respect to the whole"; that is, because of their varying velocities and direction of movement.

BELZEBUB. Thou shouldst not think on God.

LUCIFER. Think on the devil.

BELZEBUB. And his dam too.

FAUSTUS. Nor will I henceforth: pardon me in this,
And Faustus vows never to look to heaven,
Never to name God, or to pray to him,
To burn his Scriptures, slay his ministers,
And make my spirits pull his churches down.

LUCIFER. So shalt thou show thyself an obedient servant,
And we will highly gratify thee for it.

BELZEBUB. Faustus, we are come from hell in person to show thee some pastime: sit down, and thou shalt behold the Seven Deadly Sins appear to thee in their own proper shapes and likeness.

FAUSTUS. That sight will be as pleasing unto me,
As Paradise was to Adam, the first day
Of his creation.

LUCIFER. Talk not of Paradise or creation; but mark the show.

Go, Mephistophilis, fetch them in.

(*Enter the 7* DEADLY SINS *with a* PIPER.)

BELZEBUB. Now, Faustus, question them of their names and dispositions.

FAUSTUS. That shall I soon. What are thou, the first?

PRIDE. I am Pride. I disdain to have any parents. I am like to Ovid's flea;[38] I can creep into every corner of a wench;* sometimes, like a periwig, I sit upon her brow; maiden next, like a necklace I hang about her neck; then, like a fan of feathers, I kiss her lips, and then turning myself to a wrought* smock do what I list.* But, fie, what embroidered/please a smell is here! I'll not speak another word, unless the ground be perfum'd, and cover'd with cloth of arras.[39]

FAUSTUS. Thou art a proud knave, indeed! What are thou, the second?

COVETOUSNESS. I am Covetousness, begotten of an old churl in a leather bag: and might I now obtain my wish, this house, you and all, should turn to gold, that I might lock you safe into my chest. O my sweet gold!

---

[38] The *Carmen de Pulice,* a poem wrongly ascribed to Ovid.

[39] Using tapestry cloth for carpeting would be a sign of extreme ostentation.

FAUSTUS. And what art thou, the third?

ENVY. I am Envy, begotten of a chimney-sweeper and an oyster-wife. I cannot read, and therefore wish all books burn'd. I am lean with seeing others eat. O, that there would come a famine over all the world, that all might die, and I live alone! then thou should'st see how fat I'ld be. But must thou sit, and I stand? come down, with a vengeance!

FAUSTUS. Out, envious wretch!—But what art thou, the fourth?

WRATH. I am Wrath. I had neither father nor mother: I leapt out of a lion's mouth when I was scarce an hour old; and ever since have run up and down the world with these case* of rapiers, wounding myself when I could get none   pair to fight withal. I was born in hell; and look to it, for some of you shall be my father.

FAUSTUS. And what are thou, the fifth?

GLUTTONY. I am Gluttony. My parents are all dead, and the devil a penny they have left me, but a small pension, and that buys me thirty meals a day and ten bevers*—a   snacks small trifle to suffice nature. I come of a royal pedigree! my father was a Gammon of Bacon, and my mother was a Hogshead of Claret wine; my godfathers were these, Peter Pickledherring and Martin Martlemas-beef.[40] But my godmother, O she was an ancient gentlewoman; her name was Margery March-beer.[41] Now, Faustus, thou hast heard all my progeny,* wilt thou bid me to supper?   lineage

FAUSTUS. Not I.

GLUTTONY. Then the devil choke thee.

FAUSTUS. Choke thyself, glutton!—What art thou, the sixth?

SLOTH. Heigh ho! I am Sloth. I was begotten on a sunny bank, where I have lain ever since; and you have done me great injury to bring me from thence: let me be carried thither again by Gluttony and Lechery. Heigh ho! I'll not speak a word more for a king's ransom.

FAUSTUS. And what are you, Mistress Minx, the seventh and last?

LECHERY. Who, I, sir? I am one that loves an inch of raw mutton[42] better than an ell of fried stockfish,* and   dried codfish the first letter of my name begins with Lechery.

[40] The customary time for salting beef was Martinmas, November 11.

[41] A strong beer brewed in March.

[42] A pun on *mutton*, meaning prostitute.

LUCIFER. Away, to hell, away, on Piper!

(*Exeunt the 7* SINS.)

FAUSTUS. O, how this sight doth delight my soul!

LUCIFER. But, Faustus, in hell is all manner of delight.

FAUSTUS. O, might I see hell, and return again safe, how happy were I then!

LUCIFER. Faustus, thou shalt. At midnight I will send for thee.

Meanwhile peruse this book and view it thoroughly,

And thou shalt turn thyself into what shape thou wilt.

FAUSTUS. Thanks, mighty Lucifer!

This will I keep as chary* as my life.   carefully

LUCIFER. Now, Faustus, farewell.

FAUSTUS. Farewell, great Lucifer. Come, Mephistophilis.

(*Exeunt omnes several ways.*)

Scene 3

(*An inn-yard. Enter* ROBIN *with a book.*)

ROBIN. What, Dick, look to the horses there, till I come again. I have gotten one of Doctor Faustus' conjuring books, and now we'll have such knavery, as't passes.*   as beats everything

(*Enter* DICK.)

DICK. What, Robin, you must come away and walk the horses.

ROBIN. I walk the horses? I scorn't, 'faith, I have other matters in hand, let the horses walk themselves and they will. (*Reads.*) *A per se; a, t. h. e. the; o per se; o deny orgon, gorgon.*[43] Keep further from me, O thou illiterate and unlearned hostler.

DICK. 'Snails,* what hast thou got there? a book?   God's nails why, thou canst not tell ne'er a word on't.

ROBIN. That thou shalt see presently. Keep out of the circle, I say, lest I send you into the ostry* with a vengeance.   inn

DICK. That's like, 'faith: you had best leave your foolery, for an* my master come, he'll conjure you, 'faith.   if

ROBIN. My master conjure me? I'll tell thee what, an my

---

[43] Robin is reading with difficulty. *A per se* means "*a* by itself" which is followed by *the*; then comes *o* by itself; next Robin struggles over the word *demogorgon*.

master come here, I'll clap as fair a pair of horns on's head
as e'er thou sawest in thy life.

DICK. Thou need'st not do that, for my mistress hath
done it.*   that is,
                                                        cuckolded him

ROBIN. Ay, there be of us here that have waded as deep
into matters as other men, if they were disposed to talk.

DICK. A plague take you, I thought you did not sneak up
and down after her for nothing. But I prithee, tell me, in good
sadness,* Robin, is that a conjuring book?   seriously

ROBIN. Do but speak what thou'lt have me to do, and I'll
do't: If thou'lt dance naked, put off thy clothes, and I'll conjure thee about presently: or if thou'lt go but to the tavern
with me, I'll give thee white wine, red wine, claret wine, sack,
muscadine, malmesey, and whippin-crust,* hold   spiced wine
belly, hold,* and we'll not pay one penny for it.   a belly full

DICK. O brave, prithee let's to it presently, for I am as dry
as a dog.

ROBIN. Come then, let's away.

                                                        (*Exeunt.*)

ACT III

Prologue

(*Enter the* CHORUS.)

CHORUS. Learned Faustus,
To find the secrets of astronomy
Graven* in the book of Jove's high firmament,   engraved
Did mount him up to scale Olympus' top,
Where sitting in a chariot burning bright,
Drawn by the strength of yoked dragons' necks,
He views the clouds, the planets, and the stars,
The tropic zones, and quarters of the sky,
From the bright circle of the hornèd moon,
E'en to the height of *Primum Mobile:*   highest celestial
                                                              sphere
And whirling round with this circumference,
Within the concave compass of the pole;
From east to west his dragons swiftly glide,
And in eight days did bring him home again.
Not long he stayed within his quiet house,
To rest his bones after his weary toil,
But new exploits do hale him out again,

And mounted then upon a dragon's back,
That with his wings did part the subtle* air,   rarefied
He now is gone to prove* cosmography,   test
That measures coasts, and kingdoms of the earth:
And, as I guess, will first arrive at Rome,
To see the Pope and manner of his court,
And take some part of holy Peter's feast,
The which this day is highly solemniz'd.

               (*Exit.*)

Scene 1

(*The* POPE'S *privy-chamber. Enter* FAUSTUS *and* MEPHISTOPHILIS.)

FAUSTUS. Having now, my good Mephistophilis,
Pass'd with delight the stately town of Trier,
Environ'd round with airy mountain-tops,
With walls of flint, and deep entrenched lakes,*   moats
Not to be won by any conquering prince;
From Paris next, coasting the realm of France,
We saw the river Maine fall into Rhine,
Whose banks are set with groves of fruitful vines;
Then up to Naples, rich Campania,[44]
Whose buildings fair and gorgeous to the eye,
The streets straight forth,* and paved with finest   in straight lines
    brick,
Quarters the town in four equivalents;*   equal sections
There saw we learned Maro's* golden tomb,   Virgil
The way he cut, an English mile in length,
Through a rock of stone, in one night's space,[45]
From thence to Venice, Padua, and the rest,*   that is, other
                                  Venetian territories
In midst of which a sumptuous temple* stands,   St. Mark's, Venice
That threats the stars with her aspiring top,
Whose frame is paved with sundry coloured stones,
And roof'd aloft with curious work in gold.
Thus hitherto hath Faustus spent his time:
But tell me now, what resting-place is this?
Hast thou, as erst I did command,
Conducted me within the walls of Rome?

    [44] Marlowe mistook the province reference in his source as another name for Naples.
    [45] A tunnel at Posilippo which Virgil supposedly bored by magic.

MEPHISTOPHILIS. I have, my Faustus, and for proof thereof
This is the goodly Palace of the Pope;
And cause we are no common guests
I choose his privy-chamber for our use.
    FAUSTUS. I hope his Holiness will bid us welcome.
    MEPHISTOPHILIS. All's one, for we'll be bold with his veni-
      son.
But now, my Faustus, that thou may'st perceive
What Rome contains for to delight thine eyes,
Know that this city stands upon seven hills
That underprop the groundwork of the same:
Just through the midst runs flowing Tiber's stream,
With winding banks that cut it in two parts;
Over which four stately bridges lean,*   bend
That make safe passage to each part of Rome:
Upon the bridge called Ponte Angelo
Erected is a castle passing strong,
Where thou shalt see such stone of ordinance,
As that the double cannons, forg'd of brass,
Do match the number of the days contain'd
Within the compass* of one complete year: limits
Beside the gates, and high pyramides,*   obelisks
That Julius Cæsar brought from Africa.
    FAUSTUS. Now, by the kingdoms of infernal rule,
Of Styx, of Acheron,* and the fiery lake   rivers of Hell
Of ever-burning Phlegethon, I swear
That I do long to see the monuments
And situation* of bright splendent Rome: layout
Come, therefore, let's away.
    MEPHISTOPHILIS. Nay, stay, my Faustus; I know you'd see
      the Pope
And take some part of holy Peter's feast,
The which, in state and high solemnity,
This day is held through Rome and Italy,
In honour of the Pope's triumphant victory.
    FAUSTUS. Sweet Mephistophilis, thou pleasest me,
Whilst I am here on earth, let me be cloy'd
With all things that delight the heart of man.
My four-and-twenty years of liberty
I'll spend in pleasure and in dalliance,
That Faustus' name, whilst this bright frame* doth stand, body
May be admired through the furthest land.
    MEPHISTOPHILIS. 'Tis well said, Faustus, come then, stand
      by me

And thou shalt see them come immediately.

FAUSTUS. Nay, stay, my gentle Mephistophilis,
And grant me my request, and then I go.
Thou know'st within the compass of eight days
We view'd the face of heaven, of earth and hell.
So high our dragons soar'd into the air,
That looking down, the earth appear'd to me
No bigger than my hand in quantity.
There did we view the kingdoms of the world,
And what might please mine eye, I there behold,
Then in this show let me an actor be,
That this proud Pope[46] may Faustus' cunning see.

MEPHISTOPHILIS. Let it be so, my Faustus, but, first stay,
And view their triumphs,* as they pass this way.   triumphal
And then devise what best contents thy mind   procession
By cunning in thine art to cross the Pope,
Or dash the pride of this solemnity;
To make his monks and abbots stand like apes,
And point like antics* at his triple crown: grotesque figures
To beat the beads about the friars' pates,
Or clap huge horns upon the Cardinals' heads;
Or any villainy thou canst devise,
And I'll perform it, Faustus: Hark! they come:
This day shall make thee be admir'd in Rome.

(*Enter the* CARDINALS *and* BISHOPS, *some bearing crosiers,
some the pillars,* MONKS *and* FRIARS, *singing their procession.* *Then the* POPE, *and* RAYMOND, KING OF   processional
HUNGARY, *with* BRUNO *led in chains.*)   hymn

POPE. Cast down our footstool.

RAYMOND.   Saxon Bruno, stoop,
Whilst on thy back his Holiness ascends
Saint Peter's chair and state* pontifical.   throne

BRUNO. Proud Lucifer, that state belongs to me:
But thus I fall to Peter, not to thee.

POPE. To me and Peter shalt thou grovelling lie,
And crouch before the Papal dignity;
Sound trumpets, then, for thus Saint Peter's heir,
From Bruno's back, ascends Saint Peter's chair.

(*A flourish while he ascends.*)

[46] The Pope is either Adrian IV or Adrian VI. Marlowe is not
historically accurate in this scene.

Thus, as the gods creep on with feet of wool,
Long ere with iron hands they punish men,
So shall our sleeping vengeance now arise,
And smite with death thy hated enterprise.
Lord Cardinals of France and Padua,
Go forthwith to our holy Consistory,
And read amongst the Statutes Decretal,
What, by the holy Council held at Trent,[47]
The sacred synod hath decreed for him
That doth assume the Papal government
Without election, and a true consent:
Away, and bring us word with speed.
    FIRST CARDINAL. We go, my lord.

                           (*Exeunt* CARDINALS.)

    POPE. Lord Raymond.
    (*The* POPE *and* RAYMOND *converse*.)
    FAUSTUS. Go, haste thee, gentle Mephistophilis
Follow the Cardinals to the Consistory;
And as they turn their superstitious books,
Strike them with sloth, and drowsy idleness;
And make them sleep so sound, that in their shapes
Thyself and I may parley with this Pope,
This proud confronter of the Emperor:
And in despite of all his Holiness
Restore this Bruno to his liberty,
And bear him to the States of Germany.
    MEPHISTOPHILIS. Faustus, I go.
    FAUSTUS. Despatch it soon,
The Pope shall curse that Faustus came to Rome.

             (*Exeunt* FAUSTUS *and* MEPHISTOPHILIS.)

    BRUNO. Pope Adrian, let me have right of law,
I was elected by the Emperor.
    POPE. We will depose the Emperor for that deed,
And curse the people that submit to him;
Both he and thou shalt stand excommunicate,
And interdict from Church's privilege
And all society of holy men:
He grows too proud in his authority,
Lifting his lofty head above the clouds,
And like a steeple over-peers the Church:
But we'll pull down his haughty insolence.
And as Pope Alexander,* our progenitor,*   Alexander III/
                                                        predecessor

[47] The Council of Trent, 1545-63.

Trod on the neck of German Frederick,
Adding this golden sentence to our praise:—
'That Peter's heirs should tread on Emperors,
And walk upon the dreadful adder's back,
Treading the lion and the dragon down,
And fearless spurn the killing basilisk':
So will we quell that haughty schismatic;
And by authority apostolical
Depose him from his regal government.

    BRUNO. Pope Julius swore to princely Sigismond,
For him, and the succeeding Popes of Rome,
To hold the Emperors their lawful lords.[48]

    POPE. Pope Julius did abuse the Church's rites,
And therefore none of his decrees can stand.
Is not all power on earth bestowed on us?
And therefore, though we would, we cannot err.
Behold this silver belt, whereto is fix'd
Seven golden keys fast sealed with seven seals
In token of our sevenfold power from Heaven,
To bind or loose, lock fast, condemn, or judge,
Resign,* or seal, or whatso pleaseth us.   that is, unseal
Then he and thou, and all the world shall stoop,
Or be assured of our dreadful curse,
To light as heavy as the pains of hell.

    (*Enter* FAUSTUS *and* MEPHISTOPHILIS *like the Cardinals.*)

    MEPHISTOPHILIS. Now tell me, Faustus, are we rot fitted
      well?
    FAUSTUS. Yes, Mephistophilis, and two such Cardinals
Ne'er serv'd a holy Pope as we shall do.
But whilst they sleep within the Consistory,
Let us salute his reverend Fatherhood.

    RAYMOND. Behold, my Lord, the Cardinals are return'd.

    POPE. Welcome, grave Fathers, answer presently,
What have our holy Council there decreed,
Concerning Bruno and the Emperor,
In quittance of* their late conspiracy   requital for
Against our state and Papal dignity?

    FAUSTUS. Most sacred Patron of the Church of Rome
By full consent of all the synod
Of priests and prelates, it is thus decreed:
That Bruno and the German Emperor

      [48] This reference does not correspond to historical fact.

Be held as Lollards* and bold schismatics   that is, heretics
And proud disturbers of the Church's peace.
And if that Bruno, by his own assent,
Without enforcement of* the German peers,   compulsion by
Did seek to wear the triple diadem,
And by your death to climb Saint Peter's chair,
The Statutes Decretal have thus decreed,
He shall be straight condemn'd of heresy,
And on a pile of fagots burnt to death.

   POPE. It is enough: Here, take him to your charge,
And bear him straight to Ponte Angelo,
And in the strongest tower enclose him fast;
To-morrow, sitting in our Consistory
With all our college of grave Cardinals,
We will determine of his life or death.
Here, take his triple crown along with you,
And leave it in the Church's treasury.
Make haste again,* my good Lord Cardinals,   come back
And take our blessing apostolical.   quickly

   MEPHISTOPHILIS. So, so; was never devil thus blessed before.

   FAUSTUS. Away, sweet Mephistophilis, be gone,
The Cardinals will be plagu'd for this anon.

      (*Exeunt* FAUSTUS *and* MEPHISTOPHILIS, *with* BRUNO.)

   POPE. Go presently and bring a banquet forth,
That we may solemnize Saint Peter's feast,
And with Lord Raymond, King of Hungary,
Drink to our late and happy victory.

                                       (*Exeunt.*)

Scene 2

(*A sennet* while the banquet is brought in; and   that is, a
then enter* FAUSTUS *and* MEPHISTOPHILIS *in their own*   trumpet call
shapes.)

   MEPHISTOPHILIS. Now, Faustus, come, prepare thyself for
     mirth:
The sleepy Cardinals are hard at hand
To censure* Bruno, that is posted hence,   pass judgment on
And on a proud-pac'd steed, as swift as thought,
Flies o'er the Alps to fruitful Germany,
There to salute the woeful Emperor.

   FAUSTUS. The Pope will curse them for their sloth to-day,
That slept both Bruno and his crown away:

But now, that Faustus may delight his mind,
And by their folly make some merriment,
Sweet Mephistophilis, so charm me here,
That I may walk invisible to all,
And do whate'er I please, unseen of any.
    MEPHISTOPHILIS. Faustus, thou shalt, then kneel down
        presently:
Whilst on thy head I lay my hand,
And charm thee with this magic wand.
First wear this girdle, then appear
Invisible to all are here:
The Planets seven, the gloomy air,
Hell and the Furies' forked hair,
Pluto's blue fire, and Hecate's tree,
With magic spells so compass thee,
That no eye may thy body see.
So, Faustus, now for all their holiness,
Do what thou wilt, thou shalt not be discern'd.
    FAUSTUS. Thanks, Mephistophilis; now, friars, take heed,
Lest Faustus make your shaven crowns to bleed.
    MEPHISTOPHILIS. Faustus, no more: see where the Cardi-
        nals come.

(*Enter* POPE, KING RAYMOND, *the* ARCHBISHOP OF RHEIMS,
and all the LORDS. *Enter the* CARDINALS *with a book.*)

    POPE. Welcome, Lord Cardinals: come, sit down.
Lord Raymond, take your seat. Friars, attend,
And see that all things be in readiness,
As best beseems this solemn festival.
    FIRST CARDINAL. First, may it please your sacred Holiness
To view the sentence of the reverend synod,
Concerning Bruno and the Emperor?
    POPE. What needs this question? Did I not tell you,
To-morrow we could sit i' th' Consistory,
And there determine of his punishment?
You brought us word even now, it was decreed
That Bruno and the cursed Emperor
Were by the holy Council both condemn'd
For loathed Lollards and base schismatics:
Then wherefore would you have me view that book?
    FIRST CARDINAL. Your Grace mistakes, you gave us no such
        charge.
    RAYMOND. Deny it not, we all are witnesses

That Bruno here was late deliver'd you,

With his rich triple crown to be reserv'd*   preserved

And put into the Church's treasury.

　　BOTH CARDINALS. By holy Paul, we saw them not.

　　POPE. By Peter, you shall die,

Unless you bring them forth immediately:

Hale them to prison, lade their limbs with gyves:*   chains

False prelates, for this hateful treachery,

Curs'd be your souls to hellish misery.

　　　　　　　(*Exeunt* Attendants *with the two* CARDINALS.)

　　FAUSTUS. So, they are safe: now, Faustus, to the feast,

The Pope had never such a frolic* guest.   frolicsome

　　POPE. Lord Archbishop of Reames, sit down with us.

　　ARCHBISHOP. I thank your Holiness.

　　FAUSTUS. Fall to, the devil choke you an* you spare.   if

　　POPE. How now? Who's that which spake?—Friars, look
　　　about.

　　FRIAR. Here's nobody, if it like your Holiness.

　　POPE. Lord Raymond, pray fall to. I am beholding

To the Bishop of Milan for this so rare a present.

　　FAUSTUS. I thank you, sir.

　　(*Snatches the dish.*)

　　POPE. How now? who's that which snatch'd the meat from
　　　me?

Villains, why speak you not?—

My good Lord Archbishop, here's a most dainty dish,

Was sent me from a Cardinal in France.

　　FAUSTUS. I'll have that too.

　　(*Snatches the dish.*)

　　POPE. What Lollards do attend our Holiness,

That we receive such great indignity?

Fetch me some wine.

　　FAUSTUS. Ay, pray do, for Faustus is a-dry.

　　POPE. Lord Raymond, I drink unto your grace.

　　FAUSTUS. I pledge your grace.

　　(*Snatches the cup.*)

　　POPE. My wine gone too?—ye lubbers* look about   louts

And find the man that doth this villainy,

Or by our sanctitude, you all shall die,

I pray, my lords, have patience at this

Troublesome banquet.

　　ARCHBISHOP. Please it your Holiness, I think it be

Some ghost crept out of Purgatory, and now

Is come unto your Holiness for his pardon.*   indulgence

POPE. It may be so:
Go then command our priests to sing a dirge,*   requiem mass
To lay the fury of this same troublesome ghost.

> (*Exit an* ATTENDANT.)

Once again, my Lord, fall to.
> (*The* POPE *crosses himself.*)

FAUSTUS. How now?
Must every bit be spiced with a cross?
Nay then, take that.
> (*Strikes the* POPE.)

POPE. O I am slain, help me, my lords;
O come and help to bear my body hence:—
Damn'd be his soul for ever for this deed!

> (*Exeunt the* POPE *and his train.*)

MEPHISTOPHILIS. Now, Faustus, what will you do now, for
I can tell you you'll be curs'd with bell, book, and candle.[49]

FAUSTUS. Bell, book and candle,—candle, book, and bell,—
Forward and backward, to curse Faustus to hell!

(*Enter* FRIARS *with bell, book, and candle for the Dirge.*)

FIRST FRIAR. Come, brethren, let's about our business with
   good devotion.
(*Sing this.*)
Cursed be he that stole his Holiness' meat from the table!
Maledicat Dominus![50]
Cursed be he that struck his Holiness a blow on the face!
Maledicat Dominus!
Cursed be he that took Friar Sandelo a blow on the   gave
pate! Maledicat Dominus!
Cursed be he that disturbeth our holy dirge! Maledicat
Dominus!
Cursed be he that took away his Holiness' wine! Maledicat
Dominus!
     Et omnes Sancti![51] *Amen!*

(MEPHISTOPHILIS *and* FAUSTUS *beat the* FRIARS; *fling fire-*
works among them; and exeunt.)

---

[49] A reference to the ceremony of excommunication.
[50] "May the Lord curse him."
[51] "And all the saints."

Scene 3

(*A street, near an inn. Enter* ROBIN *and* DICK, *with a cup.*)

DICK. Sirrah Robin, we were best look that your devil can answer the stealing of this same cup, for the vintner's boy follows us at the hard heels.*   at our heels

ROBIN. Tis no matter! let him come; an he follow us I'll so conjure him as he was never conjured in his life. I warrant him. Let me see the cup.

(*Enter* VINTNER.)

DICK. Here 't is. Yonder he comes. Now, Robin, now or never show thy cunning.

VINTNER. O are you here? I am glad I have found you, you are a couple of fine companions; pray, where's the cup you stole from the tavern?

ROBIN. How, how? we steal a cup? Take heed what you say; we look not like cup-stealers, I can tell you.

VINTNER. Never deny 't, for I know you have it, and I'll search you.

ROBIN. Search me? Ay, and spare not. Hold the cup, Dick (*aside to* DICK). Come, come, search me, search me!

(VINTNER *searches him.*)

VINTNER (*to* DICK). Come on, sirrah, let me search you now!

DICK. Ay, ay, do! Hold the cup, Robin (*aside to* ROBIN). I fear not your searching; we scorn to steal your cups, I can tell you.

(VINTNER *searches him.*)

VINTNER. Never outface me for the matter,[52] for, sure, the cup is between you two.

ROBIN. Nay, there you lie, 'tis beyond us both.

VINTNER. A plague take you! I thought 't was your knavery to take it away; come, give it me again.

ROBIN. Ay much; when? can you tell? Dick, make me a circle, and stand close at my back, and stir not for thy life. Vintner, you shall have your cup anon. Say nothing, Dick. (*Reads.*) O per se,* o Demogorgon, Belcher and   O by itself
Mephistophilis!

[52] Brazen out the matter with me.

(*Enter* MEPHISTOPHILIS.)

MEPHISTOPHILIS. You princely legions of infernal rule,
How am I vexed by these villains' charms!
From Constantinople have they brought me now
Only for pleasure of these damned slaves.

(*Exit* VINTNER.)

ROBIN. By Lady, sir, you have had a shrewd* journey   irksome
of it. Will it please you to take a shoulder of mutton to supper,
and a tester⁵³ in your purse, and go back again? '

DICK. Aye, aye. I pray you heartily, sir, for we call'd you
but in jest, I promise you.

MEPHISTOPHILIS. To purge the rashness of this cursed deed,
First be thou turned to this ugly shape,
For apish* deeds transformed to an ape.   silly

ROBIN. O brave! an ape! I pray, sir, let me have the carrying of him about to show some tricks.

MEPHISTOPHILIS. And so thou shalt: be thou transformed
  to a dog,
And carry him upon thy back. Away, be gone!

ROBIN. A dog! that's excellent; let the maids look well to
their porridge-pots, for I'll into the kitchen presently. Come,
Dick, come.

(*Exeunt* ROBIN *and* DICK.)

MEPHISTOPHILIS. Now with the flames of ever-burning fire,
I'll wing myself, and forthwith fly amain
Unto my Faustus, to the Great Turk's Court.

(*Exit.*)

ACT IV

Prologue

(*Enter* CHORUS.)

CHORUS. When Faustus had with pleasure ta'en the view
Of rarest things, and royal courts of kings,
He stay'd his course,* and so returned home;   stopped traveling
Where such as bear his absence but with grief,
I mean his friends and near'st companions,
Did gratulate* his safety with kind words,   express joy at
And in their conference of what befell,
Touching his journey through the world and air,

---

⁵³ Slang, a sixpence.

They put forth questions of astrology,
Which Faustus answer'd with such learned skill
As they admir'd and wonder'd at his wit,
Now is his fame spread forth in every land:
Amongst the rest the Emperor is one,
Carolus the Fifth,* at whose palace now   Charles V
Faustus is feasted 'mongst his noblemen.
What there he did, in trial of his art,
I leave untold; your eyes shall see perform'd.

                                                            (*Exit.*)

Scene 1

(*A room in the* EMPEROR'S *Court at Innsbruck. Enter* MAR-
TINO *and* FREDERICK *at different doors.*)

MARTINO. What ho, officers, gentlemen,
Hie to the presence* to attend the Emperor,   presence-chamber
Good Frederick, see the rooms be voided straight,
His Majesty is coming to the hall;
Go back, and see the state* in readiness.   throne
    FREDERICK. But where is Bruno, our elected Pope,
That on a fury's back came post from Rome?
Will not his Grace consort* the Emperor?   accompany
    MARTINO. O yes, and with him comes the German conjuror,
The learned Faustus, fame* of Wittenberg,   glory
The wonder of the world for magic art;
And he intends to show great Carolus
The race of all his stout progenitors;*   predecessors,
                                                              ancestors
And bring in presence of his Majesty
The royal shapes and warlike semblances
Of Alexander and his beauteous paramour.
    FREDERICK. Where is Benvolio?
    MARTINO. Fast asleep, I warrant you,
He took his rouse with stoups* of Rhenish wine   that is,
                                                   drank tankards
So kindly yesternight to Bruno's health,
That all this day the sluggard keeps his bed.
    FREDERICK. See, see, his window's ope, we'll call to him.
    MARTINO. What ho, Benvolio!

(*Enter* BENVOLIO *above, at a window, in his night-cap; but-
toning his clothes.*)

BENVOLIO. What a devil ail you two?
MARTINO. Speak softly, sir, lest the devil hear you:

For Faustus at the court is late arriv'd,
And at his heels a thousand furies wait,
To accomplish whatsoever the Doctor please.
    BENVOLIO. What of this?
    MARTINO. Come, leave thy chamber first, and thou shalt see
This conjuror perform such rare exploits,
Before the Pope* and royal Emperor,   that is, Bruno
As never yet was seen in Germany.
    BENVOLIO. Has not the Pope enough of conjuring yet?
He was upon the devil's back late enough;
And if he be so far in love with him,
I would he would post with him to Rome again.
    FREDERICK. Speak, wilt thou come and see this sport?
    BENVOLIO. Not I.
    MARTINO. Wilt thou stand in thy window, and see it then?
    BENVOLIO. Ay, an I fall not asleep i' th' meantime.
    MARTINO. The Emperor is at hand, who comes to see
What wonders by black spells may compass'd* be.   accomplished
    BENVOLIO. Well, go you attend the Emperor: I am content
for this once to thrust my head out at a window; for they say,
if a man be drunk overnight the devil cannot hurt him in the
morning; if that be true, I have a charm in my head shall control him as well as the conjuror, I warrant you.
                  (*Exeunt* FREDERICK *and* MARTINO.)

Scene 2

(*The presence-chamber in the Court. A sennet. Enter*
CHARLES, *the* GERMAN EMPEROR, BRUNO, DUKE OF SAX-
ONY, FAUSTUS, MEPHISTOPHILIS, FREDERICK, MARTINO, *and*
ATTENDANTS.)

    EMPEROR. Wonder of men, renown'd magician,
Thrice-learned Faustus, welcome to our Court.
This deed of thine, in setting Bruno free
From his and our professed enemy,
Shall add more excellence unto thine art,
Than if by powerful necromantic spells,
Thou couldst command the world's obedience:
For ever be belov'd of Carolus,
And if this Bruno thou hast late redeem'd,
In peace possess the triple diadem,
And sit in Peter's chair, despite of chance,
Thou shalt be famous through all Italy,
And honour'd of the German Emperor.

FAUSTUS. These gracious words, most royal Carolus,
Shall make poor Faustus, to his utmost power,
Both love and serve the German Emperor,
And lay his life at holy Bruno's feet.
For proof whereof, if so your Grace be pleas'd,
The Doctor stands prepar'd by power of art
To cast his magic charms, that shall pierce through
The ebon* gates of ever-burning hell,   black
And hale the stubborn Furies from their caves,
To compass* whatsoe'er your Grace commands.   perform
 BENVOLIO (*above*).⁵⁴ 'Blood, he speaks terribly: but for all
  that
I do not greatly believe him: he looks as like a conjuror as the
  Pope to a costermonger.*   street vendor
 EMPEROR. Then, Faustus, as thou late did'st promise us,
We would behold that famous conqueror,
Great Alexander and his paramour
In their true shapes and state majestical,
That we may wonder at their excellence.
 FAUSTUS. Your Majesty shall see them presently.
Mephistophilis, away.
And with a solemn noise of trumpets' sound
Present before this royal Emperor,
Great Alexander and his beauteous paramour.
 MEPHISTOPHILIS. Faustus, I will.
 BENVOLIO. Well, Master Doctor, an your devils come not
away quickly, you shall have me asleep presently: zounds, I
could eat myself for anger, to think I have been such an ass
all this while to stand gaping after the devil's governor,*   tutor
and can see nothing.
 FAUSTUS (*aside to* BENVOLIO). I'll make you feel something
  anon, if my art fail me not.—
My lord, I must forewarn your Majesty,
That when my spirits present the royal shapes
Of Alexander and his paramour,
Your Grace demand no questions of the king,
But in dumb silence let them come and go.
 EMPEROR. Be it as Faustus please, we are content.
 BENVOLIO. Ay, ay, and I am content too; and thou bring
Alexander and his paramour before the Emperor, I'll be
Acteon and turn myself to a stag.⁵⁵

 ⁵⁴ Benvolio remains at the window from the previous scene.
 ⁵⁵ Actaeon was a huntsman who surprised Diana while she was
bathing; in punishment he was turned into a stag, with the result
that he was killed by his own hounds.

Faustus (*aside to* Benvolio). And I'll play Diana, and send you the horns presently.

(*Sennet. Enter at one door the* Emperor Alexander, *at the other* Darius; *they meet,* Darius *is thrown down,* Alexander *kills him; takes off his crown and offering to go out, his paramour meets him, he embraces her, and sets* Darius' *crown upon her head; and coming back, both salute the* Emperor, *who, leaving his state,* offers to embrace* throne *them, which,* Faustus *seeing, suddenly stays him. Then trumpets cease, and music sounds.*)

My gracious lord, you do forget yourself,
These are but shadows, not substantial.
Emperor. O pardon me, my thoughts are so ravished
With sight of this renowned Emperor,
That in mine arms I would have compass'd* him.   encircled
But, Faustus, since I may not speak to them,
To satisfy my longing thoughts at full,
Let me this tell thee: I have heard it said,
That this fair lady whilst she liv'd on earth,
Had on her neck, a little wart, or mole;
How may I prove that saying to be true?
Faustus. Your Majesty may boldly go and see.
Emperor. Faustus, I see it plain,
And in this sight thou better pleasest me,
Than if I gain'd another monarchy.
Faustus. Away, be gone!

(*Exit show.*)

See, see, my gracious lord, what strange beast is yon, that
          thrusts his head out at window?
Emperor. O wondrous sight: see, Duke of Saxony,
Two spreading horns most strangely fastened
Upon the head of young Benvolio.
Saxony. What, is he asleep, or dead?
Faustus. He sleeps, my lord, but dreams not of his horns.
Emperor. This sport is excellent; we'll call and wake him.
What ho, Benvolio.
Benvolio. A plague upon you, let me sleep a while.
Emperor. I blame thee not to sleep much, having such a
head of thine own.
Saxony. Look up, Benvolio, 'tis the Emperor calls.
Benvolio. The Emperor? where?—O zounds, my head![56]

[56] His horns prevent him from pulling his head back from the
window.

EMPEROR. Nay, and thy horns hold, 'tis no matter for thy head, for that's arm'd sufficiently.

FAUSTUS. Why, how now, Sir Knight, what, hang'd by the horns? this is most horrible: fie, fie, pull in your head for shame, let not all the world wonder at you.

BENVOLIO. Zounds, Doctor, is this your villainy?

FAUSTUS. O say not so, sir: the Doctor has no skill,
No art, no cunning, to present these lords,
Or bring before this royal Emperor
The mighty monarch, warlike Alexander.
If Faustus do it, you are straight resolv'd
In bold Acteon's shape to turn a stag.
And therefore, my lord, so please your Majesty,
I'll raise a kennel of hounds, shall hunt him so,
As all his footmanship* shall scarce prevail   skill in running
To keep his carcase* from their bloody fangs.   carcass
Ho, Belimote, Argiron, Asterote.

BENVOLIO. Hold, hold! Zounds, he'll raise up a kennel of devils,
I think, anon: good, my lord, entreat for me: 'sblood,
I am never able to endure these torments.

EMPEROR. Then, good Master Doctor,
Let me entreat you to remove his horns,
He has done penance now sufficiently.

FAUSTUS. My gracious lord, not so much for injury done to me, as to delight your Majesty with some mirth, hath Faustus justly requited this injurious* knight, which being all   insulting
I desire, I am content to remove his horns. Mephistophilis, transform him (MEPHISTOPHILIS *removes the horns*), and hereafter, sir, look you speak well of scholars.

BENVOLIO. Speak well of ye? 'sblood, and scholars be such cuckold-makers to clap horns of honest men's heads o' this order,* I'll ne'er trust smooth faces and small   in this manner
ruffs,[57] more. But an* I be not reveng'd for this, would I   if
might be turn'd to a gaping oyster, and drink nothing but salt water.

> (*Aside, and then exit above.*)

EMPEROR. Come, Faustus, while the Emperor lives,
In recompense of this thy high desert,*   meritoriousness
Thou shalt command the state of Germany,
And live belov'd of mighty Carolus.

> (*Exeunt omnes.*)

---

[57] "Beardless scholars in academic garb" (Boas).

Scene 3

(*Near a grove, outside Innsbruck. Enter* BENVOLIO, MAR-
TINO, FREDERICK, *and* SOLDIERS.)

MARTINO. Nay, sweet Benvolio, let us sway thy thoughts
From this attempt against the conjuror.
 BENVOLIO. Away, you love me not, to urge me thus.
Shall I let slip so great an injury,
When every servile groom jests at my wrongs,
And in their rustic gambols proudly say,
'Benvolio's head was graced with horns to-day'?
O may these eyelids never close again,
Till with my sword I have that conjuror slain.
If you will aid me in this enterprise,
Then draw your weapons, and be resolute:
If not, depart: here will Benvolio die,
But* Faustus' death shall quit* my infamy.   unless/requite
 FREDERICK. Nay, we will stay with thee, betide*   happen
  what may,
And kill that Doctor if he come this way.
 BENVOLIO. Then, gentle Frederick, hie thee to the grove,
And place our servants and our followers
Close* in an ambush there behind the trees.   hidden
By this (I know) the conjuror is near;
I saw him kneel and kiss the Emperor's hand,
And take his leave laden with rich rewards.
Then, soldiers, boldly fight; if Faustus die,
Take you the wealth, leave us the victory.
 FREDERICK. Come, soldiers, follow me unto the grove;
Who kills him shall have gold and endless love.
      (*Exit* FREDERICK *with the* SOLDIERS.)
 BENVOLIO. My head is lighter than it was by th' horns,
But yet my heart's more ponderous than my head,
And pants until I see that conjuror dead.
 MARTINO. Where shall we place ourselves, Benvolio?
 BENVOLIO. Here will we stay to bide the first assault.
O were that damned hell-bound but in place,*   at hand
Thou soon shouldst see me quit my foul disgrace,

(*Enter* FREDERICK.)

FREDERICK. Close,* close, the conjuror is at hand,   hide

And all alone comes walking in his gown;
Be ready then, and strike the peasant* down.   rascal
   BENVOLIO. Mine be that honour then: now, sword, strike
     home,
For horns he gave I'll have his head anon.

   (*Enter* FAUSTUS *wearing a false head.*)

   MARTINO. See, see, he comes.
   BENVOLIO.   No words: this blow ends all,
Hell take his soul, his body thus must fall.
   (*Stabs* FAUSTUS.)
   FAUSTUS. (*falling*). Oh!
   FREDERICK. Groan you, Master Doctor?
   BENVOLIO. Break may his heart with groans: dear Frederick,
     see,
Thus will I end his griefs* immediately.   wrongdoings
   MARTINO. Strike with a willing hand.
   (BENVOLIO *strikes off* FAUSTUS' *false head.*)
                          His head is off.
   BENVOLIO. The devil's head, the Furies now may laugh.
   FREDERICK. Was this that stern aspect, that awful frown,
Made the grim monarch of infernal spirits
Tremble and quake at his commanding charms?
   MARTINO. Was this that damned head, whose art conspir'd
Benvolio's shame before the Emperor?
   BENVOLIO. Ay, that's the head, and here the body lies,
Justly rewarded for his villainies.
   FREDERICK. Come, let's devise how we may add more shame
To the black scandal of his hated name.
   BENVOLIO. First, on his head, in quittance of my wrongs,
I'll nail huge forked horns, and let them hang
Within the window where he yok'd me first,
That all the world may see my first revenge.
   MARTINO. What use shall we put his beard to?
   BENVOLIO. We'll sell it to a chimney-sweeper; it will wear
out ten birchen brooms, I warrant you.
   FREDERICK. What shall his eyes do?
   BENVOLIO. We'll put out his eyes, and they shall serve for
buttons to his lips, to keep his tongue from catching cold.
   MARTINO. An excellent policy.* And now, sirs, having device
divided him, what shall the body do?
   (FAUSTUS *rises.*)

BENVOLIO. Zounds, the devil's alive again.

FREDERICK. Give him his head, for God's sake.

FAUSTUS. Nay, keep it: Faustus will have heads and hands,
Ay, all your hearts to recompense this deed.
Knew you not, traitors, I was limited*   accorded
For four-and-twenty years to breathe on earth?
And had you cut my body with your swords,
Or hew'd this flesh and bones as small as sand,
Yet in a minute had my spirit return'd,
And I had breath'd a man made free from harm.
But wherefore do I dally my revenge?
Asteroth, Belimoth, Mephistophilis,

(*Enter* MEPHISTOPHILIS *and other* DEVILS.)

Go, horse these traitors on your fiery backs,
And mount aloft with them as high as heaven,
Thence pitch them headlong to the lowest hell:
Yet, stay, the world shall see their misery,
And hell shall after plague their treachery.
Go, Belimoth, and take this caitiff hence,
And hurl him in some lake of mud and dirt:
Take thou this other, drag him through the woods,
Amongst the pricking thorns, and sharpest briers,
Whilst with my gentle Mephistophilis,
This traitor flies unto some steepy rock,
That, rolling down, may break the villain's bones,
As he intended to dismember me.
Fly hence, despatch my charge immediately.

FREDERICK. Pity us, gentle Faustus, save our lives!

FAUSTUS. Away!

FREDERICK. He must needs go that the devil drives.

(*Exeunt* SPIRITS *with the* KNIGHTS.)

(*Enter the* SOLDIERS *from their ambush.*)

FIRST SOLDIER. Come, sirs, prepare yourselves in readiness,
Make haste to help these noble gentlemen,
I heard them parley with the conjuror.

SECOND SOLDIER. See where he comes, despatch, and kill the
 slave.

FAUSTUS. What's here? an ambush to betray my life:
Then, Faustus, try thy skill: base peasants, stand:
For lo! these trees remove* at my command, change places

And stand as bulwarks 'twixt yourselves and me,
To shield me from your hated treachery:
Yet to encounter this your weak attempt,
Behold an army comes incontinent.*   immediately
> (FAUSTUS *strikes the door, and enter a devil playing on a
> drum, after him another bearing an ensign; and divers with
> weapons,* MEPHISTOPHILIS *with fireworks; they set upon the*
> SOLDIERS, *and drive them out. Exit* FAUSTUS.)

Scene 4

> (*Enter at different doors* BENVOLIO, FREDERICK, *and* MAR-
> TINO, *their heads and faces bloody, and besmear'd with mud
> and dirt, all having horns on their heads.*)

MARTINO. What ho, Benvolio!
BENVOLIO. Here, what, Frederick, ho!
FREDERICK. O help me, gentle friend; where is Martino?
MARTINO. Dear Frederick, here,
Half smother'd in a lake of mud and dirt,
Through which the furies dragg'd me by the heels
FREDERICK. Martino, see Benvolio's horns again.
MARTINO. O misery, how now, Benvolio?
BENVOLIO. Defend me, heaven, shall I be haunted still?
MARTINO. Nay, fear not, man; we have no power to kill.[58]
BENVOLIO. My friends transformed thus! O hellish spite,
Your heads are all set with horns.
FREDERICK.   You hit it right:
It is your own you mean, feel on your head.
BENVOLIO. 'Zounds, horns again!
MARTINO.   Nay, chafe not,
man, we all are sped.*   provided with them
BENVOLIO. What devil attends this damn'd magician,
That, spite of spite,* our wrongs are doubled?   despite everything
FREDERICK. What may we do, that we may hide our shames?
BENVOLIO. If we should follow him to work revenge,
He'd join long asses' ears to these huge horns,
And make us laughing-stocks to all the world.
MARTINO. What shall we then do, dear Benvolio?
BENVOLIO. I have a castle joining near these woods,
And thither we'll repair and live obscure,
Till time shall alter these our brutish shapes:

[58] That is, We will not hunt you down because you resemble
an animal. *Haunted* of the previous line may also be a pun on
hunted.

Sith* black disgrace hath thus eclips'd our fame,   since
We'll rather die with grief than live with shame. .

(*Exeunt omnes.*)

Scene 5

(*At the entrance to the house of* FAUSTUS. *Enter* FAUSTUS
and the HORSE-COURSER.*)   horse dealer

HORSE-COURSER. I beseech, your worship, accept of these
forty dollars.[59]

FAUSTUS. Friend, thou canst not buy so good a horse, for
so small a price. I have no great need to sell him, but if thou
likest him for ten dollars more take him, because I see thou
hast a good mind to him.

HORSE-COURSER. I beseech you, sir, accept of this; I am
a very poor man and have lost very much of late by horse-
flesh, and this bargain will set me up again.

FAUSTUS. Well, I will not stand* with thee, give me   haggle
the money. (HORSE-COURSER *gives* FAUSTUS *the money*.) Now,
sirrah, I must tell you that you may ride him o'er hedge and
ditch, and spare him not; but, do you hear? in any case ride
him not into the water.

HORSE-COURSER. How, sir, not into the water? Why, will he
not drink of all waters?

FAUSTUS. Yes, he will drink of all waters, but ride him not
into the water; o'er hedge and ditch, or where thou wilt, but
not into the water. Go, bid the ostler deliver him unto you,
and remember what I say.

HORSE-COURSER. I warrant you, sir. O joyful day, now am I
a made man for ever.

(*Exit.*)

FAUSTUS. What are thou, Faustus, but a man condemn'd to
die?
Thy fatal time* draws to a final end,   allotted time
Despair doth drive distrust into my thoughts.
Confound these passions with a quiet sleep.
Tush! Christ did call the thief upon the Cross;
Then rest thee, Faustus, quiet in conceit.*   in mind
(*He sits to sleep.*)

(*Re-enter the* HORSE-COURSER *wet*.)

[59] English name for the German *thaler*.

HORSE-COURSER. O what a cozening* Doctor was   cheating
this? I was riding my horse into the water, thinking some hidden mystery had been in the horse, I had nothing under me but a little straw, and had much ado to escape drowning. Well, I'll go rouse him, and make him give me my forty dollars again. Ho, sirrah Doctor, you cozening scab!* Master scoundrel
Doctor, awake and rise, and give me my money again, for your horse is turned to a bottle* of hay, master Doctor (*He*   bundle
pulls off his leg.) Alas! I am undone, what shall I do? I have pull'd off his leg.

FAUSTUS. O, help, help, the villain hath murder'd me.

HORSE-COURSER. Murder, or not murder, now he has but one leg, I'll outrun him, and cast this leg into some ditch or other.

                            (*Aside, and then runs out.*)

FAUSTUS. Stop him, stop him, stop him!—ha, ha, ha, Faustus hath his leg again, and the horse-courser a bundle of hay for his forty dollars.

(*Enter* WAGNER.)

How now, Wagner, what news with thee?

WAGNER. If it please you, the Duke of Anholt doth earnestly entreat your company, and hath sent some of his men to attend you with provision fit for your journey.

FAUSTUS. The Duke of Anholt's an honourable gentleman, and one to whom I must be no niggard of my cunning. Come away!

                                   (*Exeunt.*)

Scene 6

(*An inn. Enter* ROBIN, DICK, *the* HORSE-COURSER, *and a* CARTER.)

CARTER. Come, my masters, I'll bring you to the best beer in Europe. What ho, hostess!—where be these whores?

(*Enter* HOSTESS.)

HOSTESS. How now, what lack you? What, my old guests, welcome.

ROBIN. Sirra Dick, dost thou know why I stand so mute?

DICK. No, Robin, why is't?

ROBIN. I am eighteenpence on the score,[60] but say nothing, see if she have forgotten me.

HOSTESS. Who's this, that stands so solemnly by himself? what, my old guest?

ROBIN. O hostess, how do you? I hope my score*   bill stands still.

HOSTESS. Ay, there's no doubt of that, for methinks you make no haste to wipe it out.

DICK. Why, hostess, I say, fetch us some beer.

HOSTESS. You shall presently. Look up in th' hall there, ho![61]

(Exit.)

DICK. Come, sirs, what shall we do now till mine hostess comes?

CARTER. Marry, sir, I'll tell you the bravest tale how a conjuror served me; you know Doctor Fauster?

HORSE-COURSER. Ay, a plague take him, here's some on's have cause to know him; did he conjure thee too?

CARTER. I'll tell you how he serv'd me: As I was going to Wittenberg t'other day, with a load of hay, he met me, and asked me what he should give me for as much hay as he could eat; now, sir, I thinking that a little would serve his turn, bade him take as much as he would for three farthings; so he presently gave me my money, and fell to eating; and, as I am a cursen* man, he never left eating, till he had eat up all Christian my load of hay.

ALL. O monstrous, eat a whole load of hay!

ROBIN. Yes, yes, that may be; for I have heard of one that has eat a load of logs.

HORSE-COURSER. Now, sirs, you shall hear how villainously he serv'd me: I went to him yesterday to buy a horse of him, and he would by no means sell him under forty dollars; so, sir, because I knew him to be such a horse as would run over hedge and ditch and never tire, I gave him his money. So when I had my horse, Doctor Fauster bade me ride him night and day, and spare him no time; but, quoth he, in any case, ride him not into the water. Now, sir, I thinking the horse had had some rare quality that he would not have me know of, what did I but rid him into a great river, and when I came just in

[60] That is, I haven't enough money to pay the bill.
[61] This is an order to her staff.

the midst, my horse vanish'd away, and I sat straddling upon
a bottle* of hay.   bundle

    ALL. O brave* Doctor!   villainous

    HORSE-COURSER. But you shall hear how bravely* villainously
I serv'd him for it; I went me home to his house, and there I
found him asleep; I kept a hallooing and whooping in his ears,
but all could not wake him: I seeing that, took him by the leg,
and never rested pulling, till I had pull'd me his leg quite off,
and now 'tis at home in mine hostry.*   hostelry

    DICK. And has the Doctor but one leg then? that's excellent,
for one of his devils turn'd me into the likeness of an ape's
face.

    CARTER. Some more drink, hostess.

    ROBIN. Hark you, we'll into another room and drink a while,
and then we'll go seek out the Doctor.

                                                    (*Exeunt omnes.*)

                            Scene 7

(*The Court of the* DUKE OF ANHOLT. *Enter the* DUKE OF
ANHOLT, *his* DUCHESS, FAUSTUS, *and* MEPHISTOPHILIS.)

    DUKE. Thanks, master Doctor, for these pleasant sights. Nor
know I how sufficiently to recompense your great deserts in
erecting that enchanted castle in the air, the sight whereof so
delighted   me,
As nothing in the world could please me more.

    FAUSTUS. I do think myself, my good Lord, highly recom-
pensed in that it pleaseth your Grace to think but well of that
which Faustus hath performed. But gracious lady, it may be
that you have taken no pleasure in those sights; therefore, I
pray you tell me, what is the thing you most desire to have;
be it in the world, it shall be yours. I have heard that great-
bellied women do long for things are* rare and dainty. which are

    DUCHESS. True, master Doctor, and since I find you so kind,
I will make known unto you what my heart desires to have;
and were it now summer, as it is January, a dead time of the
winter, I would request no better meat* than a dish of   food
ripe grapes.

    FAUSTUS. This is but a small matter. Go, Mephistophilis,
away!

                                            (*Exit* MEPHISTOPHILIS.)
Madam, I will do more than this for your content.

    (*Enter* MEPHISTOPHILIS *again with the grapes.*)

Here now taste ye these, they should be good,
For they come from a far country, I can tell you.

    DUKE. This makes me wonder more than all the rest
That at this time of the year, when every tree
Is barren of his fruit, from whence you had
These ripe grapes.

    FAUSTUS. Please it your Grace the year is divided into two
circles over the whole world, so that when it is winter with us,
in the contrary circle it is likewise summer with them, as in
India, Saba* and such countries that lie far east, where   Sheba
they have fruit twice a year. From whence, by means of a swift
spirit that I have, I had these grapes brought, as you see.

    DUCHESS. And trust me, they are the sweetest grapes that
e'er I tasted.

    (*The* CLOWNS* *bounce* *at the gate within.*)   rustics/thump
    DUKE. What rude disturbers have we at the gate?
Go, pacify their fury, set it ope,*   open it
And then demand of them what they would have.

    (*They knock again, and call out to talk with* FAUSTUS.)
    A SERVANT. Why, how now, masters, what a coil* is   racket
      there?
What is the reason you disturb the Duke?

    DICK. We have no reason for it, therefore a fig for him.

    SERVANT. Why, saucy varlets, dare you be so bold?

    HORSE-COURSER. I hope, sir, we have wit enough to be more
bold than welcome.

    SERVANT. It appears so, pray be bold elsewhere,
And trouble not the Duke.

    DUKE. What would they have?

    SERVANT. They all cry out to speak with Doctor Faustus.

    CARTER. Ay, and we will speak with him.

    DUKE. Will you, sir? Commit the rascals.[62]

    DICK. Commit with us! he were as good commit with his
father as commit with us.

    FAUSTUS. I do beseech your Grace let them come in,
They are good subject for a merriment.

    DUKE. Do as thou wilt, Faustus, I give thee leave.

    FAUSTUS. I thank your Grace.

    (*Enter* ROBIN, DICK, CARTER, *and* HORSE-COURSER.)

Why, how now, my good friends?

     [62] "Send the rascals to prison." In the following line Dick
takes *commit* to mean "to have sexual intercourse."

'Faith you are too outrageous,* but come near,   violent
I have procur'd your pardons: welcome all.

ROBIN. Nay, sir, we will be welcome for our money, and we
will pay for what we take. What ho, give's half a dozen of
beer here, and be hang'd.[63]

FAUSTUS. Nay, hark you, can you tell me where you are?

CARTER. Ay, marry can I; we are under heaven.

SERVANT. Ay, but, sir sauce-box,[64] know you in what place?

HORSE-COURSER. Ay, ay, the house is good enough to drink
in: Zounds, fill us some beer, or we'll break all the barrels in
the house, and dash out all your brains with your bottles.

FAUSTUS. Be not so furious: come, you shall have beer.
My lord, beseech you give me leave a while,
I'll gage* my credit, 'twill content your Grace.   stake

DUKE. With all my heart, kind Doctor, please thyself;
Our servants and our Court's at thy command.

FAUSTUS. I humbly thank your Grace: then fetch some beer.

HORSE-COURSER. Ay, marry, there spake a Doctor indeed,
and, 'faith, I'll drink a health to thy wooden leg for that word.

FAUSTUS. My wooden leg! what dost thou mean by that?

CARTER. Ha, ha, ha, dost hear him, Dick? He has forgot his
leg.

HORSE-COURSER. Ay, ay, he does not stand much upon[65]
that.

FAUSTUS. No, 'faith not much upon a wooden leg.

CARTER. Good Lord, that flesh and blood should be so frail
with your Worship. Do not you remember a horse-courser you
sold a horse to?

FAUSTUS. Yes, I remember I sold one a horse.

CARTER. And do you remember you bid he should not ride
him into the water?

FAUSTUS. Yes, I do very well remember that.

CARTER. And do you remember nothing of your leg?

FAUSTUS. No, in good sooth.

CARTER. Then, I pray, remember your curtsy.[66]

---

[63] Robin and his companions believe they are still in the tavern
of the previous scene.

[64] Name given to a person who makes saucy remarks.

[65] That is, He doesn't consider it too important. Faustus replies
with the literal meaning of the words.

[66] The carter puns on another meaning of leg, a bow. Double
pun on penis?

FAUSTUS. I thank you, sir.

CARTER. 'Tis not so much worth; I pray you tell me one thing.

FAUSTUS. What's that?

CARTER. Be both your legs bedfellows every night together?

FAUSTUS. Wouldst thou make a Colossus[67] of me, that thou askest me such questions?

CARTER. No, truly, sir: I would make nothing of you, but I would fain* know that.   gladly

(*Enter* HOSTESS *with drink*.)

FAUSTUS. Then I assure thee certainly they are.

CARTER. I thank you, I am fully satisfied.

FAUSTUS. But wherefore dost thou ask?

CARTER. For nothing, sir: but methinks you should have a wooden bedfellow of one of 'em.

HORSE-COURSER. Why, do you hear, sir, did not I pull off one of your legs when you were asleep?

FAUSTUS. But I have it again, now I am awake: look you here, sir.

ALL. O horrible, had the Doctor three legs?

CARTER. Do you remember, sir, how you cozened me and ate up my load of——

(FAUSTUS *charms him dumb*.)

DICK. Do you remember how you made me wear an ape's——

HORSE-COURSER. You whoreson conjuring scab, do you remember how you cozened me with a ho——

ROBIN. Ha' you forgotten me? you think to carry it away[68] with your *hey-pass* and *re-pass;** do you (conjuring terms) remember the dog's fa——

(*Exeunt* CLOWNS.)

HOSTESS. Who pays for the ale? hear you, Master Doctor, now you have sent away my guests, I pray who shall pay me for my a——

(*Exit* HOSTESS.)

LADY. My lord,
We are much beholding to this learned man.

[67] It was commonly thought that the Colossus of Rhodes straddled the entrance to the harbor.

[68] Get away with it.

DUKE. So are we, Madam, which we will recompense
With all the love and kindness that we may.
His artful sport drives all sad thoughts away.

                                                    (*Exeunt.*)

ACT V

Scene 1

(*Thunder and lightning. Enter* DEVILS *with cover'd dishes.*
MEPHISTOPHILIS *leads them into* FAUSTUS' *study. Then
enter* WAGNER.)

WAGNER. I think my master means to die shortly,
He has made his will, and given me his wealth,
His house, his goods, and store of golden plate,
Besides two thousand ducats ready coin'd.
I wonder what he means; if death were nigh
He would not frolic thus. He's now at supper
With the scholars, where there's such belly-cheer
As Wagner in his life ne'er saw the like.
And see where they come, belike the feast is done.

                                                    (*Exit.*)

(*Enter* FAUSTUS, MEPHISTOPHILIS, *and three* SCHOLARS.)

FIRST SCHOLAR. Master Doctor Faustus, since our confer-
ence about fair ladies, which was the beautifullest in all the
world, we have determined with ourselves that Helen of
Greece was the admirablest lady that ever liv'd: therefore,
Master Doctor, if you will do us so much favour, as to let us
see that peerless dame of Greece, we should think ourselves
much beholding unto you.
FAUSTUS. Gentlemen,
For that I know your friendship is unfeign'd,
It is not Faustus' custom to deny
The just request of those that wish him well,
You shall behold that peerless dame of Greece,
No otherwise for pomp or majesty
Than when Sir Paris cross'd the seas with her,
And brought the spoil* to rich Dardania.*   booty/Troy
Be silent, then, for danger is in words.

(*Music sounds,* MEPHISTOPHILIS *brings in* HELEN, *she
passes over the stage.*)

SECOND SCHOLAR. Was this fair Helen, whose admired worth
Made Greece with ten years' wars afflict poor Troy?
Too simple is my wit to tell her praise,
Whom all the world admires for majesty.

THIRD SCHOLAR. No marvel though the angry Greeks pursued
With ten years' war the rape* of such a queen,   capture
Whose heavenly beauty passeth all compare.

FIRST SCHOLAR. Now we have seen the pride of Nature's work,
And only paragon of excellence,
We'll take our leaves; and for this glorious deed
Happy and blest be Faustus evermore!

FAUSTUS. Gentlemen, farewell: the same wish I to you.
(*Exeunt* SCHOLARS.)

(*Enter an* OLD MAN.)

OLD MAN. O gentle Faustus, leave this damned art,
This magic, that will charm thy soul to hell,
And quite bereave thee of salvation,
Though thou hast now offended like a man,
Do not persever in it like a devil;
Yet, yet, thou hast an amiable* soul,   worthy of love
If sin by custom grow not into nature:
Then, Faustus, will repentance come too late,
Then thou art banish'd from the sight of heaven;
No mortal can express the pains of hell.
It may be this my exhortation
Seems harsh and all unpleasant; let it not,
For, gentle son, I speak it not in wrath,
Or envy of* thee, but in tender love,   with malice toward
And pity of thy future misery.
And so have hope, that this my kind rebuke,
Checking* thy body, may amend thy soul.   reproving

FAUSTUS. Break heart, drop blood, and mingle it with tears,
Tears falling from repentant heaviness
Of thy most vile and loathesome filthiness,
The stench whereof corrupts the inward soul
With such flagitious crimes of heinous sins
As no commiseration may expel,
But mercy, Faustus, of thy Saviour sweet,
Whose blood alone must wash away thy guilt—

Where art thou, Faustus? wretch, what hast thou done?
Damn'd art thou, Faustus, damn'd; despair and die!
   (MEPHISTOPHILIS *gives him a dagger.*)
Hell claims his right, and with a roaring voice
Says, 'Faustus, come; thine hour is almost come';
And Faustus now will come to do thee right.
   (FAUSTUS *raises the dagger.*)
   OLD MAN. Oh, stay, good Faustus, stay thy desperate steps!
I see an angel hover o'er thy head,
And, with a vial full of precious grace,
Offers to pour the same into thy soul:
Then call for mercy, and avoid despair.
   FAUSTUS. O friend, I feel
Thy words to comfort my distressed soul!
Leave me a while to ponder on my sins.
   OLD MAN. Faustus, I leave thee; but with grief of heart,
Fearing the enemy of thy hapless soul.

                                                    (*Exit.*)

   FAUSTUS. Accursed Faustus, where is mercy now?
I do repent; and yet I do despair:
Hell strives with grace for conquest in my breast:
What shall I do to shun the snares of death?
   MEPHISTOPHILIS. Thou traitor, Faustus, I arrest thy soul
For disobedience to my sovereign lord:
Revolt,[69] or I'll in piecemeal tear thy flesh.
   FAUSTUS. I do repent I e'er offended him.
Sweet Mephistophilis, entreat thy lord
To pardon my unjust presumption,
And with my blood again I will confirm
The former vow I made to Lucifer.
   MEPHISTOPHILIS. Do it, then, Faustus, with unfeigned heart,
Lest greater dangers do attend thy drift.
   (FAUSTUS *stabs his arm, and writes on a paper with his blood.*)
   FAUSTUS. Torment, sweet friend, that base and aged man.
That durst* dissuade me from thy Lucifer,   dared
With greatest torments that our hell affords.
   MEPHISTOPHILIS. His faith is great; I cannot touch his soul;
But what I may afflict his body with
I will attempt, which is but little worth.
   FAUSTUS. One thing, good servant, let me crave of thee,

       [69] Return to your allegiance.

To glut the longing of my heart's desire,—
That I may have unto my paramour
That heavenly Helen which I saw of late,
Whose sweet embraces may extinguish clean
Those thoughts that do dissuade me from my vow,
And keep my oath I made to Lucifer.
    MEPHISTOPHILIS. This, or what else, my Faustus shall desire,
Shall be perform'd in twinkling of an eye.

(*Enter* HELEN *again, passing over the stage between two* CUPIDS.)

    FAUSTUS. Was this the face that launch'd a thousand ships,
And burnt the topless towers of Ilium?—
Sweet Helen, make me immortal with a kiss.—
    (*She kisses him.*)
Her lips suck forth my soul: see where it flies!—
Come, Helen, come, give me my soul again.
Here will I dwell, for heaven is in these lips,
And all is dross that is not Helena.

(*Enter* OLD MAN.)

I will be Paris, and for love of thee,
Instead of Troy, shall Wittenberg be sack'd;
And I will combat with weak Menelaus,*   Helen's husband
And wear thy colours on my plumed crest:
Yea, I will wound Achilles in the heel,
And then return to Helen for a kiss.
O thou art fairer than the evening's air
Clad in the beauty of a thousand stars;
Brighter art thou than flaming Jupiter
When he appear'd to hapless Semele;[70]
More lovely than the monarch of the sky
In wanton Arethusa's[71] azured arms;
And none but thou shalt be my paramour!
        (*Exeunt* FAUSTUS, HELEN *and* CUPIDS.)

[70] Semele wanted to see Zeus in his full magnificence; unable to stand the burning light, she died.

[71] Arethusa would have nothing to do with men. When she was pursued by Alpheus, the river god, Artemis changed her into a spring. Both Semele and Arethusa engaged in excesses of conduct which led to their destruction.

OLD MAN. Accursed Faustus, miserable man,
That from thy soul exclud'st the grace of Heaven,
And fliest the throne of his tribunal-seat!

(*Enter* DEVILS.)

Satan begins to sift* me with his pride:[72]   make trial of
As in this furnace God shall try my faith,
My faith, vile hell, shall triumph over thee.
Ambitious fiends, see how the heavens smiles
At your repulse, and laughs your state to scorn!
Hence, hell! for hence I fly unto my God.

(*Exeunt.*)

Scene 2

(FAUSTUS' *study. Thunder. Enter above* LUCIFER, BELZE-
BUB, *and* MEPHISTOPHILIS.)

LUCIFER. Thus from infernal Dis* do we ascend   Hell
To view the subjects of our monarchy,
Those souls which sin seals the black sons of hell,
'Mong which as chief, Faustus, we come to thee,
Bringing with us lasting damnation
To wait upon thy soul; the time is come
Which makes it forfeit.
　　　MEPHISTOPHILIS.   And this gloomy night,
Here in this room will wretched Faustus be.
　　　BELZEBUB. And here we'll stay,
To mark him how he doth demean himself.
　　　MEPHISTOPHILIS. How should he, but in desperate lunacy?
Fond* worldling, now his heart-blood dries with grief,   foolish
His conscience kills it and his labouring brain
Begets a world of idle fantasies,
To over-reach the Devil; but all in vain,
His store of pleasures must be sauc'd with pain.
He and his servant, Wagner, are at hand.
Both come from drawing Faustus' latest will.
See where they come!

(*Enter* FAUSTUS *and* WAGNER.)

FAUSTUS. Say, Wagner, thou hast perus'd my will,
How dost thou like it?

[72] "Display of power" (Boas).

WAGNER.   Sir, so wondrous well,
As in all humble duty, I do yield
My life and lasting service for your love.

(*Enter the* SCHOLARS.)

FAUSTUS. Gramercies, Wagner. Welcome, gentlemen.
                              (*Exit* WAGNER.)
FIRST SCHOLAR. Now, worthy Faustus, methinks your looks
are changed.
FAUSTUS. O, gentlemen!
SECOND SCHOLAR. What ails Faustus?
FAUSTUS. Ah, my sweet chamber-fellow,[73] had I liv'd with
thee, then had I lived still! but now must die eternally. Look,
sirs, comes he not? comes he not?
FIRST SCHOLAR. O my dear Faustus, what imports this fear?
SECOND SCHOLAR. Is all our pleasure turn'd to melancholy?
THIRD SCHOLAR. He is not well with being over-solitary.
SECOND SCHOLAR. If it be so, we'll have physicians, and
Faustus shall be cur'd.
THIRD SCHOLAR. 'Tis but a surfeit, sir; fear nothing.
FAUSTUS. A surfeit of deadly sin, that hath damn'd both
body and soul.
SECOND SCHOLAR. Yet, Faustus, look up to heaven; remember God's mercies are infinite.
FAUSTUS. But Faustus' offence can ne'er be pardoned: the
serpent that tempted Eve may be saved, but not Faustus. O,
gentlemen, hear me with patience, and tremble not at my
speeches! Though my heart pant and quiver to remember
that I have been a student here these thirty years, O, would
I had never seen Wittenberg, never read book! and what
wonders I have done, all Germany can witness, yea, all the
world; for which Faustus hath lost both Germany and the
world; yea, heaven itself, heaven, the seat of God, the throne
of the blessed, the kingdom of joy; and must remain in hell for
ever—hell, oh, hell for ever! Sweet friends, what shall become
of Faustus, being in hell for ever?
SECOND SCHOLAR. Yet, Faustus, call on God.
FAUSTUS. On God, whom Faustus hath abjur'd! on God,
whom Faustus hath blasphem'd! Oh, my God, I would weep!
but the devil draws in my tears. Gush forth blood, instead of

[73] "It was customary at the Universities for two or more students to occupy the same room." (Ward)

tears! yea, life and soul—Oh, he stays my tongue! I would
lift up my hands; but see, they hold 'em, they hold 'em!

ALL. Who, Faustus?

FAUSTUS. Why, Lucifer and Mephistophilis. O, gentlemen,
I gave them my soul for my cunning!*   knowledge

ALL. Oh, God forbid!

FAUSTUS. God forbade it, indeed; but Faustus hath done it:
for the vain pleasure of four and twenty years hath Faustus
lost eternal joy and felicity. I writ them a bill* with mine   deed
own blood: the date is expired; this is the time, and he will
fetch me.

FIRST SCHOLAR. Why did not Faustus tell us of this before,
that divines* might have pray'd for thee?   clergymen

FAUSTUS. Oft have I thought to have done so; but the devil
threaten'd to tear me in pieces, if I nam'd God; to fetch me,
body and soul, if I once gave ear to divinity: and now 'tis
too late. Gentlemen, away, lest you perish with me.

SECOND SCHOLAR. O, what may we do to save Faustus?

FAUSTUS. Talk not of me, but save yourselves, and depart.

THIRD SCHOLAR. God will strengthen me; I will stay with
Faustus.

FIRST SCHOLAR. Tempt not God, sweet friend; but let us into
the next room, and pray for him.

FAUSTUS. Ay, pray for me, pray for me; and what noise
soever you hear, come not unto me, for nothing can rescue
me.

SECOND SCHOLAR. Pray thou, and we will pray that God
may have mercy upon thee.

FAUSTUS. Gentlemen, farewell: if I live till morning, I'll visit
you; if not, Faustus is gone to hell.

(*Exeunt* SCHOLARS.)

ALL. Faustus, farewell.

MEPHISTOPHILIS (*above*). Ay, Faustus, now thou hast no
        hope of heaven;
Therefore despair, think only upon hell,
For that must be thy mansion, there to dwell.

FAUSTUS. O thou bewitching fiend, 'twas thy temptation
Hath robb'd me of eternal happiness.

MEPHISTOPHILIS. I do confess it, Faustus, and rejoice;
'Twas I, that when thou wert i' the way to heaven,
Damm'd up thy passage; when thou took'st the book,
To view the Scriptures, then I turn'd the leaves,
And led thine eye.—
What, weep'st thou? 'tis too late, despair, farewell!

Fools that will laugh on earth, must weep in hell.

> (*Exeunt* LUCIFER, BELZEBUB, MEPHISTOPHILIS.)

(*Enter the* GOOD ANGEL *and the* BAD ANGEL *at different doors.*)

GOOD ANGEL. Oh, Faustus, if thou hadst given ear to me,
Innumerable joys had followed thee.
But thou didst love the world.
BAD ANGEL.   Gave ear to me,
And now must taste hell's pains perpetually.
GOOD ANGEL. O what will all thy riches, pleasures, pomps,
Avail thee now?
BAD ANGEL.   Nothing but vex thee more,
To want in hell, that had on earth such store.
(*Music while the throne descends.*)[74]
GOOD ANGEL. O thou hast lost celestial happiness,
Pleasures unspeakable, bliss without end.
Hadst thou affected* sweet divinity,   preferred
Hell, or the devil, had had no power on thee.
Hadst thou kept on that way, Faustus, behold,
In what resplendent glory thou hadst sit
In yonder throne, like those bright shining saints,[75]
And triumph'd over hell: that hast thou lost:
And now, poor soul, must thy good angel leave thee,
(*The throne ascends.*)
The jaws of hell are open to receive thee.

> (*Exit.*)

(*Hell is discovered.*)[76]
BAD ANGEL. Now, Faustus, let thine eyes with horror stare
Into that vast perpetual torture-house.
There are the Furies tossing damned souls
On burning forks; their bodies boil in lead:
There are live quarters broiling on the coals,
That ne'er can die: this ever-burning chair
Is for o'er-tortured souls to rest them in;
These that are fed with sops* of flaming fire,   great quantities
Were gluttons and lov'd only delicates,*   delicacies

---

[74] On the Elizabethan stage this would have been accomplished by lowering the throne from "the heavens."

[75] Figures seated on the throne.

[76] This may have been done by drawing a curtain to reveal a painted backcloth depicting the horrors of hell or by uncovering a trap door from which smoke and flame arose or by opening the curtain of the inner stage, revealing a medieval Hell mouth.

And laugh'd to see the poor starve at their gates:
But yet all these are nothing; thou shalt see
Ten thousand tortures that more horrid be.
    FAUSTUS. O, 1 have seen enough to torture me.
    BAD ANGEL. Nay, thou must feel them, taste the smart of all:
He that loves pleasure, must for pleasure fall:
And so I leave thee, Faustus, till anon;
Then wilt thou tumble in confusion.
        (*Exit. Hell disappears. The clock strikes eleven.*)
    FAUSTUS. Ah, Faustus,
Now hast thou but one bare hour to live,
And then thou must be damn'd perpetually!
Stand still, you ever moving spheres of heaven,
That time may cease, and midnight never come;
Fair Nature's eye,* rise, rise again, and make   that is,
Perpetual day; or let this hour be but   the sun
A year, a month, a week, a natural day,
That Faustus may repent and save his soul!
O lente, lente currite, noctis equi![77]
The stars move still, time runs, the clock will strike,
The devil will come, and Faustus must be damn'd.
O, I'll leap up to my God!—Who pulls me down?—
See, see, where Christ's blood streams in the firmament!
One drop would save my soul, half a drop: ah, my Christ!—
Ah, rend not my heart for naming of my Christ!
Yet will I call on him: O, spare me, Lucifer!—
Where is it now? 'tis gone: and see, where God
Stretcheth out his arm, and bends his ireful brows!
Mountains and hills, come, come, and fall on me,
And hide me from the heavy wrath of God!
No, no!
Then will I headlong run into the earth:
Earth, gape! O, no, it will not harbour me!
You stars that reign'd at my nativity,
Whose influence hath allotted death and hell,
Now draw up Faustus, like a foggy mist,
Into the entrails of yon lab'ring cloud
That, when you vomit forth into the air,
My limbs may issue from your smoky mouths,
So* that my soul may but ascend to heaven!   provided
    (*The clock strikes.*)

        [77] "O run slowly, slowly, horses of the night." (Adapted from
Ovid's *Amores.*)

Ah, half the hour is past! 'twill all be passed anon.
O God,
If thou wilt not have mercy on my soul,
Yet for Christ's sake, whose blood hath ransom'd me,
Impose some end to my incessant pain;
Let Faustus live in hell a thousand years,
A hundred thousand, and at last be sav'd!
O, no end is limited* to damned souls!   assigned
Why wert thou not a creature wanting* soul?   lacking
Or why is this immortal that thou hast?
Ah, Pythagoras' *metempsychosis*,[78] were that true,
This soul should fly from me, and I be changed
Unto some brutish beast! all beasts are happy,
For, when they die,
Their souls are soon dissolved in elements;
But mine must live still to be plagu'd in hell.
Curs'd be the parents that engender'd me!
No, Faustus, curse thyself, curse Lucifer
That hath depriv'd thee of the joys of heaven.
   (*The clock strikes twelve.*)
O, it strikes, it strikes! Now, body, turn to air,
Or Lucifer will bear thee quick* to hell!   living
O soul, be changed into little water-drops,
And fall into the ocean, ne'er be found!

   (*Thunder and enter the* DEVILS.)

My God, my God, look not so fierce on me!
Adders and serpents, let me breathe a while!
Ugly hell, gape not! come not, Lucifer!
I'll burn my books!—Ah, Mephistophilis!
                           (*Exeunt with him.*)

Scene 3

(*A room next to* FAUSTUS' *study. Enter the* SCHOLARS.)

FIRST SCHOLAR. Come, gentlemen, let us go visit Faustus,
For such a dreadful night was never seen,
Since first the world's creation did begin.
Such fearful shrieks and cries were never heard:
Pray heaven the Doctor have escap'd the danger.

---

[78] The doctrine of transmigration of souls promulgated by
Pythagoras of Samos.

SECOND SCHOLAR. O help us heaven! see, here are Faustus'
    limbs,
All torn asunder by the hand of death.
    THIRD SCHOLAR. The devils whom Faustus serv'd have torn
    him thus:
For 'twixt the hours of twelve and one, methought
I heard him shriek and call aloud for help:
At which self time the house seem'd all on fire,
With dreadful horror of these damned fiends.
    SECOND SCHOLAR. Well, gentlemen, though Faustus' end
    be such
As every Christian heart laments to think on,
Yet for he was a scholar, once admired
For wondrous knowledge in our German schools,
We'll give his mangled limbs due burial;
And all the students, clothed in mourning black,
Shall wait upon* his heavy* funeral.   attend/sad
                                        (*Exeunt.*)

EPILOGUE

(*Enter* CHORUS.)

    CHORUS. Cut is the branch that might have grown full
    straight,
And burned is Apollo's laurel-bough,
That sometime* grew within this learned man.   at one time
Faustus is gone: regard his hellish fall,
Whose fiendful fortune may exhort the wise,
Only to wonder at unlawful things,
Whose deepness* doth entice such forward wits   obscurity
To practise more than heavenly power permits.
                                          (*Exit.*)

    Terminat hora diem; terminat Author opus.[79]

---

[79] "The hour ends the day; the author ends his work."—This
may be a printer's addition.

Edward II

BY CHRISTOPHER MARLOWE

There are two radically different estimates of *Edward II*. One view stresses Marlowe's inferiority to Shakespeare in the area of historical drama; the other points to the maturity and control apparent in this historical play after the exuberance manifested in *Tamburlaine* and in the other plays believed to have preceded *Edward II*. Not only is this work free from the turgid rhetoric that often afflicted the Elizabethan theatre, but it is also relatively well-organized for a "chronicle history," a genre that tended to sprawl quite unconscionably; the text also escaped the mutilations from which other Marlowe plays, including *Doctor Faustus,* suffered severely. It is noteworthy that Marlowe compressed nearly a quarter of a century of history into about a year, and that although he suppressed important events of the inglorious reign of Edward II, such as the failure of his military venture in Scotland in the battle of Bannockburn, one feels no gaps in the story or plot. The dramatic pattern is satisfying and meaningful. Without departing from the "horizontal" structure of the Elizabethan chronicle play as a sequence of contiguous episodes, *Edward II* is a more complex drama than Marlowe's *Tamburlaine*.

The play traces the alternate rise and fall of its two protagonists, Edward II and Mortimer ("Young Mortimer"), with retribution overtaking the latter for his part in destroying the former. Mortimer's story sustains the medieval *De Casibus* theme of the fall of princes, illustrated in the account of Mortimer in *The Mirror for Magistrates,* with the accompanying moral that men should refrain from incriminating themselves with their "high climbing." Caught up in this rivalry, moreover, are several other characters, chiefly the King's principal favorite, Gaveston, and Queen Isabella, Edward's neglected wife who, under extreme pressure, transfers her affections from her husband to his major opponent among the nobility.

The play's objectvity is one of its outstanding merits. Marlowe confines himself to presenting, without comment, Edward's bankruptcy as a husband and as a ruler. In the political arena he traces the course of conflict when a self-indulgent and capricious monarch insists upon pitting his will against that of the feudal nobility in circumstances that amount to civil war. Man is shown to be the victim of forces he himself unleashes, and Edward's tragic flaw appears both in his irrational attachment to male favorites who exploit the kingdom and antagonize the feudal barons and in his insistence on wielding absolute power which he neither deserves to possess nor is capable of exercising. Mortimer's *hamartia* resides in his Machiavellian lust for power. Though Queen Isabella may have been driven into Mortimer's arms by the King's neglect, she is not without personal culpability, especially in assenting to Edward's murder.

Fluctuations of fortune and dynamism in the manifest struggle for power contribute strongly to the development of character in this tragedy. Edward II manifests a vainglorious arbitrariness in defying the nobles and exalting his favorites, but when life humbles him, he grows in humanity and dies in command of our sympathy. (The King's brother, Kent, is also a well-drawn minor character who understandably vacillates between loyalty to Edward and sympathy for the rebellious barons and then repents his assistance to the barons.) Edward, too much the esthete to be effective ruler of a turbulent kingdom, has a glaring tragic flaw in his openly declared homosexuality, yet he manifests high spirits along with his obsessiveness, especially when he resolves to avenge the nobles' murder of his favorite, Gaveston. At the conclusion of his life, moreover, he reveals a rich sensibility that he must have had all along and that manifested itself, albeit perversely, in his attachment to Gaveston.

Young Mortimer stalwartly begins his dramatic course as a patriot and ends as a usurper responsible for murdering his sovereign. Isabella, Edward II's unimpeachable queen, as the result of provocation from Edward and attraction to Mortimer at a time when his conduct is still admirable, becomes an adulteress, but a very human one; once the love-starved consort of a homosexual king, Isabella pathetically pleads with her own son, the young Edward III, for her lover Mortimer's life. Her character in the play is astutely softened by Marlowe, since the historical Isabella led the fight against Edward in France. Early in the play Marlowe's queen even pleads with the nobles for Gaveston in the hope of pleasing her husband.

For all its chronicle character and political detail, *Edward II* is true tragedy. The chief antagonists are not unworthy men with whom it is impossible to identify, and even the upstart favorites Gaveston and Spencer, who use Edward for their own advancement, reveal an emotional attachment to him in critical situations. Young Mortimer reveals a stoic dignity when condemned to death which, after his moral decline in commissioning the secret murder of the King, reconstitutes him as a tragic hero. Mortimer, well described by Henry W. Wells as "an English Achilles" (*Elizabethan and Jacobean Playwrights,* 1939), announces no profound discovery at the end, but his resort to the cliche of "Fortune's wheel" culminates in a spirited acceptance of his fate:

> Base Fortune, now I see that in thy wheel
> There is a point to which men aspire,
> They tumble headlong down: that point I touched,
> And seeing there was no place to mount up higher,
> Why should I grieve at my declining fall?
> Farewell, fair queen, weep not for Mortimer,
> That scorns the world and, as a traveler,
> Goes to discover countries yet unknown.

The result is, to a degree, *tragedy of character.* Harry Levin put the case pointedly (in *The Overreacher,* p. 77) when he declared that in *Edward II,* by contrast with such other plays as *The Jew of Malta* and *The Massacre at Paris,* the maturing Marlowe "sets forth his discovery that tragic life needs no villains; that plots are spun by passions; that men betray themselves."

To complain that Edward's obsession with his favorites "assumes a disproportionate and independent psychological interest for Marlowe" (*The Age of Shakespeare,* Pelican Guide to English Literature, p. 175) is hardly a serious charge against *Edward II* from a twentieth-century point of view. By now, moreover, the historical interest of the subject is bound to be subordinated to the clinical. At the same time, the play nevertheless transcends psychopathology and, in spite of Edward's inadequacies as husband to Isabella and king of England, culminates in heroic tragedy. If Isabella's transformation seems too abrupt (she actually connives with Mortimer in the murder of Edward), as does Mortimer's moral deterioration, the rapidity of the action bridges the discontinuity of characterization. If there is structural weakness in duplicating Edward's infatuation with young men when after Gaves-

ton's death he turns to young Spencer, the thematic repetition
nevertheless serves to establish the fateful pattern of his be
havior. If, finally, Marlowe's dialogue in *Edward II* has a
more even tenor and manifests less brilliance than it does in
Tamburlaine and *Doctor Faustus,* it is also more convincing
and efficient while still managing to sparkle at the appropriate
moments. Even Gaveston, the King's somewhat Machiavellian
minion, has such moments, as in the famous couplet:

> What need the arctic people love starlight,
> To whom the sun shines both by day and night?

One can easily agree with Eugene M. Waith's warning in his
closely considered essay "Edward II: The Shadow of Action"
(*Tulane Drama Review,* Summer 1964) that "it is a mistake
to underestimate Marlowe's achievement in this play."

A sound analysis of the merits and defects of *Edward II*
is Willard Farnham's conclusion (in *The Medieval Heritage
of Elizabethan Tragedy*) that although Marlowe achieved "a
concentration upon a central tragic figure . . . such as no
dramatist before him had achieved"—that is, since classic
tragedy—he was unfortunate in having chosen a protagonist
thoroughly deficient in dynamic quality, "whom he cannot
make us admire until the end of the play, and then merely
as a man capable of some final dignity in hopeless suffering." Yet, as Farnham observes, Edward's tragedy "has a
rising and falling action curiously similar to that of a *De
Casibus* tragedy of ambition," at least as his fortunes rise and
fall with his consuming desire for Gaveston. Despite his worth-
lessness, Gaveston is an object of more than debauchery on
the King's part and is identified by Edward II with his ideal
of kingship and its prerogatives *vis à vis* the feudal nobles
who challenge his power.

J. G.

Date. Scholarly consensus recognizes *Edward II* as late
Marlowe. Since the playwright died in May 1593, the range
of dating has been narrowed to 1591-93, with 1591-92 emerg-
ing as the most likely date.

Text and Publishing Data. William Jones entered the play
in the Stationers' Register on July 6, 1593. The earliest extant
edition is the octavo printing of 1594; however, there is strong
evidence that an earlier edition had appeared in 1593. In 1598,
Q (Quarto) 2 appeared, followed by Q3 in 1612 and Q4 in
1622. These quarto editions are reprints of the 1594 text—a

good text probably derived from a playhouse manuscript. The early editions are not divided into acts or scenes.

Sources. Holinshed's *Chronicles* is the primary source, some supplementary details coming from Fabyan's *Chronicle* and Stow's *Annals of England.*

Stage History. The early history is unknown. The number of early editions would indicate that the play was popular. The 1594 edition states that *Edward II* was acted by the Earl of Pembroke's Men "sundrie times." Q4 notes a revival by the Queen Anne's Men at the Red Bull, probably between 1612 and 1617. The play has not been particularly favored with modern revivals, although William Poel produced it for the Elizabethan Stage Society at Oxford in 1903. The first known American performance took place at Barnard College, Columbia University, in December 1943, with an all-female cast.

Miscellaneous Information. *Edward II* is no longer regarded as the precursor of Shakespeare's *Henry VI* plays. If anything, Marlowe appears to have been under the influence of Shakespeare. The parallel passages in *Edward II* and *2* and *3 Henry VI* probably stem from Marlowe's echoing passages from the Shakespearean originals and the faulty memory of the pirates who turned out the quarto editions of *2* and *3 Henry VI* (which appeared after *Edward II*) and who turned to *Edward II* to fill in the gaps. The investigations of Peter Alexander have shown *2* and *3 Henry VI* to be "bad" quartos; the Folio edition is the authoritative source for the texts of these two plays.

W. G.

DRAMATIS PERSONAE

KING EDWARD THE SECOND
PRINCE EDWARD, his son, afterwards King Edward the Third
EARL OF KENT, brother of King Edward the Second
PIERS GAVESTON
EARL OF WARWICK
EARL OF LANCASTER
EARL OF PEMBROKE
EARL OF ARUNDEL
EARL OF LEICESTER
SIR THOMAS BERKELEY
LORD ROGER MORTIMER, the elder
LORD ROGER MORTIMER, the younger, his nephew
SPENCER, the elder
SPENCER, the younger, his son
ARCHBISHOP OF CANTERBURY
BISHOP OF COVENTRY
BISHOP OF WINCHESTER
ROBERT BALDOCK, a scholar
HENRY DE BEAUMONT
SIR WILLIAM TRUSSEL
GURNEY
MATREVIS
LIGHTBORN
SIR JOHN OF HAINAULT
LEVUNE
RICE AP HOWELL
JAMES
Abbot, Monks, Herald, Lords, Poor Men, Mower, Champion,
    Messengers, Soldiers, and Attendants
QUEEN ISABELLA, wife of King Edward the Second
NIECE to King Edward the Second, daughter of the Duke of
    Gloucester
Ladies

ACT I

Scene 1

(*A street in London. Enter* GAVESTON, *reading a letter from the King.*)

GAVESTON. "My father is deceased! Come, Gaveston,
And share the kingdom with thy dearest friend."
Ah! words that make me surfeit with delight!
What greater bliss can hap to Gaveston
Than live and be the favourite of a king!
Sweet prince, I come; these, these thy amorous lines
Might have enforced me to have swum from France,
And, like Leander,[1] gasped upon the sand,
So* thou would'st smile, and take me in thine arms.   provided that
The sight of London to my exiled eyes
Is as Elysium to a new-come soul;
Not that I love the city, or the men,
But that it harbours him I hold so dear—
The king, upon whose bosom let me lie,
And with the world be still at enmity.
What need the arctic people love starlight,
To whom the sun shines both by day and night?
Farewell base stooping to the lordly peers!
My knee shall bow to none but to the king.
As for the multitude, that are but sparks,
Raked up in embers of their poverty;—
*Tanti,** I'll fawn first on the wind   so much for them
That glanceth at my lips, and flieth away.
But how now, what are these?

(*Enter three* POOR MEN.)

MEN. Such as desire your worship's service.
GAVESTON. What canst thou do?

---

[1] Leander nightly swam the Hellespont in order to visit Hero, a priestess of Aphrodite.

FIRST POOR MAN. I can ride.

GAVESTON. But I have no horse. What art thou?

SECOND POOR MAN. A traveller.

GAVESTON. Let me see—thou would'st do well
To wait at my trencher* and tell me lies at dinner wooden platter
    time
And as I like your discoursing, I'll have you.
And what art thou?

THIRD POOR MAN. A soldier, that hath served against the
    Scot.

GAVESTON. Why, there are hospitals* for such as almshouses
    you;
I have no war, and therefore, sir, begone.

THIRD POOR MAN. Farewell, and perish by a soldier's hand,
That would'st reward them with an hospital.

GAVESTON (*aside*). Ay, ay, these words of his move me
    as much
As if a goose would play the porcupine,
And dart her plumes, thinking to pierce my breast.
But yet it is no pain to speak men fair;
I'll flatter these, and make them live in hope.—
You know that I came lately out of France,
And yet I have not viewed my lord the king;
If I speed well, I'll entertain* you all.   take into service

ALL. We thank your worship.

GAVESTON. I have some business. Leave me to myself.

ALL. We will wait here about the court.

                                                               (*Exeunt.*)

GAVESTON. Do; these are not men for me:
I must have wanton poets, pleasant wits,
Musicians, that with touching of a string
May draw the pliant king which way I please.
Music and poetry is his delight;
Therefore I'll have Italian masks by night,
Sweet speeches, comedies, and pleasing shows;
And in the day, when he shall walk abroad,
Like sylvan nymphs my pages shall be clad;
My men, like satyrs grazing on the lawns,
Shall with their goat-feet dance the antic hay.*   country dance
Sometime a lovely boy in Dian's shape,[2]
With hair that gilds the water as it glides,
Crownets* of pearl about his naked arms,   coronets

---

[2] The following lines relate the story of Diana and Actaeon.

And in his sportful hands an olive-tree,
To hide those parts which men delight to see,
Shall bathe him in a spring; and there hard by,
One like Actæon peeping through the grove,
Shall by the angry goddess be transformed,
And running in the likeness of an hart
By yelping hounds pulled down, shall seem to die;—
Such things as these best please his majesty;
Here comes my lord the king, and the nobles
From the parliament. I'll stand aside.
    (*Retires.*)

(*Enter* KING EDWARD, LANCASTER, *the* ELDER MORTIMER,
YOUNG MORTIMER, KENT, WARWICK, PEMBROKE, *and* AT-
TENDANTS.)

KING EDWARD. Lancaster!
LANCASTER. My lord.
GAVESTON (*aside*). That Earl of Lancaster do I abhor.
KING EDWARD. Will you not grant me this? (*Aside.*) In spite
    of them
I'll have my will; and these two Mortimers,
That cross me thus, shall know I am displeased.
    ELDER MORTIMER. If you love us, my lord, hate Gaveston.
    GAVESTON (*aside*). That villain Mortimer! I'll be his death.
    YOUNG MORTIMER. Mine uncle here, this earl, and I myself,
Were sworn to your father at his death,
That he should ne'er return into the realm:
And know, my lord, ere I will break my oath,
This sword of mine, that should offend your foes,
Shall sleep within the scabbard at thy need,
And underneath thy banners march who will,
For Mortimer will hang his armour up.
    GAVESTON (*aside*). *Mort Dieu!*
    KING EDWARD. Well, Mortimer, I'll make thee rue these
    words.
Beseems it thee to contradict thy king?
Frown'st thou thereat, aspiring Lancaster?
The sword shall plane the furrows of thy brows,
And hew these knees that now are grown so stiff.
I will have Gaveston; and you shall know
What danger 'tis to stand against your king.
    GAVESTON (*aside*). Well done, Ned!

LANCASTER. My lord, why do you thus incense your peers,
That naturally would love and honour you
But for that base and obscure Gaveston?
Four earldoms have I, besides Lancaster—
Derby, Salisbury, Lincoln, Leicester,—
These will I sell, to give my soldiers pay,
Ere Gaveston shall stay within the realm;
Therefore, if he be come, expel him straight.

   KENT. Barons and earls, your pride hath made me mute;
But now I'll speak, and to the proof, I hope.
I do remember, in my father's days,
Lord Percy of the north, being highly moved,
Braved Moubery* in presence of the king;   Mowbray
For which, had not his highness loved him well,
He should have lost his head; but with his look
The undaunted spirit of Percy was appeased,
And Moubery and he were reconciled:
Yet dare you brave the king unto his face.—
Brother, revenge it, and let these their heads
Preach upon poles, for trespass of their tongues.

   WARWICK. O, our heads!

   KING EDWARD. Ay, yours; and therefore I would wish you
     grant*—   yield

   WARWICK. Bridle thy anger, gentle Mortimer.

   YOUNG MORTIMER. I cannot, nor I will not; I must speak.—
Cousin, our hands I hope shall fence* our heads,   protect
And strike off his that makes you threaten us.
Come, uncle, let us leave the brain-sick king,
And henceforth parley with our naked swords.

   ELDER MORTIMER. Wiltshire hath men enough to save our
     heads.

   WARWICK. All Warwickshire will love him for my sake.

   LANCASTER. And northward Gaveston hath many friends.—
Adieu, my lord; and either change your mind,
Or look to see the throne, where you should sit,
To float in blood; and at thy wanton head,
The glozing* head of thy base minion thrown.   flattering
                  (*Exeunt all except* KING EDWARD, KENT,
                      GAVESTON *and* ATTENDANTS.)

   KING EDWARD. I cannot brook these haughty menaces;
Am I a king, and must be overruled?—
Brother, display my ensigns in the field;
I'll bandy* with the barons and the earls,   contend
And either die or live with Gaveston.

GAVESTON. I can no longer keep me from my lord.
(*Comes forward.*)
KING EDWARD. What, Gaveston! welcome!—Kiss not my
 hand—
Embrace me, Gaveston, as I do thee.
Why should'st thou kneel? know'st thou not who I am?
Thy friend, thyself, another Gaveston!
Not Hylas was more mourned of Hercules,[3]
Than thou hast been of me since thy exile.
 GAVESTON. And since I went from hence, no soul in hell
Hath felt more torment than poor Gaveston.
 KING EDWARD. I know it.—Brother, welcome home my
 friend.
Now let the treacherous Mortimers conspire,
And that high-minded* Earl of Lancaster: arrogant
I have my wish, in that I joy thy sight;
And sooner shall the sea o'erwhelm my land,
Than bear the ship that shall transport thee hence.
I here create thee Lord High Chamberlain,
Chief Secretary to the state and me,
Earl of Cornwall, King and Lord of Man.*   Isle of Man
 GAVESTON. My lord, these titles far exceed my worth.
 KENT. Brother, the least of these may well suffice
For one of greater birth than Gaveston.
 KING EDWARD. Cease, brother: for I cannot brook these
 words.
Thy worth, sweet friend, is far above my gifts,
Therefore, to equal it, receive my heart;
If for these dignities thou be envied,
I'll give thee more; for, but to honour thee,
Is Edward pleased with kingly regiment.*   rule
Fear'st thou thy person? thou shalt have a guard:
Wantest thou gold? go to my treasury:
Wouldst thou be loved and feared? receive my seal;
Save or condemn, and in our name command
Whatso thy mind affects,* or fancy likes.   seeks
 GAVESTON. It shall suffice me to enjoy your love,
Which whiles I have, I think myself as great
As Cæsar riding in the Roman street,
With captive kings at his triumphant car.

  [3] Hercules left the ship *Argo* at Mysia during the expedition
for the golden fleece in order to find his armor-bearer Hylas,
who had disappeared searching for water. Meanwhile, the *Argo*
sailed without Hercules.

(*Enter the* BISHOP OF COVENTRY.)

KING EDWARD. Whither goes my lord of Coventry so fast?
BISHOP OF COVENTRY. To celebrate your father's exequies.
But is that wicked Gaveston returned?
KING EDWARD. Ay, priest, and lives to be revenged on thee,
That wert the only cause of his exile.
GAVESTON. 'Tis true; and but for reverence of these robes,
Thou should'st not plod one foot beyond this place,
BISHOP OF COVENTRY. I did no more than I was bound to
  do;
And, Gaveston, unless thou be reclaimed,*   reformed
As then I did incense the parliament,
So will I now, and thou shalt back to France.
GAVESTON. Saving your reverence, you must pardon me.
KING EDWARD. Throw off his golden mitre, rend his stole,
And in the channel* christen him anew.   gutter
KENT. Ah, brother, lay not violent hands on him!
For he'll complain unto the see of Rome.
GAVESTON. Let him complain unto the see of hell;
I'll be revenged on him for my exile.
KING EDWARD. No, spare his life, but seize upon his goods:
Be thou lord bishop and receive his rents,
And make him serve thee as thy chaplain:
I give him thee—here, use him as thou wilt.
GAVESTON. He shall to prison, and there die in bolts.*   fetters
KING EDWARD. Ay, to the Tower, the Fleet, or where thou
  wilt.
BISHOP OF COVENTRY. For this offence, be thou accurst of
  God!
KING EDWARD. Who's there? Convey this priest to the
  Tower.
BISHOP OF COVENTRY. True, true.[4]
KING EDWARD. But in the meantime, Gaveston, away,
And take possession of his house and goods.
Come, follow me, and thou shalt have my guard
To see it done, and bring thee safe again.
GAVESTON. What should a priest do with so fair a house?
A prison may beseem his holiness.

(*Exeunt.*)

    [4] An ironic comment on the King's *convey*, which also means
steal.

Scene 2

(*Westminster. Enter on one side the two* MORTIMERS; *on the other*, WARWICK *and* LANCASTER.)

WARWICK. 'Tis true, the bishop is in the Tower,
And goods and body given to Gaveston.
LANCASTER. What! will they tyrannise upon the church?
Ah, wicked king! accursèd Gaveston!
This ground, which is corrupted with their steps,
Shall be their timeless* sepulchre or mine.   untimely
  YOUNG MORTIMER. Well, let that peevish Frenchman guard
    him sure;
Unless his breast be sword-proof he shall die.
  ELDER MORTIMER. How now! why droops the Earl of
    Lancaster?
  YOUNG MORTIMER. Wherefore is Guy of Warwick discon-
    tent?
  LANCASTER. That villain Gaveston is made an earl.
  ELDER MORTIMER. An earl!
  WARWICK. Ay, and besides Lord Chamberlain of the realm,
And Secretary too, and Lord of Man.
  ELDER MORTIMER. We may not, nor we will not suffer this.
  YOUNG MORTIMER. Why post we not from hence to levy
    men?
  LANCASTER. "My Lord of Cornwall," now at every word!
And happy is the man whom he vouchsafes,
For vailing of his bonnet,* one good look.   doffing
Thus, arm in arm, the king and he doth march:
Nay more, the guard upon his lordship waits;
And all the court begins to flatter him.
  WARWICK. Thus leaning on the shoulder of the king,
He nods and scorns and smiles at those that pass.
  ELDER MORTIMER. Doth no man take exceptions at the
    slave?
  LANCASTER. All stomach* him, but none dare speak   resent
    a word.
  YOUNG MORTIMER. Ah, that bewrays* their baseness,   reveals
    Lancaster!
Were all the earls and barons of my mind,
We'd hale him from the bosom of the king,
And at the court-gate hang the peasant up,
Who, swoln with venom of ambitious pride,

Will be the ruin of the realm and us.
    WARWICK. Here comes my lord of Canterbury's grace.
    LANCASTER. His countenance bewrays he is displeased.

    (*Enter the* ARCHBISHOP OF CANTERBURY *and an* ATTEND-
ANT.)

    ARCHBISHOP OF CANTERBURY. First were his sacred gar-
       ments rent and torn,
Then laid they violent hands upon him; next
Himself imprisoned, and his goods asseized:
This certify the Pope;—away, take horse.
                      (*Exit* ATTENDANT.)
    LANCASTER. My lord, will you take arms against the king?
    ARCHBISHOP OF CANTERBURY. What need I? God himself
      is up in arms,
When violence is offered to the church.
    YOUNG MORTIMER. Then will you join with us, that be his
      peers,
To banish or behead that Gaveston?
    ARCHBISHOP OF CANTERBURY. What else, my lords? for it
      concerns me near;—
The bishopric of Coventry is his.

    (*Enter* QUEEN ISABELLA.)

    YOUNG MORTIMER. Madam, whither walks your majesty
      so fast?
    QUEEN ISABELLA. Unto the forest, gentle Mortimer,
To live in grief and baleful discontent;
For now, my lord, the king regards me not,
But dotes upon the love of Gaveston.
He claps* his cheeks, and hangs about his neck,   pats
Smiles in his face, and whispers in his ears;
And when I come he frowns, as who should say,
"Go whither thou wilt, seeing I have Gaveston."
    ELDER MORTIMER. Is it not strange that he is thus be-
      witched?
    YOUNG MORTIMER. Madam, return unto the court again:
That sly inveigling Frenchman we'll exile,
Or lose our lives; and yet, ere that day come,
The king shall lose his crown; for we have power,
And courage too, to be revenged at full.

QUEEN ISABELLA. But yet lift not your swords against the
    king.
LANCASTER. No; but we will lift Gaveston from hence.
WARWICK. And war must be the means, or he'll stay still.
QUEEN ISABELLA. Then let him stay; for rather than my
    lord
Shall be oppressed with civil mutinies,
I will endure a melancholy life,
And let him frolic with his minion.
ARCHBISHOP OF CANTERBURY. My lords, to ease all this,
    but hear me speak:—
We and the rest, that are his counsellors,
Will meet, and with a general consent
Confirm his banishment with our hands and seals.
LANCASTER. What we confirm the king will frustrate.
YOUNG MORTIMER. Then may we lawfully revolt from him.
WARWICK. But say, my lord, where shall this meeting be?
ARCHBISHOP OF CANTERBURY. At the New Temple.
YOUNG MORTIMER. Content.
ARCHBISHOP OF CANTERBURY. And, in the meantime, I'll
    entreat you all
To cross to Lambeth, and there stay with me.
LANCASTER. Come then, let's away.
YOUNG MORTIMER. Madam, farewell!
QUEEN ISABELLA. Farewell, sweet Mortimer; and, for my
    sake,
Forbear to levy arms against the king.
YOUNG MORTIMER. Ay, if words will serve; if not, I must.
                                               (*Exeunt.*)

Scene 3

(*The same. Enter* GAVESTON *and* KENT.)

GAVESTON. Edmund, the mighty Prince of Lancaster,
That hath more earldoms than an ass can bear,
And both the Mortimers, two goodly men,
With Guy of Warwick, that redoubted knight,
Are gone toward Lambeth—
    KENT. There let them remain.
                                               (*Exeunt.*)

Scene 4

(*The New Temple. Appearing on the scene are* LANCASTER,
WARWICK, PEMBROKE, *the* ELDER MORTIMER, YOUNG
MORTIMER, *the* ARCHBISHOP OF CANTERBURY, *and* ATTEND-
ANTS.)

LANCASTER. Here is the form* of Gaveston's exile: draft
May it please your lordship to subscribe your name.
ARCHBISHOP OF CANTERBURY. Give me the paper.
(*He subscribes, as do the others after him.*)
LANCASTER. Quick, quick, my lord; I long to write my name.
WARWICK. But I long more to see him banished hence.
YOUNG MORTIMER. The name of Mortimer shall fright the
    king,
Unless he be declined* from that base peasant.   turned away

(*Enter* KING EDWARD, GAVESTON, *and* KENT.)

KING EDWARD. What, are you moved that Gaveston sits
    here?
It is our pleasure; we will have it so.
LANCASTER. Your grace doth well to place him by your side,
For nowhere else the new earl is so safe.
ELDER MORTIMER. What man of noble birth can brook this
    sight?
Quam male conveniunt![5]
See what a scornful look the peasant casts!
PEMBROKE. Can kingly lions fawn on creeping ants?
WARWICK. Ignoble vassal, that like Phaeton*   son of Phoebus
Aspired unto the guidance of the sun!
YOUNG MORTIMER. Their downfall is at hand, their forces
    down:
We will not thus be faced and over-peered.*   looked down on
KING EDWARD. Lay hands on that traitor Mortimer!
ELDER MORTIMER. Lay hands on that traitor Gaveston!
KENT. Is this the duty that you owe your king?
WARWICK. We know our duties—let him know his peers.
KING EDWARD. Whither will you bear him? Stay, or ye
    shall die.

      ⁵ How ill they agree!

ELDER MORTIMER. We are no traitors; therefore threaten not.

GAVESTON. No, threaten not, my lord, but pay them home!
Were I a king—

YOUNG MORTIMER. Thou villain, wherefore talk'st thou of a king,
That hardly art a gentleman by birth?

KING EDWARD. Were he a peasant, being my minion,
I'll make the proudest of you stoop to him.

LANCASTER. My lord, you may not thus disparage us.—
Away, I say, with hateful Gaveston!

ELDER MORTIMER. And with the Earl of Kent that favours him.

(ATTENDANTS *remove* KENT *and* GAVESTON.)

KING EDWARD. Nay, then, lay violent hands upon your king,
Here, Mortimer, sit thou in Edward's throne:
Warwick and Lancaster, wear you my crown:
Was ever king thus over-ruled as I?

LANCASTER. Learn then to rule us better, and the realm.

YOUNG MORTIMER. What we have done, our heart-blood shall maintain.

WARWICK. Think you that we can brook this upstart's pride?

KING EDWARD. Anger and wrathful fury stops my speech.

ARCHBISHOP OF CANTERBURY. Why are you moved? be patient my lord
And see what we your counsellors have done.

YOUNG MORTIMER. My lords, now let us all be resolute,
And either have our wills, or lose our lives.

KING EDWARD. Meet you for this, proud overbearing peers?
Ere my sweet Gaveston shall part from me,
This isle shall fleet* upon the ocean,   float
And wander to the unfrequented Inde.

ARCHBISHOP OF CANTERBURY. You know that I am legate to the Pope;
On your allegiance to the see of Rome,
Subscribe, as we have done, to his exile.

YOUNG MORTIMER. Curse him, if he refuse; and then may we
Depose him and elect another king.

KING EDWARD. Ay, there it goes! but yet I will not yield:
Curse me, depose me, do the worst you can.

LANCASTER. Then linger not, my lord, but do it straight.

ARCHBISHOP OF CANTERBURY. Remember how the bishop was abused!

Either banish him that was the cause thereof,
Or I will presently* discharge these lords   immediately
Of duty and allegiance due to thee.
   KING EDWARD (*aside*). It boots me not to threat—I must
     speak fair:
The legate of the Pope will be obeyed.
My lord, you shall be Chancellor of the realm;
Thou, Lancaster, High Admiral of our fleet;
Young Mortimer and his uncle shall be earls;
And you, Lord Warwick, President of the North;
And thou* of Wales. If this content you not,   Pembroke
Make several kingdoms of this monarchy,
And share it equally amongst you all,
So I may have some nook or corner left,
To frolic with my dearest Gaveston.
   ARCHBISHOP OF CANTERBURY. Nothing shall alter us—we
     are resolved.
   LANCASTER. Come, come, subscribe.
   YOUNG MORTIMER. Why should you love him whom the
     world hates so?
   KING EDWARD. Because he loves me more than all the world.
Ah, none but rude and savage-minded men
Would seek the ruin of my Gaveston;
You that be noble-born should pity him.
   WARWICK. You that are princely-born should shake him off:
For shame subscribe, and let the lown* depart.   rogue
   ELDER MORTIMER. Urge him, my lord.
   ARCHBISHOP OF CANTERBURY. Are you content to banish
     him the realm?
   KING EDWARD. I see I must, and therefore am content:
Instead of ink I'll write it with my tears.
   (*Subscribes.*)
   YOUNG MORTIMER. The king is love-sick for his minion.
   KING EDWARD. 'Tis done—and now, accursèd hand, fall off!
   LANCASTER. Give it me—I'll have it published in the streets.
   YOUNG MORTIMER. I'll see him presently despatched away.
   ARCHBISHOP OF CANTERBURY. Now is my heart at ease.
   WARWICK. And so is mine.
   PEMBROKE. This will be good news to the common
     sort.*   people
   ELDER MORTIMER. Be it or no, he shall not linger here.
             (*Exeunt all except* KING EDWARD.)
   KING EDWARD. How fast they run to banish him I love!
They would not stir, were it to do me good.

Why should a king be subject to a priest?
Proud Rome! that hatchest such imperial* grooms,   imperious
For these thy superstitious taper-lights,
Wherewith thy antichristian churches blaze,
I'll fire thy crazed* buildings, and enforce*   infirm/force
The papal towers to kiss the lowly ground!
With slaughtered priests make Tiber's channel swell,
And banks raised higher with their sepulchres!
As for the peers, that back the clergy thus,
If I be king, not one of them shall live.

   (*Re-enter* GAVESTON.)

  GAVESTON. My lord, I hear it whispered everywhere,
That I am banished, and must fly the land.
  KING EDWARD. 'Tis true, sweet Gaveston—O! were it false!
The legate of the Pope will have it so,
And thou must hence, or I shall be deposed.
But I will reign to be revenged of them;
And therefore, sweet friend, take it patiently.
Live where thou wilt, I'll send thee gold enough;
And long thou shalt not stay, or if thou dost,
I'll come to thee; my love shall ne'er decline.
  GAVESTON. Is all my hope turned to this hell of grief?
  KING EDWARD. Rend not my heart with thy too-piercing
    words:
Thou from this land, I from myself am banished.
  GAVESTON. To go from hence grieves not poor Gaveston;
But to forsake you, in whose gracious looks
The blessedness of Gaveston remains:
For nowhere else seeks he felicity.
  KING EDWARD. And only this torments my wretched soul
That, whether I will or no, thou must depart.
Be governor of Ireland in my stead,
And there abide till fortune call thee home.
Here take my picture, and let me wear thine;
  (*They exchange pictures.*)
O, might I keep thee here as I do this,
Happy were I! but now most miserable!
  GAVESTON. 'Tis something to be pitied of a king.
  KING EDWARD. Thou shalt not hence—I'll hide thee,
    Gaveston.
  GAVESTON. I shall be found, and then 'twill grieve me
    more.*   I'll be hurt more

KING EDWARD. Kind words and mutual talk makes our grief
    greater:
Therefore, with dumb embracement, let us part—
Stay, Gaveston, I cannot leave thee thus.

GAVESTON. For every look, my lord drops down a tear:
Seeing I must go, do not renew my sorrow.

KING EDWARD. The time is little that thou hast to stay,
And, therefore, give me leave to look my fill:
But come, sweet friend, I'll bear thee on thy way.

GAVESTON. The peers will frown.

KING EDWARD. I pass* not for their anger—come,   care
    let's go;
O that we might as well return as go.

(*Enter* QUEEN ISABELLA.)

QUEEN ISABELLA. Whither goes my lord?

KING EDWARD. Fawn not on me, French strumpet! get thee
    gone!

QUEEN ISABELLA. On whom but on my husband should
    I fawn?

GAVESTON. On Mortimer! with whom, ungentle queen—
I say no more—judge you the rest, my lord.

QUEEN ISABELLA. In saying this, thou wrong'st me, Gav-
    eston;
Is't not enough that thou corrup'st my lord,
And art a bawd to his affections,
But thou must call mine honour thus in question?

GAVESTON. I mean not so; your grace must pardon me.

KING EDWARD. Thou art too familiar with that Mortimer,
And by thy means is Gaveston exiled;
But I would wish thee reconcile the lords,
Or thou shalt ne'er be reconciled to me.

QUEEN ISABELLA. Your highness knows it lies not in my
    power.

KING EDWARD. Away thee! touch me not—Come, Gaveston.

QUEEN ISABELLA. Villain! 'tis thou that robb'st me of my
    lord.

GAVESTON. Madam, 'tis you that rob me of my lord.

KING EDWARD. Speak not unto her; let her droop and pine.

QUEEN ISABELLA. Wherein, my lord, have I deserved these
    words?
Witness the tears that Isabella sheds,
Witness this heart, that sighing for thee, breaks,

How dear my lord is to poor Isabel.

    KING EDWARD. And witness Heaven how dear thou art to
    me:

There weep: for till my Gaveston be repealed,*   recalled
Assure thyself thou com'st not in my sight.

                         (*Exeunt* EDWARD *and* GAVESTON.)

    QUEEN ISABELLA. O miserable and distressèd queen!
Would, when I left sweet France and was embarked,
That charming* Circe walking on the waves,   the enchantress
Had changed my shape, or at the marriage-day
The cup of Hymen* had been full of poison,   god of marriage
Or with those arms that twined about my neck
I had been stifled, and not lived to see
The king my lord thus to abandon me!
Like frantic Juno will I fill the earth
With ghastly murmur of my sighs and cries;
For never doted Jove on Ganymede[6]
So much as he on cursèd Gaveston:
But that will more exasperate his wrath;
I must entreat him, I must speak him fair;
And be a means to call home Gaveston:
And yet he'll ever dote on Gaveston;
And so am I for ever miserable.

    (*Re-enter* LANCASTER, WARWICK, PEMBROKE, *the* ELDER
MORTIMER, *and* YOUNG MORTIMER.)

    LANCASTER. Look where the sister of the King of France
Sits wringing of her hands, and beats her breast!

    WARWICK. The king, I fear, hath ill-entreated* her.   ill-treated

    PEMBROKE. Hard is the heart that injures such a saint.

    YOUNG MORTIMER. I know 'tis 'long* of Gaveston   because
    she weeps.

    ELDER MORTIMER. Why, he is gone.

    YOUNG MORTIMER. Madam, how fares your grace?

    QUEEN ISABELLA. Ah, Mortimer! now breaks the king's hate
    forth,
And he confesseth that he loves me not.

    YOUNG MORTIMER. Cry quittance, madam, then; and love
    not him.

    QUEEN ISABELLA. No, rather will I die a thousand deaths:
And yet I love in vain;—he'll ne'er love me.

      [6] A Trojan boy, made cup-bearer to the gods.

LANCASTER. Fear ye not, madam; now his minion's gone,
His wanton humour will be quickly left.
QUEEN ISABELLA. O never, Lancaster! I am enjoined
To sue upon you all for his repeal;
This wills my lord, and this must I perform,
Or else be banished from his highness' presence.
LANCASTER. For his repeal, madam! he comes not back,
Unless the sea cast up his shipwrecked body.
WARWICK. And to behold so sweet a sight as that,
There's none here but would run his horse to death.
YOUNG MORTIMER. But, madam, would you have us call
    him home?
QUEEN ISABELLA. Ay, Mortimer, for till he be restored,
The angry king hath banished me the court;
And, therefore, as thou lov'st and tender'st* me,   care for
Be thou my advocate unto these peers.
YOUNG MORTIMER. What! would you have me plead for
    Gaveston?
ELDER MORTIMER. Plead for him that will, I am resolved.
LANCASTER. And so am I, my lord: dissuade the queen.
QUEEN ISABELLA. O Lancaster! let him dissuade the king,
For 'tis against my will he should return.
WARWICK. Then speak not for him, let the peasant go.
QUEEN ISABELLA. 'Tis for myself I speak, and not for him.
PEMBROKE. No speaking will prevail, and therefore cease.
YOUNG MORTIMER. Fair queen, forbear to angle for the fish
Which, being caught, strikes him that takes it dead;
I mean that vile torpedo* Gaveston,   electric ray
That now, I hope, floats on the Irish seas.
QUEEN ISABELLA. Sweet Mortimer, sit down by me awhile,
And I will tell thee reasons of such weight
As thou wilt soon subscribe to his repeal.
YOUNG MORTIMER. It is impossible; but speak your mind.
QUEEN ISABELLA. Then thus, but none shall hear it but
    ourselves.
(*Talks to* YOUNG MORTIMER *apart.*)
LANCASTER. My lords, albeit the queen win Mortimer,
Will you be resolute, and hold with me?
ELDER MORTIMER. Not I, against my nephew.
PEMBROKE. Fear not, the queen's words cannot alter him.
WARWICK. No? do but mark how earnestly she pleads!
LANCASTER. And see how coldly his looks make denial!
WARWICK. She smiles; now for my life his mind is changed!
LANCASTER. I'll rather lose his friendship, I, than grant.

Young Mortimer. Well, of necessity it must be so.
My lords, that I abhor base Gaveston,
I hope your honours make no question,
And therefore, though I plead for his repeal,
'Tis not for his sake, but for our avail;
Nay for the realm's behoof, and for the king's.
   Lancaster. Fie, Mortimer, dishonour not thyself!
Can this be true, 'twas good to banish him?
And is this true, to call him home again?
Such reasons make white black, and dark night day.
   Young Mortimer. My lord of Lancaster, mark the
     respect.*   reason
   Lancaster. In no respect can contraries be true.
   Queen Isabella. Yet, good my lord, hear what he can
     allege.
   Warwick. All that he speaks is nothing; we are resolved.
   Young Mortimer. Do you not wish that Gaveston were
     dead?
   Pembroke. I would he were!
   Young Mortimer. Why then, my lord, give me but leave
     to speak.
   Elder Mortimer. But, nephew, do not play the soph-
     ister.*   sophist
   Young Mortimer. This which I urge is of a burning zeal
To mend the king, and do our country good.
Know you not Gaveston hath store of gold,
Which may in Ireland purchase him such friends
As he will front* the mightiest of us all?   confront
And whereas* he shall live and be beloved,   where
'Tis hard for us to work his overthrow.
   Warwick. Mark you but that, my lord of Lancaster.
   Young Mortimer. But were he here, detested as he is,
How easily might some base slave be suborned
To greet his lordship with a poniard,
And none so much as blame the murderer,
But rather praise him for that brave attempt,
And in the chronicle enrol his name
For purging of the realm of such a plague!
   Pembroke. He saith true.
   Lancaster. Ay, but how chance this was not done before?
   Young Mortimer. Because, my lords, it was not thought
     upon.
Nay, more, when he shall know it lies in us
To banish him, and then to call him home,

'Twill make him vail* the top-flag of his pride,   lower
And fear to offend the meanest* nobleman.   lowliest

    ELDER MORTIMER. But how if he do not, nephew?

    YOUNG MORTIMER. Then may we with some colour*   excuse
        rise in arms;
For howsoever we have borne it out,
'Tis treason to be up against the king;
So we shall have the people of* our side,   on
Which for his father's sake lean to the king,
But cannot brook a night-grown mushroom,
Such a one as my lord of Cornwall is,
Should bear us down of the nobility.
And when the commons and the nobles join,
'Tis not the king can buckler* Gaveston;   shield
We'll pull him from the strongest hold he hath.
My lords, if to perform this I be slack,
Think me as base a groom as Gaveston.

    LANCASTER. On that condition, Lancaster will grant.

    PEMBROKE. And so will Pembroke.

    WARWICK. And I.

    ELDER MORTIMER. And I.

    YOUNG MORTIMER. In this I count me highly
        gratified,*   greatly obliged
And Mortimer will rest at your command.

    QUEEN ISABELLA. And when this favour Isabel forgets,
Then let her live abandoned and forlorn.—
But see, in happy time,* my lord the king,   that is,
Having brought the Earl of Cornwall on his way,   propitiously
Is new returned; this news will glad him much;
Yet not so much as me; I love him more
Than he can Gaveston; would he love me
But half so much, then were I treble-blessed!
    (*They withdraw.*)

    (*Re-enter* KING EDWARD *in mourning.*)

    KING EDWARD. He's gone, and for his absence thus I mourn.
Did never sorrow go so near my heart
As doth the want of my sweet Gaveston;
And could my crown's revenue bring him back,
I would freely give it to his enemies,
And think I gained, having bought so dear a friend.

    QUEEN ISABELLA. Hark! how he harps upon his minion.

    KING EDWARD. My heart is as an anvil unto sorrow.

Which beats upon it like the Cyclops' hammers,[7]
And with the noise turns up my giddy brain,
And makes me frantic for my Gaveston.
Ah! had some bloodless Fury rose from hell,
And with my kingly sceptre struck me dead,
When I was forced to leave my Gaveston!

LANCASTER (*aside*). *Diablo!* What passions call you these?

QUEEN ISABELLA (*advancing*). My gracious lord, I come
to bring you news.

KING EDWARD. That you have parleyed with your Mortimer!

QUEEN ISABELLA. That Gaveston, my lord, shall be repealed.

KING EDWARD. Repealed? the news is too sweet to be true?

QUEEN ISABELLA. But will you love me, if you find it so?

KING EDWARD. If it be so, what will not Edward do?

QUEEN ISABELLA. For Gaveston, but not for Isabel.

KING EDWARD. For thee, fair queen if thou lov'st Gaveston;
I'll hang a golden tongue* about thy neck,   type of jewel
Seeing thou hast pleaded with so good success.

QUEEN ISABELLA. No other jewels hang about my neck
Than these,* my lord; nor let me have more wealth   that is, his arms
Than I may fetch from this rich treasury*—   that is, his mouth
O how a kiss revives poor Isabel!

KING EDWARD. Once more receive my hand; and let this be
A second marriage 'twixt thyself and me.

QUEEN ISABELLA. And may it prove more happy than the
first!
My gentle lord, bespeak these nobles fair,
That wait attendance for a gracious look,
And on their knees salute your majesty.

KING EDWARD. Courageous Lancaster, embrace thy king!
And, as gross vapours perish by the sun,
Even so let hatred with thy sovereign's smile.
Live thou with me as my companion.

LANCASTER. This salutation overjoys my heart.

KING EDWARD. Warwick shall be my chiefest counsellor:
These silver hairs will more adorn my court
Than gaudy silks, or rich embroidery.
Chide me, sweet Warwick, if I go astray.

WARWICK. Slay me, my lord, when I offend your grace.

KING EDWARD. In solemn triumphs, and in public shows,
Pembroke shall bear the sword before the king.

---

[7] The Cyclopes assisted Vulcan in forging Jupiter's thunder-bolts.

PEMBROKE. And with this sword Pembroke will fight for
you.

KING EDWARD. But wherefore walks young Mortimer aside?
Be thou commander of our royal fleet;
Or, if that lofty office like thee not,
I make thee here Lord Marshal of the realm.

YOUNG MORTIMER. My lord, I'll marshal so your enemies,
As England shall be quiet, and you safe.

KING EDWARD. And as for you, Lord Mortimer of Chirke,
Whose great achievements in our foreign war
Deserves no common place, nor mean reward;
Be you the general of the levied troops,
That now are ready to assail the Scots.

ELDER MORTIMER. In this your grace hath highly honoured
me,
For with my nature war doth best agree.

QUEEN ISABELLA. Now is the King of England rich and
strong,
Having the love of his renownèd peers.

KING EDWARD. Ay, Isabel, ne'er was my heart so light.
Clerk of the crown, direct our warrant forth
For Gaveston to Ireland:

(*Enter* BEAUMONT *with warrant.*)

                              Beaumont, fly
As fast as Iris or Jove's Mercury.*   messengers of
                                                         the gods
BEAUMONT. It shall be done, my gracious lord.

                                              (*Exit.*)

KING EDWARD. Lord Mortimer, we leave you to your charge.
Now let us in, and feast it royally.
Against our friend the Earl of Cornwall comes,
We'll have a general tilt and tournament;
And then his marriage shall be solemnised.
For wot* you not that I have made him sure*   know/betrothed
Unto our cousin, the Earl of Gloucester's heir?

LANCASTER. Such news we hear, my lord.

KING EDWARD. That day, if not for him, yet for my sake,
Who* in the triumph* will be challenger,   whoever/
Spare for no cost; we will requite your love.   tournament

WARWICK. In this, or aught your highness shall command us.

KING EDWARD. Thanks, gentle Warwick: come, let's in and
revel.

                    (*Exeunt all except the* MORTIMERS.)

ELDER MORTIMER. Nephew, I must to Scotland; thou stayest
    here.
Leave now t'oppose thyself against the king.
Thou seest by nature he is mild and calm,
And, seeing his mind so dotes on Gaveston,
Let him without controlment have his will.
The mightiest kings have had their minions:
Great Alexander loved Hephaestion;
The conquering Hercules for Hylas wept;
And for Patroclus stern Achilles drooped
And not kings only, but the wisest men:
The Roman Tully loved Octavius;
Grave Socrates wild Alcibiades.
Then let his grace, whose youth is flexible,
And promiseth as much as we can wish,
Freely enjoy that vain, light-headed earl;
For riper years will wean him from such toys.
    YOUNG MORTIMER. Uncle, his wanton humour grieves not
    me;
But this I scorn, that one so basely born
Should by his sovereign's favour grow so pert,
And riot it with the treasure of the realm.
While soldiers mutiny for want of pay,
He wears a lord's revenue on his back,
And Midas-like, he jets* it in the court,   struts
With base outlandish cullions* at his heels,   foreign rascals
Whose proud fantastic liveries make such show,
As if that Proteus, god of shapes, appeared.
I have not seen a dapper Jack so brisk;
He wears a short Italian hooded cloak,
Larded* with pearl, and, in his Tuscan cap,   embroidered
A jewel of more value than the crown.
While others walk below, the king and he
From out a window laugh at such as we,
And flout our train, and jest at our attire.
Uncle, 'tis this makes me impatient.
    ELDER MORTIMER. But, nephew, now you see the king is
    changed.
    YOUNG MORTIMER. Then so am I, and live to do him service:
But whiles I have a sword, a hand, a heart,
I will not yield to any such upstart.
You know my mind; come, uncle, let's away.

                                            (*Exeunt.*)

ACT II

Scene 1

(*A room in Gloucester's castle. Enter* YOUNG SPENCER *and* BALDOCK.)

BALDOCK. Spencer,
Seeing that our lord the Earl of Gloucester's dead,
Which of the nobles dost thou mean to serve?
YOUNG SPENCER. Not Mortimer, nor any of his side;
Because the king and he are enemies.
Baldock, learn this of me, a factious lord
Shall hardly do himself good, much less us;
But he that hath the favour of a king,
May with one word advance us while we live:
The liberal Earl of Cornwall is the man
On whose good fortune Spencer's hopes depends.
BALDOCK. What, mean you then to be his follower?
YOUNG SPENCER. No, his companion; for he loves me well,
And would have once preferred* me to the king.   recommended
BALDOCK. But he is banished; there's small hope of him.
YOUNG SPENCER. Ay, for a while; but, Baldock, mark the
    end.
A friend of mine told me in secrecy
That he's repealed, and sent for back again;
And even now a post came from the court
With letters to our lady from the king;
And as she read she smiled, which makes me think
It is about her lover Gaveston.
BALDOCK. 'Tis like enough; for since he was exiled
She neither walks abroad, nor comes in sight.
But I had thought the match had been broke off,
And that his banishment had changed her mind.
YOUNG SPENCER. Our lady's first love is not wavering;
My life for thine she will have Gaveston.
BALDOCK. Then hope I by her means to be preferred,
Having read unto her since she was a child.
YOUNG SPENCER. Then, Baldock, you must cast the scholar
    off,
And learn to court it like a gentleman.
'Tis not a black coat and a little band,*   clerical collar
A velvet-caped coat, faced before with serge,

And smelling to a nosegay all the day,
Or holding of a napkin in your hand,
Or saying a long grace at a table's end,
Or making low legs* to a nobleman,   bows
Or looking downward with your eyelids close,
And saying, "Truly, an't may please your honour,"
Can get you any favour with great men;
You must be proud, bold, pleasant, resolute,
And now and then stab, as occasion serves.
    BALDOCK. Spencer, thou know'st I hate such formal
        toys,*   tricks
And use them but of mere hypocrisy.
Mine old lord whiles he lived was so precise,*   Puritanical
That he would take exceptions at my buttons,
And being like pin's heads, blame me for the bigness;
Which made me curate-like in mine attire,
Though inwardly licentious enough,
And apt for any kind of villany.
I am none of these comman pedants, I,
That cannot speak without *propterea quod.**   because
    YOUNG SPENCER. But one of those that saith, *quandoqui-*
        dem,*   since
And hath a special gift to form a verb.
    BALDOCK. Leave off this jesting, here my lady comes.
    (*They withdraw.*)

(*Enter* KING EDWARD'S NIECE.)

    NIECE. The grief for his exile was not so much,
As is the joy of his returning home.
This letter came from my sweet Gaveston:
What need'st thou, love, thus to excuse thyself?
I know thou could'st not come and visit me:
(*Reads.*) "I will not long be from thee, though I die."
This argues the entire love of my lord;
(*Reads.*) "When I forsake thee, death seize on my heart:"
But stay thee here where Gaveston shall sleep.
    (*Puts the letter into her bosom.*)
Now to the letter of my lord the king.—
He wills me to repair unto the court,
And meet my Gaveston. Why do I stay,
Seeing that he talks thus of my marriage-day?
Who's there? Baldock!

See that my coach be ready, I must hence.
    BALDOCK. It shall be done, madam.
    NIECE. And meet me at the park-pale presently.
                                   (*Exit* BALDOCK.)

Spencer, stay you and bear me company,
For I have joyful news to tell thee of;
My lord of Cornwall is a-coming over,
And will be at the court as soon as we.
    YOUNG SPENCER. I knew the king would have him home
        again.
    NIECE. If all things sort* out, as I hope they will,   turn
Thy service, Spencer, shall be thought upon.
    YOUNG SPENCER. I humbly thank your ladyship.
    NIECE. Come, lead the way; I long till I am there.
                                     (*Exeunt.*)

Scene 2

(*Tynemouth Castle. Enter* KING EDWARD, QUEEN ISABELLA,
KENT, LANCASTER, YOUNG MORTIMER, WARWICK, PEM-
BROKE, *and* ATTENDANTS.)

KING EDWARD. The wind is good, I wonder why he stays;
I fear me he is wrecked upon the sea.
    QUEEN ISABELLA. Look, Lancaster, how passionate*   sorrowful
        he is,
And still his mind runs on his minion!
    LANCASTER. My lord,—
    KING EDWARD. How now! what news? is Gaveston arrived?
    YOUNG MORTIMER. Nothing but Gaveston! what means
        your grace?
You have matters of more weight to think upon;
The King of France sets foot in Normandy.
    KING EDWARD. A trifle! we'll expel him when we please.
But tell me, Mortimer, what's thy device*   heraldic emblem
Against* the stately triumph we decreed?   for use in
    YOUNG MORTIMER. A homely one, my lord, not worth the
        telling.
    KING EDWARD. Pray thee let me know it.
    YOUNG MORTIMER. But, seeing you are so desirous, thus it is
A lofty cedar-tree, fair flourishing,
On whose top-branches kingly eagles perch,
And by the bark a canker* creeps me up,   canker-worm
And gets into the highest bough of all:

The motto, *Æque tandem.** Justly at length

    KING EDWARD. And what is yours, my lord of Lancaster?

    LANCASTER. My lord, mine's more obscure than Mortimer's.
Pliny reports there is a flying fish
Which all the other fishes deadly hate,
And therefore, being pursued, it takes the air.
No sooner is it up, but there's a fowl
That seizeth it; this fish, my lord, I bear,
The motto this: *Undique mors est.** Death is
everywhere

    KENT. Proud Mortimer! ungentle Lancaster.
Is this the love you bear your sovereign?
Is this the fruit your reconcilement bears?
Can you in words make show of amity,
And in your shields display your rancorous minds!
What call you this but private libelling
Against the Earl of Cornwall and my brother?

    QUEEN ISABELLA. Sweet husband, be content, they all love
      you.

    KING EDWARD. They love me not that hate my Gaveston.
I am that cedar, shake me not too much;
And you the eagles; soar ye ne'er so high,
I have the jesses[8] that will pull you down;
And *Æque tandem* shall that canker cry
Unto the proudest peer of Britainy.
Though thou compar'st him to a flying fish,
And threatenest death whether he rise or fall,
'Tis not the hugest monster of the sea,
Nor foulest harpy that shall swallow him.

    YOUNG MORTIMER. If in his absence thus he favours him,
What will he do whenas* he shall be present? when

    LANCASTER. That shall we see; look where his lordship
      comes.

    (*Enter* GAVESTON.)

    KING EDWARD. My Gaveston!
Welcome to Tynemouth! welcome to thy friend!
Thy absence made me droop and pine away;
For, as the lovers of fair Danae,[9]

---

    [8] Straps fastened to the legs of a hawk to control him.

    [9] Danae, daughter of King Acrisius, was buried in a bronze
house to keep her from marrying and having children. The roof,
however, was above ground. Through an opening Zeus entered
in a shower of gold and seduced the maiden. Perseus was the
son of this union.

When she was locked up in a brazen* tower,   bronze
Desired her more, and waxed outrageous,
So did it fare with me: and now thy sight
Is sweeter far than was thy parting hence
Bitter and irksome to my sobbing heart.

    GAVESTON. Sweet lord and king, your speech
      preventeth* mine,   anticipates
Yet have I words left to express my joy:
The shepherd nipt with biting winter's rage
Frolics not more to see the painted spring,
Then I do to behold your majesty.

    KING EDWARD. Will none of you salute my Gaveston?
    LANCASTER. Salute him? yes; welcome, Lord Chamberlain!
    YOUNG MORTIMER. Welcome is the good Earl of Cornwall!
    WARWICK. Welcome, Lord Governor of the Isle of Man!
    PEMBROKE. Welcome, Master Secretary!
    KENT. Brother, do you hear them?
    KING EDWARD. Still will these earls and barons use me thus?
    GAVESTON. My lord, I cannot brook these injuries.
    QUEEN ISABELLA (*aside*). Ay me, poor soul, when these
      begin to jar.
    KING EDWARD. Return it to their throats, I'll be thy warrant.
    GAVESTON. Base, leaden earls, that glory in your birth,
Go sit at home and eat your tenant's beef;
And come not here to scoff at Gaveston,
Whose mounting thoughts did never creep so low
As to bestow a look on such as you.

    LANCASTER. Yet I disdain not to do this for you.
    (*Draws his sword and offers to stab* GAVESTON.)
    KING EDWARD. Treason! treason! where's the traitor?
    PEMBROKE. Here! here!
    KING EDWARD. Convey hence Gaveston; they'll murder him.
    GAVESTON. The life of thee shall salve this foul disgrace.
    YOUNG MORTIMER. Villain! thy life, unless I miss mine aim.
    (*Wounds* GAVESTON.)
    QUEEN ISABELLA. Ah! Furious Mortimer, what hast thou
      done?
    YOUNG MORTIMER. No more than I would answer, were he
      slain.

                (*Exit* GAVESTON *with* ATTENDANTS.)
    KING EDWARD. Yes, more than thou canst answer, though he
      live;
Dear shall you both abide this riotous deed.

Out of my presence! come not near the court.

YOUNG MORTIMER. I'll not be barred the court for Gaveston.

LANCASTER. We'll hale him by the ears unto the block.

KING EDWARD. Look to your own heads; his is sure enough.

WARWICK. Look to your own crown, if you back him thus.

KENT. Warwick, these words do ill beseem thy years

KING EDWARD. Nay, all of them conspire to cross me thus;

But if I live, I'll tread upon their heads

That think with high looks thus to tread me down.

Come, Edmund, let's away and levy men,

'Tis war that must abate these barons' pride.

(*Exeunt* KING EDWARD, QUEEN ISABELLA, *and* KENT.)

WARWICK. Let's to our castles, for the king is moved.

YOUNG MORTIMER. Moved may he be, and perish in his wrath!

LANCASTER. Cousin, it is no dealing with him now,

He means to make us stoop by force of arms;

And therefore let us jointly here protest,*   swear

To prosecute that Gaveston to the death.

YOUNG MORTIMER. By heaven, the abject villain shall not live!

WARWICK. I'll have his blood, or die in seeking it.

PEMBROKE. The like oath Pembroke takes.

LANCASTER. And so doth Lancaster.

Now send our heralds to defy the king;

And make the people swear to put him down.

(*Enter a* MESSENGER.)

YOUNG MORTIMER. Letters! from whence?

MESSENGER. From Scotland, my lord.

(*Giving letters to* MORTIMER.)

LANCASTER. Why, how now, cousin, how fares all our friends?

YOUNG MORTIMER. My uncle's taken prisoner by the Scots.

LANCASTER. We'll have him ransomed, man; be of good cheer.

YOUNG MORTIMER. They rate his ransom at five thousand pound.

Who should defray the money but the king,

Seeing he is taken prisoner in his wars?

I'll to the king.

LANCASTER. Do, cousin, and I'll bear thee company.

WARWICK. Meantime, my lord of Pembroke and myself

Will to Newcastle here, and gather head.*   an army

YOUNG MORTIMER. About it then, and we will follow you.
LANCASTER. Be resolute and full of secrecy.
WARWICK. I warrant you.

(*Exit with* PEMBROKE.)

YOUNG MORTIMER. Cousin, and if he will not ransom him,
I'll thunder such a peal into his ears,
As never subject did unto his king.
LANCASTER. Content, I'll bear my part—Holla! who's there?

(*Enter* GUARD.)

YOUNG MORTIMER. Ay, marry, such a guard as this doth
    well.
LANCASTER. Lead on the way.
GUARD. Whither will your lordships?
YOUNG MORTIMER. Whither else but to the king.
GUARD. His highness is disposed to be alone.
LANCASTER. Why, so he may, but we will speak to him.
GUARD. You may not in, my lord.
YOUNG MORTIMER. May we not?

(*Enter* KING EDWARD *and* KENT.)

KING EDWARD. How now!
What noise is this? who have we there, is't you?
    (*Going.*)
YOUNG MORTIMER. Nay, stay, my lord, I come to bring you
    news;
Mine uncle's taken prisoner by the Scots.
KING EDWARD. Then ransom him.
LANCASTER. 'Twas in your wars; you should ransom him.
YOUNG MORTIMER. And you shall ransom him, or else——
KENT. What! Mortimer, you will not threaten him?
KING EDWARD. Quiet yourself, you shall have the broad seal,
To gather* for him throughout the realm.   collect money
LANCASTER. Your minion Gaveston hath taught you this.
YOUNG MORTIMER. My lord, the family of the Mortimers
Are not so poor, but, would they sell their land,
'Twould levy men enough to anger you.
We never beg, but use such prayers as these.
KING EDWARD. Shall I still be haunted thus?
YOUNG MORTIMER. Nay, now you're here alone, I'll speak
    my mind.

LANCASTER. And so will I, and then, my lord, farewell.

YOUNG MORTIMER. The idle triumphs, masks, lascivious
    shows,
And prodigal gifts bestowed on Gaveston,
Have drawn thy treasury dry, and made thee weak;
The murmuring commons, overstretchèd, break.

LANCASTER. Look for rebellion, look to be deposed;
Thy garrisons are beaten out of France,
And, lame and poor, lie groaning at the gates.
The wild O'Neill, with swarms of Irish kerns,*   foot soldiers
Lives uncontrolled within the English pale.
Unto the walls of York the Scots make road,*   inroad
And unresisted drive away rich spoils.

YOUNG MORTIMER. The haughty Dane commands the nar-
    row seas,*   English Channel
While in the harbour ride thy ships unrigged.

LANCASTER. What foreign prince sends thee ambassadors?

YOUNG MORTIMER. Who loves thee, but a sort* of   band
    flatterers?

LANCASTER. Thy gentle queen, sole sister to Valois,
Complains that thou hast left her all forlorn.

YOUNG MORTIMER. Thy court is naked, being bereft of those
That make a king seem glorious to the world;
I mean the peers, whom thou should'st dearly love:
Libels are cast again thee in the street:
Ballads and rhymes made of thy overthrow.

LANCASTER. The Northern borderers seeing their houses
    burnt,
Their wives and children slain, run up and down,
Cursing the name of thee and Gaveston.

YOUNG MORTIMER. When wert thou in the field with banner
    spread,
But once? and then thy soldiers marched like players,
With garish robes, not armour; and thyself,
Bedaubed with gold, rode laughing at the rest,
Nodding and shaking of thy spangled crest,
Where women's favours hung like labels down.

LANCASTER. And therefore came it, that the fleering*   jeering
    Scots,
To England's high disgrace, have made this jig;[10]

[10] From Fabyan's *Chronicle*. The Battle of Bannocksbourn was
fought in 1314, two years after Gaveston's death.

"Maids of England, sore may you mourn,—
    For your lemans* you have lost at Bannocks-   lovers
        bourn,—
    With a heave and a ho!
    What weeneth the King of England,
    So soon to have won Scotland?—
        With a rombelow!"

YOUNG MORTIMER. Wigmore shall fly,[11] to set my uncle
    free.

LANCASTER. And when 'tis gone, our swords shall purchase
    more.

If ye be moved, revenge it as you can;
Look next to see us with our ensigns spread.

                                    (*Exit with* YOUNG MORTIMER.)

KING EDWARD. My swelling heart for very anger breaks!
How oft have I been baited by these peers,
And dare not be revenged, for their power is great!
Yet, shall the crowing of these cockerels
Affright a lion? Edward, unfold thy paws,
And let their lives' blood slake thy fury's hunger.
If I be cruel and grow tyrannous,
Now let them thank themselves, and rue too late.

KENT. My lord, I see your love to Gaveston
Will be the ruin of the realm and you,
For now the wrathful nobles threaten wars,
And therefore, brother, banish him for ever.

KING EDWARD. Art thou an enemy to my Gaveston?

KENT. Ay, and it grieves me that I favoured him.

KING EDWARD. Traitor, begone! whine thou with Mortimer.

KENT. So will I, rather than with Gaveston.

KING EDWARD. Out of my sight, and trouble me no more!

KENT. No marvel though thou scorn thy noble peers,
When I thy brother am rejected thus.

KING EDWARD. Away!

                                                    (*Exit* KENT.)

Poor Gaveston, that has no friend but me,
Do what they can, we'll live in Tynemouth here,
And, so I walk with him about the walls,
What care I though the earls begirt us round?—
Here cometh she that's cause of all these jars.

---

[11] That is, I'll put my estate up for sale.

(*Enter* QUEEN ISABELLA *with* KING EDWARD'S NIECE, *two*
LADIES, GAVESTON, BALDOCK *and* YOUNG SPENCER.)

QUEEN ISABELLA. My lord, 'tis thought the earls are up in
arms.

KING EDWARD. Ay, and 'tis likewise thought you favour 'em.

QUEEN ISABELLA. Thus do you still suspect me without
cause?

NIECE. Sweet uncle! speak more kindly to the queen.

GAVESTON. My lord, dissemble with her, speak her fair.

KING EDWARD. Pardon me, sweet, I had forgot myself.

QUEEN ISABELLA. Your pardon is quickly got of Isabel.

KING EDWARD. The younger Mortimer is grown so brave,
That to my face he threatens civil wars.

GAVESTON. Why do you not commit him to the Tower?

KING EDWARD. I dare not, for the people love him well.

GAVESTON. Why, then we'll have him privily made away.

KING EDWARD. Would Lancaster and he had both caroused
A bowl of poison to each other's health!
But let them go, and tell me what are these.

NIECE. Two of my father's servants whilst he liv'd,—
May't please your grace to entertain them now.

KING EDWARD. Tell me, where wast thou born? what is thine
arms?

BALDOCK. My name is Baldock, and my gentry
I fetch from Oxford, not from heraldry.

KING EDWARD. The fitter thou art, Baldock, for my turn.
Wait on me, and I'll see thou shall not want.

BALDOCK. I humbly thank your majesty.

KING EDWARD. Knowest thou him, Gaveston?

GAVESTON. Ay, my lord;
His name is Spencer, he is well allied;[12]
For my sake, let him wait upon your grace;
Scarce shall you find a man of more desert.

KING EDWARD. Then, Spencer, wait upon me; for his sake
I'll grace thee with a higher style* ere long.   title

YOUNG SPENCER. No greater titles happen unto me,
Than to be favoured of your majesty!

KING EDWARD. Cousin, this day shall be your marriage-feast.
And, Gaveston, think that I love thee well,
To wed thee to our niece, the only heir
Unto the Earl of Gloucester late deceased.

[12] That is, comes from a good family.

GAVESTON. I know, my lord, many will stomach* me,   resent
But I respect neither their love nor hate.

KING EDWARD. The headstrong barons shall not limit me;
He that I list to favour shall be great.
Come, let's away; and when the marriage ends,
Have at the rebels, and their 'complices!

(*Exeunt.*)

Scene 3

(*Near Tynemouth Castle. Enter* KENT, LANCASTER, YOUNG
MORTIMER, WARWICK, PEMBROKE, *and others.*)

KENT. My lords, of love to this our native land
I come to join with you and leave the king;
And in your quarrel and the realm's behoof
Will be the first that shall adventure life.

LANCASTER. I fear me, you are sent of policy,
To undermine us with a show of love.

WARWICK. He is your brother, therefore have we cause
To cast* the worst, and doubt of your revolt.   calculate

KENT. Mine honour shall be hostage of my truth:
If that will not suffice, farewell, my lords.

YOUNG MORTIMER. Stay, Edmund; never was Plantagenet
False of his word, and therefore trust we thee.

PEMBROKE. But what's the reason you should leave him
   now?

KENT. I have informed the Earl of Lancaster.

LANCASTER. And it sufficeth. Now, my lords, know this,
That Gaveston is secretly arrived,
And here in Tynemouth frolics with the king.
Let us with these our followers scale the walls,
And suddenly surprise them unawares.

YOUNG MORTIMER. I'll give the onset.

WARWICK. And I'll follow thee.

YOUNG MORTIMER. This tottered* ensign of my   tattered
   ancestors,
Which swept the desert shore of that dead sea
Whereof we got the name of Mortimer,
Will I advance upon this castle's walls.
Drums, strike alarum, raise them from their sport,
And ring aloud the knell of Gaveston!

LANCASTER. None be so hardy as to touch the king;
But neither spare you Gaveston nor his friends.

(*Exeunt.*)

Scene 4

(*The same. Enter* KING EDWARD *and* YOUNG SPENCER.)

KING EDWARD. O tell me, Spencer, where is Gaveston?
SPENCER. I fear me he is slain, my gracious lord.
KING EDWARD. No, here he comes; now let them spoil and
    kill.

(*Enter* QUEEN ISABELLA, KING EDWARD'S NIECE, GAVES-
TON, *and Nobles.*)

Fly, fly, my lords, the earls have got the hold;*   stronghold
Take shipping and away to Scarborough;
Spencer and I will post away by land.
    GAVESTON. O stay, my lord, they will not injure you.
    KING EDWARD. I will not trust them; Gaveston, away!
    GAVESTON. Farewell, my lord.
    KING EDWARD. Lady, farewell.
    NIECE. Farewell, sweet uncle, till we meet again.
    KING EDWARD. Farewell, sweet Gaveston; and farewell,
        niece.
    QUEEN ISABELLA. No farewell to poor Isabel thy queen?
    KING EDWARD. Yes, yes, for Mortimer, your lover's sake.
    QUEEN ISABELLA. Heaven can witness I love none but you:
               (*Exeunt all but* QUEEN ISABELLA.)
From my embracements thus he breaks away.
O that mine arms could close this isle about,
That I might pull him to me where I would!
Or that these tears, that drizzle from mine eyes,
Had power to mollify his stony heart,
That when I had him we might never part.

(*Enter* LANCASTER, WARWICK, YOUNG MORTIMER, *and others. Alarums within.*)

LANCASTER. I wonder how he 'scaped!
YOUNG MORTIMER. Who's this? the queen!
    QUEEN ISABELLA. Ay, Mortimer, the miserable queen,
Whose pining heart her inward sighs have blasted,
And body with continual mourning wasted:
These hands are tired with haling of my lord

From Gaveston, from wicked Gaveston,
And all in vain; for, when I speak him fair,
He turns away, and smiles upon his minion.

    YOUNG MORTIMER. Cease to lament, and tell us where's the
      king?

    QUEEN ISABELLA. What would you with the king? is't him
      you seek?

    LANCASTER. No, madam, but that cursèd Gaveston.
Far be it from the thought of Lancaster
To offer violence to his sovereign.
We would but rid the realm of Gaveston:
Tell us where he remains, and he shall die.

    QUEEN ISABELLA. He's gone by water unto Scarborough;
Pursue him quickly, and he cannot 'scape;
The king hath left him and his train is small.

    WARWICK. Foreslow* no time, sweet Lancaster; let's   delay
      march.

    YOUNG MORTIMER. How comes it that the king and he is
      parted?

    QUEEN ISABELLA. That thus your army, going several ways,
Might be of lesser force: and with the power
That he intendeth presently to raise,
Be easily suppressed; therefore be gone.

    YOUNG MORTIMER. Here in the river rides a Flemish
      hoy;*   small ship
Let's all aboard, and follow him amain.

    LANCASTER. The wind that bears him hence will fill our sails:
Come, come aboard, 'tis but an hour's sailing.

    YOUNG MORTIMER. Madam, stay you within this castle here.

    QUEEN ISABELLA. No, Mortimer, I'll to my lord the king.

    YOUNG MORTIMER. Nay, rather sail with us to Scarborough.

    QUEEN ISABELLA. You know the king is so suspicious,
As if he hear I have but talked with you,
Mine honor will be called in question;
And therefore, gentle Mortimer, be gone.

    YOUNG MORTIMER. Madam, I cannot stay to answer you,
But think of Mortimer as he deserves.

                    (*Exeunt all except* QUEEN ISABELLA.)

    QUEEN ISABELLA. So well hast thou deserved, sweet
      Mortimer,
As Isabel could live with thee for ever.
In vain I look for love at Edward's hand,
Whose eyes are fixed on none but Gaveston.
Yet once more I'll importune him with prayer:

If he be strange* and not regard my words,   cold
My son and I will over into France,
And to the king my brother there complain,
How Gaveston hath robbed me of his love:
But yet I hope my sorrows will have end,
And Gaveston this blessèd day be slain.

                                                    (*Exit.*)

Scene 5

(*Open country near Scarborough. Enter* GAVESTON, *pursued.*)

GAVESTON. Yet, lusty lords, I have escaped your hands,
Your threats, your 'larums,* and your hot   danger warnings
      pursuits;
And though divorced from King Edward's eyes,
Yet liveth Pierce of Gaveston unsurprised,*   uncaptured
Breathing, in hope (malgrado* all your beards,   in spite of
That muster rebels thus against your king),
To see his royal sovereign once again.

(*Enter* WARWICK, LANCASTER, PEMBROKE, YOUNG MORTI-
MER, SOLDIERS, JAMES, *and other* ATTENDANTS *of* PEM-
BROKE.)

WARWICK. Upon him, soldiers, take away his weapons.
YOUNG MORTIMER. Thou proud disturber of thy country's
      peace,
Corrupter of thy king; cause of these broils,*   quarrels
Base flatterer, yield! and were it not for shame,
Shame and dishonour to a soldier's name,
Upon my weapon's point here should'st thou fall,
And welter* in thy gore.   roll
      LANCASTER. Monster of men!
That, like the Greekish strumpet,* trained* to arms Helen/enticed
And bloody wars so many valiant knights;
Look for no other fortune, wretch, than death!
King Edward is not here to buckler* thee.   defend
      WARWICK. Lancaster, why talk'st thou to the slave?
Go, soldiers, take him hence, for, by my sword,
His head shall off: Gaveston, short warning
Shall serve thy turn: it is our country's cause,
That here severely we will execute

Upon thy person. Hang him at a bough.
 GAVESTON. My lord!—
 WARWICK. Soldiers, have him away;—
But for* thou wert the favourite of a king,   because
Thou shalt have so much honour at our hands[13]—
 GAVESTON. I thank you all, my lords: then I perceive,
That heading is one, and hanging is the other,
And death is all.

   (*Enter* ARUNDEL.)

 LANCASTER. How now, my lord of Arundel?
 ARUNDEL. My lords, King Edward greets you all by me.
 WARWICK. Arundel, say your message.
 ARUNDEL. His majesty.
Hearing that you had taken Gaveston,
Entreateth you by me, yet but he may
See him before he dies; for why* he says,   because
And sends you word, he knows that die he shall;
And if you gratify his grace so far,
He will be mindful of the courtesy.
 WARWICK. How now?
 GAVESTON. Renownèd Edward, how thy name
Revives poor Gaveston!
 WARWICK. No, it needeth not;
Arundel, we will gratify the king
In other matters; he must pardon us in this.
Soldiers, away with him!
 GAVESTON. Why, my lord of Warwick,
Will not these delays beget my hopes?
I know it, lords, it is this life you aim at,
Yet grant King Edward this.
 YOUNG MORTIMER. Shalt thou appoint
What we shall grant? Soldiers, away with him!
Thus we'll gratify the king,
We'll send his head by thee; let him bestow
His tears on that, for that is all he gets
Of Gaveston, or else his senseless trunk.
 LANCASTER. Not so, my lords, lest he bestow more cost
In burying him than he hath ever earned.
 ARUNDEL. My lords, it is his majesty's request,
And in the honour of a king he swears,

   [13] To be beheaded like a gentleman instead of hanged.

He will but talk with him, and send him back.

WARWICK. When? can you tell? Arundel, no; we wot,*   know
He that the care of his realm remits,
And drives his nobles to these exigents*   extremes
For Gaveston, will, if he sees him once,
Violate any promise to possess him.

ARUNDEL. Then if you will not trust his grace in
    keep,*   as keeper
My lords, I will be pledge for his return.

YOUNG MORTIMER. 'Tis honourable in thee to offer this;
But for we know thou art a noble gentleman,
We will not wrong thee so, to make away
A true man for a thief.

GAVESTON. How mean'st thou, Mortimer? that is over-base.

YOUNG MORTIMER. Away, base groom, robber of king's
    renown!
Question with thy companions and mates.

PEMBROKE. My Lord Mortimer, and you, my lords, each
    one,
To gratify the king's request therein.
Touching the sending of this Gaveston,
Because his majesty so earnestly
Desires to see the man before his death,
I will upon mine honour undertake
To carry him, and bring him back again;
Provided this, that you my lord of Arundel
Will join with me.

WARWICK. Pembroke, what wilt thou do?
Cause yet more bloodshed? is it not enough
That we have taken him, but must we now
Leave him on "had I wist,"[14] and let him go?

PEMBROKE. My lords, I will not over-woo your honours,
But if you dare trust Pembroke with the prisoner,
Upon mine oath, I will return him back.

ARUNDEL. My lord of Lancaster, what say you in this?

LANCASTER. Why, I say, let him go on Pembroke's word.

PEMBROKE. And you, Lord Mortimer?

YOUNG MORTIMER. How say you, my lord of Warwick?

WARWICK. Nay, do your pleasures, I know how 'twill prove.

PEMBROKE. Then give him me.

GAVESTON. Sweet sovereign, yet I come
To see thee ere I die.

---

[14] " 'Had I known'—the exclamation of those who repent of
what they have rashly done" (Dyce).

WARWICK (*aside*). Yet not perhaps,
If Warwick's wit and policy* prevail.   cunning
   YOUNG MORTIMER. My lord of Pembroke, we deliver him
    you;
Return him on your honour. Sound, away!
(*Exeunt all except* PEMBROKE, ARUNDEL, GAVESTON, JAMES,
             and other ATTENDANTS *of* PEMBROKE.)
   PEMBROKE. My lord of Arundel, you shall go with me.
My house is not far hence; out of the way
A little, but our men shall go along.
We that have pretty wenches to our wives,
Sir, must not come so near to baulk* their lips.   pass by
   ARUNDEL. 'Tis very kindly spoke, my lord of Pembroke;
Your honour hath an adamant of power*   powerful magnet
To draw a prince.
   PEMBROKE. So, my lord. Come hither, James:
I do commit this Gaveston to thee,
Be thou this night his keeper; in the morning
We will discharge thee of thy charge: be gone.
   GAVESTON. Unhappy Gaveston, whither goest thou now?
         (*Exit with* JAMES *and the other* ATTENDANTS.)
   HORSE-BOY. My lord, we'll quickly be at Cobham.
                          (*Exeunt.*)

ACT III

Scene 1

(*Open country. Enter* GAVESTON *mourning,* JAMES, *and
other* ATTENDANTS *of* PEMBROKE.)

   GAVESTON. O treacherous Warwick! thus to wrong thy
    friend.
   JAMES. I see it is your life these arms pursue.
   GAVESTON. Weaponless must I fall, and die in bands?*   bonds
O! must this day be period of my life?
Centre of all my bliss! An* ye be men,   if
Speed to the king.

(*Enter* WARWICK *and* SOLDIERS.)

   WARWICK. My lord of Pembroke's men,
Strive you no longer—I will have that Gaveston.

JAMES. Your lordship does dishonour to yourself,
And wrong our lord, your honourable friend.
WARWICK. No, James, it is my country's cause I follow.
Go, take the villain; soldiers, come away.
We'll make quick work. Commend me to your master,
My friend, and tell him that I watched it well.
Come, let thy shadow* parley with King Edward.   ghost
    GAVESTON. Treacherous earl, shall I not see the king?
    WARWICK. The king of Heaven perhaps, no other king.
Away!

        (*Exeunt* WARWICK *and* Soldiers *with* GAVESTON.)
    JAMES. Come, fellows, it booted* not for us to strive, availed
We will in haste go certify* our lord.   inform
                                (*Exeunt.*)

Scene 2

(*Near Boroughbridge, Yorkshire. Enter* KING EDWARD *and*
YOUNG SPENCER, BALDOCK, *and* NOBLES *of the* KING'S *side,
and* SOLDIERS *with drums and fifes.*)

    KING EDWARD. I long to hear an answer from the barons
Touching my friend, my dearest Gaveston.
Ah! Spencer, not the riches of my realm
Can ransom him! ah, he is marked to die!
I know the malice of the younger Mortimer,
Warwick I know is rough, and Lancaster
Inexorable, and I shall never see
My lovely Pierce of Gaveston again!
The barons overbear me with their pride.
    YOUNG SPENCER. Were I King Edward, England's sovereign,
Son to the lovely Eleanor of Spain,
Great Edward Longshanks' issue, would I bear
These braves,* this rage, and suffer uncontrolled   defiances
These barons thus to beard* me in my land,   affront
In mine own realm? My lord, pardon my speech:
Did you retain your father's magnanimity,
Did you regard the honour of your name,
You would not suffer thus your majesty
Be counterbuft of* your nobility.   to be rebuffed by
Strike off their heads, and let them preach on poles!
No doubt, such lessons they will teach the rest,
As by their preachments they will profit much,
And learn obedience to their lawful king.

KING EDWARD. Yea, gentle Spencer, we have been too mild,
Too kind to them; but now have drawn our sword,
And if they send me not my Gaveston,
We'll steel it* on their crest, and poll* their tops.   use steel/trim
    BALDOCK. This haught* resolve becomes your majesty   proud
Not to be tied to their affection,
As though your highness were a schoolboy still,
And must be awed and governed like a child.

(*Enter the* ELDER SPENCER, *with his truncheon**   staff of
and SOLDIERS.)   authority

    ELDER SPENCER. Long live my sovereign, the noble
        Edward—
In peace triumphant, fortunate in wars!
    KING EDWARD. Welcome, old man, com'st thou in Edward's
        aid?
Then tell thy prince of whence, and what thou art.
    ELDER SPENCER. Lo, with a band of bowmen and of pikes,
Brown bills* and targeteers,* four hundred strong,   halberdiers/
Sworn to defend King Edward's royal right,   foot soldiers
I come in person to your majesty,
Spencer, the father of Hugh Spencer there,
Bound to your highness everlastingly,
For favour done, in him, unto us all.
    KING EDWARD. Thy father, Spencer?
    YOUNG SPENCER. True, an it like your grace,
That pours, in lieu of* all your goodness shown,   in recompense for
His life, my lord, before your princely feet.
    KING EDWARD. Welcome ten thousand times, old man,
        again.
Spencer,* this love, this kindness to thy king,   the younger
Argues thy noble mind and disposition.   Spencer
Spencer, I here create thee Earl of Wiltshire,
And daily will enrich thee with our favour,
That, as the sunshine, shall reflect o'er thee.
Beside, the more to manifest our love,
Because we hear Lord Bruce doth sell his land,
And that the Mortimers are in hand withal,*   are negotiating
Thou shalt have crowns of us t' outbid the barons: for it
And, Spencer, spare them not, lay it on.
Soldiers, a largess, and thrice welcome all!
    YOUNG SPENCER. My lord, here comes the queen.

(*Enter* QUEEN ISABELLA, PRINCE EDWARD, *and* LEVUNE.)

KING EDWARD. Madam, what news?

QUEEN ISABELLA. News of dishonour, lord, and discontent.
Our friend Levune, faithful and full of trust,
Informeth us, by letters and by words,
That Lord Valois our brother, King of France,
Because your highness hath been slack in homage,
Hath seizèd Normandy into his hands.
These be the letters, this the messenger.

KING EDWARD. Welcome, Levune. Tush, Sib, if this be all
Valois and I will soon be friends again.—
But to my Gaveston; shall I never see,
Never behold thee now?—Madam, in this matter,
We will employ you and your little son;
You shall go parley with the King of France.—
Boy, see you bear you bravely to the king,
And do your message with a majesty.

PRINCE EDWARD. Commit not to my youth things of more
    weight
Than fits a prince so young as I to bear,
And fear not, lord and father, Heaven's great beams*   supports
On Atlas' shoulder[15] shall not lie more safe,
Than shall your charge committed to my trust.

QUEEN ISABELLA. Ah, boy! this towardness* makes   docility
    thy mother fear
Thou art not marked to many days on earth.

KING EDWARD. Madam, we will that you with speed be
    shipped.
And this our son; Levune shall follow you
With all the haste we can despatch him hence.
Choose of our lords to bear you company;
And go in peace, leave us in wars at home.

QUEEN ISABELLA. Unnatural wars, where subjects
    brave* their king;   defy
God end them once! My lord, I take my leave,
To make my preparation for France.

                  (*Exit with* PRINCE EDWARD.)

(*Enter* ARUNDEL.)

KING EDWARD. What, Lord Arundel, dost thou come alone?

[15] For defying the gods, Atlas was changed into a mountain
and made to bear the heavens on his shoulders.

ARUNDEL. Yea, my good lord, for Gaveston is dead.

KING EDWARD. Ah, traitors! have they put my friend to
death?

Tell me, Arundel, died he ere thou cam'st,

Or didst thou see my friend to take his death?

ARUNDEL. Neither, my lord; for as he was surprised,* captured

Begirt with weapons and with enemies round,

I did your highness' message to them all;

Demanding him of them, entreating rather,

And said, upon the honour of my name,

That I would undertake to carry him

Unto your highness, and to bring him back.

KING EDWARD. And tell me, would the rebels deny me that?

YOUNG SPENCER. Proud recreants!

KING EDWARD. Yea, Spencer, traitors all.

ARUNDEL. I found them at the first inexorable;

The Earl of Warwick would not bide the hearing,

Mortimer hardly; Pembroke and Lancaster

Spake least: and when they flatly had denied,

Refusing to receive me pledge for him,

The Earl of Pembroke mildly thus bespake;

"My lords, because our sovereign sends for him,

And promiseth he shall be safe returned,

I will this undertake, to have him hence,

And see him re-delivered to your hands."

KING EDWARD. Well, and how fortunes it that he came not?

YOUNG SPENCER. Some treason, or some villany, was the
cause.

ARUNDEL. The Earl of Warwick seized him on his way;

For being delivered unto Pembroke's men,

Their lord rode home thinking his prisoner safe;

But ere he came, Warwick in ambush lay,

And bare* him to his death; and in a trench   bore

Strake* off his head, and marched unto the camp.   struck

YOUNG SPENCER. A bloody part, flatly 'gainst law of arms!

KING EDWARD. O shall I speak, or shall I sigh and die!

YOUNG SPENCER. My lord, refer your vengeance to the
sword

Upon these barons; hearten up your men;

Let them not unrevenged murder your friends!

Advance your standard, Edward, in the field,

And march to fire them from their starting holes.16

16 "As hunted animals are driven from their holes by fire" (H.
Spencer).

KING EDWARD (*kneeling*). By earth, the common mother
    of us all,
By Heaven, and all the moving orbs thereof,
By this right hand, and by my father's sword,
And all the honours 'longing to my crown,
I will have heads, and lives for him, as many
As I have manors, castles, towns, and towers!—
    (*Rises.*)
Treacherous Warwick! traitorous Mortimer!
If I be England's king, in lakes of gore
Your headless trunks, your bodies will I trail,
That you may drink your fill, and quaff in blood,
And stain my royal standard with the same,
That so my bloody colours may suggest
Remembrance of revenge immortally
On your accursèd traitorous progeny,
You villains, that have slain my Gaveston!
And in this place of honour and of trust,
Spencer, sweet Spencer, I adopt thee here:
And merely* of our love we do create thee   absolutely
Earl of Gloucester, and Lord Chamberlain,
Despite of times, despite of enemies.
    YOUNG SPENCER. My lord, here's a messenger from the
      barons
Desires access unto your majesty.
    KING EDWARD. Admit him near.

(*Enter the* HERALD, *with his coat of arms.*)

HERALD. Long live King Edward, England's lawful lord!
    KING EDWARD. So wish not they, I wis,* that sent   I know
    thee hither.
Thou com'st from Mortimer and his 'complices,
A ranker rout* of rebels never was.   band
Well, say thy message.
    HERALD. The barons up in arms, by me salute
Your highness with long life and happiness;
And bid me say, as plainer* to your grace,   complainer
That if without effusion of blood
You will* this grief have ease and remedy,   desire that
That from your princely person you remove
This Spencer, as a putrifying branch,
That deads the royal vine, whose golden leaves
Empale your princely head, your diadem,

Whose brightness such pernicious upstarts dim
Say they; and lovingly advise your grace,
To cherish virtue and nobility,
And have old servitors in high esteem,
And shake off smooth dissembling flatterers:
This granted, they, their honours, and their lives,
Are to your highness vowed and consecrate.

    Young Spencer. Ah, traitors! will they still display their
      pride?

    King Edward. Away, tarry no answer, but be gone!
Rebels, will they appoint their sovereign
His sports, his pleasures, and his company?
Yet, ere thou go, see how I do divorce
    (*Embraces* Spencer.)
Spencer from me.—Now get thee to thy lords,
And tell them I will come to chastise them
For murdering Gaveston; hie thee, get thee gone!
Edward with fire and sword follows at thy heels.

                        (*Exit* Herald.)

My lords, perceive you how these rebels swell?
Soldiers, good hearts, defend your sovereign's right,
For now, even now, we march to make them stoop.
Away!

    (*Exeunt. Alarums, excursions, a great fight, and a retreat
    sounded, within. Re-enter* King Edward, *the* Elder Spen-
    cer, Young Spencer, *and* Noblemen *of the* King's *side*.)

    King Edward. Why do we sound retreat? upon them, lords!
This day I shall pour vengeance with my sword
On those proud rebels that are up in arms,
And do confront and countermand* their king.   oppose

    Young Spencer. I doubt it not, my lord, right will prevail.

    Elder Spencer. 'Tis not amiss, my liege, for either part
To breathe awhile; our men, with sweat and dust
All choked, well near* begin to faint for heat;   almost
And this retire refresheth horse and man.

    Young Spencer. Here come the rebels.

    (*Enter* Young Mortimer, Lancaster, Warwick, Pem-
    broke, *and others*.)

    Young Mortimer. Look, Lancaster, yonder is Edward
Among his flatterers.

    Lancaster. And there let him be
Till he pay dearly for their company.

WARWICK. And shall, or Warwick's sword shall smite in vain.

KING EDWARD. What, rebels, do you shrink and sound retreat?

YOUNG MORTIMER. No, Edward, no, thy flatterers faint and fly.

LANCASTER. They'd best betimes* forsake thee,   soon
and their trains*   stratagems
For they'll betray thee, traitors as they are.

YOUNG SPENCER. Traitor on thy face, rebellious Lancaster!

PEMBROKE. Away, base upstart, bravest thou nobles thus?

ELDER SPENCER. A noble attempt, and honourable deed,
Is it not, trow ye, to assemble aid,
And levy arms against your lawful king!

KING EDWARD. For which ere long their heads shall satisfy,
To appease the wrath of their offended king.

YOUNG MORTIMER. Then, Edward, thou wilt fight it to the last,
And rather bathe thy sword in subjects' blood,
Than banish that pernicious company?

KING EDWARD. Ay, traitors all, rather than thus be braved,
Make England's civil towns huge heaps of stones,
And ploughs to go about our palace-gates.

WARWICK. A desperate and unnatural resolution!
Alarum!—to the fight!
Saint George for England, and the barons' right.

KING EDWARD. Saint George for England, and King Edward's right.

    (*Alarums, Exeunt the two parties severally.**)   separately

Scene 3

(*Another part of the battle-field. Enter* KING EDWARD *and his followers, with the* BARONS *and* KENT, *captives.*)

KING EDWARD. Now, lusty lords, now, not by chance of war,
But justice of the quarrel and the cause,
Vailed* is your pride; methinks you hang the heads   humbled
But we'll advance* them, traitors; now 'tis time   raise
To be avenged on you for all your braves,*   defiance
And for the murder of my dearest friend,
To whom right well you knew our soul was knit,
Good Pierce of Gaveston, my sweet favourite.

Ah, rebels! recreants! you made him away.

KENT. Brother, in regard of thee, and of thy land,

Did they remove that flatterer from thy throne.

KING EDWARD. So, sir, you have spoke; away, avoid our
   presence!

                                              (*Exit* KENT.)

Accursèd wretches, was't in regard of us,

When we had sent our messenger to request

He might be spared to come to speak with us,

And Pembroke undertook for his return,

That thou, proud Warwick, watched* the prisoner,   ambushed

Poor Pierce, and headed* him 'gainst law of arms?   beheaded

For which thy head shall overlook the rest,

As much as thou in rage outwent'st the rest.

WARWICK. Tyrant, I scorn thy threats and menaces;

It is but temporal that thou canst inflict.

LANCASTER. The worst is death, and better die to
   live*   that is,
                                            become eternal
Than live in infamy under such a king.

KING EDWARD. Away with them, my lord of
   Winchester!*   elder Spencer

These lusty* leaders, Warwick and Lancaster,   insolent

I charge you roundly—off with both their heads!

Away!

WARWICK. Farewell, vain world!

LANCASTER. Sweet Mortimer, farewell.

YOUNG MORTIMER. England, unkind to thy nobility,

Groan for this grief, behold how thou art maimed!

KING EDWARD. Go, take that haughty Mortimer to the
   Tower,

There see him safe bestowed; and for the rest

Do speedy execution on them all.

Begone!

YOUNG MORTIMER. What, Mortimer! can ragged stony
   walls

Immure thy virtue that aspires to Heaven?

No, Edward, England's scourge, it may not be;

Mortimer's hope surmounts his fortune far.

                          (*The captive* Barons *are led off.*)

KING EDWARD. Sound drums and trumpets! March with me,
   my friends,

Edward this day hath crowned him king anew.

(*Exeunt all except* YOUNG SPENCER, LEVUNE, *and* BALDOCK.)

YOUNG SPENCER. Levune, the trust that we repose in thee,
Begets the quiet of King Edward's land.
Therefore begone in haste, and with advice
Bestow that treasure on the lords of France,
That, therewith all enchanted, like the guard
That suffered Jove to pass in showers of gold[17]
To Danae, all aid may be denied
To Isabel, the queen, that now in France
Makes friends, to cross the seas with her young son,
And step into his father's regiment.*   rule
    LEVUNE. That's it these barons and the subtle queen
Long levelled* at.   aimed
    BALDOCK. Yea, but, Levune, thou seest
These barons lay their heads on blocks together;
What they intend, the hangman frustrates clean.
    LEVUNE. Have you no doubt, my lords, I'll clap so
      close*   that is,
                                                         effectively plant
Among the lords of France with England's gold,
That Isabel shall make her plaints* in vain,   complaints
And France shall be obdurate with her tears.
    YOUNG SPENCER. Then make for France, amain—Levune,
      away!
Proclaim King Edward's wars and victories.

                                         (*Exeunt.*)

ACT IV

Scene 1

(*Near the Tower of London. Enter* KENT.)

KENT. Fair blows the wind for France; blow gentle gale,
Till Edmund be arrived for England's good!
Nature, yield to my country's cause in this.
A brother? no, a butcher of thy friends!
Proud Edward, dost thou banish me thy presence?
But I'll to France, and cheer the wrongèd queen,
And certify what Edward's looseness is.
Unnatural king! to slaughter noblemen
And cherish flatterers! Mortimer, I stay*   await
Thy sweet escape: stand gracious, gloomy night,
To his device.

    [17] See note 9.

(*Enter* YOUNG MORTIMER, *disguised.*)

YOUNG MORTIMER. Holla! who walketh there?
Is't you, my lord?
KENT. Mortimer, 'tis I;
But hath thy potion wrought so happily?
YOUNG MORTIMER. It hath, my lord; the warders all asleep,
I thank them, gave me leave to pass in peace.
But hath your grace got shipping unto France?
KENT. Fear it not.

(*Exeunt.*)

Scene 2

(*Paris. Enter* QUEEN ISABELLA *and* PRINCE EDWARD.)

QUEEN ISABELLA. Ah, boy! our friends do fail us all in
France;
The lords are cruel, and the king unkind;
What shall we do?
PRINCE EDWARD. Madam, return to England,
And please my father well, and then a fig
For all my uncle's friendship here in France.
I warrant you, I'll win his highness quickly;
'A loves me better than a thousand Spencers.
QUEEN ISABELLA. Ah, boy, thou art deceived, at least in this,
To think that we can yet be tuned together;
No, no, we jar too far. Unkind Valois!
Unhappy Isabel! when France rejects,
Whither, oh! whither dost thou bend thy steps?

(*Enter* SIR JOHN OF HAINAULT.)

SIR JOHN. Madam, what cheer?
QUEEN ISABELLA. Ah! good Sir John of Hainault,
Never so cheerless, nor so far distrest.
SIR JOHN. I hear, sweet lady, of the king's unkindness;
But droop not, madam; noble minds contemn
Despair: will your grace with me to Hainault,
And there stay time's advantage with your son?
How say you, my lord, will you go with your friends,
And shake off all our fortunes equally?
PRINCE EDWARD. So pleaseth the queen, my mother, me it
likes:

The King of England, nor the court of France,
Shall have me from my gracious mother's side,
Till I be strong enough to break a staff;*   lance
And then have at the proudest Spencer's head.
   SIR JOHN. Well said, my lord.
   QUEEN ISABELLA. O, my sweet heart, how do I moan thy
     wrongs,
Yet triumph in the hope of thee, my joy!
Ah, sweet Sir John! even to the utmost verge
Of Europe, or the shore of Tanais,*   Don River
We will with thee to Hainault—so we will:—
The marquis is a noble gentleman;
His grace, I dare presume, will welcome me.
But who are these?

    (*Enter* KENT *and* YOUNG MORTIMER.)

   KENT. Madam, long may you live,
Much happier than your friends in England do!
   QUEEN ISABELLA. Lord Edmund and Lord Mortimer alive!
Welcome to France! the news was here, my lord,
That you were dead, or very near your death.
   YOUNG MORTIMER. Lady, the last was truest of the twain:
But Mortimer, reserved for better hap,
Hath shaken off the thraldom of the Tower,
And lives t' advance your standard, good my lord.
   PRINCE EDWARD. How mean you? and the king, my father,
     lives!
No, my Lord Mortimer, not I, I trow.
   QUEEN ISABELLA. Not, son! why not? I would it were no
     worse.
But, gentle lords, friendless we are in France.
   YOUNG MORTIMER. Monsieur le Grand, a noble friend of
     yours,
Told us, at our arrival, all the news—
How hard the nobles, how unkind the king
Hath showed himself; but, madam, right makes room
Where weapons want; and, though a many friends
Are made away, as Warwick, Lancaster,
And others of our party and faction;
Yet have we friends, assure your grace, in England
Would cast up caps, and clap their hands for joy,
To see us there, appointed* for our foes.   equipped
   KENT. Would all were well, and Edward well reclaimed,

For England's honour, peace, and quietness.
    YOUNG MORTIMER. But by the sword, my lord, 't must be
    deserved;
The king will ne'er forsake his flatterers.
    SIR JOHN. My lords of England, sith* th' ungentle king _{since}
Of France refuseth to give aid of arms
To this distressèd queen his sister here,
Go you with her to Hainault; doubt ye not,
We will find comfort, money, men and friends
Ere long, to bid the English king a base.[18]
How say'st, young prince? what think you of the match?
    PRINCE EDWARD. I think King Edward will outrun us all.
    QUEEN ISABELLA. Nay, son, not so; and you must not dis-
    courage
Your friends, that are so forward in your aid.
    KENT. Sir John of Hainault, pardon us, I pray;
These comforts that you give our woful queen
Bind us in kindness all at your command.
    QUEEN ISABELLA. Yea, gentle brother; and the God of
    heaven
Prosper your happy motion,* good Sir John.   _{proposal}
    YOUNG MORTIMER. This noble gentleman, forward in arms,
Was born, I see, to be our anchor-hold.
Sir John of Hainault, be it thy renown,
That England's queen, and nobles in distress,
Have been by thee restored and comforted.
    SIR JOHN. Madam, along, and you my lords, with me,
That England's peers may Hainault's welcome see.
                             (*Exeunt.*)

Scene 3

(EDWARD'S *palace in London. Enter* KING EDWARD, ARUN-
DEL, *the* ELDER *and* YOUNGER SPENCER, *and others.*)

    KING EDWARD. Thus after many threats of wrathful war,
Triumpheth England's Edward with his friends;
And triumph, Edward, with his friends uncontrolled!
My lord of Gloucester, do you hear the news?
    YOUNG SPENCER. What news, my lord?
    KING EDWARD. Why, man, they say there is great execution
Done through the realm; my lord of Arundel,

    [18] A challenge. The reference is from the game of prisoner's
base.

You have the note, have you not?

    ARUNDEL. From the Lieutenant of the Tower, my lord.

    KING EDWARD. I pray let us see it. (*Takes the note.*) What
      have we there?

Read it, Spencer.

    (*Hands the note to* YOUNG SPENCER, *who reads the names.*)

Why, so; they barked apace a month ago:

Now, on my life, they'll neither bark nor bite.

Now, sirs, the news from France? Gloucester, I trow

The lords of France love England's gold so well

As* Isabella gets no aid from thence. What now remains?   that

      have you proclaimed, my lord,

Reward for them can bring in Mortimer?

    YOUNG SPENCER. My lord, we have; and if he be in Eng-
      land,

'A will be had ere long, I doubt it not.

    KING EDWARD. If, dost thou say? Spencer, as true as death

He is in England's ground; our portmasters

Are not so careless of their king's command.

    (*Enter a* MESSENGER.)

How now, what news with thee? from whence come these?

    MESSENGER. Letters, my lord, and tidings forth of France;—

To you, my lord of Gloucester, from Levune.

    (*Gives letters to* YOUNG SPENCER.)

    KING EDWARD. Read.

    YOUNG SPENCER (*reads*).

    "My duty to your honour premised, &c., I have, according
to instructions in that behalf, dealt with the King of France
his lords, and effected, that the queen, all discontented and dis-
comforted, is gone: whither, if you ask, with Sir John of
Hainault, brother to the marquis, into Flanders. With them are
gone Lord Edmund, and the Lord Mortimer, having in their
company divers of your nation, and others; and, as constant
report goeth, they intend to give King Edward battle in England, sooner than he can look for them. This is all the news
of import.

                  Your honour's in all service, LEVUNE."

    KING EDWARD. Ah, villains! hath that Mortimer escaped?

With him is Edmund gone associate?

And will Sir John of Hainault lead the round?*   dance

Welcome, a God's name, madam, and your son;

England shall welcome you and all your rout.*   troop

Gallop apace, bright Phœbus, through the sky,
And dusky night, in rusty iron car,
Between you both shorten the time, I pray,
That I may see that most desirèd day,
When we may meet these traitors in the field.
Ah, nothing grieves me, but my little boy
Is thus misled to countenance their ills.*   evil acts
Come, friends, to Bristow,* there to make us strong;   Bristol
And, winds, as equal* be to bring them in,   impartial
As you injurious were to bear them forth!

                                                        (*Exeunt.*)

Scene 4

(*Near Harwich. Enter* QUEEN ISABELLA, PRINCE EDWARD,
KENT, YOUNG MORTIMER, *and* SIR JOHN *of* HAINAULT.)

QUEEN ISABELLA. Now, lords, our loving friends and coun-
    trymen,
Welcome to England all, with prosperous winds!
Our kindest friends in Belgia* have we left,   Belgium
To cope with friends at home; a heavy case
When force to force is knit, and sword and glaive*   lance
In civil broils* make kin and countrymen   quarrels
Slaughter themselves in others, and their sides
With their own weapons gore! But what's the help?
Misgoverned kings are cause of all this wreck;
And, Edward, thou art one among them all,
Whose looseness hath betrayed thy land to spoil,
Who made the channel overflow with blood
Of thine own people; patron shouldst thou be,
But thou——
    YOUNG MORTIMER. Nay, madam, if you be a warrior,
You must not grow so passionate in speeches.
Lords,
Sith* that we are by sufferance of Heaven   since
Arrived, and armèd in this prince's right,
Here for our country's cause swear we to him
All homage, fealty, and forwardness;
And for the open wrongs and injuries
Edward hath done to us, his queen and land,
We come in arms to wreak it with the sword;
That England's queen in peace may repossess
Her dignities and honours: and withal
We may remove these flatterers from the king,

That havoc England's wealth and treasury.

    SIR JOHN. Sound trumpets, my lord, and forward let us
      march.

Edward will think we come to flatter him.

    KENT. I would he never had been flattered more!

(Exeunt.)

Scene 5

(*Near Bristol. Enter* KING EDWARD, BALDOCK, *and* YOUNG
SPENCER.)

    YOUNG SPENCER. Fly, fly, my lord! the queen is over-strong;
Her friends do multiply, and yours do fail.
Shape we our course to Ireland, there to breathe.

    KING EDWARD. What! was I born to fly and run away,
And leave the Mortimers conquerors behind?
Give me my horse, and let's reinforce our troops:
And in this bed of honour die with fame.

    BALDOCK. O no, my lord, this princely resolution
Fits not the time; away! we are pursued.

(Exeunt.)

(*Enter* KENT, *with sword and target.**)   shield

    KENT. This way he fled, but I am come too late.
Edward, alas! my heart relents for thee.
Proud traitor, Mortimer, why dost thou chase
Thy lawful king, thy sovereign, with thy sword?
Vile wretch! and why hast thou, of all unkind,* most unnaturally
Borne arms against thy brother and thy king?
Rain showers of vengeance on my cursèd head,
Thou God, to whom in justice it belongs
To punish this unnatural revolt!
Edward, this Mortimer aims at thy life!
O fly him, then! But, Edmund, calm this rage,
Dissemble, or thou diest; for Mortimer
And Isabel do kiss, while they conspire:
And yet she bears a face of love forsooth.
Fie on that love that hatcheth death and hate!
Edmund, away! Bristow to Longshanks' blood
Is false; be not found single for suspect:[19]
Proud Mortimer pries near unto thy walks.

---

[19] Don't be found alone as you may arouse suspicion.

(*Enter* QUEEN ISABELLA, PRINCE EDWARD, YOUNG MORTI-
MER, *and* SIR JOHN *of* HAINAULT.)

QUEEN ISABELLA. Successful battle gives the God of kings
To them that fight in right and fear his wrath.
Since then successfully we have prevailed,
Thankèd be Heaven's great architect, and you.
Ere farther we proceed, my noble lords,
We here create our well-belovèd son,
Of love and care unto his royal person,
Lord Warden of the realm, and sith* the fates   since
Have made his father so infortunate,
Deal you, my lords, in this, my loving lords,
As to your wisdoms fittest seems in all.
  KENT. Madam, without offence, if I may ask,
How will you deal with Edward in his fall?
    PRINCE EDWARD. Tell me, good uncle, what Edward do you
      mean?
    KENT. Nephew, your father: I dare not call him king.
    YOUNG MORTIMER. My lord of Kent, what needs these
      questions?
'Tis not in her controlment, nor in ours,
But as the realm and parliament shall please,
So shall your brother be disposèd of.—
(*Aside to the* QUEEN.) I like not this relenting mood in
      Edmund.
Madam, 'tis good to look to him betimes.
    QUEEN ISABELLA. My lord, the Mayor of Bristow knows
      our mind.
    YOUNG MORTIMER. Yea, madam, and they 'scape not easily
That fled the field.
    QUEEN ISABELLA. Baldock is with the king.
A goodly chancellor, is he not, my lord?
    SIR JOHN. So are the Spencers, the father and the son.
    KENT. This Edward is the ruin of the realm.

(*Enter* RICE AP HOWELL, *with the* ELDER SPENCER *prisoner,
and* ATTENDANTS.)

RICE. God save Queen Isabel, and her princely son!
Madam, the mayor and citizens of Bristow,
In sign of love and duty to this presence,
Present by me this traitor to the state,
Spencer, the father to that wanton Spencer,

That, like the lawless Catiline of Rome,
Revelled in England's wealth and treasury.
  QUEEN ISABELLA. We thank you all.
  YOUNG MORTIMER. Your loving care in this
Deserveth princely favours and rewards.
But where's the king and the other Spencer fled?
  RICE. Spencer the son, created Earl of Gloucester,
Is with that smooth-tongued scholar Baldock gone,
And shipped but late for Ireland with the king.
  YOUNG MORTIMER (*aside*). Some whirlwind fetch him back
    or sink them all!—
They shall be started* thence, I doubt it not.   flushed out
  PRINCE EDWARD. Shall I not see the king my father yet?
  KENT (*aside*). Unhappy Edward, chased from England's
    bounds.
  SIR JOHN. Madam, what resteth,* why stand you in a remains
    muse?
  QUEEN ISABELLA. I rue my lord's ill-fortune; but alas!
Care of my country called me to this war.
  YOUNG MORTIMER. Madam, have done with care and sad
    complaint;
Your king hath wronged your country and himself,
And we must seek to right it as we may.
Meanwhile, have hence this rebel to the block.
Your lordship cannot privilege your head.
  ELDER SPENCER. Rebel is he that fights against the prince;
So fought not they that fought in Edward's right.
  YOUNG MORTIMER. Take him away, he prates;
        (*Exeunt* Attendants *with the* ELDER SPENCER.)
                    You, Rice ap Howell,
Shall do good service to her majesty,
Being of countenance* in your country here,   authority
To follow these rebellious runagates.*   runaways
We in meanwhile, madam, must take advice,
How Baldock, Spencer, and their complices,*   accomplices
May in their fall be followed to their end.
                         (*Exeunt.*)

Scene 6

(*Neath abbey. Enter the* ABBOT, MONKS, KING EDWARD,
YOUNG SPENCER, *and* BALDOCK [*the three latter disguised*].)

  ABBOT. Have you no doubt, my lord; have you no fear;
As silent and as careful we will be,

To keep your royal person safe with us,
Free from suspect, and fell invasion
Of such as have your majesty in chase,
Yourself, and those your chosen company,
As danger of this stormy time requires.
    KING EDWARD. Father, thy face should harbour no deceit.
O! hadst thou ever been a king, thy heart,
Pierced deeply with a sense of my distress,
Could not but take compassion of my state.
Stately and proud, in riches and in train,
Whilom* I was, powerful, and full of pomp: formerly
But what is he whom rule and empery
Have not in life or death made miserable?
Come, Spencer; come, Baldock, come, sit down by me;
Make trial now of that philosophy,
That in our famous nurseries of arts
Thou suck'dst from Plato and from Aristotle.
Father, this life contemplative is Heaven.
O that I might this life in quiet lead!
But we, alas! are chased; and you, my friends,
Your lives and my dishonour they pursue.
Yet, gentle monks, for treasure, gold nor fee,
Do you betray us and our company.
    MONK. Your grace may sit secure, if none but we
Do wot* of your abode.   know
    YOUNG SPENCER. Not one alive, but shrewdly I suspect
A gloomy fellow in a mead below.
'A gave a long look after us, my lord;
And all the land I know is up in arms,
Arms that pursue our lives with deadly hate.
    BALDOCK. We were embarked for Ireland, wretched we!
With awkward winds and sore tempests driven
To fall on shore, and here to pine in fear
Of Mortimer and his confederates.
    KING EDWARD. Mortimer! who talks of Mortimer?
Who wounds me with the name of Mortimer,
That bloody man? Good father, on thy lap
Lay I this head, laden with mickle* care.   much
O might I never open these eyes again!
Never again lift up this drooping head!
O never more lift up this dying heart!
    YOUNG SPENCER. Look up, my lord.—Baldock, this drowsi-
       ness
Betides no good; here even we are betrayed.

(*Enter, with Welsh hooks,* RICE AP HOWELL, *a* MOWER, *and* LEICESTER.)

MOWER. Upon my life, these be the men ye seek.

RICE. Fellow, enough.—My lord, I pray be short,
A fair commission warrants what we do.

LEICESTER. The queen's commission, urged by Mortimer;
What cannot gallant Mortimer with the queen?
Alas! see where he sits, and hopes unseen
To escape their hands that seek to reave* his life.   take
Too true it is, *Quem dies vidit veniens superbum,*
Hunc dies vidit fugiens jacentem.[20]
But, Leicester, leave to grow so passionate.
Spencer and Baldock, by no other names,
I do arrest you of high treason here.
Stand not on titles, but obey the arrest;
'Tis in the name of Isabel the queen.
My lord, why droop you thus?

KING EDWARD. O day the last of all my bliss on earth!
Centre of all misfortune! O my stars,
Why do you lour* unkindly on a king?   frown
Comes Leicester, then, in Isabella's name
To take my life, my company from me?
Here, man, rip up this panting breast of mine,
And take my heart in rescue of my friends!

RICE. Away with them!

YOUNG SPENCER. It may become thee yet
To let us take our farewell of his grace.

ABBOT (*aside*). My heart with pity earns* to see   is deeply
    this sight,   moved
A king to bear these words and proud commands.

KING EDWARD. Spencer, ah, sweet Spencer, thus then must
    we part?

YOUNG SPENCER. We must, my lord, so will the angry
    Heavens.

KING EDWARD. Nay, so will hell and cruel Mortimer;
The gentle Heavens have not to do in this.

BALDOCK. My lord, it is in vain to grieve or storm.
Here humbly of your grace we take our leaves;
Our lots are cast; I fear me, so is thine.

---

[20] "Whom the dawning day sees proud, the departing day sees prostrate" (Seneca, *Thyestes*, l. 613).

KING EDWARD. In Heaven we may, in earth ne'er shall
  we meet:
And, Leicester, say, what shall become of us?
  LEICESTER. Your majesty must go to Killingworth.* Kenilworth
  KING EDWARD. Must! it is somewhat hard, when kings
  "must" go.
  LEICESTER. Here is a litter ready for your grace,
That waits your pleasure, and the day grows old.
  RICE. As good be gone, as stay and be benighted.
  KING EDWARD. A litter hast thou? lay me in a hearse,
And to the gates of hell convey me hence;
Let Pluto's bells ring out my fatal knell,
And hags howl for my death at Charon's* shore,   Hell's ferryman
For friends hath Edward none but these and these,*   that is,
                                                    the monks
And these* must die under a tyrant's sword.   Spencer and Baldock
  RICE. My lord, be going; care not for these,
For we shall see them shorter by the heads.
  KING EDWARD. Well, that shall be, shall be: part we must!
Sweet Spencer, gentle Baldock, part we must!
Hence feignèd weeds!* unfeignèd are my woes;   garments
  (*Throws off his disguise.*)
Father, farewell! Leicester, thou stay'st for me,
And go I must. Life, farewell, with my friends.
                    (*Exeunt* KING EDWARD *and* LEICESTER.)
  YOUNG SPENCER. O! is he gone? is noble Edward gone?
Parted from hence? never to see us more?
Rend, sphere of Heaven! and, fire, forsake thy orb!
Earth, melt to air! gone is my sovereign,
Gone, gone, alas! never to make return.
  BALDOCK. Spencer, I see our souls are fleeting hence;
We are deprived the sunshine of our life:
Make for a new life, man; throw up thy eyes,
And heart and hands to Heaven's immortal throne;
Pay nature's debt with cheerful countenance;
Reduce we all our lessons unto this,
To die, sweet Spencer, therefore live we all;
Spencer, all live to die, and rise to fall.
  RICE. Come, come, keep these preachments till you come
to the place appointed. You, and such as you are, have made
wise work in England; will your lordships away?
  MOWER. Your lordship, I trust, will remember me?
  RICE. Remember thee, fellow! what else? Follow me to
  the town.
                                              (*Exeunt.*)

ACT V

Scene 1

(*A room in Kenilworth Castle. Enter* KING EDWARD, LEICESTER, BISHOP OF WINCHESTER, *and* TRUSSEL.)

LEICESTER. Be patient, good my lord, cease to lament,
Imagine Killingworth Castle were your court,
And that you lay for pleasure here a space,
Not of compulsion or necessity.
    KING EDWARD. Leicester, if gentle words might comfort me,
Thy speeches long ago had eased my sorrows;
For kind and loving hast thou always been.
The griefs of private men are soon allayed,
But not of kings. The forest deer, being struck,
Runs to an herb* that closeth up the wounds;   dittany
But, when the imperial lion's flesh is gored,
He rends and tears it with his wrathful paw,
And highly scorning that the lowly earth
Should drink his blood, mounts up to the air.
And so it fares with me, whose dauntless mind
The ambitious Mortimer would seek to curb,
And that unnatural queen, false Isabel,
That thus hath pent and mewed* me in a prison;   shut
For such outrageous passions cloy my soul,
As with the wings of rancour and disdain,
Full often am I soaring up to Heaven,
To plain* me to the gods against them both.   complain
But when I call to mind I am a king,
Methinks I should revenge me of my wrongs,
That Mortimer and Isabel have done.
But what are kings, when regiment* is gone,   rule
But perfect shadows in a sunshine* day?   sunny
My nobles rule, I bear the name of king;
I wear the crown, but am controlled by them,
By Mortimer, and my unconstant queen,
Who spots my nuptial bed with infamy;
Whilst I am lodged within this cave of care,
Where sorrow at my elbow still attends,
To company my heart with sad laments,
That bleeds within me for this strange exchange.

But tell me, must I now resign my crown,
To make usurping Mortimer a king?
    BISHOP OF WINCHESTER. Your grace mistakes; it is for
    England's good,
And princely Edward's right we crave the crown.
    KING EDWARD. No, 'tis for Mortimer, not Edward's head;
For he's a lamb, encompassèd by wolves,
Which in a moment will abridge his life.
But if proud Mortimer do wear this crown,
Heavens turn it to a blaze of quenchless fire
Or like the snaky wreath of Tisiphon,*   Tisiphone,
                                                a Fury
Engirt the temples of his hateful head;
So shall not England's vine be perishèd,
But Edward's name survives, though Edward dies.
    LEICESTER. My lord, why waste you thus the time away?
They stay your answer; will you yield your crown?
    KING EDWARD. Ah, Leicester, weigh how hardly I can brook
To lose my crown and kingdom without cause;
To give ambitious Mortimer my right,
That like a mountain overwhelms my bliss,
In which extreme my mind here murdered is.
But what the heavens appoint, I must obey!
Here, take my crown; the life of Edward too;
    (*Taking off the crown.*)
Two kings in England cannot reign at once.
But stay awhile, let me be king till night,
That I may gaze upon this glittering crown;
So shall my eyes receive their last content,
My head, the latest honour due to it,
And jointly both yield up their wishèd right.
Continue ever thou celestial sun;
Let never silent night possess this clime;
Stand still you watches of the element;*   that is,
                                      heavenly bodies
All times and seasons, rest you at a stay,
That Edward may be still fair England's king!
But day's bright beam doth vanish fast away,
And needs I must resign my wishèd crown.
Inhuman creatures! nursed with tiger's milk!
Why gape you for your sovereign's overthrow!
My diadem I mean, and guiltless life.
See, monsters, see, I'll wear my crown again!
    (*He puts on the crown.*)
What, fear you not the fury of your king?

But, hapless Edward, thou art fondly* led;　　　　　foolishly
They pass* not for thy frowns as late they did,　　　care
But seek to make a new-elected king;
Which fills my mind with strange despairing thoughts,
Which thoughts are martyrèd with endless torments,
And in this torment comfort find I none,
But that I feel the crown upon my head;
And therefore let me wear it yet awhile.

　　TRUSSEL. My lord, the parliament must have
　　　　present* news,　　　　　　　　　　　immediate
And therefore say, will you resign or no?
　　(*The* KING *rageth.*)
　　KING EDWARD. I'll not resign, but whilst I live be king.
Traitors, be gone! and join you with Mortimer!
Elect, conspire, install, do what you will:—
Their blood and yours shall seal these treacheries!
　　BISHOP OF WINCHESTER. This answer we'll return, and so
　　　　farewell.
　　(*Going with* TRUSSEL.)
　　LEICESTER. Call them again, my lord, and speak them fair;
For if they go, the prince shall lose his right.
　　KING EDWARD. Call thou them back, I have no power to
　　　　speak.
　　LEICESTER. My lord, the king is willing to resign.
　　BISHOP OF WINCHESTER. If he be not, let him choose.
　　KING EDWARD. O would I might! but heavens and earth
　　　　conspire
To make me miserable! Here receive my crown;
Receive it? no, these innocent hands of mine
Shall not be guilty of so foul a crime.
He of you all that most desires my blood,
And will be called the murderer of a king,
Take it. What, are you moved? pity you me?
Then send for unrelenting Mortimer,
And Isabel, whose eyes, being turned to steel,
Will sooner sparkle fire than shed a tear.
Yet stay, for rather than I'll look on them,
Here, here!
　　(*Gives the crown.*)
　　　　　　　Now, sweet God of Heaven,
Make me despise this transitory pomp,
And sit for aye* enthronizèd in Heaven!　　　　　ever
Come, death, and with thy fingers close my eyes,
Or if I live, let me forget myself.

BISHOP OF WINCHESTER. My lord—
KING EDWARD. Call me not lord; away—out of my sight:
Ah, pardon me: grief makes me lunatic!
Let not that Mortimer protect* my son;   be guardian of
More safety there is in a tiger's jaws,
Than his embracements. Bear this to the queen,
Wet with my tears, and dried again with sighs;
    (*Gives a handkerchief.*)
If with the sight thereof she be not moved,
Return it back and dip it in my blood.
Commend me to my son, and bid him rule
Better than I. Yet how have I transgressed,
Unless it be with too much clemency?
    TRUSSEL. And thus most humbly do we take our leave.
    KING EDWARD. Farewell;
        (*Exeunt the* BISHOP OF WINCHESTER *and* TRUSSEL.)
                        I know the next news that they bring
Will be my death; and welcome shall it be;
To wretched men, death is felicity.

(*Enter* BERKELEY, *who gives a paper to* LEICESTER.)

LEICESTER. Another post! what news brings he?
KING EDWARD. Such news as I expect—come, Berkeley,
    come.
And tell thy message to my naked breast.
    BERKELEY. My lord, think not a thought so villainous
Can harbour in a man of noble birth.
To do your highness service and devoir,*   duty
And save you from your foes, Berkeley would die.
    LEICESTER. My lord, the council of the queen commands
That I resign my charge.
    KING EDWARD. And who must keep me now? Must you,
    my lord?
    BERKELEY. Ay, my most gracious lord—so 'tis decreed.
    KING EDWARD (*taking the paper.*) By Mortimer, whose
    name is written here!
Well may I rend his name that rends my heart!
    (*Tears it.*)
This poor revenge has something* eased my mind.   somewhat
So may his limbs be torn, as is this paper!
Hear me, immortal Jove, and grant it too!
    BERKELEY. Your grace must hence with me to Berkeley
    straight.

KING EDWARD. Whither you will; all places are alike,
And every earth is fit for burial.

LEICESTER. Favour him, my lord, as much as lieth in you.

BERKELEY. Even so betide my soul as I use him.

KING EDWARD. Mine enemy* hath pitied my   that is, Leicester
estate,
And that's the cause that I am now removed.

BERKELEY. And thinks your grace that Berkeley will be
cruel?

KING EDWARD. I know not; but of this am I assured,
That death ends all, and I can die but once.
Leicester, farewell!

LEICESTER. Not yet, my lord; I'll bear you on your way.
                               (*Exeunt.*)

Scene 2

(*London, the royal palace. Enter* QUEEN ISABELLA *and*
YOUNG MORTIMER.)

YOUNG MORTIMER. Fair Isabel, now have we our desire;
The proud corrupters of the light-brained king
Have done their homage to the lofty gallows,
And he himself lies in captivity.
Be ruled by me, and we will rule the realm.
In any case take heed of childish fear,
For now we hold an old wolf by the ears,
That, if he slip, will seize upon us both,
And gripe the sorer, being griped himself.
Think therefore, madam, that imports us much
To erect your son with all the speed we may,
And that I be protector* over him;   that is,
                                    Lord Protector
For our behoof will bear the greater sway
Whenas* a king's name shall be under writ.   when

QUEEN ISABELLA. Sweet Mortimer, the life of Isabel,
Be thou persuaded that I love thee well,
And therefore, so the prince my son be safe,
When I esteem as dear as these mine eyes,
Conclude against his father what thou wilt,
And I myself will willingly subscribe.

YOUNG MORTIMER. First would I hear news he were
deposed,
And then let me alone to handle him.

(*Enter* MESSENGER.)

Letters! from whence?

    MESSENGER. From Killingworth, my lord.

    QUEEN ISABELLA. How fares my lord the king?

    MESSENGER. In health, madam, but full of pensiveness.

    QUEEN ISABELLA. Alas, poor soul, would I could ease his
        grief!

(*Enter the* BISHOP OF WINCHESTER *with the crown.*)

Thanks, gentle Winchester. (*To the* MESSENGER.) Sirrah, be
    gone.

(Exit MESSENGER.)

    BISHOP OF WINCHESTER. The king hath willingly resigned
        his crown.

    QUEEN ISABELLA. O happy news! send for the prince, my
        son.

    BISHOP OF WINCHESTER. Further, or* this letter was   before
        sealed, Lord Berkeley came,

So that he now is gone from Killingworth;

And we have heard that Edmund laid a plot

To set his brother free; no more but so.

The lord of Berkeley is as pitiful*   full of pity

As Leicester that had charge of him before.

    QUEEN ISABELLA. Then let some other be his guardian.

    YOUNG MORTIMER. Let me alone, here is the privy seal.

(Exit the BISHOP OF WINCHESTER.)

Who's there?—Call hither Gurney and Matrevis.

(*To* Attendants *within.*)

To dash the heavy-headed Edmund's drift,*   plot

Berkeley shall be discharged, the king removed,

And none but we shall know where he lieth.

    QUEEN ISABELLA. But, Mortimer, as long as he survives,

What safety rests for us, or for my son?

    YOUNG MORTIMER. Speak, shall he presently be despatched
        and die?

    QUEEN ISABELLA. I would he were, so 'twere not by my
        means.

(*Enter* MATREVIS *and* GURNEY.)

    YOUNG MORTIMER. Enough.—

Matrevis, write a letter presently*   immediately

Unto the lord of Berkeley from ourself
That he resign the king to thee and Gurney;
And when 'tis done, we will subscribe our name.
   (*Writes.*)
   MATREVIS. It shall be done, my lord.
   YOUNG MORTIMER. Gurney.
   GURNEY. My lord.
   YOUNG MORTIMER. As thou intend'st to rise by Mortimer,
Who now makes Fortune's wheel turn as he please,
Seek all the means thou canst to make him* droop,   that is, the King
And neither give him kind word nor good look.
   GURNEY. I warrant you, my lord.
   YOUNG MORTIMER. And this above the rest: because we
     hear
That Edmund casts* to work his liberty,   plots
Remove him still* from place to place by night,   always
Till at the last he come to Killingworth,
And then from thence to Berkeley back again;
And by the way, to make him fret the more,
Speak curstly* to him; and in any case   viciously
Let no man comfort him if he chance to weep,
But amplify his grief with bitter words.
   MATREVIS. Fear not, my lord, we'll do as you command.
   `YOUNG MORTIMER. So now away; post thitherwards
     amain.*   at full speed
   QUEEN ISABELLA. Whither goes this letter? to my lord the
     king?
Commend me humbly to his majesty,
And tell him that I labour all in vain
To ease his grief, and work his liberty;
And bear him this as witness of my love.
   (*Gives a ring.*)
   MATREVIS. I will, madam.
                         (*Exit with* GURNEY.)
   YOUNG MORTIMER. Finely dissembled. Do so still, sweet
     queen.
Here comes the young prince with the Earl of Kent.
   QUEEN ISABELLA. Something he whispers in his childish
     ears.
   YOUNG MORTIMER. If he have such access unto the prince,
Our plots and stratagems will soon be dashed.
   QUEEN ISABELLA. Use Edmund friendly as if all were well.

(*Enter* Prince Edward, *and* Kent *talking with him.*)

Young Mortimer. How fares my honourable lord of Kent?

Kent. In health, sweet Mortimer: how fares your grace?

Queen Isabella. Well, if my lord your brother were enlarged.*   freed

Kent. I hear of late he hath deposed himself.

Queen Isabella. The more my grief.

Young Mortimer. And mine.

Kent (*aside*). Ah, they do dissemble!

Queen Isabella. Sweet son, come hither, I must talk with
thee.

Young Mortimer. You being his uncle, and the next of
blood,

Do look to be protector o'er the prince.

Kent. Not I, my lord; who should protect the son,

But she that gave him life? I mean the queen.

Prince Edward. Mother, persuade me not to wear the
crown:

Let him be king—I am too young to reign.

Queen Isabella. But be content, seeing 'tis his highness'
pleasure.

Prince Edward. Let me but see him first, and then I will.

Kent. Ay, do, sweet nephew.

Queen Isabella. Brother, you know it is impossible.

Prince Edward. Why, is he dead?

Queen Isabella. No, God forbid.

Kent. I would those words proceeded from your heart.

Young Mortimer. Inconstant Edmund, dost thou favour
him,

That wast a cause of his imprisonment?

Kent. The more cause have I now to make amends.

Young Mortimer (*aside to* Queen Isabella). I tell thee,
'tis not meet that one so false

Should come about the person of a prince.—

My lord, he hath betrayed the king his brother,

And therefore trust him not.

Prince Edward. But he repents, and sorrows for it now.

Queen Isabella. Come, son, and go with this gentle lord
and me.

Prince Edward. With you I will, but not with Mortimer.

Young Mortimer. Why, youngling, 'sdain'st thou so of
Mortimer?

Then I will carry thee by force away.

    PRINCE EDWARD. Help, uncle Kent! Mortimer will wrong
    me.

    QUEEN ISABELLA. Brother Edmund, strive not; we are his
    friends;

Isabel is nearer than the Earl of Kent.

    KENT. Sister, Edward is my charge, redeem him.

    QUEEN ISABELLA. Edward is my son, and I will keep him.

    KENT. Mortimer shall know that he hath wrongèd me!—

(*Aside.*) Hence will I haste to Killingworth Castle,

And rescue aged* Edward from his foes,   the older

To be revenged on Mortimer and thee.

    (*Exeunt on one side* QUEEN ISABELLA, PRINCE EDWARD, *and*
                YOUNG MORTIMER; *on the other* KENT.)

Scene 3

(*Near Kenilworth Castle. Enter* MATREVIS *and* GURNEY *and*
SOLDIERS, *with* KING EDWARD.)

    MATREVIS. My lord, be not pensive, we are your friends;

Men are ordained to live in misery,

Therefore come,—dalliance dangereth our lives.

    KING EDWARD. Friends, whither must unhappy Edward go?

Will hateful Mortimer appoint no rest?

Must I be vexèd like the nightly bird,

Whose sight is loathsome to all wingèd fowls?

When will the fury of his mind assuage?

When will his heart be satisfied with blood?

If mine will serve, unbowel straight this breast,

And give my heart to Isabel and him;

It is the chiefest mark they level* at.   aim

    GURNEY. Not so my liege, the queen hath given this charge

To keep your grace in safety;

Your passions make your dolours to increase.

    KING EDWARD. This usage makes my misery to increase.

But can my air of life continue long

When all my senses are annoyed with stench?

Within a dungeon England's king is kept,

Where I am starved for want of sustenance.

My daily diet is heart-breaking sobs,

That almost rent* the closet of my heart;   rend

Thus lives old Edward not relieved by any,

And so must die, though pitièd by many.

O, water, gentle friends, to cool my thirst,

And clear my body from foul excrements!

MATREVIS. Here's channel* water, as your charge is   gutter
    given

Sit down, for we'll be barbers to your grace.

KING EDWARD. Traitors, away! what, will you murder me,
Or choke your sovereign with puddle water?

GURNEY. No; but wash your face, and shave away your
    beard,

Lest you be known and so be rescuèd.

MATREVIS. Why strive you thus? your labour is in vain!

KING EDWARD. The wren may strive against the lion's
    strength,

But all in vain: so vainly do I strive
To seek for mercy at a tyrant's hand.

(*They wash him with puddle water, and shave off his
beard.*)

Immortal powers! that knows the painful cares
That wait upon my poor distressèd soul,
O level all your looks upon these daring men,
That wrongs their liege and sovereign, England's king!
O Gaveston, 'tis for thee that I am wronged,
For me, both thou and both the Spencers died!
And for your sakes a thousand wrongs I'll take.
The Spencers' ghosts, wherever they remain,
Wish well to mine; then tush, for them I'll die.

MATREVIS. 'Twixt theirs and yours shall be no enmity.
Come, come away; now put the torches out,
We'll enter in by darkness to Killingworth.

(*Enter* KENT.)

GURNEY. How now, who comes there?

MATREVIS. Guard the king sure: it is the Earl of Kent.

KING EDWARD. O gentle brother, help to rescue me!

MATREVIS. Keep them asunder; thrust in the king.

KENT. Soldiers, let me but talk to him one word.

GURNEY. Lay hands upon the earl for his assault.

KENT. Lay down your weapons, traitors! yield the king!

MATREVIS. Edmund, yield thou thyself, or thou shalt die.

KENT. Base villains, wherefore do you gripe me thus?

GURNEY. Bind him and so convey him to the court.

KENT. Where is the court but here? here is the king;
And I will visit him; why stay you me?

MATREVIS. The court is where Lord Mortimer remains;

Thither shall your honour go; and so farewell.

(*Exeunt* MATREVIS *and* GURNEY, *with* KING EDWARD.)

KENT. O miserable is that commonweal,
Where lords keep courts, and kings are locked in prison!

SOLDIER. Wherefore stay we? on, sirs, to the court!

KENT. Ay, lead me whither you will, even to my death,
Seeing that my brother cannot be released.

(*Exeunt.*)

Scene 4

(*London, the royal palace. Enter* YOUNG MORTIMER.)

YOUNG MORTIMER. The king must die, or Mortimer goes
   down;
The commons now begin to pity him:
Yet he that is the cause of Edward's death,
Is sure to pay for it when his son's of age;
And therefore will I do it cunningly.
This letter, written by a friend of ours,
Contains his death, yet bids them save his life.
   (*Reads.*)
"*Edwardum occidere nolite timere, bonum est*
Fear not to kill the king, 'tis good he die."
But read it thus, and that's another sense:
"*Edwardum occidere nolite, timere bonum est*
Kill not the king, 'tis good to fear the worst."
Unpointed* as it is, thus shall it go,   unpunctuated
That, being dead, if it chance to be found,
Matrevis and the rest may bear the blame,
And we be quit that caused it to be done.
Within this room is locked the messenger
That shall convey it, and perform the rest:
And by a secret token that he bears,
Shall he be murdered when the deed is done.—
Lightborn, come forth!

(*Enter* LIGHTBORN.)

Art thou so resolute as thou wast?

LIGHTBORN. What else, my lord? and far more resolute.

YOUNG MORTIMER. And hast thou cast* how to   planned
   accomplish it?

LIGHTBORN. Ay, ay, and none shall know which way he died.

YOUNG MORTIMER. But at his looks, Lightborn, thou wilt
relent.

LIGHTBORN. Relent! ha, ha! I use much to relent.

YOUNG MORTIMER. Well, do it bravely,* and be   splendidly
secret.

LIGHTBORN. You shall not need to give instructions;
'Tis not the first time I have killed a man.
I learned in Naples how to poison flowers;
To strangle with a lawn* thrust down the throat;   linen cloth
To pierce the windpipe with a needle's point;
Or whilst one is asleep, to take a quill
And blow a little powder in his ears:
Or open his mouth and pour quicksilver down.
And yet I have a braver way than these.

YOUNG MORTIMER. What's that?

LIGHTBORN. Nay, you shall pardon me; none shall know my
tricks.

YOUNG MORTIMER. I care not how it is, so it be not spied.
Deliver this to Gurney and Matrevis.
(*Gives letter.*)
At every ten mile end thou hast a horse.
Take this; (*gives money*) away! and never see me more.

LIGHTBORN. No!

YOUNG MORTIMER. No;
Unless thou bring me news of Edward's death.

LIGHTBORN. That will I quickly do. Farewell, my lord.
                                                (*Exit.*)

YOUNG MORTIMER. The prince I rule, the queen do I com-
mand,
And with a lowly congé* to the ground,   bow
The proudest lords salute me as I pass;
I seal, I cancel, I do what I will.
Feared am I more than loved;—let me be feared,
And when I frown, make all the court look pale.
I view the prince with Aristarchus'[21] eyes,
Whose looks were as a breeching* to a boy.   flogging
They thrust upon me the protectorship,
And sue to me for that that I desire.
While at the council-table, grave enough,
And not unlike a bashful puritan,
First I complain of imbecility,*   incompetency
Saying it is *onus quam gravissimum;*[22]

---

[21] An Alexandrian grammarian and critic.
[22] "A very heavy burden."

Till being interrupted by my friends,
Suscepi that *proviniciam*[23] as they term it;
And to conclude, I am Protector now.
Now is all sure: the queen and Mortimer
Shall rule the realm, the king; and none rules us.
Mine enemies will I plague, my friends advance;
And what I list* command who dare control?   desire to
Major sum quam cui possit fortuna nocere.[24]
And that this be the coronation-day,
It pleaseth me, and Isabel the queen.
    (*Trumpets within.*)
The trumpets sound, I must go take my place.

    (*Enter* KING EDWARD THE THIRD, *formerly* PRINCE EDWARD, QUEEN ISABELLA, *the* ARCHBISHOP OF CANTERBURY, CHAMPION *and* NOBLES.)

    ARCHBISHOP OF CANTERBURY. Long live King Edward, by
      the grace of God,
King of England and Lord of Ireland!
    CHAMPION. If any Christian, Heathen, Turk, or Jew,
Dare but affirm that Edward's not true king,
And will avouch his saying with the sword,
I am the champion that will combat him.
    YOUNG MORTIMER. None comes, sound trumpets.
    (*Trumpets sound.*)
    KING EDWARD THIRD. Champion, here's to thee.
    (*Gives a purse.*)
    QUEEN ISABELLA. Lord Mortimer, now take him to your
      charge.

    (*Enter* SOLDIERS, *with* KENT *prisoner.*)

    YOUNG MORTIMER. What traitor have we there with blades
      and bills?
    SOLDIER. Edmund, the Earl of Kent.
    KING EDWARD THIRD. What hath he done?
    SOLDIER. 'A would have taken the king away perforce,* by force
As we were bringing him to Killingworth.
    YOUNG MORTIMER. Did you attempt his rescue, Edmund?
      speak.

       [23] "I have undertaken the office."
       [24] "I am too great for fortune to harm me" (Ovid, *Metamorphoses*, vi, 195).

KENT. Mortimer, I did; he is our king,
And thou compell'st this prince to wear the crown.
YOUNG MORTIMER. Strike off his head! he shall have martial
law.
KENT. Strike off my head! base traitor, I defy thee!
KING EDWARD THIRD. My lord, he is my uncle, and shall live.
YOUNG MORTIMER. My lord, he is your enemy, and shall
die.
KENT. Stay, villains!
KING EDWARD THIRD. Sweet mother, if I cannot pardon him,
Entreat my Lord Protector for his life.
QUEEN ISABELLA. Son, be content; I dare not speak a word.
KING EDWARD THIRD. Nor I, and yet methinks I should
command;
But, seeing I cannot, I'll entreat for him—
My lord, if you will let my uncle live,
I will requite it when I come to age.
YOUNG MORTIMER. 'Tis for your highness' good, and for the
realm's.—
How often shall I bid you bear him hence?
KENT. Art thou king? must I die at thy command?
YOUNG MORTIMER. At our command.—Once more away
with him.
KENT. Let me but stay and speak; I will not go.
Either my brother or his son is king,
And none of both them thirst for Edmund's blood:
And therefore, soldiers, whither will you hale me?
               (SOLDIERS *hale* KENT *away, to be beheaded.*)
KING EDWARD THIRD. What safety may I look for at his
hands,
If that my uncle shall be murdered thus?
QUEEN ISABELLA. Fear not, sweet boy, I'll guard thee from
thy foes;
Had Edmund lived, he would have sought thy death.
Come, son, we'll ride a-hunting in the park.
KING EDWARD THIRD. And shall my uncle Edmund ride with
us?
QUEEN ISABELLA. He is a traitor; think not on him; come.
                                              (*Exeunt.*)

Scene 5

(*Berkeley Castle. Enter* MATREVIS *and* GURNEY.)

MATREVIS. Gurney, I wonder the king dies not,
Being in a vault up to the knees in water,
To which the channels* of the castle run,   gutters
From whence a damp continually ariseth,
That were enough to poison any man,
Much more a king brought up so tenderly.
 GURNEY. And so do I, Matrevis: yesternight
I opened but the door to throw him meat,
And I was almost stifled with the savour.
 MATREVIS. He hath a body able to endure
More than we can inflict: and therefore now
Let us assail his mind another while.
 GURNEY. Send for him out thence, and I will anger him.
 MATREVIS. But stay, who's this?

(*Enter* LIGHTBORN.)

LIGHTBORN. My lord Protector greets you.
(*Gives letter.*)
 GURNEY. What's here? I know not how to construe it.
 MATREVIS. Gurney, it was left unpointed for the
  nonce;*   purposely
             for this occasion
"*Edwardum occidere nolite timere,*"
That's his meaning.
 LIGHTBORN. Know ye this token? I must have the king.
(*Gives token.*)
 MATREVIS. Ay, stay awhile, thou shalt have answer straight.
(*Aside.*) This villain's sent to make away the king.
 GURNEY (*aside*). I thought as much.
 MATREVIS (*aside*). And when the murder's done,
See how he must be handled for his labour.
*Pereat iste!** Let him have the king.   Let him perish
What else? here is the key, this is the lock,
Do as you are commanded by my lord.
 LIGHTBORN. I know what I must do. Get you away.
Yet be not far off, I shall need your help;
See that in the next room I have a fire,
And get me a spit, and let it be red-hot.

MATREVIS. Very well.

GURNEY. Need you anything besides?

LIGHTBORN. What else? A table and a feather-bed.

GURNEY. That's all?

LIGHTBORN. Ay, ay; so, when I call you, bring it in.

MATREVIS. Fear not thou that.

GURNEY. Here's a light, to go into the dungeon.

(*Gives a light, and then exit with* MATREVIS.)

LIGHTBORN. So now
Must I about this gear;* ne'er was there any   affair
So finely handled as this king shall be.
    (*Enters dungeon.*)[25]
Foh, here's a place indeed, with all my heart!

   KING EDWARD. Who's there? what light is that? wherefore
      com'st thou?

   LIGHTBORN. To comfort you, and bring you joyful news.

   KING EDWARD. Small comfort finds poor Edward in thy
      looks.
Villain, I know thou com'st to murder me.

   LIGHTBORN. To murder you, my most gracious lord!
Far is it from my heart to do you harm.
The queen sent me to see how you were used,
For she relents at this your misery:
And what eyes can refrain from shedding tears,
To see a king in this most piteous state?

   KING EDWARD. Weep'st thou already? list awhile to me.
And then thy heart, were it as Gurney's is,
Or as Matrevis', hewn from the Caucasus,
Yet will it melt, ere I have done my tale.
This dungeon where they keep me is the sink
Wherein the filth of all the castle falls.

   LIGHTBORN. O villains!

   KING EDWARD. And there in mire and puddle have I stood
This ten days' space; and, lest that I should sleep,
One plays continually upon a drum.
They give me bread and water, being a king;
So that, for want of sleep and sustenance,
My mind's distempered, and my body's numbed,
And whether I have limbs or no I know not.
O, would my blood dropped out from every vein,

     [25] In the Elizabethan theater this scene would have been played
on the inner stage.

As doth this water from my tattered robes.
Tell Isabel, the queen, I looked not thus,
When for her sake I ran at tilt in France,
And there unhorsed the Duke of Cleremont.

LIGHTBORN. O speak no more, my lord! this breaks my
heart.

Lie on this bed,[26] and rest your self awhile.

KING EDWARD. These looks of thine can harbour nought but
death:

I see my tragedy written in thy brows.
Yet stay; awhile forbear thy bloody hand,
And let me see the stroke before it comes,
That even then when I shall lose my life,
My mind may be more steadfast on my God.

LIGHTBORN. What means your highness to mistrust me thus?

KING EDWARD. What mean'st thou to dissemble with me
thus?

LIGHTBORN. These hands were never stained with innocent
blood,

Nor shall they now be tainted with a king's.

KING EDWARD. Forgive my thought for having such a
thought.

One jewel have I left; receive thou this.

(*Giving him the jewel.*)

Still fear I, and I know not what's the cause,
But every joint shakes as I give it thee.
O, if thou harbourest murder in thy heart,
Let this gift change thy mind, and save thy soul.
Know that I am a king: O, at that name
I feel a hell of grief! where is my crown?
Gone, gone! and do I still remain alive?

LIGHTBORN. You're overwatched,* my lord; lie overexhausted
down and rest.

KING EDWARD. But that grief keeps me waking, I should
sleep;

For not these ten days have these eye-lids closed.
Now as I speak they fall, and yet with fear
Open again. O wherefore sitt'st thou here?

LIGHTBORN. If you mistrust me, I'll begone, my lord.

KING EDWARD. No, no, for if thou mean'st to murder me,
Thou wilt return again, and therefore stay.

(*Sleeps.*)

[26] The bed provided by Matrevis and Gurney.

LIGHTBORN. He sleeps.
KING EDWARD (*waking*). O let me not die yet! O stay a
    while!
LIGHTBORN. How now, my lord?
KING EDWARD. Something still buzzeth in mine ears,
And tells me if I sleep I never wake;
This fear is that which makes me tremble thus.
And therefore tell me, wherefore art thou come?
LIGHTBORN. To rid thee of thy life.—Matrevis, come!

(*Enter* MATREVIS *and* GURNEY.)

KING EDWARD. I am too weak and feeble to resist:—
Assist me, sweet God, and receive my soul!
LIGHTBORN. Run for the table.
KING EDWARD. O spare me, or despatch me in a trice.
(MATREVIS *brings in a table*.)
LIGHTBORN. So, lay the table down, and stamp on it,
But not too hard, lest that you bruise his body.
(KING EDWARD *is murdered*.)
MATREVIS. I fear me that this cry will raise the town,
And therefore, let us take horse and away.
LIGHTBORN. Tell me, sirs, was it not bravely* done? splendidly
GURNEY. Excellent well: take this for thy reward.
(GURNEY *stabs* LIGHTBORN, *who dies*.)
Come, let us cast the body in the moat,
And bear the king's to Mortimer our lord:
Away!
                                    (*Exeunt with the bodies*.)

Scene 6

(*London, the royal palace. Enter* YOUNG MORTIMER *and*
MATREVIS.)

YOUNG MORTIMER. Is't done, Matrevis, and the murderer
    dead?
MATREVIS. Ay, my good lord; I would it were undone!
YOUNG MORTIMER. Matrevis, if thou now growest penitent
I'll be thy ghostly father;* therefore choose,   father confessor
Whether thou wilt be secret in this,
Or else die by the hand of Mortimer.

MATREVIS. Gurney, my lord, is fled, and will, I fear
Betray us both, therefore let me fly.
    YOUNG MORTIMER. Fly to the savages!
    MATREVIS. I humbly thank your honour.
                                      (*Exit.*)
    YOUNG MORTIMER. As for myself, I stand as Jove's huge
      tree,*   that is, the oak
And others are but shrubs compared to me.
All tremble at my name, and I fear none;
Let's see who dare impeach me for his death!

(*Enter* QUEEN ISABELLA.)

QUEEN ISABELLA. Ah, Mortimer, the king my son hath news
His father's dead, and we have murdered him!
    YOUNG MORTIMER. What if he have? the king is yet a child.
    QUEEN ISABELLA. Ay, but he tears his hair, and wrings his
      hands,
And vows to be revenged upon us both.
Into the council-chamber he is gone,
To crave the aid and succour of his peers.
Ay me! see where he comes, and they with him;
Now, Mortimer, begins our tragedy.

(*Enter* KING EDWARD THE THIRD, LORDS, *and* ATTENDANTS.)

FIRST LORD. Fear not, my lord, know that you are a king.
    KING EDWARD THIRD. Villain!—
    YOUNG MORTIMER. Ho, now, my lord!
    KING EDWARD THIRD. Think not that I am frighted with thy
      words!
My father's murdered through thy treachery;
And thou shalt die; and on his mournful hearse*   coffin
Thy hateful and accursèd head shall lie,
To witness to the world, that by thy means
His kingly body was too soon interred.
    QUEEN ISABELLA. Weep not, sweet son!
    KING EDWARD THIRD. Forbid me not to weep; he was my
      father;
And, had you loved him half so well as I,
You could not bear his death thus patiently.
But you, I fear, conspired with Mortimer.
    FIRST LORD. Why speak you not unto my lord the king?

YOUNG MORTIMER. Because I think it scorn to be accused.
Who is the man dares say I murdered him?
KING EDWARD THIRD. Traitor! in me my loving father
  speaks,
And plainly saith, 'twas thou that murder'dst him.
YOUNG MORTIMER. But has your grace no other proof than
  this?
KING EDWARD THIRD. Yes, if this be the hand of Mortimer.
  (*Showing letter.*)
YOUNG MORTIMER (*aside to the* QUEEN). False Gurney
  hath betrayed me and himself.
QUEEN ISABELLA (*aside*). I feared as much; murder cannot
  be hid.
YOUNG MORTIMER. It is my hand; what gather you by this?
KING EDWARD THIRD. That thither thou didst send a mur-
  derer.
YOUNG MORTIMER. What murderer? Bring forth the man I
  sent.
KING EDWARD THIRD. Ah, Mortimer, thou knowest that he
  is slain;
And so shalt thou be too—Why stays he here?
Bring him unto a hurdle,* drag him forth;   that is,
Hang him, I say, and set his quarters up;   execution cart
But bring his head back presently to me.
QUEEN ISABELLA. For my sake, sweet son, pity Mortimer.
YOUNG MORTIMER. Madam, entreat not, I will rather die,
Than sue for life unto a paltry boy.
KING EDWARD THIRD. Hence with the traitor! with the mur-
  derer!
YOUNG MORTIMER. Base Fortune, now I see, that in thy
  wheel
There is a point, to which when men aspire,
They tumble headlong down: that point I touched,
And, seeing there was no place to mount up higher,
Why should I grieve at my declining fall?—
Farewell, fair queen; weep not for Mortimer,
That scorns the world, and, as a traveller,
Goes to discover countries yet unknown.
KING EDWARD THIRD. What! suffer you the traitor to delay?
                    (YOUNG MORTIMER *is taken away by*
                    FIRST LORD *and* ATTENDANTS.)
QUEEN ISABELLA. As thou receivedest thy life from me,
Spill not the blood of gentle Mortimer!

KING EDWARD THIRD. This argues that you spilt my father's
blood,
Else would you not entreat for Mortimer.
QUEEN ISABELLA. I spill his blood? no.
KING EDWARD THIRD. Ay, madam, you; for so the rumour
runs.
QUEEN ISABELLA. That rumour is untrue; for loving thee,
Is this report raised on poor Isabel.
KING EDWARD THIRD. I do not think her so unnatural.
SECOND LORD. My lord, I fear me it will prove too true.
KING EDWARD THIRD. Mother, you are suspected for his
death
And therefore we commit you to the Tower
Till farther trial may be made thereof;
If you be guilty, though I be your son,
Think not to find me slack or pitiful.
QUEEN ISABELLA. Nay, to my death, for too long I have
lived,
Whenas* my son thinks to abridge my days.   when
KING EDWARD THIRD. Away with her, her words enforce
these tears,
And I shall pity her if she speak again.
QUEEN ISABELLA. Shall I not mourn for my belovèd lord,
And with the rest accompany him to his grave?
SECOND LORD. Thus, madam, 'tis the king's will you shall
hence.
QUEEN ISABELLA. He hath forgotten me; stay, I am his
mother.
SECOND LORD. That boots* not; therefore, gentle   avails
madam, go.
QUEEN ISABELLA. Then come, sweet death, and rid me of
this grief.

                                                      (*Exit.*)

(*Re-enter* FIRST LORD, *with the head of* YOUNG MORTIMER.)

FIRST LORD. My lord, here is the head of Mortimer.
KING EDWARD THIRD. Go fetch my father's hearse,*   coffin
where it shall lie;
And bring my funeral robes.

                                        (*Exeunt* ATTENDANTS.)
                    Accursèd head,
Could I have ruled thee then, as I do now,

Thou had'st not hatched this monstrous treachery!—
Here comes the hearse; help me to mourn, my lords.

(*Re-enter* ATTENDANTS *with hearse and funeral robes.*)

Sweet father, here unto thy murdered ghost
I offer up this wicked traitor's head;
And let these tears, distilling from mine eyes,
Be witness of my grief and innocency.

(*Exeunt.*)

Every Man in His Humour

BY BEN JONSON

Ben Jonson's career straddles the reigns of Elizabeth and James I, but most of his major works belong to the Jacobean period. Strictly speaking, however, he is an Elizabethan playwright by early conditioning and in contributing to the development of a so-called comedy of humours which combined realism and imagination, characterization and exaggeration, in late-sixteenth-century comedy. This species of comedy was based on Elizabethan "psychology," in which the humours, held to the body fluids loosely comparable to endocrine secretions, were supposed to affect temperament to the extent of producing characteristics and idiosyncrasies that dominated the individual's personality.

The first comedy devoted totally to "comedy of humours" was Ben Jonson's *Every Man in His Humour*, produced in 1598 by Shakespeare's company, the Lord Chamberlain's Men. It exemplifies the paradox of comic realism encompassed by exaggeration, for Jonson managed to sharpen comic depiction of character traits and manners by stressing his characters' humours. At the same time he took London for his scene and effectuated a paradox in using comic "realism" of environment ("social drama," so to speak) while employing imaginatively stretched characters, who may be rightly considered caricatures, and placing them in farcically invented situations. The result in this play and in Jonson's next comedy, *Every Man out of His Humour*, produced a year later, is a special genre of satirical comedy, to be distinguished from the romantic genre of court comedies initiated by John Lyly and brought to delightful pre-eminence by the charm of Shakespeare's writing in *As You Like It, Much Ado About Nothing, Twelfth Night,* and *A Midsummer Night's Dream*.

Jonson (1572-1637) came to the Elizabethan theatre well prepared for the realistic observation and vigorous invention achieved in his "comedy of humours." Born in London, the stepson of a master bricklayer who for a time apprenticed him to his trade, he experienced common life at an early age. Running away from an occupation he found uncongenial, Jonson enlisted in the British army then lending support to the revolt of the Netherlands against the imperialism of Spain. After a brief period of service, during which the doughty ex-bricklayer slew a soldier in single combat, he returned to England and plunged at once into the turbulent life of London. At the age of twenty he married and then appears to have become an actor; according to tradition he played the part of Hieronimo in a touring company's production of *The Spanish Tragedy*. While still identified (in Henslowe's *Diary* for 1597) as a player, Jonson became associated with the writers furnishing plays to Henslowe; and he is known to have completed a now lost play, *The Isle of Dogs*, started by the satirist Thomas Nashe, which was subsequently produced at the Swan, Jonson playing one of the parts. The production, which gave offense to the government, resulted in a short prison term for Jonson and the other actors. Released from prison in the early fall of 1597, he returned to writing for Henslowe, and shortly thereafter he gave *Every Man in His Humour* to Shakespeare's company. The comedy proved successful and Jonson could congratulate himself on the outcome of the expertly staged production by 1598, which included in the cast Richard Burbage, the comedian Will Kemp, and Shakespeare himself.

Jonson's spirits were hardly dampened by a second brief imprisonment for fighting a duel with one of Henslowe's valuable actors, Gabriel Spencer, whom Jonson killed after himself having been wounded in the arm. (He would have suffered the death penalty if he had not been able to plead "benefit of clergy"—that is, the right, as a cleric, not to be tried by a civil court—by reading some Latin to the authorities.) After his release from prison he quickly made his peace with Gabriel Spencer's employer and resumed writing for Henslowe, who advanced sums of money as previously. About the same time Jonson wrote another comedy, *Every Man out of His Humour*, for the rival Lord Chamberlain's Men, who produced it in the fall of 1599 at the recently opened Globe Theatre but without winning as much success as had his earlier comedy of humours. Jonson went ahead with other projects—with *Cynthia's Revels* in 1600 and *The Poetaster* in 1601, both written for the newly established children's acting company, the Chapel Children at the "private" Blackfriars theatre; with possibly making additions to the still popular melodrama *The Spanish Tragedy* in 1602; with *Richard Crookback*, a play about RIchard III, in the same year, for Henslowe; and a year later, with another historical drama, the Roman tragedy *Sejanus*, for the Lord Chamberlain's Men.

A second long career followed for Jonson after Queen Elizabeth's death during which he wrote masques for production at court in association with England's first great scene designer, Inigo Jones. He also collaborated with Marston and Chapman on one of the best city comedies of the period, *Eastward Ho!* and wrote his comic masterpieces *Volpone* (1606), *The Silent Woman* (1609), *The Alchemist* (1610), and *Bartholomew Fair* (1614). Jonson became the leading literary figure of his time, was nearly knighted by James I, and although he had never gone beyond three years of schooling at the Westminster grammar school in London, was given an honorary Master of Art degree by Oxford University.

It is important to realize that Jonson took an exalted view of playwriting as a legitimate branch of the profession of letters. In fact, he took the extraordinary step in those days of publishing his plays in 1616 under the title of "Works": *The Works of Benjamin Jonson*. He also thought of comedy in classical terms as a social corrective, adopted that view early in his work, and expressed it vigorously in the Induction, or introduction, he added to the published text of *Every Man out of His Humour* (1599) in which the character, Asper, obviously speaking for Jonson himself, declares:

> ...with an armed and resolved hand,
> I'll strip the ragged follies of the time
> Naked as at their birth.

Asper proceeds to describe at some length the nature of a "humour" as a secretion of "the choler, melancholy, phlegm, and blood" in the human body:

> ...Now thus far
> It may, by metaphor, apply itself
> Unto the general disposition:
> As when some one peculiar quality
> Doth so possess a man that it doth draw
> All his affects, his spirits, and his powers,
> In their confluxions, all to run one way,
> This may be truly said to be a humour.

By exposing these "humours" Jonson's alter ego intends to

> . . . scourge those apes
> And to these courteous eyes oppose a mirror
> As large as is the stage whereon we act,
> Where they shall see the time's deformity
> Anatomized in every nerve and sinew,
> With constant courage and contempt of fear.

Every Man in His Humour anticipated these intentions by
about a year, but it would be a mistake to measure this play
solely by Asper's proclaimed aims. Too exuberant and mirthful a work to be appreciated merely as a purge of manners,
this comedy simply bubbles over with the spontaneous overflow
of its author's zest for life; this despite Jonson's observance of
the neoclassical principles of unity of place and time, which
confines the action, without debilitating it, to a period of
twelve hours. In fact, Jonson greatly increased the vitality of
his play by domesticating it. Originally set in Florence with
characters bearing Italian names, in its revised form *Every
Man in His Humour* became a comedy with contemporary
characters bearing English names and speaking vivid English
speech. The pleasure Jonson takes in his exaggerations can
prove infectious. Professor Henry W. Wells (in *Elizabethan
and Jacobean Playwrights,* New York, 1939, p. 271) makes
an illuminating observation in writing that Jonson, who took
pride in his acquired classicism, had "a Gothic (that is, medieval) weakness for eccentricity" and that he could be "as
broad and goliardic a humorist as Chaucer."

J. G.

Genre. In this, his first produced play, Jonson became the
foremost exponent of the newly popular comedy of humours
in the Elizabethan theatre. The prologue to *Every Man in His
Humour,* which gives some insight into Jonson's dramatic
theories, was not part of the original version.

Date. The first—or Italianate—version appeared in 1598.
This date is confirmed by a statement on the title page of the
Folio version and by reference to the play as "new" in a letter
from Tobie Matthew to Dudley Carlton dated September 20,
1598. The second—or English—version was probably under-
taken about 1612. Although now known only in this later
version, the play is included in this volume because it was
originally written and produced during Elizabeth's reign.

Text and Publishing Data. On August 4, 1600, the play was
entered in the Stationers' Register along with *As You Like It,
King Henry V,* and *Much Ado About Nothing* as plays of the

Lord Chamberlain's Company "to be stayed"—a move by the company to prevent unauthorized publication. The strategy failed, for ten days later Cuthbert Burly and Walter Burre entered *Every Man in His Humour* in the Register, Burre printing the play the following year, 1601. In 1616 the revised version appeared as one of the plays in the Jonson folio edition of his "Works" printed by William Stansby. Inasmuch as Jonson personally supervised the printing of his folio, accurate texts were reproduced. The folio (F) version of *Every Man in His Humour* was probably prepared from a collation of the 1601 quarto and from Jonson's own manuscript corrections rather than from a playhouse copy. In the quarto version, which is set in Florence, the characters bear Italian names. In revising the play, Jonson transferred the locale to London and so gave the script a decided contemporary English flavor.

Sources. The story is original; however, the prototypes of the characters may be found in the comedies of Plautus.

Stage History. The play was first acted by the Lord Chamberlain's Men at the Curtain with a cast which included Shakespeare, as Jonson notes in his 1616 edition, where he lists the players in the original production. In 1605 the play was presented at court before King James I. It was produced during the Restoration period by the Duke of York's Company at the Drury Lane in 1675, with a prologue written for the occasion by Lord Dorset. Among noteworthy later productions were Garrick's in 1751, Cooke's in 1800, and Edmund Kean's in 1816.

Structure. The original follows the classical pattern of indicating a new scene whenever a new character or characters appeared. Jonson also lists at the head of each scene all characters in the scene in order of speech or appearance. The present edition has modified both practices, indicating a new scene only when a change of place occurs and listing characters only where they actually enter the scene.

W. G.

DRAMATIS PERSONAE

KNOWELL, an old gentleman
EDWARD KNOWELL, his son
BRAINWORM, the father's man
MASTER STEPHEN, a country gull[1]
GEORGE DOWNRIGHT, a plain squire
WELLBRED, his half-brother
THOMAS KITELY, a merchant, their brother-in-law
THOMAS CASH, his cashier
MASTER MATTHEW, a town gull
CAPTAIN BOBADILL, a Paul's man[2]
OLIVER COB, a water-bearer
JUSTICE CLEMENT, an old, merry magistrate
ROGER FORMAL, his clerk
DAME KITELY, Kitely's wife
MISTRESS BRIDGET, his sister
TIB, Cob's wife
Servant to Wellbred, other servants

THE SCENE—London

---

[1] A fool.
[2] One who frequented the central aisle of St. Paul's Cathedral, at that time a lounging place as well as a meeting place for business appointments; Bobadill is a loafer.

PROLOGUE

Though need make many poets, and some such
As art, and nature have not bettered much;
Yet ours, for want, hath not so loved the stage,
As he dare serve the ill customs of the age,
Or purchase your delight at such a rate,
As, for it, he himself must justly hate.
To make a child, now swaddled, to proceed
Man, and then shoot up, in one beard and weed,*   garment
Past threescore years: or, with three rusty swords,
And help of some few foot-and-half-foot words,
Fight over York and Lancaster's long jars,³
And in the tiring-house* brings wounds to scars.   dressing room
He rather prays you will be pleased to see
One such to-day, as other plays should be;
Where neither chorus wafts you o'er the seas;⁴
Nor creaking throne comes down, the boys to please;⁵
Nor nimble squib* is seen, to make afeard   firecracker
The gentlewomen; nor rolled bullet* heard   cannon ball
To say, it thunders; nor tempestuous drum
Rumbles, to tell you when the storm doth come;
But deeds and language such as men do use:
And persons such as comedy would choose
When she would show an image of the times,
And sport with human follies, not with crimes.
Except we make 'hem such, by loving still
Our popular errors, when we know they're ill.
I mean such errors as you'll all confess,
By laughing at them, they deserve no less:
Which when you heartily do, there's hope left then,
You, that have so graced* monsters, may like men. shown favor to

³ Quarrels. The line probably refers to Shakespeare's *Henry VI* trilogy.
⁴ As in Shakespeare's *Henry V* or Heywood's *The Four Prentices of London*.
⁵ As in Lodge and Greene's *A Looking Glass for London and England* or Greene's *Alphonsus*.

ACT I

Scene 1

(*Before* KNOWELL'S *house. Enter* KNOWELL *from the house.*)

KNOWELL. A goodly day toward! and a fresh morning.—
  Brainworm,

(*Enter* BRAINWORM.)

Call up your young master: bid him rise, sir.
Tell him, I have some business to employ him.
  BRAINWORM. I will, sir, presently.*   at once
  KNOWELL.   But hear you, sirrah!
If he be 't* tis book disturb him not.   at
  BRAINWORM.   Well, sir.
                                                         (*Exit.*)

  KNOWELL. How happy yet should I esteem myself,
Could I, by any practice,* wean the boy   scheming
From one vain course of study he affects.
He is a scholar, if a man may trust
The liberal voice of fame in her report,
Of good account in both our Universities,
Either of which hath favoured him with graces:*   degrees
But their indulgence must not spring in me
A fond* opinion that he cannot err.   foolish
Myself was once a student; and indeed,
Fed with the self-same humour* he is now,   disposition
Dreaming on nought but idle poetry,
That fruitless and unprofitable art,
Good unto none but least to the professors,*   practitioners
Which then I thought the mistress of all knowledge.
But since, time and the truth have waked my judgment,
And reason taught me better to distinguish
The vain from the useful learnings.

(*Enter* STEPHEN.)

                                        Cousin Stephen,

What news with you, that you are here so early?

STEPHEN. Nothing, but e'en come to see how you do, uncle.

KNOWELL. That's kindly done; you are welcome, coz.

STEPHEN. Ay, I know that, sir; I would not ha' come else.
How does my cousin Edward, uncle?

KNOWELL. O, well, coz, go in and see; I doubt he be scarce
stirring yet.

STEPHEN. Uncle, afore I go in, can you tell me, an*   *if*
he have e'er a book of the sciences of hawking and hunting?
I would fain* borrow it.   *gladly*

KNOWELL. Why, I hope you will not a hawking now, will
you?

STEPHEN. No, wusse;* but I'll practise against next   *certainly*
year, uncle: I have bought me a hawk, and a hood, and
bells, and all; I lack nothing but a book to keep it by.

KNOWELL. O, most ridiculous!

STEPHEN. Nay, look you now, you are angry, uncle:
why you know, an a man have not skill in the hawking
and hunting languages[6] now-a-days, I'll not give a rush for
him. They are more studied than the Greek, or the Latin.
He is for no gallants' company without 'hem. And by gads-
lid* I scorn it, I, so I do, to be a consort for   every *God's eyelid*
humdrum;* hang 'hem, scroyles,* there's   *commonplace fellow/*
nothing in 'hem i' the world. What do you talk on   *scoundrels*
it? Because I dwell at Hogsden,* I shall keep com-   *Hoxton*
pany with none but the archers of Finsbury? or the citizens
that come a ducking* to Islington ponds? A fine   *duck hunting*
jest, i' faith! 'Slid, a gentleman mun* show himself like   *must*
a gentleman. Uncle, I pray you be not angry; I know what I
have to do, I trow; I am no novice.

KNOWELL. You are a prodigal, absurd coxcomb; go to!
Nay, never look at me, it's I that speak.
Take't as you will sir, I'll not flatter you.
Ha' you not yet found means enow* to waste   *enough*
That which your friends have left you, but you must
Go cast away your money on a kite,*   *hawk*
And know not how to keep it, when you ha' done?
O, it's comely! this will make you a gentleman!
Well, cousin, well! I see you are e'en past hope
Of all reclaim.—Ay, so now you're told on it,
You look another way.

STEPHEN.   What would you ha' me do?

---

6 Knowledge of the technical terms.

KNOWELL. What would I have you do? I'll tell you, kins-
man.
Learn to be wise, and practise how to thrive,
That would I have you do: and not to spend
Your coin on every bauble that you fancy,
Or every foolish brain that humours you.
I would not have you to invade each place,
Nor thrust yourself on all societies,
Till men's affections, or your own desert,
Should worthily invite you to your rank.
He that is so respectless* in his courses,*   heedless/behavior
Oft sells his reputation at cheap market.
Nor would I you should melt away yourself
In flashing bravery,* lest, while you affect   flashy clothes
To make a blaze of gentry to the world,
A little puff of scorn extinguish it,
And you be left like an unsav'ry snuff,
Whose property is only to offend.
I'ld ha' you sober, and contain yourself,
Not that your sail be bigger than your boat;
But moderate your expenses now, at first,
As* you may keep the same proportion still: so that
Nor stand so much on your gentility,
Which is an airy, and mere borrowed thing,
From dead men's dust and bones; and none of yours,
Except you make, or hold it.—Who comes here?

(*Enter a* SERVANT.)

SERVANT. Save you, gentlemen!
STEPHEN. Nay, we don't stand much on our gentility,
friend; yet you are welcome; and I assure you, mine uncle
here is a man of a thousand a year, Middlesex land. He has
but one son in all the world, I am his next heir, at the common law, Master Stephen, as simple as I stand here, if my
cousin die, as there's hope he will. I have a pretty living o'
mine own too, beside, hard by here.
SERVANT. In good time, sir.[7]
STEPHEN. "In good time, sir?" Why! And in very good
time, sir! You do not flout,* friend, do you?   mock

---

[7] "A formula of polite acquiescence . . . But it could be ironical
or incredulous . . ." (Simpson). Stephen, in the next line, takes
it as an insulting implication that his "living" is yet to come to
him.

SERVANT. Not I, sir.

STEPHEN. Not you, sir? You were not best, sir; an* you   if
should, here be them can perceive it, and that quickly too;
go to. And they can give it again soundly too, an need be.

SERVANT. Why, sir, let this satisfy you; good faith, I had no
such intent.

STEPHEN. Sir, an I thought you had, I would talk with
you, and that presently.*   immediately

SERVANT. Good Master Stephen, so you may, sir, at your
pleasure.

STEPHEN. And so I would, sir, good my saucy companion!
An you were out o' mine uncle's ground, I can tell you; though
I do "not stand upon my gentility," neither, in't.

KNOWELL. Cousin, will this ne'er be left?

STEPHEN. Whoreson-base fellow! A mechanical*   menial
servingman! By this cudgel, an 'twere not for shame, I would—

KNOWELL. What would you do, you peremptory*   absolute
    gull?
If you cannot be quiet, get you hence.
You see the honest man demeans himself
Modestly towards you, giving no reply
To your unseasoned, quarrelling, rude fashion;
And still you huff* it, with a kind of carriage   swagger
As void of wit, as of humanity.
Go, get you in; 'fore Heaven, I am ashamed
Thou hast a kinsman's interest in me.

                          (*Exit* STEPHEN.)

SERVANT. I pray you, sir, is this Master Knowell's house?

KNOWELL. Yes, marry is it, sir.

SERVANT. I should inquire for a gentleman here, one Master
Edward Knowell. Do you know any such, sir, I pray you?

KNOWELL. I should forget myself else, sir.

SERVANT. Are you the gentleman? Cry you mercy, sir. I
was required by a gentleman i' the city, as I rode out at this
end o' the town, to deliver you this letter, sir.

KNOWELL. To me, sir! What do you mean? Pray you remember your court'sy.⁸ (*Reads.*) "To his most selected friend,
Master Edward Knowell." What might the gentleman's name
be, sir, that sent it? Nay, pray you be covered.

SERVANT. One Master Wellbred, sir.

KNOWELL. Master Wellbred! A young gentleman, is he not?

    ⁸ Put on your hat.

SERVANT. The same, sir; Master Kitely married his sister—
the rich merchant i' the Old Jewry.
KNOWELL. You say very true.—Brainworm!

(*Re-enter* BRAINWORM.)

BRAINWORM. Sir.
KNOWELL. Make this honest friend drink here. Pray you,
go in.
                              (*Exeunt* BRAINWORM *and* Servant.)
This letter is directed to my son:
Yet I am Edward Knowell too, and may,
With the safe conscience of good manners, use
The fellow's error to my satisfaction.
Well, I will break it ope (old men are curious),
Be it but for the style's sake, and the phrase;
To see if both do answer my son's praises,
Who is almost grown the idolater
Of this young Wellbred. What have we here? What's this?
(*Reads.*) Why, Ned, I beseech thee, hast thou forsworn all
thy friends i' the Old Jewry? Or dost thou think us all Jews
that inhabit there yet? If thou dost, come over and but see
our frippery;* change an old shirt for a whole   old clothes shop
smock* with us. Do not conceive that antipathy be-   woman
tween us and Hogsden as was between Jews and hogs' flesh.
Leave thy vigilant father alone to number over his green apricots, evening and morning, o' the north-west wall. An* I   if
had been his son, I had saved him the labour, long since, if
taking in all the young wenches that pass by at the back-door,
and coddling* every kernel of the fruit for 'hem,   stewing
would ha' served. But, pr'y thee, come over to me quickly this
morning; I have such a present for thee!—our Turkey company[9] never sent the like to the Grand Signior. One is a
rhymer, sir, o' your own batch, your own leaven; but doth
think him himself poet-major o' the town, willing to be shown,
and worthy to be seen. The other, I will not venture his description with you till you come because I would ha' you
make hither with an appetite. If the worst of 'hem be not
worth your journey, draw your bill of charges, as unconscion-
able* as any Guildhall verdict will give it you, and   excessive
you shall be allowed your viaticum.*   travel expenses
                              From the Windmill.[10]

[9] Merchant trading company for the Levant.
[10] A wine tavern, formerly a synagogue.

From the Bordello it might come as well,
The Spittle,[11] or Pict-hatch.[12] Is this the man
My son hath sung so for the happiest wit,
The choicest brain the times hath sent us forth!
I know not what he may be in the arts,
Nor what in schools; but, surely, for his manners,
I judge him a profane and dissolute wretch;
Worse by possession of such great good gifts,
Being the master of so loose a spirit.
Why, what unhollowed ruffian would have writ
In such a scurrilous manner to a friend!
Why should he think I tell* my apricots,   count
Or play the Hesperian dragon[13] with my fruit,
To watch it? Well, my son, I'd thought
Y'd had more judgment t' have made election
Of your companions than t' have ta'en on trust
Such petulant, jeering gamesters that can spare
No argument or subject from their jest.
But I perceive affection make a fool
Of any man too much the father.—Brainworm!

(*Re-enter* BRAINWORM.)

BRAINWORM. Sir.
KNOWELL. Is the fellow gone that brought this letter?
BRAINWORM. Yes, sir, a pretty while since.
KNOWELL. And where's your young master?
BRAINWORM. In his chamber, sir.
KNOWELL. He spake not with the fellow, did he?
BRAINWORM. No, sir, he saw him not.
KNOWELL. Take you this letter, and deliver it my son;
But with no notice that I have opened it, on your life.
BRAINWORM. O Lord, sir! that were a jest indeed.

(*Exit.*)

KNOWELL. I am resolved I will not stop his journey;
Nor practise any violent mean to stay
The unbridled course of youth in him; for that,
Restrained, grows more impatient; and in kind,*   nature

---

[11] Hospital for the treatment of venereal disease.
[12] Red-light district.
[13] The dragon who assisted the daughters of Hesperus in guarding the golden apples Juno had received at her wedding from the goddess of the Earth.

Like to the eager, but the generous* greyhound,   well-bred
Who ne'er so little from his game withheld,
Turns head and leaps up at his holder's throat.
There is a way of winning more by love
And urging of the modesty than fear:
Force works on servile natures, not the free.
He that's compelled to goodness may be good,
But 'tis but for that fit;* where others, drawn   minute
By softness and example, get a habit.
Then, if they stray, but warn 'hem, and the same
They should for virtue 've done, they'll do for shame.

(*Exit.*)

Scene 2

(*A room in* KNOWELL'*s house. Enter* EDWARD KNOWELL,
with a letter in his hand, followed by BRAINWORM.)

EDWARD KNOWELL. Did he open it, say'st thou?
BRAINWORM. Yes, o' my word, sir, and read the contents.
E. KNOWELL. That scarce contents me.—what countenance,
prithee, made he i' the reading of it? was he angry, or pleased?
BRAINWORM. Nay sir, I saw him not read it, nor open it, I
assure your worship.
E. KNOWELL. No? How know'st thou then that he did
either?
BRAINWORM. Marry, sir, because he charged me, on my life,
to tell nobody that he opened it; which, unless he had done,
he would never fear to have it revealed.
E. KNOWELL. That's true: well, I thank thee, Brainworm.
(*Moves aside to read letter.*)

(*Enter* STEPHEN.)

STEPHEN. O, Brainworm, didst thou not see a fellow here
in a what-sha-call-him doublet? he brought mine uncle a
letter e'en now.
BRAINWORM. Yes, Master Stephen, what of him?
STEPHEN. O, I ha' such a mind to beat him. Where is he,
canst thou tell?
BRAINWORM. Faith, he is not of that mind: he is gone,
Master Stephen.
STEPHEN. Gone! which way? When went he? How long
since?

BRAINWORM. He is rid hence; he took horse at the street-door.

STEPHEN. And I staid i' the fields! Whoreson Scanderbag[14] rogue! Oh that I had but a horse to fetch him back again!

BRAINWORM. Why, you may ha' my master's gelding, to save your longing, sir.

STEPHEN. But I ha' no boots, that's the spite on't.

BRAINWORM. Why, a fine wisp of hay, rolled hard, Master Stephen.

STEPHEN. No faith, it's no boot to follow him now. Let him e'en go and hang. 'Pray thee, help to truss[15] me a little. He does so vex me—

BRAINWORM. You'll be worse vexed when you are trussed,[16] Master Stephen. Best keep unbraced,* and walk yourself unlaced till you be cold; your choler may founder you else.

STEPHEN. By my faith, and so I will, now thou tell'st me on't. How dost thou like my leg, Brainworm?

BRAINWORM. A very good leg, Master Stephen! But the woolen stocking does not commend it so well.

STEPHEN. Foh! the stockings be good enough, now summer is coming on, for the dust. I'll ha' a pair of silk again* winter, that* I go to dwell i' the town. in preparation for/ when
I think my leg would show in a silk hose.

BRAINWORM. Believe me, Master Stephen, rarely well.

STEPHEN. In sadness,* I think it would. I have a seriously reasonable good leg.

BRAINWORM. You have an excellent good leg, Master Stephen, but I cannot stay to praise it longer now, and I am very sorry for't.

(*Exit.*)

STEPHEN.   Another time will serve, Brainworm. Gra-mercy* for this.   many thanks

E. KNOWELL. Ha, ha, ha!

(*Laughs having read the letter.*)

STEPHEN. 'Slid,* I hope he laughs not at me; an* God's lid/if he do—

---

[14] A corruption of Iskander Bey, Turkish name of the Albanian hero George Castroita, who freed Albania from Turkish control in the fifteenth century. Books about his exploits received English translations in 1562 and 1596.

[15] Tie the laces which hold up the breeches.

[16] Brainworm puns on *truss* meaning beaten.

E. KNOWELL. Here was a letter indeed to be intercepted by a man's father and do him good with him! he cannot but think most virtuously, both of me and the sender, sure, that make the careful costermonger* of him in   fruit dealer our familiar epistles. Well, if he read this with patience, I'll be gelt,* and troll* ballads for Master John   that is, disinherited/ Trundle[17] yonder, the rest of my mortality. It is true, and   sing likely, my father may have as much patience as another man; for he takes much physic, and oft taking physic makes a man very patient. But would your packet, Master Wellbred, had arrived at him in such a minute of his patience! Then we had known the end of it, which now is doubtful, and threatens— (*Sees* STEPHEN.) What, my wise cousin! nay then, I'll furnish our feast with one gull more to'ard the mess.[18] He writes to me of a brace, and here's one, that's three: oh, for a fourth, Fortune! if ever thou'lt use thine eyes, I entreat thee—

STEPHEN. Oh, now I see who he laughed at. He laughed at somebody in that letter. By this good light, an* he had   if laughed at me—

E. KNOWELL. How now, cousin Stephen, melancholy?

STEPHEN. Yes, a little. I thought you had laughed at me, cousin.

E. KNOWELL. Why, what an* I had, coz? what would   if you ha' done?

STEPHEN. By this light I would ha' told mine uncle.

E. KNOWELL. Nay, if you would ha' told your uncle, I did laugh at you, coz.

STEPHEN. Did you, indeed?

E. KNOWELL. Yes, indeed.

STEPHEN. Why, then—

E. KNOWELL. Well then?

STEPHEN. I am satisfied; it is sufficient.

E. KNOWELL. Why, be so, gentle coz. And, I pray you, let me entreat a courtesy of you. I am sent for this morning by a friend i' the Old Jewry, to come to him; it's but crossing over the fields to Moorgate: Will you bear me company? I protest it is not to draw you into bond or any plot against the state, coz.

STEPHEN. Sir, that's all one an 'twere; you shall command me twice so far as Moorgate, to do you good in such a matter. Do you think I would leave you? I protest—

---

[17] A publisher of ballads, active from 1603 to 1626.
[18] Group of diners; originally four made "a mess."

E. KNOWELL. No, no, you shall not protest, coz.

STEPHEN. By my fackins,* but I will, by your leave: faith I'll protest more to my friend than I'll speak of at this time.

E. KNOWELL. You speak very well, coz.

STEPHEN. Nay, not so neither, you shall pardon me: but I speak to serve my turn.

E. KNOWELL. Your turn, coz? do you know what you say? A gentleman of your sort,* parts, carriage, and estimation rank to talk o' your turn[19] i' this company, and to me alone, like a tankard-bearer at a conduit! Fie! A wight that, hitherto, his every step hath left the stamp of a great foot behind him, as every word the savour of a strong spirit; and he! this man! so graced, gilded, or, to use a more fit metaphor, so tin-foiled by nature, as not ten housewives' pewter, again a good time,[20] shows more bright to the world than he! and he! (as I said last, so I say again, and still shall say it) this man! to conceal such real ornaments as these, and shadow their glory, as a milliner's[21] wife does her wrought stomacher, with a smoky lawn,* or a black cypress!* Oh, coz! it cannot be linen/crêpe answered; go not about it. Drake's old ship* at the Golden Hind Deptford may sooner circle the world again. Come, wrong not the quality of your desert with looking downward, coz; but hold up your head, so; and let the idea of what you are, be portrayed i' your face that men may read i' your physnomy, "Here within this place is to be seen the true, rare, and accomplished monster, or miracle of nature," which is all one. What think you of this, cos?

STEPHEN. Why, I do think of it; and I will be more proud, and melancholy, and gentlemanlike, than I have been, I'll insure you.

E. KNOWELL. Why, that's resolute, Master Stephen! (*Aside.*) Now, if I can but hold him up to his height, as it is happily begun, it will do well for a suburb humour. We may hap have a match with the city, and play him for forty pound.— Come, coz.

STEPHEN. I'll follow you.

E. KNOWELL. Follow me! You must go before.[22]

---

[19] A trip in which a water bearer carried a tankard of water from the conduit to his customer and then returned to the conduit was called a turn.

[20] In preparation for a festival.

[21] A vendor of articles of apparel.

[22] That is, like a serving man.

STEPHEN. Nay, an* I must, I will. Pray you, show me,   if
good cousin.

(*Exeunt.*)

Scene 3

(*The lane before* COB'S *house. Enter* MATTHEW.)

MATTHEW. I think this be the house. What, ho!

(COB *opening door.*)

COB. Who's there? O Master Matthew! Give your worship
good morrow.

MATTHEW. What, Cob? how dost thou, good Cob? dost thou
inhabit here, Cob?

COB. Ay, sir, I and my lineage ha' kept a poor house here,
in our days.

MATTHEW. Thy lineage, Monsieur Cob! What lineage, what
lineage?

COB. Why, sir, an ancient lineage, and a princely. Mine ance'try came from a king's belly, no worse man; and yet no
man neither—by your worship's leave, I did lie in that—but
Herring, the king of fish (from his belly, I proceed), one o'
the monarchs o' the world, I assure you. The first red herring
that was broiled in Adam and Eve's kitchen do I fetch my pedigree from, by the harrot's* book. His cob*   herald's/herring-head
was my great-great-mighty-great grandfather.

MATTHEW. Why mighty? why mighty, I pray thee?

COB. O, it was a mighty while ago, sir, and a mighty great
cob.

MATTHEW. How know'st thou that?

COB. How know I? Why, I smell his ghost, ever and anon.

MATTHEW. Smell a ghost! O unsavoury jest! And the ghost
of a herring cob?

COB. Ay sir. With favour of your worship's nose, Master
Matthew, why not the ghost of a herring-cob, as well as the
ghost of rasher-bacon?

MATTHEW. Roger Bacon, thou would'st say.

COB. I say rasher-bacon. They were both broiled o' the
coals; and a man may smell broiled meat, I hope? You are a
scholar; upsolve* me that, now.   clear up

MATTHEW (*aside*). O raw ignorance!—Cob, canst thou show
me of a gentlemen, one Captain Bobadill, where his lodging is?

Cob. O, my guest, sir, you mean.

Matthew. Thy guest, alas! ha, ha!

Cob. Why do you laugh, sir? Do you not mean Captain Bobadill?

Matthew. Cob, 'pray thee advise thyself well. Do not wrong the gentleman, and thyself too. I dare be sworn, he scorns thy house; he! He lodge in such a base, obscure place as thy house! Tut, I know his disposition so well, he would not lie in thy bed if thou'dst gi' it him.

Cob. I will not give it him, though, sir. Mass, I thought somewhat was in't, we could not get him to bed, all night! Well, sir; though he lie not o' my bed, he lies o' my bench. In't please you to go up, sir, you shall find him with two cushions under his head, and his cloak wrapt about him, as though he had neither won nor lost, and yet, I warrant, he ne'er cast[23] better in his life, than he has done to-night.*   last night

Matthew. Why, was he drunk?

Cob. Drunk, sir! You hear not me say so. Perhaps he swallowed a tavern-token,[24] or some such device, sir; I have nothing to do withal. I deal with water and not with wine. Gi' me my tankard there, ho! God b' wi' you, sir. It's six o'clock. I should ha' carried two turns by this. What ho! my stopple! come.

(*Enter* Tib *with water tankard.*)

Matthew. Lie in a water-bearer's house! a gentleman of his havings? Well, I'll tell him my mind.

Cob. What, Tib, show this gentleman up to the captain.

(*Exeunt* Tib *and* Matthew.)

O, an my house were the Brazen-head[25] now! Faith it would e'en speak "Moe* fools yet." You should have some now   more would take this Master Matthew to be a gentleman, at the least. His father's an honest man, a worshipful fish-monger,[26] and so forth; and now does he creep and wriggle into acquaintance with all the brave gallants about the town, such as

---

[23] A pun on *cast*, meaning to throw dice and to vomit.

[24] Got drunk. This euphemism comes from the practice of tavern keepers of issuing low-denomination tokens at a time when currency was in short supply.

[25] See Greene's *Friar Bacon and Friar Bungay*.

[26] A member of the Company of Fishmongers.

my guest is (O, my guest is a fine man!), and they flout him
invincibly.* He useth* every day to a merchant's   exceedingly/
house where I serve water, one Master Kitely's, i' the   that is, goes
Old Jewry; and here's the jest, he is in love with my master's
sister, Mistress Bridget, and calls her "mistress,"*   that is, beloved
and there he will sit you a whole afternoon sometimes, reading
o' these same abominable, vile (a pox on 'hem! I cannot abide
them,) rascally verses, poyetry, poyetry, and speaking of en-
terludes, 'twill make a man burst to hear him. And the
wenches, they do so jeer, and ti-he at him—Well, should they
do so much to me, I'ld forswear them all, "by the foot of
Pharaoh!" There's an oath! How many water-bearers shall
you hear swear such an oath? O, I have a guest—he teaches
me—he does swear the legiblest of any man christened. "By
St. George! The foot of Pharaoh! The body of me! As I am
a gentleman and a soldier!" Such dainty oaths! And withal he
does take this same filthy roguish tobacco, the finest, and
cleanliest! It would do a man good to see the fume come forth
at's tonnels.*—Well, he owes me forty shillings—   tunnels; that
my wife lent him out of her purse, by six-pence at a   is, nostrils
time—besides his lodging. I would I had it! I shall ha' it, he
says, the next action.* Helter skelter, hang sorrow,   campaign
care'll kill a cat, up-tails all, and a louse for the hangman.

                                                        (*Exit.*)

Scene 4

(*A room in* COB's *house.* BOBADILL *lying on a bench.*)

BOBADILL. Hostess, hostess!

(*Enter* TIB.)

TIB. What say you, sir?
BOBADILL. A cup o' thy small beer, sweet hostess.
TIB. Sir, there's a gentleman below, would speak with you.
BOBADILL. A gentleman! 'odso, I am not within.
TIB. My husband told him you were, sir.
BOBADILL. What a plague, What meant he?
MATTHEW (*below*). Captain Bobadill!
BOBADILL. Who's there?—Take away the bason, good host-
ess.—Come up, sir.
TIB. He would desire you to come up, sir. You come into a
cleanly house, here!

(*Enter* MATTHEW.)

MATTHEW. 'Save you, sir; 'save you, captain!

BOBADILL. Gentle Master Matthew! Is it you, sir? please
you to sit down.

MATTHEW. Thank you, good captain; you may see, I am
somewhat audacious.

BOBADILL. Not so, sir. I was requested to supper last night
by a sort* of gallants, where you were wished for, and   company
drunk to, I assure you.

MATTHEW. Vouchsafe me, by whom, good captain?

BOBADILL. Marry, by young Wellbred, and others.——Why,
hostess, a stool here, for this gentleman.

MATTHEW. No haste, sir, 'tis very well.

BOBADILL. Body of me! it was so late ere we parted last
night, I can scarce open my eyes yet; I was but new risen, as
you came. How passes the day abroad, sir? You can tell.

MATTHEW. Faith, some half hour to seven. Now, trust me,
you have an exceeding fine lodging here, very neat, and private.

BOBADILL. Ay, sir. Sit down, I pray you. Master Matthew,
in any case, possess no gentlemen of our acquaintance with
notice of my lodging.

MATTHEW. Who? I, sir? no.

BOBADILL. Not that I need to care who know it, for the
cabin[27] is convenient; but in regard I would not be too popular, and generally visited, as some are.

MATTHEW. True, captain, I conceive you.

BOBADILL. For, do you see, sir, by the heart of valour in me,
except it be to some peculiar and choice spirits, to whom I
am extraordinarily engaged, as yourself, or so, I could not ex-
tend thus far.

MATTHEW. O Lord, sir! I resolve so.[28]

BOBADILL. I confess I love a cleanly and quiet privacy above
all the tumult and roar of fortune. What new book ha' you
there? What! "Go by, Hieronymo"?[29]

MATTHEW. Ay: did you ever see it acted? Is't not well
penned?

BOBADILL. Well penned? I would fain see all the poets of
these times pen such another play as that was! they'll prate

----

[27] Military term; a soldier's tent.
[28] I am sure of it.
[29] An allusion to Kyd's *The Spanish Tragedy.*

and swagger, and keep a stir of art and devices, when, as I am
a gentleman, read 'hem, they are the most shallow, pitiful,
barren fellows that live upon the face of the earth again.

(*While* MATTHEW *reads,* BOBADILL *makes himself ready.*)

MATTHEW. Indeed, here are a number of fine speeches in
this book.[30] "O eyes, no eyes, but fountains fraught with tears!"
There's a conceit! "Fountains fraught with tears!" "O life, no
life, but lively form of death!" Another—"O world, no world,
but mass of public wrongs!" A third—"Confused and filled
with murder and misdeeds!" A fourth. O, the Muses! Is't not
excellent? Is't not simply the best that you ever heard, captain?
Ha! how do you like it?

BOBADILL. 'Tis good.

MATTHEW. "To thee, the purest object to my sense,
     The most refinèd essence Heaven covers,
     Send I these lines, wherein I do commence
     The happy state of turtle-billing lovers.
     If they prove rough, unpolished, harsh, and rude,
     Haste made the waste: thus, mildly, I conclude."

BOBADILL. Nay proceed, proceed. Where's this?

MATTHEW. This, sir! a toy* o' mine own, in my   trifle
nonage; the infancy of my muses. But when will you come and
see my study? Good faith? I can show you some very good
things, I have done of late.—That boot becomes your leg passing well, captain, methinks.

BOBADILL. So, so; it's the fashion gentlemen now use.

MATTHEW. Troth, captain, and now you speak o' the fashion, Master Wellbred's elder brother and I are fallen out exceedingly. This other day I happened to enter into some discourse of a hanger,[31] which, I assure you, both for fashion and
workmanship was most peremptory* beautiful and   absolutely
gentlemanlike; yet he condemned and cried it down for the
most pied* and ridiculous that ever he saw.   variegated

BOBADILL. Squire Downright, the half-brother, was't not?

MATTHEW. Ay sir, he.

BOBADILL. Hang him, rook!* He! Why he has no   simpleton
more judgment than a malt-horse. By St. George, I wonder
you'ld lose a thought upon such an animal; the most peremptory absurd clown of Christendom this day he is holden. I protest to you, as I am a gentleman and a soldier, I ne'er

---

[30] *The Spanish Tragedy,* III, ii, 1-4.
[31] Strap for hanging a sword from its belt.

changed* words with his like. By his discourse, he   exchanged
should eat nothing but hay; he was born for the manger, pan-
nier or pack-saddle. He has not so much as a good phrase in
his belly, but all old iron and rusty proverbs: a good commodity for some smith to make hob-nails of.

MATTHEW. Ay, and he thinks to carry it away*   carry it off
with his manhood still, where he comes. He brags he will gi'
me the bastinado, as I hear.

BOBADILL. How! He the bastinado! How came he by that
word, trow?*   do you suppose

MATTHEW. Nay, indeed, he said cudgel me; I termed it so,
for my more grace.

BOBADILL. That may be! For I was sure it was none of his
word. But when, when said he so?

MATTHEW. Faith, yesterday, they say; a young gallant, a
friend of mine, told me so.

BOBADILL. By the foot of Pharaoh, an* 'twere my case   if
now, I should send him a chartel* presently. The   challenge
bastinado! A most proper and sufficient dependence,[32] war-
ranted by the great Caranza.[33] Come hither, you shall chartel
him; I'll show you a trick or two you shall kill him with, at
pleasure; the first stoccata,* if you will, by this air.   thrust

MATTHEW. Indeed, you have absolute knowledge i' the mystery,* I have heard, sir.   that is, of
the secrets

BOBADILL. Of whom? Of whom, ha' you heard it, I
beseech you?

MATTHEW. Troth, I have heard it spoken of divers*   by many
that you have very rare, and up-in-one-breath-utter-able skill,
sir.

BOBADILL. By Heaven, no, not I; so skill i' the earth; some
small rudiments i' the science, as to know my time, distance, or
so. I have professed it more for noblemen and gentlemen's
use than mine own practice, I assure you.—Hostess, accommodate us with another bed-staff[34] here quickly. (*Enter* TIB.)
Lend us another bed-staff. (*Exit* TIB.) The woman does not
understand the words of action.—Look you, sir: exalt not your
point above this state, at any hand, and let your poniard maintain your defence, thus. (*Re-enter* TIB.)—Give it the gentle-

---

[32] Ground for a quarrel.

[33] Jeronimo de Carranza, sixteenth-century Spanish authority on
dueling.

[34] Staff used for beating the bed in making it.

man and leave us. (*Exit* TIB.) So, sir. Come on. O, twine your body more about that you may fall to a more sweet, comely, gentleman-like guard. So, indifferent. Hollow your body more, sir, thus. Now, stand fast o' your left leg, note your distance, keep your due proportion of time. Oh, you disorder your point most irregularly.

MATTHEW. How is the bearing of it now sir?

BOBADILL. O, out of measure ill! A well-experienced hand would pass upon you at pleasure.

MATTHEW. How mean you, sir, pass upon me?[35]

BOBADILL. Why, thus, sir. Make a thrust at me. Come in upon the answer, control your point, and make a full career at the body. The best-practised gallants of the time name it the passada;[36] a most desperate thrust, believe it.

MATTHEW. Well, come, sir.

BOBADILL. Why, you do not manage your weapon with any facility or grace to invite me. I have no spirit to play with you; your dearth of judgment renders you tedious.

MATTHEW. But one venue,* sir.   bout

BOBADILL.   "Venue!" Fie; most gracious denomina-
tion* as ever I heard.[37] O, the "stoccata," while you   appellation
live, sir; note that.—Come, put on your cloak, and we'll go to some private place where you are acquainted; some tavern, or so—and have a bit. I'll send for one of these fencers, and he shall breathe* you, by my direction; and then, I will   exercise
teach you your trick. You shall kill him with it, at the first, if you please. Why, I will learn you by the true judgment of the eye, hand, and foot to control any enemy's point i' the world. Should your adversary confront you with a pistol 'twere nothing, by this hand; you should, by the same rule, control his bullet, in a line,—except it were hail-shot and spread. What money ha' you about you, Master Matthew?

MATTHEW. Faith, I ha' not past a two shillings or so.

BOBADILL. 'Tis somewhat with the least; but come. We will have a bunch of radish and salt to taste our wine; and a pipe of tobacco to close the orifice of the stomach; and then we'll call upon young Wellbred. Perhaps we shall meet the Cory-
don* his brother there, and put him to the question.   rustic

(*Exeunt.*)

[85] Matthew takes the phrase in its unfavorable senses of pass sentence upon or impose upon.

[86] A forward thrust made with one foot advanced.

[87] Matthew uses the French term, no longer considered fashionable.

ACT II

Scene 1

(*A hall in* KITELY'S *house. Enter* KITELY, CASH, *and* DOWNRIGHT.)

KITELY. Thomas, come hither.
There lies a note within upon my desk.
Here take my key. It is no matter neither.
Where is the boy?
    CASH. Within, sir, i'th' warehouse.
    KITELY. Let him tell over straight that Spanish gold,
And weigh it, with th' pieces of eight. Do you
See the delivery of those silver stuffs
To Master Lucar. Tell him, if he will,
He shall ha' the grograns[38] at the rate I told him,
And I will meet him on the Exchange anon.
    CASH. Good, sir.

                                  (*Exit.*)
    KITELY.   Do you see that fellow, brother Downright?
    DOWNRIGHT. Ay, what of him?
    KITELY.   He is a jewel, brother.
I took him of a child up at my door,
And christened him, gave him mine own name, Thomas;
Since bred him at the Hospital;[39] where proving
A toward imp,* I called him home and taught   promising child
    him
So much as I have made him my cashier,
And given him, who had none, a surname, Cash;
And find him in his place, so full of faith,
That I durst trust my life into his hands.
    DOWNRIGHT. So would not I in any bastard's, brother,
As it is like he is, although I knew
Myself his father. But you said y' had somewhat
To tell me, gentle brother, what is't? what is't?

      [38] Coarse fabric of silk or silk blended with other fabrics.
      [39] Christ's Hospital, a famous London school.

KITELY. Faith, I am very loath to utter it,
As fearing it may hurt your patience;
But that I know your judgment is of strength,
Against the nearness of affection——
  DOWNRIGHT. What need this circumstance?[40] Pray you, be
  direct.
KITELY. I will not say how much I do ascribe
Unto your friendship, nor in what regard
I hold your love, but let my past behaviour,
And usage of your sister, but confirm
How well I've been affected to your——
  DOWNRIGHT. You are too tedious; come to the matter, the
  matter.
KITELY. Then, without further ceremony, thus.
My brother Wellbred, sir, I know not how,
Of late is much declined in what he was,
And greatly altered in his disposition.
When he came first to lodge here in my house,
Ne'er trust me if I were not proud of him;
Methought he bare himself in such a fashion,
So full of man, and sweetness in his carriage,
And—what was chief—it showed not borrowed in him,
But all he did became him as his own,
And seemed as perfect, proper, and possessed,
As breath with life, or colour with the blood.
But now, his course is so irregular,
So loose, affected, and deprived of grace,
And he himself withal so far fallen off
From that first place as scarce no note remains,
To tell men's judgments where he lately stood.
He's grown a stranger to all due respect,
Forgetful of his friends; and not content
To stale himself* in all societies,   make himself cheap
He makes my house here common as a mart,
A theatre, a public receptacle
For a giddy humour and diseasèd riot;
And here, as in a tavern or a stews,
He and his wild associates spend their hours,
In repetition of lascivious jests,
Swear, leap, drink, dance, and revel night by night,
Control my servants; and, indeed, what not?

  [40] Beating about the bush.

DOWNRIGHT. 'Sdeins,* I know not what I should God's dignity
say to him, i' the whole world! He values me at a cracked
three-farthings, for aught I see. It will never out o' the flesh
that's bred i' the bone. I have told him enough, one would
think, if that would serve; but counsel to him is as good as a
shoulder of mutton to a sick horse. Well! He knows what to
trust to, for George.[41] Let him spend and spend and domineer,
till his heart ache; an he think to be relieved by me, when he
is got into one o' your city-pounds, the Counters,* London prisons
he has the wrong sow by the ear, i' faith; and claps his dish* begs
at the wrong man's door. I'll lay my hand o' my halfpenny ere
I part with 't to fetch him out, I'll assure you.

KITELY. Nay, good brother, let it not trouble you thus.

DOWNRIGHT. 'Sdeath! he mads me; I could eat my very spur-
leathers for anger! But, why are you so tame? Why do not you
speak to him and tell him how he disquiets your house?

KITELY. O, there are divers reasons to dissuade, brother,
But would yourself vouchsafe to travail in it,
(Though but with plain and easy circumstance,)
It would both come much better to his sense,
And savour less of stomach* or of passion. anger
You are his elder brother, and that title
Both gives and warrants you authority,
Which, by your presence seconded, must breed
A kind of duty in him, and regard;
Whereas, if I should intimate the least,
It would but add contempt to his neglect,
Heap worse on ill, make up a pile of hatred,
That, in the rearing, would come tottering down,
And in the ruin bury all our love.
Nay, more than this, brother; if I should speak,
He would be ready, from his heat of humour* hot temper
And overflowing of the vapour in him,
To blow the ears of his familiars
With the false breath of telling what disgraces
And low disparagements I had put upon him.
Whilst they, sir, to relieve him in the fable,* narrative
Make their loose comments upon every word,
Gesture, or look I use; mock me all over,
From my flat cap unto my shining shoes;[42]

[41] 'fore George; that is, for all I care.
[42] Both were marks of the tradesman.

And, out of their impetuous rioting phant'sies,
Beget some slander that shall dwell with me.
And what would that be, think you? marry, this:
They would give out—because my wife is fair,
Myself but lately married, and my sister
Here sojourning a virgin in my house—
That I were jealous!—Nay as sure as death,
That they would say; and how that I had quarrelled*   quarrelled with
My brother purposely, thereby to find
An apt pretext to banish them my house.
    DOWNRIGHT. Mass, perhaps so; they're like enough to do it.
    KITELY. Brother, they would, believe it; so should I,
Like one of these penurious quack-salvers,
But set the bills up* to mine own disgrace,   advertise
And try experiments upon myself;
Lend scorn and envy, opportunity
To stab my reputation and good name——

    (*Enter* MATTHEW *struggling with* BOBADILL.)

    MATTHEW. I will speak to him——
    BOBADILL. Speak to him! By the foot of Pharaoh, you shall
not! You shall not do him that grace.—The time of day to
you, gentleman o' the house. Is Master Wellbred stirring?
    DOWNRIGHT. How then? What should he do?
    BOBADILL. Gentleman of the house, it is to you. Is he with-
in, sir?
    KITELY. He came not to his lodging to-night,* sir,   last night
I assure you.
    DOWNRIGHT. Why, do you hear? You!
    BOBADILL. The gentleman-citizen hath satisfied me; I'll talk
to no scavenger.
    (*Exeunt* BOBADILL *and* MATTHEW.)
    DOWNRIGHT. How! Scavenger? Stay, sir, stay!
    KITELY. Nay, brother Downright.
    DOWNRIGHT. 'Heart! Stand you away, an* you love me.   if
    KITELY. You shall not follow him now, I pray you, brother.
Good faith you shall not; I will overrule you.
    DOWNRIGHT. Ha! scavenger? Well, go to, I say little; but, by
this good day (God forgive me I should swear), if I put it up
so,* say I am the rankest cow that ever pist. 'Sdeins,   tolerate it
an I swallow this, I'll ne'er draw my sword in the sight of Fleet-
street again, while I live; I'll sit in a barn with madge-howlet,
and catch mice first. Scavenger? 'Heart!—and I'll go near to

fill that huge tumbrel-slop⁴³ of yours with somewhat, and I
have good luck; your Garagantua breech cannot carry it away.

KITELY. Oh, do not fret yourself thus; never think on't.

DOWNRIGHT. These are my brother's consorts, these! These
are his cam'rades, his walking mates! He's a gallant, a cava-
liero too, right hangman cut!* Let me not   that is,
                                             hanging material
live an I could not find in my heart to
swinge* the whole ging* of 'hem one after another, beat/company
and begin with him first. I am grieved it should be said he is
my brother and take these courses. Well, as he brews, so shall
he drink, for George, again. Yet he shall hear on't, and that
tightly* too, an I live, i' faith.   vigorously

KITELY. But, brother, let your reprehension, then,
Run in an easy current, not o'er-high
Carried with rashness or devouring choler;
But rather use the soft persuading way,
Whose powers will work more gently, and compose
The imperfect thoughts you labour to reclaim;
More winning than enforcing the consent.

DOWNRIGHT. Ay, ay, let me alone for that, I warrant you.
(*Bell rings.*)

KITELY. How now! Oh, the bell rings to breakfast.
Brother, I pray you go in, and bear my wife
Company till I come; I'll but give order
For some despatch of business to my servants.
                                            (*Exit* DOWNRIGHT.)

(*Enter* COB *with his tankard.*)

KITELY. What, Cob! Our maids will have you by the back,
      i' faith,
For coming so late this morning.

COB. Perhaps so, sir; take heed somebody have not them
by the belly for walking so late in the evening.
                                                    (*Exit.*)

KITELY. Well, yet my troubled spirit's somewhat eased,
Though not reposed in that security
As I could wish; but I must be content,
Howe'er I set a face on't to the world.
Would I had lost this finger at a venture,
So Wellbred had ne'er lodged within my house.
Why't cannot be, where there is such resort

---

⁴³ Large puffed breeches, an extravagant fashion of the day.

Of wanton gallants and young revellers,
That any woman should be honest* long.   chaste
Is't like that factious beauty will preserve
The public weal of chastity unshaken,
When such strong motives muster and make head*   gather forces
Against her single peace? No, no. Beware
When mutual appetite doth meet to treat,
And spirits of one kind and quality
Come once to parley in the pride of blood,
It is no slow conspiracy that follows.
Well, to be plain, if I but thought the time
Had answered their affections,* all the world   suited their desires
Should not persuade me but I were a cuckold.
Marry, I hope they ha' not got that start;
For opportunity hath balked 'hem yet,
And shall do still, while I have eyes and ears
To attend the impositions of my heart.
My presence shall be as an iron bar
'Twixt the conspiring motions of desire;
Yea, every look or glance mine eye ejects
Shall check occasion, as one doth his slave,
When he forgets the limits of prescription.

(*Enter* DAME KITELY *and* BRIDGET.)

DAME KITELY. Sister Bridget, pray you fetch down the rose-
water above in the closet.
(*Exit* BRIDGET.)
Sweetheart, will you come in to breakfast?
KITELY (*aside*). An* she have overheard me now!   if
DAME KITELY. I pray thee, good muss,* we stay*   mouse/
for you.   wait
KITELY (*aside*). By Heaven, I would not for a thousand
angels!*   gold coins
DAME KITELY. What ail you, sweetheart? Are you not well?
Speak, good muss.
KITELY. Troth my head aches extremely on a sudden.[44]
DAME KITELY (*putting her hand to his forehead*). Oh, the
Lord!
KITELY. How now? What?
DAME KITELY. Alas, how it burns! Muss, keep you warm;

[44] A reference to the horns of a cuckold.

good truth it is this new disease;[45] there's a number are troubled withal. For love's sake, sweetheart, come in out of the air.

KITELY. How simple and how subtle are her answers!
A new disease, and many troubled with it?
Why true; she heard me, all the world to nothing.*   *that is, I'll wager everything*
    DAME KITELY. I pray thee, good sweetheart,
come in; the air will do you harm, in troth.
    KITELY. "The air!" She has me i' the wind!*   *scents my thoughts*
     —Sweetheart,
I'll come to you presently; 'twill away, I hope.
    DAME KITELY. Pray Heaven it do.

                                 (*Exit.*)

    KITELY. A new disease? I know not, new or old,
But it may well be called poor mortals' plague;
For, like a pestilence, it doth infect
The houses of the brain.[46] First, it begins
Solely to work upon the phantasy,
Filling her seat with such pestiferous air
As soon corrupts the judgment; and from thence
Sends like contagion to the memory;
Still each to other giving the infection,
Which, as a subtle vapour, spreads itself
Confusedly through every sensitive part,
Till not a thought or motion in the mind
Be free from the black poison of suspect.*   *suspicion*
Ah! but what misery is it to know this?
Or, knowing it, to want the mind's erection*   *that is, elevation*
In such extremes? Well, I will once more strive,
In spite of this black cloud, myself to be,
And shake the fever off that thus shakes me.

                                   (*Exit.*)

Scene 2

(*Moorfields. Enter* BRAINWORM *disguised as a soldier.*)

BRAINWORM. 'Slid I cannot choose but laugh to see myself

---

    [45] A term for various fevers whose courses could not be diagnosed.

    [46] According to contemporary anatomical theory, the brain was divided into three houses or ventricles: imagination, reason, and memory.

translated thus from a poor creature to a creator; for now
must I create an intolerable sort* of lies or my present   pack
profession loses the grace; and yet the lie, to a man of my coat,
is as ominous a fruit as the fico.[47] O, sir, it holds for good
polity ever to have that outwardly in vilest estimation that inwardly is most dear to us; so much for my borrowed shape.
Well, the troth is my old master intends to follow my young
master, dry-foot,* over Moorfields to London this   by the scent
morning; now I knowing of this hunting-match, or rather conspiracy, and to insinuate with my young master (for so must
we that are blue waiters,[48] and men of hope and service do,
or perhaps we may wear motley* at the year's   costume of Fools
end, and who wears motley, you know), have got me afore, in
this disguise, determining here to live in ambuscado, and intercept him in the midway. If I can but get his cloak, his purse,
his hat, nay, any thing to cut him off, that is, to stay his journey, *Veni, vidi, vici,*[49] I may say with Captain Cæsar, I am
made for ever, i' faith. Well, now must I practise to get the
true garb* of one of these lance-knights,* my arm   bearing/
here, and my—young master! And his cousin,   mercenary
Master Stephen, as I am a true counterfeit man of war, and   foot soldiers
no soldier!
     (*Retires.*)

     (*Enter* E. KNOWELL *and* STEPHEN.)

     E. KNOWELL. So sir, and how then, coz?
     STEPHEN. 'Sfoot! I have lost my purse, I think.
     E. KNOWELL. How! Lost your purse? Where? When had
you it?
     STEPHEN. I cannot tell;—stay.
     BRAINWORM. 'Slid, I am afeard they will know me; would I
could get by them!
     E. KNOWELL. What? Ha' you it?
     STEPHEN. No; I think I was bewitched, I——
     (*Weeps.*)
     E. KNOWELL. Nay, do not weep the loss; hang it, let it go.
     STEPHEN. Oh, it's here: No, an it had been lost, I had not
cared, but for a jet ring Mistress Mary sent me.

> [47] The fig. "To give the fico" was considered an obscene gesture.
> [48] Serving men then wore blue livery.
> [49] "I came, I saw, I conquered."

E. KNOWELL. A jet ring! O the posy,* the posy?   poetic motto
STEPHEN. Fine, i' faith.—

"Though Fancy sleep,
My love is deep."

Meaning that though I did not fancy her, yet she loved me dearly.
E. KNOWELL. Most excellent!
STEPHEN. And then I sent her another, and my posy was,

"The deeper the sweeter,
I'll be judged by St. Peter."

E. KNOWELL. How, by St. Peter? I do not conceive that.
STEPHEN. Marry, St. Peter, to make up the metre.
E. KNOWELL. Well, there the saint was your good patron, he helped you at your need. Thank him, thank him.
BRAINWORM (*aside*). I cannot take leave on 'hem so; I will venture, come what will. (*Comes forward.*) Gentlemen, please you change a few crowns for a very excellent good blade here? I am a poor gentleman, a soldier; on that, in the better state of my fortunes, scorned so mean a refuge; but now it is the humour* of necessity to have it so. You seem to be gen-   whim tlemen well affected to martial men, else should I rather die with silence than live with shame; however, vouchsafe to re-member, it is my want speaks, not myself; this condition agrees not with my spirit——
E. KNOWELL. Where hast thou served?
BRAINWORM. May it please you, sir, in all the late wars of Bohemia, Hungaria, Dalmatia, Poland; where not, sir? I have been a poor servitor by sea and land any time this fourteen years, and followed the fortunes of the best commanders in Christendom. I was twice shot at the taking of Aleppo, once at the relief of Vienna; I have been at Marseilles, Naples, and the Adriatic gulf; a gentleman-slave in the gallies, thrice, where I was most dangerously shot in the head, through both the thighs; and yet, being thus maimed, I am void of maintenance, nothing left me but my scars, the noted marks of my resolu-tion.
STEPHEN. How will you sell this rapier, friend?
BRAINWORM. Generous sir, I refer it to your own judg-ment; you are a gentleman, give me what you please.

STEPHEN. True, I am a gentleman, I know that, friend; but what though? I pray you say, what would you ask?

BRAINWORM. I assure you, the blade may become the side or thigh of the best prince in Europe.

E. KNOWELL. Ay, with a velvet scabbard, I think.

STEPHEN. Nay, an't be mine, it shall have a velvet scabbard, coz, that's flat; I'd not wear it as 'tis, an you would give me an angel.

BRAINWORM. At your worship's pleasure, sir. (STEPHEN *examines the blade.*) Nay, 'tis a most pure Toledo.

STEPHEN. I had rather it were a Spaniard; but tell me, what shall I give you for it? An it had a silver hilt—

E. KNOWELL. Come, come, you shall not buy it. Hold, there's a shilling, fellow; take thy rapier.

STEPHEN. Why, but I will buy it now because you say so, and there's another shilling, fellow, I scorn to be outbidden. What, shall I walk with a cudgel, like Higginbottom,[50] and may have a rapier for money!

E. KNOWELL. You may buy one in the city.

STEPHEN. Tut! I'll buy this i' the field, so I will; I have a mind to't because 'tis a field rapier.—Tell me your lowest price.

E. KNOWELL. You shall not buy it, I say.

STEPHEN. By this money, but I will, though I give more than 'tis worth.

E. KNOWELL. Come away, you are a fool.

STEPHEN. Friend, I am a fool, that's granted; but I'll have it, for that word's sake. Follow me for your money.

BRAINWORM. At your service, sir.

(*Exeunt.*)

Scene 3

(*Another part of Moorfield. Enter* KNOWELL.)

KNOWELL. I cannot lose the thought yet of this letter
Sent to my son; nor leave t' admire* the change   wonder at
Of manners and the breeding of our youth
Within the kingdom since myself was one.
When I was young, he lived not in the stews*   brothels
Durst have conceived a scorn, and uttered it,
On a gray head; age was authority

---

[50] An unidentified topical allusion.

Against a buffoon; and a man had then
A certain reverence paid unto his years,
That had none due unto his life; so much
The sanctity of some prevailed for others.
But now, we all are fallen; youth, from their fear;
And age, from that which bred it, good example.[51]
Nay, would ourselves were not the first, e'en parents,
That did destroy the hopes in our own children;
Or they not learned our vices in their cradles,
And sucked in our ill customs with their milk;
Ere all their teeth be born, or they can speak,
We make their palates cunning! the first words
We form their tongues with are licentious jests!
Can it call whore? Cry bastard? O, then, kiss it!
A witty child! can't swear? The father's darling!
Give it two plums. Nay, rather than't shall learn
No bawdy song, the mother herself will teach it!
But this is in the infancy, the days
Of the long coat; when it puts on the breeches,
It will put off all this. Ay, it is like,
When it is gone into the bone already!
No, no; this dye goes deeper than the coat,
Or shirt, or skin; it stains into the liver
And heart,[52] in some; and, rather than it should not,
Note what we fathers do! Look, how we live!
What mistresses we kept! At what expense!
In our sons' eyes! Where they may handle our gifts,
Hear our lascivious courtships, see our dalliance,
Taste of the same provoking meats with us,
To ruin of our states!* Nay, when our own   estates
Portion is fled, to prey on their remainder
We call them into fellowship of vice!
Bait 'hem with the young chambermaid, to seal![53]
And teach 'hem all bad ways to buy affliction.
This is one path, but there are millions more
In which we spoil our own with leading them.
Well, I thank Heaven, I never yet was he
That travelled with my son, before sixteen,

[51] The following twenty lines are from Quintilian's *Institutio Oratoria*, I, ii, 6-8.
[52] The liver was the supposed seat of the passions; the heart was the seat of knowledge.
[53] To agree to the sale of family property (?).

To show him the Venetian courtezans;
Nor read the grammar of cheating I had made,
To my sharp boy, at twelve, repeating still
The rule,[54] "Get money; still* get money, boy;   always
No matter by what means; money will do
More, boy, than my lord's letter." Neither have I
Dressed snails, or mushrooms curiously before him,
Perfumed my sauces, and taught him to make 'hem;
Preceding still, with my gray gluttony,
At all the ordinaries,* and only feared   eating houses
His palate should degenerate, not his manners.
These are the trade of fathers now; however,
My son, I hope, hath met within my threshold
None of these household precedents, which are strong
And swift, to rape youth to their precipice.
But, let the house at home be ne'er so clean-
Swept, or kept sweet from filth, nay dust and cobwebs,
If he will live abroad with his companions,
In dung and leystals,* it is worth a fear;   dung heaps
Nor is the danger of conversing less
Than all that I have mentioned of example.

(*Enter* BRAINWORM, *disguised.*)

BRAINWORM (*aside*). My master! Nay, faith, have at you;
I am fleshed* now, I have sped* so well.———   initiated/succeeded
Worshipful sir, I beseech you, respect* the estate of a   regard
poor soldier; I am ashamed of this base course of life—God's
my comfort—but extremity provokes me to't; what remedy?
KNOWELL. I have not for you now.
BRAINWORM. By the faith I bear unto truth, gentlemen, it
is no ordinary custom in me, but only to preserve manhood.
I protest to you, a man I have been; a man I may be, by
your sweet bounty.
KNOWELL. 'Pray thee, good friend, be satisfied.
BRAINWORM. Good sir, by that hand you may do the part
of a kind gentleman in lending a poor soldier the price of
two cans of beer,* a matter of small value; the   that is, twopence
King of Heaven shall pay you, and I shall rest thankful; sweet
worship.———
KNOWELL. Nay, an you be so importunate———

[54] The rest of the speech is based on passages from Horace's
first epistle and Juvenal's satires.

BRAINWORM. Oh, tender sir! Need will have its course; I was not made to this vile use! Well, the edge of the enemy could not have abated me so much; it's hard when a man hath served in his prince's cause, and be thus—(*Weeps.*) Honourable worship, let me derive a small piece of silver from you; it shall not be given in the course of time;[55] by this good ground, I was fain to pawn my rapier last night for a poor supper; I had sucked the hilts long before, I am a pagan else. Sweet honour——

KNOWELL. Believe me, I am taken with some wonder,
To think a fellow of thy outward presence,
Should, in the frame and fashion of his mind,
Be so degenerate, and sordid-base!
Art thou a man? And sham'st thou not to beg?
To practise such a servile kind of life?
Why, were thy education ne'er so mean,
Having thy limbs, a thousand fairer courses
Offer themselves to thy election.
Either the wars might still supply thy wants,
Or service of some virtuous gentleman,
Or honest labour; nay, what can I name,
But would become thee better than to beg.
But men of thy condition feed on sloth,
As doth the beetle on the dung she breeds in;
Not caring how the metal of your minds
Is eaten with the rust of idleness.
Now, afore me, whate'er he be that should
Relieve a person of thy quality
While thou insist'st in this loose desperate course,
I would esteem the sin not thine, but his.

BRAINWORM. Faith, sir, I would gladly find some other course, if so——

KNOWELL. Ay.
You'ld gladly find it, but you will not seek it.

BRAINWORM. Alas, sir, where should a man seek? In the wars, there's no ascent by desert in these days; but——and for service, would it were as soon purchased* as obtained wished for! The air's my comfort!—I know what I would say—

KNOWELL. What's thy name?

BRAINWORM. Please you, Fitz-Sword, sir.

KNOWELL.   Fitz-Sword!

[55] That is, it will be repaid.

Say that a man should entertain* thee now,   hire
Wouldst thou be honest, humble, just, and true?

BRAINWORM. Sir, by the place and honour of a soldier——

KNOWELL. Nay, nay, I like not those affected oaths. Speak
plainly, man; what think'st thou of my words?

BRAINWORM. Nothing, sir, but wish my fortunes were as
happy as my service should be honest.

KNOWELL. Well, follow me; I'll prove* thee, if thy   test
deeds will carry a proportion to thy words.

(*Exit.*)

BRAINWORM. Yes, sir, straight; I'll but garter my hose. O
that my belly were hooped now, for I am ready to burst with
laughing! Never was bottle or bagpipe fuller. 'Slid, was there
ever seen a fox in years to betray himself thus! Now shall I
be possessed of all his counsels; and, by that conduit, my
younger master. Well, he is resolved to prove my honesty;
faith, and I'm resolved to prove his patience; oh, I shall abuse
him intolerably. This small piece of service will bring him
clean out of love with the soldier for ever. He will never
come within the sign of it, the sight of a cassock*   soldier's cloak
or a musket-rest again. He will hate the musters at Mile-end[56]
for it to his dying day. It's no matter; let the world think me
a bad counterfeit, if I cannot give him the slip[57] at an instant.
Why, this is better than to have staid* his journey!   prevented
Well, I'll follow him. Oh, how I long to be employed!

(*Exit.*)

ACT III

Scene 1

(*A room in the Windmill Tavern. Enter* MATTHEW, WELL-
BRED, *and* BOBADILL.)

MATTHEW. Yes faith, sir, we were at your lodging to seek
you too.

WELLBRED. Oh, I came not there to-night.*   last night

BOBADILL. Your brother delivered us as much.

WELLBRED. Who, my brother Downright?

BOBADILL. He! Master Wellbred; I know not in what kind

---

[56] The training ground for the London militia.
[57] With a pun on *slip* meaning counterfeit coin.

you hold me, but let me say to you this: as sure as honour, I esteem it so much out of the sunshine of reputation to throw the least beam of regard upon such a——

WELLBRED. Sir, I must hear no ill words of my brother.

BOBADILL. I protest to you, as* I have a thing to   *as surely as* be saved about me, I never saw any gentleman-like part——

WELLBRED. Good captain, "faces about"* to some   *about face* other discourse.

BOBADILL. With your leave, sir, an there were no more men living upon the face of the earth, I should not fancy him, by St. George!

MATTHEW. Troth, nor I; he is a rustical cut, I know not how; he doth not carry himself like a gentleman of fashion.

WELLBRED. Oh, Master Matthew, that's a grace peculiar but to a few, *quos æquus amavit Jupiter.*[58]

MATTHEW. I understand you, sir.

WELLBRED. No question you do, (*Aside.*) or you do not, sir.

(*Enter* E. KNOWELL *and* STEPHEN.)

Ned Knowell! By my soul, welcome. How dost thou, sweet spirit, my genius? 'Slid, I shall love Apollo and the mad Thespian girls* the better, while I live, for this, my   *the muses* dear Fury; now, I see there's some love in thee. (*Aside to* KNOWELL.) Sirrah, these be the two I writ to thee of. Nay, what a drowsy humour is this now! Why dost thou not speak?

E. KNOWELL. Oh, you are a fine gallant, you sent me a rare letter!

WELLBRED. Why, was't not rare?

E. KNOWELL. Yes, I'll be sworn, I was ne'er guilty of reading the like; match it in all Pliny,[59] or Symmachus'[60] epistles, and I'll have my judgment burned in the ear for a rogue;[61] make much of thy vein, for it is inimitable. But I mar'le*   *marvel* what camel[62] it was that had the carriage of it; for doubtless he was no ordinary beast that brought it!

---

[58] Whom impartial Jupiter loved (Virgil).

[59] Pliny the Younger (A.D. 62–c. 114), noted for his epistolatory style.

[60] Famous fourth-century Roman statesman and letter writer, who modeled his style on Pliny.

[61] Criminals were commonly punished in this manner.

[62] Noted as a dull beast.

WELLBRED. Why?

E. KNOWELL. "Why," say'st thou? Why, dost thou think that any reasonable creature, especially in the morning, the sober time of the day too, could have mista'en my father for me?

WELLBRED. 'Slid, you jest, I hope?

E. KNOWELL. Indeed, the best use we can turn it to is to make a jest on't, now; but I'll assure you, my father had the full view o' your flourishing style some hour before I saw it.

WELLBRED. What a dull slave was this! But, sirrah, what said he to it, i' faith?

E. KNOWELL. Nay, I know not what he said; but I have a shrewd guess what he thought.

WELLBRED. What, what?

E. KNOWELL. Marry, that thou art some strange, dissolute young fellow, and I a grain or two better for keeping thee company.

WELLBRED. Tut, that thought is like the moon in her last quarter; 'twill change shortly. But, sirrah, I pray thee be acquainted with my two hang-by's here; thou wilt take exceeding pleasure in 'hem, if thou hear'st 'hem once go; my wind-instruments; I'll wind 'hem up. But what strange piece of silence is this? The sign of the Dumb Man?

E. KNOWELL. Oh, sir, a kinsman of mine, one that may make your music the fuller, an he please; he has his humour sir.

WELLBRED. Oh, what is't, what is't?

E. KNOWELL. Nay, I'll neither do your judgment, nor his folly that wrong as to prepare your apprehension. I'll leave him to the mercy o' your search; if you can take him, so!

WELLBRED. Well, Captain Bobadill, Master Matthew, pray you know this gentleman here; he is a friend of mine, and one that will deserve your affection.—(*To* STEPHEN.) I know not your name, sir, but I shall be glad of any occasion to render me more familiar to you.

STEPHEN. My name is Master Stephen, sir; I am this gentleman's own cousin, sir; his father is mine uncle, sir: I am somewhat melancholy, but you shall command me, sir, in whatsoever is incident to a gentleman.

BOBADILL. Sir, I must tell you this, I am no general man;[63] but for Master Wellbred's sake, (you may embrace it at what height of favour you please) I do communicate with you, and

[63] I am a very particular person.

conceive you to be a gentleman of some parts; I love few words.

E. KNOWELL. And I fewer, sir; I have scarce enow* _{enough} to thank you.

MATTHEW. But are you, indeed, sir, so given to it?

STEPHEN. Ay, truly, sir, I am mightily given to melancholy.

MATTHEW. Oh it's your only fine humour, sir! Your true melancholy breeds your perfect fine wit, sir. I am melancholy myself, divers times, sir, and then do I no more but take pen and paper presently,* and overflow you half _{instantly} a score, or a dozen of sonnets at a sitting.

E. KNOWELL (*aside*). Sure he utters* them _{puts into circulation} then by the gross.

STEPHEN. Truly, sir, and I love such things out of measure.*

_{very much}

E. KNOWELL (*aside*). I'faith, better than in measure, I'll undertake.

MATTHEW. Why, I pray you, sir, make use of my study; it's at your service.

STEPHEN. I thank you, sir, I shall be bold, I warrant you; have you a stool there to be melancholy upon?

MATTHEW. That I have, sir, and some papers there of mine own doing, at idle hours, that you'll say there's some sparks of wit in 'hem when you see them.

WELLBRED (*aside*). Would the sparks would kindle once and become a fire amongst 'hem! I might see self-love burnt for her heresy.

STEPHEN. Cousin, is it well? am I melancholy enough?

E. KNOWELL. Oh ay, excellent.

WELLBRED. Captain Bobadill, why muse you so?

E. KNOWELL. He is melancholy too.

BOBADILL. Faith, sir, I was thinking of a most honourable piece of service, was performed to-morrow, being St. Mark's day, shall be some ten years now.

E. KNOWELL. In what place, captain?

BOBADILL. Why at the beleaguering of Strigonium,[64] where, in less than two hours, seven hundred resolute gentlemen, as any were in Europe, lost their lives upon the breach. I'll tell you, gentlemen, it was the first, but the best leaguer* _{siege} that ever I beheld with these eyes, except the taking in of*—what do you call it, last year, by the Genoways;* _{capture/ Genoese} but that, of all other, was the most fatal and dangerous exploit

[64] Graan in Hungary, retaken from the Turks in 1595.

that ever I was ranged in, since I first bore arms before the
face of the enemy, as I am a gentleman and soldier.

STEPHEN. 'So! I had as lief as an angel I could swear as
well as that gentleman!

E. KNOWELL. Then, you were a servitor at both, it seems;
at Strigonium? and "What-do-you-call't"?

BOBADILL. O Lord, sir! By St. George, I was the first man
that entered the breach; and had I not effected it with resolution, I had been slain, if I had had a million of lives.

E. KNOWELL (*aside*). 'Twas pity you had not ten; a cat's
and your own i'faith. But, was it possible?

MATTHEW (*aside to* STEPHEN). 'Pray you mark this discourse, sir.

STEPHEN. So I do.

BOBADILL. I assure you, upon my reputation, 'tis true, and
yourself shall confess.

E. KNOWELL (*aside*). You must bring me to the rack, first.

BOBADILL. Observe me, judicially, sweet sir; they had
planted me three demi-culverins* just in the mouth small cannon
of the breach; now sir, as we were to give on,* their   charge
master-gunner (a man of no mean skill and mark, you must
think) confronts me with his linstock,[65] ready to give fire; I,
spying his intendment, discharged my petronel* in his   carbine
bosom, and with these single arms, my poor rapier, ran violently upon the Moors that guarded the ordnance, and put 'hem
pellmell to the sword.

WELLBRED. To the sword! To the rapier, captain.

E. KNOWELL. Oh, it was a good figure observed, sir. But did
you all this, captain, without hurting your blade?

BOBADILL. Without any impeach o' the earth;* you   harm
shall perceive, sir. (*Shows his rapier.*) It is the most fortunate
weapon that ever rid on poor gentleman's thigh. Shall I tell
you sir? You talk of Morglay, Excalibur, Durindana[66] or so;
tut! I lend no credit to that is fabled of 'hem; I know the virtue
of mine own, and therefore I dare the boldlier maintain it.

STEPHEN. I mar'le whether it be a Toledo or no.

BOBADILL. A most perfect Toledo, I assure you, sir.

STEPHEN. I have a countryman of his here.

MATTHEW. 'Pray you, let's see, sir; yes, faith, it is.

BOBADILL. This a Toledo! Pish!

---

[65] Staff used to hold the lighted match when firing a cannon.
[66] The swords of Bevis, Arthur, and Orlando.

STEPHEN. Why do you pish, captain?

BOBADILL. A Fleming, by Heaven! I'll buy them for a guilder[67] apiece, an I would have a thousand of them.

E. KNOWELL. How say you, cousin? I told you thus much.

WELLBRED. Where bought you it, Master Stephen?

STEPHEN. Of a scurvy rogue soldier. A hundred of lice go with him! he swore it was a Toledo.

BOBADILL. A poor provant[68] rapier, no better.

E. KNOWELL. Nay, the longer you look on't, the worse. Put it up, put it up.

STEPHEN. Well, I will put it up! But by—I have forgot the captain's oath, I thought to have sworn by it—an e'er I meet him——

WELLBRED. O, it is past help now, sir; you must have patience.

STEPHEN. Whoreson, coney-catching* rascal! I could   cheating eat the very hilts for anger.

E. KNOWELL. A sign of good digestion! you have an ostrich stomach,[69] cousin.

STEPHEN. A stomach? Would I had him here, you should see an I had a stomach.*   the courage

WELLBRED. It's better as 'tis.—Come, gentlemen, shall we go?

(*Enter* BRAINWORM *still disguised.*)

E. KNOWELL. A miracle, cousin; look here, look here!

STEPHEN. Oh—od's lid! By your leave, do you know me, sir?

BRAINWORM. Ay, sir, I know you by sight.

STEPHEN. You sold me a rapier did you not?

BRAINWORM. Yes, marry did I, sir.

STEPHEN. You said it was a Toledo, ha?

BRAINWORM. True, I did so.

STEPHEN. But it is none.

BRAINWORM. No, sir, I confess it; it is none.

STEPHEN. Do you confess it? Gentlemen, bear witness; he

---

[67] A Dutch coin worth about twenty-five cents.

[68] A government issued rapier, and therefore supposedly inferior.

[69] The ostrich is noted for its ability to swallow and digest metal.

has confessed it. Od's will, an you had not confessed it——

E. KNOWELL. Oh, cousin, forbear, forbear!

STEPHEN. Nay, I have done, cousin.

WELLBRED. Why, you have done like a gentleman; he has confessed it. What would you more?

STEPHEN. Yet, by his leave, he is a rascal, under his favour, do you see.

E. KNOWELL (*aside to* WELLBRED). Ay, "by his leave," he is and "under favour"; a pretty piece of civility! Sirrah, how dost thou like him?

WELLBRED. Oh it's a most precious fool; make much on him. I can compare him to nothing more happily than a drum, for every one may play upon him.

E. KNOWELL. No, no, a child's whistle were far the fitter.

BRAINWORM. Sir, shall I entreat a word with you?

(*They move aside.*)

E. KNOWELL. With me, sir? You have not another Toledo to sell, ha' you?

BRAINWORM. You are conceited,* sir. Your name is   witty Master Knowell, as I take it?

E. KNOWELL. You are i' the right; you mean not to proceed in the catechism, do you?

BRAINWORM. No sir: I am none of that coat.* that is, clergyman

E. KNOWELL. Of as bare a coat, though. Well, say sir.

BRAINWORM. Faith, sir, I am but servant to the drum extraordinary,[70] and indeed, this smoky varnish being washed off, and three or four patches removed, I appear—your worship's in reversion, after the decease of your good father, Brainworm.

E. KNOWELL. Brainworm! 'Slight, what breath of a conjurer hath blown thee hither in this shape?

BRAINWORM. The breath o' your letter, sir, this morning; the same that blew you to the Windmill, and your father after you.

E. KNOWELL. My father?

BRAINWORM. Nay, never start; 'tis true; he has followed you over the fields by the foot, as you would do a hare i' the snow.

E. KNOWELL. Sirrah Wellbred, what shall we do, sirrah? My father is come over after me.

WELLBRED. Thy father! Where is he?

BRAINWORM. At Justice Clement's house, in Coleman-street, where he but stays my return; and then——

[70] That is, I am not a regular soldier.

WELLBRED. Who's this? Brainworm!

BRAINWORM. The same, sir.

WELLBRED. Why how, in the name of wit, com'st thou transmuted thus?

BRAINWORM. Faith, a device,* a device. Nay, for the trick love of reason, gentlemen, and avoiding the danger, stand not here; withdraw, and I'll tell you all.

WELLBRED. But, art thou sure, he will stay thy return?

BRAINWORM. Do I live, sir? What a question is that!

WELLBRED. We'll prorogue his expectation, then, a little. Brainworm, thou shalt go with us.—— Come on, gentlemen.—— Nay, I pray thee, sweet Ned, droop not; 'heart, an our wits be so wretchedly dull that one old plodding brain can outstrip us all, would we were e'en pressed* to impressed make porters of, and serve out the remnant of our days in Thames Street, or at Custom-house Quay, in a civil war against the carmen!* carters

BRAINWORM. Amen, amen, amen, say I.

(*Exeunt.*)

Scene 2

(KITELY'S *warehouse. Enter* KITELY *and* CASH.)

KITELY. What says he, Thomas? Did you speak with him?

CASH. He will expect you, sir, within this half-hour.

KITELY. Has he the money ready, can you tell?

CASH. Yes, sir, the money was brought in last night.

KITELY. O, that is well; fetch me my cloak, my cloak!—

(*Exit* CASH.)

Stay, let me see; an hour to go and come;
Ay, that will be the least; and then 'twill be
An hour before I can despatch with him,
Or very near; well, I will say two hours.
Two hours? ha! things never dreamt of yet,
May be contrived, ay, and effected too,
In two hours' absence; well I will not go.
Two hours! No, fleering Opportunity,
I will not give your subtilty that scope.
Who will not judge him worthy to be robbed
That sets his doors wide open to a thief,
And shows the felon where his treasure lies?
Again, what earthly spirit but will attempt
To taste the fruit of beauty's golden tree,

When leaden sleep seals up the dragon's eyes?
I will not go. Business, "go by" for once.
No, beauty, no; you are of too good caract,*   caret, value
To be left so, without a guard, or open!
Your lustre too, 'll inflame at any distance,
Draw courtship to you, as a jet doth straws;
Put motion in a stone, strike fire from ice,
Nay, make a porter leap you with his burden.
You must be then kept up, close, and well watched,
For, give you opportunity, no quick-sand
Devours or swallows swifter! He that lends
His wife—if she be fair—or* time or place,   either
Compels her to be false. I will not go.
The dangers are too many.—And then the dressing
Is a most main attractive!* Our great heads   great attraction
Within the city never were in safety
Since our wives wore these little caps.[71] I'll change 'hem;
I'll change 'hem straight in mine; mine shall no more
Wear three-piled* acorns to make my horns ache.   that is,
                                                      best quality
Nor will I go. I am resolved for that.

   (*Re-enter* CASH *with cloak.*)

Carry in my cloak again.—Yet stay.—Yet do, too;
I will defer going, on all occasions.
   CASH. Sir, Snare, your scrivener, will be there with th'
bonds.
   KITELY. That's true! Fool on me! I had clean forgot it;
I must go. What's a-clock?
   CASH.   Exchange time,* sir.   10 A.M.
   KITELY. 'Heart, then will Wellbred presently be here, too,
With one or other of his loose consorts.
I am a knave if I know what to say,
What course to take, or which way to resolve.
My brain, methinks, is like an hour-glass,
Wherein my imaginations run like sands,
Filling up time; but then are turned and turned,
So that I know not what to stay upon,
And less, to put in act.—It shall be so.
Nay, I dare build upon his secrecy,
He knows not to deceive me.—Thomas!

   [71] Fashionable velvet caps.

CASH.   Sir.

KITELY. Yet now I have bethought me too, I will not.—
Thomas, is Cob within?

CASH.   I think he be, sir.

KITELY (*aside*). But he'll prate too; there is no speech
    of him.

No, there were no man o' the earth to* Thomas,   comparable to
If I durst trust him; there is all the doubt.
But, should he have a chink in him, I were gone,
Lost i' my fame for ever, talk for th' Exchange!
The manner he hath stood with till this present
Doth promise no such change! What should I fear then?
Well, come what will, I'll tempt my fortune once.
Thomas—you may deceive me, but I hope
Your love to me is more——

CASH.   Sir, if a servant's
Duty, with faith, may be called love, you are
More than in hope; you are possessed of it.

KITELY. I thank you, heartily, Thomas; gi' me your hand.
With all my heart, good Thomas. I have, Thomas,
A secret to impart unto you——but,
When once you have it, I must seal your lips up:——
So far I tell you, Thomas.

CASH.   Sir, for that——

KITELY. Nay, hear me out. Think I esteem you, Thomas,
When I will let you in, thus, to my private.*   private thoughts
It is a thing sits nearer to my crest*   head
Than thou art 'ware of, Thomas. If thou should'st
Reveal it, but——

CASH.   How! I reveal it?

KITELY.   Nay,
I do not think thou would'st; but if thou should'st,
'Twere a great weakness.

CASH.   A great treachery;
Give it no other name.

KITELY.   Thou wilt not do't, then?

CASH. Sir, if I do, mankind disclaim me ever!

KITELY (*aside*). He will not swear; he has some reservation,
Some concealed purpose, and close* meaning, sure;   secret
Else, being urged so much, how should he choose
But lend an oath to all this protestation?
He's no precisian,* that I am certain of,   Puritan

Nor rigid Roman Catholic. He'll play
At fayles and tick-tack;[72] I have heard him swear.
What should I think of it? Urge him again,
And by some other way? I will do so.——
Well, Thomas, thou hast sworn not to disclose—
Yes, you did swear?
    CASH.   Not yet, sir, but I will.
Please you——
    KITELY.   No, Thomas, I dare take thy word;
But, if thou wilt swear, do as thou think'st good;
I am resolved without it. At thy pleasure.
    CASH. By my soul's safety then, sir, I protest
My tongue shall ne'er take knowledge of a word
Delivered me in nature of your trust.
    KITELY.   It's too much; these ceremonies need
        not.*   are not necessary
I know thy faith to be as firm as rock.
Thomas, come hither, near; we cannot be
Too private in this business. So it is,——
(*Aside.*) Now he has sworn, I dare the safelier venture.—
I have of late, by divers observations—
(*Aside.*) But, whether his oath can bind him, yea or no,
Being not taken lawfully?[73] Ha?—Say you?—
(*Aside.*) I will ask counsel ere I do proceed——
Thomas, it will be now too long to stay;
I'll spy some fitter time soon, or tomorrow.
    CASH. Sir, at your pleasure.
    KITELY.   I will think.—And, Thomas,
I pray you search che books 'gainst my return
For the receipts 'twixt me and Traps.
    CASH.   I will, sir.
    KITELY. And hear you, if your mistress's brother, Wellbred,
Chance to bring hither any gentlemen
Ere I come back, let one straight bring me word.
    CASH. Very well, sir.
    KITELY.   To the Exchange, do you hear?
Or here in Coleman Street, to Justice Clement's.
Forget it not, nor be not out of the way.
    CASH. I will not, sir.
    KITELY.   I pray you have a care on't.

---

[72] Varieties of backgammon.

[73] Before a magistrate.

Or, whether he come or no, if any other,
Stranger or else; fail not to send me word.
    CASH. I shall not, sir.
    KITELY.   Be't your special business
Now to remember it.
    CASH.   Sir, I warrant you.
    KITELY. But, Thomas, this is not the secret, Thomas,
I told you of.
    CASH.   No, sir; I do suppose it.
    KITELY. Believe me, it is not.
    CASH.   Sir, I do believe you.
    KITELY. By Heaven it is not; that's enough. But, Thomas,
I would not you should utter it, do you see,
To any creature living, yet, I care not.
Well, I must hence. Thomas, conceive thus much;
It was a trial of you when I meant
So deep a secret to you; I mean not this,
But that I have to tell you; this is nothing, this.
But, Thomas, keep this from my wife, I charge you,
Locked up in silence, midnight, buried here.—
    (*Touches his temple.*)
(*Aside.*) No greater hell than to be slave to fear.
                             (*Exit.*)
    CASH. "Locked up in silence, midnight, buried here!"
Whence should this flood of passion, trow, take head? Ha?
Best dream no longer of this running humour,
For fear I sink! The violence of the stream
Already hath transported me so far
That I can feel no ground at all! but soft—
Oh, 'tis our water-bearer; somewhat has crossed him now.

    (*Enter* COB.)

    COB. Fasting days! What tell you me of fasting days? 'Slid,
would they were all on a light fire* for me! They say the   ablaze
whole world shall be consumed with fire one day, but would
I had these Ember-weeks and villanous Fridays[74] burnt in
the mean time, and then——
    CASH. Why, how now, Cob? What moves thee to this choler,
ha?
    COB. Collar, Master Thomas! I scorn your collar; I, sir,

    [74] An allusion to the statutes against eating meat on these and
other special days.

I am none o' your cart-horse, though I carry and draw water. An you offer to ride me, with your collar or halter either, I may hap show you a jade's trick, sir.

CASH. O, you'll slip your head out of the collar? Why, goodman Cob, you mistake me.

COB. Nay, I have my rheum, and I can be angry as well as another, sir.

CASH. Thy rheum, Cob? Thy humour, thy humour—thou mistak'st.[75]

COB. Humour! mack,* I think it be so indeed, what is   mass that humour? Some rare thing, I warrant.

CASH. Marry, I'll tell thee, Cob. It is a gentleman-like monster, bred in the special gallantry of our time by affectation and fed by folly.

COB. How! Must it be fed?

CASH. Oh ay, humour is nothing if it be not fed. Did'st thou never hear that? It's a common phrase, "Feed my humour."

COB. I'll none on it; humour, avaunt! I know you not, be gone! Let who will make hungry meals for your monstership, it shall not be I. Feed you, quoth he! 'Slid, I ha' much ado to feed myself, especially on these lean rascally days, too; an't had been any other day but a fasting day—a plague on them all for me—by this light, one might have done the commonwealth good sevice, and have drowned them all i' the flood two or three hundred thousand years ago. O, I do stomach* them hugely. I have a maw* now, and   resent/appetite 'twere for Sir Bevis his horse,[76] against 'hem.

CASH. I pray thee, good Cob, what makes thee so out of love with fasting days?

COB. Marry, that which will make any man out of love with 'hem, I think; their bad conditions, as you will needs know. First they are of a Flemish breed, I am sure on't, for they raven up* more butter than all the days of the   devour week beside; next, they stink of fish and leek-porridge miserably; thirdly, they'll keep a man devoutly hungry all day and at night send him supperless to bed.

CASH. Indeed, these are faults, Cob.

COB. Nay, an this were all, 'twere something, but they are the only known enemies to my generation. A fasting day no

---

[75] *Rheum* was no longer the fashionable word for whim.

[76] "*I. e.,* comparable to that of Sir Bevis's horse" (H. Spencer).

sooner comes, but my lineage goes to wrack; poor cobs! they smoke for it, they are made martyrs o' the gridiron, they melt in passion; and your maids too know this, and yet would have me turn Hannibal,* and eat my own fish and   that is, cannibal blood. My princely coz, (*Pulls out a red herring.*) fear nothing: I have not the heart to devour you and I might be made as rich as King Cophetua.[77] Oh, that I had room for my tears, I could weep salt-water enough now to preserve the lives of ten thousand of my kin. But I may curse none but these filthy almanacs; for an't were not for them, these days of persecution would ne'er be known. I'll be hanged an some fishmonger's son do not make of* 'hem, and puts in more make fasting days than he should do, because he would utter*   sell his father's dried stock-fish and stinking conger.

CASH. 'Slight peace! Thou'lt be beaten like a stock-fish[78] else; here's Master Matthew. (*Aside.*) Now must I look out for a messenger to my master.   (*Exeunt.*)

(*Enter* WELLBRED, E. KNOWELL, BRAINWORM, MATTHEW, BOBADILL, *and* STEPHEN.)

WELLBRED. Beshrew me, but it was an absolute good jest, and exceedingly well carried!

E. KNOWELL. Ay, and our ignorance maintained it as well, did it not?

WELLBRED. Yes faith; but was't possible thou shouldst not know him? I forgive Master Stephen, for he is stupidity itself.

E. KNOWELL. 'Fore God, not I, an I might have been joined patten[79] with one of the Seven Wise Masters for knowing him. He had so writhen* himself into the habit of   twisted one of your poor infantry, your decayed, ruinous worm-eaten gentlemen of the round;* such as have vowed to   military patrol sit on* the skirts* of the city, let your provost and stay on/outskirts his half-dozen of halberdiers do what they can; and have translated begging out of the old hackney pace to a fine easy amble, and made it run as smooth off the tongue as a shove-groat shilling.[80] Into the likeness of one of these reformados[81] had

[77] In balladry, a rich African king who married a beggar maid.
[78] Dried codfish that became so hard from salting that it had to be beaten before cooking.
[79] "Sharing by letters patent in a privilege or office" (Simpson).
[80] A smooth shilling used to play shovel-board.
[81] Officers of disbanded companies.

he moulded himself so perfectly, observing every trick of their
action, as, varying the accent, swearing with an emphasis,
indeed, all, with so special and exquisite a grace that hadst
thou seen him, thou wouldst have sworn he might have been
sergeant-major,* if not lieutenant-colonel to the   that is, major
regiment.

WELLBRED. Why, Brainworm, who would have thought
thou hadst been such an artificer?

E. KNOWELL. An artificer? An architect! Except a man had
studied begging all his life time, and been a weaver of language from his infancy, for the clothing of it, I never saw
his rival.

WELLBRED. Where got'st thou this coat, I mar'le?

BRAINWORM. Of a Hounsditch man, sir, one of the devil's
near kinsmen, a broker.*   pawnbroker

WELLBRED. That cannot be, if the proverb hold, for "A
crafty knave needs no broker."

BRAINWORM. True, sir; but I did "need a broker," ergo—

WELLBRED. Well put off: "no crafty knave," you'll say.

E. KNOWELL. Tut, he has more of these shifts.

BRAINWORM. And yet, where I have one the broker has
ten,[82] sir.

(*Re-enter* CASH.)

CASH. Francis! Martin! Ne'er a one to be found, now? What
a spite's this!

WELLBRED. How now, Thomas? Is my brother Kitely
within?

CASH. No sir, my master went forth e'en now; but Master
Downright is within.—Cob! what, Cob! Is he gone too?

WELLBRED. Whither went your master? Thomas, canst thou
tell?

CASH. I know not; to Justice Clement's, I think, sir—Cob!
                                                    (*Exit.*)

E. KNOWELL. Justice Clement! What's he?

WELLBRED. Why, dost thou not know him? He is a city-
magistrate, a justice here, an excellent good lawyer, and a
great scholar; but the only mad, merry old fellow in Europe.
I showed him you the other day.

E. KNOWELL. Oh, is that he? I remember him now. Good
faith, and he has a very strange presence, methinks; it shows
as if he stood out of the rank from other men. I have heard

___
[82] Punning on *shifts,* meaning tricks and suits of clothes.

many of his jests i' the University. They say he will commit a
man for taking the wall of his horse.[83]

WELLBRED. Ay, or wearing his cloak of one shoulder, or
serving of God; any thing, indeed, if it come in the way of
his humour.

(CASH *comes in and out, calling.*)

CASH. Gasper!—Martin!—Cob! 'Heart, where should they
be, trow?

BOBADILL. Master Kitely's man, pray thee vouchsafe us the
lighting of this match.

CASH (*aside*). Fire on your match! No time but now to
"vouchsafe"?—Francis—Cob!

(*Exit.*)

BOBADILL. Body o' me! here's the remainder of seven
pound since yesterday was seven-night. 'Tis your right Trinidado!* Did you never take any, Master Stephen?   that is, the
best tobacco

STEPHEN. No truly, sir; but I'll learn to take it now, since
you commend it so.

BOBADILL. Sir, believe me, upon my relation, for what I tell
you, the world shall not reprove.* I have been in the   disprove
Indies, where this herb grows, where neither myself, nor a
dozen gentlemen more, of my knowledge, have received the
taste of any other nutriment in the world for the space of one
and twenty weeks but the fume of this simple* only;   herb
therefore, it cannot be but 'tis most divine! Further, take it in
the nature, in the true kind, so, it makes an antidote that,
had you taken the most deadly poisonous plant in all Italy,
it should expel it and clarify you with as much ease as I
speak. And for your green wound, your balsamum and your
St. John's wort are all mere gulleries* and trash to it,   frauds
especially your Trinidado. Your Nicotian[84] is good too. I
could say what I know of the virtue of it for the expulsion
of rheums, raw humours, crudities, obstructions, with a thousand of this kind; but I profess myself no quacksalver. Only
thus much, by Hercules, I do hold it, and will affirm it, before
any prince in Europe to be the most sovereign, and precious
weed that ever the earth tendered to the use of man.

---

[83] An allusion to the custom of yielding the position closest to
the wall to one's superior in rank when walking on the London
streets.

[84] Tobacco named after Jacques Nicot, who introduced it into
France in 1560.

E. KNOWELL. This speech would ha' done decently in a tobacco-trader's mouth.

(Re-enter CASH *wnth* COB.)

CASH. At Justice Clement's he is, in the middle of Coleman Street.

COB. Oh, oh!

BOBADILL. Where's the match I gave thee, Master Kitely's man?

CASH *(aside)*. Would this match, and he, and pipe, and all, were at Sancto Domingo! I had forgot it.

(Exit.)

COB. By God's me,* I mar'le what pleasure or felic-   (an oath)
ity they have in taking this roguish tobacco! It's good for nothing but to choke a man and fill him full of smoke and embers. There were four died out of one house last week with taking of it, and two more the bell went for, yesternight; one of them, they say, will ne'er scape it. He voided a bushel of soot yesterday, upward and downward. By the stocks, an there were no wiser men than I, I'ld have it present whipping, man or woman, that should but deal with a tobacco pipe. Why, it will stifle them all in the end, as many as use it; it's little better than ratsbane or rosaker.[85]

(BOBADILL cudgels him.)

ALL. Oh, good captain, hold, hold!

BOBADILL. You base cullion,* you!   rascal

(Re-enter CASH.)

CASH. Sir, here's your match.——Come, thou must needs be talking too; thou'rt well enough served.

COB. Nay, he will not meddle with his match, I warrant you. Well, it shall be a dear beating, an I live.

BOBADILL. Do you prate? Do you murmur?

E. KNOWELL. Nay, good captain, will you regard the humour of a fool?——Away, knave.

WELLBRED. Thomas, get him away.

(Exit CASH *with* COB.)

BOBADILL. A whoreson filthy slave, a dung-worm, an excrement! Body o' Cæsar, but that I scorn to let forth so mean a spirit, I'ld ha' stabbed him to the earth.

[85] Preparations of arsenic.

WELLBRED. Marry, the law forbid, sir.

BOBADILL. By Pharaoh's foot, I would have done it.

STEPHEN (*aside*). Oh, he swears most admirably! "By Pharaoh's foot!"—"Body o' Cæsar!" I shall never do it, sure. "Upon mine honour, and by St. George!"—No, I ha' not the right grace.

MATTHEW. Master Stephen, will you any? By this air, the most divine tobacco that ever I drunk.*   smoked

STEPHEN. None, I thank you, sir. (*Aside.*) O, this gentleman does it rarely too; but nothing like the other. (*Practising to the post.*) "By this air!"—"As I am a gentleman!" "By——"

BRAINWORM. Master, glance, glance!—Master Wellbred!

                            (*Exeunt* BOBADILL *and* MATTHEW.)

STEPHEN. "As I have somewhat to be saved, I protest—"

WELLBRED (*aside*). You are a fool; it needs no affidavit.

E. KNOWELL. Cousin, will you any tobacco?

STEPHEN. I, sir! Upon my reputation——

E. KNOWELL. How now, cousin!

STEPHEN. I protest, as I am a gentleman, but no soldier, indeed——

WELLBRED. No, Master Stephen? As I remember, your name is entered in the artillery-garden.[86]

STEPHEN. Ay, sir, that's true. Cousin, may I swear, "as I am a soldier" by that?

E. KNOWELL. O yes, that you may; it's all you have for your money.

STEPHEN. Then, as I am a gentleman, and a soldier, it is "divine tobacco!"

WELLBRED. But soft, where's Master Matthew? Gone?

BRAINWORM. No, sir, they went in here.

WELLBRED. O, let's follow them. Master Matthew is gone to salute his mistress in verse. We shall have the happiness to hear some of his poetry now. He never comes unfurnished. —Brainworm!

STEPHEN. Brainworm? Where? Is this Brainworm?

E. KNOWELL. Ay, cousin; no words of it, upon your gentility.

STEPHEN. Not I, a body o' me! By this air! St. George! And the foot of Pharaoh!

WELLBRED. Rare! Your cousin's discourse is simply drawn out with oaths.

      [86] Training ground for the Honourable Artillery Company, located in Tassell Close near Bishopsgate.

E. KNOWELL. 'Tis larded with 'hem; a kind of French dressing,[87] if you love it.

(*Exeunt.*)

Scene 3

(*A room in* Justice CLEMENT'S *house. Enter* KITELY *and* COB.)

KITELY. Ha! how many are there, say'st thou?

COB. Marry, sir, your brother, Master Wellbred——

KITELY. Tut, beside him. What strangers are there, man?

COB. Strangers? Let me see, one, two;—mass, I know not well, there are so many.

KITELY. How! so many?

COB. Ay, there's some five or six of them, at the most.

KITELY (*aside*). A swarm, a swarm!
Spite of the devil, how they sting my head
With forkèd stings, thus wide and large!——But, Cob,
How long hast thou been coming hither, Cob?

COB. A little while, sir.

KITELY.   Didst thou come running?

COB.   No, sir,

KITELY (*aside*). Nay, then I am familiar with thy haste!
Bane to my fortunes; what meant I to marry?
I, that before was ranked in such content,
My mind at rest too in so soft a peace,
Being free master of mine own free thoughts,
And now become a slave? What? Never sigh,
Be of good cheer, man; for thou art a cuckold;
'Tis done, 'tis done! Nay, when such flowing store,
Plenty itself, falls in my wife's lap,
The cornucopiæ[88] will be mine, I know.——But, Cob,
What entertainment had they? I am sure
My sister and my wife would bid them welcome. Ha?

COB. Like enough, sir; yet I heard not a word of it.

KITELY. No. (*Aside.*) Their lips were sealed with kisses,
and the voice—
Drowned in a flood of joy at their arrival—
Had lost her motion, state, and faculty.——

---

[87] The French were noted for their swearing.

[88] Horns of plenty, with a play on horns of the cuckold.

Cob, which of them was't that first kissed my wife?
My sister, I should say; my wife, alas!
I fear not her. Ha? Who was it, say'st thou?
COB. By my troth, sir, will you have the troth of it?
KITELY. Oh ay, good Cob, I pray thee, heartily.
COB. Then I am a vagabond, and fitter for Bridewell*   that is, the workhouse
than your worship's company, if I saw any body to be kissed,
unless they would have kissed the post in the middle of the
warehouse;* for there I left them all at their tobacco,   shop
with a pox!
KITELY. How? Were they not gone in, then, ere thou cam'st?
COB. O no, sir.
KITELY. Spite of the devil! What do I stay here then? Cob,
follow me.

                                (*Exit.*)

COB. Nay, soft and fair; I have eggs on the spit,* I   I'm busy
cannot go yet, sir. Now am I, for some five and fifty reasons,
hammering, hammering revenge. Oh, for three or four gallons
of vinegar to sharpen my wits! Revenge, vinegar revenge, vinegar and mustard revenge! Nay, and he had not lien* in   lain
my house, 'twould never have grieved me, but being my guest,
one, that I'll be sworn, my wife has lent him her smock off her
back while his one shirt has been at washing; pawned her neck-
kerchers for clean bands* for him! sold almost all my   collars
platters to buy him tobacco; and he to turn monster of ingratitude and strike his lawful host! Well, I hope to raise up an
host of fury for't. Here comes Justice Clement.

(*Enter* CLEMENT, KNOWELL, *and* FORMAL.)

CLEMENT. What's Master Kitely gone? Roger?
FORMAL. Ay, sir.
CLEMENT. 'Heart of me! What made him leave us so
abruptly?—How now, sirrah? What make* you here?   do
What would you have, ha?
COB. An't please your worship, I am a poor neighbour of
your worship's——
CLEMENT. A poor neighbour of mine! Why, speak, poor
neighbour.
COB. I dwell, sir, at the sign of the Water-tankard, hard by
the Green Lattice.* I have paid scot and lot[89] there   a tavern
any time this eighteen years.

[89] Parish assessments.

CLEMENT. To the Green Lattice?

COB. No, sir, to the parish. Marry, I have seldom scaped scot-free at the Lattice.

CLEMENT. O, well! what business has my poor neighbour with me?

COB. An't like your worship, I am come to crave the peace of your worship.[90]

CLEMENT. Of me, knave? Peace of me, knave! Did I ever hurt thee? Or threaten thee? Or wrong thee, ha?

COB. No, sir, but your worship's warrant for one that has wronged me, sir; his arms are at too much liberty; I would fain have them bound to a treaty of peace, an my credit could compass it with your worship.

CLEMENT. Thou goest far enough about for't, I'm sure.

KNOWELL. Why, dost thou go in danger of thy life for him, friend?

COB. No, sir; but I go in danger of my death every hour by his means; an I die within a twelve-month and a day,[91] I may swear, by the law of the land, that he killed me.

CLEMENT. How? How, knave? Swear he killed thee? And by the law? What pretence? What colour* hast thou for   reason that?

COB. Marry, an't please your worship, both black and blue; colour enough, I warrant you. I have it here, to show your worship.

(*Shows his arm.*)

CLEMENT. What is he that gave you this, sirrah?

COB. A gentleman and a soldier, he says he is, o' the city here.

CLEMENT. A soldier o' the city! What call you him?

COB. Captain Bobadill.

CLEMENT. Bobadill! And why did he bob* and beat   strike you, sirrah? How began the quarrel betwixt you, ha? Speak truly, knave, I advise you.

COB. Marry, indeed, an't please your worship, only because I spake against their vagrant tobacco as I came by 'hem when they were taking on't; for nothing else.

CLEMENT. Ha! you speak against tobacco? Formal, his name.

---

[90] To petition for a surety of the peace from one who has injured a person or threatened injury.

[91] The legal time limit for determining the cause of death from bodily injury.

FORMAL. What's your name, sirrah?

COB. Oliver, sir, Oliver Cob, sir.

CLEMENT. Tell Oliver Cob he shall go to the jail, Formal.

FORMAL. Oliver Cob, my master, Justice Clement says you shall go to the jail.

COB. O, I beseech your worship, for God's sake, dear Master Justice!

CLEMENT. Nay God's precious! And such drunkards and tankards as you are, come to dispute of tobacco once, I have done. Away with him!

COB. O, good Master Justice! (*To* KNOWELL.) Sweet old gentleman!

KNOWELL. Sweet Oliver, would I could do thee any good!— Justice Clement, let me entreat you, sir.

CLEMENT. What? A thread-bare rascal! A beggar! A slave that never drunk out of better than pisspot metal* in   pewter his life! And he to deprave* and abuse the virtue of   disparage an herb so generally received in the courts of princes, the chambers of nobles, the bowers of sweet ladies, the cabins* of soldiers!—Roger, away with him! By God's   tents precious—(*To* COB.)—I say, go to.

COB. Dear Master Justice, let me be beaten again; I have deserved it; but not the prison, I beseech you.

KNOWELL. Alas, poor Oliver!

CLEMENT. Roger, make him a warrant.—(*Aside.*) He shall not go, I but fear* the knave.   frighten

FORMAL. Do not stink, sweet Oliver; you shall not go. My master will give you a warrant.

COB. O, the Lord maintain his worship, his worthy worship!

CLEMENT. Away, dispatch him.

                (*Exeunt* FORMAL *with* COB.)

How now, Master Knowell, in dumps, in dumps! Come, this becomes not.

KNOWELL. Sir, would I could not feel my cares—

CLEMENT. Your cares are nothing; they are like my cap, soon put on, and as soon put off. What! Your son is old enough to govern himself. Let him run his course; it's the only way to make him a staid man. If he were an unthrift, a ruffian, a drunkard, or a licentious liver, then you had reason; you had reason to take care: but being none of these, mirth's my witness, an I had twice so many cares as you have, I'd drown them all in a cup of sack. Come, come, let's try it. I muse* your parcel* of a soldier returns not all this while.   wonder/ piece

                                    (*Exeunt.*)

ACT IV

Scene 1

(*A room in* KITELY'S *house. Enter* DOWNRIGHT *and* DAME KITELY.)

DOWNRIGHT. Well, sister, I tell you true; and you'll find it so in the end.

DAME KITELY. Alas, my brother, what would you have me to do? I cannot help it; you see my brother brings 'hem in here; they are his friends.

DOWNRIGHT. His friends? His fiends. 'Slud! They do nothing but haunt him up and down like a sort* of unlucky   company sprites, and tempt him to all manner of villainy that can be thought of. Well, by this light, a little thing would make me play the devil with some of 'hem. And 'twere not more for your husband's sake than anything else, I'd make the house too hot for the best on 'hem. They should say and swear hell were broken loose, ere they went hence. But, by God's will, 'tis nobody's fault but yours; for an you had done as you might have done, they should have been perboiled*   boiled thoroughly and baked too, every mother's son, ere they should ha' come in, e'er a one of 'hem.

DAME KITELY. God's my life! Did you ever hear the like? What a strange man is this! Could I keep out all them, think you? I should put myself against half a dozen men, should I? Good faiths, you'ld mad the patient'st body in the world, to hear you talk so, without any sense or reason!

(*Enter* Mistress BRIDGET, Master MATTHEW, *and* BOBADILL *followed, at a little distance, by* WELLBRED, E. KNOWELL, STEPHEN, *and* BRAINWORM.)

BRIDGET. Servant,* in troth, you are too prodigal   lover
Of your wit's treasure, thus to pour it forth
Upon so mean a subject as my worth!

MATTHEW. You say well, mistress; and I mean as well.

DOWNRIGHT (*aside*). Hoy-day, here is stuff!

WELLBRED. O, now stand close;* pray Heaven, she   aside can get him to read! He should do it of his own natural impudency.

BRIDGET. Servant, what is this same, I pray you?

MATTHEW. Marry, an elegy, an elegy, an odd toy——

DOWNRIGHT (*aside*). "To mock an ape withal!"[92] O, I could sew up his mouth, now.

DAME KITELY. Sister, I pray you let's hear it.

DOWNRIGHT (*aside*). Are you rhyme-given too?

MATTHEW. Mistress, I'll read it, if you please.

BRIDGET. Pray you do, servant.

DOWNRIGHT (*aside*). O, here's no foppery! Death! I can endure the stocks better.

(Exit.)

E. KNOWELL. What ails thy brother? Can he not hold his water at reading of a ballad?

WELLBRED. O, no; a rhyme to him is worse than cheese or a bag-pipe. But mark; you lose the protestation.

MATTHEW. Faith, I did it in a humour; I know not how it is; but—please you come near, sir. This gentleman has judgment, he knows how to censure of a——pray you, sir, you can judge.

STEPHEN. Not I, sir; upon my reputation, and by the foot of Pharaoh.

WELLBRED. O, chide your cousin for swearing.

E. KNOWELL. Not I, so long as he does not forswear himself.

BOBADILL. Master Matthew, you abuse the expectation of your dear mistress and her fair sister. Fie! While you live, avoid this prolixity.

MATTHEW. I shall, sir; well, *incipere dulce.*[93]

E. KNOWELL. How! *Insipere dulce?* "A sweet thing to be a fool," indeed!

WELLBRED. What, do you take *insipere* in that sense?

E. KNOWELL. You do not? You? This was your villainy to gull him with a *mot.** word

WELLBRED. O, the benchers'* phrase: *"pauca verba,* pauca verba!"* tavern loafers / few words

MATTHEW (*reads*). "Rare creature, let me speak without offence,

Would God my rude words had the influence

To rule thy thoughts, as thy fair looks do mine,

Then shouldst thou be his prisoner, who is thine."

[92] Dupe a simpleton with.

[93] It is sweet to begin.

E. KNOWELL (*aside*). This is in "Hero and Leander."[94]

WELLBRED (*aside*). O, ay! Peace, we shall have more of this.

MATTHEW. "Be not unkind and fair: misshapen stuff
Is of behaviour boisterous and rough."

WELLBRED. How like you that, sir?

(STEPHEN *nods affirmatively*.)

E. KNOWELL. 'Slight, he shakes his head like a bottle, to feel an there be any brain in it.

MATTHEW. But observe "the catastrophe" now:
"And I in duty will exceed all other,
As you in beauty do excel Love's mother."

E. KNOWELL (*aside*). Well, I'll have him free of the wit-brokers,[95] for he utters nothing but stolen remnants.

WELLBRED (*aside*.) O, forgive it him.

E. KNOWELL (*aside*). A filching rogue; hang him! And from the dead! It's worse than sacrilege.

(WELLBRED, E. KNOWELL, *and* STEPHEN *come forward*.)

WELLBRED. Sister, what ha' you here? Verses? 'Pray you, let's see. Who made these verses? They are excellent good.

MATTHEW. O, Master Wellbred, 'tis your disposition to say so, sir. They were good i' the morning; I made 'hem *extempore* this morning.

WELLBRED. How? *Extempore?*

MATTHEW. Ay, would I might be hanged else; ask Captain Bobadill. He saw me write them, at the——pox on it!—the Star, yonder.

BRAINWORM (*aside*). Can he find in his heart to curse the stars so?

E. KNOWELL (*aside*). Faith, his are even with him; they ha' curst him enough already.

STEPHEN. Cousin, how do you like this gentleman's verse?

E. KNOWELL. O, admirable! the best that ever I heard, coz.

STEPHEN. Body o' Cæsar, they are admirable!
The best that ever I heard, as I'm a soldier!

(*Re-enter* DOWNRIGHT.)

DOWNRIGHT (*aside*). I am vext; I can hold ne'er a bone of me still! 'Heart, I think they mean to build and breed here.

---

[94] By Christopher Marlowe. The lines are slightly misquoted.

[95] That is, made a member of. The phrase was used in reference to admittance to a City company.

WELLBRED. Sister, you have a simple servant here, that crowns your beauty with such encomiums, and devices. You may see what it is to be the mistress of a wit that can make your perfections so transparent that every blear eye may look through them, and see him drowned, over head and ears, in the deep well of desire. Sister Kitely, I marvel you get you not a servant* that can rhyme, and do tricks, too.   lover

DOWNRIGHT (*aside*). Oh monster! Impudence itself! Tricks.[96]

DAME KITELY. Tricks, brother? What tricks?

BRIDGET. Nay, speak, I pray you, what tricks?

DAME KITELY. Ay, never spare any body here; but say, what tricks.

BRIDGET. Passion of my heart! Do tricks!

WELLBRED. 'Slight, here's a trick vied and revied![97] Why, you monkeys, you. What a caterwauling do you keep! Has he not given you rhymes, and verses, and tricks?

DOWNRIGHT (*aside*). O, the fiend!

WELLBRED. Nay, you lamp of virginity, that take it in snuff* so, come, and cherish this tame poetical fury   take offense at in your servant; you'll be begged else shortly for a conceal-ment.[98] Go to, reward his muse. You cannot give him less than a shilling, in conscience, for the book he had it out of, cost him a teston* at least. How now, gallants? Master Mat-   sixpence thew? Captain? What, all sons of silence? No spirit?

DOWNRIGHT. Come, you might practise your ruffian trick somewhere else, and not here. I wuss,* this is no   to be sure tavern, nor drinking-school, to vent your exploits in.

WELLBRED. How now! whose cow has calved?*   what's the
                                                    matter
DOWNRIGHT. Marry, that has mine, sir. Nay, boy, never look askance at me for the matter; I'll tell you of it, I, sir; you and your companions mend yourselves when I ha' done.

WELLBRED. My companions?

DOWNRIGHT. Yes sir, your companions, so I say. I am not

---

[96] Simpson notes, "The word acquired an equivocal meaning from punning on the Latin *Meretrix*" = *wantonness* and on *merry tricks*.

[97] From card playing, to bet and raise.

[98] When the monasteries and other properties had been seques-tered by the Crown, certain lands remained in private hands. Queen Elizabeth I appointed commissions to seek out such prop-erties or "concealments." Courtiers often begged for the com-missions of search. Abuses led Elizabeth to revoke the commis-sions in 1572 and 1579.

afraid of you, nor them neither; your hangbyes here. You
must have your poets and your potlings,* your soldados tipplers
and foolados to follow you up and down the city; and here
they must come to domineer and swagger.—Sirrah, you
ballad-singer, and Slops* your fellow there, get   that is, Bobadill
you out, get you home; or, by this steel, I'll cut off your ears
and that presently.*   immediately

WELLBRED. 'Slight, stay, let's see what he dare do. Cut off
his ears? Cut a whetstone! You are an ass, do you see! Touch
any man here, and, by this hand, I'll run my rapier to the
hilts in you.

DOWNRIGHT. Yea, that would I fain see, boy.

(*They all draw.*)

DAME KITELY. O Jesu ! Murder! Thomas! Gasper!

BRIDGET. Help, help! Thomas!

(*Enter CASH and some of the house to part them.*)

E. KNOWELL. Gentlemen, forbear, I pray you.

BOBADILL. Well, sirrah, you Holofernes; by my hand, I will
pink your flesh full of holes with my rapier for this; I will, by
this good Heaven!—Nay, let him come, let him come, gentlemen; by the body of St. George, I'll not kill him.

(*They offer to fight again, and are parted.*)

CASH. Hold, hold, good gentlemen.

DOWNRIGHT. You whoreson, bragging coystrill!*   knave

(*Enter KITELY.*)

KITELY. Why, how now? What's the matter, what's the stir
    here?
Whence springs the quarrel? Thomas! Where is he?
Put up your weapons, and put off this rage:
My wife and sister, they are cause of this.
What, Thomas?—Where is this knave?

CASH. Here, Sir.

WELLBRED. Come, let's go. This is one of my brother's
ancient humours, this.

STEPHEN. I am glad nobody was hurt by his "ancient
humour."

(*Exeunt* WELLBRED, STEPHEN, MATTHEW, E. KNOWELL,
          BOBADILL, BRAINWORM, *and* SERVANTS.)

KITELY. Why, how now, brother, who enforced this brawl?

DOWNRIGHT. A sort* of lewd rake-hells that care   pack
neither for God nor the devil. And they must come here to
read ballads, and roguery, and trash! I'll mar the knot of 'hem
ere I sleep, perhaps; especially Bob there, he that's all manner
of shapes; and "Songs and Sonnets," his fellow.

BRIDGET. Brother, indeed you are too violent,
Too sudden, in your humour. And you know
My brother Wellbred's temper will not bear
Any reproof, chiefly in such a presence,
Where every slight disgrace he should receive
Might wound him in opinion, and respect.

DOWNRIGHT. Respect! What talk you of respect 'mong such
As ha' no spark of manhood, nor good manners?
'Sdeins, I am ashamed to hear you! Respect!

                                                  (*Exit.*)

BRIDGET. Yes, there was one a civil gentleman,
And very worthily demeaned himself.

KITELY. O, that was some love of yours, sister.

BRIDGET. A love of mine? I would it were no worse, brother!
You'ld pay my portion, sooner than you think for.

DAME KITELY. Indeed he seemed to be a gentleman of an
exceeding fair disposition, and of very excellent good parts.

                    (*Exeunt* DAME KITELY *and* BRIDGET.)

KITELY. Here love, by Heaven! My wife's minion!
"Fair disposition!" "Excellent good parts!"
Death! These phrases are intolerable.
"Good parts!" How should she know his parts?
His parts! Well, well, well, well, well, well!
It is too plain, too clear.—Thomas, come hither.
What, are they gone?

CASH.   Ah, sir, they went in.
My mistress and your sister——

KITELY. Are any of the gallants within?

CASH. No, sir, they are all gone.

KITELY. Art thou sure of it?

CASH. I can assure you, sir.

KITELY. What gentleman was that they praised so, Thomas?

CASH. One, they call him Master Knowell, a handsome
     young gentleman, sir.

KITELY. Ay, I thought so; my mind gave me as much.

I'll die but* they have hid him i' the house   if not
Somewhere; I'll go and search. Go with me, Thomas.
Be true to me, and thou shalt find me a master!

(*Exeunt.*)

Scene 2

(*The lane before* COB's *house. Enter* COB.)

COB (*knocking*). What, Tib! Tib, I say!

TIB (*within*). How now, what cuckold is that knocks so
hard? (*She opens.*) O, husband! is't you? What's the news?

COB. Nay, you have stunned me, i'faith! you ha' given
me a knock o' the forehead will stick by me. Cuckold! 'Slid,
cuckold!

TIB. Away, you fool! did I know it was you that knocked?
Come, come, you may call me as bad, when you list.*   please

COB. May I?—Tib, you are a whore.

TIB. You lie in your throat, husband.

COB. How, the lie? And in my throat too! Do you long to
be stabbed, ha?

TIB. Why, you are no soldier,[99] I hope.

COB. O, must you be stabbed by a soldier? Mass, that's
true! When was Bobadill here, your captain? That rogue, that
foist,* that fencing Burgullion?* I'll tickle him,   pickpocket/bully
i'faith.

TIB. Why, what's the matter, trow?

COB. O, he has basted me rarely, sumptuously! But I have
it here in black and white. (*Shows the warrant.*) For his black
and blue, shall* pay him. O, the Justice! the honestest   I shall
old brave Trojan in London! I do honour the very flea of his
dog. A plague on him though; he put me once in a villanous
filthy fear; marry, it vanished away like the smoke of tobacco;
but I was smoked* soundly first. I thank the devil,   ridiculed
and his good angel, my guest. Well, wife, or Tib, which you
will, get you in, and lock the door; I charge you, let nobody in
to you, wife, nobody in, to you; those are my words. Not Captain Bob himself, nor the fiend, in his likeness. You are a woman; you have flesh and blood enough in you to be tempted;
therefore, keep the door shut upon all comers.

[99] Soldiers were supposed to answer accusations of lying by
stabbing their accusers.

Tib. I warrant you, there shall nobody enter here, without my consent.

Cob. Nor with your consent, sweet Tib, and so I leave you.

Tib. It's more than you know, whether you leave me so.

Cob. How?

Tib. Why, "sweet."

Cob. Tut, sweet or sour, thou art a flower. Keep close thy door; I ask no more.

(*Exeunt.*)

Scene 3

(*A room in the Windmill Tavern. Enter* E. Knowell, Wellbred, Stephen, *and* Brainworm, *disguised as before.*)

E. Knowell. Well, Brainworm, perform this business happily,* and thou makest a purchase of my love for ever.   successfully

Wellbred. I'faith, now let thy spirits use their best faculties. But, at any hand, remember the message to my brother; for there's no other means to start him.

Brainworm. I warrant you, sir, fear nothing. I have a nimble soul has waked all forces of my phant'sie by this time, and put 'hem in true motion. What you have possessed* instructed me withal, I'll discharge it amply, sir. Make it no question.

Wellbred. Forth, and prosper, Brainworm. (*Exit* Brainworm.)—Faith, Ned, how dost thou approve of my abilities in this device?

E. Knowell. Troth, well, howsoever; but it will come excellent, if it take.

Wellbred. Take, man? Why it cannot choose but take, if the circumstances miscarry not. But tell me, ingenuously, dost thou affect my sister Bridget, as thou pretend'st*   profess

E. Knowell. Friend am I worth belief?

Wellbred. Come, do not protest. In faith, she is a maid of good ornament and much modesty; and, except I conceived very worthily of her, thou shouldest not have her.

E. Knowell. Nay, that, I am afraid, will be a question yet, whether I shall have her, or no.

Wellbred. 'Slid, thou shalt have her; by this light thou shalt.

E. Knowell. Nay, do not swear.

Wellbred. By this hand, thou shalt have her; I'll go fetch

her presently.* 'Point but where to meet, and as I   at once
am an honest man, I'll bring her.

E. KNOWELL. Hold, hold, be temperate.

WELLBRED. Why, by——what shall I swear by? Thou shalt
have her, as I am——

E. KNOWELL. 'Pray thee, be at peace; I am satisfied, and
do believe thou wilt omit no offered occasion to make my
desires complete.

WELLBRED. Thou shalt see and know I will not.

(Exeunt.)

Scene 4

(The Old Jewry. Enter FORMAL *and* KNOWELL.)

FORMAL. Was your man a soldier, sir?

KNOWELL. Ay, a knave; I took him begging o' the way,
This morning, as I came over Moorfields.

(Enter BRAINWORM.)

O, here he is!—You've made fair speed, believe me.
Where, i' the name of sloth, could you be thus?

BRAINWORM. Marry, peace be my comfort, where I thought
I should have had little comfort of your worship's service.

KNOWELL. How so?

BRAINWORM. O, sir! Your coming to the city, your entertainment of me, and your sending me to watch——indeed
all the circumstances either of your charge or my employment, are as open to your son as to yourself!

KNOWELL. How should that be, unless that villain, Brain-
worm,
Have told him of the letter, and discovered*   revealed
All that I strictly charged him to conceal? 'Tis so.

BRAINWORM. I am, partly, o' the faith 'tis so, indeed.

KNOWELL. But, how should he know thee to be my man?

BRAINWORM. Nay, sir, I cannot tell, unless it be by the
black art! Is not your son a scholar, sir?

KNOWELL. Yes, but I hope his soul is not allied
Unto such hellish practice. If it were,
I had just cause to weep my part in him,
And curse the time of his creation.
But, where did'st thou find them, Fitz-Sword?

BRAINWORM. You should rather ask, where they found me,

sir; for I'll be sworn, I was going along in the street thinking nothing, when, of a sudden, a voice calls, "Master Knowell's man!" Another cries "Soldier!" And thus half a dozen
of them, till they had called me within a house, where I no
sooner came, but they seemed men,[100] and out flew all their
rapiers at my bosom, with some three or fourscore oaths to
accompany 'hem; and all to tell me I was but a dead man
if I did not confess where you were, and how I was employed,
and about what; which when they could not get out of me
(as, I protest, they must ha' dissected, and made an
anatomy* o' me first, and so I told 'hem), they locked   skeleton
me up into a room i' the top of a high house, whence, by great
miracle (having a light heart) I slid down by a bottom* of ball
packthread into the street, and so 'scaped. But, sir, thus much
I can assure you, for I heard it while I was locked up. There
was a great many rich merchants and brave*   richly dressed
citizens' wives with 'hem at a feast, and your son, Master
Edward, withdrew with one of 'hem, and has 'pointed to meet
her anon, at one Cob's house, a water-bearer, that dwells by
the Wall. Now, there your worship shall be sure to take him,
for there he preys, and fail he will not.

KNOWELL. Nor, will I fail to break his match, I doubt not.
Go thou, along with Justice Clement's man,
And stay there for me. At one Cob's house, say'st thou?

BRAINWORM. Ay, sir, there you shall have him.

                                   (*Exit* KNOWELL.)

Yes!—invisible? Much wench, or much son! 'Slight, when
he has staid there three or four hours, travailing with the
expectation of wonders, and at length be delivered of air, oh,
the sport that I should then take to look on him, if I durst!
But now I mean to appear no more afore him in this shape.
I have another trick to act yet. O, that I were so happy as
to light on a nupson,* now, of* this justice's   simpleton/in
novice!——Sir, I make you stay somewhat long.

FORMAL. Not a whit, sir. 'Pray you what do you mean, sir?

BRAINWORM. I was putting up some papers——

FORMAL. You ha' been lately in the wars, sir, it seems.

BRAINWORM. Marry have I, sir, to my loss; and expense of
all, almost——

FORMAL.   Troth, sir, I would be glad to bestow a
pottle* of wine o' you, if it please you to accept it—— two quarts

---

[100] There is no satisfactory explanation for this expression.
H. Spencer suggests it means that they "displayed their manly
valor."

BRAINWORM. O, sir——

FORMAL. But to hear the manner of your services and your devices in the wars; they say they be very strange, and not like those a man reads in the Roman histories, or sees at Mile-end.[101]

BRAINWORM. No, I assure you. sir; why, at any time when it please you, I shall be ready to discourse to you all I know. (*Aside.*) And more too somewhat.

FORMAL. No better time than now, sir; we'll go to the Windmill. There we shall have a cup of neat grist,* _{that is, malt liquor} we call it. I pray you, sir, let me request you to the Windmill.

BRAINWORM. I'll follow you, sir; (*Aside.*) and make grist o' you, if I have good luck.

(*Exeunt.*)

Scene 5

(*Moorfields. Enter* MATTHEW, E. KNOWELL, BOBADILL, *and* STEPHEN.)

MATTHEW. Sir, did your eyes ever taste the like clown of him where we were to-day, Master Wellbred's half-brother? I think the whole earth cannot show his parallel, by this daylight.

E. KNOWELL. We were now speaking of him. Captain Bobadill tells me, he is fallen foul o' you too.

MATTHEW.   O, ay, sir, he threatened me with the bastinado.*   _{a beating}

BOBADILL. Ay, but I think I taught you prevention this morning for that.—You shall kill him, beyond question; if you be so generously minded.

MATTHEW. Indeed, it is a most excellent trick. (*Fences.*)

BOBADILL. O, you do not give spirit enough to your motion; you are too tardy, too heavy! O, it must be done like lightning. Hay![102]

(*Practices at a post.*)

MATTHEW. Rare captain!

BOBADILL. Tut! 'Tis nothing, an't be not done in a— punto.*   _{instant}

---

[101] Training ground for the London militia.

[102] A fencing term uttered upon hitting one's opponent. From the Italian *hai*, "you have it."

E. KNOWELL. Captain, did you ever prove yourself upon any of our masters of defence here?

MATTHEW. O, good sir! Yes, I hope, he has.

BOBADILL. I will tell you, sir. Upon my first coming to the city after my long travail* for knowledge (in that   travel; labor mystery only), there came three or four of 'hem to me, at a gentleman's house where it was my chance to be resident at that time, to entreat my presence at their schools; and withal so much importuned me that—I protest to you as I am a gentleman—I was ashamed of their rude demeanour, out of all measure. Well, I told 'hem that to come to a public school, they should pardon me, it was opposite (in diameter) to my humour; but, if so be they would give their attendance at my lodging, I protested to do them what right of favour I could, as I was a gentleman, and so forth.

E. KNOWELL. So, sir, then you tried their skill?

BOBADILL. Alas, soon tried! You shall hear, sir. Within two or three days after, they came; and, by honesty, fair sir, believe me, I graced them exceedingly, showed them some two or three tricks of prevention have purchased 'hem since, a credit to admiration! They cannot deny this. And yet now they hate me, and why? Because I am excellent! And for no other vile reason on the earth.

E. KNOWELL. This is strange and barbarous, as ever I heard!

BOBADILL. Nay, for a more instance of their preposterous natures, but note, sir. They have assaulted me some three, four, five, six of them together, as I have walked alone in divers skirts* i' the town as Turnbull, White-chapel,   outskirts Shoreditch,[103] which were then my quarters; and since, upon the Exchange, at my lodging, and at my ordinary;* where I have driven them afore me, the   public dining place whole length of a street, in the open view of all our gallants, pitying to hurt them, believe me. Yet all this lenity will not o'ercome their spleen; they will be doing with the pismire,* raising a hill a man may spurn abroad with his   ant foot at pleasure. By myself, I could have slain them all, but I delight not in murder. I am loth to bear any other than this bastinado for 'hem; yet I hold it good polity not to go disarmed, for though I be skillful, I may be oppressed with multitudes.

E. KNOWELL. Ay, believe me, may you, sir: and, in my

---

[103] All notorious areas.

conceit, our whole nation should sustain the loss by it, if it were so.

BOBADILL. Alas, no! What's a peculiar* man to a   individual
nation? Not seen.

E. KNOWELL. O, but your skill, sir.

BOBADILL. Indeed, that might be some loss; but who respects it? I will tell you, sir, by the way of private, and under seal; I am a gentleman, and live here obscure, and to myself. But, were I known to her Majesty and the Lords,—observe me,—I would undertake—upon this poor head, and life—for the public benefit of the state, not only to spare the entire lives of her subjects in general, but to save the one half, nay, three parts of her yearly charge in holding war, and against what enemy soever. And how would I do it, think you?

E. KNOWELL. Nay, I know not, nor can I conceive.

BOBADILL. Why thus, sir. I would select nineteen more to myself throughout the land; gentlemen they should be, of good spirit, strong, and able constitution. I would choose them by an instinct, a character that I have; and I would teach these nineteen the special rules as your punto, your reverso, your stoccata, your imbroccata, your passada, your montanto[104] till they could all play very near or altogether as well as myself. This done, say the enemy were forty thousand strong, we twenty would come into the field the tenth of March, or thereabouts; and we would challenge twenty of the enemy. They could not, in their honour, refuse us. Well, we would kill them, challenge twenty more, kill them; twenty more, kill them; twenty more, kill them too; and thus, would we kill, every man, his twenty a day. That's twenty score; twenty score, that's two hundred;[105] two hundred a day, five days a thousand; forty thousand; forty times five, five times forty, two hundred days kills them all up, by computation. And this, will I venture my poor gentleman-like carcass to perform (provided there be no treason practised upon us) by fair, and discreet, manhood; that is, civilly by the sword.

E. KNOWELL. Why, are you so sure of your hand, captain, at all times?

BOBADILL. Tut! Never miss thrust, upon my reputation with you.

E. KNOWELL. I would not stand in Downright's state then,

---

[104] These are technical fencing terms.

[105] "Bobadill is too much of a borrower to be an accurate reckoner" (Gifford).

an* you meet him, for the wealth of any one street in   if
London.

BOBADILL. Why, sir, you mistake me! If he were here now,
by this welkin, I would not draw my weapon on him! Let this
gentleman do his mind; but, I will bastinado him, by the bright
sun, wherever I meet him.

MATTHEW. Faith, and I'll have a fling at him, at my distance.

E. KNOWELL. Gods so, look where he is! Yonder he goes.

(DOWNRIGHT *crosses over the stage.*)

DOWNRIGHT. What peevish luck have I, I cannot meet with
these bragging rascals?

BOBADILL. It's not he, is it?

E. KNOWELL.   Yes, faith, it is he.

MATTHEW. I'll be hanged then, if that were he.

E. KNOWELL. Sir, keep your hanging good for some greater
matter, for I assure you that was he.

STEPHEN. Upon my reputation, it was he.

BOBADILL. Had I thought it had been he, he must not have
gone so; but I can hardly be induced to believe it was he, yet.

E. KNOWELL. That I think, sir.

(*Re-enter* DOWNRIGHT.)

                              But see, he is come again.

DOWNRIGHT. O, "Pharaoh's foot," have I found you? Come,
draw, to your tools.* Draw, gipsy,* or I'll thrash   weapons/rogue
you.

BOBADILL. Gentleman of valour, I do believe in thee, hear
me—

DOWNRIGHT. Draw your weapon then.

BOBADILL. Tall* man, I never thought on it till now;   bold
body of me, I had a warrant of the peace served on me, even
now as I came along, by a water-bearer; this gentleman saw
it, Master Matthew.

DOWNRIGHT. 'Sdeath! You will not draw then?

          (*Beats him and disarms him;* MATTHEW *runs away.*)

BOBADILL. Hold, hold, under thy favour, forbear!

DOWNRIGHT. Prate again, as you like this, you whoreson
foist* you! You'll "control* the point," you!   rogue/check
(*Looking about.*) Your consort is gone? Had he stayed he had
shared with you, sir.

                                             (*Exit.*)

BOBADILL. Well, gentlemen, bear witness; I was bound to
the peace, by this good day.

E. KNOWELL. No faith, it's an ill day, captain; never reckon
it other. But, say you were bound to the peace, the law allows
you to defend yourself. That'll prove but a poor excuse.

BOBADILL. I cannot tell, sir. I desire good construction, in
fair sort. I never sustained the like disgrace, by Heaven! Sure
I was struck with* a planet thence, for I had no power to   by
touch my weapon.

E. KNOWELL. Ay, like enough; I have heard of many that
have been beaten under a planet: go, get you to a surgeon.
(*Exit* BOBADILL.) 'Slid! an these be your tricks, your passadas,
and your montantos, I'll none of them. O, manners! That this
age should bring forth such creatures! That nature should be
at leisure to make 'hem! Come, coz.

STEPHEN. Mass, I'll ha' this cloak.

E. KNOWELL. Gods will, 'tis Downright's.

STEPHEN. Nay, it's mine now; another might have ta'en't
up as well as I. I'll wear it, so I will.

  E. KNOWELL. How, an he see it? He'll challenge it, assure
yourself.

STEPHEN. Ah, but he shall not ha' it; I'll say I bought it.

E. KNOWELL. Take heed you buy it not too dear, coz.

(*Exeunt.*)

Scene 6

(*A room in* KITELY'S *house. Enter* KITELY, WELLBRED,
DAME KITELY, *and* BRIDGET.)

KITELY. Now, trust me, brother, you were much to blame
T'incense his anger and disturb the peace
Of my poor house, where there are sentinels
That every minute watch to give alarms
Of civil war, without adjection*   addition
Of your assistance or occasion.

WELLBRED. No harm done, brother, I warrant you, since
there is no harm done. Anger costs a man nothing; and a
tall* man is never his own man till he be angry. To keep   bold
his valour in obscurity is to keep himself, as it were, in a cloak-
bag. What's a musician unless he play? What's a tall man unless he fight? For indeed, all this my wise brother stands upon
absolutely; and that made me fall in with him so resolutely.

DAME KITELY. Ay, but what harm might have come of it,
brother?

WELLBRED. Might, sister? So might the good warm clothes

your husband wears be poisoned, for any thing he knows, or
the wholesome wine he drunk even now at the table——
KITELY (*aside*). Now, God forbid! O me! Now I remember
My wife drunk to me last and changed the cup;
And bade me wear this cursèd suit to-day.
See, if Heaven suffer murder undiscovered!—
I feel me ill; give me some mithridate,[106]
Some mithridate and oil, good sister, fetch me;
O, I am sick at heart! I burn, I burn.
If you will save my life, go fetch it me.
WELLBRED. O strange humour! My very breath has poisoned
him.
BRIDGET. Good brother, be content. What do you mean?
The strength of these extreme conceits* will kill you.   fancies
DAME KITELY. Beshrew* your heart-blood, brother   curse
    Wellbred, now,
For putting such a toy* into his head!   foolish idea
WELLBRED. Is a fit simile a toy? Will he be poisoned with a
simile? Brother Kitely, what a strange and idle* imagi-   trifling
nation is this! For shame, be wiser. O' my soul, there's no such
matter.
KITELY. Am I not sick? How am I, then, not poisoned? Am
I not poisoned? How am I, then, so sick?
DAME KITELY. If you be sick, your own thoughts make you
sick.
WELLBRED. His jealousy is the poison he has taken.

(*Enter* BRAINWORM *disguised in* FORMAL'S *clothes.*)

BRAINWORM. Master Kitely, my master, Justice Clement,
salutes you, and desires to speak with you with all possible
speed.
KITELY. No time but now? When I think I am sick? Very
sick! Well, I will wait upon his worship.—Thomas? Cob?
(*Aside.*) I must seek them out, and set 'hem sentinels till I
return.—Thomas? Cob? Thomas?
                                 (*Exit.*)
WELLBRED (*takes him aside*). This is perfectly rare, Brainworm! But how got'st thou this apparel of the Justice's man?
BRAINWORM (*aside*). Marry, sir, my proper fine penman
would needs bestow the grist o' me at the Windmill to hear

---

[106] An antidote.

some martial discourse; where so I marshalled* him   guided
that I made him drunk—with admiration! And, because too
much heat was the cause of his distemper, I stripped him stark
naked as he lay along asleep, and borrowed his suit to deliver
this counterfeit message in, leaving a rusty armour and an old
brown bill* to watch him till my return, which shall be   pike
when I ha' pawned his apparel, and spent the better part o' the
money, perhaps.

WELLBRED (*aside*). Well, thou art a successful merry knave,
Brainworm; his absence will be a good subject for more mirth.
I pray thee, return to thy young master, and will him to meet
me and my sister Bridget at the Tower[107] instantly; for, here,
tell him, the house is so stored with jealousy there is no room
for love to stand upright in. We must get our fortunes committed to some larger prison, say; and, than the Tower, I know no
better air; nor where the liberty of the house may do us more
present service. Away.

(*Exit* BRAINWORM.)

(*Re-enter* KITELY, CASH *following.*)

KITELY. Come hither, Thomas. Now, my secret's ripe,
And thou shalt have it. Lay to both thine ears.
Hark, what I say to thee. I must go forth, Thomas.
Be careful of thy promise, keep good watch,
Note every gallant, and observe him well
That enters in my absence to thy mistress.
If she would show him rooms, the jest is stale,
Follow 'hem, Thomas, or else hang on him
And let him not go after. Mark their looks;
Note if she offer but to see his band,
Or any other amorous toy about him;
But praise his leg or foot; or if she say
The day is hot, and bid him feel her hand,
How hot it is—oh, that's a monstrous thing!
Note me all this, good Thomas; mark their sighs,
And, if they do but whisper, break 'hem off.
I'll bear thee out in it. Wilt thou do this?
Wilt thou be true, my Thomas?
      CASH. As truth's self, sir.
      KITELY. Why, I believe thee.—Where is Cob now? Cob?
                                                          (*Exit.*)

---

[107] Since the Tower of London was not located in any parish,
a marriage could be performed there at once.

DAME KITELY. He's ever calling for Cob! I wonder how he employs Cob so!

WELLBRED. Indeed, sister, to ask how he employs Cob is a necessary question for you that are his wife, and a thing not very easy for you to be satisfied in. But this I'll assure you, Cob's wife is an excellent bawd, sister, and oftentimes your husband haunts her house. Marry, to what end? I cannot altogether accuse him; imagine you what you think convenient. But I have known fair hides have foul hearts ere now, sister.

DAME KITELY. Never said you truer than that, brother; so much I can tell you for your learning.—Thomas, fetch your cloak and go with me. (*Exit* CASH.) I'll after him presently.* I would to fortune I could take him there; immediately i' faith, I'ld return him his own, I warrant him!

(*Exit.*)

WELLBRED. So, let 'hem go; this may make sport anon. Now, my fair sister-in-law, that you knew but how happy a thing it were to be fair and beautiful.

BRIDGET. That touches not me, brother.

WELLBRED. That's true; that's even the fault of it; for indeed, beauty stands a woman in no stead unless it procure her touching. But sister, whether it touch you or no, it touches your beauties; and I am sure they will abide the touch. An they do not, a plague of all ceruse,[108] say I! And it touches me too in part, though not in the—— Well, there's a dear and respected friend of mine, sister, stands very strongly and worthily affected toward you, and hath vowed to inflame whole bonfires of zeal at his heart in honour of your perfections. I have already engaged my promise to bring you where you shall hear him confirm much more. Ned Knowell is the man, sister. There's no exception against the party. You are ripe for a husband; and a minute's loss to such an occasion is a great trespass in a wise beauty. What say you, sister? On my soul, he loves you. Will you give him the meeting?

BRIDGET. Faith, I had very little confidence in mine own constancy, brother, if I durst not meet a man; but this motion* of yours savours of an old knight adventurer's serv- plan ant a little too much, methinks.

WELLBRED. What's that, sister?

BRIDGET. Marry, of the squire.* apple-squire, pander

WELLBRED. No matter if it did; I would be such an one for my friend. But see who is returned to hinder us!

[108] A cosmetic of white lead.

(*Re-enter* KITELY.)

KITELY. What villany is this? Called out a false message?
This was some plot! I was not sent for.—Bridget,
Where's your sister?
    BRIDGET.   I think she be gone forth, sir.
    KITELY. How! Is my wife gone forth? Whither, for God's
sake?
    BRIDGET. She's gone abroad with Thomas.
    KITELY. Abroad with Thomas! Oh, that villain dors* deceives
    me.
He hath discovered all unto my wife!
Beast that I was to trust him! Whither, I pray you,
Went she?
    BRIDGET. I know not, sir.
    WELLBRED.   I'll tell you, brother,
Whither I suspect she's gone.
    KITELY.   Whither, good brother?
    WELLBRED. To Cob's house, I believe. But keep my counsel.
    KITELY. I will, I will. To Cob's house? Doth she haunt
    Cob's?
She's gone a purpose now to cuckold me
With that lewd rascal who, to win her favour,
Hath told her all.

                                      (*Exit.*)

    WELLBRED.   Come, he is once more gone.
Sister, let's lose no time; the affair is worth it.

                                  (*Exeunt.*)

Scene 7

(*A street. Enter* MATTHEW *and* BOBADILL.)

MATTHEW. I wonder, Captain, what they will say of my
going away? Ha?
    BOBADILL. Why, what should they say? But as of a discreet
gentleman! Quick, wary, respectful of nature's fair lineaments;
and that's all.
    MATTHEW. Why, so! But what can they say of your beat-
ing?
    BOBADILL. A rude part, a touch with soft wood, a kind of
gross battery used, laid on strongly, borne most patiently; and
that's all.

MATTHEW. Ay, but would any man have offered it in
Venice? As you say?

BOBADILL. Tut! I assure you, no; you shall have there your
Nobilis, your *Gentilezza,** come in bravely upon your   gentry
"reverse," stand you close, stand you firm, stand you fair, save
your "retricato" with his left leg, come to the "assalto" with
the right, thrust with brave steel, defy your base wood! But,
wherefore do I awake this remembrance? I was fascinated, by
Jupiter, fascinated;* but I will be unwitched and re-   bewitched
venged by law.

MATTHEW. Do you hear? Is't not best to get a warrant, and
have him arrested and brought before Justice Clement?

BOBADILL. It were not amiss; would we had it!

(*Enter* BRAINWORM *still as* FORMAL.)

MATTHEW. Why, here comes his man; let's speak to him.

BOBADILL. Agreed; do you speak.

MATTHEW. 'Save you, sir!

BRAINWORM. With all my heart, sir.

MATTHEW. Sir, there is one Downright hath abused this
gentleman and myself, and we determine to make our amends
by law; now, if you would do us the favour to procure a warrant to bring him afore your master, you shall be well considered, I assure you, sir.

BRAINWORM. Sir, you know my service is my living; such
favours as these, gotten of my master, is his only prefer-
ment;[109] and therefore you must consider me as* I may   so that
make benefit of my place.

MATTHEW. How is that, sir?

BRAINWORM. Faith sir, the thing is extraordinary, and the
gentleman may be of great account; yet, be what he will, if you
will lay me down a brace of angels, in my hand, you shall have
it; otherwise not.

MATTHEW. How shall we do, Captain? He asks a brace of
angels. You have no money?

BOBADILL. Not a cross,[110] by fortune.

MATTHEW. Nor I, as I am a gentleman; but twopence left
of my two shillings in the morning for wine and radish. Let's
find him some pawn.

BOBADILL. Pawn? We have none to the value of his demand.

---

[109] The only pay he gives me.

[110] That is, nothing. The silver penny and halfpenny were
marked with a cross.

MATTHEW. O, yes. I'll pawn this jewel in my ear, and you may pawn your silk stockings and pull up your boots; they will ne'er be missed. It must be done now.

BOBADILL. Well, an there be no remedy. I'll step aside and pull 'hem off.

(*Withdraws.*)

MATTHEW. Do you hear, sir? We have no store of money at this time, but you shall have good pawns—look you, sir, this jewel and that gentleman's silk stockings—because we would have it dispatched ere we went to our chambers.

BRAINWORM. I am content, sir; I will get you the warrant presently,* what's his name, say you? Downright?   immediately

MATTHEW. Ay, ay, George Downright.

BRAINWORM. What manner of man is he?

MATTHEW. A tall big man, sir; he goes in a cloak most commonly of silk-russet, laid about with russet lace.

BRAINWORM. 'Tis very good, sir.

MATTHEW. Here, sir, here's my jewel.

BOBADILL (*returning*). And here—are stockings.

BRAINWORM. Well, gentlemen, I'll procure you this warrant presently; but, who will you have to serve it?

MATTHEW. That's true, Captain; that must be considered.

BOBADILL. Body o' me. I know not! 'Tis service of danger!

BRAINWORM. Why, you were best get one o' the varlets* o' the city, a serjeant; I'll appoint you one, if that is, officers you please.

MATTHEW. Will you, sir? Why, we can wish no better.

BOBADILL. We'll leave it to you, sir.

(*Exeunt* BOBADILL *and* MATTHEW.)

BRAINWORM. This is rare! Now will I go pawn this cloak of the justice's man's at the broker's for a varlet's suit, and be the varlet myself; and get either more pawns, or more money of Downright for* the arrest.   instead of

(*Exit.*)

Scene 8

(*Before* COB'S *house. Enter* KNOWELL.)

KNOWELL. Oh, here it is; I am glad I have found it now. Ho! Who is within here?

TIB (*within*). I am within, sir; what's your pleasure?

KNOWELL. To know who is within besides yourself.

TIB. Why, sir, you are no constable, I hope?

KNOWELL. O, fear you the constable? Then I doubt not
You have some guests within deserve that fear;
I'll fetch him straight.
(TIB *opens*.)
TIB.   O' God's name, sir!
KNOWELL. Go to. Come, tell me, is not young Knowell
here?
TIB. Young Knowell? I know none such, sir, o'mine honesty.
KNOWELL. Your honesty? Dame, it flies too lightly from
you. There is no way but fetch the constable.
TIB. The constable? The man is mad, I think.

                                         (*Exit.*)

(*Enter* DAME KITELY *and* CASH. KNOWELL *conceals himself.*)

CASH. Ho! Who keeps house here?
KNOWELL. O, this's the female copesmate* of my   paramour
son.
Now shall I meet him straight.
DAME KITELY.   Knock, Thomas, hard.
CASH. Ho, goodwife!

(*Re-enter* TIB.)

TIB.   Why, what's the matter with you?
DAME KITELY. Why, woman, grieves it you to ope your
door?
Belike you get something to keep it shut.
TIB. What mean these questions, 'pray ye?
DAME KITELY. So strange you make it! Is not my husband
here?
KNOWELL. Her husband!
DAME KITELY.   My tried husband, Master Kitely?
TIB. I hope he needs not to be tried here.
DAME KITELY. No dame; he does it not for need, but pleasure.
TIB. Neither for need nor pleasure, is he here.
KNOWELL. This is but a device to baulk me withal.

(*Enter* KITELY, *muffled in his cloak.*)

Soft, who is this? 'Tis not my son disguised?

DAME KITELY (*spies her husband, and runs to him*). O, sir,
  have I forestalled your honest market?
Found your close* walks? You stand amazed now, do   secret
  you?
I'faith, I'm glad I have smoked* you yet at last.   exposed
What is your jewel, trow? In; come, let's see her;—
Fetch forth your housewife, dame;—if she be fairer,
In any honest judgment, than myself,
I'll be content with it; but, she is change,
She feeds you fat, she soothes your appetite,
And you are well! Your wife, an honest woman,
Is meat twice sod* to you, sir! O, you treacher!*   boiled/traitor
  KNOWELL. She cannot counterfeit thus palpably.
  KITELY. Out on thy more than strumpet's impudence!
Steal'st thou thus to thy haunts? And have I taken
Thy bawd and thee, and thy companion,
This hoary-headed lecher, this old goat,
Close* at your villainy; and wouldst thou 'scuse it   secretly
With this stale harlot's jest, accusing me?——
O, old incontinent, [*To* KNOWELL.] dost not thou shame,
When all thy powers in chastity is spent,
To have a mind so hot? And to entice,
And feed the enticements of a lustful woman?
  DAME KITELY. Out, I defy thee, I, dissembling wretch!
  KITELY. Defy me, strumpet? Ask thy pander here,
  (*Indicating* CASH.)
Can he deny it? Or that wicked elder?
  KNOWELL. Why, hear you, sir.
  KITELY.   Tut, tut, tut; never speak.
Thy guilty conscience will discover thee.
  KNOWELL. What lunacy is this that haunts this man?
  KITELY. Well, good wife B A 'D,[111] Cob's wife, and you,
That make your husband such a hoddy-doddy*—— that is, cuckold
And you, young apple-squire,* and old cuckold-maker; pander
I'll ha' you every one before a justice.
Nay, you shall answer it; I charge you go.
  KNOWELL. Marry, with all my heart, sir. I go willingly,
Though I do taste this as a trick put on me
To punish my impertinent search, and justly;
And half forgive my son for the device.*   trick
  KITELY. Come, will you go?
  DAME KITELY.   Go? To thy shame believe it.

---

[111] With a pun on *bawd*.

(*Enter* COB.)

COB. Why, what's the matter here; what's here to do?

KITELY. O, Cob, art thou come? I have been abused,
And i' thy house. Never was man so wronged!

COB. 'Slid, in my house? My Master Kitely? Who wrongs
you in my house?

KITELY. Marry, young lust in old, and old in young here.
Thy wife's their bawd; here have I taken 'hem.

COB. How? Bawd? Is my house come to that? Am I preferred thither? (*Beats his wife.*) Did I charge you to keep your
doors shut, Is'bel? And do you let 'hem lie open for all
comers?

KNOWELL. Friend, know some cause before thou beat'st thy
  wife;
This's madness in thee.

COB.   Why? is there no cause?

KITELY. Yes, I'll show cause before the Justice, Cob.
Come, let her go with me.

COB.   Nay, she shall go.

TIB. Nay, I will go. I'll see an* you may be allowed to   if
make a bundle o' hemp[112] o' your right and lawful wife thus,
at every cuckoldy knave's pleasure. Why do you not go?

KITELY. A bitter quean!* Come, we'll ha' you tamed.   hussy

                                        (*Exeunt.*)

Scene 9

(*A street. Enter* BRAINWORM *as a City Sergeant.*)

BRAINWORM. Well, of all my disguises yet, now am I most
like myself, being in this sergeant's gown. A man of my
present profession never counterfeits till he lays hold upon a
debtor, and says, he 'rests him; for then he brings him to
all manner of unrest. A kind of little kings we are, bearing
the diminutive of a mace,[113] made like a young artichoke,
that always carries pepper and salt in itself.[114] Well, I know
not what danger I undergo by this exploit; 'pray Heaven I
come well off!

[112] Hemp is prepared by beating.

[113] Badge of the city sergeant.

[114] Jonson plays on the word *mace*, the spice.

(*Enter* MATTHEW *and* BOBADILL.)

MATTHEW. See, I think yonder is the varlet, by his gown.

BOBADILL. Let's go in quest of him.

MATTHEW. 'Save you, friend! Are not you here by appointment of Justice Clement's man?

BRAINWORM. Yes, an't please you, sir; he told me two gentlemen had willed him to procure a warrant from his master (which I have about me) to be served on one Downright.

MATTHEW. It is honestly done of you both; and see, where the party comes you must arrest; serve it upon him, quickly, afore he be aware.

BOBADILL. Bear back, Master Matthew.

(*Enter* STEPHEN *in* DOWNRIGHT'S *cloak.*)

BRAINWORM. Master Downright, I arrest you i' the queen's name, and must carry you afore a justice by virtue of this warrant.

STEPHEN. Me, friend? I am no Downright, I. I am Master Stephen; you do not well to arrest me, I tell you truly. I am in nobody's bonds, nor books; I would you should know it. A plague on you heartily for making me thus afraid afore my time!

BRAINWORM. Why, now are you deceived, gentlemen!

BOBADILL. He wears such a cloak, and that deceived us; but see, here a'* comes indeed! This is he, officer.   he

(*Enter* DOWNRIGHT.)

DOWNRIGHT. Why, how now, Signior gull! Are you turned filcher of late? Come, deliver my cloak.

STEPHEN. Your cloak, sir? I bought it, even now, in open market.

BRAINWORM. Master Downright, I have a warrant I must serve upon you—procured by these two gentlemen.

DOWNRIGHT. These gentlemen? These rascals!

(*Tries to beat them.*)

BRAINWORM. Keep the peace, I charge you, in Her Majesty's name.

DOWNRIGHT. I obey thee. What must I do, officer?

BRAINWORM. Go before Master Justice to answer what they can object against you, sir. I will use you kindly, sir.

MATTHEW. Come, let's before, and make* the Justice, prepare
Captain.

BOBADILL. The varlet's a tall* man, afore Heaven!   brave
                       (*Exeunt* BOBADILL *and* MATTHEW.)

DOWNRIGHT. Gull, you'll gi' me my cloak.

STEPHEN. Sir, I bought it, and I'll keep it.

DOWNRIGHT. You will.

STEPHEN. Ay, that I will.

DOWNRIGHT. Officer, there's thy fee. Arrest him.

BRAINWORM. Master Stephen, I must arrest you.

STEPHEN. Arrest me! I scorn it. There take your cloak; I'll
none on't.

DOWNRIGHT. Nay, that shall not serve your turn now, sir.
Officer, I'll go with thee to the justice's. Bring him along.

STEPHEN. Why, is not here your cloak? What would you
have?

DOWNRIGHT. I'll ha' you answer it, sir.

BRAINWORM. Sir, I'll take your word, and this gentleman's
too, for his appearance.

DOWNRIGHT. I'll ha' no words taken; bring him along.

BRAINWORM. Sir. I may choose to do that; I may take bail.

DOWNRIGHT. 'Tis true, you may take bail, and choose, at
another time. But you shall not, now, varlet. Bring him along
or I'll swinge* you.   beat

BRAINWORM. Sir, I pity the gentleman's case. Here's your
money again.

DOWNRIGHT. 'Sdeins, tell not me of my money; bring him
away, I say.

BRAINWORM. I warrant you he will go with you of himself, sir.

DOWNRIGHT. Yet more ado.

BRAINWORM (*aside*). I have made a fair mash* on't. muddle

STEPHEN. Must I go?

BRAINWORM. I know no remedy, Master Stephen.

DOWNRIGHT. Come along afore me here; I do not love your
hanging look behind.

STEPHEN. Why, sir, I hope you cannot hang me for it.—
Can he, fellow?

BRAINWORM. I think not, sir; it is but a whipping matter,
sure.

STEPHEN. Why, then, let him do his worst; I am resolute.
                                    (*Exeunt.*)

ACT V

Scene 1

(*A hall in* Justice CLEMENT'S *house. Enter* CLEMENT, KNOWELL, KITELY, Dame KITELY, TIB, CASH, COB, *and* SERVANTS.)

CLEMENT. Nay, but stay, stay, give me leave.—My chair, sirrah.—You, Master Knowell, say you went thither to meet your son?

KNOWELL. Ay, sir.

CLEMENT. But who directed you thither?

KNOWELL. That did mine own man, sir.

CLEMENT. Where is he?

KNOWELL. Nay, I know not now; I left him with your clerk, and appointed him to stay here for me.

CLEMENT. My clerk? About what time was this?

KNOWELL. Marry, between one and two, as I take it.

CLEMENT. And what time came my man with the false message to you, Master Kitely?

KITELY. After two, sir.

CLEMENT. Very good. But, Mistress Kitely, how chance that you were at Cob's? Ha?

DAME KITELY. An please you, sir, I'll tell you; my brother Wellbred told me that Cob's house was a suspected place——

CLEMENT. So it appears, methinks; but on.

DAME KITELY. And that my husband used*   regularly went thither daily.

CLEMENT. No matter, so he used himself well, mistress.

DAME KITELY. True sir, but you know what grows by such haunts oftentimes.

CLEMENT. I see rank fruits of a jealous brain, Mistress Kitely. But did you find your husband there, in that case, as you suspected?

KITELY. I found her there, sir.

CLEMENT. Did you so? That alters the case. Who gave you knowledge of your wife's being there?

KITELY. Marry, that did my brother Wellbred.

CLEMENT. How? Wellbred first tell her? Then tell you after? Where is Wellbred?

KITELY. Gone with my sister, sir, I know not whither.

CLEMENT. Why, this is a mere trick, a device; you are gulled in this most grossly, all!—Alas, poor wench, wert thou beaten for this?

TIB. Yes, most pitifully, an't please you.

COB. And worthily, I hope, if it shall prove so.

CLEMENT. Ay, that's like, and a piece of a sentence.—

(Enter a SERVANT.*)*

How now, sir? What's the matter?

SERVANT. Sir, there's a gentleman i' the court without desires to speak with your worship.

CLEMENT. A gentleman! What's he?

SERVANT. A soldier, sir, he says.

CLEMENT. A soldier? Take down my armour, my sword, quickly. A soldier speak with me! Why when;[115] knaves? Come on, come on, *(Arming himself.)* hold my cap there, so; give my my gorget,* my sword.——Stand by; I will throat armor end your matters anon.—Let the soldier enter.

(Exit SERVANT.*)*

(Enter BOBADILL *and* MATTHEW.*)*

Now sir, what ha' you to say to me?

BOBADILL. By your worship's favour——

CLEMENT. Nay, keep out, sir; I know not your pretence;* you send me word, sir, you are a soldier. intention Why, sir, you shall be answered here; here be them have been amongst soldiers. Sir, your pleasure.

BOBADILL. Faith, sir, so it is; this gentleman and myself have been most uncivilly wronged and beaten by one Downright, a coarse fellow about the town here; and for mine own part, I protest, being a man in no sort given to this filthy humour of quarrelling, he hath assaulted me in the way of my peace; despoiled me of mine honour; disarmed me of my weapons; and rudely laid me along* in the knocked me down open streets when I not so much as once offered to resist him.

CLEMENT. O God's precious! Is this the soldier? Here, take my armour off quickly; 'twill make him swoon, I fear; he is not fit to look on't that will put up* a blow. put up with

MATTHEW. An't please your worship, he was bound to the peace.

---

115 "How long are you going to be?" (Nicholson).

CLEMENT. Why, an he were, sir, his hands were not bound, were they?

(*Re-enter* SERVANT.)

SERVANT. There's one of the varlets of the city, sir, has brought two gentlemen here; one, upon your worship's warrant.

CLEMENT. My warrant?

SERVANT. Yes, sir. The officer says procured by these two.

CLEMENT. Bid him come in. (*Exit* SERVANT.) Set by this picture.[116]

(*Enter* DOWNRIGHT, STEPHEN, *and* BRAINWORM.)

What, Master Downright! Are you brought at Master Freshwater's[117] suit here?

DOWNRIGHT. I'faith, sir. And here's another brought at my suit.

CLEMENT. What are you, sir?

STEPHEN. A gentleman, sir.—Oh, uncle!

CLEMENT. Uncle? Who? Master Knowell?

KNOWELL. Ay, sir! This is a wise kinsman of mine.

STEPHEN. God's my witness, uncle, I am wronged here, monstrously. He charges me with stealing of his cloak, and would I might never stir if I did not find it in the street by chance.

DOWNRIGHT. O, did you "find it," now? You said, "you bought it" erewhile.

STEPHEN. And you said I stole it; nay, now my uncle is here, I'll do well enough with you.

CLEMENT. Well, let this breathe* awhile.—You that   rest
have cause to complain there, stand forth. Had you my warrant for this gentleman's apprehension?

BOBADILL. Ay, an't please your worship.

CLEMENT. Nay, do not speak in passion* so.   sorrowfully
Where had you it?

BOBADILL. Of your clerk, sir.

CLEMENT. That's well! An* my clerk can make war-   and
rants and my hand not at 'hem! Where is the warrant?—
Officer, have you it?

[116] This semblance of a soldier, referring to Bobadill's dress.
[117] A contemptuous term for a soldier who had never had overseas duty.

BRAINWORM. No sir, your worship's man, Master Formal, bid me do it for these gentlemen, and he would be my discharge.

CLEMENT. Why, Master Downright, are you such a novice to be served and never see the warrant?

DOWNRIGHT. He did not serve it on me.

CLEMENT. No? How then?

DOWNRIGHT. Marry, sir, he came to me and said he must serve it, and he would use me kindly, and so——

CLEMENT. O, God's pity was it so, sir? "He must serve it!" Give me my long sword there, and help me off. So. Come on, sir varlet, I "must" cut off your legs, sirrah. (BRAINWORM *kneels.*) Nay, stand up, "I'll use you kindly";—I "must" cut off your legs, I say.

(*Flourishes over him with his long sword.*)

BRAINWORM (*kneeling again*). O, good sir, I beseech you; nay, good Master Justice!

CLEMENT. I "must" do it; there is no remedy. I "must" cut off your legs, sirrah; I "must" cut off your ears, you rascal, I must do it; I "must" cut off your nose; I "must" cut off your head.

BRAINWORM. O, good your worship!

CLEMENT. Well, rise. How dost thou do now? Dost thou feel thyself well? Hast thou no harm?

BRAINWORM. No, I thank your good worship, sir.

CLEMENT. Why, so! I said "I must cut off thy legs," and, "I must cut off thy arms," and, "I must cut off thy head"; but, I did not do it. So you said, "You must serve this gentleman with my warrant," but, you did not serve him. You knave, you slave, you rogue, do you say you "must?"—Sirrah, away with him to the jail; I'll teach you a trick for your "must," sir.

BRAINWORM. Good sir, I beseech you, be good to me.

CLEMENT. Tell him he shall to the jail. Away with him, I say.

BRAINWORM. Nay, sir, if you will commit me it shall be for committing more than this. I will not lose by my travail any grain of my fame, certain.

(*Takes off his disguise.*)

CLEMENT. How is this!

KNOWELL. My man Brainworm!

STEPHEN. O yes, uncle. Brainworm has been with my cousin Edward and I all this day.

CLEMENT. I told you all there was some device.*   trick
BRAINWORM. Nay, excellent Justice, since I have laid myself thus open to you, now stand strong for me—both with
your sword and your balance.
CLEMENT. Body o' me, a merry knave!—Give me a bowl of
sack.—If he belong to you, Master Knowell, I bespeak your
patience.
BRAINWORM. That is it I have most need of. Sir, if you'll
pardon me only, I'll glory in all the rest of my exploits.
KNOWELL. Sir, you know I love not to have my favours
come hard from me. You have your pardon, though I suspect you shrewdly for being of counsel with my son against
me.
BRAINWORM. Yes, faith, I have, sir, though you retained
me doubly this morning for yourself: first, as Brainworm;
after, as Fitz-Sword. I was your reformed soldier, sir. 'Twas
I sent you to Cob's upon the errand without end.
KNOWELL. Is it possible! Or that thou shouldst disguise thy
language so as I should not know thee?
BRAINWORM. O, sir, this has been the day of my metamorphosis. It is not that shape alone that I have run through
today. I brought this gentleman, Master Kitely, a message too,
in the form of Master Justice's man here, to draw him out
o' the way, as well as your worship, while Master Wellbred
might make a conveyance of Mistress Bridget to my young
master.
KITELY. How! My sister stolen away?
KNOWELL. My son is not married, I hope!
BRAINWORM. Faith, sir, they are both as sure* as   contracted
love, a priest and three thousand pound—which is her portion—can make 'hem; and by this time are ready to bespeak
their wedding supper at the Windmill, except some friend
here prevent* 'hem and invite 'hem home.   anticipate
CLEMENT. Marry, that will I (I thank thee for putting me
in mind on't).—Sirrah, go you and fetch 'hem hither, "upon
my warrant." (*Exit* SERVANT.) Neither's friends have cause
to be sorry, if I know the young couple aright.—Here, I
drink to thee for thy good news. But, I pray thee, what hast
thou done with my man Formal?
BRAINWORM. Faith, sir, after some ceremony past, as making him drunk, first with story and then with wine,—but all
in kindness—and stripping him to his shirt, I left him in that
cool vein departed, sold "your worship's warrant" to these
two, pawned his livery for that valet's gown to serve it in;

and thus have brought myself, by my activity, to your worship's consideration.

CLEMENT. And I will consider thee in another cup of sack. Here's to thee, which having drunk off, this is my sentence: Pledge me. Thou hast done or assisted to nothing, in my judgment, but deserves to be pardoned for the wit o' the offence. If thy master, or any man here, be angry with thee, I shall suspect his ingine* while I know him, for't.——How wit now, what noise is that?

(*Enter* SERVANT.)

SERVANT. Sir, it is Roger is come home.

CLEMENT. Bring him in, bring him in.

(*Enter* FORMAL *in a suit of armour.*)

What! drunk in arms, against me? Your reason, your reason for this?

FORMAL. I beseech your worship to pardon me; I happened into ill company by chance that cast me into a sleep and stript me of all my clothes——

CLEMENT. Well, tell him I am Justice Clement, and do pardon him. But what is this to your armour? What may that signify?

FORMAL. An't please you, sir, it hung up i' the room where I was stript; and I borrowed it of one o' the drawers* to waiters come home in because I was loth to do penance through the street i' my shirt.

CLEMENT. Well, stand by a while.

(*Enter* E. KNOWELL, WELLBRED, *and* BRIDGET.)

Who be these? O, the young company. Welcome, welcome! Gi' you joy.[118] Nay, Mistress Bridget, blush not; you are not so fresh a bride but the news of it is come hither afore you. Master bridegroom, I ha' made your peace; give me your hand. So will I for all the rest ere you forsake my roof.

E. KNOWELL. We are the more bound to your humanity sir.

CLEMENT. Only these two (*Indicating* BOBADILL *and* MAT-THEW.) have so little of man in 'hem they are no part of my care.

[118] Traditional greeting to the bridal couple.

WELLBRED. Yes, sir, let me pray you for this gentleman;* he belongs to my sister, the bride.   that is, Matthew
     CLEMENT. In what place, sir.
     WELLBRED. Of her delight, sir; below the stairs, and in
public. Her poet, sir.
     CLEMENT. A poet? I will challenge him myself presently
at extempore.

> Mount up thy Phlegon,[119] Muse, and testify
>   How Saturn, sitting in an ebon cloud,
> Disrobed his podex,* white as ivory,   rump
>   And, through the welkin, thundered all aloud.

     WELLBRED. He is not for extempore, sir. He is all for the
pocket muse; please you command a sight of it.
     CLEMENT. Yes, yes, search him for a taste of his vein.
     (*They search* MATTHEW'S *pockets.*)
     WELLBRED. You must not deny the Queen's Justice, sir,
under a writ o' rebellion.
     CLEMENT. What! All this verse? Body o' me, he carries a
whole ream,[120] a commonwealth of paper in 's hose; let's see
some of his subjects.
     (*Reads.*)

> "Unto the boundless ocean of thy face,
>   Runs this poor river, charged with streams of eyes."

How? This is stolen.[121]
     E. KNOWELL. A parody! A parody, with a kind of miracu-
lous gift to make it absurder than it was.
     CLEMENT. Is all the rest of this batch?—Bring me a torch;
lay it together, and give fire. Cleanse the air. (*Sets the papers
on fire.*) Here was enough to have infected the whole city, if
it had not been taken in time. See, see, how our poet's glory
shines! Brighter, and brighter! Still it increases! Oh, now it's
at the highest: and now, it declines as fast. You may see. *Sic
transit gloria mundi!*[122]

---

[119] One of the horses of the sun.

[120] Pun on *realm*, which was written and pronounced *ream*.

[121] From the opening lines of Samuel Daniel's first sonnet to
Delia.

[122] "Thus passes the glory of the world."

KNOWELL. There's an emblem[123] for you, son, and your studies!

CLEMENT. Nay, no speech or act of mine be drawn against such as profess it worthily. They are not born every year, as an alderman. There goes more to the making of a good poet than a sheriff, Master Kitely. You look upon me! Though I live i' the city here amongst you, I will do more reverence to him, when I meet him, than I will to the mayor—out of his year.[124] But, these paper-peddlers! These ink-dabblers! They cannot expect reprehension or reproach. They have it with the fact.

E. KNOWELL. Sir, you have saved me the labour of a defence.

CLEMENT. It shall be discourse for supper between your father and me, if he dare undertake me. But, to dispatch away these. You sign o' the soldier, and picture o' the poet (but both so false I will not ha' you hanged out at my door till midnight[125]), while we are at supper you two shall penitently fast it out in my court without; and, if you will, you may pray there that we may be so merry within as to forgive, or forget you, when we come out. Here's a third,* because we   that is, Formal tender your safety, shall watch you; he is provided for the purpose.[126] Look to your charge, sir.

STEPHEN. And what shall I do?

CLEMENT. O! I had lost a sheep, and he had not bleated!— Why, sir, you shall give Master Downright his cloak; and I will entreat him to take it. A trencher and a napkin you shall have, i' the buttery, and keep Cob and his wife company here —whom I will entreat first to be reconciled—and you to endeavour with your wit to keep 'hem so.

STEPHEN. I'll do my best.

COB. Why, now I see thou art honest, Tib, I receive thee as my dear and mortal wife again.

TIB. And I you, as my loving and obedient husband.

CLEMENT. Good complement! It will be their bridal night too. They are married anew. Come, I conjure the rest to put off all discontent. You, Master Downright, your anger; you Master Knowell, your cares; Master Kitely and his wife, their jealousy.

---

[123] "A picture and short posie [motto] expressing some particular conceit" (Cotsgrave).

[124] That is, when his term of office is over.

[125] "When no one can see you" (Nicholson).

[126] Because he is wearing armor.

> For, I must tell you both, while that is fed,
> Horns i' the mind are worse than o' the head.

KITELY. Sir, thus they go from me. Kiss me, sweetheart.

> "See what a drove of horns fly in the air,
> Winged with my cleansed and my cred'lous breath!
> Watch 'hem, suspicious eyes, watch where they fall.
> See, see! On heads that think they've none at all!
> O, what a plenteous world of this will come!
> When air rains horns, all may be sure of some."

I ha' learned so much verse out of a jealous man's part in a play.

CLEMENT. 'Tis well, 'tis well! This night we'll dedicate to friendship, love, and laughter. Master bridegroom, take your bride and lead; everyone, a fellow. Here is my mistress, Brainworm, to whom all my addresses of courtship shall have their reference—whose adventures this day, when our grandchildren shall hear to be made a fable, I doubt not, but it shall find both spectators and applause.

                                          (*Exeunt.*)

The Shoemaker's Holiday

BY THOMAS DEKKER

Thomas Dekker (*circa* 1572–1632), one of the most assiduous hack writers of the Elizabethan stage, was also one of its most attractive and gifted creators. *The Shoemaker's Holiday*, a comedy both folksy and romantic, is the most satisfying product of his congenial temperament. Apparently born in London and educated in one of its grammar schools, where a student was bound to acquire more Latin than in most American colleges, Dekker became a member of the bank of playwrights who "serviced" the Lord Admiral's Men with plays and who received advances for them from the company's business manager Philip Henslowe. It is calculated that Dekker wrote and collaborated in the writing of at least forty plays in addition to supplying London publishers with about twenty pamphlets, one of which, a satire on the city's fashionable dandies, sharpers, and dupes, is the well-known *Gull's Hornbook*. Despite his prodigious labors he appears to have been in an almost constant state of penury and indebtedness; committed to prison for debt in 1613, he languished there for six years. On his release he quietly resumed his labors for the theatre in collaboration with younger playwrights, and later he drew a commission to write the Lord Mayor's pageants of 1628 and 1629.

Dekker revealed his genial vein early in *Old Fortunatus* (1596), a charming folk play written in pleasant verse. A revised version is known to have been performed at Elizabeth's court during the Christmas season of 1599. About half a decade later, in 1604, he reached a high point in his literary career with a collaboration, the two-part drama *The Honest Whore*. Characteristically Dekker was able to infuse a story of witchcraft, *The Witch of Edmonton*, with sympathy for both the Witch and the wife-murderer Frank.

It is, however, his less ambitiously planned play, *The Shoemaker's Holiday*, based on a book about the "gentle craft" of cobblers, which has chiefly carried Dekker's name down the

ages. The play combines a congenial picture of London life
and manners with the romantic comedy of a young nobleman's
wooing of the Lord Mayor's daughter in the disguise of a
Dutch shoemaker. Another romantic story element tells of a
conscripted young shoemaker's recovering his wife from the
man about to marry her after a report that her soldier husband
is dead. Exuberant in action and speech, vital and vigorous in
characterization, *The Shoemaker's Holiday* combines hearty
humor with sympathy and realism of manners with romanticism of sentiments. It is a comedy both of milieu and character. Outstanding among the captivating character sketches is
the portrait of master-cobbler Simon Eyre, destined to become
Lord Mayor of London. The success of the young nobleman in
love does not detract from the historically most important
quality of the play—its democratic verve and partiality for a
middle-class world of energetic masters and plucky apprentices. Much life and liveliness remain in this play even today,
as many an amateur production has shown and as a professional production of the play by Orson Welles at his Mercury
Theatre in 1938 made triumphantly evident.

J. G.

Author. Although all early editions of the play appeared
without an author's name on the title page, Thomas Dekker's
authorship is authenticated by a record of payment in Henslowe's *Diary.*

Date. The play may safely be dated 1599. The payment
entry in Henslowe's *Diary* bears the date July 15, 1599. On
January 1, 1600, the play received a court performance.

Text and Publishing Data. The first quarto, printed by Val-
entine Simmes, appeared in 1600. There is no Stationers' Register entry for the play, but Simmes seems to have had the
publishing rights, because he transferred control of the play
to John Wright on April 19, 1610. Wright brought out four
editions: 1610, 1618, 1624, and 1631. These are no more
than reprints of the first quarto (Q1) with minor changes.
Wright, in turn, transferred his copyright to his brother
Edward, who subsequently transferred it to William Gilbertson. In 1617 Gilbertson issued a sixth quarto (Q6). Whether
Q1 was based on the author's manuscript or upon a playhouse
copy cannot be determined; Q1, however, is a good text. None
of these early quartos bears act or scene divisions.

Sources. The play was based on three tales about shoemakers from Thomas Deloney's *The Gentle Craft,* published in

1598. The historical Simon Eyre was an early fifteenth-century Londoner who had been an upholsterer and draper before rising to become Lord Mayor of London. Deloney changed him to a shoemaker.

Early Stage History. Originally the play was produced by the Lord Admiral's Men. The first known performance took place before the Queen at court on New Year's Day, 1600.

W. G.

DRAMATIS PERSONAE

THE KING
THE EARL OF CORNWALL
SIR HUGH LACY, Earl of Lincoln
ROWLAND LACY, otherwise HANS
ASKEW } his nephews
SIR ROGER OTELEY, Lord Mayor of London
Master HAMMON,
Master WARNER, } citizens of London
Master SCOTT,
SIMON EYRE, the shoemaker
ROGER, commonly called
    HODGE,
FIRK, } EYRE's journeymen
RALPH,
LOVELL, a courtier
DODGER, servant to the EARL OF LINCOLN
A DUTCH SKIPPER
A BOY
Courtiers, Attendants, Officers, Soldiers, Hunters, Shoemakers,
    Apprentices, Servants
ROSE, daughter of SIR ROGER
SYBIL, her maid
MARGERY, wife of SIMON EYRE
JANE, wife of RALPH
           SCENE—London and Old Ford

THE PROLOGUE

As It Was Pronounced Before the Queen's Majesty

As wretches in a storm (expecting day),
With trembling hands and eyes cast up to heaven,
Make prayers the anchor of their conquered hopes,
So we, dear goddess, wonder of all eyes,
Your meanest vassals, through mistrust and fear
To sink into the bottom of disgrace
By our imperfect pastimes, prostrate thus
On bended knees, our sails of hope do strike,
Dreading the bitter storms of your dislike.
Since then, unhappy men, our hap* is such,   fortune
That to ourselves ourselves no help can bring,
But needs must perish, if your saint-like ears
(Locking the temple where all mercy sits)
Refuse the tribute of our begging tongues:
Oh grant, bright mirror of true chastity,
From those life-breathing stars, your sun-like eyes
One gracious smile: for your celestial breath
Must send us life, or sentence us to death.

ACT I

Scene 1

(*A street in London. Enter the* LORD MAYOR *and the* EARL OF LINCOLN.)

LINCOLN. My lord mayor, you have sundry times
Feasted myself and many courtiers more:
Seldom or never can we be so kind
To make requital of your courtesy.
But leaving this, I hear my cousin* Lacy   nephew
Is much affected to* your daughter Rose.   loves
    LORD MAYOR. True, my good lord, and she loves him so
  well
That I mislike her boldness in the chase.
    LINCOLN. Why, my lord mayor, think you it then a shame,
To join a Lacy with an Oteley's name?
    LORD MAYOR. Too mean is my poor girl for his high birth;
Poor citizens must not with courtiers wed,
Who will in silks and gay apparel spend
More in one year than I am worth, by far:
Therefore your honor need not doubt* my girl.   worry about
    LINCOLN. Take heed, my lord, advise you what you do!
A verier unthrift lives not in the world,
Than is my cousin; for I'll tell you what:
'Tis now almost a year since he requested
To travel countries for experience;
I furnished him with coin, bills of exchange,
Letters of credit, men to wait on him,
Solicited my friends in Italy
Well to respect him. But to see the end:
Scant had he journeyed through half Germany,
But all his coin was spent, his men cast off,
His bills embezzled,* and my jolly coz,   squandered
Ashamed to show his bankrupt presence here,
Became a shoemaker in Wittenberg,
A goodly science for a gentleman
Of such descent! Now judge the rest by this:
Suppose your daughter have a thousand pound,

He did consume me more in one half year;
And make him heir to all the wealth you have,
One twelvemonth's rioting will waste it all.
Then seek, my lord, some honest citizen
To wed your daughter to.
   LORD MAYOR. I thank your lordship.
(*Aside.*) Well, fox, I understand your subtilty.—
As for your nephew, let your lordship's eye
But watch his actions, and you need not fear,
For I have sent my daughter far enough.
And yet your cousin Rowland might do well,
Now he hath learned an occupation;
And yet I scorn to call him son-in-law.
   LINCOLN. Ay, but I have a better trade for him:
I thank his grace,* he hath appointed him   majesty
Chief colonel of all those companies
Mustered in London and the shires about,
To serve his highness in those wars of France.
See where he comes!—

   (*Enter* LOVELL, LACY, *and* ASKEW.)

                   Lovell, what news with you?
   LOVELL. My lord of Lincoln, 'tis his highness' will,
That presently* your cousin ship for France   immediately
With all his powers; he would not for a million,
But they should land at Dieppe within four days.
   LINCOLN. Go certify his grace, it shall be done.
                     (*Exit* LOVELL.)
Now, cousin Lacy, in what forwardness
Are all your companies?
   LACY. All well prepared.
The men of Hertfordshire lie at Mile-end,
Suffolk and Essex train in Tothill-fields,
The Londoners and those of Middlesex,
All gallantly prepared in Finsbury,
With frolic spirits long for their parting hour.
   LORD MAYOR. They have their imprest,* coats,   advance pay
     and furniture;*   equipment
And, if it please your cousin Lacy come
To the Guildhall, he shall receive his pay;
And twenty pounds besides my brethren*   that is, city officials
Will freely give him, to approve* our loves   prove
We bear unto my lord, your uncle here.

LACY. I thank your honor.

LINCOLN. Thanks, my good lord mayor.

LORD MAYOR. At the Guildhall we will expect* your   await
   coming.

                                                 (Exit.)

LINCOLN. To approve your loves to me? No subtilty!
Nephew, that twenty pounds he doth bestow
For joy to rid you from his daughter Rose.
But, cousins both, now here are none but friends.
I would not have you cast an amorous eye
Upon so mean a project as the love
Of a gay, wanton, painted citizen.
I know, this churl even in the height of scorn
Doth hate the mixture of his blood with thine.
I pray thee, do thou so! Remember, coz,
What honorable fortunes wait on thee:
Increase the king's love, which so brightly shines,
And gilds thy hopes. I have no heir but thee,—
And yet not thee, if with a wayward spirit
Thou start* from the true bias* of my love.   turn away/inclination

    LACY. My lord, I will for honor, not desire
Of land or livings, or to be your heir,
So guide my actions in pursuit of France,
As shall add glory to the Lacys' name.

        LINCOLN. Coz, for those words here's thirty
            Portuguese,*   gold coins
And, Nephew Askew, there a few for you.
Fair Honor, in her loftiest eminence,
Stays in France for you, till you fetch her thence.
Then, nephews, clap swift wings on your designs:
Begone, begone, make haste to the Guildhall;
There presently I'll meet you. Do not stay:
Where honor beckons, shame attends delay.

                                              (Exit.)

    ASKEW. How gladly would your uncle have you gone!

    LACY. True, coz, but I'll o'erreach his policies.
I have some serious business for three days,
Which nothing but my presence can dispatch.
You, therefore, cousin, with the companies,
Shall haste to Dover; there I'll meet with you:
Or, if I stay past my prefixèd time,
Away for France; we'll meet in Normandy.
The twenty pounds my lord mayor gives to me
You shall receive, and these ten Portuguese,

Part of mine uncle's thirty. Gentle coz,
Have care to our great charge; I know, your wisdom
Hath tried itself in higher consequence.

ASKEW. Coz, all myself am yours: yet have this care,
To lodge in London with all secrecy;
Our uncle Lincoln hath, besides his own,
Many a jealous eye, that in your face
Stares only to watch means for your disgrace.

LACY. Stay, cousin, who be these?

(*Enter* SIMON EYRE, MARGERY *his wife*, HODGE, FIRK, JANE, *and* RALPH *with a pair of shoes.*)

EYRE. Leave whining, leave whining! Away with this whimpering, this puling, these blubbering tears, and these wet eyes! I'll get thy husband discharged, I warrant thee, sweet Jane; go to!

HODGE. Master, here be the captains.

EYRE. Peace, Hodge; husht, ye knave, husht!

FIRK. Here be the cavaliers and the colonels, master.

EYRE. Peace, Firk; peace, my fine Firk! Stand by with your pishery-pashery,* away! I am a man of the best   trifling talk
presence; I'll speak to them, an they were Popes.—Gentlemen, captains, colonels, commanders! Brave men, brave leaders, may it please you to give me audience. I am Simon Eyre, the mad shoemaker of Tower Street; this wench with the mealy mouth that will never tire is my wife, I can tell you; here's Hodge, my man and my foreman; here's Firk, my fine firk-ing* journeyman, and this is blubbered Jane. All   that is, lively
we come to be suitors for this honest Ralph. Keep him at home, and as I am a true shoemaker and a gentleman of the Gentle Craft, buy spurs yourselves, and I'll find* ye   provide
boots these seven years.

MARGERY. Seven years, husband?

EYRE. Peace, midriff, peace! I know what I do. Peace!

FIRK. Truly, master cormorant,* you shall do   that is, colonel
God good service to let Ralph and his wife stay together. She's a young new-married woman; if you take her husband away from her a-night, you undo her; she may beg in the daytime; for he's as good a workman at a prick and an awl, as any is in our trade.

JANE. O let him stay, else I shall be undone.

FIRK. Ay, truly, she shall be laid at one side like a pair of old shoes else, and be occupied for no use.

LACY. Truly, my friends, it lies not in my power:
The Londoners are pressed,* paid, and set forth   impressed
By the lord mayor, I cannot change a man.

HODGE. Why, then you were as good be a corporal as a
colonel, if you cannot discharge one good fellow; and I tell
you true, I think you do more than you can answer, to press
a man within a year and a day of his marriage.

EYRE. Well said, melancholy Hodge; gramercy, my fine
foreman.

MARGERY. Truly, gentlemen, it were ill done for such as
you, to stand so stiffly against a poor young wife; considering
her case, she is new-married, but let that pass: I pray, deal
not roughly with her; her husband is a young man, and but
newly entered, but let that pass.

EYRE. Away with your pishery-pashery, your pols and your
edipols!* Peace, midriff; silence, Cicely   that is, exclamations
Bumtrinket! Let your head speak.

FIRK. Yea, and the horns too, master.

EYRE. Too soon, my fine Firk, too soon! Peace, scoundrels!
See you this man? Captains, you will not release him? Well,
let him go; he's a proper shot; let him vanish! Peace, Jane,
dry up thy tears, they'll make his powder dankish. Take him,
brave men; Hector of Troy was an hackney* to him,   drudge
Hercules and Termagant[1] scoundrels, Prince Arthur's Round-
table—by the Lord of Ludgate—ne'er fed such a tall,*   valiant
such a dapper swordsman; by the life of Pharaoh, a brave
resolute swordsman! Peace, Jane! I say no more, mad knaves.

FIRK. See, see, Hodge, how my master raves in commenda-
tion of Ralph!

HODGE. Ralph, th' art a gull,* by this hand, an* thou   fool/if
goest not.

ASKEW. I am glad, good Master Eyre, it is my hap
To meet so resolute a soldier.
Trust me, for your report and love to him,
A common slight regard shall not respect him.[2]

LACY. Is thy name Ralph?

RALPH.   Yes, sir.

LACY. Give me thy hand;
Thou shalt not want, as I am a gentleman.

---

[1] An overbearing character from medieval drama thought to be
an Islamic deity.

[2] He will receive special consideration.

Woman, be patient; God, no doubt, will send
Thy husband safe again; but he must go,
His country's quarrel says it shall be so.

HODGE. Th' art a gull, by my stirrup,[3] if thou dost not go.
I will not have thee strike thy gimlet into these weak vessels;
prick thine enemies, Ralph.

(*Enter* DODGER.)

DODGER. My lord, your uncle on the Tower-hill
Stays with the lord mayor and the aldermen,
And doth request you with all speed you may,
To hasten thither.

ASKEW.   Cousin, come let's go.

LACY. Dodger, run you before, tell them we come.—
                                (*Exit* DODGER.)
This Dodger is mine uncle's parasite.
The arrant'st varlet that e'er breathed on earth;
He sets more discord in a noble house
By one day's broaching of his pickthank* tales,   tattle
Than can be salved again in twenty years,
And he, I fear, shall go with us to France,
To pry into our actions.

ASKEW.   Therefore, coz,
It shall behove you to be circumspect.

LACY. Fear not, good cousin.—Ralph, hie to your colors.

RALPH. I must, because there is no remedy;
But, gentle master and my loving dame,
As you have always been a friend to me,
So in my absence think upon my wife.

JANE. Alas, my Ralph.

MARGERY.   She cannot speak for weeping.

EYRE. Peace, you cracked groats,* you   that is, worthless ones
mustard tokens,* disquiet not the brave sol-   —for both expressions
dier. Go thy ways, Ralph!

JANE. Ay, ay, you bid him go; What shall I do
When he is gone?

FIRK. Why, be doing with me or my fellow Hodge; be not
idle.

EYRE. Let me see thy hand, Jane. This fine hand, this white
hand, these pretty fingers must spin, must card, must work;

---

[3] The strap by which a shoemaker steadies his last on his knee.

work, you bombast-cotton-candle-quean,* work that is, plump lass
for your living, with a pox to you.—Hold thee, Ralph, here's
five sixpences for thee; fight for the honor of the Gentle Craft,
for the gentlemen shoemakers, the courageous cordwainers,
the flower of St. Martin's, the mad knaves of Bedlam, Fleet
Street, Tower Street and Whitechapel; crack me the crowns
of the French knaves; a pox on them, crack them; fight, by the
Lord of Ludgate; fight, my fine boy!

FIRK. Here, Ralph, here's three twopences: two carry into
France, the third shall wash our souls at parting, for sorrow
is dry. For my sake, firk* the *Basa mon cues.*[4]   beat

HODGE. Ralph, I am heavy* at parting; but here's a   sad
shilling for thee. God send* thee to cram thy   grant
slops* with French crowns, and thy enemies'   breeches
bellies with bullets.

RALPH. I thank you, master, and I thank you all.
Now, gentle wife, my loving lovely Jane,
Rich men, at parting, give their wives rich gifts,
Jewels and rings, to grace their lily hands.
Thou know'st our trade makes rings for women's heels:
Here take this pair of shoes, cut out by Hodge.
Stitched by my fellow Firk, seamed by myself.
Made up and pinked* with letters for thy name.   perforated
Wear them, my dear Jane, for thy husband's sake,
And every morning, when thou pull'st them on,
Remember me, and pray for my return.
Make much of them; for I have made them so,
That I can know them from a thousand mo.

(*Drum sounds. Enter the* LORD MAYOR, *the* EARL OF LIN-
COLN, LACY, ASKEW, DODGER, *and* SOLDIERS. *They pass
over the stage;* RALPH *falls in amongst them;* FIRK *and the
rest cry 'Farewell,' etc., and so exeunt.*)

---

[4] That is, the French. Cf. *baisez ma queue.*

ACT II

Scene 1

(A garden at Old Ford. Enter ROSE, *alone, making a garland.)*

ROSE. Here sit thou down upon this flow'ry bank,
And make a garland for thy Lacy's head.
These pinks, these roses, and these violets,
These blushing gilliflowers, these marigolds,
The fair embroidery of his coronet,
Carry not half such beauty in their cheeks,
As the sweet countenance of my Lacy doth.
O my most unkind father! O my stars,
Why lowered* you so at my nativity,   dimmed
To make me love, yet live robbed of my love?
Here as a thief am I imprisonèd
For my dear Lacy's sake within those walls,
Which by my father's cost were builded up
For better purposes; here must I languish
For him that doth as much lament, I know,
Mine absence, as for him I pine in woe.

(Enter SYBIL.)

SYBIL. Good morrow, young mistress. I am sure you make
that garland for me; against* I shall be Lady of the   when
Harvest.

ROSE. Sybil, what news at London?

SYBIL. None but good; my lord mayor, your father, and
Master Philpot, your uncle, and Master Scott, your cousin,
and Mistress Frigbottom by Doctors' Commons, do all, by my
troth, send you most hearty commendations.

ROSE. Did Lacy send kind greetings to his love?

SYBIL. O yes, out of cry,* by my troth. I   beyond description
scant knew him; here 'a* wore a scarf; and here a scarf,   he
here a bunch of feathers, and here precious stones and jewels,
and a pair of garters,—O, monstrous! like one of our yellow
silk curtains at home here in Old Ford house, here in Master
Bellymount's chamber. I stood at our door in Cornhill, looked

at him, he at me indeed, spake to him, but he not to me, not
a word; marry go-up, thought I, with a wanion!* with a vengeance
He passed by me as proud—Marry foh! are you grown
humorous,* thought I; and so shut the door, and in   capricious
I came.

ROSE. O Sybil, how dost thou my Lacy wrong!
My Rowland is as gentle as a lamb,
No dove was ever half so mild as he.

SYBIL. Mild? yea, as a bushel of stamped
    crabs.*   crushed
                                                  crab apples
He looked upon me as sour as verjuice.5 Go thy ways, thought
I; thou may'st be much in my gaskins,* but nothing   breeches
in my netherstocks.* This is your fault, mistress, to   stockings
love him that loves not you; he thinks scorn to do as he's done
to; but if I were as you, I'd cry: Go by, Jeronimo, go by!6
I'd set mine old debts against my new driblets,
And the hare's foot against the goose giblets,7
For if ever I sigh, when sleep I should take,
Pray God I may lose my maidenhead when I wake.

ROSE. Will my love leave me then, and go to France?

SYBIL. I know not that, but I am sure I see him stalk
before the soldiers. By my troth, he is a proper* man;   handsome
but he is proper* that proper doth. Let him go   worthy
snick-up,* young mistress.   hang

ROSE. Get thee to London, and learn perfectly,
Whether my Lacy go to France, or no.
Do this, and I will give thee for thy pains
My cambric apron and my Romish gloves,
My purple stockings and a stomacher.
Say, wilt thou do this, Sybil, for my sake?

SYBIL. Will I, quotha? At whose suit? By my troth, yes
I'll go. A cambric apron, gloves, a pair of purple stockings,
and a stomacher! I'll sweat in purple, mistress, for you; I'll
take anything that comes a God's name. O rich! a cambric
apron! Faith, then have at 'up tails all'.8 I'll go jiggy-joggy to
London, and be here in a trice, young mistress.

(*Exit.*)

---

  5 Juice from sour green fruit.
  6 This is a line from Kyd's *Spanish Tragedy*.
  7 According to Lange, this couplet may be paraphrased, "off
with the old love, on with the new; an even exchange."
  8 A card game; also a dance tune.

ROSE. Do so, good Sybil. Meantime wretched I
Will sit and sigh for his lost company.

(Exit.)

Scene 2

(*A street in London. Enter* ROWLAND LACY, *like a Dutch
shoemaker.*)

LACY. How many shapes have gods and kings devised,
Thereby to compass* their desired loves!   encircle
It is no shame for Rowland Lacy, then,
To clothe his cunning with the Gentle Craft,
That, thus disguised, I may unknown possess
The only happy presence of my Rose.
For her have I forsook my charge in France,
Incurred the king's displeasure, and stirred up
Rough hatred in mine uncle Lincoln's breast.
O love, how powerful art thou, that canst change
High birth to baseness, and a noble mind
To the mean semblance of a shoemaker!
But thus it must be. For her cruel father,
Hating the single union of our souls,
Hath secretly conveyed my Rose from London,
To bar me of her presence; but I trust,
Fortune and this disguise will further me
Once more to view her beauty, gain her sight.
Here in Tower Street with Eyre the shoemaker
Mean I a while to work; I know the trade,
I learnt it when I was in Wittenberg.
Then cheer thy hoping spirits, be not dismayed,
Thou canst not want: do Fortune what she can,
The Gentle Craft is living for a man.

(Exit.)

Scene 3

(*An open yard before Eyre's house. Enter* EYRE, *making
himself ready.**)   dressing

EYRE. Where be these boys, these girls, these drabs, these
scoundrels? They wallow in the fat brewis* of my bounty,   broth
and lick up the crumbs of my table, yet will not rise to see
my walks cleansed. Come out, you powder-beef*   salt beef

queans! What, Nan! what, Madge Mumble-crust! Come out, you fat midriff-swag-belly-whores, and sweep me these ken- nels* that the noisome stench offend not the noses of my   gutters neighbors. What, Firk, I say; what, Hodge! Open my shop- windows! What, Firk, I say!

(*Enter* FIRK.)

FIRK. O master, is't you that speak bandog* and   furiously Bedlam* this morning? I was in a dream, and mused   madly what madman was got into the street so early; have you drunk this morning that your throat is so clear?

EYRE. Ah, well said, Firk; well said, Firk. To work, my fine knave, to work! Wash thy face, and thou'lt be more blest.

FIRK. Let them wash my face that will eat it. Good mas- ter, send for a souse-wife,* if you will have my face   pig pickler cleaner.

(*Enter* HODGE.)

EYRE. Away, sloven! avaunt, scoundrel!—Good-morrow, Hodge; good-morrow, my fine foreman.

HODGE. O master, good-morrow; y'are an early stirrer. Here's a fair morning.—Good-morrow, Firk, I could have slept this hour. Here's a brave day towards.

EYRE. O, haste to work, my fine foreman, haste to work.

FIRK. Master, I am dry as dust to hear my fellow Roger talk of fair weather; let us pray for good leather, and let clowns* and ploughboys and those that work in the   rustics fields pray for brave* days. We work in a dry shop;   splendid what care I if it rain?

(*Enter* MARGERY.)

EYRE. How now, Dame Margery, can you see to rise? Trip and go, call up the drabs, your maids.

MARGERY. See to rise? I hope 'tis time enough, 'tis early enough for any woman to be seen abroad. I marvel how many wives in Tower Street are up so soon. Gods me, 'tis not noon,—here's a yowling!

EYRE. Peace, Margery, peace! Where's Cicely Bumtrinket, your maid? She has a privy fault, she farts in her sleep. Call

the quean up; if my men want* shoe-thread, I'll   lack
swinge* her in a stirrup.   beat

FIRK. Yet, that's but a dry beating; here's still a sign of
drought.

(*Enter* LACY, *as* HANS, *singing.*)

HANS.   *Der was een bore van Gelderland*
      Frolick sie byen;
   He was als dronck he cold nyet stand,
      Upsolce sie byen.
   Tap eens de canneken,
   Drincke, schone mannekin.[9]

FIRK. Master, for my life, yonder's a brother of the Gentle
Craft; if he bear not Saint Hugh's bones,[10] I'll forfeit my
bones; he's some uplandish* workman: hire him, good provincial
master, that I may learn some gibble-gabble; 'twill make us
work the faster.

EYRE. Peace, Firk! A hard world! Let him pass, let him
vanish; we have journeymen enow.* Peace, my fine   enough
Firk!

MARGERY (*sarcastically*). Nay, nay, y' are best follow your
man's counsel; you shall see what will come on't: we have
not men enow, but we must entertain* every butter-   hire
box;* but let that pass.   Dutchman

HODGE. Dame, 'fore God, if my master follow your counsel, he'll consume little beef. He shall be glad of men,
an* he can catch them.   if

FIRK. Ay, that he shall.

HODGE. 'Fore God, a proper man, and I warrant, a fine
workman. Master, farewell; dame, adieu; if such a man as he
cannot find work, Hodge is not for you.

(*Offers to go.*)

[9] There was a boor from Gelderland,
    Merry they be;
He was so drunk he could not stand,
    Drunken [?] they be.
Tap once the cannikin,
Drink, pretty mannikin.

[10] In return for kindnesses from the shoemakers, St. Hugh be-
queathed them his bones. These were supposedly made into shoemakers' tools.

ītay, my fine Hodge.

aith, an your foreman go, dame, you must take a
ʌɹɪney to seek a new journeyman; if Roger remove, Firk
follows. If Saint Hugh's bones shall not be set a-work, I may
prick mine awl in the walls, and go play. Fare ye well, master;
goodbye, dame.

EYRE. Tarry, my fine Hodge, my brisk foreman! Stay,
Firk!—Peace, pudding-broth! By the Lord of Ludgate, I love
my men as my life. Peace, you gallimaufry*—   hodge-podge
Hodge, if he want work, I'll hire him. One of you to him;
stay,—he comes to us.

HANS. *Goeden dach, meester, ende u vro oak.*[11]

FIRK. Nails, if I should speak after him without drinking, I
should choke. And you, friend Oake, are you of the Gentle
Craft?

HANS. *Yaw, yaw, ick bin den skomawker.*

FIRK. *Den skomaker*, quotha! And mark you, *skomaker*,
have you all your tools, a good rubbing-pin, a good stopper,
a good dresser, your four sorts of awls, and your two balls of
wax, your paring knife, your hand- and thumb-leathers, and
good St. Hugh's bones to smooth up your work?

HANS. *Yaw, yaw; be niet vorveard. Ick hab all de dingen
voour mack skooes groot and cleane.*[12]

FIRK. Ha, ha! Good master, hire him; he'll make me laugh
so that I shall work more in mirth than I can in earnest.

EYRE. Hear ye, friend, have ye any skill in the mystery* of cordwainers?   trade

HANS. *Ick weet niet wat yow seg; ick verstaw you niet.*[13]

FIRK. Why, thus, man: (*Imitating by gesture a shoemaker
at work.*) *Ick verste u niet*, quotha.

HANS. *Yaw, yaw, yaw; ick can dat wel doen.*

FIRK. *Yaw, yaw!* He speaks yawing like a jackdaw that
gapes to be fed with cheese-curds. O, he'll give a villanous pull
at a can of double-beer; but Hodge and I have the vantage,
we must drink first, because we are the eldest journeymen.

EYRE. What is thy name?

HANS. Hans—Hans Meulter.

EYRE. Give me thy hand; th' art welcome.—Hodge, entertain him; Firk, bid him welcome; come, Hans. Run, wife, bid

[11] "Good day, master, and your wife also."

[12] "Yes, yes; do not be afraid. I have all the things to make
shoes large and small."

[13] "I don't know what you are saying; I don't understand you."

your maids, your trullibubs,* make ready my fine ^that is,^ men's breakfasts. To him, Hodge! useless charges

HODGE. Hans, th' art welcome; use thyself friendly, for we are good fellows; if not, thou shalt be fought with, wert thou bigger than a giant.

FIRK. Yea, and drunk with, wert thou Gargantua. My master keeps no cowards, I tell thee.—Ho, boy, bring him an heel-block, here's a new journeyman.

(*Enter* BOY.)

HANS. *O, ick wersto you; ick moet een halve dossen cans betaelen; here, boy, nempt dis skilling, tap eens freelicke.*[14]

(*Exit* BOY.)

EYRE. Quick, snipper-snapper, away! Firk, scour thy throat, thou shalt wash it with Castilian liquor.

(*Enter* BOY.)

Come, my last of the fives,[15] give me a can. Have to thee, Hans; here, Hodge; here, Firk; drink, you mad Greeks, and work like true Trojans, and pray for Simon Eyre, the shoemaker.—Here, Hans, and th' art welcome.

FIRK. Lo, dame, you would have lost a good fellow that will teach us to laugh. This beer came hopping in well.

MARGERY. Simon, it is almost seven.

EYRE. Is't so, Dame Clapper-dudgeon?* Is't seven ^that is,^ a clock, and my men's breakfast not ready? Trip and go, you chatter box soused conger,* away! Come, you mad Hyper- ^pickled conger-eel^ boreans; follow me, Hodge; follow me, Hans; come after, my fine Firk; to work, to work a while, and then to breakfast!

FIRK. Soft! *Yaw, yaw,* good Hans, though my master have no more wit but to call you afore me, I am not so foolish to go behind you, I being the elder journeyman.

(*Exeunt.*)

Scene 4

(*A field near Old Ford. Halloaing within. Enter* MASTER WARNER *and* MASTER HAMMON, *attired as* HUNTERS.)

---

[14] "Oh, I understand you; I must pay for half a dozen cans; here boy, take this shilling; tap once freely."

[15] That is, little lad. Number-five last is the smallest.

HAMMON. Cousin, beat every brake, the game's not far.
This way with wingèd feet he fled from death,
Whilst the pursuing hounds, scenting his steps,
Find out his highway to destruction.
Besides, the miller's boy told me even now,
He saw him take soil,* and he halloaed him,   take to
                                                               the water
Affirming him to have been so embost*   exhausted
That long he could not hold.
WARNER.   If it be so,
'Tis best we trace these meadows by Old Ford.

(A noise of HUNTERS *within. Enter a* BOY.)

HAMMON. How now, boy? Where's the deer? speak, saw'st
      thou him?
BOY. O yea; I saw him leap through a hedge, and then over
a ditch, then at my lord mayor's pale. Over he skipped me, and
in he went me, and 'holla' the hunters cried, and 'there, boy;
there, boy!' But there he is, 'a mine honesty.
HAMMON. Boy, Godamercy.* Cousin, let's away;   thanks
I hope we shall find better sport to-day.

                                                  (*Exeunt.*)

Scene 5

(Another part of the field. Hunting within. Enter ROSE *and*
SYBIL.)

ROSE. Why, Sybil, wilt thou prove a forester?   that is,
SYBIL. Upon some, no;* forester, go by; no, faith,   heavens no!
mistress. The deer came running into the barn through the
orchard and over the pale; I wot* well, I looked as pale   know
as a new cheese to see him. But whip, says goodman Pinclose,
up with his flail, and our Nick with a prong, and down he fell,
and they upon him, and I upon them. By my troth, we had
such sport; and in the end we ended him; his throat we cut,
flayed him, unhorned him, and my lord mayor shall eat of
him anon, when he comes.
(Horns sound within.)
ROSE. Hark, hark, the hunters come; y' are best take heed,
They'll have a saying to you for this deed.

(Enter MASTER HAMMON, MASTER WARNER, HUNTSMEN,
and BOY.)

HAMMON. God save you, fair ladies.

SYBIL. Ladies! O gross!* _{gross flattery} ^{that is,}

WARNER. Came not a buck this way?

ROSE. No, but two does.

HAMMON. And which way went they? Faith, we'll hunt
at those.

SYBIL. At those? upon some, no: when, can you tell?

WARNER. Upon some, ay.

SYBIL. Good Lord!

WARNER. Wounds! Then farewell!

HAMMON. Boy, which way went he?

BOY. This way, sir, he ran.

HAMMON. This way he ran indeed, fair Mistress Rose;
Our game was lately in your orchard seen.

WARNER. Can you advise which way he took his flight?

SYBIL. Follow your nose; his horns will guide you right.

WARNER. Th' art a mad wench.

SYBIL. O, rich!

ROSE. Trust me, not I.
It is not like that the wild forest-deer
Would come so near to places of resort;
You are deceived, he fled some other way.

WARNER. Which way, my sugar-candy, can you show?

SYBIL. Come up, good honeysops, upon some, no.

ROSE. Why do you stay, and not pursue your game?

SYBIL. I'll hold* my life, their hunting-nags be lame. _{wager}

HAMMON. A deer more dear is found within this place.

ROSE. But not the deer, sir, which you had in chase.

HAMMON. I chased the deer, but this dear chaseth me.

ROSE. The strangest hunting that ever I see.
But where's your park?

(*She offers to go away.*)

HAMMON. 'Tis here: O stay!

ROSE. Impale me,* and then I will not stray. _{fence me in}

WARNER. They wrangle, wench; we are more kind than
they.

SYBIL. What kind of hart is that dear heart, you seek?

WARNER. A hart, dear heart.

SYBIL. Who ever saw the like?

ROSE. To lose your heart, is't possible you can?

HAMMON. My heart is lost.

ROSE. Alack, good gentleman!

HAMMON. This poor lost heart would I wish you might find.
ROSE. You, by such luck, might prove your hart a hind.
HAMMON. Why, Luck had horns, so have I heard some say.
ROSE. No. God, an't be his will, send Luck into your way.

(*Enter the* LORD MAYOR *and* SERVANTS.)

LORD MAYOR. What, Master Hammon? Welcome to Old
   Ford!
SYBIL. Gods pittikins,* hands off, sir! Here's my   God's pity
   lord.
LORD MAYOR. I hear you had ill luck, and lost your game.
HAMMON. 'Tis true, my lord.
LORD MAYOR.   I am sorry for the same.
What gentleman is this?
HAMMON.   My brother-in-law.
LORD MAYOR. Y' are welcome both; sith* Fortune   since
   offers you
Into my hands, you shall not part from hence
Until you have refreshed your wearied limbs.—
Go, Sybil, cover the board!—You shall be guest
To no good cheer, but even a hunter's feast.
   HAMMON. I thank your lordship.—Cousin, on my life,
For our lost venison I shall find a wife.
                                        (*Exeunt.*)
   LORD MAYOR. In, gentlemen; I'll not be absent long.—
This Hammon is a proper gentleman.
A citizen by birth, fairly allied;
How fit an husband were he for my girl!
Well, I will in, and do the best I can,
To match my daughter to this gentleman.
                                         (*Exit.*)

ACT III

Scene 1

(*A room in* EYRE'S *house. Enter* HANS, SKIPPER, HODGE,
and FIRK.)

SKIPPER. *Ick sal yow wat seggen, Hans; dis skip, dat comen
from Candy, is al vol, by Got's sacrament, van sugar, civet,
almonds, cambrick, end alle dingen, towsand towsand ding.*

*Nempt it, Hans, nempt it vor v meester. Daer be de bils van
laden. Your meester Simon Eyre sal hae good copen. Wat
seggen yow, Hans?*[16]

FIRK. *Wat segen de reggen, de copen slopen*—laugh, Hodge,
laugh!

HANS. *Mine liever broder Firk, bringt Meester Eyre tot det
signe vn Swannekin; daer sal yow finde dis skipper end me.
Wat seggen yow, broder Firk? Doot it, Hodge.*[17] Come,
Skipper.

(*Exeunt* HANS *and* SKIPPER.)

FIRK. Bring him, quoth you? Here's no knavery, to bring my
master to buy a ship worth of lading of two or three hundred
thousand pounds. Alas, that's nothing; a trifle, a bauble,
Hodge.

HODGE. The truth is, Firk, that the merchant owner of the
ship dares not show his head, and therefore this skipper that
deals for him, for the love he bears to Hans, offers my master
Eyre a bargain in the commodities. He shall have a reasonable
day of payment; he may sell the wares by that time, and be
an huge gainer himself.

FIRK. Yea, but can my fellow Hans lend my master twenty
porpentines as an earnest penny?

HODGE. Portuguese, thou wouldst say; here they be, Firk;
hark, they jingle in my pocket like St. Mary Overy's bells.

(*Enter* EYRE *and* MARGERY.)

FIRK. Mum, here comes my dame and my master. She'll
scold, on my life, for loitering this Monday; but all's one, let
them all say what they can, Monday's our holiday.

MARGERY. You sing, Sir Sauce, but I beshrew* your   curse
    heart,
    I fear, for this your singing we shall smart.

FIRK. Smart for me, dame; why, dame, why?

HODGE. Master, I hope you'll not suffer my dame to take
down your journeymen.

[16] "I'll tell you what, Hans; this ship that comes from Candia,
is all full, by God's sacrament, of sugar, civet, almonds, cambric,
and all things, a thousand thousand things. Take it, Hans, take
it for your master. There are the bills of lading. Your master,
Simon Eyre, shall have a good bargain. What do you say, Hans?"

[17] "My dear brother Firk, bring Master Eyre to the sign of the
Swan; there shall you find this skipper and me. What say you,
brother Firk? Do it, Hodge."

FIRK. If she take me down, I'll take her up; yea, and take her down too, a button-hole lower.

EYRE. Peace, Firk; not I, Hodge; by the life of Pharaoh, by the Lord of Ludgate, by this beard, every hair whereof I value at a king's ransom, she shall not meddle with you.— Peace, you bombast-cotton-candle-quean; away, queen of clubs; quarrel not with me and my men, with me and my fine Firk; I'll firk* you, if you do.   beat

MARGERY. Yea, yea, man, you may use me as you please; but let that pass.

EYRE. Let it pass, let it vanish away; peace! Am I not Simon Eyre? Are not these my brave men, brave shoemakers, all gentlemen of the Gentle Craft? Prince am I none, yet am I nobly born, as being the sole son of a shoemaker. Away, rubbish! vanish, melt; melt like kitchen-stuff.*   grease

MARGERY. Yea, yea, 'tis well; I must be called rubbish kitchen-stuff, for a sort* of knaves.   pack

FIRK. Nay, dame, you shall not weep and wail in woe for me. Master, I'll stay no longer; here's an inventory of my shop-tools. Adieu, master; Hodge, farewell.

HODGE. Nay, stay, Firk, thou shalt not go alone.

MARGERY. I pray, let them go; there be more maids than Mawkin, more men than Hodge, and more fools than Firk,

FIRK. Fools? Nails! if I tarry now, I would my guts might be turned to shoe-thread.

HODGE. And if I stay, I pray God I may be turned to a Turk, and set in Finsbury[18] for boys to shoot at.—Come, Firk.

EYRE. Stay, my fine knaves, you arms of my trade, you pillars of my profession. What, shall a tittle-tattle's words make you forsake Simon Eyre?—Avaunt, kitchen-stuff! Rip,*   move on you brown-bread Tannikin,* out of my sight! Move Dutchwoman me not! Have not I ta'en you from selling tripes in Eastcheap, and set you in my shop, and made you hail-fellow with Simon Eyre, the shoemaker? And now do you deal thus with my journeymen? Look, you powder-beef-queen, on the face of Hodge, here's a face for a lord.

FIRK. And here's a face for any lady in Christendom.

EYRE. Rip, you chitterling,* avaunt! Boy, bid the   sausage tapster of the Boar's Head fill me a dozen cans of beer for my journeymen.

FIRK. A dozen cans? O brave! Hodge, now I'll stay.

EYRE (*aside to the* BOY). An* the knave fills any more   if

---

[18] An archery practice ground in London.

than two, he pays for them. (*Exit* Boy. *Aloud.*) A dozen cans
of beer for my journeymen. (*Re-enter* Boy.) Here, you mad
Mesopotamians, wash your livers with this liquor. Where be
the odd ten? (*Aside.*) No more, Madge, no more.—Well said.
Drink and to work!—What work dost thou, Hodge? what
work?

HODGE. I am a-making a pair of shoes for my lord mayor's
daughter, Mistress Rose.

FIRK. And I a pair of shoes for Sybil, my lord's maid. I deal
with her.

EYRE. Sybil? Fie, defile not thy fine workmanly fingers with
the feet of kitchen-stuff and basting-ladles. Ladies of the
court, fine ladies, my lads, commit their feet to our apparell-
ing; put gross work to Hans. Yark* and seam, yark   stitch tightly
and seam!

FIRK. For yarking and seaming let me alone, an I come
to 't.

HODGE. Well, Master, all this is from the bias.* Do   tangential
you remember the ship my fellow Hans told you of? The
Skipper and he are both drinking at the Swan. Here be the
Portuguese to give earnest. If you go through with it, you
cannot choose but be a lord at least.

FIRK. Nay, dame, if my master prove not a lord, and you a
lady, hang me.

MARGERY. Yea, like enough, if you may loiter and tipple
thus.

FIRK. Tipple, dame? No, we have been bargaining with
Skellum Skanderbag:* can you Dutche spreaken for   that is, a
a ship of silk Cyprus, laden with sugar-candy?   Dutch rascal

(*Enter the* BOY *with a velvet coat and an Alderman's gown.*
EYRE *puts them on.*)

EYRE. Peace, Firk; silence, Tittle-tattle! Hodge, I'll go
through with it. Here's a seal-ring, and I have sent for a
guarded* gown and a damask cassock. See where   ornamentally
it comes; look here, Maggy; help me, Firk; apparel me, Hodge;   bordered
silk and satin, you mad Philistines, silk and satin.

FIRK. Ha, ha, my master will be as proud as a dog in a
doublet, all in beaten* damask and velvet.   stamped

EYRE. Softly, Firk, for rearing of* the nap, and   raising
wearing threadbare my garments. How dost thou like me,
Firk. How do I look, my fine Hodge?

HODGE. Why, now you look like yourself, master. I warrant you, there's few in the city, but will give you the wall,[19] and come upon you with the "right worshipful."

FIRK. Nails, my master looks like a threadbare cloak new turned and dressed. Lord, Lord, to see what good raiment doth! Dame, dame, are you not enamored?

EYRE. How say'st thou, Maggy, am I not brisk? Am I not fine?

MARGERY. Fine? By my troth, sweetheart, very fine! By my troth, I never liked thee so well in my life, sweetheart; but let that pass. I warrant, there be many women in the city have not such handsome husbands, but only for their apparel; but let that pass too.

(*Re-enter* HANS *and* SKIPPER.)

HANS. *Godden day, mester. Dis be de skipper dat heb de skip van marchandice; de commodity ben good; nempt**   take *it, master, nempt it.*

EYRE. Godamercy, Hans; welcome, skipper. Where lies this ship of merchandise?

SKIPPER. *De skip ben in revere,* dor be van sugar,* river *cyvet, almonds, cambrick, and a towsand towsand tings, Gotz sacrament; nempt it, mester: ye sal heb good copen.** bargain

FIRK. To him, master! O sweet master! O sweet wares! Prunes, almonds, sugar-candy, carrot-roots, turnips, O brave fatting meat! Let not a man buy a nutmeg but yourself.

EYRE. Peace, Firk! Come, skipper, I'll go aboard with you. —Hans, have you made him drink?

SKIPPER. *Yaw, yaw, ick heb veale gedrunck.*[20]

EYRE. Come, Hans, follow me. Skipper, thou shalt have my countenance in the city.

(*Exeunt.*)

FIRK. *Yaw, heb veale gedrunck,* quotha. They may well be called butter-boxes, when they drink fat veal and thick beer too. But come, dame, I hope you'll chide us no more.

MARGERY. No, faith, Firk; no, perdy,* Hodge. I do that is, by God feel honor creep upon me, and which is more, a certain rising in my flesh; but let that pass.

FIRK. Rising in your flesh do you feel, say you? Ay, you may be with child, but why should not my master feel a ris-

ing in his flesh, having a gown and a gold ring on? But you
are such a shrew, you'll soon pull him down.

MARGERY. Ha, ha! prithee, peace! Thou mak'st my worship
laugh; but let that pass. Come, I'll go in; Hodge, prithee, go
before me; Firk, follow me.

FIRK. Firk doth follow: Hodge, pass out in state.

(Exeunt.)

Scene 2

(*London: a room in* LINCOLN'S *house. Enter the* EARL OF
LINCOLN *and* DODGER.)

LINCOLN. How now, good Dodger, what's the news in
    France?

DODGER. My lord, upon the eighteenth day of May
The French and English were prepared to fight;
Each side with eager fury gave the sign
Of a most hot encounter. Five long hours
Both armies fought together; at the length
The lot of victory fell on our sides.
Twelve thousand of the Frenchmen that day died,
Four thousand English, and no man of name
But Captain Hyam and young Ardington,
Two gallant gentlemen, I knew them well.

LINCOLN. But, Dodger, prithee, tell me, in this fight
How did my cousin Lacy bear himself?

DODGER. My lord, your cousin Lacy was not there.

LINCOLN. Not there?

DODGER.   No, my good lord.

LINCOLN.   Sure, thou mistakest.
I saw him shipped, and a thousand eyes beside
Were witnesses of the farewells which he gave,
When I, with weeping eyes, bid him adieu.
Dodger, take heed.

DODGER.   My lord, I am advised,
That what I spake is true: to prove it so,
His cousin Askew, that supplied his place,
Sent me for him from France, that secretly
He might convey himself thither.

LINCOLN.   Is't even so?
Dares he so carelessly venture his life
Upon the indignation of a king?
Has he despised my love, and spurned those favors

Which I with prodigal hand poured on his head?
He shall repent his rashness with his soul;
Since of my love he makes no estimate,
I'll make him wish he had not known my hate.
Thou hast no other news?
    DODGER.   None else, my lord.
    LINCOLN. None worse I know thou hast.—Procure the king
To crown his giddy brows with ample honors,
Send him chief colonel, and all my hope
Thus to be dashed! But 'tis in vain to grieve,
One evil cannot a worse relieve.
Upon my life, I have found out his plot;
That old dog, Love, that fawned upon him so,
Love to that puling girl, his fair-cheeked Rose,
The lord mayor's daughter, hath distracted him,
And in the fire of that love's lunacy
Hath he burnt up himself, consumed his credit.
Lost the king's love, yea, and I fear, his life,
Only to get a wanton to his wife.
Dodger, it is so.
    DODGER.   I fear so, my good lord.
    LINCOLN. It is so—nay, sure it cannot be!
I am at my wits' end. Dodger!
    DODGER.   Yea, my lord.
    LINCOLN. Thou art acquainted with my nephew's haunts;
Spend this gold for thy pains; go seek him out;
Watch at my lord mayor's—there if he live,
Dodger, thou shalt be sure to meet with him.
Prithee, be diligent.—Lacy, thy name
Lived once in honor, now dead in shame.—
Be circumspect.

                                   (Exit.)
    DODGER.   I warrant you, my lord.
                                     (Exit.)

Scene 3

(London: a room in the LORD MAYOR'S *house. Enter the* LORD MAYOR *and* MASTER SCOTT.)

    LORD MAYOR. Good Master Scott, I have been bold with
        you,
To be a witness to a wedding-knot
Betwixt young Master Hammon and my daughter.
O, stand aside; see where the lovers come.

(*Enter* MASTER HAMMON *and* ROSE.)

ROSE. Can it be possible you love me so?
No, no, within those eyeballs I espy
Apparent likelihoods of flattery.
Pray now, let go my hand.
    HAMMON.   Sweet Mistress Rose,
Misconstrue not my words, nor misconceive
Of my affection, whose devoted soul
Swears that I love thee dearer than my heart.
    ROSE. As dear as your own heart? I judge it right,
Men love their hearts best when th' are out of sight.
    HAMMON. I love you, by this hand.
    ROSE.   Yet hands off now!
If flesh be frail, how weak and frail's your vow!
    HAMMON. Then by my life I swear.
    ROSE.   Then do not brawl;
One quarrel loseth wife and life and all.
Is not your meaning thus?
    HAMMON.   In faith, you jest.
    ROSE. Love loves to sport; therefore leave love, y' are best.
    LORD MAYOR. What? square* they, Master Scott?   quarrel
    SCOTT.   Sir, never doubt,
Lovers are quickly in, and quickly out.
    HAMMON. Sweet Rose, be not so strange in fancying me.
Nay, never turn aside, shun not my sight:
I am not grown so fond,* to fond* my love   foolish/that
On any that shall quit* it with disdain;   is, found
If you will love me, so—if not, farewell.   requite
    LORD MAYOR. Why, how now, lovers, are you both agreed?
    HAMMON. Yes, faith, my lord.
    LORD MAYOR. 'Tis well, give me your hand.
Give me yours, daughter.—How now, both pull back?
What means this, girl?
    ROSE.   I mean to live a maid.
    HAMMON (*aside*). But not to die one; pause, ere that be
    said.
    LORD MAYOR. Will you still cross me, still be obstinate?
    HAMMON. Nay, chide her not, my lord, for doing well;
If she can live an happy virgin's life,
'Tis far more blessed than to be a wife.
    ROSE. Say, sir, I cannot: I have made a vow,
Whoever be my husband, 'tis not you.

LORD MAYOR. Your tongue is quick; but Master Hammon,
   know,
I bade you welcome to another end.
   HAMMON. What, would you have me pule and pine and
      pray,
            With 'lovely lady', 'mistress of my heart',
            'Pardon your servant', and the rhymer play,
            Railing on Cupid and his tyrant's-dart;
Or shall I undertake some martial spoil,
Wearing your glove at tourney and at tilt,
And tell how many gallants I unhorsed—
Sweet, will this pleasure you?
   ROSE.   Yea, when wilt begin?
What, love rhymes, man? Fie on that deadly sin!
   LORD MAYOR. If you will have her, I'll make her agree.
   HAMMON. Enforced love is worse than hate to me.
(*Aside.*) There is a wench keeps shop in the Old Change.
To her will I; it is not wealth I seek,
I have enough, and will prefer her love
Before the world.—(*Aloud.*) My good lord mayor, adieu.
Old love for me, I have no luck with new.
                                                         (*Exit.*)

   LORD MAYOR. Now, mammet,* you have well   puppet
      behaved yourself,
But you shall curse your coyness if I live.—
Who's within there? See you convey your mistress
Straight to th' Old Ford! I'll keep you straight enough.
Fore God, I would have sworn the puling girl
Would willingly accepted Hammon's love;
But banish him, my thoughts!—Go, minion, in!
                                                   (*Exit* ROSE.)
Now tell me, Master Scott, would you have thought
That Master Simon Eyre, the shoemaker,
Had been of wealth to buy such merchandise?
   SCOTT. 'Twas well, my lord, your honor and myself
Grew partners with him; for your bills of lading
Shew that Eyre's gains in one commodity
Rise at the least to full three thousand pound
Besides like gain in other merchandise.
   LORD MAYOR. Well, he shall spend some of his thousands
      now.
For I have sent for him to the Guildhall.

(*Enter* EYRE.)

See, where he comes. Good morrow, Master Eyre.

EYRE. Poor Simon Eyre, my lord, your shoemaker.

LORD MAYOR. Well, well, it likes yourself to term you so.

(*Enter* DODGER.)

Now, Master Dodger, what's the news with you?

DODGER. I'd gladly speak in private to your honor.

LORD MAYOR. You shall, you shall.—Master Eyre and Master Scott,
I have some business with this gentleman;
I pray, let me entreat you to walk before
To the Guildhall; I'll follow presently.
Master Eyre, I hope ere noon to call you sheriff.

EYRE. I would not care, my lord, if you might call me
King of Spain.—Come, Master Scott.

(*Exeunt* EYRE *and* SCOTT.)

LORD MAYOR. Now, Master Dodger, what's the news you bring?

DODGER. The Earl of Lincoln by me greets your lordship,
And earnestly requests you, if you can,
Inform him, where his nephew Lacy keeps.

LORD MAYOR. Is not his nephew Lacy now in France?

DODGER. No, I assure your lordship, but disguised
Lurks here in London.

LORD MAYOR.   London? is't even so?
It may be; but upon my faith and soul,
I know not where he lives, or whether he lives:
So tell my Lord of Lincoln.—Lurks in London?
Well, Master Dodger, you perhaps may start him;
Be but the means to rid him into France,
I'll give you a dozen angels* for your pains: gold coins
So much I love his honor, hate his nephew.
And, prithee, so inform thy lord from me.

DODGER. I take my leave.

(*Exit* DODGER.)

LORD MAYOR.   Farewell, good Master Dodger.
Lacy in London? I dare pawn my life,
My daughter knows thereof, and for that cause
Denied young Master Hammon in his love.
Well, I am glad I sent her to Old Ford.
Gods Lord, 'tis late; to Guildhall I must hie;
I know my brethren stay* my company.   await

(*Exit.*)

Scene 4

(*London: a room in* EYRE'S *house. Enter* FIRK, MARGERY, HANS, *and* HODGE.)

MARGERY. Thou goest too fast for me, Roger. O, Firk!

FIRK. Ay, forsooth.

MARGERY. I pray thee, run—do you hear?—run to Guildhall, and learn if my husband, Master Eyre, will take that worshipful vocation of Master Sheriff upon him. Hie thee, good Firk.

FIRK. Take it? Well, I go; an he should not take it, Firk swears to forswear him. Yes, forsooth, I go to Guildhall.

MARGERY. Nay, when? thou art too compendious and tedious.

FIRK. O rare, your excellence is full of eloquence. (*Aside.*) How like a new cart-wheel my dame speaks, and she looks like an old musty ale-bottle* going to scalding.   a leather bottle

MARGERY. Nay, when? thou wilt make me melancholy.

FIRK. God forbid your worship should fall into that humor;—I run.

                                                        (*Exit.*)

MARGERY. Let me see now, Roger and Hans.

HODGE. Ay, forsooth, dame—mistress I should say, but the old term so sticks to the roof of my mouth, I can hardly lick it off.

MARGERY. Even what thou wilt, good Roger; dame is a fair name for any honest Christian; but let that pass. How dost thou, Hans?

HANS. *Mee tanck you, vro.**   mistress

MARGERY. Well, Hans and Roger, you see, God hath blest your master, and, perdy, if ever he comes to be Master Sheriff of London—as we are all mortal—you shall see, I will have some odd thing or other in a corner for you: I will not be your back-friend;* but let that pass. Hans, pray thee,   false friend tie my shoe.

HANS. *Yaw, ick sal, vro.*

MARGERY. Roger, thou know'st the length of my foot; as it is none of the biggest, so I thank God, it is handsome enough; prithee, let me have a pair of shoes made, cork, good Roger, wooden heel too.

HODGE. You shall.

MARGERY. Art thou acquainted with never a farthingale-maker, nor a French hood-maker? I must enlarge my bum, ha, ha! How shall I look in a hood, I wonder! Perdy, oddly, I think.

HODGE (*aside*). As a cat out of* a pillory.—Very well, I warrant you, mistress.　　　　　　　　　　　　　　　　in

MARGERY. Indeed, all flesh is grass; and, Roger, canst thou tell where I may buy a good hair?

HODGE. Yes, forsooth, at the poulterer's in Gracious Street.

MARGERY. Thou art an ungracious wag; perdy, I mean a false hair for my periwig.

HODGE. Why, mistress, the next time I cut my beard, you shall have the shavings of it; but they are all true hairs.

MARGERY. It is very hot, I must get me a fan or else a mask.

HODGE (*aside*). So you had need, to hide your wicked face.

MARGERY. Fie upon it, how costly this world's calling is; perdy, but that it is one of the wonderful works of God, I would not deal with it. Is not Firk come yet? Hans, be not so sad, let it pass and vanish, as my husband's worship says.

HANS. *Ick bin vrolicke, lot see yow soo.*[21]

HODGE. Mistress, will you drink* a pipe of tobacco?　　　smoke

MARGERY. O, fie upon it, Roger, perdy! These filthy tobacco-pipes are the most idle slavering baubles that ever I felt. Out upon it! God bless us, men look not like men that use them.

(*Enter* RALPH, *being lame.*)

HODGE. What, fellow Ralph? Mistress, look here, Jane's husband! Why, how now, lame? Hans, make much of him, he's a brother of our trade, a good workman, and a tall*　　　brave soldier.

HANS. You be welcome, *broder.*

MARGERY. Perdy, I knew him not. How dost thou, good Ralph? I am glad to see thee well.

RALPH. I would to God you saw me, dame, as well As when I went from London into France.

MARGERY. Trust me, I am sorry, Ralph, to see thee impotent. Lord, how the wars have made him sunburnt! The left leg is not well; 'twas a fair gift of God the infirmity took not hold a little higher, considering thou camest from France; but let that pass.

RALPH. I am glad to see you well, and I rejoice

---

²¹ "I am merry. Let's see you so."

To hear that God hath blest my master so
Since my departure.

MARGERY. Yea, truly, Ralph, I thank my Maker; but let
that pass.

HODGE. And, sirrah Ralph, what news, what news in
France?

· RALPH. Tell me, good Roger, first, what news in England?
How does my Jane? When didst thou see my wife?
Where lives my poor heart? She'll be poor indeed,
Now I want* limbs to get whereon to feed.   lack

HODGE. Limbs? Hast thou not hands, man?
Thou shalt never see a shoemaker want bread, though he
have but three fingers on a hand.

RALPH. Yet all this while I hear not of my Jane.

MARGERY. O Ralph, your wife,—perdy, we know not what's
become of her. She was here a while, and because she was
married, grew more stately than became her, I checked her,
and so forth; away she flung, never returned, nor did bye
nor bah; and, Ralph, you know, "ka me, ka thee."22 And
so, as I tell ye—Roger, is not Firk come yet?

HODGE. No, forsooth.

MARGERY. And so, indeed, we heard not of her, but I
hear she lives in London; but let that pass. If she had wanted,
she might have opened her case to me or my husband, or to
any of my men; I am sure, there's not any of them, perdy,
but would have done her good to his power. Hans, look if
Firk be come.

HANS. *Yaw, ick sal, vro.*

(*Exit* HANS.)

MARGERY. And so, as I said—but, Ralph, why dost thou
weep? Thou knowest that naked we came out of our mother's
womb, and naked we must return; and, therefore, thank God
for all things.

HODGE. No, faith, Jane is a stranger here; but, Ralph, pull
up a good heart, I know thou hast one. Thy wife, man, is in
London; one told me, he saw her awhile ago very
brave* and neat; we'll ferret her out, an* London   finely dressed/if
hold her.

MARGERY. Alas, poor soul, he's overcome with sorrow;
he does but as I do, weep for the loss of any good thing. But,
Ralph, get thee in, call for some meat and drink, thou shalt
find me worshipful towards thee.

22 That is, you help me and I'll help you.

RALPH. I thank you, dame; since I want limbs and lands,
I'll trust to God, my good friends, and my hands.

(*Exit.*)

(*Enter* HANS *and* FIRK *running.*)

FIRK. Run, good Hans! O Hodge, O mistress! Hodge, heave
up thine ears; mistress, smug* up your looks; on with   smarten
your best apparel; my master is chosen, my master is called,
nay, condemned by the cry of the country to be sheriff of the
city for this famous year now to come. And time now being,
a great many men in black gowns were asked for their
voices* and their hands, and my master had all their   votes
fists about his ears presently, and they cried 'Ay, ay, ay, ay',—
and so I came away—

> Wherefore without all other grieve
> I do salute you, Mistress Shrieve.*   sheriff

HANS. *Yaw, my mester is de groot man, de shrieve.*

HODGE. Did not I tell you, mistress? Now I may boldly
say: Good-morrow to your worship.

MARGERY. Good-morrow, good Roger. I thank you, my
good people all.—Firk, hold up thy hand: here's a three-
penny piece for thy tidings.

FIRK. 'Tis but three-half-pence, I think. Yes, 'tis threepence, I smell the rose.[23]

HODGE. But, mistress, be ruled by me, and do not speak
so pulingly.

FIRK. 'Tis her worship speaks so, and not she. No, faith
mistress, speak me in the old key: 'To it, Firk'; 'there, good
Firk'; 'ply your business, Hodge'; 'Hodge, with a full mouth';
'I'll fill your bellies with good cheer, till they cry twang'.

(*Enter* EYRE *wearing a gold chain.*)

HANS. *See, myn liever broder, heer compt my meester.*

MARGERY. Welcome home, Master Shrieve; I pray God continue you in health and wealth.

EYRE. See here, my Maggy, a chain, a gold chain for
Simon Eyre. I shall make thee a lady; here's a French hood

---

[23] H. Spencer notes, "The silver threepence of Elizabeth had
the Queen's head and a rose on the obverse side. It was not in
general circulation, but was used for maundy money. Margery is
acting the rôle of a sovereign dispensing alms."

for thee; on with it, on with it! dress thy brows with this flap
of a shoulder of mutton,* to make thee look lovely. sheep's wool
Where be my fine men? Roger, I'll make over my shop and
tools to thee; Firk, thou shalt be the foreman; Hans, thou shalt
have an hundred for twenty.[24] Be as mad knaves as your
master Sim Eyre hath been, and you shall live to be Sheriffs of
London.—How dost thou like me, Margery? Prince am I none,
yet am I princely born. Firk, Hodge, and Hans!

ALL THREE. Ay, forsooth, what says your worship, Master Sheriff?

EYRE. Worship and honor, you Babylonian knaves, for the
Gentle Craft. But I forgot myself; I am bidden by my lord
mayor to dinner to Old Ford; he's gone before, I must after.
Come, Madge, on with your trinkets! Now, my true Trojans,
my fine Firk, my dapper Hodge, my honest Hans, some device,* some odd crotchets, some morris,* or such   entertainment/
like, for the honor of the gentlemen shoemakers. Meet me at   morris dance
Old Ford, you know my mind. Come, Madge, away. Shut up
the shop, knaves, and make holiday.

(*Exeunt.*)

FIRK. O rare! O brave! Come, Hodge; follow me, Hans;
We'll be with them for a morris-dance.

(*Exeunt.*)

Scene 5

(*A room at Old Ford. Enter the* LORD MAYOR, ROSE, EYRE,
MARGERY *in a French hood,* SYBIL, *and other* SERVANTS.)

LORD MAYOR. Trust me, you are as welcome to Old Ford
As I myself.

MARGERY.   Truly, I thank your lordship.

LORD MAYOR. Would our bad cheer were worth the thanks
  you give.

EYRE. Good cheer, my lord mayor, fine cheer! A fine house,
fine walls, all fine and neat.

LORD MAYOR. Now, by my troth, I'll tell thee, Master Eyre,
It does me good, and all my brethren,
That such a madcap fellow as thyself
Is entered into our society.

MARGERY. Ay, but, my lord, he must learn now to put on
gravity.

²⁴ The return on Hans' loan of twenty Portuguese.

EYRE. Peace, Maggy, a fig for gravity! When I go to Guild-hall in my scarlet gown, I'll look as demurely as a saint, and speak as gravely as a justice of peace; but now I am here at Old Ford, at my good lord mayor's house, let it go by, van-ish, Maggy, I'll be merry; away with flip-flap, these fooleries, these gulleries! What, honey? Prince am I none, yet am I princely born. What says my lord mayor?

LORD MAYOR. Ha, ha, ha! I had rather than a thousand pound,
I had an heart but half so light as yours.

EYRE. Why, what should I do, my lord? A pound of care pays not a dram of debt. Hum, let's be merry, whiles we are young; old age, sack and sugar will steal upon us, ere we be aware.

THE FIRST THREE-MAN'S SONG[25]

O the month of May, the merry month of May,
　So frolick, so gay, and so green, so green, so green!
O, and then did I unto my true love say:
　'Sweet Peg, thou shalt be my summer's queen!

'Now the nightingale, the pretty nightingale,
　The sweetest singer in all the forest's choir,
Entreats thee, sweet Peggy, to hear thy true love's tale;
　Lo, yonder she sitteth, her breast against a brier.

'But O, I spy the cuckoo, the cuckoo, the cuckoo;
　See where she sitteth: come away, my joy;
Come away, I prithee: I do not like the cuckoo
　Should sing where my Peggy and I kiss and toy.'

O the month of May, the merry month of May,
　So frolick, so gay, and so green, so green, so green!
And then did I unto my true love say:
　'Sweet Peg, thou shalt be my summer's queen!'

LORD MAYOR. It's well done; Mistress Eyre, pray, give good counsel
To my daughter.

MARGERY. I hope, Mistress Rose will have the grace to take nothing that's bad.

LORD MAYOR. Pray God she do; for i' faith, Mistress Eyre,

---

[25] The quarto editions print both songs (see V, 4) before the play, without any indication of where they belong in the script.

I would bestow upon that peevish girl
A thousand marks more than I mean to give her
Upon condition she'd be ruled by me.
The ape still crosseth me. There came of late
A proper gentleman of fair revenues,
Whom gladly I would call son-in-law:
But my fine cockney would have none of him.
You'll prove a coxcomb for it, ere you die:
A courtier, or no man must please your eye.

EYRE. Be ruled, sweet Rose: th' art ripe for a man. Marry
not with a boy that has no more hair on his face than thou
hast on thy cheeks. A courtier? wash, go by! stand not upon
pishery-pashery: those silken fellows are but painted images,
outsides, outsides, Rose; their inner linings are torn. No, my
fine mouse, marry me with a gentleman grocer like my lord
mayor, your father; a grocer is a sweet trade: plums, plums.
Had I a son or daughter should marry out of the generation
and blood of the shoemakers, he should pack; what, the Gentle Trade is a living for a man through Europe, through the
world.

(*A noise within of a tabor and a pipe.*)

LORD MAYOR. What noise is this?

EYRE. O my lord mayor, a crew of good fellows that for
love to your honor are come hither with a morris-dance.
Come in, my Mesopotamians, cheerily.

(*Enter* HODGE, HANS, RALPH, FIRK, *and other* Shoemakers,
in a morris; after a little dancing the LORD MAYOR *speaks.*)

LORD MAYOR. Master Eyre, are all these shoemakers?

EYRE. All cordwainers, my good lord mayor.

ROSE (*aside*). How like my Lacy looks yond' shoemaker!

HANS (*aside*). O that I durst but speak unto my love!

LORD MAYOR. Sybil, go fetch some wine to make these
drink.
You are all welcome.

ALL.   We thank your lordship.

(ROSE *takes a cup of wine and goes to* HANS.)

ROSE. For his sake whose fair shape thou represent'st,
Good friend, I drink to thee.

HANS. *Ick bedancke, good frister.**   miss

MARGERY. I see, Mistress Rose, you do not want judgment;
you have drunk to the properest man I keep.

FIRK. Here be some have done their parts to be as proper
as he.

LORD MAYOR. Well, urgent business calls me back to Lon-
don:
Good fellows, first go in and taste our cheer;
And to make merry as you homeward go,
Spend these two angels in beer at Stratford-Bow.

EYRE. To these two, my mad lads, Sim Eyre adds another;
then cheerily, Firk; tickle it, Hans, and all for the honor of
shoemakers.

(*All go dancing out.*)

LORD MAYOR. Come, Master Eyre, let's have your company.

(*Exeunt.*)

ROSE. Sybil, what shall I do?

SYBIL.   Why, what's the matter?

ROSE. That Hans the shoemaker is my love Lacy,
Disguised in that attire to find me out.
How should I find the means to speak with him?

SYBIL. What, mistress, never fear; I dare venture my maidenhead to nothing, and that's great odds, that Hans the Dutchman, when we come to London, shall not only see and speak
with you, but in spite of all your father's policies steal you
away and marry you. Will not this please you?

ROSE. Do this, and ever be assured of my love.

SYBIL. Away, then, and follow your father to London, lest
your absence cause him to suspect something:
Tomorrow, if my counsel be obeyed,
I'll bind you prentice to the Gentle Trade.

(*Exeunt.*)

ACT IV

Scene 1

(*A street in London.* JANE *in a seamster's shop, working.
Enter* MASTER HAMMON, *muffled; he stands aloof.*)

HAMMON. Yonder's the shop, and there my fair love sits.
She's fair and lovely, but she is is not mine.
O, would she were! Thrice have I courted her,
Thrice hath my hand been moistened with her hand,
Whilst my poor famished eyes do feed on that

Which made them famish. I am infortunate:
I still love one, yet nobody loves me.
I muse* in other men what women see,   wonder
That I so want! Fine Mistress Rose was coy,
And this too curious!* Oh, no, she is chaste,   careful
And for* she thinks me wanton, she denies   because
To cheer my cold heart with her sunny eyes.
How prettily she works, oh pretty hand!
Oh happy work! It doth me good to stand
Unseen to see her. Thus I oft have stood
In frosty evenings, a light burning by her,
Enduring biting cold, only to eye her.
One only look hath seemed as rich to me
As a king's crown; such is love's lunacy.
Muffled I'll pass along, and by that try
Whether she know me.
    JANE.   Sir, what is't you buy?
What is't you lack, sir, calico, or lawn,*   linenlike material
Fine cambric shirts, or bands, what will you buy?
    HAMMON (*aside*). That which thou wilt not sell.
      Faith, yet I'll try;
How do you sell this handkerchief?
    JANE.   Good cheap.*   at a bargain
    HAMMON. And how these ruffs?
    JANE.   Cheap too.
    HAMMON.   And how this band?
    JANE. Cheap too.
    HAMMON.   All cheap; how sell you then this hand?
    JANE. My hands are not to be sold.
    HAMMON.   To be given then!
Nay, faith, I come to buy.
    JANE.   But none knows when.
    HAMMON. Good sweet, leave work a little while; let's play.
    JANE. I cannot live by keeping holiday.
    HAMMON. I'll pay you for the time which shall be lost.
    JANE. With me you shall not be at so much cost.
    HAMMON. Look how you wound this cloth, so you wound
    me.
    JANE. It may be so.
    HAMMON.   'Tis so.
    JANE.   What remedy?
    HAMMON. Nay, faith, you are too coy.
    JANE.   Let go my hand.
    HAMMON. I will do any task at your command;

I would let go this beauty, were I not
In mind to disobey you by a power
That controls kings: I love you!
  JANE.   So, now part.
  HAMMON. With hands I may, but never with my heart.
In faith, I love you.
  JANE.   I believe you do.
  HAMMON. Shall a true love in me breed hate in you?
  JANE. I hate you not.
  HAMMON.   Then you must love?
  JANE.   I do.
What are you better now? I love not you.
  HAMMON. All this, I hope, is but a woman's fray,
That means: "Come to me," when she cries: "Away!"
In earnest, mistress, I do not jest,
A true chaste love hath entered in my breast.
I love you dearly, as I love my life,
I love you as a husband loves a wife;
That, and no other love, my love requires.
Thy wealth, I know, is little; my desires
Thirst not for gold. Sweet, beauteous Jane, what's mine
Shall, if thou make myself thine, all be thine.
Say, judge, what is thy sentence, life or death?
Mercy or cruelty lies in thy breath.
  JANE. Good sir, I do believe you love me well;
For 'tis a silly conquest, silly pride
For one like you—I mean a gentleman—
To boast that by his love-tricks he hath brought
Such and such women to his amorous lure;
I think you do not so, yet many do,
And make it even a very trade to woo.
I could be coy, as many women be,
Feed you with sunshine smiles and wanton looks,
But I detest witchcraft; say that I
Do constantly believe you, constant have——
  HAMMON. Why dost thou not believe me?
  JANE.   I believe you;
But yet, good sir, because I will not grieve you
With hopes to taste fruit which will never fall,
In simple truth this is the sum of all:
My husband lives, at least, I hope he lives.
Pressed was he to these bitter wars in France;
Bitter they are to me by wanting him.
I have but one heart, and that heart's his due.

How can I then bestow the same on you?
Whilst he lives, his I live, be it ne'er so poor,
And rather be his wife than a king's whore.
    HAMMON. Chaste and dear woman, I will not abuse thee,
Although it cost my life, if thou refuse me.
Thy husband, pressed for France, what was his name?
    JANE. Ralph Damport.
    HAMMON.   Damport?—Here's a letter sent
From France to me, from a dear friend of mine,
A gentleman of place; here he doth write
Their names that have been slain in every fight.
    JANE. I hope death's scroll contains not my love's name.
    HAMMON. Cannot you read?
    JANE.   I can.
    HAMMON.   Peruse the same.
To my remembrance such a name I read
Amongst the rest. See here!
    JANE.   Ay me, he's dead!
He's dead! if this be true, my dear heart's slain!
    HAMMON. Have patience, dear love.
    JANE.   Hence, hence!
    HAMMON.   Nay, sweet Jane,
Make not poor sorrow proud with these rich tears.
I mourn thy husband's death, because thou mourn'st.
    JANE. That bill is forged; 'tis signed by forgery.
    HAMMON. I'll bring thee letters sent besides to many,
Carrying the like report: Jane, 'tis too true.
Come, weep not: mourning, though it rise from love,
Helps not the mournèd, yet hurts them that mourn.
    JANE. For God's sake, leave me.
    HAMMON.   Whither dost thou turn?
Forget the dead, love them that are alive:
His love is faded, try how mine will thrive.
    JANE. 'Tis now no time for me to think on love.
    HAMMON. 'Tis now best time for you to think on love,
Because your love lives not.
    JANE.   Though he be dead,
My love to him shall not be buried;
For God's sake, leave me to myself alone.
    HAMMON. 'Twould kill my soul, to leave thee drowned in
        moan.
Answer me to my suit, and I am gone;
Say to me yea or no.
    JANE.   No.

HAMMON.   Then farewell!
One farewell will not serve, I come again;
Come, dry these wet cheeks; tell me, faith, sweet Jane,
Yea or no, once more.
JANE.   Once more I say, no;
Once more be gone, I pray; else will I go.
HAMMON. Nay, then I will grow rude, by this white hand,
Until you change that cold "no"; here I'll stand
Till by your hard heart——
JANE.   Nay, for God's love, peace!
My sorrows by your presence more increase.
Not that you thus are present, but all grief
Desires to be alone; therefore in brief
Thus much I say, and saying bid adieu:
If ever I wed man, it shall be you.
HAMMON. O blessed voice! Dear Jane, I'll urge no more;
Thy breath hath made me rich.
JANE.   Death makes me poor.
                                   (*Exeunt.*)

Scene 2

(*London: a street before* HODGE'S *shop.* HODGE, *at his shop-
board,** RALPH, FIRK, HANS, *and a* BOY *at work.*) tradesman's
                                                      table

ALL. Hey, down a down derry.
HODGE. Well said, my hearts; ply your work today, we loi-
tered yesterday; to it pell-mell, that we may live to be lord
mayors, or aldermen at least.
FIRK. Hey, down a down, derry.
HODGE. Well said, i' faith! How say'st thou, Hans, doth not
Firk tickle it?
HANS. *Yaw, mester.*
FIRK. Not so neither, my organ-pipe squeaks this morning
for want of liquoring. Hey, down a down, derry!
HANS. *Forward, Firk, tow best un jolly yongster. Hort, ay,
mester, ick bid you, cut me un pair vampres vor Mester Jeffre's
boots.*[26]
HODGE. Thou shalt, Hans.
FIRK. Master!
HODGE. How now, boy?
FIRK. Pray, now you are in the cutting vein, cut me out a

        [26] "Forward, Firk, you are a jolly youngster. Hark, ay, master,
I bid you; cut me a pair of vamps for Master Jeffrey's boots."

pair of counterfeits,* or else my work will not pass   patterns
current; hey, down a down!

HODGE. Tell me, sirs, are my cousin Mistress Priscilla's
shoes done?

FIRK. Your cousin? No, master; one of your aunts,*prostitutes
hang her; let them alone.

RALPH. I am in hand with them; she gave charge that none
but I should do them for her.

FIRK. Thou do for her? then 'twill be a lame doing, and that
she loves not. Ralph, thou might'st have sent her to me, in
faith, I would have yearked and firked your Priscilla. Hey,
down a down, derry. This gear* will not hold.   rubbish

HODGE. How say'st thou, Firk, were we not merry at Old
Ford?

FIRK. How, merry? why, our buttocks went jiggy-joggy like
a quagmire. Well, Sir Roger Oatmeal, if I thought all meal of
that nature, I would eat nothing but bagpuddings.

RALPH. Of all good fortunes my fellow Hans had the best.

FIRK. 'Tis true, because Mistress Rose drank to him.

HODGE. Well, well, work apace. They say, seven of the aldermen be dead, or very sick.

FIRK. I care not, I'll be none.

RALPH. No, nor I; but then my Master Eyre will come
quickly to be lord mayor.

(*Enter* SYBIL.)

FIRK. Whoop, yonder comes Sybil.

HODGE. Sybil, welcome, i' faith; and how dost thou, mad
wench?

FIRK. Syb-whore, welcome to London.

SYBIL. Godamercy, sweet Firk; good lord, Hodge, what a
delicious shop you have got! You tickle it, i' faith.

RALPH. Godamercy, Sybil, for our good cheer at Old Ford.

SYBIL. That you shall have, Ralph.

FIRK. Nay, by the mass, we had tickling cheer, Sybil; and
how the plague dost thou and Mistress Rose and my lord
mayor? I put the women in first.

SYBIL. Well, Godamercy; but God's me, I forget myself,
where's Hans the Fleming?

FIRK. Hark, butter-box, now you must yelp out some
spreken.

HANS. *Wat begaie you? Vat vod you, Frister?*[27]

    [27] "What do you want? What would you, Miss?"

SYBIL. Marry, you must come to my young mistress, to pull on her shoes you made last.

HANS. *Vare ben your egle fro, vare ben your mistris?*[28]

SYBIL. Marry, here at our London house in Cornhill.

FIRK. Will nobody serve her turn but Hans?

SYBIL. No, sir. Come, Hans, I stand upon needles.

HODGE. Why then, Sybil, take heed of pricking.

SYBIL. For that let me alone. I have a trick in my budget.[29] Come, Hans.

HANS. *Yaw, yaw, ick sall meete yo gane.*[30]

(*Exeunt* HANS *and* SYBIL.)

HODGE. Go, Hans, make haste again. Come, who lacks work?

FIRK. I, master, for I lack my breakfast; 'tis munching-time and past.

HODGE. Is't so? why, then leave work, Ralph. To breakfast! Boy, look to the tools. Come, Ralph; come, Firk.

(*Exeunt.*)

Scene 3

(*The same. Enter a* SERVING-MAN.)

SERVING-MAN. Let me see now, the sign of the Last in Tower Street. Mass, yonder's the house. What, haw! Who's within?

(*Enter* RALPH.)

RALPH. Who calls there? What want you, sir?

SERVING-MAN. Marry, I would have a pair of shoes made for a gentlewoman against tomorrow morning. What, can you do them?

RALPH. Yes, sir, you shall have them. But what's length her foot?

SERVING-MAN. Why, you must make them in all parts like this shoe; but, at any hand, fail not to do them, for the gentlewoman is to be married very early in the morning.

RALPH. How? by this shoe must it be made? by this? Are you sure, sir, by this?

SERVING-MAN. How, by this? Am I sure, by this? Art thou in thy wits? I tell thee, I must have a pair of shoes, dost thou

[28] "Where is your noble mistress, where is your lady?"
[29] That is, I have an ace up my sleeve.
[30] "Yes, yes, I shall go with you."

mark me? a pair of shoes, two shoes, made by this very shoe,
this same shoe, against tomorrow morning by four a clock.
Dost understand me? Canst thou do 't?

RALPH. Yes, sir, yes—ay, ay!—I can do 't. By this shoe, you
say? I should know this shoe. Yes, sir, yes, by this shoe, I
can do 't. Four a clock, well. Whither shall I bring them?

SERVING-MAN. To the sign of the Golden Ball in Watling
Street; enquire for one Master Hammon, a gentleman, my
master.

RALPH. Yea, sir, by this shoe, you say?

SERVING-MAN. I say, Master Hammon at the Golden Ball;
he's the bridegroom, and those shoes are for his bride.

RALPH. They shall be done by this shoe; well, well, Master Hammon at the Golden Shoe—I would say, the Golden
Ball; very well, very well. But I pray you, sir, where must Master Hammon be married?

SERVING-MAN. At Saint Faith's Church, under Paul's. But
what's that to thee? Prithee, dispatch those shoes, and so farewell.

(*Exit.*)

RALPH. By this shoe, said he. How am I amazed
At this strange accident! Upon my life,
This was the very shoe I gave my wife,
When I was pressed for France; since when, alas!
I never could hear of her: 'tis the same,
And Hammon's bride no other but my Jane.

(*Enter* FIRK.)

FIRK. 'Snails, Ralph, thou hast lost thy part of three pots,
a countryman of mine gave me to breakfast.

RALPH. I care not; I have found a better thing.

FIRK. A thing? away! Is it a man's thing, or a woman's
thing?

RALPH. Firk, dost thou know this shoe?

FIRK. No, by my troth; neither doth that know me! I have
no acquaintance with it, 'tis a mere stranger to me.

RALPH. Why, then I do; this shoe, I durst be sworn,
Once covered the instep of my Jane.
This is her size, her breadth, thus trod my love;
These true-love knots I pricked; I hold my life,
By this old shoe I shall find out my wife.

FIRK. Ha, ha! Old shoe, that wert new! How a mur-

rain* came this ague-fit of foolishness upon thee?   plague
  RALPH. Thus, Firk: even now here came a serving-man;
By this shoe would he have a new pair made
Against tomorrow morning for his mistress,
That's to be married to a gentleman.
And why may not this be my sweet Jane?
  FIRK. And why may'st not thou be my sweet ass? Ha, ha!
  RALPH. Well, laugh and spare not! But the truth is this:
Against tomorrow morning I'll provide
A lusty crew of honest shoemakers,
To watch the going of the bride to church.
If she prove Jane, I'll take her in despite
From Hammon and the devil, were he by.
If it be not my Jane, what remedy?
Hereof I am sure, I shall live till I die,
Although I never with a woman lie.

                          (Exit.)

  FIRK. Thou lie with a woman, to build nothing but Cripple-
gates! Well, God sends fools fortune, and it may be, he may
light upon his matrimony* by such a device; for wedding   wife
and hanging goes by destiny.

                          (Exit.)

Scene 4

(London: a room in the LORD MAYOR'S *house in Cornhill.
Enter* HANS *and* ROSE, *arm in arm.)*

  HANS. How happy am I by embracing thee!
Oh, I did fear such cross mishaps did reign,
That I should never see my Rose again.
  ROSE. Sweet Lacy, since fair opportunity
Offers herself to further our escape,
Let not too over-fond esteem of me
Hinder that happy hour. Invent the means,
And Rose will follow thee through all the world.
  HANS. Oh, how I surfeit with excess of joy,
Made happy by thy rich perfection!
But since thou pay'st sweet interest to my hopes,
Redoubling love on love, let me once more
Like to a bold-faced debtor crave of thee,
This night to steal abroad, and at Eyre's house,
Who now by death of certain aldermen
Is mayor of London, and my master once,

Meet thou thy Lacy, where in spite of change,
Your father's anger, and mine uncle's hate,
Our happy nuptials will we consummate.

(*Enter* SYBIL.)

SYBIL. O God, what will you do, mistress? Shift for yourself,
your father is at hand! He's coming, he's coming! Master Lacy,
hide yourself in my mistress! For God's sake, shift for yourselves!

HANS. Your father come, sweet Rose—what shall I do?
Where shall I hide me? How shall I escape?

ROSE. A man, and want wit in extremity?
Come, come, be Hans still, play the shoemaker,
Pull on my shoe.

(*Enter the* LORD MAYOR.)

HANS.   Mass, and that's well remembered.

SYBIL. Here comes your father.

HANS. *Forware, metresse, 'tis un good skow, it sal vel dute,
or ye sal neit betallen.*[31]

ROSE. O God, it pincheth me; what will you do?

HANS (*aside*). Your father's presence pincheth, not the
shoe.

LORD MAYOR. Well done; fit my daughter well, and she shall
please thee well.

HANS. *Yaw, yaw, ick weit dat well; forware, 'tis un good
skoo, 'tis gimait van neits leither; see euer, mine here.*[32]

(*Enter a* PRENTICE.)

LORD MAYOR. I do believe it.—What's the news with you?

PRENTICE. Please you, the Earl of Lincoln at the gate
Is newly 'lighted, and would speak with you.

LORD MAYOR. The Earl of Lincoln come to speak with me?
Well, well, I know his errand. Daughter Rose,
Send hence your shoemaker, dispatch, have done!
Syb, make things handsome! Sir boy, follow me.

(*Exit.*)

---

[31] "Indeed, mistress, it is a good shoe; it shall well do it, or you
shall not pay."

[32] "Yes, yes, I know that well; indeed, it is a good shoe; it is
made of neat's leather; take a look, sir."

HANS. Mine uncle come! O, what may this portend?
Sweet Rose, this of our love threatens an end.
　　ROSE. Be not dismayed at this; whate'er befall,
Rose is thine own. To witness I speak truth,
Where thou appoint'st the place, I'll meet with thee.
I will not fix a day to follow thee,
But presently* steal hence. Do not reply:　　　immediately
Love which gave strength to bear my father's hate,
Shall now add wings to further our escape.

　　　　　　　　　　　　　　　　　　　　(*Exeunt.*)

Scene 5

(*Another room in the same house. Enter the* LORD MAYOR
and the EARL OF LINCOLN.)

　　LORD MAYOR. Believe me, on my credit, I speak truth:
Since first your nephew Lacy went to France,
I have not seen him. It seemed strange to me,
When Dodger told me that he stayed behind,
Neglecting the high charge the king imposed.
　　LINCOLN. Trust me, Sir Roger Oteley, I did think
Your counsel had given head to this attempt,
Drawn to it by the love he bears your child.
Here I did hope to find him in your house;
But now I see mine error, and confess,
My judgment wronged you by conceiving so.
　　LORD MAYOR. Lodge in my house, say you? Trust me, my
　　　　lord,
I love your nephew Lacy too too dearly,
So much to wrong his honor; and he hath done so,
That first gave him advice to stay from France.
To witness I speak truth, I let you know,
How careful I have been to keep my daughter
Free from all conference or speech of him;
Not that I scorn your nephew, but in love
I bear your honor, lest your noble blood
Should by my mean worth be dishonored.
　　LINCOLN (*aside*). How far the churl's tongue wanders from
　　　　his heart!
—Well, well, Sir Roger Oteley, I believe you,
With more than many thanks for the kind love
So much you seem to bear me. But, my lord,
Let me request your help to seek my nephew,

Whom if I find, I'll straight embark for France.
So shall your Rose be free, my thoughts at rest,
And much care die which now lies in my breast.

(*Enter* SYBIL.)

SYBIL. O Lord! Help, for God's sake! my mistress; oh, my
young mistress!
    LORD MAYOR. Where is thy mistress? What's become of her?
    SYBIL. She's gone, she's fled!
    LORD MAYOR.   Gone! Whither is she fled?
    SYBIL. I know not, forsooth; she's fled out of doors with
Hans the shoemaker; I saw them scud, scud, scud, apace,
apace!
    LORD MAYOR. Which way? What, John! Where be my men?
        Which way?
    SYBIL. I know not, an* it please your worship.   if
    LORD MAYOR. Fled with a shoemaker? Can this be true?
    SYBIL. O Lord, sir, as true as God's in Heaven.
    LINCOLN (*aside*). Her love turned shoemaker? I am glad
    of this.
    LORD MAYOR. A Fleming butter-box, a shoemaker!
Will she forget her birth, requite my care
With such ingratitude? Scorned she young Hammon
To love a honnikin,* a needy knave?   low fellow
Well, let her fly, I'll not fly after her,
Let her starve, if she will; she's none of mine.
    LINCOLN. Be not so cruel, sir.

(*Enter* FIRK *with shoes.*)

SYBIL (*aside*).   I am glad, she's 'scaped.
    LORD MAYOR. I'll not account of her as of my child.
Was there no better object for her eyes
But a foul drunken lubber, swill-belly,
A shoemaker? That's brave!
    FIRK. Yea, forsooth; 'tis a very brave shoe, and as fit as a
pudding.
    LORD MAYOR. How now, what knave is this? From whence
comest thou?
    FIRK. No knave, sir. I am Firk the shoemaker, lusty Roger's
chief lusty journeyman, and I come hither to take up the pretty
leg of sweet Mistress Rose, and thus hoping your worship is in

as good health, as I was at the making hereof, I bid you farewell, yours, Firk.

LORD MAYOR. Stay, stay, Sir Knave!

LINCOLN.   Come hither, shoemaker!

FIRK. 'Tis happy the knave is put before the shoemaker, or
else I would not have vouchsafed to come back to you. I am
moved, for I stir.

LORD MAYOR. My lord, this villain calls us knaves by craft.

FIRK. Then 'tis by the Gentle Craft, and to call one knave
gently, is no harm. Sit your worship merry! (*Aside to* SYBIL.)
Syb, your young mistress—I'll so bob* them, now my   fool
Master Eyre is lord mayor of London.

LORD MAYOR. Tell me, sirrah, whose man are you?

FIRK. I am glad to see your worship so merry. I have no
maw* to this gear,* no stomach as yet to a red   appetite/matter
petticoat.

(*Pointing to* SYBIL.)

LINCOLN. He means not, sir, to woo you to his maid,
But only doth demand whose man you are.

FIRK. I sing now to the tune of Rogero. Roger, my fellow,
is now my master.

LINCOLN. Sirrah, know'st thou one Hans, a shoemaker?

FIRK. Hans, shoemaker? O yes, stay, yes, I have him. I tell
you what, I speak it in secret: Mistress Rose and he are by
this time—no, not so, but shortly are to come over one another with 'Can you dance the shaking of the sheets?' It is
that Hans—(*Aside.*) I'll so gull these diggers!*   questioners

LORD MAYOR. Know'st thou, then, where he is?

FIRK. Yes, forsooth; yea, marry!

LINCOLN. Canst thou, in sadness*—   without jesting

FIRK. No, forsooth; no marry!

LORD MAYOR. Tell me, good honest fellow, where he is.
And thou shalt see what I'll bestow of* thee.   on

FIRK. Honest fellow? No, sir; not so, sir; my profession is
the Gentle Craft; I care not for seeing, I love feeling; let me
feel it here; *aurium tenus,*[33] ten pieces of gold; *genuum tenus,*[34]
ten pieces of silver; and then Firk is your man—(*Aside.*) in a
new pair of stretchers.[35]

LORD MAYOR. Here is an angel, part of thy reward,
Which I will give thee; tell me where he is.

---

[33] "Up to the ears."
[34] "Up to the knees."
[35] Shoe stretchers; also a pun on *lies.*

FIRK. No point!* Shall I betray my brother? no!   certainly not
Shall I prove Judas to Hans? no! Shall I cry treason to my cor-
poration? no, I shall be firked and yerked* then. But   beaten
give me your angel; your angel shall tell you.

LINCOLN. Do so, good fellow; 'tis no hurt to thee.

FIRK. Send Simpering Syb away.

LORD MAYOR. Huswife, get you in.

(Exit SYBIL.)

FIRK. Pitchers have ears, and maids have wide mouths; but
for Hauns-prauns, upon my word, tomorrow morning he and
young Mistress Rose go to this gear, they shall be married together, by this rush,* or else turn Firk to a firkin   rush
of butter, to tan leather withal.   floor-covering

LORD MAYOR. But art thou sure of this?

FIRK. Am I sure that Paul's steeple is a handful higher than
London Stone or that the Pissing-Conduit leaks nothing but
pure Mother Bunch?* Am I sure I am lusty Firk?   a famous ale
God's nails, do you think I am so base to gull you?

LINCOLN. Where are they married? Dost thou know the
church?

FIRK. I never go to church, but I know the name of it; it is
a swearing church—stay a while, 'tis—Ay, by the mass, no, no,
—tis—Ay, by my troth, no, nor that; 'tis—Ay, by my faith,
that, that, 'tis, Ay, by my Faith's Church under Paul's Cross.
There they shall be knit like a pair of stockings in matrimony;
there they'll be inconie.*   that is, a
                                                             pretty pair
LINCOLN. Upon my life, my nephew Lacy walks
In the disguise of this Dutch shoemaker.

FIRK. Yes, forsooth.

LINCOLN. Doth he not, honest fellow?

FIRK. No, forsooth; I think Hans is nobody but Hans, no
spirit.

LORD MAYOR. My mind misgives me now, 'tis so, indeed.

LINCOLN. My cousin speaks the language, knows the trade.

LORD MAYOR. Let me request your company, my lord;
Your honorable presence may, no doubt,
Refrain their headstrong rashness, when myself
Going alone perchance may be o'erborne.
Shall I request this favor?

LINCOLN.   This, or what else.

FIRK. Then you must rise betimes,* for they mean to   early

fall to their hey-pass and repass,[36] pindy-pandy, which hand
will you have,[37] very early.

LORD MAYOR. My care shall every way equal their haste.
This night accept your lodging in my house,
The earlier shall we stir, and at Saint Faith's
Prevent this giddy hare-brained nuptial.
This traffic of hot love shall yield cold gains:
They ban our loves, and we'll forbid their banns.

(Exit.)

LINCOLN. At Saint Faith's Church thou say'st?
FIRK. Yes, by their troth.
LINCOLN. Be secret, on thy life.

(Exit.)

FIRK. Yes, when I kiss your wife! Ha, ha, here's no craft
in the Gentle Craft. I came hither of purpose with shoes to
Sir Roger's worship, whilst Rose, his daughter, be cony-
catched* by Hans. Soft now; these two gulls will be at   duped
Saint Faith's Church tomorrow morning, to take Master Bridegroom and Mistress Bride napping, and they, in the meantime,
shall chop up the matter at the Savoy. But the best sport is,
Sir Roger Oteley will find my fellow lame Ralph's wife going
to marry a gentleman, and then he'll stop her instead of his
daughter. O, brave! there will be fine tickling sport. Soft now,
what have I to do? O, I know; now a mess* of shoe-   group
makers meet at the Woolsack in Ivy Lane, to cozen* my   cheat
gentleman of lame Ralph's wife, that's true.

> Alack, alack!
> Girls, hold out tack!*   resist
> For now smocks for this jumbling
> Shall go to wrack.

(Exit.)

ACT V

Scene 1

(A room in EYRE'S *house. Enter* EYRE, MARGERY, HANS,
and ROSE.*)*

EYRE. This is the morning, then, say, my bully, my honest
Hans, is it not?

---

[36] Juggling terms.
[37] From the child's game of handy-dandy.

HANS. This is the morning, that must make us two happy
or miserable; therefore, if you—

EYRE. Away with these ifs and ans, Hans, and these *et
caeteras!* By mine honor, Rowland Lacy, none but the king
shall wrong thee. Come, fear nothing, am not I Sim Eyre?
Is not Sim Eyre lord mayor of London? Fear nothing, Rose:
let them all say what they can; dainty, come thou to me—
laughest thou?

MARGERY. Good my lord, stand her friend in what thing
you may.

EYRE. Why, my sweet Lady Madgy, think you Simon Eyre
can forget his fine Dutch journeyman? No, vah! Fie, I scorn it,
it shall never be cast in my teeth, that I was unthankful. Lady
Madgy, thou had'st never covered thy Saracen's head with this
French flap, nor loaden thy bum with this farthingale ('tis
trash, trumpery, vanity); Simon Eyre had never walked in a
red petticoat, nor wore a chain of gold, but for my fine journeyman's Portuguese.—And shall I leave him? No! Prince am
I none, yet bear a princely mind.

HANS. My lord, 'tis time for us to part from hence.

EYRE. Lady Madgy, Lady Madgy, take two or three of my
pie-crust-eaters, my buff-jerkin varlets, that do walk in black
gowns at Simon Eyre's heels; take them, good Lady Madgy;
trip and go, my brown queen of periwigs, with my delicate
Rose and my jolly Rowland to the Savoy; see them linked,
countenance the marriage; and when it is done, cling, cling together, you Hamborow* turtle-doves. I'll bear you out, Hamburg
come to Simon Eyre; come, dwell with me, Hans, thou shalt
eat minced-pies and marchpane.* Rose, away, cricket;   marzipan
trip and go, my Lady Madgy, to the Savoy; Hans, wed, and to
bed; kiss, and away! Go, vanish!

MARGERY. Farewell, my lord.

ROSE. Make haste, sweet love.

MARGERY.   She'd fain the deed were done.

HANS. Come, my sweet Rose; faster than deer we'll run.

                              (*Exeunt all but* EYRE.)

EYRE. Go, vanish, vanish! Avaunt, I say! By the Lord of
Ludgate, it's a mad life to be a lord mayor; it's a stirring life,
a fine life, a velvet life, a careful life. Well, Simon Eyre, yet
set a good face on it, in the honor of Saint Hugh. Soft, the
king this day comes to dine with me, to see my new buildings;
his majesty is welcome, he shall have good cheer, delicate
cheer, princely cheer. This day, my fellow prentices of London

come to dine with me too; they shall have fine cheer, gentle-manlike cheer. I promised the mad Cappadocians, when we all served at the Conduit together,[38] that if ever I came to be mayor of London, I would feast them all, and I'll do 't, I'll do 't, by the life of Pharaoh; by this beard, Sim Eyre will be no flincher. Besides, I have procured that upon every Shrove Tues-day, at the sound of the pancake bell,[39] my fine dapper As-syrian lads shall clap up their shop windows, and away. This is the day, and this day they shall do 't, they shall do 't.

Boys, that day are you free, let masters care,
And prentices shall pray for Simon Eyre.

(*Exit.*)

Scene 2

(*A street near St. Faith's Church.* Enter HODGE, FIRK, RALPH, *and five or six* SHOEMAKERS, *all with cudgels or such weapons.*)

HODGE. Come, Ralph; stand to it, Firk. My masters, as we are the brave bloods of the shoemakers, heirs apparent to Saint Hugh, and perpetual benefactors to all good fellows, thou shalt have no wrong; were Hammon a king of spades, he should not delve in thy close[40] without thy sufferance.* permission But tell me, Ralph, art thou sure 'tis thy wife?

RALPH. Am I sure this is Firk? This morning, when I stroked on her shoes, I looked upon her, and she upon me, and sighed, asked me if ever I knew one Ralph. Yes, said I. For his sake, said she—tears standing in her eyes—and for thou art some-what like him, spend this piece of gold. I took it; my lame leg and my travel beyond sea made me unknown. All is one for that: I know she's mine.

FIRK. Did she give thee this gold? O glorious glittering gold! She's thine own, 'tis thy wife, and she loves thee; for I'll stand to 't, there's no woman will give gold to any man, but she thinks better of him, than she thinks of them she gives silver to. And for Hammon, neither Hammon nor hangman shall wrong thee in London. Is not our old master Eyre, lord mayor? Speak, my hearts.

ALL. Yes, and Hammon shall know it to his cost.

[38] The apprentices had to carry water from the conduit as one of their duties.
[39] The approach of Lent was celebrated with pancake feasts.
[40] That is, dig in your garden.

(*Enter* Hammon, *his* Serving-man, Jane, *and others.*)

Hodge. Peace, my bullies; yonder they come.

Ralph. Stand to 't, my hearts. Firk, let me speak first.

Hodge. No, Ralph, let me.—Hammon, whither away so early?

Hammon. Unmannerly, rude slave, what's that to thee?

Firk. To him, sir? Yes, sir, and to me, and others. Good-morrow, Jane, how dost thou? Good Lord, how the world is changed with you! God be thanked!

Hammon. Villains, hands off! How dare you touch my love?

All the Shoemakers. Villains? Down with them! Cry clubs for prentices![41]

Hodge. Hold, my hearts! Touch her, Hammon? Yea, and more than that: we'll carry her away with us. My masters and gentlemen, never draw your bird-spits; shoemakers are steel to the back, men every inch of them, all spirit.

Those of Hammon's side. Well, and what of all this?

Hodge. I'll show you.—Jane, dost thou know this man? 'Tis Ralph, I can tell thee; nay, 'tis he in faith, though he be lamed by the wars. Yet look not strange, but run to him, fold him about the neck and kiss him.

Jane. Lives then my husband? O God, let me go, Let me embrace my Ralph.

Hammon.   What means my Jane?

Jane. Nay, what meant you, to tell me, he was slain?

Hammon. Pardon me, dear love, for being misled.

(*To Ralph.*) 'Twas rumored here in London, thou wert dead.

Firk. Thou seest he lives. Lass, go, pack home with him. Now, Master Hammon, where's your mistress, your wife?

Serving-man. 'Swounds, master, fight for her! Will you thus lose her?

Shoemakers. Down with that creature! Clubs! Down with him!

Hodge. Hold, hold!

Hammon. Hold, fool! Sirs, he shall do no wrong. Will my Jane leave me thus, and break her faith?

Firk. Yea, sir! She must, sir! She shall, sir! What then? Mend it!

Hodge. Hark, fellow Ralph, follow my counsel: set the

───────────

[41] The rallying cry of the apprentice.

wench in the midst, and let her choose her man, and let her
be his woman.

JANE. Whom should I choose? Whom should my thoughts
affect
But him whom Heaven hath made to be my love?
Thou art my husband, and these humble weeds*   clothes
Make thee more beautiful than all his wealth.
Therefore, I will but put off his attire,
Returning it into the owner's hand,
And after ever be thy constant wife.

HODGE. Not a rag, Jane! The law's on our side; he that
sows in another man's ground, forfeits his harvest. Get thee
home, Ralph; follow him, Jane; he shall not have so much as
a busk-point* from thee.   corset lace

FIRK. Stand to that, Ralph; the appurtenances are thine
own. Hammon, look not at her!

SERVING-MAN. O, 'swounds, no!

FIRK. Blue-coat,[42] be quiet, we'll give you a new livery else;
we'll make Shrove Tuesday Saint George's Day for you.[43]
Look not, Hammon, leer not! I'll firk* you! For thy head   beat
now, not one glance, one sheep's eye, anything, at her! Touch
not a rag, lest I and my brethren beat you to clouts.

SERVING-MAN. Come, Master Hammon, there's no striving
here.

HAMMON. Good fellows, hear me speak; and, honest Ralph,
Whom I have injured most by loving Jane,
Mark what I offer thee: here in fair gold
Is twenty pound, I'll give it for thy Jane;
If this content thee not, thou shalt have more.

HODGE. Sell not thy wife, Ralph; make her not a whore.

HAMMON. Say, wilt thou freely cease thy claim in her,
And let her be my wife?

ALL THE SHOEMAKERS.   No, do not, Ralph.

RALPH. Sirrah Hammon, Hammon, dost thou think a shoemaker is so base to be a bawd to his own wife for commodity? Take thy gold, choke with it! Were I not lame, I
would make thee eat thy words.

FIRK. A shoemaker sell his flesh and blood? O, indignity!

HODGE. Sirrah, take up your pelf,* and be packing.   money

[42] The usual color for servants' livery.
[43] That is, we'll beat you black and blue.

HAMMON. I will not touch one penny, but in lieu
Of that great wrong I offerèd thy Jane,
To Jane and thee I give that twenty pound.
Since I have failed of her, during my life,
I vow, no woman else shall be my wife.
Farewell, good fellows of the Gentle Trade:
Your morning mirth my mourning day hath made.

                              (*Exeunt* HAMMON *and companions.*)

FIRK (*to the* SERVING-MAN). Touch the gold, creature, if
you dare! Y' are best be trudging. (*Exit the* SERVING-MAN.)
Here, Jane, take thou it. Now let's home, my hearts.

HODGE. Stay! Who comes here? Jane, on again with thy
mask!

(*Enter the* EARL OF LINCOLN, *the* LORD MAYOR, *and*
SERVANTS.)

LINCOLN. Yonder's the lying varlet mocked us so.

LORD MAYOR. Come hither, sirrah!

FIRK. I, sir? I am sirrah? You mean me, do you not?

LINCOLN. Where is my nephew married?

FIRK. Is he married? God give him joy, I am glad of it.
They have a fair day, and the sign is in a good planet, Mars
in Venus.

LORD MAYOR. Villain, thou toldst me that my daughter Rose
This morning should be married at Saint Faith's;
We have watched there these three hours at the least,
Yet see we no such thing.

FIRK. Truly, I am sorry for 't; a bride's a pretty thing.

HODGE. Come to the purpose. Yonder's the bride and bridegroom you look for, I hope. Though you be lords, you are
not to bar by your authority men from women, are you?

LORD MAYOR. See, see, my daughter's masked.

LINCOLN.   True, and my nephew,
To hide his guilt, counterfeits him lame.

FIRK. Yea, truly; God help the poor couple, they are lame
and blind.

LORD MAYOR. I'll ease her blindness.

LINCOLN.   I'll his lameness cure.

FIRK (*aside to the Shoemakers*). Lie down, sirs, and laugh!
My fellow Ralph is taken for Rowland Lacy, and Jane for
Mistress Damask Rose. This is all my knavery.

LORD MAYOR. What, have I found you, minion?

LINCOLN. O base wretch!
Nay, hide thy face, the horror of thy guilt
Can hardly be washed off. Where are thy powers?* troops
What battles have you made? O yes, I see,
Thou fought'st with Shame, and Shame hath conquered thee.
This lameness will not serve.

LORD MAYOR. Unmask yourself.

LINCOLN. Lead home your daughter.

LORD MAYOR. Take your nephew hence.

RALPH. Hence! 'Swounds, what mean you? Are you mad?
I hope you cannot enforce my wife from me. Where's Hammon?

LORD MAYOR. Your wife?

LINCOLN. What Hammon?

RALPH. Yea, my wife; and, therefore, the proudest of you
that lays hands on her first, I'll lay my crutch 'cross his pate.

FIRK. To him, lame Ralph! Here's brave sport!

RALPH. Rose call you her? Why, her name is Jane. Look
here else; do you know her now?

(*Unmasking* JANE.)

LINCOLN. Is this your daughter?

LORD MAYOR. No, nor this your nephew.
My Lord of Lincoln, we are both abused* deceived
By this base, crafty varlet.

FIRK. Yea, forsooth, no varlet; forsooth, no base; forsooth,
I am but mean;[44] no crafty neither, but of the Gentle Craft.

LORD MAYOR. Where is my daughter Rose? Where is my
child?

LINCOLN. Where is my nephew Lacy married?

FIRK. Why, here is good laced mutton,[45] as I promised you.

LINCOLN. Villain, I'll have thee punished for this wrong.

FIRK. Punish the journeyman villain, but not the journeyman shoemaker.

(*Enter* DODGER.)

DODGER. My lord, I come to bring unwelcome news.
Your nephew Lacy and your daughter Rose
Early this morning wedded at the Savoy,

[44] Tenor, with a pun on bass as a musical term.

[45] Prostitute. Firk is punning on Lacy's name rather than com-
menting on Jane's character.

None being present but the lady mayoress.
Besides, I learnt among the officers,
The lord mayor vows to stand in their defense
'Gainst any that shall seek to cross the match.

LINCOLN. Dares Eyre the shoemaker uphold the deed?

FIRK. Yes, sir, shoemakers dare stand in a woman's quarrel, I warrant you, as deep as another, and deeper too.

DODGER. Besides, his grace today dines with the mayor;
Who on his knees humbly intends to fall
And beg a pardon for your nephew's fault.

LINCOLN. But I'll prevent him! Come, Sir Roger Oteley;
The king will do us justice in this cause.
Howe'er their hands have made them man and wife,
I will disjoin the match, or lose my life.

                                        (*Exeunt.*)

FIRK. Adieu, Monsieur Dodger! Farewell, fools! Ha, ha!
Oh, if they had stayed, I would have so lambed* them   lambasted
with flouts! O heart, my codpiece-point is ready to fly in pieces
every time I think upon Mistress Rose; but let that pass, as
my lady mayoress says.

HODGE. This matter is answered. Come, Ralph; home with
thy wife. Come, my fine shoemakers, let's to our master's, the
new lord mayor, and there swagger this Shrove Tuesday.[46]
I'll promise you wine enough, for Madge keeps the cellar.

ALL. O rare! Madge is a good wench.

FIRK. And I'll promise you meat enough, for simp'ring
Susan keeps the larder. I'll lead you to victuals, my brave
soldiers; follow your captain. O brave! Hark, hark!

(*Bell rings.*)

ALL. The pancake-bell rings, the pancake-bell! Trilill, my
hearts!

FIRK. O brave! O sweet bell! O delicate pancakes! Open
the doors, my hearts, and shut up the windows! keep in the
house, let out the pancakes! Oh, rare, my hearts! Let's march
together for the honor of Saint Hugh to the great new
hall* in Gracious Street-corner, which master,   Leadenhall
the new lord mayor hath built

RALPH. O the crew of good fellows that will dine at my
lord mayor's cost today!

HODGE. By the Lord, my lord mayor is a most brave man.
How shall prentices be bound to pray for him and the honor

_____
[46] The apprentices' holiday.

of the gentlemen shoemakers! Let's feed and be fat with my lord's bounty.

FIRK. O musical bell, still! O Hodge, O my brethren! There's cheer for the heavens: venison-pasties walk up and down piping hot, like sergeants; beef and brewis* comes   broth marching in dry-fats,* fritters and pancakes come   casks trowling in in wheel-barrows; hens and orange hopping in porters'-baskets, collops* and eggs in scuttles,* and slices of meat/ tarts and custards come quavering in in malt-shovels.   baskets

(*Enter more* PRENTICES.)

ALL. Whoop, look here, look here!

HODGE. How now, mad lads, whither away so fast?

FIRST PRENTICE. Whither? Why, to the great new hall, know you not why? The lord mayor hath bidden all the prentices in London to breakfast this morning.

ALL. Oh, brave shoemaker, Oh, brave lord of incomprehensible good fellowship! Whoo! Hark you! The pancake-bell rings.

(*Cast up caps.*)

FIRK. Nay, more, my hearts! Every Shrove Tuesday is our year of jubilee; and when the pancake-bell rings, we are as free as my lord mayor; we may shut up our shops, and make holiday. I'll have it called Saint Hugh's Holiday.

ALL. Agreed, agreed! Saint Hugh's Holiday.

HODGE. And this shall continue for ever.

ALL. Oh, brave! Come, come, my hearts! Away, away!

FIRK. O eternal credit to us of the Gentle Craft! March fair, my hearts! Oh, rare!

(*Exeunt.*)

Scene 3

(*A street in London. Enter the* KING *and his* TRAIN *over the stage.*)

KING. Is our lord mayor of London such a gallant?

NOBLEMAN. One of the merriest madcaps in your land.
Your grace will think, when you behold the man,
He's rather a wild ruffian than a mayor,
Yet thus much I'll ensure your majesty.
In all his actions that concern his state,

He is as serious, provident, and wise,
As full of gravity amongst the grave,
As any mayor hath been these many years.

    KING. I am with child,* till I behold this   impatient
       huffcap.*   swaggerer
But all my doubt is, when we come in presence,
His madness will be dashed clean out of countenance.

    NOBLEMAN. It may be so, my liege.

    KING.   Which to prevent
Let some one give him notice, 'tis our pleasure
That he put on his wonted merriment.
Set forward!

    ALL.   On afore!

                                  (*Exeunt.*)

Scene 4

(*A great hall. Enter* EYRE, HODGE, FIRK, RALPH, *and other* SHOEMAKERS, *all with napkins on their shoulders.*)

    EYRE. Come, my fine Hodge, my jolly gentlemen shoemakers; soft, where be these cannibals, these varlets, my officers? Let them all walk and wait upon my brethren; for my meaning is, that none but shoemakers, none but the livery of my company shall in their satin hoods wait upon the trencher of my sovereign.

    FIRK. O my lord, it will be rare!

    EYRE. No more, Firk; come, lively! Let your fellow prentices want no cheer; let wine be plentiful as beer, and beer as water. Hang these penny-pinching fathers, that cram wealth in innocent lambskins.* Rip, knaves, avaunt! Look to   purses my guests!

    HODGE. My lord, we are at our wits' end for room; those hundred tables will not feast the fourth part of them.

    EYRE. Then cover me those hundred tables again, and again, till all my jolly prentices be feasted. Avoid, Hodge! Run, Ralph! Frisk about, my nimble Firk! Carouse me fathom-healths to the honor of the shoemakers. Do they drink lively, Hodge? Do they tickle it, Firk?

    FIRK. Tickle it? Some of them have taken their liquor standing so long that they can stand no longer; but for meat, they would eat it, an* they had it.   if

    EYRE. Want they meat? Where's this swag-belly, this greasy

kitchenstuff cook? Call the varlet to me! Want meat? Firk, Hodge, lame Ralph, run, my tall men, beleaguer the sham-bles,* beggar all Eastcheap, serve me whole oxen   butcher shops in chargers,* and let sheep whine upon the tables   large platters like pigs for want of good fellows to eat them. Want meat? Vanish, Firk! Avaunt, Hodge!

HODGE. Your lordship mistakes my man Firk; he means, their bellies want meat, not the boards; for they have drunk so much, they can eat nothing.

THE SECOND THREE-MAN'S SONG

Cold's the wind, and wet's the rain,
  Saint Hugh be our good speed:
Ill is the weather that bringeth no gain,
  Nor helps good hearts in need.

Trowl* the bowl, the jolly nut-brown bowl,   pass around
  And here, kind mate, to thee:
Let's sing a dirge for Saint Hugh's soul,
  And down it merrily.

Down a down heydown a down,
  Hey derry derry, down a down.
Ho, well done; to me let come!
  Ring compass,* gentle joy.   that is, circulate
                                  the drinks

Trowl the bowl, the nut-brown bowl,
  And here, kind mate, to thee:
Let's sing a dirge for Saint Hugh's soul,
  And down it merrily.

Cold's the wind, and wet's the rain,
  Saint Hugh be our good speed:
Ill is the weather that bringeth no gain,
  Nor helps good hearts in need.

(*Enter* HANS, ROSE, *and* MARGERY.)

MARGERY. Where is my lord?
EYRE. How now, Lady Madgy?
MARGERY. The king's most excellent majesty is new come;

he sends me for thy honor; one of his most worshipful peers
bade me tell thou must be merry, and so forth; but let that
pass.

EYRE. Is my sovereign come? Vanish, my tall shoemakers,
my nimble brethren; look to my guests, the prentices. Yet
stay a little! How now, Hans? How looks my little Rose?

HANS. Let me request you to remember me.
I know, your honor easily may obtain
Free pardon of the king for me and Rose,
And reconcile me to my uncle's grace.

EYRE. Have done, my good Hans, my honest journeyman;
look cheerily! I'll fall upon both my knees, till they be as
hard as horn, but I'll get thy pardon.

MARGERY. Good my lord, have a care what you speak to
his grace.

EYRE. Away, you Islington whitepot!⁴⁷ hence, you hop-
perarse! you barley-pudding, full of maggots! you broiled car-
bonado!* avaunt, avaunt, avoid, Mephistophilus! Shall   steak
Sim Eyre learn to speak of you, Lady Madgy? Vanish, Mother
Miniver*-cap; vanish, go, trip and go; meddle with   fur-lined
your partlets* and your pishery-pashery, your   neckerchiefs
flewes* and your whirligigs; go, rub,* out of   flapping skirts/
  obstacle (bowling)
mine alley! Sim Eyre knows how to speak to a Pope, to Sultan
Soliman, to Tamburlaine,⁴⁸ an* he were here, and shall I   if
melt, shall I droop before my sovereign? No, come, my Lady
Madgy! Follow me, Hans! About your business, my frolic
free-booters! Firk, frisk about, and about, and about, for the
honor of mad Simon Eyre, lord mayor of London.

FIRK. Hey, for the honor of the shoemakers.

                                   (*Exeunt.*)

Scene 5

(*An open yard before the hall. A long flourish, or two.
Enter the* KING, NOBLES, EYRE, MARGERY, LACY, ROSE.
LACY *and* ROSE *kneel.*)

KING. Well, Lacy, though the fact was very foul
Of your revolting from our kingly love
And your own duty, yet we pardon you.

---

    ⁴⁷ A mixture of milk, eggs, raisins, and sugar.
    ⁴⁸ Mongolian emperor Timur (1336–1405). See Marlowe's
Tamburlaine.

Rise both, and, Mistress Lacy, thank my lord mayor
For your young bridegroom here.

EYRE. So, my dear liege, Sim Eyre and my brethren, the
gentlemen shoemakers, shall set your sweet majesty's image
cheek by jowl by Saint Hugh for this honor you have done
poor Simon Eyre. I beseech your grace, pardon my rude be-
havior; I am a handicraftsman, yet my heart is without craft;
I would be sorry at my soul, that my boldness should offend
my king.

KING. Nay, I pray thee, good lord mayor, be even as merry
As if thou wert among thy shoemakers;
It does me good to see thee in this humor.

EYRE. Say'st thou me so, my sweet Dioclesian?*   that is,
                                                      emperor
Then, humph! Prince am I none, yet am I princely born. By
the Lord of Ludgate, my liege, I'll be as merry as a pie.* magpie

KING. Tell me, in faith, mad Eyre, how old thou art.

EYRE. My liege, a very boy, a stripling, a younker,* youngster
you see not a white hair on my head, not a grey in this beard.
Every hair, I assure thy majesty, that sticks in this beard, Sim
Eyre values at the King of Babylon's ransom, Tamar
Cham's* beard was a rubbing brush to 't: yet I'll   Tamburlaine
shave it off, and stuff tennis-balls with it, to please my bully
king.

KING. But all this while I do not know your age.

EYRE. My liege, I am six and fifty year old, yet I can cry
humph! with a sound heart for the honor of Saint Hugh.
Mark this old wench, my king: I danced the shaking of the
sheets with her six and thirty years ago, and yet I hope to
get two or three young lord mayors, ere I die. I am lusty still,
Sim Eyre still. Care and cold lodgings brings white hairs. My
sweet Majesty, let care vanish, cast it upon thy nobles, it will
make thee look always young like Apollo, and cry humph!
Prince am I none, yet am I princely born.

KING. Ha, ha!
Say, Cornwall, didst thou ever see his like?

CORNWALL. Not I, my lord.

(*Enter the* EARL OF LINCOLN *and the* LORD MAYOR.)

KING.   Lincoln, what news with you?
LINCOLN. My gracious lord, have care unto yourself,
For there are traitors here.

ALL.   Traitors? Where? Who?

EYRE. Traitors in my house? God forbid! Where be my
officers? I'll spend my soul, ere my king feel harm.

KING. Where is the traitor, Lincoln?

LINCOLN.   Here he stands.

KING. Cornwall, lay hold on Lacy!—Lincoln, speak,
What canst thou lay unto thy nephew's charge?

LINCOLN. This, my dear liege: your Grace, to do me honor,
Heaped on the head of this degenerous* boy   degenerate
Desertless* favors; you made choice of him,   undeserved
To be commander over powers* in France.   troops
But he—

KING. Good Lincoln, prithee, pause a while!
Even in thine eyes I read what thou wouldst speak.
I know how Lacy did neglect our love,
Ran himself deeply, in the highest degree,
Into vile treason——

LINCOLN.   Is he not a traitor?

KING. Lincoln, he was; now have we pardoned him.
'Twas not a base want of true valor's fire,
That held him out of France, but love's desire.

LINCOLN. I will not bear his shame upon my back.

KING. Nor shalt thou, Lincoln; I forgive you both.

LINCOLN. Then, good my liege, forbid the boy to wed
One whose mean birth will much disgrace his bed.

KING. Are they not married?

LINCOLN.   No, my liege.

BOTH.   We are.

KING. Shall I divorce them then? O be it far,
That any hand on earth should dare untie
The sacred knot, knit by God's majesty;
I would not for my crown disjoin their hands,
That are conjoined in holy nuptial bands.
How say'st thou, Lacy, wouldst thou lose thy Rose?

LACY. Not for all India's wealth, my sovereign.

KING. But Rose, I am sure, her Lacy would forgo?

ROSE. If Rose were asked that question, she'd say no.

KING. You hear them, Lincoln?

LINCOLN.   Yea, my liege, I do.

KING. Yet canst thou find i' th' heart to part these two?
Who seeks, besides you, to divorce these lovers?

LORD MAYOR. I do, my gracious lord, I am her father.

KING. Sir Roger Oteley, our last mayor, I think?

NOBLEMAN. The same, my liege.

KING.   Would you offend Love's laws?
Well, you shall have your wills. You sue to me,
To prohibit the match. Soft, let me see—
You both are married, Lacy, art thou not?
   LACY. I am, dread sovereign.
   KING.   Then, upon thy life,
I charge thee not to call this woman wife.
   LORD MAYOR. I thank your grace.
   ROSE.   O my most gracious lord!
(Kneels.)
   KING. Nay, Rose, never woo me; I tell you true,
Although as yet I am a bachelor,
Yet I believe, I shall not marry you.
   ROSE. Can you divide the body from the soul,
Yet make the body live?
   KING.   Yea, so profound?
I cannot, Rose, but you I must divide.
This fair maid, bridegroom, cannot be your bride.
Are you pleased, Lincoln? Oteley, are you pleased?
   BOTH. Yes, my lord.
   KING.   Then must my heart be eased;
For, credit me, my conscience lives in pain
Till these whom I divorced, be joined again.
Lacy, give me thy hand; Rose, lend me thine!
Be what you would be! Kiss now? So, that's fine.
At night, lovers, to bed!—Now, let me see,
Which of you mislikes this harmony.
   LORD MAYOR. Will you then take from me my child per-
      force?*   <small>through force</small>
   KING. Why, tell me, Oteley: shines not Lacy's name
As bright in the world's eye as the gay beams
Of any citizen?
   LINCOLN.   Yea, but, my gracious lord,
I do mislike the match far more than he;
Her blood is too too base.
   KING.   Lincoln, no more.
Dost thou not know that love respects no blood,
Cares not for difference of birth or state?
The maid is young, well born, fair, virtuous,
A worthy bride for any gentleman.
Besides, your nephew for her sake did stoop
To bare necessity, and, as I hear,
Forgetting honors and all courtly pleasures,

To gain her love, became a shoemaker.
As for the honor which he lost in France,
Thus I redeem it: Lacy, kneel thee down!—
Arise, Sir Rowland Lacy! Tell me now,
Tell me in earnest, Oteley, canst thou chide,
Seeing thy Rose a lady and a bride?

LORD MAYOR. I am content with what your grace hath done.

LINCOLN. And I, my liege, since there's no remedy.

KING. Come on, then, all shake hands: I'll have you friends;
Where there is much love, all discord ends.
What says my mad lord mayor to all this love?

EYRE. O my liege, this honor you have done to my fine
journeyman here, Rowland Lacy, and all these favors which
you have shown to me this day in my poor house, will make
Simon Eyre live longer by one dozen of warm summers more
than he should.

KING. Nay my mad lord mayor, that shall be thy name,
If any grace of mine can length thy life,
One honor more I'll do thee: that new building,
Which at thy cost in Cornhill is erected,
Shall take a name from us; we'll have it called
The Leadenhall, because in digging it
You found the lead that covereth the same.

EYRE. I thank your majesty.

MARGERY. God bless your grace!

KING. Lincoln, a word with you!

(*Enter* HODGE, FIRK, RALPH, *and more* SHOEMAKERS.)

EYRE. How now, my mad knaves? Peace, speak softly,
yonder is the king.

KING. With the old troop which there we keep in pay,
We will incorporate a new supply.
Before one summer more pass o'er my head,
France shall repent England was injured.
What are all those?

LACY.   All shoemakers, my liege,
Sometime* my fellows; in their companies   formerly
I lived as merry as an emperor.

KING. My mad lord mayor, are all these shoemakers?

EYRE. All shoemakers, my liege; all gentlemen of the Gentle
Craft, true Trojans, courageous cordwainers; they all kneel
to the shrine of holy Saint Hugh.

ALL THE SHOEMAKERS. God save your majesty!

KING. Mad Simon, would they anything with us?

EYRE. Mum, mad knaves! Not a word! I'll do 't; I warrant you.—They are all beggars, my liege; all for themselves, and I for them all, on both my knees do entreat, that for the honor of poor Simon Eyre and the good of his brethren, these mad knaves, your grace would vouchsafe some privilege to my new Leadenhall, that it may be lawful for us to buy and sell leather there two days a week.

KING. Mad Sim, I grant your suit; you shall have patent
To hold two market-days in Leadenhall,
Mondays and Fridays, those shall be the times.
Will this content you?

ALL.   Jesus bless your grace!

EYRE. In the name of these my poor brethren shoemakers, I most humbly thank your grace. But before I rise, seeing you are in the giving vein and we in the begging, grant Sim Eyre one boon more.

KING. What is it, my lord mayor?

EYRE. Vouchsafe to taste of a poor banquet that stands sweetly waiting for your sweet presence.

KING. I shall undo thee, Eyre, only with feasts;
Already have I been too troublesome;
Say, have I not?

EYRE. O my dear king, Sim Eyre was taken unawares upon a day of shroving,* which I promised long ago to   merrymaking the prentices of London.

> For, an* 't please your highness, in time past,   if
> I bare the water-tankard,[49] and my coat
> Sits not a whit the worse upon my back;
> And then, upon a morning, some mad boys
> (It was Shrove Tuesday, even as 'tis now)

Gave me my breakfast, and I swore then by the stopple of my tankard, if ever I came to be lord mayor of London, I would feast all the prentices. This day, my liege, I did it, and the slaves had an hundred tables five times covered; they are gone home and vanished;

> Yet add more honor to the Gentle Trade,
> Taste of Eyre's banquet, Simon's happy made.

[49] As an apprentice. See note 38.

KING. Eyre, I will taste of thy banquet, and will say,
I have not met more pleasure on a day.
Friends of the Gentle Craft, thanks to you all,
Thanks, my kind lady mayoress, for our cheer.—
Come, lords, a while let's revel it at home!
When all our sports and banquetings are done,
Wars must right wrongs which Frenchmen have begun.

(Exeunt.)

A Woman Killed with Kindness

BY THOMAS HEYWOOD

A prolific virtuoso of both Elizabethan and Jacobean drama, Thomas Heywood (*c.* 1573-74 to 1641) was remarkable for the variety of the more than 200 plays he wrote alone and in collaboration with others. Although no more than about 10 per cent of his work has survived, it includes histories, romances, adventures, tragicomedies (when those came into vogue) and treatments of classical and mythological subjects as well as themes concerning English contemporary life. Heywood contributed something noteworthy in each category of the playwriting of his time.

Heywood, a cultivated man who came of a good country family, was university-educated at Cambridge and earned the appellation in later years of "learned author." In his early twenties he became an actor (for Henslowe) and continued to act long after he became a successful playwright. Heywood also wrote numerous books, mostly historical and biographical in character, but for the most part he busied himself with writing for the theater and subsequently, in his official capacity as City Poet, with annual pageants for the Lord Mayor's municipal shows.

In the long run Heywood's interest in domestic tragedy contributed most to his reputation, largely because of the effectiveness of one relatively early play, *A Woman Killed with Kindness.* The drama was unusual in its radical revision of the conventions of dramas of marital infidelity, its reversal of the expected conduct of an outraged husband, the conventional view of which appeared even in an otherwise to remarkable play as *Othello.* In Heywood's play the husband, Frankford, forgives his unfaithful wife instead of conforming

to the bloody pattern of vengeance which was standard for the
English and Spanish theatres. Although Frankford's first impulse is to kill his wife's seducer, his anger passes and he
forgives his wife, from whom he then separates more in sorrow than in anger. His wife punishes herself and dies of remorse, killed more by kindness, so to speak, than by wrath.

Although *A Woman Killed with Kindness* is essentially
concerned with pathos rather than tragedy, it carries not only
conviction and a sense of reality, but also an enlightened
viewpoint rather than the conventional heroics. Coming after
the vogue of the romantic drama of the 1590's, the play
antedates an attitude that became familiar on the English-
speaking stage only in the late nineteenth century, with the
advent of Ibsen's "enlightened" realism. *A Woman Killed
with Kindness* was certainly a radical departure from the
Renaissance genre of "revenge tragedy," which was bound
up with aristocratic codes of honor while Heywood's play
reflects the less presumptuous and more humane orientation
of middle-class realism, to which Heywood was uncommonly
attached. It was this congenial temperament that two centuries
later attracted Charles Lamb when he attributed to Heywood
"generosity, courtesy, temperance in the depth of passion,
sweetness, in a word, and gentleness" (*Specimens of the
English Dramatic Poets*, 1808, 1823) and called him, on the
strength of his "natural and affecting" scenes, "a sort of prose
Shakespeare."

                                                                         J. G.

Date. The date of 1603 is verified by payment to Heywood
recorded in Henslowe's *Diary*, dated February 12 and March
6, 1603.

Text and Publishing Data. The play was never entered in
the Stationers' Register. In 1607 the first known edition appeared, printed by William Jaggard. Another edition was published in 1617 bearing on its title page the phrase "the third
edition." Since no copy of a second edition has come to light,
there is no way of telling whether an edition appeared before
1607 (making the 1607 quarto edition Q2) or whether the
play had been republished between 1607 and 1617. Some
scholars, therefore, arbitrarily assign the label Q1 to the 1607
edition and Q2 to that of 1617. The textual relationship between these two extant editions is difficult to establish. Each
appears to be independent of the other; whether their common source was an author's manuscript or a prompt copy

cannot be ascertained. Neither early edition was divided into acts and scenes.

Sources. The Mountford-Acton subplot comes from an early sixteenth-century Sienese *novella* by Illicini. Retold by Bandello and Belleforest, it was rendered into English by William Painter for his *Palace of Pleasure* (1566) and by Geoffrey Fenton for his *Tragical Discourses* (1567). Heywood appears to have used Painter as his source. No single direct source has been pinpointed for the main plot. Although resemblances to other tales in the *Palace of Pleasure* have been noted, there is a possibility that Heywood invented the main plot. The English atmosphere of both parts is definitely the work of Heywood.

Stage History. Apparently the play was popular in its own day. First performed by the Earl of Worcester's Men in March 1603, it held the stage over the next several years in revivals by the Queen's Majesty's Servants, as the title page of the 1617 edition notes. Several early seventeenth-century literary allusions further attest to its popularity. After its own time, the play disappears from sight—except for two eighteenth-century adaptations that were never acted—until the late nineteenth-century when it was revived in London in 1887. Since then the play has received a sprinkling of productions in Europe and America. Jacques Copeau chose *A Woman Killed with Kindness* as his opening production at the Théâtre du Vieux-Colombier in Paris in October 1913.

W. G.

DRAMATIS PERSONAE

SIR FRANCIS ACTON
SIR CHARLES MOUNTFORD
JOHN FRANKFORD
WENDOLL } Frankford's friends
CRANWELL }
MALBY, friend to Sir Francis
OLD MOUNTFORD, uncle to Sir Charles
TIDY, cousin to Sir Charles
SANDY, former friend to Sir Charles
RODER, former tenant to Sir Charles
SHAFTON, false friend to Frankford
NICHOLAS } servants to Frankford
JENKIN }
SPIGGOT, butler to Frankford
ROGER BRICKBAT } country fellows
JACK SLIME }
Sheriff
Keeper of the Prison
Sergeant
Officers, Falconers, Huntsmen, Coachman, Carters, Musicians,
    Servants, and Children
ANNE, wife to Frankford and sister to Sir Francis
SUSAN, sister to Sir Charles
CICELY MILKPAIL, servingwoman to Frankford
JOAN MINIVER }
JANE TRUBKIN } country girls
ISBEL MOTLEY }

THE SCENE—*Yorkshire*

Prologue

I come but like a harbinger,* being sent   messenger
To tell you what these preparations[1] mean.
Look for no glorious state; our Muse is bent
Upon a barren subject, a bare scene.
We could afford this twig a timber-tree,[2]
Whose strength might boldly on your favours build;
Our russet, tissue;* drone, a honey-bee;   coarse cloth,
                                                     fine cloth
Our barren plot, a large and spacious field;
Our coarse fare, banquets; our thin water, wine;
Our brook, a sea; our bat's eyes, eagle's sight;
Our Poet's dull and earthy Muse, divine;
Our ravens, doves; our crow's black feathers, white.
   But gentle thoughts, when they may give the foil,*   overthrow
   Save them that yield, and spare where they may spoil.*   hurt

---

[1] Preparations for presenting a play.

[2] Could wish this twig (this little play) were a large tree (a high tragedy or play about great characters and momentous events).

Scene 1

(FRANKFORD'S *house. Enter* MASTER JOHN FRANKFORD, MIS-
TRESS ANNE, SIR FRANCIS ACTON, SIR CHARLES MOUNT-
FORD, MASTER MALBY, MASTER WENDOLL, *and* MASTER
CRANWELL.)

SIR FRANCIS. Some music there! None lead the bride a
  dance?
SIR CHARLES. Yes, would she dance "The Shaking of the
  Sheets";[3]
But that's the dance her husband means to lead her.
  WENDOLL. That's not the dance that every man must dance,
According to the ballad.
  SIR FRANCIS.   Music ho!
By your leave, sister—by your husband's leave
I should have said—(*To* FRANKFORD.) the hand that but
  this day
Was given you in the church I'll borrow. Sound!
This marriage music hoists me from the ground.
  FRANKFORD. Ay, you may caper, you are light and free;
Marriage hath yoked my heels, pray then pardon me.[4]
  SIR FRANCIS. I'll have you dance too, brother.
  SIR CHARLES.   Master Frankford,
You are a happy man, sir; and much joy
Succeed your marriage mirth, you have a wife
So qualified,[5] and with such ornaments
Both of the mind and body. First, her birth
Is noble, and her education such
As might become the daughter of a prince.
Her own tongue speaks all tongues, and her own hand
Can teach all strings to speak in their best grace,
From the shrill treble to the hoarsest bass.
To end her many praises in one word,
She's Beauty and Perfection's eldest daughter,
Only found by yours, though many a heart hath sought her.
  FRANKFORD. But that I know your virtues and chaste
    thoughts,
I should be jealous of your praise, Sir Charles.

----

[3] A popular Elizabethan ballad, also known as "The Dance of
Death."
  [4] Marriage has tied my feet, so please excuse me from dancing.
  [5] So endowed with good qualities.

CRANWELL. He speaks no more than you approve.
MALBY. Nor flatters he that gives to her her due.
ANNE. I would your praise could find a fitter theme
Than my imperfect beauty to speak on.
Such as they be, if they my husband please,
They suffice me now I am married.
His sweet content is like a flattering glass,
To make my face seem fairer to mine eye;
But the least wrinkle from his stormy brow
Will blast the roses in my cheeks that grow.
SIR FRANCIS. A perfect wife already, meek and patient.
How strangely the word "husband" fits your mouth,
Not married three hours since, sister. 'Tis good:
You that begin betimes* thus, must needs prove   early
Pliant and duteous in your husband's love.
Godamercies, brother [have you] wrought her to it already?
"Sweet husband," and a curtsey the first day!
Mark this, mark this, you that are bachelors,
And never took the grace of honest man,[6]
Mark this against you marry, this one phrase:
"In a good time that man both wins and woos
That takes his wife down in her wedding shoes."[7]
FRANKFORD. Your sister takes not after you, Sir Francis.
All his wild blood your father spent on you;
He got her in his age when he grew civil.
All his mad tricks were to his land entailed,
And you are heir to all; your sister, she
Hath to her dower her mother's modesty.
SIR CHARLES. Lord, sir, in what a happy state live you.
This morning, which to many seems a burden
Too heavy to bear, is unto you a pleasure.
This lady is no clog, as many are;
She doth become you like a well-made suit
In which the tailor hath used all his art,
Not like a thick coat of unseasoned frieze,*   coarse
Forc'd on your back in summer. She's no chain   woolen cloth
To tie your neck and curb you to the yoke;
But she's a chain of gold to adorn your neck.
You both adorn each other, and your hands
Methinks are matches. There's equality
In this fair combination; you are both scholars,

---

[6] "Assumed the honorable estate of husband" (Bates).
[7] That is, shows his wife that he's the boss.

Both young, both being descended nobly.
There's music in this sympathy; it carries
Consort[8] and expectation of much joy,
Which God bestow on you from this first day
Until your dissolution—that's for aye.
    SIR FRANCIS. We keep you here too long, good brother
    Frankford.
Into the hall! Away, go, cheer your guests!
What, bride and bridegroom both withdrawn at once?
If you be missed, the guests will doubt their welcome,
And charge you with unkindness.
    FRANKFORD.   To prevent it,
I'll leave you here, to see the dance within.
    ANNE. And so will I.
                  (*Exeunt* FRANKFORD *and* ANNE.)
    SIR FRANCIS.   To part you it were sin.
Now gallants, while the town musicians
Finger their frets within, and the mad lads
And country lasses, every mother's child
With nosegays and bride-laces* in their hats,   lace streamers
Dance all their country measures, rounds, and jigs,
What shall we do? Hark, they are all on the hoigh;*   excited
They toil like mill-horses, and turn as round—
Marry, not on the toe.* Ay, and they caper,   that is,
But without cutting.[9] You shall see to-morrow   not gracefully
The hall floor peck'd and dinted like a millstone,
Made with their high shoes; though their skill be small,
Yet they tread heavy where their hobnails fall.
    SIR CHARLES. Well, leave them to their sports. Sir Francis
    Acton,
I'll make a match with you. Meet me to-morrow
At Chevy Chase; I'll fly my hawk with yours.
    SIR FRANCIS. For what? For what?
    SIR CHARLES.   Why, for a hundred pound.
    SIR FRANCIS. Pawn* me some gold of that.   pledge
    SIR CHARLES.   Here are ten angels;
I'll make them good a hundred pound tomorrow
Upon my hawk's wing.
    SIR FRANCIS.   'Tis a match, 'tis done.
Another hundred pound upon your dogs,

---

    [8] Both harmony and companionship.
    [9] That is, they are making the steps improperly.

Dare you, Sir Charles?

SIR CHARLES. I dare. Were I sure to lose
I durst do more than that. Here's my hand;
The first course* for a hundred pound. event

SIR FRANCIS. A match.

WENDOLL. Ten angels on Sir Francis Acton's hawk;
As much upon his dogs.

CRANWELL. I am for Sir Charles Mountford; I have seen
His hawk and dog both tried. What, clap you
hands?* shake hands
Or is't no bargain?

WENDOLL. Yes, and stake them down.
Were they five hundred they were all my own.

SIR FRANCIS. Be stirring early with the lark to-morrow;
I'll raise into my saddle ere the sun
Rise from his bed.

SIR CHARLES. If there you miss me, say
I am no gentleman; I'll hold my day.* keep my
appointment

SIR FRANCIS. It holds on all sides. Come, tonight let's dance.
Early tomorrow let's prepare to ride;
We had need be three hours up before the bride.

(*Exeunt.*)

Scene 2

(*The yard of* FRANKFORD'S *house. Enter* NICHOLAS, JENKIN,
JACK SLIME, *and* ROGER BRICKBAT *with four country girls
and two or three musicians.*)

JENKIN. Come, Nick, take you Joan Miniver to trace* dance
withal; Jack Slime, traverse* you with Cicely Milk- dance
pail; I will take Jane Trubkin, and Roger Brickbat shall have
Isbel Motley; and now that they are busy in the parlour, come,
strike up, we'll have a crash* here in the yard. revel

(CICELY *and* JANE *switch partners.*)

NICHOLAS. My humour* is not compendious;* that is, talent/
dancing I possess not, though I can foot it; yet since I am fall'n all-encompassing
into the hands of Cicely Milkpail, I assent.

JACK. Truly, Nick, though we were never brought up like
serving courtiers, yet we have been brought up with serving
creatures, ay and God's creatures too, for we have been
brought up to serve sheep, oxen, horses, and hogs, and such
like; and though we be but country fellows, it may be in the

way of dancing we can do the horse-trick* as well   *a dance step*
as servingmen.

ROGER. Ay, and the crosspoint,* too.   *a dance step*

JENKIN. O Slime, O Brickbat, do not you know that comparisons are odious? Now we are odious ourselves, too; therefore there are no comparisons to be made betwixt us.

NICHOLAS. I am sudden,* and not superfluous;   *prompt*
I am quarrelsome, and not seditious;
I am peaceable, and not contentious;
I am brief, and not compendious.
Slime, foot it quickly. If the music overcome not my melancholy, I shall quarrel; and if they suddenly* do not   *promptly*
strike up, I shall presently* strike thee down.   *immediately*

JENKIN. No quarrelling, for God's sake! Truly, if you do, I
shall set a knave* between you.   *servant*

JACK. I come to dance, not to quarrel. Come, what shall it
be? "Rogero"?[10]

JENKIN. "Rogero"? No. We will dance "The Beginning of
the World"!

CICELY. I love no dance so well as "John, Come Kiss Me
Now."

NICHOLAS. I, that have ere now deserv'd a cushion,* call for "The Cushion Dance."   *deserved*
                               some comfort

ROGER. For my part, I like nothing so well as
"Tom Tyler."

JENKIN. No, we'll have "The Hunting of the Fox."

JACK. "The Hay," "The Hay," there's nothing like "The
Hay."

NICHOLAS. I have said, I do say, and I will say again—

JENKIN. Every man agree to have it as Nick says.

ALL. Content.

NICHOLAS. It hath been, it now is, and it shall be—

CICELY. What, Master Nicholas, what?

NICHOLAS. "Put on Your Smock a Monday."

JENKIN. So the dance will come cleanly off. Come, for God's
sake agree of something. If you like not that, put it to the musicians, or let me speak for all, and we'll have "Sellenger's
Round."

ALL. That, that, that!

NICHOLAS. No, I am resolv'd thus it shall be:
First take hands, then take you to your heels.

---

[10] "Rogero" and the titles cited in the following set of lines
refer to popular Elizabethan tunes and dances.

JENKIN. Why, would you have us run away?

NICHOLAS. No, but I would have you shake your heels.

Music, strike up.

(*They dance;* NICHOLAS, *dancing, speaks stately and scurvily,*[11] *the rest after the country fashion.*)

JENKIN. Hey! Lively, my lasses! Here's a turn for thee!

(*Exeunt.*)

Scene 3

(*Chevy Chase. Wind horns. Enter* SIR CHARLES, SIR FRANCIS, MALBY, CRANWELL, WENDOLL, *Falconers, and Huntsmen.*)

SIR CHARLES. So! Well cast off. Aloft, aloft! Well flown!

O now she takes her at the souse,* and strikes her   swoop

Down to the earth, like a swift thunder clap.

WENDOLL. She hath struck ten angels out of my way.

SIR FRANCIS. A hundred pound from me.

SIR CHARLES.   What, falconer?

FALCONER. At hand, sir.

SIR CHARLES. Now she hath seized the fowl, and 'gins to

plume* her.   pluck

Rebeck her not; rather stand still and cherk her.[12]

So! seize her gets, her jesses,[13] and her bells.

Away!

SIR FRANCIS. My hawk killed, too.

SIR CHARLES.   Ay, but 'twas at the querre,[14]

Not at the mount like mine.

SIR FRANCIS.   Judgement, my masters.

CRANWELL. Yours missed her at the ferre.[15]

WENDOLL. Ay, but our merlin* first had plumed the   hawk

fowl,

And twice renewed* her from the river too.   driven

---

[11] That is, makes a sorry attempt to speak in an elevated manner (?).

[12] The falconry terms here refer to the calming of the bird by chirping to her. The falconry terms in this scene are from the *Boke of Saynt Albans.*

[13] Falconry equipment. The gets were part of the hawk's harness and the jesses, the leg straps.

[14] While the quarry was still on the ground.

[15] Meaning uncertain; both "at the higher point" and "on the opposite bank of a river" have been suggested.

Her bells, Sir Francis, had not both one weight,
Nor was one semitune above the other.
Methinks these Milan bells do sound too full,
And spoil the mounting of your hawk.
    SIR CHARLES.   'Tis lost.
    SIR FRANCIS. I grant it not. Mine likewise seized a fowl
Within her talents,* and you saw her paws   talons
Full of the feathers; both her petty singles*   outer claws
And her long singles* gripped her more than other. middle claws
The terrials[16] of her legs were stained with blood;
Not of the fowl only she did discomfit*   destroy
Some of her feathers, but she* brake   that is,
    away.   the fowl
Come, come, your hawk is but a rifler.*   that is, bungler
    SIR CHARLES.   How?
    SIR FRANCIS. Ay, and your dogs are trindle-tails* curly-tailed
    and curs.
    SIR CHARLES. You stir my blood.
You keep not a good hound in all your kennel,
Nor one good hawk upon your perch.
    SIR FRANCIS.   How, knight?
    SIR CHARLES. So, knight? You will not swagger,* be insolent
    sir?
    SIR FRANCIS. Why, say I did?
    SIR CHARLES. Why, sir, I say you would gain as much by
    swagg'ring
As you have got by wagers on your dogs.
You will come short in all things.
    SIR FRANCIS.   Not in this!
Now I'll strike home.
    SIR CHARLES.   Thou shalt to thy long home,* that is, grave
Or I will want my will.
    SIR FRANCIS. All they that love Sir Francis follow me.
    SIR CHARLES. All that affect Sir Charles draw on my part.
    CRANWELL. On this side heaves my hand.
    WENDOLL.   Here goes my heart.

(*They divide themselves.*)

(SIR CHARLES, CRANWELL, *Falconer, and Huntsman fight*
against SIR FRANCIS, WENDOLL, *his Falconer, and Huntsman;*
SIR CHARLES *overcomes them and beats them away, killing*
both of SIR FRANCIS' *men. Exeunt all except* SIR CHARLES.)

     [16] Possibly talons or terrets (leather straps for tying the bells
to the hawk's legs).

SIR CHARLES. My God! What have I done? What have I
done?
My rage hath plunged into a sea of blood,
In which my soul lies drowned. Poor innocents,
For whom we are to answer. Well, 'tis done,
And I remain the victor. A great conquest,
When I would give this right hand, nay, this head,
To breathe in them new life whom I have slain.
Forgive me, God; 'twas in the heat of blood,
And anger quite removes me from myself.
It was not I, but rage, did this vile murder;
Yet I, and not my rage, must answer it.
Sir Francis Acton he is fled the field;
With him, all those that did partake his quarrel;*   fight for him
And I am left alone with sorrow dumb,
And in my height of conquest, overcome.

(*Enter* SUSAN.)

SUSAN. O God, my brother wounded among the dead;
Unhappy jest* that in such earnest ends.   action
The rumour of this fear* stretched to my ears,   fearful event
And I am come to know if you be wounded.
SIR CHARLES. O sister, sister, wounded at the heart.
SUSAN. My God forbid!
SIR CHARLES. In doing that thing which he forbade,
I am wounded, sister.
SUSAN.   I hope not at the heart.
SIR CHARLES. Yes, at the heart.
SUSAN.   O God! A surgeon there!
SIR CHARLES. Call me a surgeon, sister, for my soul;
The sin of murder it hath pierced my heart
And made a wide wound there; but for these scratches,
They are nothing, nothing.
SUSAN.   Charles, what have you done?
Sir Francis hath great friends, and will pursue you
Unto the utmost danger* of the law.   penalty
SIR CHARLES. My conscience is become my enemy,
And will pursue me more than Acton can.
SUSAN. O fly, sweet brother.
SIR CHARLES.   Shall I fly from thee?
What, Sue, art weary of my company?
SUSAN. Fly from your foe.

SIR CHARLES.   You, sister, are my friend,
And flying you, I shall pursue my end.
    SUSAN. Your company is as my eyeball dear;
Being far from you, no comfort can be near.
Yet fly to save your life. What would I care
To spend my future age in black despair,
So you were safe? And yet to live one week
Without my brother Charles, through every* cheek   either
My streaming tears would downwards run so rank*   abundantly
Till they could set on either side a bank,
And in the midst a channel; so my face
For two salt water brooks shall still* find place.   always
    SIR CHARLES. Thou shalt not weep so much, for I will stay
In spite of danger's teeth. I'll live with thee,
Or I'll not live at all. I will not sell
My country and my father's patrimony,
Nor thy sweet sight, for a vain hope of life.

    (*Enter Sheriff with Officers.*)

    SHERIFF. Sir Charles, I am made the unwilling instrument
Of your attach* and apprehension.   arrest
I am sorry that the blood of innocent men
Should be of you exacted. It was told me
That you were guarded with a troop of friends,
And therefore I come armed.
    SIR CHARLES.   O master Sheriff,
I came into the field with many friends,
But, see, they all have left me; only one
Clings to my sad misfortune, my dear sister.
I know you for an honest gentleman;
I yield my weapons and submit to you.
Convey me where you please.
    SHERIFF.   To prison then,
To answer for the lives of these dead men.
    SUSAN. O God! O God!
    SIR CHARLES.   Sweet sister, every strain
Of sorrow from your heart augments my pain.
Your grief abounds* and hits against my breast.   overflows
    SHERIFF. Sir, will you go?
    SIR CHARLES.   Even where it likes* you best. pleases
                                                        (*Exeunt.*)

Scene 4

(FRANKFORD's *house. Enter* MASTER FRANKFORD *in thought.*)

FRANKFORD. How happy am I amongst other men
That in my mean* estate embrace content.   moderate
I am a gentleman, and by my birth
Companion with a king; a king's no more.
I am possessed of many fair revenues,
Sufficient to maintain a gentleman.
Touching my mind, I am studied in all arts,
The riches of my thoughts; and of my time
Have been a good proficient.[17] But the chief
Of all the sweet felicities on earth,
I have a fair, a chaste, and loving wife,
Perfection all, all truth, all ornament.
If man on earth may truly happy be,
Of these at once* possessed, sure I am he.   simultaneously

(*Enter* NICHOLAS.)

NICHOLAS. Sir, there's a gentleman attends without to speak
with you.
FRANKFORD. On horseback?
NICHOLAS. Ay, on horseback.
FRANKFORD. Entreat him to alight; I will attend him.
Knowest thou him, Nick?
NICHOLAS.   I know him; his name's Wendoll.
It seems he comes in haste. His horse is booted*   covered
Up to the flank in mire, himself all spotted
And stained with plashing.* Sure he rid in fear   splashing
Or for a wager. Horse and man both sweat;
I ne'er saw two in such a smoking heat.
FRANKFORD. Entreat him in. About it instantly!
                                        (*Exit* NICHOLAS.)
This Wendoll I have noted, and his carriage
Hath pleased me much. By observation
I have noted many good deserts in him—
He's affable and seen* in many things,   skilled
Discourses well, a good companion,

        [17] That is, I have used my time well.

And though of small means, yet a gentleman
Of a good house, somewhat pressed by want.
I have preferred him to a second place
In my opinion and my best regard.

(*Enter* WENDOLL, ANNE, *and* NICHOLAS.)

ANNE. O Master Frankford, Master Wendoll here
Brings you the strangest news that e'er you heard.
    FRANKFORD. What news, sweet wife? What news, good
      Master Wendoll?
    WENDOLL. You knew the match made 'twixt Sir Francis
      Acton
And Sir Charles Mountford.
    FRANKFORD.   True, with their hounds and hawks.
    WENDOLL. The matches were both played.
    FRANKFORD.   Ha! And which won?
    WENDOLL. Sir Francis, your wife's brother, had the worst
And lost the wager.
    FRANKFORD.   Why, the worse his chance;
Perhaps the fortune of some other day
Will change his luck.
    ANNE.   O, but you hear not all.
Sir Francis lost, and yet was loath to yield;
In brief the two knights grew to difference,
From words to blows, and so to banding sides,*   forming parties
Where valorous Sir Charles slew in his spleen*   wrath
Two of your brother's men—his falconer
And his good huntsman, whom he loved so well.
More men were wounded, no more slain outright.
    FRANKFORD. Now trust me I am sorry for the knight;
But is my brother* safe?   that is,
    WENDOLL.   All whole and sound,   brother-in-law
His body not being blemished with one wound.
But poor Sir Charles is to the prison led,
To answer at th' assize for them that's dead.
    FRANKFORD. I thank your pains, sir; had the news been
      better,
Your will was to have brought it, Master Wendoll.
Sir Charles will find hard friends; his case is heinous,
And will be most severely censured on.*   judged
I am sorry for him. Sir, a word with you.
I know you, sir, to be a gentleman
In all things, your possibilities* but mean;   resources

Please you to use my table and my purse;
They are yours.
    WENDOLL.   O Lord, sir, I shall never deserve it.
    FRANKFORD. O sir, disparage not your worth too much;
You are full of quality* and fair desert.   accomplishments
Choose of my men which shall attend on you,
And he is yours. I will allow you, sir,
Your man, your gelding, and your table, all
At my own charge; be my companion.
    WENDOLL. Master Frankford, I have oft been bound to you
By many favours; this exceeds them all
That I shall never merit your least favour.
But when your last remembrance I forget,
Heaven at my soul exact that weighty debt.
    FRANKFORD. There needs no protestation, for I know you
Virtuous, and therefore grateful. Prithee, Nan,
Use him with all thy loving'st courtesy.
    ANNE. As far as modesty may well extend,
It is my duty to receive your friend.
    FRANKFORD. To dinner. Come, sir, from this present day
Welcome to me forever. Come, away.
        (*Exeunt* MASTER FRANKFORD, WENDOLL, *and* ANNE.)
    NICHOLAS. I do not like this fellow by no means;
I never see him but my heart still earns.*   grieves
Zounds! I could fight with him, yet know not why;
The Devil and he are all one in my eye.

(*Enter* JENKIN.)

    JENKIN. O Nick, what gentleman is that comes to lie at our
house? My master allows him one to wait on him, and I
believe it will fall to thy lot.
    NICHOLAS. I love my master—by these hilts I do[18]—
But rather than I'll ever come to serve him,
I'll turn away my master.

(*Enter* CICELY.)

    CICELY. Nich'las, where are you, Nich'las? You must come
in, Nich'las, and help the young gentleman off with his boots.
    NICHOLAS. If I pluck off his boots, I'll eat the spurs,
And they shall stick fast in my throat like burrs.
        (*Exit.*)

---

[18] Nicholas carries a dagger.

CICELY. Then, Jenkin, come you.

JENKIN. 'Tis no boot* for me to deny it. My master   avail
hath given me a coat here, but he takes pains himself to
brush it once or twice a day with a holly wand.

CICELY. Come, come, make haste, that you may wash your
hands again and help to serve in dinner.

(*Exit.*)

JENKIN (*to the audience*). You may see, my masters, though
it be afternoon with you, 'tis but early days with us, for we
have not dined yet. Stay but a little, I'll but go in and help
to bear up the first course and come to you again presently.

(*Exit.*)

Scene 5

(*The jail. Enter* MALBY *and* CRANWELL.)

MALBY. This is the sessions day; pray, can you tell me
How young Sir Charles hath sped?* Is he acquit,   succeeded
Or must he try* the law's strict penalty?   undergo

CRANWELL. He's cleared of all, 'spite of his enemies,
Whose earnest labours was to take his life;
But in this suit of pardon he hath spent
All the revenues that his father left him,
And he is now turned a plain countryman,
Reformed* in all things. See, sir, here he comes.   transformed

(*Enter* SIR CHARLES *and his* KEEPER.)

KEEPER. Discharge your fees, and you are then at freedom.

SIR CHARLES. Here, master Keeper, take the poor remainder
Of all the wealth I have. My heavy foes
Have made my purse light, but, alas, to me,
'Tis wealth enough that you have set me free.

MALBY. God give you joy of your delivery;
I am glad to see you abroad, Sir Charles.

SIR CHARLES. The poorest knight in England, Master Malby.
My life hath cost me all the patrimony
My father left his son. Well, God forgive them
That are the authors of my penury.

(*Enter* SHAFTON.)

SHAFTON. Sir Charles! A hand, a hand! At liberty?
Now by the faith I owe,* I am glad to see it.   own

What want you? Wherein may I pleasure you?

SIR CHARLES. O me! O most unhappy gentleman!
I am not worthy to have friends stirred up
Whose hands may help me in this plunge of want.[19]
I would I were in Heaven, to inherit there
Th' immortal birthright which my Saviour keeps,
And by no unthrift* can be bought and sold;   spendthrift or
For here on earth, what pleasures should we trust?   unthriftiness

SHAFTON. To rid you from these contemplations,
Three hundred pounds you shall receive of me—
Nay, five for fail.[20] Come, sir, the sight of gold
Is the most sweet receipt for melancholy,
And will revive your spirits. You shall hold law[21]
With your proud adversaries. Tush, let Frank Acton
Wage with knighthood-like expense[22] with me,
And he will sink, he will. Nay, good Sir Charles,
Applaud your fortune and your fair escape
From all these perils.

SIR CHARLES.   O sir, they have undone me.
Two thousand and five hundred pound a year
My father at his death possessed me of,
All which the envious* Acton made me spend,   malicious
And notwithstanding all this large expense,
I had much ado to gain my liberty;
And I have now only a house of pleasure,*   summerhouse
With some five hundred pounds, reserved
Both to maintain me and my loving sister.

SHAFTON (*aside*). That must I have; it lies convenient
for me.
If I can fasten but one finger on him,
With my full hand I'll gripe him to the heart.
'Tis not for love I proffered him this coin,
But for my gain and pleasure. (*To* SIR CHARLES.) Come, Sir
Charles,
I know you have need of money; take my offer.

SIR CHARLES. Sir, I accept it, and remain indebted
Even to the best of my unable* power.   feeble
Come, gentlemen, and see it tendered* down.   paid
(*Exeunt.*)

---

[19] That is, in my financial difficulties.
[20] That is, if three hundred may not be enough.
[21] Enter in litigation.
[22] That is, venture the sums a knight is able to expend.

Scene 6

(FRANKFORD'S *house. Enter* WENDOLL, *melancholy.*)

WENDOLL. I am a villain if I apprehend*   conceive
But such a thought; then to attempt the deed—
Slave, thou art damned without redemption.
I'll drive away this passion with a song.
A song! Ha, ha! A song, as if, fond* man,   foolish
Thy eyes could swim in laughter when thy soul
Lies drenched and drowned in red tears of blood.
I'll pray, and see if God within my heart
Plant better thoughts. Why, prayers are meditations,
And when I meditate—O God, forgive me—
It is on her divine perfections.
I will forget her; I will arm myself
Not to entertain a thought of love to her;
And when I come by chance into her presence,
I'll hale* these balls* until my eyestrings crack   pull away/eyeballs
From being pulled and drawn to look that way.

(*Enter, cross over the stage* FRANKFORD, ANNE, *and* NICH-
OLAS, *and exeunt.*)

O God! O God! With what a violence
I am hurried to my own destruction.
There goest thou the most perfect'st man
That ever England bred a gentleman,
And shall I wrong his bed? Thou God of thunder,
Stay in Thy thoughts of vengeance and of wrath
Thy great almighty and all-judging hand
From speedy execution on a villain,
A villain and a traitor to his friend.

(*Enter* JENKIN [*behind*].)

JENKIN. Did your worship call?
WENDOLL (*not noticing* JENKIN). He doth maintain me; he
    allows me largely*   generously
Money to spend—
    JENKIN (*aside*). By my faith, so do not you me; I cannot
    get a cross* of you.   that is, coin

WENDOLL.   My gelding and my man.

JENKIN. That's Sorrel and I.

WENDOLL. This kindness grows of no alliance*   relationship
   twixt us—

JENKIN (*aside*). Nor is my service of any great acquaintance.

WENDOLL. I never bound him to me by desert.
Of a mere stranger, a poor gentleman,
A man by whom in no kind* he could gain,   way
He hath placed me in the height of all his thoughts,
Made me companion with the best and chiefest
In Yorkshire. He cannot eat without me,
Nor laugh without me. I am to his body
As necessary as his digestion,
And equally do make him whole* or sick.   healthy
And shall I wrong this man? Base man! Ingrate!
Hast thou the power straight with thy gory hands
To rip thy image from his bleeding heart?
To scratch thy name from out the holy book
Of his remembrance, and to wound his name
That holds thy name so dear, or rend his heart
To whom thy heart was joined and knit together?
And yet I must. Then, Wendoll, be content!
Thus villains, when they would, cannot repent.

JENKIN (*aside*). What a strange humour is my new master
in. Pray God he be not mad. If he should be so, I should
never have any mind to serve him in Bedlam.[23] It may be
he is mad for missing of me.

WENDOLL (*seeing* JENKIN). What, Jenkin? Where's your
mistress?

JENKIN. Is your worship married?

WENDOLL. Why dost thou ask?

JENKIN. Because you are my master, and if I have a mistress, I would be glad like a good servant to do my duty to
her.

WENDOLL. I mean where's Mistress Frankford?

JENKIN. Marry, sir, her husband is riding out of town, and
she went very lovingly to bring him on his way to horse. Do
you see, sir, here she comes, and here I go.

WENDOLL. Vanish.

                              (*Exit* JENKIN.)

[23] Bethlehem hospital, famous London insane asylum.

(*Enter* ANNE.)

ANNE. You are well met, sir. Now in troth my husband
Before he took horse had a great desire
To speak with you. We sought about the house,
Hallooed into the fields, sent every way,
But could not meet you. Therefore he enjoined me
To do unto you his most kind commends.*   greetings
Nay, more, he wills you as you prize his love,
Or hold in estimation his kind friendship,
To make bold in his absence and command
Even as himself were present in the house;
For you must keep his table, use his servants,
And be a present Frankford in his absence.
WENDOLL. I thank him for his love.
(*Aside*). Give me a name, you whose infectious tongues
Are tipped with gall and poison. As you would
Think on a man that had your father slain,
Murdered thy children, made your wives base strumpets,
So call me, call me so! Print in my face
The most stigmatic* title of a villain   ignominious
For hatching treason to so true a friend.
ANNE. Sir, you are much beholding* to my husband;   beholden
You are a man most dear in his regard.
WENDOLL. I am bound unto your husband and you too.
(*Aside*.) I will not speak to wrong a gentleman
Of that good estimation,* my kind friend.   reputation
I will not! Zounds, I will not! I may choose,
And I will choose. Should I be so misled?
Or shall I purchase* to my father's crest   add
The motto of a villain? If I say
I will not do it, what thing can enforce me?
Who can compel me? What sad destiny
Hath such command upon my yielding thoughts?
I will not. Ha! Some fury pricks me on;
The swift Fates drag me at their chariot wheel
And hurry me to mischief. Speak I must;
Injure myself, wrong her, deceive his trust.
ANNE. Are you not well, sir, that you seem thus troubled?
There is sedition in your countenance.
WENDOLL. And in my heart, fair angel, chaste and wise.
I love you. Start not, speak not, answer not.
I love you—nay, let me speak the rest.

Bid me to swear, and I will call to record
The host of Heaven.

ANNE. The host of Heaven forbid
Wendoll should hatch such a disloyal thought.

WENDOLL. Such is my fate; to this suit I was born,
To wear rich Pleasure's crown, or Fortune's scorn.

ANNE. My husband loves you.

WENDOLL. I know it.

ANNE. He esteems you
Even as his brain, his eyeball, or his heart.

WENDOLL. I have tried* it. tested

ANNE. His purse is your exchequer, and his table
Doth freely serve you.

WENDOLL. So I have found it.

ANNE. O with what face of brass, what brow of steel,
Can you unblushing speak this to the face
Of the espoused wife of so dear a friend?
It is my husband that maintains your state.
Will you dishonour him? I am his wife
That in your power hath left his whole affairs.
It is to me you speak!

WENDOLL. O speak no more,
For more than this I know and have recorded
Within the red-leaved table* of my heart. notebook
Fair, and of all beloved, I was not fearful
Bluntly to give my life into your hand,
And at one hazard²⁴ all my earthly means.
Go, tell your husband; he will turn me off,
And I am then undone. I care not, I—
'Twas for your sake. Perchance in rage he'll kill me.
I care not. 'Twas for you. Say I incur
The general name of villain through the world,
Of traitor to my friend; I care not, I.
Beggary, shame, death, scandal, and reproach—
For you I'll hazard all. What care I?
For you I'll live, and in your love I'll die.

ANNE. You move me, sir, to passion* and to pity. anger
The love I bear my husband is as precious
As my soul's health.

WENDOLL. I love your husband too,
And for his love I will engage my life.
Mistake me not; the augmentation

²⁴ That is, in the same stake.

Of my sincere affection borne to you
Doth no whit lessen my regard of him.
I will be secret, lady, close as night,
And not the light of one small glorious* star   boastful
Shall shine here in my forehead to bewray*   disclose
That act of night.
    ANNE (*aside*). What shall I say?
My soul is wand'ring and hath lost her way.
(*To him.*) O Master Wendoll, O.
    WENDOLL.   Sigh not, sweet saint,
For every sigh you breathe draws from my heart
A drop of blood.[25]
    ANNE.   I ne'er offended yet.
My fault, I fear, will in my brow be writ.
Women that fall not quite bereft of grace
Have their offences noted in their face.
I blush and am ashamed. O Master Wendoll,
Pray God I be not born to curse your tongue,
That hath enchanted me. This maze I am in
I fear will prove the labyrinth of sin.

(*Enter* NICHOLAS *behind.*)

    WENDOLL. The path of pleasure and the gate to bliss,
Which on your lips I knock at with a kiss. (*Kisses her.*)
    NICHOLAS (*aside*). I'll kill the rogue.
    WENDOLL. Your husband is from home, your bed's no
    blab—*   tattle-tale
Nay, look not down and blush.
                    (*Exeunt* WENDOLL *and* ANNE.)
    NICHOLAS.   Zounds, I'll stab.
Ay, Nick, was it thy chance to come just in the nick?
I love my master, and I hate that slave;
I love my mistress, but these tricks I like not.
My master shall not pocket up* this wrong;   swallow
I'll eat my fingers first. (*Drawing his dagger.*) What say'st thou,
    metal?
Does not the rascal Wendoll go* on legs   walk
That thou must cut off? Hath he not hamstrings
That thou must hock?* Nay, metal,[26] thou shalt stand   cut
To all I say. I'll henceforth turn a spy,

    [25] "It was supposed that every sigh cost the sigher's heart a
drop of blood" (H. Spencer).
    [26] Dagger, with a play on *mettle.*

And watch them in their close conveyances.*   secret dealings
I never looked for better of that rascal
Since he came miching* first into our house.   sneaking
It is that Satan hath corrupted her,
For she was fair and chaste. I'll have an eye
In all their gestures.* Thus I think of them.   movements
If they proceed as they have done before,
Wendoll's a knave, my mistress is a ——.

                                (*Exit.***)**

Scene 7

(*Before* SIR CHARLES MOUNTFORD'S *house. Enter* SIR
CHARLES *and* SUSAN.)

SIR CHARLES. Sister, you see we are driven to hard shift
To keep this poor house we have left unsold.
I am now enforced to follow husbandry,
And you to milk. And do we not live well?
Well, I thank God.
    SUSAN.   O brother, here's a change
Since old Sir Charles died in our father's house.
    SIR CHARLES. All things on earth thus change, some up,
    some down;
Content's a kingdom, and I wear that crown.

(*Enter* SHAFTON *with a Sergeant.*)

SHAFTON. Good morrow, good morrow, Sir Charles. What,
    with your sister
Plying your husbandry?—Sergeant, stand off.
You have a pretty house here, and a garden,
And goodly ground about it. Since it lies
So near a lordship* that I lately bought,   estate
I would fain* buy it of you. I will give you—   gladly
    SIR CHARLES. O pardon me; this house successively
Hath 'longed* to me and my progenitors   belonged
Three hundred year. My great-great-grandfather,
He in whom first our gentle style* began,   title to gentility
Dwelt here, and in this ground increased this molehill
Unto that mountain which my father left me.
Where he the first of all our house begun,
I now the last will end and keep this house,
This virgin title never yet deflowered

By any unthrift of the Mountfords' line.
In brief, I will not sell it for more gold
Than you could hide or pave the ground withal.
 SHAFTON. Ha, ha! A proud mind and a beggar's purse.
Where's my three hundred pounds—beside the use?*   interest
I have brought it to an execution
By course of law. What, is my money ready?
 SIR CHARLES. An execution, sir, and never tell me
You put my bond in suit? You deal extremely.*   severely
 SHAFTON. Sell me the land and I'll acquit you straight.
 SIR CHARLES. Alas, alas! 'Tis all trouble hath left me
To cherish me and my poor sister's life.
If this were sold, our names should then be quite
Razed from the bead-roll* of gentility.   list
You see what hard shift we have made to keep it
Allied still to our own name. This palm you see
Labour hath glowed within;[27] her silver brow,
That never tasted a rough winter's blast
Without a mask or fan, doth with a grace
Defy cold winter and his storms outface.
 SUSAN. Sir, we feed sparing, and we labour hard;
We lie uneasy,[28] to reserve to us
And our succession* this small plot of ground. descendants
 SIR CHARLES. I have so bent my thoughts to husbandry
That I protest I scarcely can remember
What a new fashion is, how silk or satin
Feels in my hand. Why, pride is grown to us
A mere,* mere stranger. I have quite forgot   absolute
The names of all that ever waited on me;
I cannot name ye any of my hounds,
Once from whose echoing mouths I heard all the music
That e'er my heart desired. What should I say?
To keep this place I have changed myself away.[29]
  SHAFTON (*to the Sergeant*). Arrest him at my suit. (*To*
  SIR CHARLES.) Actions and actions.
Shall keep thee in perpetual bondage fast.
Nay, more, I'll sue thee by a late appeal,* further accusation
And call thy former life in question.[30]

   [27] That is, has become red from work.
   [28] That is, rest in physical discomfort.
   [29] Changed completely my style of living.
   [30] That is, "put in jeopardy the life which you formerly saved"
(H. Spencer).

The Keeper is my friend; thou shalt have irons,
And usage such as I'll deny to dogs.
Away with him!
    SIR CHARLES. You are too timorous;* but trouble is   terrible
    my master,
And I will serve him truly. My kind sister,
Thy tears are of no force to mollify
This flinty man. Go to my father's brother,
My kinsmen and allies; entreat them from me
To ransom me from this injurious man
That seeks my ruin.
    SHAFTON.   Come, irons, irons, away!
I'll see thee lodged far from the sight of day.

                    (*Exeunt all except* SUSAN.)

    (*Enter* SIR FRANCIS *and* MALBY.)

    SUSAN. My heart's so hardened with the frost of grief
Death cannot pierce it through. Tyrant too fell!*   cruel
So lead the fiends condemned souls to Hell.
    SIR FRANCIS. Again to prison! Malby, hast thou seen
A poor slave better tortured? Shall we hear
The music of his voice cry from the grate*   prison grating
'Meat for the Lord's sake'? No, no, yet I am not
Throughly* revenged. They say he hath a pretty   thoroughly
    wench
Unto his sister. Shall I, in mercy sake
To him and to his kindred, bribe the fool
To shame herself by lewd, dishonest lust?
I'll proffer largely,* but, the deed being done,   generously
I'll smile to see her base confusion.*   ruin
    MALBY. Methinks, Sir Francis, you are full revenged
For greater wrongs than he can proffer you.
See where the poor sad gentlewoman stands.
    SIR FRANCIS. Ha, ha! Now I will flout her poverty,
Deride her fortunes, scoff her base estate;
My very soul the name of Mountford hates.
(*Aside.*) But stay, my heart! O what a look did fly
To strike my soul through with thy piercing eye.
I am enchanted; all my spirits are fled,
And with one glance my envious spleen* struck   malicious anger
    dead.

SUSAN (*seeing them*). Acton, that seeks our blood!
                                              (*Runs away.*)
SIR FRANCIS.   O chaste and fair!
MALBY. Sir Francis, why Sir Francis, zounds, in a trance?
Sir Francis, what cheer, man? Come, come, how is't?
SIR FRANCIS. Was she not fair? Or else this judging eye
Cannot distinguish beauty.
MALBY.   She was fair.
SIR FRANCIS. She was an angel in a mortal's shape,
And ne'er descended from old Mountford's line.
But soft, soft,* let me call my wits together.   that is,
                                                       go easily
A poor, poor wench, to my great adversary
Sister, whose very souls denounce stern war
One against other. How now, Frank, turned fool
Or madman, whether?* But no! Master of   which one
My perfect senses and directest wits.
Then why should I be in this violent humour*   disposition
Of passion and of love? And with a person
So different every way, and so opposed
In all contractions* and still-warring actions?   dealings
Fie, fie, how I dispute against my soul.
Come, come, I'll gain her, or in her fair quest
Purchase my soul free and immortal rest.
                                              (*Exeunt.*)

Scene 8

(FRANKFORD'S *house. Enter 3 or 4 Servingmen* [*including*
SPIGGOT *the Butler and* NICHOLAS], *one with a voider*[31] *and
a wooden knife to take away all; another the salt and
bread; another the tablecloth and napkins; another the carpet.* JENKIN *with two lights after them.*)   table covering

JENKIN. So, march in order and retire in battle 'ray.*   array
My master and the guests have supped already; all's taken
away. Here, now spread for the servingmen in the hall. Butler,
it belongs to your office.
SPIGGOT. I know it, Jenkin. What do you call the gentleman
that supped there to-night?
JENKIN. Who, my master?
SPIGGOT. No, no, Master Wendoll, he is a daily guest. I
mean the gentleman that came but this afternoon.

---

[31] A tray or basket for clearing the remains of a meal.

JENKIN. His name is Master Cranwell. God's light! Hark, within there, my master calls to lay more billets* on the ~~logs~~ fire. Come, come! Lord how we that are in office* here ~~service~~ in the house are troubled. One spread the carpet in the parlour and stand ready to snuff the lights; the rest be ready to prepare their stomachs.* More lights in the hall there. ~~appetites~~ Come, Nich'las.

> (*Exeunt except* NICHOLAS.)

NICHOLAS. I cannot eat, but had I Wendoll's heart
I would eat that; the rogue grows impudent.
O I have seen such vild* notorious tricks,   ~~vile~~
Ready to make my eyes dart from my head.
I'll tell my master, by this air I will;
Fall what may fall, I'll tell him. Here he comes.

> (*Enter* FRANKFORD, *brushing the crumbs from his clothes with a napkin, and newly risen from supper.*)

FRANKFORD. Nich'las, what make* you here? Why are ~~do~~ not you
At supper in the hall there with your fellows?
NICHOLAS. Master, I stayed* your rising from the ~~awaited~~ board
To speak with you.
FRANKFORD.   Be brief, then, gentle Nich'las.
My wife and guests attend* me in the parlour.   ~~wait for~~
Why dost thou pause? Now, Nich'las, you want* money, ~~lack~~
And unthrift-like would eat into your wages
Ere you have earned it. Here's, sir, half a crown;
Play the good husband,* and away to supper.   ~~that is, be thrifty~~
NICHOLAS (*aside*). By this hand, an honourable gentleman.
I will not see him wronged. (*To him.*) Sir, I have served you
long; you entertained* me seven years before your   ~~hired~~
beard. You knew me, sir, before you knew my mistress.
FRANKFORD. What of this, good Nich'las?
NICHOLAS. I never was a make-bate* or a knave; ~~trouble-maker~~
I have no fault but one—I am given to quarrel,
But not with women. I will tell you, master,
That which will make your heart leap from your breast,
Your hair to startle* from your head, your ears to tingle. ~~start~~
FRANKFORD. What preparation's this to dismal news?
NICHOLAS. 'Sblood, sir, I love you better than your wife—
I'll make it good.

FRANKFORD. Thou art a knave, and I have much ado
With wonted patience to contain my rage
And not to break thy pate. Thou art a knave;
I'll turn you with your base comparisons
Out of my doors.

NICHOLAS. Do, do. There's not room for Wendoll and me
too both in one house. O master, master, that Wendoll is a
villain.

FRANKFORD (*striking him*). Ay, saucy!

NICHOLAS. Strike, strike, do strike! Yet hear me; I am no
fool!
I know a villain when I see him act
Deeds of a villain. Master, master, that base slave
Enjoys my mistress and dishonours you.

FRANKFORD. Thou hast killed me with a weapon whose
sharpened point
Hath pricked quite through and through my shivering heart.
Drops of cold sweat sit dangling on my hairs
Like morning's dew upon the golden flowers,
And I am plunged into a strange agony.
What didst thou say? If any word that touched
His credit or her reputation,
It is as hard to enter my belief
As Dives into Heaven.[32]

NICHOLAS.   I can gain nothing;
They are two that never wronged me. I knew before
'Twas but a thankless office, and perhaps
As much as is my service or my life
Is worth. All this I know; but this and more,
More by a thousand dangers could not hire me
To smother such a heinous wrong from you.
I saw, and I have said.

FRANKFORD (*aside*). 'Tis probable. Though blunt, yet he is
honest.
Though I durst pawn my life, and on their faith
Hazard the dear salvation of my soul,
Yet in my trust I may be too secure.
May this be true? O may it? Can it be?
Is it by any wonder possible?
Man, woman, what thing mortal may we trust

[32] In the parable of Dives and Lazarus, Dives is the rich man
sent to Hell (Luke, xvi:19–31).

When friends and bosom wives prove so unjust?
(*To him.*) What instance* hast thou of this strange   evidence
  report?
  NICHOLAS. Eyes, eyes.
  FRANKFORD. Thy eyes may be deceived I tell thee,
For should an angel from the heavens drop down
And preach this to me that thyself hast told,
He should have much ado to win belief,
In both their loves I am so confident.
  NICHOLAS. Shall I discourse the same by
        circumstance?*   with circumstantial
  FRANKFORD. No more! To supper, and command   evidence
    your fellows
To attend us and the strangers.* Not a word,   visitors
I charge thee on thy life! Be secret then,
For I know nothing.
  NICHOLAS. I am dumb, and now that I have eased my stom-
ach,[33] I will go fill my stomach.

                                                    (*Exit.*)

  FRANKFORD. Away, begone.
She is well born, descended nobly;
Virtuous her education; her repute
Is in the general voice of all the country
Honest and fair; her carriage, her demeanour
In all her actions that concern the love
To me her husband, modest, chaste, and godly.
Is all this seeming gold plain copper?
But he, that Judas that hath borne my purse,
And sold me for a sin—O God, O God,
Shall I put up* these wrongs? No! Shall I trust   put up with
The bare report of this suspicious groom
Before the double gilt,[34] the well-hatched* ore   richly inlaid
Of their two hearts? No, I will loose these thoughts;
Distraction I will banish from my brow
And from my looks exile sad discontent.
Their wonted favours* in my tongue shall flow;   usual kindnesses
Till I know all, I'll nothing seem to know.—
Lights and a table there. Wife, Master Wendoll, and Master
    Cranwell—

        [33] Revealed my inner thoughts.
        [34] With a pun on *guilt*.

(*Enter* ANNE, MASTER WENDOLL, MASTER CRANWELL,
NICHOLAS, *and* JENKIN, *with cards, carpet, stools, and other
necessaries.*)

FRANKFORD. O Master Cranwell, you are a stranger here,
And often balk* my house; faith, you are a churl.   avoid
Now we have supped, a table and to cards.

JENKIN. A pair* of cards, Nich'las, and a carpet to   deck
cover the table. Where's Cicely with her counters and her box?
Candles and candlesticks there! (*Enter* CICELY *and a serving-
man with counters and candles.*) Fie, we have such a household of serving creatures! Unless it be Nick and I, there's not
one amongst them all can say 'bo' to a goose. (*To* NICHOLAS.)
Well said,* Nick.   done
(*They spread a carpet, set down lights and cards. Exeunt all
                      the servants except* NICHOLAS.)

ANNE. Come, Master Frankford, who shall take my
part?*   *   be my partner

FRANKFORD. Marry, that will I, sweet wife.

WENDOLL. No, by my faith, sir, when you are together I sit
out; it must be Mistress Frankford and I, or else it is no match.

FRANKFORD. I do not like that match.

NICHOLAS (*aside*). You have no reason, marry, knowing all.

FRANKFORD. 'Tis no great matter, neither. Come, Master
Cranwell, shall you and I take them up?*   play against them

CRANWELL. At your pleasure, sir.

FRANKFORD. I must look to you, Master Wendoll, for you
will be playing false.* Nay, so will my wife, too.   improperly

NICHOLAS (*aside*). Ay, I will be sworn she will.

ANNE. Let them that are taken playing false forfeit the set.

FRANKFORD. Content; it shall go hard but I'll take you.

CRANWELL. Gentlemen, what shall our game be?

WENDOLL. Master Frankford, you play best at noddy.[35]

FRANKFORD. You shall not find it so; indeed you shall not!

ANNE. I can play at nothing so well as double ruff.[36]

FRANKFORD. If Master Wendoll and my wife be together,
there's no playing against them at double hand.*   a card game

NICHOLAS. I can tell you, sir, the game that Master Wendoll
is best at.

[35] A game similar to cribbage; *noddy* also means fool. Heywood
employs double entendres in the names of these card games.
[36] A game resembling whist; *ruff* also means passion.

WENDOLL. What game is that, Nick?

NICHOLAS. Marry, sir, knave out of doors.*   a card game

WENDOLL. She and I will take you at lodam.[37]

ANNE. Husband, shall we play at saint?[38]

FRANKFORD (*aside*). My saint's turned devil! (*To her.*) No, we'll none of saint. You're best at new-cut,[39] wife; you'll play at that!

WENDOLL.   If you play at new-cut, I am soonest hitter* of any here, for a wager.   winner

FRANKFORD (*aside*). 'Tis me they play on. Well, you may draw out,[40]
For all your cunning; 'twill be to your shame.
I'll teach you at your new-cut a new game.
(*To them.*) Come, come.

CRANWELL. If you cannot agree upon the game, to post and pair.[41]

WENDOLL. We shall be soonest pairs, and my good host,
When he comes late home, he must kiss the post.*   be shut out

FRANKFORD. Whoever wins, it shall be to thy cost.

CRANWELL. Faith, let it be vide-ruff,[42] and let's make honours.

FRANKFORD. If you make honours, one thing let me crave:
Honour the king and queen; except* the knave.*   exclude/jack

WENDOLL. Well, as you please for that. Lift who shall deal.*   cut for deal

ANNE. The least* in sight. What are you, Master Wendoll?   lowest

WENDOLL (*cutting the cards*). I am a knave.

NICHOLAS (*aside*).   I'll swear it.

ANNE (*cutting*).   I a queen.

FRANKFORD (*aside*). A quean* thou should'st say.   prostitute
(*To them.*) Well, the cards are mine.
They are the grossest pair[43] that e'er I felt.*   handled, probed

ANNE. Shuffle, I'll cut. (*Aside.*) Would I had never dealt!

---

[37] An old card game comparable to the Italian *carica l'asino* (load the ass).

[38] The game *cent*, in which one hundred points were needed to win.

[39] An old card game.

[40] That is, "so pick your cards as to lose the game" (Van Fossen).

[41] An old card game.

[42] Another variant of whist.

[43] Thickest deck, with a play on "monstrous couple."

FRANKFORD (*deals*). I have lost my dealing.*   misdealt
WENDOLL.   Sir, the fault's in me.
This queen I have more than my own, you see.
Give me the stock.* (*Deals.*)   deck
    FRANKFORD.   My mind's not on my game.
(*Aside.*) Many a deal I have lost, the more's your shame.
(*To them.*) You have served me a bad trick, Master Wendoll.
    WENDOLL. Sir, you must take your lot. To end this strife,
I know I have dealt better with your wife.
    FRANKFORD. (*aside*). Thou hast dealt falsely, then.
    ANNE. What's trumps?
    WENDOLL. Hearts. Partner, I rub.[44]
    FRANKFORD (*aside*). Thou robb'st me of my soul, of her
        chaste love;
In thy false dealing thou hast robbed my heart.
Booty you play;[45] I like a loser stand,
Having no heart, or* here or in my hand.   either
(*To them.*) I will give o'er the set; I am not well.
Come, who will hold my cards?
    ANNE. Not well, sweet Master Frankford?
Alas, what ail you? 'Tis some sudden qualm.
    WENDOLL. How long have you been so, Master Frankford?
    FRANKFORD. Sir, I was lusty* and I had my health,   vigorous
But I grew ill when you began to deal.—
Take hence this table.

        (*The servants enter and remove the table, cards, etc.*)

                        Gentle Master Cranwell,
You are welcome; see your chamber at your pleasure.
I am sorry that this megrim* takes me so   migraine
I cannot sit and bear you company.—
Jenkin, some lights, and show him to his chamber.
                        (*Exeunt* CRANWELL *and* JENKIN.)
    ANNE. A nightgown* for my husband, quickly   dressing gown
        there.

        (*Enter a servant with a gown, and exit.*)

It is some rheum or cold.
    WENDOLL.   Now, in good faith,
This illness you have got by sitting late
Without your gown.

            [44] Take all the cards of one suit.
            [45] That is, you have joined together to victimize me.

FRANKFORD.   I know it, Master Wendoll.
Go, go to bed, lest you complain like me.
Wife, prithee wife, into my bedchamber.
The night is raw and cold and rheumatic.
Leave me my gown and light; I'll walk away my fit.
WENDOLL. Sweet sir, good night.
FRANKFORD. Myself, good night.

(Exit WENDOLL.)

ANNE.   Shall I attend you, husband?
FRANKFORD. No, gentle wife, thou'lt catch cold in thy head;
Prithee, begone, sweet, I'll make haste to bed.
ANNE. No sleep will fasten on mine eyes, you know,
Until you come.
FRANKFORD.   Sweet Nan, I prithee, go.

(Exit ANNE.)

(*To* NICHOLAS.) I have bethought me. Get me by degrees
The keys of all my doors, which I will mould
In wax, and take their fair impression,
To have by them new keys. This being compassed,
At a set hour a letter shall be brought me,
And when they think they may securely play,
They are nearest to danger. Nick, I must rely
Upon thy trust and faithful secrecy.
NICHOLAS. Build on my faith.
FRANKFORD.   To bed then, not to rest;
Care lodges in my brain, grief in my breast.

(Exeunt.)

Scene 9

(*Near* OLD MOUNTFORD'S *house. Enter* SUSAN, OLD MOUNT-
FORD, SANDY, RODER, *and* TIDY.)

OLD MOUNTFORD. You say my nephew is in great distress.
Who brought it to him but his own lewd* life?   wicked
I cannot spare a cross. I must confess
He was my brother's son; why, niece, what then?
This is no world in which to pity men.
SUSAN.   I was not born a beggar, though his ex-
          tremes*   extremities
Enforce this language from me. I protest
No fortune of mine own could lead my tongue
To this base key. I do beseech you, uncle,
For the name's sake,* for Christianity,   family name

Nay, for God's sake, to pity his distress.
He is denied the freedom of the prison,
And in the hole* is laid with men condemned;   worst cell
Plenty he hath of nothing but of irons,
And it remains in you to free him thence.
  OLD MOUNTFORD. Money I cannot spare; men should take
    heed.
He lost my kindred when he fell to need.
                    (Exit.)

  SUSAN. Gold is but earth; thou earth enough shalt have
When thou hast once took measure of thy grave.
You know me, Master Sandy, and my suit.
  SANDY. I knew you, lady, when the old man lived;
I knew you ere your brother sold his land.
Then you were Mistress Sue, tricked up in jewels;
Then you sung well, played sweetly on the flute;
But now I neither know you nor your suit.
                    (Exit.)

  SUSAN. You, Master Roder, was my brother's tenant.
Rent-free he placed you in that wealthy farm
Of which you are possessed.
  RODER.   True, he did;
And have I not there dwelt still for his sake?
I have some business now, but without doubt
They that have hurled him in will help him out.
                    (Exit.)

  SUSAN. Cold comfort still. What say you, cousin Tidy?
  TIDY. I say this comes of roisting,* swagg'ring.   revelling
Call me not cousin; each man for himself!
Some men are born to mirth and some to sorrow;
I am no cousin unto them that borrow.
                    (Exit.)

  SUSAN. O Charity, why art thou fled to Heaven,
And left all things on this earth uneven?*   unjust
Their scoffing answers I will ne'er return,[46]
But to myself his grief in silence mourn.

  (Enter SIR FRANCIS *and* MALBY.*)*

  SIR FRANCIS. She is poor; I'll therefore tempt her with this
    gold.
Go, Malby, in my name deliver it,
And I will stay* thy answer.   await

  [46] To Sir Charles.

MALBY. Fair Mistress, as I understand your grief
Doth grow from want, so I have here in store*   abundance
A means to furnish you, a bag of gold
Which to your hands I freely tender you.
 SUSAN. I thank you, Heavens; I thank you, gentle sir!
God make me able to requite this favour.
 MALBY. This gold Sir Francis Acton sends by me,
And prays you—
 SUSAN. Acton! O God, that name I am born to curse.
Hence, bawd; hence, broker!* See, I spurn his gold; pander
My honour never shall for gain be sold.
 SIR FRANCIS. Stay, lady, stay!
 SUSAN.   From you I'll posting* hie, hurriedly
Even as the doves from feathered eagles fly.

                 (Exit.)

 SIR FRANCIS. She hates my name, my face. How should
  I woo?
I am disgraced in everything I do.
The more she hates me and disdains my love,
The more I am rapt in admiration
Of her divine and chaste perfections.
Woo her with gifts I cannot, for all gifts
Sent in my name she spurns. With looks I cannot,
For she abhors my sight. Nor yet with letters,
For none she will receive. How then? How then?
Well, I will fasten such a kindness on her
As shall o'ercome her hate and conquer it.
Sir Charles, her brother, lies in execution* imprisoned
For a great sum of money; and, besides,
The appeal is sued still for my huntsmen's death,[47]
Which only I have power to reverse.
In her I'll bury all my hate of him.
Go seek the Keeper, Malby; bring me to him.
To save his body, I his debts will pay;
To save his life, I his appeal will stay.

                (Exeunt.)

 [47] That is, the lawsuit over my huntsmen's death is still pending.

Scene 10

(York Castle. Enter Sir Charles *in irons, his feet bare, his garments all ragged and torn.)*

Sir Charles. Of all on the earth's face most miserable,
Breathe in this hellish dungeon thy laments.
Thus like a slave ragged, like a felon gyved.*   chained
O unkind uncle! O my friends ingrate!
That hurls thee headlong to this base estate.
Unthankful kinsmen! Mountfords all too base,
To let thy name lie fettered in disgrace.
A thousand deaths here in this grave I die.
Fear, hunger, sorrow, cold—all threat my death
And join together to deprive my breath.
But that which most torments me—my dear sister
Hath left* to visit me, and from my friends   ceased
Hath brought no hopeful answer; therefore I
Divine they will not help my misery.
If it be so, shame, scandal, and contempt
Attend their covetous thoughts, need make their graves.
Usurers they live, and may they die like slaves!

(Enter Keeper.)

Keeper. Knight, be of comfort, for I bring thee freedom
From all thy troubles.
     Sir Charles.   Then I am doomed to die;
Death is th'end of all calamity.
     Keeper. Live! your appeal is stayed, the execution
Of all your debts discharged, your creditors
Even to the utmost penny satisfied,
In sign whereof your shackles I knock off. (*Unchains him.*)
You are not left so much indebted to us
As for your fees; all is discharged, all paid.
Go freely to your house or where you please;
After long miseries embrace your ease.
     Sir Charles. Thou grumblest out the sweetest music to me
That ever organ played. Is this a dream?
Or do my waking senses apprehend
The pleasing taste of these applausive* news?   happy

Slave that I was to wrong such honest friends,
My loving kinsmen and my near allies.
Tongue, I will bite thee for the scandal breath
Against such faithful kinsmen; they are all
Composed of pity and compassion,
Of melting charity and of moving ruth.*   pity
That which I spake before was in my rage;
They are my friends, the mirrors* of this age,   models
Bounteous and free.* The noble Mountfords' race magnanimous
Ne'er bred a covetous thought or humour* base.   disposition

(*Enter* SUSAN.)

SUSAN (*aside*). I can no longer stay from visiting
My woeful brother; while I could I kept
My hapless tidings from his hopeful ear.
    SIR CHARLES. Sister, how much am I indebted to thee
And to thy travail!
    SUSAN.   What, at liberty?
    SIR CHARLES. Thou seest I am, thanks to thy industry.
O unto which of all my courteous friends
Am I thus bound? My uncle Mountford, he
Even of an infant loved me; was it he?
So did my cousin Tidy; was it he?
So Master Roder, Master Sandy too.
Which of all these did this high kindness do?
    SUSAN. Charles, can you mock me in your poverty,
Knowing your friends deride your misery?
Now I protest I stand so much amazed
To see your bonds free and your irons knocked off
That I am rapt into a maze of wonder,
The rather for I know not by what means
This happiness hath chanced.
    SIR CHARLES.   Why, by my uncle,
My cousins, and my friends. Who else, I pray,
Would take upon them all my debts to pay?
    SUSAN. O brother, they are men all of flint,
Pictures of marble,* and as void of pity   statues
As chased bears. I begged, I sued, I kneeled,
Laid open all your griefs and miseries,
Which they derided—more than that, denied us
A part in their alliance, but in pride
Said that our kindred with our plenty died.

SIR CHARLES. Drudges too much!* What, did they?   base slaves
    O known evil!
Rich fly the poor as good men shun the Devil.
Whence should my freedom come? Of whom alive,
Saving of those, have I deserved so well?
Guess, sister, call to mind, remember* me.   remind
These I have raised,* these follow the world's guise,   named
Whom, rich in honour, they in woe despise.[48]
    SUSAN. My wits have lost themselves; let's ask the Keeper.
    SIR CHARLES. Gaoler!
    KEEPER. At hand, sir.
    SIR CHARLES. Of courtesy resolve me one demand.[49]
What was he took the burden of my debts
From off my back, stayed my appeal to death,
Discharged my fees, and brought me liberty?
    KEEPER. A courteous knight, one called Sir Francis Acton.
    SUSAN. Acton!
    SIR CHARLES. Ha! Acton! O me, more distressed in this
Than all my troubles. Hale me back,
Double my irons, and my sparing meals
Put into halves, and lodge me in a dungeon
More deep, more dark, more cold, more comfortless.
By Acton freed! Not all thy manacles
Could fetter so my heels as this one word
Hath thralled* my heart, and it must now lie bound   enslaved
In more strict prison than thy stony gaol.
I am not free, I go but under bail.
    KEEPER. My charge is done, sir, now I have my fees;
As we get little, we will nothing leese.*   lose
                                                         (*Exit.*)

    SIR CHARLES. By Acton freed, my dangerous
        opposite.*   enemy
Why, to what end? Or what occasion? Ha!
Let me forget the name of enemy
And with indifference balance* this high   impartially consider
    favour. Ha!
    SUSAN (*aside*). His love to me. Upon my soul, 'tis so!
That is the root from whence these strange things grow.
    SIR CHARLES. Had this proceeded from my father, he
That by the law of nature is most bound

----

[48] That is, "those who are honorable but unfortunate they despise" (Baskervill).
[49] Answer one question.

In offices of love, it had deserved
My best employment to requite that grace.
Had it proceeded from my friends, or him,*   that is,
his father
From them this action had deserved my life—
And from a stranger more, because from such
There is less execution of good deeds.
But he—nor father, nor ally, nor friend,
More than a stranger—both remote in blood
And in his heart opposed my enemy,
That this high bounty should proceed from him—
O there I lose myself. What should I say,
What think, what do, his bounty to repay?

   SUSAN. You wonder, I am sure, whence this strange kindness
Proceeds in Acton. I will tell you, brother:
He dotes on me and oft hath sent me gifts,
Letters, and tokens. I refused them all.

   SIR CHARLES. I have enough; though poor, my heart is set
In one rich gift to pay back all my debt.

(Exeunt.)

Scene 11

(FRANKFORD'S *house. Enter* FRANKFORD *with a letter in his hand, and* NICHOLAS *with keys.*)

   FRANKFORD. This is the night, and I must play
      the touch,*   touchstone
To try* two seeming angels. Where's my keys?   test
   NICHOLAS. They are made according to your mould in wax.
I bade the smith be secret, gave him money,
And there they are. The letter, sir.
   FRANKFORD. True, take it; there it is.
And when thou seest me in my pleasant'st vein
Ready to sit to supper, bring it me.
   NICHOLAS. I'll do't; make no more question but I'll do't.

(Exit.)

(*Enter* ANNE, CRANWELL, WENDOLL, *and* JENKIN.)

   ANNE. Sirra, 'tis six o'clock already struck.
Go bid them spread the cloth and serve in supper.
   JENKIN. It shall be done forsooth, mistress. Where is Spiggot
the butler to give us out salt and trenchers?*   plates

(Exit.)

WENDOLL. We that have been a-hunting all the day
Come with prepared stomachs, Master Frankford.
We wished you at our sport.
FRANKFORD. My heart was with you, and my mind was
    on you.
Fie, Master Cranwell, you are still thus sad.—
A stool, a stool! Where's Jenkin, and where's Nick?
'Tis supper time at least an hour ago.
What's the best news abroad?
WENDOLL.   I know none good.
FRANKFORD (*aside*). But I know too much bad.

(*Enter* SPIGGOT *the Butler and* JENKIN *with a tablecloth,
bread, trenchers, and salt; then exeunt.*)

CRANWELL. Methinks, sir, you might have that interest
In* your wife's brother to be more remiss*   influence with/lenient
In this hard dealing against poor Sir Charles,
Who, as I hear, lies in York Castle, needy,
And in great want.
FRANKFORD. Did not more weighty business of my own
Hold me away, I would have laboured peace
Betwixt them with all care; indeed I would, sir.
ANNE. I'll write unto my brother earnestly
In that behalf.
WENDOLL.   A charitable deed,
And will beget the good opinion
Of all your friends that love you, Mistress Frankford.
FRANKFORD. That's you for one; I know you love Sir
    Charles.
(*Aside*.) And my wife too well.
WENDOLL.   He deserves the love
Of all true gentlemen; be yourselves judge.
FRANKFORD. But supper, ho! Now as thou lovest me,
    Wendoll,
Which I am sure thou dost, be merry, pleasant,
And frolic it to-night. Sweet Master Cranwell,
Do you the like. Wife, I protest, my heart
Was ne'er more bent on sweet alacrity.*—   pleasure
Where be those lazy knaves to serve in supper?

(*Enter* NICHOLAS.)

NICHOLAS. Sir, here's a letter.
FRANKFORD. Whence comes it? And who brought it?

NICHOLAS. A stripling that below attends your answer,
And as he tells me it is sent from York.
FRANKFORD. Have him into the cellar; let him taste
A cup of our March beer. Go, make him drink.
(*Reads the letter.*)
NICHOLAS. I'll make him drunk, if he be a Trojan.*   drunkard
(*Exit.*)
FRANKFORD. My boots and spurs! Where's Jenkin? God
forgive me,
How I neglect my business. Wife, look here;
I have a matter to be tried tomorrow
By eight o'clock, and my attorney writes me
I must be there betimes* with evidence,   early
Or it will go against me. Where's my boots?

(*Enter* JENKIN *with boots and spurs.*)

ANNE. I hope your business craves no such dispatch
That you must ride tonight.
WENDOLL (*aside*).   I hope it doth.
FRANKFORD. God's me! No such dispatch?—
Jenkin, my boots. Where's Nick? Saddle my roan,
And the gray dapple for himself.—Content ye,*   be assured
It much concerns me. (*Exit* JENKIN.) Gentle Master Cranwell
And Master Wendoll, in my absence use
The very ripest pleasure of my house.
WENDOLL. Lord, Master Frankford, will you ride to-night?
The ways are dangerous.
FRANKFORD.   Therefore will I ride
Appointed* well, and so shall Nick, my man.   armed
ANNE. I'll call you up by five o'clock tomorrow.
FRANKFORD. No, by my faith, wife, I'll not trust to that;
'Tis not such easy rising in a morning
From one I love so dearly. No, by my faith,
I shall not leave so sweet a bedfellow
But with much pain. You have made me a sluggard
Since I first knew you.
ANNE.   Then if you needs will go
This dangerous evening—Master Wendoll,
Let me entreat you bear him company.
WENDOLL. With all my heart, sweet mistress. My boots there!
FRANKFORD. Fie, fie, that for my private business
I should disease* my friend and be a trouble   inconvenience
To the whole house. Nick!

NICHOLAS (*offstage*). Anon, sir.

FRANKFORD. Bring forth my gelding—(*To* WENDOLL.) As
  you love me, sir,
Use no more words. A hand, good Master Cranwell.

CRANWELL. Sir, God be your good speed.

FRANKFORD. Good night, sweet Nan; nay, nay, a kiss and
  part!
(*Aside.*) Dissembling lips, you suit not with my heart.

(Exit.)

WENDOLL (*aside*). How business, time, and hours all gra-
  cious proves
And are the furtherers to my newborn love.
I am husband now in Master Frankford's place
And must command the house. (*To* ANNE.) My pleasure is
We will not sup abroad so publicly,
But in your private chamber, Mistress Frankford.

ANNE (*to* WENDOLL). O sir, you are too public in your love,
And Master Frankford's wife—

CRANWELL.   Might I crave favour.
I would entreat you I might see my chamber;
I am on the sudden grown exceeding ill
And would be spared from supper.

WENDOLL.   Light there, ho!
See you want nothing, sir, for if you do,
You injury that good man, and wrong me too.

CRANWELL. I will make bold. Good night.

(Exit.)

WENDOLL.   How all conspire
To make our bosom* sweet and full entire.*   intimacy/complete
Come, Nan, I prithee let us sup within.

ANNE. O what a clog unto the soul is sin.
We pale offenders are still* full of fear;   always
Every suspicious eye brings danger near,
When* they whose clear heart from offence are free,   whereas
Despise report, base scandals to outface,
And stand at mere* defiance with disgrace.   absolute

WENDOLL. Fie, fie, you talk too like a Puritan.

ANNE. You have tempted me to mischief, Master Wendoll;
I have done I know not what. Well, you plead custom;*   habit
That which for want of wit I granted erst*   originally
I now must yield through fear. Come, come, let's in.
Once o'er shoes, we are straight o'er head in sin.

WENDOLL. My jocund soul is joyful above measure;
I'll be profuse in Frankford's richest treasure.

(*Exeunt.*)

Scene 12

(*Another room in the house.* Enter CICELY, JENKIN, SPIG-
GOT *the Butler, and other servingmen.*)

JENKIN. My mistress and Master Wendoll, my master, sup
in her chamber to-night. Cicely, you are preferred*   promoted
from being the cook to be chambermaid. Of all the loves betwixt thee and me, tell me what thou thinkest of this.

CICELY. Mum; there's an old proverb, "When the cat's away
the mouse may play."

JENKIN. Now you talk of a cat, Cicely, I smell a rat.

CICELY. Good words, Jenkin, lest you be called to answer
them.

JENKIN. Why, "God make my mistress an honest*   chaste
woman." Are not these good words? "Pray God my new master play not the knave with my old master." Is there any hurt
in this? "God send no villainy intended, and if they do sup together, pray God they do not lie together. God keep my mistress chaste and make us all His servants." What harm is there
in all this? Nay, more, here is my hand; thou shalt never have
my heart unless thou say "Amen."

CICELY. "Amen, I pray God," I say.

(*Enter servingmen.*)

SERVANT. My mistress sends that you should make less noise,
to lock up the doors, and see the household all got to bed; you,
Jenkin, for this night are made the porter, to see the gates
shut in.*   closed

JENKIN. Thus by little and little I creep into office. Come to
kennel, my masters, to kennel; 'tis eleven o'clock already.

SERVANT. When you have locked the gates in, you must send
up the keys to my mistress.

CICELY. Quickly, for God's sake, Jenkin; for I must carry
them. I am neither pillow nor bolster, but I know more than
both.

JENKIN. To bed, good Spiggot; to bed, good honest serving
creatures, and let us sleep as snug as pigs in pease-straw.

(*Exeunt.*)

Scene 13

(*Before and within* FRANKFORD'S *house. Enter* FRANKFORD *and* NICHOLAS.)

FRANKFORD. Soft, soft. We have tied our geldings to a tree
Two flight-shoot* off, lest by their thund'ring hooves   bow-shots
They blab our coming back. Hear'st thou no noise?

NICHOLAS. Hear? I hear nothing but the owl and you.

FRANKFORD. So; now my watch's hand points upon twelve,
And it is dead midnight. Where are my keys?

NICHOLAS. Here, sir.

FRANKFORD. This is the key that opes my outward gate;
This is the hall door; this my withdrawing chamber.
But this, that door that's bawd unto my shame,
Fountain and spring of all my bleeding thoughts,
Where the most hallowed order and true knot
Of nuptial sanctity hath been profaned.
It leads to my polluted bedchamber,
Once my terrestrial heaven, now my earth's hell,
The place where sins in all their ripeness dwell.—
But I forget myself; now to my gate.

NICHOLAS. It must ope with far less noise than Cripplegate,⁵⁰ or your plot's dashed.

FRANKFORD. So, reach me my dark-lantern to the
rest.*   that is,
                                       of the doors
Tread softly, softly.

NICHOLAS.   I will walk on eggs this pace.

FRANKFORD. A general silence hath surprised* the   taken over
house,
And this is the last door. Astonishment,
Fear, and amazement play against my heart,
Even as a madman beats upon a drum.
O keep my eyes, you Heavens, before I enter,
From any sight that may transfix my soul;
Or if there be so black a spectacle,
O strike mine eyes stark blind; or if not so,
Lend me such patience to digest my grief
That I may keep this white and virgin hand
From any violent outrage or red murder.
And with that prayer I enter.

                                                (*Exit.*)

---

⁵⁰ A London gate.

NICHOLAS. Here's a circumstance!*   an act
A man may be made cuckold in the time
That he's about it. And* the case were mine   if
As 'tis my master's—'sblood, that he makes me swear—
I would have placed his action,[51] entered there;
I would, I would.

(*Enter* FRANKFORD.)

FRANKFORD. O, O!
NICHOLAS. Master, 'sblood, master, master!
FRANKFORD. O me unhappy, I have found them lying
Close in each other's arms, and fast asleep.
But that I would not damn two precious souls
Bought with my Saviour's blood and send them laden
With all their scarlet sins upon their backs
Unto a fearful Judgement, their two lives
Had met upon my rapier.
NICHOLAS. 'Sblood, master, have you left them sleeping still?
Let me go wake them.
FRANKFORD. Stay, let me pause awhile.
O God, O God, that it were possible
To undo things done, to call back yesterday;
That Time could turn up his swift sandy glass,
To untell* the days, and to redeem these hours;   count in
Or that the Sun   reverse
Could, rising from the west, draw his coach backward,
Take from the account of time so many minutes,
Till he had all these seasons called again,
Those minutes and those actions done in them,
Even from her first offence that I might take her
As spotless as an angel in my arms.
But O! I talk of things impossible,
And cast beyond the moon.* God give me patience,   rave
For I will in to wake them.

(*Exit.*)

NICHOLAS. Here's patience perforce;
He needs must trot afoot that tires his horse.

(*Enter* WENDOLL, *running over the stage in a night gown,*
FRANKFORD *after him with his sword drawn;* CICELY *in her*

---

[51] "Established his case" (Ward).

*smock stays his hand and clasps hold on him. He pauses
awhile.)*

FRANKFORD. I thank thee, maid; thou like the angel's hand
Hast stayed me from a bloody sacrifice.—
Go, villain, and my wrongs sit on thy soul
As heavy as this grief doth upon mine.
When thou record'st my many courtesies
And shalt compare them with thy treacherous heart,
Lay them together, weigh them equally,
'Twill be revenge enough. Go, to thy friend
A Judas; pray, pray, lest I live to see
Thee Judas-like, hanged on an elder tree.

(Enter ANNE *in her smock, nightgown, and night attire.)*

ANNE. O by what word, what title, or what name
Shall I entreat your pardon? Pardon! O
I am as far from hoping such sweet grace
As Lucifer from Heaven. To call you husband—
O me most wretched, I have lost that name;
I am no more your wife.
NICHOLAS.   'Sblood, sir, she swoons.
FRANKFORD. Spare thou thy tears, for I will weep for thee;
And keep thy countenance, for I'll blush for thee.
Now I protest I think 'tis I am tainted,
For I am most ashamed, and 'tis more hard
For me to look upon thy guilty face
Than on the sun's clear brow. What! Wouldst thou speak?
ANNE. I would I had no tongue, no ears, no eyes,
No apprehension, no capacity.[52]
When do you spurn me like a dog? When tread me
Under your feet? When drag me by the hair?
Though I deserve a thousand thousand fold
More than you can inflict, yet, once my husband,
For womanhood—to which I am a shame
Though once an ornament—even for His sake
That hath redeem'd our souls, mark not my face
Nor hack me with your sword, but let me go
Perfect and undeformed to my tomb!
I am not worthy that I should prevail
In the least suit, no, not to speak to you,

[52] That is, no powers of reason.

Nor look on you, nor to be in your presence;
Yet as an abject* this one suit I crave,   outcast
This granted I am ready for my grave.
 FRANKFORD. My God with patience arm me. Rise, nay, rise,
And I'll debate with thee. Was it for want
Thou playedst the strumpet? Wast thou not supplied
With every pleasure, fashion, and new toy*—— trinket
Nay, even beyond my calling?*   position
 ANNE.   I was.
 FRANKFORD. Was it then disability in me?
Or in thine eye seemed he a properer* man? worthier,
 ANNE. O no.   handsomer
 FRANKFORD. Did I not lodge thee in my bosom?
Wear thee here in my heart?
 ANNE.   You did.
 FRANKFORD. I did indeed; witness my tears I did.——
Go bring my infants hither.

   (*Exit* CICELY *and return with two children.*)

        O Nan, O Nan,
If either fear or shame, regard of honour,
The blemish of my house, nor my dear love
Could have withheld thee from so lewd a fact,* deed
Yet for these infants, these young harmless souls,
On whose white brows thy shame is charactered,
And grows in greatness as they wax in years——
Look but on them, and melt away in tears.
Away with them, lest as her spotted body
Hath stained their names with stripe of bastardy,
So her adult'rous breath may blast their spirits
With her infectious thoughts. Away with them!
      (*Exeunt* CICELY *and children.*)
 ANNE. In this one life I die ten thousand deaths.
 FRANKFORD. Stand up, stand up! I will do nothing rashly.
I will retire awhile into my study,
And thou shalt hear thy sentence presently.* immediately
             (*Exit.*)
 ANNE. 'Tis welcome, be it death. O me, base strumpet,
That having such a husband, such sweet children
Must enjoy neither. O to redeem my honour
I would have this hand cut off, these my breasts seared,
Be racked, strappadoed,* put to any torment; tortured

Nay, to whip but this scandal out, I would hazard
The rich and dear redemption of my soul.
He cannot be so base as to forgive me,
Nor I so shameless to accept his pardon.
(*To the audience.*) O women, women, you that have yet kept
Your holy matrimonial vow unstained,
Make me your instance.* When you tread awry,   example
Your sins like mine will on your conscience lie.

(*Enter in night clothes* CICELY, SPIGGOT, *all the servingmen,
and* JENKIN.)

ALL. O mistress, mistress, what have you done, mistress?
NICHOLAS. 'Sblood, what a caterwauling keep you here!
JENKIN. O Lord, mistress, how comes this to pass? My
master is run away in his shirt, and never so much as called
me to bring his clothes after him.
ANNE. See what guilt is! Here stand I in this place,
Ashamed to look my servants in the face.

(*Enter* MASTER FRANKFORD *and* CRANWELL, *whom seeing
she falls on her knees.*)

FRANKFORD. My words are registered in Heaven already.
With patience hear me: I'll not martyr thee
Nor mark thee for a strumpet, but with usage
Of more humility torment thy soul
And kill thee even with kindness.
CRANWELL.   Master Frankford—
FRANKFORD. Good Master Cranwell—woman, hear thy
      judgement:
Go make thee ready in thy best attire,
Take with thee all thy gowns, all thy apparel;
Leave nothing that did ever call thee mistress,
Or by whose sight being left here in the house
I may remember such a woman by.
Choose thee a bed and hangings for a chamber;
Take with thee everything that hath thy mark,
And get thee to my manor seven mile off,
Where live. 'Tis thine; I freely give it thee.
My tenants by* shall furnish thee with wains*   nearby/wagons
To carry all thy stuff within two hours;
No longer will I limit* thee my sight.   allow

Choose which of all my servants thou likest best,
And they are thine to attend thee.

ANNE.   A mild sentence.

FRANKFORD. But as thou hop'st for Heaven, as thou believ'st
Thy name's recorded in the Book of Life,
I charge thee never after this sad day
To see me, or to meet me, or to send
By word, or writing, gift, or otherwise
To move me, by thyself or by thy friends,
Nor challenge any part in my two children.
So farewell, Nan, for we will henceforth be
As we had never seen, ne'er more shall see.

ANNE. How full my heart is in my eyes appears;
What wants in words, I will supply in tears.

FRANKFORD. Come, take your coach, your stuff; all must
    along.
Servants and all make ready, all be gone.
It was thy hand cut two hearts out of one.

                                 (*Exeunt.*)

Scene 14

(*Before* SIR FRANCIS ACTON'S *house. Enter* SIR CHARLES,
dressed like a gentleman, and SUSAN, *dressed like a gentlewoman.*)

SUSAN. Brother, why have you tricked* me   decked
like a bride?
Bought me this gay attire, these ornaments?
Forget you our estate, our poverty?

SIR CHARLES. Call me not brother, but imagine me
Some barbarous outlaw or uncivil kern,*   peasant
For if thou shut'st thy eye and only hear'st
The words that I shall utter, thou shalt judge me
Some staring* ruffian, not thy brother Charles.   wild
O Susan!

SUSAN. O brother, what doth this strange language mean?

SIR CHARLES. Dost love me, sister? Wouldst thou see me live
A bankrupt beggar in the world's disgrace
And die indebted to my enemies?
Wouldst thou behold me stand like a huge beam
In the world's eye, a byword and a scorn?
It lies in thee of these to acquit me free,
And all my debt I may outstrip by thee.

Susan. By me? Why I have nothing, nothing left;
I owe even for the clothes upon my back;
I am not worth—
    Sir Charles.   O sister, say not so.
It lies in you my downcast state to raise,
To make me stand on even points with the world.
Come, sister, you are rich! Indeed you are,
And in your power you have without delay
Acton's five hundred pound back to repay.
    Susan. Till now I had thought you loved me. By mine
        honour—
Which I had kept as spotless as the moon—
I ne'er was mistress of that single doit[53]
Which I reserved not to supply your wants.
And do you think that I would hoard from you?
Now by my hopes in Heaven, knew I the means
To buy you from the slavery of your debts,
Especially from Acton, whom I hate,
I would redeem it with my life or blood.
    Sir Charles. I challenge it, and kindred set apart,
Thus ruffian-like I lay siege to your heart.
What do I owe to Acton?
    Susan. Why, some five hundred pounds, toward which I
        swear
In all the world I have not one denier.*   penny
    Sir Charles. It will not prove so. Sister, now resolve*   tell
    me:
What do you think—and speak your conscience—
Would Acton give might he enjoy your bed?
    Susan. He would not shrink to spend a thousand pound
To give the Mountfords' name so deep a wound.
    Sir Charles. A thousand pound! I but five hundred owe;
Grant him your bed, he's paid with interest so.
    Susan. O brother!
    Sir Charles.   O sister! Only this one way,
With that rich jewel you my debts may pay.
In speaking this my cold heart shakes with shame,
Nor do I woo you in a brother's name,
But in a stranger's. Shall I die in debt
To Acton, my grand foe, and you still wear
The precious jewel that he holds so dear?

[53] Dutch coin worth less than a penny.

SUSAN. My honour I esteem as dear and precious
As my redemption.
 SIR CHARLES.   I esteem you, sister,
As dear for so dear prizing it.
 SUSAN.   Will Charles
Have me cut off my hands and send them Acton?
Rip up my breast, and with my bleeding heart
Present him as a token?
 SIR CHARLES.   Neither, sister,
But hear me in my strange* assertion.   abnormal
Thy honour and my soul are equal in my regard,
Nor will thy brother Charles survive thy shame.
His kindness like a burden hath surcharged me,
And under his good deeds I stooping go,
Not with an upright soul. Had I remained
In prison still, there doubtless I had died;
Then unto him that freed me from that prison
Still do I owe that life. What moved my foe
To enfranchise me? 'Twas, sister, for your love!
With full five hundred pounds he bought your love,
And shall he not enjoy it? Shall the weight
Of all this heavy burden lean on me,
And will not you bear part? You did partake
The joy of my release; will you not stand
In joint-bond bound to satisfy the debt?
Shall I be only charged?
 SUSAN.   But that I know
These arguments come from an honoured mind,
As in your most extremity of need
Scorning to stand in debt to one you hate—
Nay, rather would engage your unstained honour
Than to be held ingrate—I should condemn you.
I see your resolution and assent;
So Charles will have me, and I am content.
 SIR CHARLES. For this I tricked you up.
 SUSAN.   But here's a knife
To save mine honour shall slice out my life.
 SIR CHARLES. I know thou pleasest me a thousand times
More in that resolution than thy grant.
(*Aside.*) Observe her love: to soothe them in my suit
Her honour she will hazard though not lose;
To bring me out of debt, rigorous hand
Will pierce her heart. O wonder, that will choose

Rather than stain her blood her life to lose.
(*To her.*) Come, you sad sister to a woeful brother,
This is the gate; I'll bear him such a present,
Such an acquittance* for the knight to seal,   release
As will amaze his senses and surprise
With admiration* all his fantasies.   wonder

(*Enter* SIR FRANCIS *and* MALBY.)

SUSAN. Before his unchaste thoughts shall seize on me,   that is,
'Tis here* shall my imprisoned soul set free.   the knife
  SIR FRANCIS. How! Mountford with his sister hand in hand!
What miracle's afoot?
  MALBY.   It is a sight
Begets in me much admiration.
  SIR CHARLES. Stand not amazed to see me thus attended.
Acton, I owe thee money, and being unable
To bring thee the full sum in ready coin,
Lo! for thy more assurance here's a pawn,
My sister, my dear sister, whose chaste honour
I prize above a million. Here—nay, take her;
She's worth your money, man; do not forsake her.
  SIR FRANCIS. I would he were in earnest!
  SUSAN. Impute it not to my immodesty.
My brother being rich in nothing else
But in his interest that he hath in me,
According to his poverty hath brought you
Me, all his store, whom howsoe'er you prize
As forfeit to your hand, he values highly,
And would not sell but to acquit your debt
For any emperor's ransom.
  SIR FRANCIS (*aside*).   Stern heart, relent;
Thy former cruelty at length repent.
Was ever known in any former age
Such honourable wrested* courtesy?   dragged forth
Lands, honours, lives, and all the world forgo
Rather than stand engaged to such a foe.
  SIR CHARLES. Acton, she is too poor to be thy bride,
And I too much opposed to be thy brother.
There, take her to thee. If thou hast the heart
To seize her as a rape or lustful prey,
To blur our house that never yet was stained,
To murder her that never meant thee harm,
To kill me now whom once thou savedst from death,

Do them at once; on her all these rely,
And perish with her spotted chastity.

SIR FRANCIS. You overcome me in your love, Sir Charles.
I cannot be so cruel to a lady
I love so dearly. Since you have not spared
To engage your reputation to the world,
Your sister's honour, which you prize so dear,
Nay, all the comforts which you hold on earth,
To grow out of my debt, being your foe,—
Your honoured thoughts, lo, thus I recompense.
Your metamorphosed foe receives your gift
In satisfaction of all former wrongs.
This jewel I will wear here in my heart,
And where* before I thought her for her wants*   whereas/poverty
Too base to be my bride, to end all strife,
I seal you my dear brother, her my wife.

SUSAN. You still exceed us. I will yield to fate
And learn to love where I till now did hate.

SIR CHARLES. With that enchantment you have charmed my
    soul
And made me rich even in those very words.
I pay no debt but am indebted more;
Rich in your love I never can be poor.

SIR FRANCIS. All's mine is yours; we are alike in state.
Let's knit in love what was opposed in hate.
Come, for our nuptials we will straight* provide,   immediately
Blessed only in our brother and fair bride.

                                                 (*Exeunt.*)

Scene 15

(FRANKFORD'S *house. Enter* CRANWELL, FRANKFORD, *and*
NICHOLAS.)

CRANWELL. Why do you search each room about your
    house,
Now that you have dispatched your wife away?

FRANKFORD. O sir, to see that nothing may be left
That ever was my wife's. I loved her dearly,
And when I do but think of her unkindness,
My thoughts are all in Hell; to avoid which torment,
I would not have a bodkin or a cuff,
A bracelet, necklace, or rebato wire,[54]

---

[54] Wire used to support a ruff.

Nor anything that ever was called hers
Left me, by which I might remember her.
Seek round about.

NICHOLAS. 'Sblood, master, here's her lute flung in a corner.

FRANKFORD. Her lute! O God, upon this instrument
Her fingers have run quick division,*   melodic passages
Sweeter than that which now divides our hearts.
These frets have made me pleasant,* that have now   merry
Frets of my heartstrings made. O Master Cranwell,
Oft hath she made this melancholy wood,
Now mute and dumb for* her disastrous chance,*   because of/
Speak sweetly many a note, sound many a strain   fortune
To her own ravishing voice, which being well strung,
What pleasant, strange airs have they jointly sung.—
Post with it after her.—Now nothing's left;
Of her and hers I am at once bereft.

NICHOLAS. I'll ride and overtake her, do my message,
And come back again.

                                        (*Exit.*)

CRANWELL.   Meantime, sir, if you please,
I'll to Sir Francis Acton and inform him
Of what hath passed betwixt you and his sister.

FRANKFORD. Do as you please. How ill am I bestead
To be a widower ere my wife be dead.

                                        (*Exeunt.*)

                    Scene 16

(*A road. Enter* ANNE, *with* JENKIN, *her maid* CICELY, *her
coachman, and three carters.*)

ANNE. Bid my coach stay. Why should I ride in state,
Being hurled so low down by the hand of fate?
A seat like to my fortunes let me have,
Earth for my chair, and for my bed a grave.

JENKIN. Comfort, good mistress; you have watered your
coach with tears already. You have but two mile to go to
your manor. A man cannot say by my old Master Frankford
as he may say by me, that he wants manors, for he hath
three or four, of which this is one that we are going to.

CICELY. Good mistress, be of good cheer. Sorrow you see
hurts you, but helps you not; we all mourn to see you so sad.

CARTER. Mistress, I spy one of my landlord's men
Come riding post,* tis like he brings some news.   speedily

ANNE. Comes he from Master Frankford, he is welcome;
So are his news, because they come from him.

(*Enter* NICHOLAS.)

NICHOLAS (*presenting the lute.*) There.
ANNE. I know the lute. Oft have I sung to thee;
We both are out of tune, both out of time.
NICHOLAS. Would that had been the worst instrument that
e'er you played on. My master commends him to ye; there's
all he can find that was ever yours. He hath nothing left that
ever you could lay claim to but his own heart—and he could
afford you that. All that I have to deliver you is this: he
prays you to forget him, and so he bids you farewell.
ANNE. I thank him; he is kind and ever was.
All you that have true feeling of my grief,
That know my loss, and have relenting hearts,
Gird me about, and help me with your tears
To wash my spotted sins. My lute shall groan;
It cannot weep, but shall lament my moan.
(*She plays.*)

(*Enter* WENDOLL *behind.*)

WENDOLL. Pursued with horror of a guilty soul
And with the sharp scourge of repentance lashed,
I fly from my own shadow. O my stars!
What have my parents in their lives deserved
That you should lay this penance on their son?
When I but think of Master Frankford's love
And lay it to my treason, or compare
My murd'ring him for his relieving me,
It strikes a terror like a lightning's flash
To scorch my blood up. Thus I, like the owl
Ashamed of day, live in these shadowy woods
Afraid of every leaf or murmuring blast,
Yet longing to receive some perfect* knowledge   correct
How he hath dealt with her. (*Sees* ANNE.) O my sad fate!
Here, and so far from home, and thus attended!
O God, I have divorced the truest turtles*   turtle doves
That ever lived together, and being divided
In several* places, make their several moan;   separate
She in the fields laments and he at home.
So poets write that Orpheus made the trees

And stones to dance to his melodious harp,
Meaning the rustic and the barbarous hinds,*   folk
That had no understanding part in them;
So she from these rude carters tears extracts,
Making their flinty hearts with grief to rise
And draw down rivers from their rocky eyes.
    ANNE (*to* NICHOLAS). If you return unto your master, say—
Though not from me, for I am all unworthy
To blast his name so with a strumpet's tongue—
That you have seen me weep, wish myself dead.
Nay, you may say too—for my vow is passed*—   made
Last night you saw me eat and drink my last.
This to your master you may say and swear,
For it is writ in Heaven and decreed here.
    NICHOLAS. I'll say you wept; I'll swear you made me sad.
Why how now, eyes? What now? What's here to do?
I am gone, or I shall straight turn baby too.
    WENDOLL (*aside*). I cannot weep; my heart is all on fire.
Cursed be the fruits of my unchaste desire.
    ANNE. Go break this lute upon my coach's wheel,
As the last music that I e'er shall make—
Not as my husband's gift, but my farewell
To all earth's joy; and so your master tell.
    NICHOLAS. If I can for crying.
    WENDOLL (*aside*).   Grief, have done,
Or like a madman I shall frantic run.
    ANNE. You have beheld the woefullest wretch on earth,
A woman made of tears. Would you had words
To express but what you see! My inward grief
No tongue can utter, yet unto your power[55]
You may describe my sorrow and disclose
To thy sad master my abundant woes.
    NICHOLAS. I'll do your commendations.*   deliver your greetings
    ANNE.   O no.
I dare not so presume; nor to my children.
I am disclaimed in both; alas, I am.
O never teach them when they come to speak
To name the name of mother; chide their tongue
If they by chance light on that hated word;
Tell them 'tis nought, for when that word they name,
Poor pretty souls, they harp on their own shame.

    [55] That is, to the best of your ability.

WENDOLL (*aside*). To recompense her wrongs, what canst thou do?
Thou hast made her husbandless and childless too.
ANNE. I have no more to say. Speak not for me,
Yet you may tell your master what you see.
NICHOLAS. I'll do't.

(*Exit.*)

WENDOLL. I'll speak to her and comfort her in grief.
O, but her wound cannot be cured with words.
No matter though, I'll do my best good will
To work a cure on her whom I did kill.
ANNE. So, now unto my coach, then to my home,
So to my deathbed, for from this sad hour
I never will nor eat, nor drink, nor taste
Of any cates* that may preserve my life;   food
I never will nor smile, nor sleep, nor rest,
But when my tears have washed my black soul white,
Sweet Saviour, to Thy hands I yield my sprite.*   spirit
WENDOLL (*coming forward*). O Mistress Frankford—
ANNE.   O for God's sake fly!
The Devil doth come to tempt me ere I die.
My coach! This sin that with an angel's face
Courted mine honour till he sought my wrack,*   ruin
In my repentant eyes seems ugly black.

(*Exeunt all except* WENDOLL *and* JENKIN,
the carters whistling.[56])

JENKIN. What, my young master that fled in his shirt! How come you by your clothes again? You have made our house in a sweet pickle, have you not, think you? What, shall I serve you still or cleave to the old house?
WENDOLL. Hence, slave! Away with thy unsea-
    soned* mirth;   inappropriate
Unless thou canst shed tears, and sigh, and howl,
Curse thy sad fortunes, and exclaim on fate,
Thou art not for my turn.
JENKIN. Marry, and* you will not, another will; farewell   if
and be hanged. Would you had never come to have kept this
coil* within our doors. We shall ha' you run away made trouble
like a sprite again.

(*Exit.*)

---

[56] Elizabethan carters were noted for their whistling.

WENDOLL. She's gone to death; I live to want and woe,
Her life, her sins, and all upon my head.
And I must now go wander like a Cain
In foreign countries and remoted climes,
Where the report of my ingratitude
Cannot be heard. I'll over, first to France,
And so to Germany, and Italy,
Where when I have recovered, and by travel
Gotten those perfect tongues,[57] and that* these rumours   when
May in their height abate, I will return;
And I divine, however now dejected,
My worth and parts being by some great man praised,
At my return I may in court be raised.

                                                (*Exit.*)

Scene 17

(*Before the manor house. Enter* SIR FRANCIS, SIR CHARLES,
CRANWELL, MALBY, *and* SUSAN.)

SIR FRANCIS. Brother, and now my wife, I think these
     troubles
Fall on my head by justice of the Heavens
For being so strict to you in your extremities;
But we are now atoned.* I would my sister   reconciled
Could with like happiness o'ercome her griefs
As we have ours.
     SUSAN. You tell us, Master Cranwell, wondrous things
Touching the patience of that gentleman,
With what strange virtue he demeans* his grief.   expresses
     CRANWELL. I told you what I was witness of;
It was my fortune to lodge there that night.
     SIR FRANCIS. O that same villain Wendoll! 'Twas his tongue
That did corrupt her; she was of herself
Chaste and devoted well.* Is this the house?   faithful
     CRANWELL. Yes sir, I take it here your sister lies.*   lives
     SIR FRANCIS. My brother Frankford showed too mild a spirit
In the revenge of such a loathed crime;
Less than he did, no man of spirit could do.
I am so far from blaming his revenge
That I commend it. Had it been my case,
Their souls at once had from their breasts been freed;
Death to such deeds of shame is the due meed!

     [57] Learned the languages well.

(*Enter* JENKIN *and* CICELY.)

JENKIN. O my mistress, my mistress, my poor mistress!
CICELY. Alas that ever I was born! What shall I do for my
poor mistress?
SIR CHARLES. Why, what of her?
JENKIN. O Lord, sir, she no sooner heard that her brother
and his friends were come to see how she did, but she for
very shame of her guilty conscience fell into a swoon, and
we had much ado to get life into her.
SUSAN. Alas that she should bear so hard a fate;
Pity it is repentance comes too late.
SIR FRANCIS. Is she so weak in body?
JENKIN. O sir, I can assure you there's no help of life in her,
for she will take no sustenance. She hath plainly starved herself, and now she is as lean as a lath. She ever looks for the
good hour. Many gentlemen and gentlewomen of the country are come to comfort her.

(*Exeunt.*)

Scene 18

(ANNE's *bedchamber.* ANNE *in bed. Enter* SIR FRANCIS, SIR
CHARLES, CRANWELL, MALBY, SUSAN, JENKIN, *and*
CICELY.)

MALBY. How fare you, Mistress Frankford?
ANNE. Sick, sick, O sick! Give me some air I pray you.
Tell me, O tell me, where's Master Frankford?
Will not he deign to see me ere I die?
MALBY. Yes, Mistress Frankford. Divers* gentlemen,   several
Your loving neighbours, with that just request
Have moved* and told him of your weak estate,*   acted/condition
Who, though with much ado to get belief,
Examining of the general circumstance,*   situation
Seeing your sorrow and your penitence,
And hearing therewithal the great desire
You have to see him ere you left the world,
He gave to us his faith* to follow us,   promise
And sure he will be here immediately.
ANNE. You half revived me with the pleasing news.
Raise me a little higher in my bed.
Blush I not, brother Acton? Blush I not, Sir Charles?

Can you not read my fault writ in my cheek?
Is not my crime there? Tell me, gentlemen.
   SIR CHARLES. Alas, good mistress, sickness hath not left you
Blood in your face enough to make you blush.
   ANNE. Then sickness like a friend my fault would hide.
Is my husband come? My soul but tarries
His arrive* and I am fit for Heaven.   arrival
   SIR FRANCIS. I came to chide you, but my words of hate
Are turned to pity and compassionate grief;
I came to rate* you, but my brawls,* you see,   chide/scolding
Melt into tears, and I must weep by thee.

   (*Enter* FRANKFORD.)

Here's Master Frankford now.
   FRANKFORD. Good morrow, brother; good morrow, gentle-
   men.
God, that hath laid this cross upon our heads,
Might, had He pleased, have made our cause of meeting
On a more fair and a more contented ground;
But He that made us, made us to this woe.
   ANNE. And is he come? Methinks that voice I know.
   FRANKFORD. How do you, woman?
   ANNE. Well, Master Frankford, well; but shall be better
I hope within this hour. Will you vouchsafe,
Out of your grace and your humanity,
To take a spotted strumpet by the hand?
   FRANKFORD. That hand once held my heart in faster bonds
Than now 'tis gripped by me. God pardon them
That made us first break hold.
   ANNE.   Amen, amen.
Out of my zeal to Heaven, whither I am now bound,
I was so impudent to wish you here,
And once more beg your pardon. O good man,
And father to my children, pardon me.
Pardon, O pardon me! My fault so heinous is
That if you in this world forgive it not,
Heaven will not clear it in the world to come.
Faintness hath so usurped upon my knees
That kneel I cannot; but on my heart's knees
My prostrate soul lies thrown down at your feet
To beg your gracious pardon. Pardon, O pardon me!
   FRANKFORD. As freely from the low depth of my soul
As my Redeemer hath forgiven His death,

I pardon thee. I will shed tears for thee,
Pray with thee, and in mere* pity   absolute
Of thy weak state I'll wish to die with thee.
 ALL. So do we all.
 NICHOLAS (*aside*). So will not I;
I'll sigh and sob, but, by my faith, not die.
 SIR FRANCIS. O Master Frankford, all the near alliance
I lose by her shall be supplied in thee.
You are my brother by the nearest way;
Her kindred hath fallen off, but yours doth stay.
 FRANKFORD. Even as I hope for pardon at that day
When the Great Judge of Heaven in scarlet sits,
So be thou pardoned. Though thy rash offence
Divorced our bodies, thy repentant tears
Unite our souls.
 SIR CHARLES.   Then comfort, Mistress Frankford.
You see your husband hath forgiven your fall;
Then rouse your spirits and cheer your fainting soul.
 SUSAN. How is it with you?
 SIR FRANCIS.   How do you feel yourself?
 ANNE. Not of this world.
 FRANKFORD. I see you are not, and I weep to see it.
My wife, the mother of my pretty babes,
Both those lost names I do restore thee back,
And with this kiss I wed thee once again.
Though thou art wounded in thy honoured name,
And with that grief upon thy deathbed liest,
Honest* in heart, upon my soul, thou diest. chaste
 ANNE. Pardoned on earth, soul, thou in Heaven art free;
Once more thy wife, dies* thus embracing thee. that is, I die
 (*Dies.*)
 FRANKFORD. New married and new widowed! O, she's dead,
And a cold grave must be our nuptial bed.
 SIR CHARLES. Sir, be of good comfort, and your heavy sor-
  row
Part equally amongst us. Storms divided
Abate their force, and with less rage are guided.
 CRANWELL. Do, Master Frankford; he that hath least part
Will find enough to drown one troubled heart.
 SIR FRANCIS. Peace with thee, Nan. Brothers and gentlemen,
All we that can plead interest in her grief,
Bestow upon her body funeral tears.
Brother, had you with threats and usage bad
Punished her sin, the grief of her offence

Had not with such true sorrow touched her heart.

FRANKFORD. I see it had not; therefore on her grave
I will bestow this funeral epitaph,
Which on her marble tomb shall be engraved.
In golden letters shall these words* be filled: that is,
"Here lies she whom her husband's kindness killed."   the epitaph

Epilogue

An honest crew, disposed to be merry,
Came to a tavern by* and called for wine.   nearby
The drawer brought it, smiling like a cherry,
And told them it was pleasant, neat,* and fine.   pure
   "Taste it," quoth one. He did so. "Fie!" quoth he,
   "This wine was good; now 't runs too near the lee."

Another sipped, to give the wine his due,
And said unto the rest it drunk too flat.
The third said it was old, the fourth too new.
"Nay," quoth the fifth, "the sharpness likes me not."
   Thus, gentlemen, you see how in one hour
   The wine was new, old, flat, sharp, sweet, and sour.

Unto this wine we do allude* our play,   compare
Which some will judge too trivial, some too grave.
You as our guests we entertain this day
And bid you welcome to the best we have.
   Excuse us, then; good wine may be disgraced
   When every several* mouth hath sundry taste.   separate

Appendix

Glossary of Allusions

Chief source for all place names: *A Topographical Dictionary to the Works of Shakespeare and His Fellow Dramatists*, by Edward H. Sugden. Manchester Univ. Press, 1925.

Centuries not specifically identified as B.C. are to be understood as A.D.; thus, 1st century poet means 1st century *A.D.*

AESOP. A sixth-century B.C. Greek to whom a collection of fables—*Aesop's Fables*—came to be attributed.

ALDERSGATE STREET. Runs south from Aldersgate to Cheapside in London.

BILLINGSGATE. Chief of the old water-gates of London on north side of Thames east of London bridge.

BLACKFRIAR'S. Area and buildings on north bank of Thames, east of Water Lane, having the right of sanctuary.

DIANA. Goddess of the moon.

EDWARD VI. Son of Henry VIII, king of England 1547–1553.

ENDYMION. Mortal loved by the goddess Diana.

FLOWER-DE-LUCE. An inn in Feversham.

FLUSHING. Seaport in Holland.

FURIES. Three goddesses who punished by secret stings those who escaped or defied public justice.

HERCULES. Greek hero of great strength who killed his friend in a fit of madness.

HORNSBY. Cuckold.

HOUGH-MONDAY. Hock Monday, a festival day coming shortly after Easter.

HYDRA. A many-headed monster.

HYMEN. God of marriage.

MOUNT LATMUS. Where Diana fell in love with Endymion.

OSBRIDGE. Village in Kent a mile southwest of Feversham.

ROCHESTER. Village in Kent on the old pilgrim's road from London to Canterbury.

ST. PAUL'S. The Cathedral Church of London east of Ludgate Hill and west of Cheapside.

SHEPPY, ISLE OF. Island in Kent on south side of Thames estuary, just opposite to Feversham.

SHORLOW. Residence of Lord Cheiny in Kent, not far from Feversham.

SITTINBURGH. Town in Kent nine miles east of Feversham on the pilgrim's road to Canterbury.

SMITHFIELD. Open place near the Tower of London.

SOMERSET, DUKE OF, gave the lands of the Abbey of Feversham to Arden.

SOUTHWARK. Borough on the south side of the Thames in Surrey.

THAMES STREET runs along the north bank of the Thames from Blackfriars to the Tower.

TISIPHONE. One of the Furies.

THE SPANISH TRAGEDY

ACHERON. River in Hell.

ACHILLES. Greek hero in the Trojan War.

AEACUS. One of the judges in Hell.

AENEAS. Trojan hero, legendary first settler of Rome.

AENEID. The Latin epic poem by Virgil.

AETNA. Volcano in Sicily.

AJAX. Greek hero of Trojan War.

ALBION. England.

ALCIDES. Hercules.

APOLLO. Greek God of music and light, lord of the bow and of healing.

ARACHNE. Maiden skilled in weaving, changed to a spider by Minerva for daring to compete with her.

ARIADNE. Daughter of King Minos who helped Theseus slay the Minotaur.

ATHENA. Greek Goddess of wisdom.

AVERNUS. Lake at the entrance to Hell.

BELLONA. Goddess of war.

CERBERUS. Three-headed dog, guard of Hell.

CHAOS. Original confusion, personified by Greeks as the most ancient of the gods.

CHARON. Ferryman in Hell.

CHIMAERA. Fire-breathing monster.

CLAUDIAN. Fourth-century Latin poet.

CORSIC. Corsican.

CUPID. Child of Venus and God of love.

DIANA. Goddess of the chase.

DIDO. Queen of Carthage.

EDMUND, EARL OF KENT. Edmund Langley, Earl during the reign of Richard II.

ELYSIAN PLAINS. A favored land to which the blessed pass without dying.

EREBUS. Son of Chaos.

ERICHTHO. A Thessalian sorceress.

FLORA. Goddess of flowers.

FURIES. Three goddesses who punish by secret stings those who escape or defy public justice.

HECATE. Goddess of the dark of the moon and of evil magic.

HECTOR. Trojan champion in the Trojan War.

HERCULES. Greek hero of great strength.

HYMEN. God of marriage.

IXION. Punished in Hell by being lashed to a continuously turning wheel.

JOHN OF GAUNT. Duke of Lancaster, 1340–1399; son of Edward III.

JUNO. Wife of Jupiter, queen of the gods.

KING STEPHEN. King of England, 1135–1154.

MARSYAS. Inventor of the flute who challenged Apollo to a musical competition.

MINOS. One of the judges in Hell.

MYRMIDONS. Subjects of Achilles.

NEMESIS. Goddess of retribution.

ORPHEUS. Great musician, son of Apollo.

PALLAS. Son of Evander, slain by Turnus and avenged by Aeneas.

PALLAS ATHENE. Goddess of learning and wisdom.

PAN. God of nature and the universe.

PERGAMUS. Troy.

PHLEGETHON. River of fire in Hell.

PHOEBE. Goddess of the moon.

PLUTO. God of Hell.

PRIAM. King of Troy.

PROSERPINE. Goddess of Hell.

RHADAMANTH. One of the judges in Hell.

ROBERT, EARL OF GLOUCESTER. Earl at the time of King Stephen.

SARACEN. Name applied to the Mohammedans of Palestine against whom the Crusaders fought.

SCYLLA. Treacherous rock on the Italian coast; also the monster living on the rock.

SISYPHUS. Condemned in Hell to roll a huge rock uphill which rolled down again when he reached the top.

SOLIMON AND PERSEDA. Anonymous tragedy attributed to Kyd.

STYX. River bordering Hades to be crossed by all the dead.

TERCEIRA. Island in the Azores.

THESEUS. Legendary King of Athens and hero of many adventures.

THETIS. Sea goddess.

TITYUS. Giant in Hell.

VENUS. Goddess of beauty and love.

VESPER. The evening star.

VIRGIL. First-century B.C. Roman poet, author of the *Aeneid*.

WATSON, THOMAS. English neo-Latin poet, c1557–92.

FRIAR BACON AND FRIAR BUNGAY

AEOLUS. King of the Winds.

AESOP. 6th Century B.C. Greek, supposed author of a collection of fables.

AGENOR. Father of Europa.

ALBION. England.

ALCIMENA. Mother of Hercules by Jupiter.

ALMAIN. German.

APHRODITE. Greek goddess of beauty and love.

APOLLO. Greek god of music, light, and truth, whose oracle at Delphi answered questions.

ARES. Greek god of war.

ARTEMIS. Courtly aspect of the moon goddess.

ASMENOTH. Infernal god.

ASPASIA. Greek courtesan, noted for her wisdom, who became the mistress of Pericles.

BABEL (BABYLON). Ancient city on the Euphrates, capital of Mesopotamia.

BARCLAY. Translator of Brandt's *Ship of Fools.*

BECCLES. Town in Suffolk 109 miles northeast of London.

BELCEPHON. Infernal god.

BOCARDO. A prison in Oxford.

BOREAS. The north wind.

BROADGATES HALL. College at Oxford for students of law.

BRUTES. Britons; from Brutus of Troy, legendary first king of Britain.

CANDIA. Crete.

CRATFIELD. Village in Suffolk.

CYRUS. Sixth-century B.C. founder of the Persian Empire.

DAMASCUS. Ancient city in Syria.

DANAE. Mother of Perseus by Jupiter.

DAPHNE. Maiden loved by Apollo and changed into a laurel tree.

DEMOGORGON. A fearful and mysterious god or demon of the underworld.

DIANA. Virgin goddess of the moon and the chase.

DOVER. Chief of the Cinque Ports on the English channel.

EUPHRATES. Asian river supposed to rise in the Garden of Eden.

EUROPA. Phoenician princess carried off by Zeus, who had taken the form of a white bull.

EXCHEQUER collects and administers royal revenues; located in Westminster.

GIHON. One of the rivers of Paradise.

HAMPTON COURT. Palace on the north bank of the Thames, fifteen miles west of London.

HAPSBURG. *i.e.,* Germany.

HECATE. Goddess of the dark of the moon and of evil magic; the underworld aspect of Artemis.

HELEN. Wife of Menelaus of Sparta; her elopement with Paris began the Trojan War.

HENLEY. Town in Oxfordshire on the north bank of the Thames, west of London.

HERA. Wife of Zeus and queen of the Greek gods.

HERCULES. Greek hero of great strength.

HERMES TRISMEGISTUS. Founder of alchemy and other occult sciences.

HESPERIAN. Used as adjective of Hesperides.

HESPERIDES. Name commonly given by Elizabethans to gardens where Hera's golden apples were guarded.

JOVE. Chief deity of gods.

JUDGMENT OF PARIS. Paris awarded a golden apple inscribed "To the fairest" to Venus.

JUNO. Roman name for queen of the gods.

LATONA. Mother of Apollo.

LAXFIELD. Village in Suffolk about ninety miles northeast of London.

LEMPSTER. Town in Herefordshire famous for the quality of its wool.

LUCIFER. Name for Satan before his fall.

LUCIUS TARQUINIUS COLLATINUS. Sixth century B.C., last of the old kings of Rome.

LUCRETIA. In revenge for her rape, the family of Tarquins were exiled and Roman government changed from kings to consuls.

LUNA. Goddess of the moon.

LYNCEUS. Argonaut famed for his sharp eyesight.

MARS. God of war and lover of Venus.

MELCHIE, PORPHYRY (MALCHUS). A neo-Platonist.

MERCURY (HERMES). Messenger of the gods.

MORPHEUS. Son of sleep and god of dreams.

NEPTUNE. Greek god of the sea.

NINUS. Legendary founder of Nineveh and the Assyrian Empire.

OCEANUS. Titan who ruled the element of water.

OENONE. Beloved of Paris before he abandoned her for Helen.

OXFORD. Great English university northwest of London.

PALLAS ATHENE. Goddess of wisdom and learning.

PARIS. Prince of Troy; he eloped with Helen of Sparta.

PHOBETOR. Son of Morpheus.

PHOEBUS. Another name for Apollo.

PLANTAGENET. Ruling family of England in the middle ages.

PYREN MOUNTS. Pyrenees, high mountains dividing France and Spain.

PYTHAGORAS. Sixth-century B.C. Greek philosopher and mathematician.

ROSCIUS. Famous actor of ancient Rome.

RYE. One of Cinque Ports, thirty miles southwest of Dover.

SAINT JAMES' DAY. July 25.

SARACEN. Name applied to Mohammedans of Palestine against whom the Crusaders fought.

SELENE. Moon; heavenly aspect of Artemis.

SEMELE. Mother of Bacchus by Zeus.

SEMIRAMIS. Legendary Babylonian queen and wife of Ninus.

SEXTUS TARQUINIUS. Son of Tarquin; he raped Lucretia.

SUFFOLK. Agricultural county on east coast of England.

THETIS. Mother of Achilles.

TROYNOVANT. London (*see* Brutes).

VENUS. Goddess of love and beauty.

VESTA. Goddess of the hearth.

WINDSOR. Town in Berkshire; site of Windsor Castle, a royal residence.

DOCTOR FAUSTUS

ACHERON. River of woe, one of the rivers bounding the underworld.

ACHILLES. Greek champion of the Trojan War.

ACTEON. Huntsman who saw Diana bathing, was changed by her to a stag and killed by his own dogs.

ADRIAN IV, V. The only English pope (1154–59).

AGRIPPA. Henry Cornelius Agrippa von Nettesheim (1486–1535), humanist and reputed magician.

ALBERTUS MAGNUS. German Dominican philosopher and scientist, 1193–1280.

ALEXANDER (PARIS). Name Homer often calls Paris, the lover of Oenone and Helen.

ALEXANDER III. Pope 1159–81.

ALMAINE. German.

ALPHEUS. River god pursuing Arethusa, who escaped by being changed to a fountain.

AMPHION. Son of Zeus, musician and king of Thebes; he fortified his city by moving rocks into a wall by his music.

ANTWERPE BRIDGE. Built by Parma to complete the blockade of Antwerp and shattered by a fireship, April 1585.

APOLLO (PHOEBUS). God of music, light, truth, lord of the bow and of healing.

ARETHUSA. Nymph of Artemis, changed to a fountain.

ARISTOTLE. Fourth-century B.C. Greek philosopher, author of *Analytics,* two works on proof in argument.

ARTEMIS (DIANA). Virgin goddess of the moon and the chase.

ASTEROTH. Astarte, Phoenician goddess of moon, fertility and love.

BACON, Roger. Thirteenth-century English Franciscan philosopher interested in experimental science.

BELIMOTH. Possibly Behemoth, in the Bible the name of a great beast.

BELZEBUB. Chief devil, Satan.

CARMEN DE PULICE. Late Latin poem falsely ascribed to Ovid.

CARTHEGENS. Carthagenians, led by Hannibal in his attempt to conquer Rome.

CHARLES V. Holy Roman Emperor, 1519–56.

COLOSSUS. Gigantic statue, especially one at harbor of Rhodes.

COUNCIL OF TRENT. Church Council (1545–1563) held to condemn the Reformation and to undertake Catholic reform.

DARDANIA. Name often given to Troy.

DELPHIAN ORACLE. A shrine sacred to Apollo; as the reputed center of the world it was frequented by pilgrims.

DIANA (ARTEMIS). Virgin goddess of the moon and the chase.

DIS (PLUTO, HADES). God of the underworld.

ELYSIUM. A happy land where favored heroes pass when dying.

EMDEN. Port in northwest Germany, headquarters of Europe's largest merchant fleet in the sixteenth century.

FURIES (ERINNYES). Three goddesses who punished by secret stings those who escaped or defied public justice.

GALEN. Second-century Greek physician and writer.

HECATE. Goddess of the dark of the moon, of the place where three roads meet, of evil magic.

HOMER. Greek epic poet, ca. eighth century B.C., author of the oldest extant Greek writings, *The Iliad* and *The Odyssey*.

JEROME. Fourth-century monk and church scholar, author of the Latin translation of the Bible called the Vulgate.

JOVE (ZEUS, JUPITER). Chief god of Greek and Roman mythology: lord of the sky, man, clouds, and the thunderbolt.

JUPITER. Largest planet in solar system, completes orbit in 11.86 years.

JUSTINIAN. Sixth-century Byzantine Emperor who codified the Roman law.

LOLLARD. Member of group of political and religious reformers of fourteenth- and fifteenth-century England, followers of John Wyclif.

LUCIFER (LIGHT-BRINGER). Satan as the leader of the revolt of the angels before his fall.

MARO, PUBLIUS VERGILIUS. Roman poet (70–19 B.C.), author of an *Aeneid*, buried in Naples.

MARS. Planet in solar system, completes orbit in 686.9 days.

MARTINMAS. November 11, customary time for slaughter of cattle for winter consumption.

MENELAUS. King of Sparta, husband of Helen.

MERCURY. Smallest planet in solar system, completes orbit in 88 days.

MUSAEUS. Legendary Greek poet and pupil of Orpheus.

MUSES. Nine Greek goddesses who presided over literature, art, and science.

OENON. Oenone, a nymph loved by Paris before he abandoned her for Helen.

OLYMPUS. Greek mountain on top of which was the home of the gods.

ORION. A constellation; a sign of stormy weather when it rises late.

OVID. First-century Roman poet, author of *Metamorphoses*.

PARIS. Prince of Troy. The Trojan war began when he eloped with Helen.

PENELOPE. Wife of Odysseus, who put off all suitors for twenty years waiting for his return.

PHLEGETHON. River of fire, one of the rivers bounding the underworld.

PONTE ANGELO. Bridge in Rome; the castle by it.

PRINCE OF PARMA. Spanish governor-general of the Netherlands (1579–92), foremost soldier of his time.

PURGATORY. State or place of suffering for sins.

PYTHAGORAS OF SAMOS. *C.* sixth century B.C., regarded as author of the doctrine of the transmigration of souls.

RHODE. Roda (Stadtroda), town in central Germany.

SABA. Queen of Sheba who came to hear the wisdom of Solomon.

SATURN. Second-largest planet in solar system, completes its orbit in 29.5 years.

ST. MARK'S. Church in Venice.

SEMELE. She asked Zeus to appear to her in his divine splendor and was consumed by his radiance.

SEVEN DEADLY SINS. Pride, avarice, lust, anger, gluttony, envy, and sloth; causing spiritual death.

SIGISMOND. Holy Roman Emperor, 1411–37.

STYX. One of the rivers bounding the underworld.

THEBES. Grecian city, the walls of which were built by the music of Amphion's lyre.

THRASINEN. Lake Trasimeno in central Italy, scene of a victory by Hannibal over the Romans, 217 B.C.

VIRGIL. Publius Vergilius Maro, Roman poet (70–19 B.C.), author of the *Aeneid*.

WYCLIF, JOHN. English religious reformer, 1320–84; first translator of the Bible into English.

EDWARD II

ACHILLES. Greek champion of the Trojan War.

ACTAEON. Huntsman who saw Diana bathing, was changed by her into a stag and killed by his own dogs.

ALCIBIADES. Friend of Socrates, general in Peloponnesian War.

ALEXANDER. Fourth-century B.C. conqueror and King of Macedonia.

APHRODITE. Greek goddess of beauty and love.

ARGO. Built Jason's ship for the quest of the Golden Fleece.

ARISTARCHUS. Alexandrian grammarian.

ARISTOTLE. Fourth-century B.C. Greek philosopher.

ATLAS. Titan condemned by Zeus to hold up the heavens.

CATILINE. Roman politician and conspirator, first century B.C.

CAUCASUS. Mountain range in Southeastern Europe.

CHARON. Ferryman in the underworld.

CHIRKE. Village in Denbighshire, Wales.

CIRCE. Goddess and enchantress who changed men into beasts.

CYCLOP. Giant with only one eye in the middle of his forehead.

DANAE. Mother of Perseus by Jupiter; she was locked up by her father to keep her unwed.

DIAN, DIANA. Virgin goddess of the moon and the chase.

ELYSIUM. Favored land, to which the blessed pass without dying.

FABYAN. Author of an English historical tract known as Fabyan's *Chronicle* (1516).

FURIES. Three goddesses who punished by secret stings those who escaped public justice.

GANYMEDE. Beautiful youth carried off to Olympus by Jove to be his cupbearer.

HELEN. Wife of Menelaus of Sparta; her elopement with Paris began the Trojan War.

HEPHESTION. Friend of Alexander the Great.

HERCULES. Hero of great strength, one of the heroes accompanying Jason on the Argosy.

HERO. Priestess of Aphrodite loved by Leander.

HYLAS accompanied Hercules on the Argosy; he was carried off by nymphs when he went ashore for water.

HYMEN. Roman god of marriage.

IRIS. Goddess of the rainbow, messenger of Hera and Zeus.

JOVE. Supreme god of Roman mythology.

LAMBETH. City residence of the Archbishop of Canterbury.

LEANDER swam the Hellespont nightly to visit his beloved, Hero.

MERCURY. Messenger of the gods.

MIDAS. Legendary king whose touch turned everything to gold.

NEW TEMPLE. Piece of land in London between the west end of Fleet Street and the Thames, belonging to the Knights Templar.

OCTAVIUS. Friend of Cicero.

OVID. First-century Roman poet, author of *Metamorphoses*.

PATROCLUS. Friend of Achilles.

PERSEUS. Hero who killed the Medusa and rescued Andromeda.

PHAETON. Son of Helios, struck down by Zeus as he drove the sun chariot too close to earth.

PHOEBUS. God of light (Apollo).

PLATO. Fifth-century B.C. Greek philosopher.

PLUTO. God of the underworld.

PROTEUS. Sea god who could change his own form at will.

SENECA. Roman statesman, writer, and Stoic philosopher, 4 B.C.–65 A.D.

THYESTES. Brother of Atreus and son of Pelops.

TIBER. River flowing through Rome.

TISIPHONE. One of the Furies.

TOWER OF LONDON. Complex of buildings on the Thames including a jail for political prisoners.

TULLY. Cicero. Roman orator.

VULCAN. God of fire and the forge.

ZEUS. Chief Greek god.

EVERY MAN IN HIS HUMOUR

ALEPPO, BATTLE OF. Won by the Turks in 1516.

APOLLO. Greek god of music.

ARTHUR. Legendary king of England and hero of many romances.

ARTILLERY-GARDEN. Training ground for Honorable Artillery Company.

BALSAMUM. An herb.

BEVIS. Knight in the Arthurian legends.

BEY, ISKANDER. Another name for the Albanian patriot Castriota.

BRIDEWELL. The workhouse.

BURGILLION. Bully.

CAESAR, JULIUS. First-century B.C. Roman statesman and general.

CARRANZA, JERONIMO DE. Author of *The Philosophy of Arms.*

CASTRIOTA, GEORGE. Albanian patriot.

COLEMAN ST. London street, a haunt of puritans.

COPHETUA. Legendary king proud of his wealth.

COUNTERS. Debtors' prisons.

DANIEL, SAMUEL. English poet, 1562–1619.

"DELIA." Sonnet series by Samuel Daniel.

DURINDANA. Sword of Orlando in the romances.

EMBER-WEEKS. Days of prayer and fasting occurring in each of four seasons.

EXCALIBUR. Sword of Arthur.

EXCHANGE. Place of business and the changing of foreign coins.

FRIDAYS, VILLANOUS. No meat was eaten on Fridays.

GENOWAYS. Genoese.

GOLDEN HIND. Sir Francis Drake's ship.

GREEN LATTICE. A tavern.

HERO. Priestess of Aphrodite loved by Leander.

"HERO AND LEANDER." Poem by Christopher Marlowe.

HESPERIAN DRAGON guarded the golden apples belonging to the goddess Hera.

HESPERINE. Western.

HIERONIMO. Protagonist of *The Spanish Tragedy.*

HORACE. First-century B.C. Roman poet.

HOSPITAL. Christ's Hospital, London school.

HOUNSDITCH. Area in London frequented by dealers in old clothes.

HUMOURS. From medieval physiology, the four fluids considered responsible for one's health and disposition (by the 1590's the term was used to explain any eccentricity of character).

Fluid	*Disposition resulting from an excess of this fluid*
Yellow bile	choleric
Blood	sanguine
Phlegm	phlegmatic
Black bile	melancholic

JUPITER. Chief god of Greek and Roman deities.

JUVENAL. First-century Roman satirical poet.

LANCASTER, HOUSE OF. Ruling family of England (1399–1461), fought in Wars of the Roses (1455–85).

LEANDER. Swam the Hellespont nightly to visit his beloved, Hero.

MILE-END. Training ground for militia outside London.

MOORFIELDS. Marshy area.

MORGLAY. Sword of Bevis in the romances.

MUSES. Goddess who presided over literature, the arts and sciences: Calliope, epic poetry; Clio, history; Euterpe, lyric poetry; Melpomene, tragedy; Terpsichore, choral dance; Erato, love poetry; Polyhymnia, sacred poetry; Urania, astronomy; Thalia, comedy.

NICOT, JACQUES, introduced tobacco into France in 1560.

ORLANDO. Hero of *Orlando Furioso,* a romance by Ariosto.

PHARAOH, foot of. A mild oath; Pharaoh was the title of rulers of ancient Egypt.

PHLEGON. One of the horses of the sun.

PICT-HATCH. Haunt of prostitutes in London.

PLINY THE YOUNGER. Roman statesman and writer, 62–113.

PRECISIAN. Puritan.

QUINTILIAN. First-century Roman rhetorician and critic.

ST. GEORGE. Patron saint of England.

ST. JOHN'S WORT. An herb.

SANCTO DOMINGO. Country in the West Indies.

SATURN. Titan, father of Jupiter.

SHOREDITCH. Disreputable part of London.

SPITTLE. Hospital for venereal diseases.

STRIGONIUM. Town in Hungary.

SYMMACHUS. Fourth-century Roman orator.

THESPIAN GIRLS. The Muses.

TOLEDO. City in Spain famous for its fine sword blades.

TOWER OF LONDON. Series of buildings including a castle and a prison.

TRINIDADO. Trinidad was the source of the best tobacco.

TRUNDLE, MASTER JOHN. Publisher of ballads.

TURKEY COMPANY. Chartered in 1581 for trade in the Levant.

TURNBULL. Disreputable quarter of London.

VIENNA, relief of. Vienna was unsuccessfully besieged by the Turks in 1529.

VIRGIL. First-century B.C. Roman poet, author of the *Aeneid*.

WHITECHAPEL. Parish east of Aldgate, a resort of thieves and prostitutes.

WINDMILL. A tavern.

YORK, HOUSE OF. Ruling family of England, 1461–85; fought in civil war with House of Lancaster.

THE SHOEMAKER'S HOLIDAY

APOLLO. Greek god, type of manly youth and beauty.
ASSYRIANS. Fanciful name Simon gives his workers.
BEDLAM. Bethlehem hospital for the insane in London.
BOAR'S HEAD. Tavern at the west end of Eastcheap.
CAPPADOCIANS. Fanciful name Simon gives his workers.
DIEPPE. Port in northern France on the English Channel.
DIOCLESIAN. Roman emperor.
EASTCHEAP. London street, a flesh market of butchers.
FINSBURY. Practice ground for archers.
FLEET STREET. London street running west from bottom of Ludgate Hill to Temple Bar, site of many taverns and shops, including shoemakers' shops.
GARGANTUA. The giant king of Rabelais' *Gargantua and Pantagruel.*
GRACIOUS STREET. Originally Grass Street, running south from the juncture of Cornhill and Leadenhall to Eastcheap.
GUILDHALL. Common hall of the City of London, place of the Lord Mayor's banquet November 9.
HAMBOROW. Hamburg, Germany.
HECTOR. Trojan champion in the Trojan War.
HERCULES. Greek hero of great strength.
IVY LANE. London street running north from Paternoster Row to Newgate Street.
JERONIMO. Protagonist of *The Spanish Tragedy.*
JUDAS. Betrayer of Christ.
LONDON STONE. Roman mile stone in Cannon Street.
MARS IN VENUS. Position of the planet Mars.
MEPHISTOPHILUS. Satan.
MESOPOTAMIANS. Fanciful name Simon gives his workers.
MILE-END. Training ground for militia outside London.
MINERVA. Roman goddess of wisdom.
MOTHER BUNCH. Ale.
PAUL'S CROSS. Tops St. Paul's Cathedral in London.
PHARAOH. Title of rulers of ancient Egypt.
PORTUGUESE. Coins.
PRINCE ARTHUR. Legendary king of England in the romances.

ST. FAITH'S CHURCH. Chapel in the crypt of St. Paul's Cathedral in London.

ST. GEORGE'S DAY. April 23, the servingmen's holiday.

ST. MARTIN'S. Parish of St. Martin's Le Grand, notorious for the sale of cheap clothes and boots.

ST. MARY OVERY. Church on the south bank of the Thames, near London Bridge.

SAVOY. A hospital whose chapel was constantly used for the celebration of irregular marriages.

SHROVE TUESDAY. Day before Lent begins.

STRATFORD-BOW. Suburb of London on the Lea northeast of St. Paul's.

SULTAN SOLIMAN. Character in the anonymous play *Soliman and Perseda*.

TAMBURLAINE. Mongol warrior.

TERMAGANT. Violent god in the miracle plays.

TIMUR. Tamburlaine.

TOTHILL-FIELDS. Tuttle Fields, a large piece of open land in Westminster, on the left bank of the Thames; training ground for troops and archers.

TOWER STREET. London street running west from Tower Hill to Eastcheap.

WATHING STREET. Watling Street near St. Paul's churchyard; inhabited by wealthy drapers.

WHITECHAPEL. Parish in London east of Aldgate; many shoemakers' shops were here.

WOOLSACK. Tavern in London outside Aldgate, famous for its pies.

A WOMAN KILLED WITH KINDNESS

ANGEL. Monetary unit, gold coin depicting the archangel Michael; in use from 1465 through the 1640's.

BEDLAM. Bethlehem Hospital, famous London insane asylum.

"THE BEGINNING OF THE WORLD." Popular Elizabethan dance tune.

BOOK OF LIFE. Mentioned in the Bible as listing those intended for the joys of eternal life.

CAIN. First son of Adam and Eve, slayer of his brother Abel.

CRIPPLEGATE. City gate in north London.

DIVES. Rich man sent to Hell in the parable of Dives and Lazarus (Luke, XVI:19-31).

"THE HAY." Popular Elizabethan rustic dance.

"JOHN, COME KISS ME NOW." Popular Elizabethan dance tune.

JUDAS. Judas Iscariot, the disciple who betrayed Jesus.

LAZARUS. Poor beggar sent to heaven in the parable of Dives and Lazarus.

ORPHEUS. Thracian prince, gifted in music, who descended to the underworld to bring back his wife Eurydice.

PURITAN. Member of the Puritan sect; by extension, one with a strict sense of morality.

"PUT ON YOUR SMOCK A MONDAY." Popular Elizabethan dance tune.

"SELLENGER'S ROUND." Popular Elizabethan dance tune.

"TOM TYLER." Popular Elizabethan dance tune.

TROJAN. Slang for a drunkard.

A Selected Bibliography

GENERAL

Bentley, Gerald E., *The Jacobean and Caroline Stage*, 7 vols., Oxford, 1941-68.

————, *The Profession of the Dramatist in Shakespeare's Time, 1590-1642*, Princeton, 1971.

Bradbrook, M.C., *The Rise of the Common Player*, London, 1962.

Campbell, Lily B., *Scenes and Machines on the English Stage during the Renaissance*, Cambridge, Mass., 1923.

Carson, Neil, *A Companion to Henslowe's Diary*, Cambridge and New York, 1988.

Chambers, E. K., *The Elizabethan Stage*, 4 vols., Oxford, 1923.

Cook, Ann Jennalie, *The Privileged Playgoers of Shakespeare's London, 1576-1642*, Princeton, 1981.

Dessen, Alan C., *Elizabethan Stage Conventions and Modern Interpreters*, Cambridge, 1984.

Gair, Reavley, *The Children of Paul's: The Story of a Theatre Company, 1553-1608*, Cambridge, 1982.

Gildersleeve, Virginia C., *Government Regulation of the Elizabethan Drama*, New York, 1908.

Greg, W. W., *A Bibliography of the English Printed Drama to the Restoration*, 4 vols., London, 1939-1959.

Griswold, Wendy, *Renaissance Revivals: City Comedy and Revenge Tragedy in the London Theatre 1576-1980*, Chicago and London, 1986.

Gurr, Andrew, *Playgoing in Shakespeare's London*, Cambridge and New York, 1987.

Harbage, A., *Annals of English Drama 975-1700*, rev. by S. Schoenbaum, London, 1964.

Harrison, G. B., *The Story of Elizabethan Drama*, New York, 1924.

Hodges, C. W., *The Globe Restored, A Study of the Elizabethan Theatre*, London, 1953.

Joseph, B. L., *Elizabethan Acting*, London, 1951.

Knights, L. C., *Drama and Society in the Age of Jonson*, London, 1937.

Lawrence, W. J., *The Physical Conditions of the Elizabethan Public Playhouse*, Cambridge, 1927.

_____, *The Elizabethan Playhouse and Other Studies*, 2 vols., Stratford-upon-Avon, 1912-13.

Leggatt, Alexander, *Citizen Comedy in the Age of Shakespeare*, Toronto, 1973.

Levin, Richard, *The Multiple Plot in English Renaissance Drama*, Chicago and London, 1971.

Linthicum, M. C., *Costume in the Drama of Shakespeare and His Contemporaries*, Oxford, 1936.

Logan, Terence P. and Denzell S. Smith, eds., *The Popular School: A Survey and Bibliography of Recent Studies in English Renaissance Drama*, Lincoln, Nebr., 1975.

_____, *The Predecessors of Shakespeare: A Survey and Bibliography of Recent Studies in English Renaissance Drama*, Lincoln, Nebr., 1973.

Nungezer, Edwin, *A Dictionary of Actors and of Other Persons Associated with the Public Representation of Plays in England Before 1642*, New Haven, 1929.

Revels History of Drama in English, The, Vol. 3: 1576-1613, eds. J. Leeds Barroll, Alexander Leggatt, Richard Hosley and Alvin Kernan, London, 1975.

Reynolds, G. F., *The Staging of Elizabethan Plays at the Red Bull Theater 1605-1625*, New York and London, 1940.

Rhodes, Ernest L., *Henslowe's Rose: The Stage and Staging*, Lexington, Ky., 1976.

Rose, Mary Beth, *The Expense of Spirit: Love and Sexuality in English Renaissance Drama*, Ithaca, N.Y., 1988.

Shapiro, Michael, *Children of the Revels: The Boy Companies of Shakespeare's Time and Their Plays*, New York, 1977.

Sisson, C. J., *The Boar's Head Theatre*, London, 1972.

Smith, Irwin, *Shakespeare's Blackfriars Playhouse*, New York, 1964.

Wells, Stanley, ed., *English Drama (excluding Shakespeare)*, London, 1975.

Welsford, E., *The Court Masque: A Study in the Relationship between Poetry and the Revels*, Cambridge, 1927.

PLAYWRIGHTS
Ashley, Leonard R. N., *George Peele*, New York, 1970.

Baines, Barbara J., *Thomas Heywood*, Boston, 1984.

Bamborough, J. B., *Ben Jonson*, London and New York, 1959.

Barish, Jonas A., *Ben Jonson and the Language of Prose Comedy*, Cambridge, Mass., 1960.

Barton, Anne, *Ben Jonson, Dramatist*, Cambridge and New York, 1984.

Baskervill, C. R., *English Elements in Jonson's Early Comedies*, Austin, Texas, 1911.

Baum, Helen W., *The Satiric and Didactic in Ben Jonson's Comedy*, Chapel Hill, N. C., 1947.

Boas, Frederick S., *Christopher Marlowe: A Biographical and Critical Study*, Oxford, 1940.

Bowers, Fredson, ed., *Elizabethan Dramatists (Dictionary of Literary Biography*, Vol. 62), Detroit, 1987.

Clarke, A. M., *Thomas Heywood*, Oxford, 1931.

Cromwell, O., *Thomas Heywood*, New Haven, Conn., 1928.

Crupi, Charles W., *Robert Greene*, Boston, 1986.

Ellis-Fermor, U. N., *Christopher Marlowe*, London, 1927.

Enck, John, *Jonson and the Comic Truth*, Madison, Wis., 1957.

Feuillerat, A., *John Lyly*, Cambridge, 1910.

Freeman, Arthur, *Thomas Kyd: Facts and Problems*, Oxford, 1967.

Henderson, Philip, *Christopher Marlowe*, London, 1952.

Hunt, Mary L., *Thomas Dekker*, New York, 1911.

Jacquot, J., *George Chapman*, Paris, 1951.

Jordan, J. C., *Robert Greene*, New York, 1915.

Kernan, Alvin B., *Two Renaissance Mythmakers: Christopher Marlowe and Ben Jonson*, Baltimore and London, 1977.

Kocher, P. H., *Christopher Marlowe*, Chapel Hill, N. C., 1946.

Leech, Clifford, *Christopher Marlowe: Poet for the Stage*, New York, 1986.

Leggatt, Alexander, *Ben Jonson: His Vision and His Art*, London and New York, 1981.

Marlowe, Christopher, *Doctor Faustus: A Conjectural Reconstruction*, ed. W. W. Greg, London, 1950.

Marlowe Issue, *Tulane Drama Review*, vol. VIII, number 4, Summer 1964.

Miles, Rosalind, *Ben Jonson: His Life and Work*, London and New York, 1986.

Murray, Peter B., *Thomas Kyd*, New York, 1969.

Partridge, E. B., *The Broken Compass, A Study of the Major Comedies of Ben Jonson*, New York, 1958.

Rowse, A. L., *Christopher Marlowe: His Life and Work*, New York and London, 1964.

Wilson, John Dover, *John Lyly*, Cambridge, 1905.

PLAYS

Boas, Frederick S., *The Works of Thomas Kyd*, Oxford, 1901.

Bond, R. W., ed, *The Complete Works of John Lyly*, 3 vols., Oxford, 1902.

Bowers, Fredson, ed., *The Complete Works of Christopher Marlowe*, 2 vols., Cambridge, 1973.

_____, *The Dramatic Works of Thomas Dekker*, 4 vols., Cambridge, 1953-61.

Case, R. H., general ed., *The Works and Life of Christopher Marlowe*, 6 vols., London, 1930-33.

Collins, J. C., ed., *The Plays and Poems of Robert Greene*, 2 vols., Oxford, 1905.

Herford, C. H. and P. Simpson, *Ben Jonson*, 8 vols., Oxford, 1925-47.

Kuriyama, Constance Brown, "Dr. Greg and *Doctor Faustus*: The Supposed Originality of the 1616 Text," *English Literary Renaissance* 5 (Spring, 1975), 171-97.

Ribner, Irving, ed., *The Complete Plays of Christopher Marlowe*, New York, 1963.

Shepherd, R. H., ed., *The Dramatic Works of Thomas Heywood*, 6 vols., London, 1874.

Warren, Michael J., "*Dr. Faustus*: The Old Man and the Text," *English Literary Renaissance* 11(Spring 1981), 111-47.

CRITICISM

Adams, Henry Hitch, *English Domestic or Homiletic Tragedy: 1575 to 1642*, New York, 1943.

Allen, Don Cameron, ed., *Studies in Honor of T. W. Baldwin*, Urbana, Ill., 1958.

Bakeless, J., *The Tragical History of Christopher Marlowe*, 2 vols., Cambridge, 1942.

Baker, Howard, *Induction to Tragedy: A Study in a Development of Form in Gorboduc, The Spanish Tragedy, and Titus Andronicus*, Baton Rouge, La., 1939.

Barber, C. L., *Creating Elizabethan Tragedy*, Chicago and London, 1988.

_____, *The Idea of Honour in the English Drama 1591-1700*, Göteborg, 1957.

Bennett, Josephine, and others, *Studies in English Renaissance Drama*, New York, 1959.

Bevington, David M., *From Mankind to Marlowe: Growth of Structure in the Popular Drama of Tudor England*, Cambridge, Mass., 1962.

_____, *Tudor Drama and Politics: A Critical Approach to Topical Meaning*, Cambridge, Mass., 1968.

Bloom, Harold, ed., *Christopher Marlowe*, New York, New Haven, and Philadelphia, 1986.

Boas, Frederick S., *An Introduction to Tudor Drama*, Oxford, 1933.

_____, *Queen Elizabeth in Drama and Related Studies*, London, 1950.

_____, *Thomas Heywood*, London, 1950.

Bowers, F. T., *Elizabethan Revenge Tragedy 1587-1642*, Princeton, 1940.

Bradbrook, M. C., *The Growth and Structure of Elizabethan Comedy*, London, 1955.

_____, *Themes and Conventions of Elizabethan Tragedy*, Cambridge, 1935.

Braden, Gordon, *Renaissance Tragedy and the Senecan Tradition*, New Haven and London, 1985.

Brooke, C. F. T., *The Tudor Drama*, Boston, 1911.

Campbell, Oscar J., *Comical Satyre*, San Marino, Calif., 1938.

Carrère, F., *Le Théâtre de Thomas Kyd*, Toulouse, 1951.

Champion, Larry S., *Thomas Dekker and the Tradition of English Drama*, New York, 1985.

Cheffaud, P. H., *George Peele*, Paris, 1913.

Clemen, Wolfgang, *English Tragedy before Shakespeare: The Development of Dramatic Speech*, New York, 1961.

Cohen, Walter, *Drama of a Nation: Public Theater in Renaissance England and Spain*, 1985.

Cole, Douglas, *Suffering and Evil in the Plays of Christopher Marlowe*, Princeton, 1962.

Creizenach, Wilhelm, *The English Drama in the Age of Shakespeare*, London and Philadelphia, 1916.

Cunliffe, J. W., *The Influence of Seneca on Elizabethan Tragedy*, London, 1893.

Curry, John V., *Deception in Elizabethan Comedy*, Chicago, 1955.

Cust, Lionel, *Arden of Feversham*, London, 1920.

Davis, Herbert and Helen Gardner, eds., *Elizabethan and Jacobean Studies Presented to Frank Percy Wilson in Honour of His Seventieth Birthday*, Oxford, 1959.

Dessen, Alan C., *Jonson's Moral Comedy*, Evanston, Ill., 1971.

Dollimore, Jonathan, *Radical Tragedy: Religion, Ideology and Power in the Drama of Shakespeare and His Contemporaries*, Chicago, 1984.

Doran, M., *Endeavors of Art: A Study of Form in Elizabethan Drama*, Madison, Wis., 1954.

Eliot, T. S., *Essays on Elizabethan Drama*, New York, 1956.

Farnham, W., *The Medieval Heritage of Elizabethan Tragedy*, Berkeley, Calif., 1936.

Gassner, John, *Masters of the Drama*, New York, 1940, 1954.

Gregg, K. L., *Thomas Dekker*, Seattle, 1924.

Grivelet, Michel, *Thomas Heywood et le Drame domestique élisabéthain*, Paris, 1957.

Hallett, Charles and Elaine, *The Revenger's Madness: A Study of Revenge Tragedy*, Lincoln, Nebr., 1980.

Harrison, G. B., *Elizabethan Plays and Players*, Ann Arbor, Mich., 1956.

Hattaway, Michael, *Elizabethan Popular Theatre: Plays in Performance*, London, 1982.

Horne, D. H., *The Life and Minor Works of George Peele*, vol. I, New Haven, 1952.

Jardine, Lisa, *Still Harping on Daughters: Women and Drama in the Age of Shakespeare*, Brighton, Sussex and Totowa, N. J., 1983.

Jeffrey, Violet M., *John Lyly and the Italian Renaissance*, Paris, 1928.

Jewkes, W. T., *Act Division in Elizabethan and Jacobean Plays 1583-1616*, Hamden, Conn., 1958.

Johnson, Marilyn L., *Images of Women in the Works of Thomas Heywood*, Salzburg, 1974.

Kiefer, Frederick, *Fortune and Elizabethan Tragedy*, San Marino, Calif., 1983.

Koszul, A., ed., *The Shoemaker's Holiday: Fête chez le Cordonnier*, Collection du Théâtre de la Renaissance, Paris, 1955.

Kuriyama, Constance Brown, *Hammer or Anvil: Psychological Patterns in Christopher Marlowe's Plays*, New Brunswick, N. J., 1980.

Lea, K. M., *Italian Popular Comedy: A Study in the Commedia dell'arte, 1560-1620 with Special Reference to the English Stage*, 2 vols., Oxford, 1934.

Levin, H., *The Overreacher*, Cambridge, Mass., 1952.

Lucas, F. L., *Seneca and Elizabethan Tragedy*, Cambridge, 1922.

Mackenzier, A. M., *The Playgoer's Handbook to the English Renaissance Drama*, London, 1927.

McAlindon, T., *English Renaissance Tragedy*, Vancouver, 1986.

McManaway, James G., and others, *Joseph Quincy Adams Memorial Studies*, Washington, D. C., 1948.

Masinton, Charles G., *Christopher Marlowe's Tragic Vision: A Study in Damnation*, Athens, Ohio, 1972.

Mehl, Dieter, *The Elizabethan Dumb Show*, Cambridge, Mass., and London, 1966.

Nicoll, Allardyce, *The Elizabethans*, New York, 1957.

Parrott, Thomas Marc and Robert Hamilton Ball, *A Short View of Elizabethan Drama*, New York, 1943.

Reed, A. W., *Early Tudor Drama*, London, 1926.

Ribner, Irving, *The English History Play in the Age of Shakespeare*, Princeton, 1957.

Rossiter, Arthur Percival, *English Drama from Early Times to the Elizabethans*, London, 1950.

Rozett, Martha Tuck, *The Doctrine of Election and the Emergence of Elizabethan Tragedy*, Princeton, 1984.

Saccio, Peter, *The Court Comedies of John Lyly: A Study in Allegorical Dramaturgy*, Princeton, 1969.

Schelling, F. E., *Elizabethan Drama*, 2 vols., Boston, 1908.

Schoenbaum, Samuel, *Internal Evidence and Elizabethan Dramatic Authorship*, Evanston, Ill., 1966.

Senn, Werner, *Studies in the Dramatic Construction of Robert Greene and George Peele*, Berne, 1973.

Shepherd, Simon, *Marlowe & the Politics of Elizabethan Theatre*, Brighton, Sussex, 1986.

Sisson, Charles J., *Le Goût public et le théâtre élisabéthain jusqu' à la mort de Shakespeare*, Dijon, 1922.

Spencer, T., *Death and Elizabethan Tragedy, a study of convention and opinion in the Elizabethan drama*, Cambridge, Mass., 1936.

Steane, J. B., *Marlowe: A Critical Study*, Cambridge, 1964.

Swinburne, A. C., *The Age of Shakespeare*, New York, 1908.

Symons, Arthur, *Studies in the Elizabethan Drama*, New York, 1919.

Thorp, Willard, *The Triumph of Realism in Elizabethan Drama: 1558-1612*, Princeton, 1928.

Waith, Eugene M., *The Herculean Hero*, New York, 1962.

Watson, Robert N., *Ben Jonson's Parodic Strategy*, Cambridge, Mass., and London, 1987.

Weimann, Robert, *Shakespeare and the Popular Tradition in the Theater*, Baltimore and London, 1978.

Wells, H. W., *Elizabethan and Jacobean Playwrights*, New York, 1939.

Wickham, Glynne, *Early English Stages, 1300-1660*, 2 vols, London and New York, 1959; 1963, 1972 (Vol. 2, Parts 1 and 2).

Wilson, F. P., *Elizabethan and Jacobean*, Oxford, 1945.

_____, *Marlowe and the Early Shakespeare*, Oxford, 1953.

MEDIEVAL AND TUDOR DRAMA
Twenty-Four Plays
Edited and with
Introductions by John Gassner

The rich tapestry of medieval belief, morality and manners shines through this comprehensive anthology of the twenty-four major plays that bridge the dramatic worlds of medieval and Tudor England. Here are the plays that paved the way to the Renaissance and Shakespeare. In John Gassner's extensively annotated collection, the plays regain their timeless appeal and display their truly international character and influence.

MEDIEVAL AND TUDOR DRAMA remains the indispensable chronicle of a dramatic heritage—the classical plays of Hrotsvitha, folk and ritual drama, the passion play, the great morality play *Everyman*, the Interlude, Tudor comedies *Ralph Roister Doister* and *Gammer Gurton's Needle*, and the most famous of Tudor tragedies *Gorboduc*. The texts have been modernized for today's readers and those composed in Latin have been translated into English.

paper • ISBN: 0-936839-84-8

SHAKESCENES
SHAKESPEARE FOR TWO
Edited with an Introduction
by John Russell Brown

Shakespeare's plays are not the preserve of "Shakespearean Actors" who specialize in a remote species of dramatic life. In the Introduction, Advice to Actors, and in the notes to each of the fifty scenes, John Russell Brown offers guidance for those who have little or no experience with the formidable Bard.

The scenes are presented in newly-edited texts, with notes which clarify meanings, topical references, puns, ambiguities, etc. Each scene has been chosen for its independent life requiring only the simplest of stage properties and the barest of spaces. A brief description of characters and situation prefaces each scene, and is followed by a commentary which discusses its major acting challenges and opportunities.

Shakescenes are for small classes and large workshops, and for individual study whenever two actors have the opportunity to work together.

From the Introduction:

"Of course, a way of speaking a character's lines meaningfully and clearly must be found, but that alone will not bring any play to life. Shakespeare did not write for talking heads ... Actors need to be acutely present all the time; ... they are like boxers in a ring, who dare not lose concentration or the ability to perform at full power for fear of losing consciousness altogether."

paper • ISBN: 1-55783-049-5

APPLAUSE

SOLILOQUY
The Shakespeare Monologues
Edited by Michael Earley and Philippa Keil

At last, over 175 of Shakespeare's finest and most performable monologues taken from all 37 plays are here in two easy-to-use volumes (MEN and WOMEN). Selections travel the entire spectrum of the great dramatist's vision, from comedies, wit and romances, to tragedies, pathos and histories.

"SOLILOQUY is an excellent and comprehensive collection of Shakespeare's speeches. Not only are the monologues wide-ranging and varied, but they are superbly annotated. Each volume is prefaced by an informative and reassuring introduction, which explains the signals and signposts by which Shakespeare helps the actor on his journey through the text. It includes a very good explanation of blank verse, with excellent examples of irregularities which are specifically related to character and acting intentions. These two books are a must for any actor in search of a 'classical' audition piece."

Elizabeth Smith
Head of Voice & Speech
The Juilliard School

paper
MEN: ISBN: 0-936839-78-3
WOMEN: ISBN: 0-936839-79-1

 **APPLAUSE**

CLASSICAL TRAGEDY

Eight Plays accompanied by Critical Essays
Edited by Robert W. Corrigan

AESCHYLUS	*Prometheus Bound*
	Oresteia
SOPHOCLES	*Antigone*
	Oedipus the King
EURIPIDES	*Medea*
	The Bakkhai
SENECA	*Oedipus*
	Medea

paper • ISBN: 1-55783-046-0

CLASSICAL COMEDY

Six Plays
Edited by Robert W. Corrigan

ARISTOPHANES	*Lysistrata*
	Oresteia
MENANDER	*The Grouch*
PLAUTUS	*The Menaechmi*
	The Haunted House
TERENCE	*The Self-Tormentor*

paper • ISBN: 0-936839-85-6

ACTING IN RESTORATION COMEDY

The Applause Acting Series
Based on the BBC Master Class Series
By Simon Callow

The art of acting in Restoration Comedy, the buoyant, often bawdy romps which celebrated the reopening of the English theatres after Cromwell's dour reign, is the subject of Simon Callow's bold new investigation. There is cause again to celebrate as Callow, one of Britain's foremost actors, aims to restore the form to all its original voluptuous vigor. Callow shows the way to attain clarity and hilarity in some of the most delightful roles ever conceived for the theatre.

Callow's lively speculations do not follow the familiar route of lace-trimmed interpretations and gratuitous pageantry. He rejects camp for camp's sake, and embraces instead the magnificently perverse language as the primary seductive force in Restoration Comedy.

The actor who follows Callow into the Restoration will emerge with an invigorated palate for the theatre of every age. "Restoration comedies," writes Callow, "are bursting with life and it is the giving of life that is the job of the theatre."

paper • ISBN: 1-55783-035-5

THE MISANTHROPE
and Other French Classics
Edited by Eric Bentley

THE MISANTHROPE Molière
English version by Richard Wilbur

PHAEDRA Racine
English version by Robert Lowell

THE CID Corneille
English version by James Schevill

FIGARO'S MARRIAGE Beaumarchais
English version by Jacques Barzun

paper • ISBN: 0-936839-19-8

THE SERVANT OF TWO MASTERS
and Other Italian Classics
Edited by Eric Bentley

THE SERVANT OF TWO MASTERS Goldoni
English version by Edward Dent

THE KING STAG Gozzi
English version by Carl Wildman

THE MANDRAKE Machiavelli
English version by Frederick May and Eric Bentley

RUZZANTE RETURNS FROM THE WARS Beolco
English version by Angela Ingold &Theodore Hoffman

paper • ISBN: 0-936839-20-1

❦APPLAUSE❦